DICTIONARY
OF
TWENTIETH CENTURY BRITISH
BUSINESS LEADERS

DICTIONARY
OF
TWENTIETH CENTURY BRITISH
BUSINESS LEADERS

DAVID J. JEREMY
Manchester Metropolitan University

GEOFFREY TWEEDALE
University of Sheffield

BOWKER
SAUR

London • Melbourne • Munich • New Jersey

British Library Cataloguing in Publication Data
A catalogue record for this book is available from the British Library

Library of Congress Cataloging in Publication Data
A catalogue record for this book is available from the Library of Congress

Published by Bowker-Saur Ltd.
60 Grosvenor Street, London W1X 9DA
Tel: +44(0)71 493 5841 Fax: +44(0)71 580 4089
Bowker-Saur is a division of REED REFERENCE PUBLISHING

ISBN 0-86291-594-5

Cover design by Robin Caira
Typesetting by Typographics, Whitstable, Kent
Printed on acid-free paper
Printed and bound in Great Britain by Antony Rowe Ltd, Chippenham

CONTENTS

PREFACE

Until recently, finding biographical and historical information on British business leaders was not easy. Newspaper obituarists and national reference works, with their well-known bias (that still continues) in favour of artists, politicians and writers, have always under-represented technologists and creators of wealth. Even when an industrialist was deemed worthy of notice, the coverage of their commercial life was often superficial and disappointing.

Lately, there have been signs that this attitude has been changing. In the so-called 'enterprise culture' of the 1980s the entrepreneur was championed and interest began to grow in his (or her) lifestyle and activities. Business leaders were increasingly profiled in the supplements of the newspapers, their activities scrutinised as never before on television, and the number of published business biographies, both scholarly and popular, began to grow. On the academic side, there were two major initiatives to rectify the short-changing of the business fraternity that had occurred in such Establishment tomes as the *Dictionary of National Biography* and *Who's Who*. In the early 1980s the Business History Unit at the London School of Economics launched the *Dictionary of Business Biography*[1] (DBB), which covered individuals active between 1850 and 1950; while the University of Glasgow at about the same time also produced a *Dictionary of Scottish Business Biography*[2] (DSBB), covering a similar historical period.

Like the national reference works they were designed to complement, these dictionaries were massive in scale, produced in multi-volume sets and expensive to purchase. They were usually not readily accessible to most readers without a visit to a major library. Nor did they contain biographical information on current business personalities. We have tried to correct these shortcomings in this book, which provides concise biographies of over 750 twentieth-century business leaders in a handy *single* volume.

Most readers will have their own ideas on what constitutes a business leader and will either be enlightened (or disappointed) at what they find when they consult this volume. But providing a satisfactory definition of a business leader is not easy; it is probably impossible - just as it is extremely difficult to define a successful firm. What measure should one use: sales, profits, production, employment, capital, market share? What weight should be given to such factors as inventive ability and technological influence? How is one to encapsulate business leaders within a quantitative framework, when their influence has often stemmed from their business philosophies, religious ideals, labour policies or scientific or economics expertise? What about distinguished failures (or even outright rogues) - influential perhaps in a negative way, but important nonetheless?

Although defining business leaders is an inexact social science (if it is a science at all), we have nevertheless - if only to make things easier for ourselves over such an extended historical period - used a quantitative yardstick for selection. Benchmark dates have been chosen - 1907, 1935, 1955 - to enable a listing of the 100 largest *employers* in the UK. (The methodology and the sources underpinning this selection have been discussed elsewhere.[3]) Using this listing, the chairmen (and/or chief executives) of these companies (both public and private) were identified and biographical information was then located. For more recent times from about 1960 to the early 1990s, an employment measure for company size was deemed less satisfactory (partly because modern high-technology industries are no longer so labour intensive). We have therefore used employment, combined with other economic indicators (such as turnover and capital) to identify the top 120 or so UK companies. Not surprisingly, these methods did not capture all the individuals we wished to include (nor did they catch all the businessmen that our readers would have expected us to include). So to increase our coverage of high-profile figures, be they business successes or failures, we have therefore used an element of good old 'rule of thumb'.

Information is provided - where it is available - on the subject's birth, education, early business career, major achievements, honours, marriage, and wealth. Brief bibliographical citations are also included where appropriate, though the nature of this publication has prevented us from providing detailed notes and acknowledgements. For the most part, only major writings are cited and an abbreviated indication of whether the subject has an entry in such reference works as the *Dictionary of Business Biography*. The only exception to this is where the source information is so obscure that a clue to its location has been thought advisable.

In compiling these biographies we have used the traditional source materials of the business historian: house histories, newspapers, annual reports, academic monographs, business magazines, autobiographies, and television documentaries, to name a few. Naturally, we have found *Who's Who* (and *Who Was Who*) and *Who's Who in Industry* (editor Juliet Margetts, 1991) particularly useful. Our debt to the endeavours of scores of business historians in the pages of the *Dictionary of Business Biography* will also be apparent. But although we have been grateful to utilise the efforts of others, our methods of selection and our policy of including current businessmen mean that over half the entries in this book are not to be found in sources such as the *DBB*. Information on these individuals came from our own files and researches or from details supplied by the subject, a relative, or company. Occasionally, we have not always been able to add significantly to the written record. It is surprising how often the head of a major public company left behind nothing more than a few, relatively uninformative lines in either *Who's Who* or *The Times*. This itself is an indication that much work remains to be done on the subject of British business leaders. We hope that the present volume will be a useful and concise starting point for future work in this field.

1. David J Jeremy and Christine Shaw (eds), *Dictionary of Business Biography* (6 vols, London: Butterworths, 1984-6)
2. Anthony Slaven and Sydney Checkland (eds), *Dictionary of Scottish Business Biography* (2 vols, Aberdeen: Aberdeen University Press, 1986-90)
3. See David J Jeremy, 'The Hundred Largest Employers in the United Kingdom in Manufacturing and Non-Manufacturing Industries in 1907, 1935 and 1955', *Business History* 33 (January 1991), pp. 96-111; revised in Barry E Supple (ed), *The Rise of Big Business* (Aldershot: Edward Elgar Publishing, 1992).

ACKNOWLEDGEMENTS

Numerous individuals have placed us in their debt as we have compiled this work. First we are grateful to both the London School of Economics and Butterworths who have allowed us to draw upon the entries and files of the *Dictionary of Business Biography* (6 vols, 1984-86) which they, respectively, sponsored and published. In the International Business Unit of the Management and Business Faculty at the Manchester Metropolitan University, the Dean, Professor Andrew Lock, has facilitated research and writing for the first of the authors, and this has been admirably supported by the faculty's library (where Mrs Polly Linton must be mentioned), reprographic and computing services. John Harris, an MMU colleague, has been of crucial importance in resolving several untimely domestic computer hold-ups. For general library resources, both authors are obliged to the staffs of the Central Reference Library, Manchester; Sheffield City Library; Stockport Library (particularly David Reid); and the British Library of Political and Economic Science at the LSE. For information on many of the entries we are obliged to the following: Adrian Allan (Liverpool University Archives), Brigadier B M Archibald, G R Barbour (Scottish Record Office), Mrs Margaret Barr née Stirling, Mrs Rosemary Boynes, Michael Bywater, T A B Corley, William Davis (British Tourist Authority), John Dodds, Dr Douglas A Farnie, Mrs Hanne Gardner, Dr Francis Goodall, Dr Terry Gourvish, Edwin Green, Andrew Jackson (Strathclyde Regional Archives), David S Johnson, Dr Edgar Jones, Dr James H H Merriman, Robert Morgan, Michael Moss, Mrs Rebecca MonWilliams, Robert Murphy, A David Owen, James Porteous, Colin Price (Leeds Central Reference Library), Lady Dorothy Radley, Johnston F Robb, Professor Peter Self, Dr Christine Shaw, Professor Anthony Slaven, Mrs Alison Sharp, Diane Stobbs (IM & S, St Helens), Dr Philip W Sykes, Mrs Leonore Symons (Institution of Electrical Engineers), Alex Taft, Nick Temple (IBM UK) and Peter Traynor (Prudential Corporation). Needless to say, they are absolved from any responsibility for what follows in this book.

David J Jeremy
Manchester Metropolitan University

Geoffrey Tweedale
University of Sheffield

July 1993

A

ABELL, George Foster
(31 July 1875 - 17 March 1946)
Banker, the son of George Edmund Abell of Grafton Manor, Bromgrove. Educated at Repton, he went into banking and joined the Bromsgrove Branch of Lloyds. Within a year, he joined the inspection staff, remaining with it eight years, including two at Lombard Street. In 1902 he went to Worcester as chief clerk and in 1906 was made manager at Bridgnorth. After a short period at Stroud, he became assistant manager at Lombard Street in 1914 and manager in 1919. Seven years later he was promoted to joint general manager and in 1929 became chief general manager. He retired from Lloyds Bank in 1938 and was made a director. He was also a director of Lloyds & National Provincial Foreign Bank. A member of the councils of Charing Cross Hospital and Cheltenham College, he served on the Financial Commission of the Church Assembly. He married Jesse Elizabeth, daughter of the Reverend E B Brackenbury, and they had two sons and two daughters. One son, George E B Abell (1904-1989), became private secretary to the two last Viceroys of India. See *Dark Horse* (February 1929); *The Times*, 20 March 1946.

AITKEN, William Maxwell
1st Baron Beaverbrook
(25 May 1879 - 9 June 1964)
Newspaper proprietor, born at Maple, Ontario, the son of William Cuthbert Aitken, an immigrant Scottish Presbyterian minister, and Jane née Noble. Leaving school at sixteen, he set up his own finance company, Royal Securities Corporation, and began buying and selling companies. A sterling millionaire aged thirty, he left for England in 1910, leaving behind some questionable dealings in cement mergers. In the same year he became Unionist MP for Ashton-under-Lyne and also bought a share in the *Daily Express* for party propaganda. He bought the controlling interest in the newspaper in 1916, the year he was awarded a peerage and also made Minister of Information. During the 1920s and 1930s the profits and circulation of Beaverbrook's newspaper empire (which also now included the *Sunday Express*) grew steadily. Circulation of the *Daily Express* rose from under 250,000 in 1922 to 4 million in 1950. Much of this success was due to the ideas and energy of Beaverbrook himself, who used the newspapers for his favourite political campaigns (such as the Empire Crusade), to pursue vendettas against individuals such as Stanley Baldwin (who retaliated with his famous jibe that Beaverbrook sought "power without responsibility - the prerogative of the harlot throughout the

ages"), or simply to have fun. Regarded as a lovable naughty boy by some, he was described as malicious and evil by others. Outside the mainstream of the Conservative Party, his appearance on the centre stage of politics owed most to personal relationships: for example, his friendship with Churchill led to his appointment as Minister of Aircraft Production during the Second World War. In 1954 Beaverbrook transferred all his voting shares (worth about £1.5 million) to the Beaverbrook Foundation, with the income devoted to various charitable purposes. He married twice: first in 1906 to Gladys née Drury: they had two sons and two daughters; second in 1963 to Marcia Anastasia, 'Christofer', the widow of Sir James Dunn. Beaverbrook left £379,530. His elder son, Sir Maxwell Aitken, eventually sold the newspapers to the Trafalgar House Group in 1977. See William Maxwell Aitken, *My Early Life* (1964); Anne Chisholm and Michael Davie, *Beaverbrook: A Life* (1992); A J P Taylor, *Beaverbrook* (1972); *DBB*; *DNB*.

AKERS-DOUGLAS, Aretas
1st Viscount Chilston
(21 October 1851 - 15 January 1926)
Politician and railway company director, elder son of the Reverend Aretas Akers of Malling Abbey, Kent, and his wife Frances Maria née Brandram, he was educated at Eton and University College, Oxford, qualifying as a barrister at the Inner Temple in 1875. That year he married Adeline, elder daugher of H Austen Smith, of Hayes Court, Kent (by whom he had two sons and five daughters), and succeeded to the Scottish estates of a cousin, James Douglas Stoddart Douglas - after whom he assumed the additional surname. Elected MP for East Kent in 1880 he pursued a political career in the Conservative Party, serving inter alia as a Whip 1883-95 and Home Secretary 1902-6; he was created a viscount in 1911. His directorship of the South East & Chatham Railway in 1907 made him a member of the British business élite albeit a relatively passive one. See Eric Alexander-Akers-Douglas, *Chief Whip* (1961).

ALEXANDER, Robert Scott
Baron Alexander of Weedon
(5 September 1936 -)
Banker, the son of Samuel James Alexander, who owned a filling station in Stoke-on-Trent that grew into a garage (the Alexander Motor Co), and his wife Hannah May. He attended Brighton College and King's College, Cambridge, where he read law (BA 1959, MA 1963). He was called to the Bar, Middle Temple, in 1961. Appointed QC in 1973, he was made a Judge of the Courts of Appeal of Jersey and Guernsey in 1985. After a string of suc-

cessful briefs - GCHQ, Kerry Packer *v.* Test & County Cricket Board, Geoffrey Collier (the insider dealer), and the *Spycatcher* case - Alexander became chairman of the National Westminster Bank in 1988, when he was also made a life peer. He was also appointed a non-executive director of RTZ Corporation in 1991. He and his wife Marie have two sons and one daughter (and one son deceased).

ALLIANCE, Sir David
(June 1932 -)

Textile manufacturer, the son of a Jewish merchant in Iran. He claims to have started business in Tehran aged nine, selling yarn to shoemakers, before arriving in England in 1950 with no work permit and no money. In the early 1950s he moved into the British textile industry, with a string of acquisitions. Until 1982 there were four big UK textile companies: Carrington Viyella, Coats Patons, Courtaulds and Tootal. By 1986 Alliance had merged the first two into Coats Viyella, of which he became chairman and chief executive, and then absorbed Tootal in 1991 after a bitter £252 million takeover. By then Coats Viyella was one of the world's largest textile companies, with 100,000 staff in 30 countries. Alliance's family also owns a profitable stake in the N Brown mail order group. Awarded a CBE in 1984, he was knighted by Margaret Thatcher in 1989 for his contribution to the enterprise culture. His personal fortune was estimated at over £70 million by 1991. He is twice married, lives in Manchester and London and collects L S Lowry paintings. See Philip Beresford, *The Sunday Times Book of the Rich* (1990) (which has 15/3/32 as date of birth).

AMOS, James
(1895 - 23 January 1970)

Transport company manager, born at Whitefield, Yarrow, the son of a border shepherd, he was educated in the village school and then apprenticed to a carpenter. He saw active service with the Lothian and Border Horse in the Balkans during the First World War. Returning home he set up a truck and bus service, Brock & Amos, which covered the whole of the Borders before it was acquired by the Scottish Motor Traction Co Ltd in 1926. Amos joined the SMT as assistant traffic manager, rising to vice-chairman. When SMT was absorbed into the British Transport Commission in 1948-49 he became chairman of the Scottish Omnibuses Group of the BTC. By 1961 this Group had a capital of £30 million, operated 4,500 vehicles and employed 20,000 people. That year Amos became the first Scot to become president of the Institute of Transport. He was made CBE in 1958. Amos mar-

ried in 1949 Rachel, daughter of John Anderson of Smailholm Mains, Kelso. See *The Scotsman* 24 January 1970; *Journal of the Institute of Transport* 29 (November 1961).

ANDERSON, John
1st Viscount Waverley
(8 July 1882 - 4 January 1958)

Civil servant, politician and chairman of the Port of London Authority, born at Eskbank, Midlothian, the only son of David Alexander Pearson Anderson, printer, he was educated at George Watson's College, Edinburgh, and the University of Edinburgh and Leipzig. He went into the Civil Service, becoming chairman of the Board of the Inland Revenue in 1919 and then Permanent Under Secretary at the Home Office in 1922. After serving as Governor of Bengal 1932-37, he took up a political career in 1938 when he was elected MP. During the Second World War he served in the Cabinet under both Chamberlain (as Home Secretary 1939-40) and Churchill (as Lord President of the Council 1940-43, and then Chancellor of the Exchequer 1943-45, introducing PAYE, devised by Stanley Paul Chambers (qv), in 1944). He was chairman of the Port of London Authority 1946-58, commencing when a third of the port's facilities had been destroyed by wartime bombing. Preoccupation with repair delayed large scale investment and the reform of outdated working practices among its 12,000 employees (in 1955) during a period of growing traffic. He was made a viscount in 1952. He married twice; first in 1907, Christina (d 1920), daughter of Andrew Mackenzie of Edinburgh, by whom he had a son and a daughter; second in 1941, Ava, daughter of J E C Bodley and widow of Ralph Wigram CMG. See John W Wheeler-Bennett, *John Anderson, Viscount Waverley* (1962).

ANGUS, Sir Michael (Richardson)
(5 May 1930 -)

Soap, food and margarine conglomerate executive, the son of William Richardson Angus and Doris Margaret Breach. After attending Marling School, Stroud, he read mathematics at Bristol University (BSc), then served in the RAF 1951-54. He joined Unilever in 1954 and in 1962 moved to France to become marketing director of Unilever toiletries. In 1970 he was elected to Unilever's Dutch and English boards as Toilet Preparations Co-ordinator. A decade later he was given the task of turning round the company's North American operations. Success took him in 1984 on to Unilever's ruling triumverate - the three-man special committee - and in 1986 he duly became British chairman. Angus has taken the company through a string of acquisitions, buying Chesebrough Pond's and the Calvin Klein and Fabergé/Elizabeth Arden perfume companies. Unilever's turnover rose from £16,931 million in 1987 (pre-tax profits £1,327 million) to £23,168 million in 1991 (pre-tax profits £1,792), making it the second largest UK company in turnover behind BP. It has nearly 300,000 workers world-wide. Angus retired, like all Unilever's board members, at sixty-two in May 1992, handing over to Michael Perry (qv). He then took over the chairmanship at Whitbread. He also became deputy chairman at the Natwest Bank in 1991; and was also president of the CBI and a non-executive director at British Airways. In 1952 he married Eileen Isabel May Elliott: they have two sons and one daughter. He was knighted in 1990. See Edmund Williams, *Unilever: The First Hundred Years* (1988).

ANSON, Sir George Wilfred
(2 June 1893 - 26 February 1974)

Tobacco manufacturer, grandson of John Hopkinson who married a sister of Henry Overton Wills III (1828-1911), head of the third generation of the Bristol tobacco manufacturing family firm, and son of G E Anson and his wife Mabel; he was educated at Winchester and Trinity College, Oxford. Commissioned in the Loyal Regiment at the outbreak of war in 1914, he emerged in 1918 with the rank of major and an MC and then joined Imperial Tobacco Co, the 1901 merger between 13 firms led by Wills, Players and Churchmans. He became leaf manager in 1926, company secretary in 1936 and a director in 1941. He sat on Imperial's executive committee, 1944-56. From 1948 until his retirement in 1958 Sir George Anson (he was knighted in 1951) was deputy chairman under Sir Robert (later Lord) Sinclair (qv). He stepped down from the Imperial board in 1966. For the industry he was a member of the Board of Trade's Tobacco Manufacturers' Advisory Committee, 1940-58. He served on many public bodies including the council of Bristol University (1956-68; pro-chancellor in 1970), the Newson-Smith Committee on Training for Business Administration (1945), the council of the British Institute of Management (1952-58), and Oxford University Business Summer School committee. He married, in 1916, Dinah Maud Lillian née Bourne; they had two sons and a daughter. See *The Times*, 27 February, 6 March 1974; Bernard W E Alford, *W D & H O Wills and the Development of the UK Tobacco Industry, 1786-1965* (1972).

ARMSTRONG, Colonel Oliver Carleton
(15 October 1859 - 18 February 1932)

Engineering company director, son of Major W C Armstrong, he entered the army in 1878, rising to major in 1898 and colonel in 1907 after service in Burmah and South Africa. By this date he was a deputy secretary to the Government of India, in the Military and Finance Department, operating in London. In 1908 he was recruited by the board of Vickers as an executive director for their newly acquired subsidiary, William Beardmore & Co Ltd, the Clydeside shipbuilders then employing 4,500. Soon after, Armstrong was made joint managing director of Beardmores, in a determined attempt to control Beardmores' finances and less successfully, William Beardmore (qv) himself. Armstrong resigned in 1913 but was appointed the Vickers representative director of Greenwood & Batley, the Leeds machine tool manufacturers, the following year, serving as chairman. Armstrong was elected president of the Federation of British Industries in 1921. He married Lilian Florence, daughter of Edward Jones-Madoc of Glentworth, Shropshire, and widow of Murray Greaves-Bagshawe; they had one son. See John R Hume and Michael S Moss, *Beardmore, the History of a Scottish Industrial Giant* (1979)

ARMYTAGE, Sir George John
(26 April 1842 - 8 November 1918)

Railway director and landed proprietor, born at Kirklees, Clifton, Brighouse, the son of Sir George Armytage, 5th Bt and Eliza Matilda Mary née Radcliffe, the family having owned the Kirklees estate since the sixteenth century. He trained to be a civil engineer and as a railway director was invariably concerned about the engineering dimension of any railway question. Armytage was an associate member of the Institution of Civil Engineers, fellow of the Institution of Chartered Surveyors and a member of the Permanent Commission of the International Railway Congress. He became a director of the Lancashire & Yorkshire Railway Co in March 1879, deputy chairman in 1883 and chairman in 1887, retiring shortly before his death. During his long chairmanship the L & Y was developed into a major railway company, employing nearly 35,000 people and ranked fifth among the UK's 130 railway companies in 1907. Sir George Armytage (he succeeded to the baronetcy in 1899) was also chairman of the Deane Valley Railway and a director of the Goole Steam Shipping Co whose fleet was purchased by the L & Y to work services to the Continent. Outside business Armytage was high sheriff of Yorkshire in 1907 and thereafter a DL. He was known as an ardent antiquarian and genealogist (FSA, and a founder of the Harleian Society), a Conservative and a Churchman. Sir George married first, in 1871, Ellen (d 1890) daughter of the Reverend Ayscough Fawkes, of Farnley Hall, Yorkshire, by whom he had two sons and two daughters; second, in 1893, Mary Georgiana, daughter of Henry Littledale of Bolton Hall, Yorkshire. See *Leeds Mercury* 11, 14 November 1918; John Marshall, *The Lancashire and Yorkshire Railway* (2 vols, 1969-72); *Railway Gazette*, 15 November 1918.

ASHCROFT, John (Kevin)
(24 December 1948 -)

Wall-coverings chain store retailer, born at Upholland, near Wigan, the son of John Ashcroft, who managed a family drift mine, and his wife Cumania Manion. Educated at Upholland Grammar School and the London School of Economics (BSc Econ), in 1970 he became a marketing trainee at Tube Investments. In 1974 he joined Crown Products as a manager in international wall-coverings and then in 1978 became an export director at Coloroll, a sleepy family wallpaper business. Ashcroft became chairman in 1986, having floated the company in the previous year for £40 million, and was largely responsible for transforming Coloroll into the largest wall-coverings manufacturer in the UK (in 1978 its market share had been only 3 per cent) and the third largest in the US. Sales hit £6 million in 1978; £565 million in 1989. But massive expansion into household textiles and carpets could not be sustained once retail spending dropped and the group collapsed in debt in 1990, when Ashcroft (who held under one per cent of the shares) was sacked. He was awarded a CBE in 1990. In 1993 he runs Survival Group Ltd, a small Cumbria-based company selling outdoor clothing and equipment. He married Jennifer King in 1972: they have two sons and a daughter. See Judi Bevan and John Jay, *The New Tycoons* (1989).

ASHLEY, Laura
(7 September 1925 - 17 September 1985)

Clothes designer and chain store retailer, born at Dowlais, South Wales, the daughter of Stanley Lewis Mountney, a civil servant, and Margaret Elizabeth Davis. After attending Aberdare Secretarial School, at sixteen she became a secretary in the City of London. In 1949 she married (Sir) Bernard Ashley (b 1926, knighted 1986) and in the early 1950s they opened a small mill in Kent to produce their own fabrics. By 1963 they had moved the business to Carno, Mid-Wales. Laura Ashley's clothes, furnishings and interior decora-

tions - with their flowery, romantic patterns and yearnings for a natural lifestyle - hit a chord with middle-class Britain and by the 1980s her factories and retail chain had become an international company with £130 million annual turnover. She died after a fall, only weeks before the group was floated for £60 million, with her husband retaining the controlling interest and chairmanship. They had two sons and two daughters. See Anne Sebba, *Laura Ashley: A Life By Design* (1990); *DNB*.

ASPINALL, Sir John Audley Frederick
(25 August 1851 - 19 January 1937)

Railway engineer and manager, born in Liverpool, son of John Bridge Aspinall QC, he was educated at Beaumont College, Berkshire. He entered the London & North Western Railway Works at Crewe in 1868 as a pupil of John Ramsbottom and later F W Webb, successive chief mechanical engineers. Thereafter he was manager of the Great Southern & Western Railway Works, near Dublin and later the company's locomotive superintendent. He returned to England in 1886 as chief mechanical engineer of the Lancashire & Yorkshire Railway, and completed the removal of the firm's works to Horwich. Here he standardised locomotive manufacture and pioneered the building of large locomotives. Promoted to general manager of the L & Y he continued to innovate by electrifying suburban lines in Liverpool and Southport (to compete with trams) and to expand services to Ireland and to the Continent, upgrading dock facilities at Goole. He was consulting mechanical engineer to the Ministry of Transport 1919-27. Professionally Sir John Aspinall (he was knighted in 1917) served as president of the Institution of Mechanical Engineers 1909-10 and of the Institution of Electrical Engineers in 1919. By upbringing, marriage and adult practice he was a Roman Catholic. He married Gertrude Helen, daughter of F B Schroder, a leather factor of Liverpool; they had one son and two daughters. See *DBB*.

ASPREY, John (Rolls)
(8 November 1937 -)

Jeweller, the son of Eric Asprey, born into a family that had fled the Huguenot persecution in eighteenth-century France and then established one of the most successful and oldest family businesses in the UK. Founded in Mitcham, Surrey, in 1781 by John's ancestor, William, Asprey's are an upmarket jewellers located in London's New Bond Street (Nos 165-169), sometimes referred to as "the Queen's gift shop". Educated at Stowe and the Sorbonne, before being drilled in the Scots Guards, he joined the family business in his twenties after learning the trade at Henry Birks, a Canadian jeweller, and Patek Philippe, the Swiss watchmaker. He became chairman in 1979 in the midst of a family feud, which pitted him and his father against his uncle and cousin, while Dunhill threatened a takeover. John Asprey emerged from the crisis with 46 per cent of the equity (the family control over 50 per cent) and then launched the firm on its most expansionist phase. He took it on to the Unlisted Securities Market in 1981 and expanded the business significantly with takeovers, the chief of which was the £75 million acquisition of Mappin & Webb from Sears in 1990. With stores in New York and Geneva, Asprey's also owns Garrards and Watches of Switzerland (acquired from Ratners for L23 million). In 1991 - in a recession - Asprey's reported record profits of £25 million on sales of £100 million and had a cash pile of nearly £35 million. John Asprey is married and has three sons, one of whom, William, has joined the business. See Bevis Hillier, *Asprey of Bond Street 1781-1981* (1981).

AUSTIN, Herbert
1st Baron Austin of Longbridge
(8 November 1866 - 23 May 1941)
Motor car manufacturer, born in Little Missenden, Buckinghamshire, the son of Giles Stevens Austin, a farm bailiff, and Clara Jane née Simpson. Educated at Rotherham Grammar School and Brampton Commercial College in preparation for a career as an architect, in 1883 he decided to take up an engineering apprenticeship with an uncle in Australia. By the 1890s he was a managing a small engineering firm, the Wolseley Sheep Shearing Machine Co, moving to England with it in 1895 after a factory had been opened in Birmingham. With backing from Vickers (qv), the firm switched to car production and the Wolseley Tool & Motor Co Ltd was formed in 1901, with Austin as managing director. In 1905 he established his own company in Longbridge, near Birmingham, which went public as the Austin Motor Car Co in 1914 with a nominal capital of £650,000. In the inter-war years under Austin's chairmanship (and engineering skill) Austin became one of the Big Three UK motor manufacturers: between 1922 and 1939 turnover grew from £1.6 million to nearly £11 million, the workforce from 8,000 to 20,000. He was Conservative MP for King's Norton 1918-24 and was knighted in 1917, becoming a baronet in 1934 and a peer in 1936. He married in 1887 Helen Dron, daughter of an Australian merchant. Lord Austin left £509,712 gross. See Roy A Church, *Herbert Austin* (1979); *DBB*; *DNB*.

AWDRY, Charles
(12 February 1847 - 28 March 1912)
Partner in wholesale and retail chain of newsagents and booksellers, born in Wiltshire the sixth son of Sir John Wither Awdry, Chief Justice of Bombay, of Notton House, Chippenham, and his first wife Sarah Maria née Awdry, he was educated at Winchester and New College, Oxford. Charles Awdry joined W H Smith at 186, the Strand, London, in 1870 on the recommendation of his college tutor. The business was then owned by William Henry Smith II (1825-91), son of the founder, who needed a second partner to help oversee a rapid expansion, with employment growing from 4,000 in 1887 to 10,000 in 1911. Wholesale depots, newsagents' shops and railway station bookstalls comprised the bulk of the business, in running which Awdry was eclipsed from 1894 by Charles Harry St John Hornby (qv). Whereas Hornby was imaginative and forceful, welcoming change and conflict, Awdry preferred the world of squirarchical, hierarchical paternalism. With William Frederick Danvers Smith (qv) the partnership worked well. While Hornby dealt with external diplomacy, Awdry concentrated on personnel matters. He married Margaret Helen, daughter of the Right Reverend G Moberly, Bishop of Salisbury, in 1876; they had two sons and three daughters. See *The Times*, 23 March 1912; Charles Wilson, *First with the News: The History of W H Smith, 1792-1972* (1985).

B

BAILLIEU, Clive Latham
1st Baron Baillieu
(24 September 1889 - 18 June 1967)
Polymath businessman, born in Australia, the eldest son of William Lawrence Baillieu, a financier and politician, and Bertha Mary née Latham, a brewery owner, he attended Melbourne Church of England School, Trinity College, Melbourne, and Magdalene College, Oxford. Called to the Bar in 1915, that year he married Ruby Florence Evelyn the daughter of William Clark an Australian sharebroker and one of his father's associates, and then entered the war, serving with the Australian Flying Corps and later the RAF. After the First World War Baillieu worked in his father's London office, sitting on the boards of a number of finance, industrial and mining companies, chiefly the New Zealand Loan & Mercantile Agency Ltd, the English, Scottish & Australian Bank, the Midland Bank (from 1944) and Dunlop Rubber. After his father's mental collapse in 1932 he took over the management of the Zinc Corporation and North

Broken Hill Mining Co. In 1949 the Zinc and Imperial Smelting coporations merged to form Consolidated Zinc which in 1962 was absorbed by Rio Tinto to form Rio Tinto Zinc of which Baillieu was deputy chairman 1962-65. During the Second World War he played an important part in the procurement of metals for munitions and served on a number of government bodies. He was a president of the Federation of British Industries in 1945-47 and was instrumental in forming the British Institute of Management in 1945. He was knighted in 1938 and made a baron in 1953. See *DBB*; Charles Harvey, *The Rio Tinto Company: An Economic History of a Leading International Mining Concern, 1873-1954* (1981).

BALFOUR, Arthur
1st Baron Riverdale
(9 January 1873 - 7 July 1957)

Steel manufacturer, born in London, the son of Mary Fraser (1847-1906), the daughter of a Scottish banker. Illegitimate (the birth was not registered), Balfour never knew his father and moved to Sheffield in 1882 as an "orphan" with Mary Fraser (only in 1906 did he discover she was his mother). Educated at a Methodist school, Ashville College, Harrogate, aged fifteen he joined the Sheffield crucible steelmakers, Seebohm & Dieckstahl, as an office boy. (Meanwhile, his mother married Robert Schott, the head of the business.) After running a foundry in Buffalo, USA, Balfour took over from Schott in 1896. When Seebohm & Dieckstahl became a limited liability company in 1899 (capital £150,000) he became a director. Soon Balfour became the sole head of the firm, the name of which was changed to Arthur Balfour & Co in 1915. A workaholic, a gifted salesman and a prodigious traveller, Balfour combined the running of the business - a typical family-controlled Sheffield crucible steelmaker employing about 500 between the wars - with an immense burden of government work, chief of which was his chairmanship of the Government Committee on Industry and Trade, 1925-28. The Second World War broke his health and the Balfour influence on the business: it went public in 1950 (capital £500,000). Balfour became Master Cutler in 1911 (one of the youngest holders of the office), was created KBE in 1923, a baronet in 1929, and a baron in 1935. In 1899 he married Frances Josephine Keighley, daughter of Charles Henry Bingham, a partner in the local silverplate firm of Walker & Hall: they had two sons and three daughters. He left £87,226 gross. See "Lord Riverdale Remembers", *Quality* (May/June 1984); Arthur Balfour & Co, *A Centenary 1865-1965* (1967); *DBB*; *DNB*.

BAMFORD, Joseph Cyril
(21 June 1916 -)

Excavator equipment manufacturer, born in Uttoxeter, Staffordshire. Educated at St John's, Alton, and Stonyhurst College, he served an apprenticeship with Russell Newbury in Altrincham, Alfred Herbert in Coventry and finally with his family's old-established firm of Bamfords of Uttoxeter, makers of agricultural machinery. Impatient with the conservative family business, he decided to set up on his own. An early sideline, a haircream named "Smartfix", failed because of the product's green colour; but in 1945 Bamford rented a lock-up garage in Uttoxeter and began business as an agricultural engineer. His first product was a renovated farm trailer, eventually sold for £45. In the 1950s Bamford began specialising in the earthmoving machines - such as the Norwegian inspired all-purpose hydraulic backhoe - that were to make the JCB logo (adopted in 1953) synonymous with excavator equipment. He retired in 1976 and became a tax exile in Switzerland (his fortune in 1992 was estimated at £200 million): by then the company was the largest UK-based manufacturer of construction equipment. In 1989 pretax profits hit a peak of about £50 million on a turnover of £400 million and the group employed over 2,500. Bamford married in 1941 Marjorie Griffin: they had two sons, one of whom, Sir Anthony Bamford, was born on the day his father opened for business and now runs JCB. Joe Bamford became CBE in 1969. See Philip Beresford, *The Sunday Times Book of the Rich* (1990); Michael D J Irwin, *JCB 1945-1980* (1992).

BANHAM, Sir John (Michael Middlecott)
(22 August 1940 -)

Director-General of the Confederation of British Industry, the son of Terence Middlecott Banham, a surgeon, and Belinda Joan née Unwin, a nurse (and later CBE, JP, and a prominent figure in health care and welfare). Educated at Charterhouse and Queen's College, Cambridge (BA Natural Sciences), he began a diplomatic career with the Foreign Office, but by 1965 had joined Reed International's wall-coverings division as director of marketing. In 1969 he moved into management consultancy with McKinsey & Co, leaving in 1983 to set up the Audit Commission for Local Authorities in England and Wales. In 1987 he became director-general of the CBI and retired in July 1992, when he was succeeded by Howard Davies (qv). Banham has also served as a non-executive director of English China Clays. Since retiring from the CBI, he has picked up a string of appointments: as chairman of West Country TV,

John Labatt (Europe), ECI Ventures Ltd, and the Government Commission for England. He married in 1965 Frances Barbara Molyneux Favell: they have one son and two daughters. He was knighted in 1991. See J M M Banham, *Future of the British Car Industry* (1975).

BANKS, Sir Donald
(31 March 1891 - 11 July 1975)
Director-General of the Post Office, educated at Elizabeth College, Guernsey, who entered the Civil Service in 1909. After distinguished military service during the First World War (DSO, MC, Croix de Guerre, besides being mentioned in despatches), from 1920-23 he was private secretary to the Secretary to the GPO and to four Postmasters-General. In 1931 he was Controller of the Post Office Savings Bank and between 1934 and 1936 became the first Director-General of the GPO (it was then the leading employer in the UK with about 230,000 workers). He headed the Air Ministry until 1939, when he returned to the army and in 1943 became Major-General. He was chairman of the Anglo-Chinese Chamber of Commerce, 1946-54, and deputy chairman of the Air Transport Advisory Council, 1947-51. He was made a KCB in 1935. He married twice: in 1921 to Dorothy née Webster (d 1947) (one daughter); and in 1948 to Elizabeth née Bradley (one son and one daughter). See Donald Banks, *Flame over Britain: A Personal Narrative of Petroleum Warfare* (1946); M J Daunton, *Royal Mail: The Post Office since 1840* (1985).

BARCLAY, David
(27 October 1934 -)

BARCLAY, Frederick
(27 October 1934 -)
Hotel and property owners, identical twins, born in London, of parents who possibly came from the west of Scotland. Highly secretive, little is known of their early life, except that they began their business career as estate agents, buying up boarding houses in London. They persuaded the Crown Agents - a government agency established to help the colonies and the developing countries to do business in the UK - to back their London hotel venture in 1970. The Crown Agents lost £6.5 million on Barclays Hotels (£34 million at 1992 prices). But in 1975 the Barclays purchased the Howard Hotel in London and soon prospered, especially in the London property boom of the 1980s. In 1983 they bid £50 million for Ellerman Lines - the shipping company established by Sir John Ellerman (qv) - and then sold its brewing interests to George Walker (qv) for £240 million.

In 1992 they bought the *European*, the newspaper started by Robert Maxwell (qv). Reputed to be worth nearly £500 million in 1992, the Barclay brothers have lived in Monaco for over a decade, where they own the Mirabeau Hotel. Roman Catholics, they are a friend of Margaret Thatcher and contributors to the Conservative Party. See Philip Beresford, *The Sunday Times Book of the Rich* (1990).

BARLOW, Sir Robert
(1 September 1891 - 30 September 1976)
Packaging materials manufacturer, born in Hackney, London, son of Edward C Barlow, a tough, terrifying maker of tin boxes, and his second wife Annie Eleanor née Baverstock, he joined his father at sixteen when the firm had sales of £29,000 and a net profit of £4,800. In 1921 the Barlows set up Metal Box & Printing Industries Ltd, a holding company for a merger of medium-sized family firms in the industry. Its turnover was £1.3 million in 1929 when the American Can Co, ten times the size of Metal Box, appeared on the horizon with its mass production technology and economies of scale. Instead of being intimidated by the American giant, Robert Barlow sold his shares to Metal Box, joined its board and led it into an alliance with Continental Can Co, American Can's smaller rival. American Can gave up the attempt to dominate the British market, Barlow turned MB & PI into a public company, Metal Box, of which he became managing director in 1930 and chairman in 1941. Barlow introduced high speed machinery manufacturing 'open top' cans in preference to 'general fire' containers for biscuits, tobacco, etc. Turnover rose from £2 million in 1931 to £5 million in 1939 and £52.6 million in 1955. Employees rose from 12,813 in 1935 to 24,818 in 1955. His pricing and contracting tactics tied customers to Metal Box, to the displeasure of the Monopolies Commission in 1970. Though he gave up the managing directorship in 1947 Barlow cunningly and ferociously remained at the helm of Metal Box until 1961. Barlow married twice, his second wife being Margaret Rawlings, an actress (m 1942); had one daughter. See W J Reader, *Metal Box: A History* (1976).

BARNETSON, William Denholm
Baron Barnetson
(21 March 1917 - 12 March 1981)
Newspaper proprietor and television chairman, born in Edinburgh, the son of William Barnetson, an estate agent, and Ella Grigor née Moir. Educated at the Royal High School, Edinburgh, and Edinburgh University (MA), he became a war correspondent in the Spanish Civil War. In the

Second World War he served in Anti-Aircraft Command and then helped reorganise West German book and newspaper publishing. From 1948 to 1961 he worked his way up as manager of the *Edinburgh Evening News*. In 1962 he joined Harley Drayton's (qv) United Publishers as director, succeeding the latter as chairman in 1966. He soon doubled the size of United, while he himself became involved with over forty different organisations: from the mid-1970s, for example, he was deputy chairman of British Electric Traction and chairman of the *Observer* and Thames Television. In 1968-79 he was chairman of Reuters, a period when its turnover rose from £6 million to £7 million and the foundations of its technological development were laid. He married in 1940 Joan Fairley née Davidson: they had one son and three daughters. He was knighted in 1972 and made a life peer in 1975. See Donald Reed, *The Power of News* (1992); *DNB*.

BARNETT, Sir Ben Lewis
(20 July 1894 - 25 November 1979)
Telecommunications executive, born in London, son of Isaac and Eva Barnett, he was educated at Christ's Hospital and Trinity College, Cambridge. After service with the Royal Engineers (TA) in the First World War, winning the MC in 1918, he joined the General Post Office in 1920. By 1930 he was a Principal, then Telecommunications Controller, Scotland, 1935-39, and Assistant Secretary (HQ), 1939-45. He became Regional Director, Home Counties Region in 1945; Director, Inland Telecommunications, 1946; and Deputy Director-General, 1949-56, serving under Sir Gordon Radley (qv). After retiring, Sir Ben Barnett (he was knighted in 1952) served as chairman of the Commonwealth Communications Board, 1956-62, as a director of Pye Ltd, Telephone Manufacturing Co Ltd, and Unidare (Dublin) Ltd. He was adviser to ATV Ltd and Western Union International. In the Institution of Electrical Engineers he played a part in advancing the status of professional engineers. A bachelor and a clubbable man, he was affectionately remembered for his many endeavours on behalf of the less fortunate. See *The Times*, 27 November 1979.

BARRIE, Robert
(1856 - 6 May 1909)
Soap and food company manager, born in Roxburghshire, he left Scotland at the age of sixteen and found work in Liverpool before entering Lever Brothers Ltd in 1896. He joined the Lever Brothers board in 1898 and became a close lieutenant of William Hesketh Lever (qv). As his obituaries testified, he was one of the few directors who did not hesitate to stand up against Lever. In the firm he was responsible for purchasing raw materials, a critical role, and he chaired the Employees' Benefit Fund. In 1903 he visited Canada and the USA to review the firm's overseas factories and markets on that continent. Barrie was a trustee of Christ Church, the non-denominational church at Port Sunlight built and controlled by Lever. For some years he suffered from ill health and died prematurely, leaving a widow. See *Progress* 7 (1906), 9 (July 1909), 10 (January 1910).

BARTLETT, Sir Charles John
(12 December 1889 - 10 August 1955)
Motor car manufacturer, born in Bibury, Gloucestershire, the son of George Bartlett, a miller journeyman, and Elizabeth née Stevens. Educated at Bath Technical College, in 1919 he joined the London-based operations (at Hendon) of the General Motors (GM) Corporation of America. After GM purchased Vauxhall Motors Ltd at Luton as their UK base (in 1925), Bartlett became managing director in 1930, a post he held until 1953 when he briefly became chairman. Under Bartlett production increased from 1,278 cars per annum in 1930 to 130,000 vehicles in 1954 (when he retired) - an increase facilitated by good labour relations and by profit-sharing, welfare and leisure programmes. He was elected a fellow of the Royal Society of Arts in 1951; and appointed DL of Bedfordshire in the following year. In 1925 he married Emily May Pincombe. He left £42,485. See L D Derbyshire, *The Story of Vauxhall 1857-1946* (1946); *DBB*.

BATES, Colonel Denis Haughton
(25 August 1886 - 13 September 1959)
Shipping line chairman, born in Liverpool, the fifth son of Sir Edward Percy Bates, 2nd Bt (1845-99) and his wife Constance née Graves, he was educated at Winchester. He joined the family firm of Edward Bates & Sons, merchants and bankers of Liverpool, which in 1911 purchased half the shares in Messrs T & J Brocklebank, a line in the Indian trade. Denis Bates went to work for Brocklebanks under Sir Aubrey Brocklebank. During the First World War he served with the Duke of Lancaster's Own Yeomanry, commanding a squadron and then the regiment, being mentioned in dispatches and earning the MC. A good rider and leader of men, he was invited to become honorary colonel of the regiment. Afterwards he returned to Brocklebanks and in 1929 at a relatively young age he became chairman, steering the firm through the depression of the 1930s. Meantime, in 1919 Brocklebanks was sold to the Cunard Steam-Ship Co Ltd, which brought three sons of Sir Edward

Bates to the chairmanship of Cunard continuously from 1930 until 1959: Sir Percy Elly Bates (qv), 1930-46; Frederick Alan Bates, 1946-53; and Denis Bates, 1953-59. Denis had been a director of the Cunard and Cunard White Star boards since 1941; he retired from both Brocklebanks and Cunard in 1959, shortly before his death. His tenure at the helm of Cunard, which employed 15,000 in 1955, coincided with increasingly poor labour relations, the overriding issue of replacing the *Queen Mary* and *Queen Elizabeth*, rising costs, heavy taxation (which prevented the accumulation of revenues for replacing the *Queens*) and the threat of competition from jet aircraft (run by nationalised, hence subsidised, airlines). Winter cruising was one solution he and his general manager Frank Dawson (qv) implemented. Denis Bates was a very shy man. He took little part in public affairs, either locally or in the shipping industry; he had no entry in the standard biographical reference works; and he disliked travel, so much so that as chairman of Cunard he never crossed the Atlantic. He married, in 1922, Aline Mary née Crook; they had a son and a daughter. See Francis E Hyde, *Cunard and the North Atlantic, 1840-1973* (1975); Liverpool University Archives, Cunard papers; *The Times*, 14 September, 9 October 1959.

BATES, Sir Percy Elly
(12 May 1879 - 16 October 1946)
Passenger shipping executive, the son of Sir Edward Percy Bates (1845-99) (2nd Bt) and Constance, daughter of S R Graves MP. Educated at Winchester, where he acquired a love for classics, he became a director of the Cunard Steamship Co in 1910, deputy chairman in 1922, and chairman in 1930. He was appointed chairman of Cunard White Star when it was formed in 1934. Under Bates, Cunard began the famous 'express' weekly transatlantic service between Southampton and New York, with the specially commissioned *Queen Mary* and *Queen Elizabeth*. Bates was also deputy chairman of Thomas & Juno Brocklebank and the Port Line; a director of the Midland Bank, the Great Western Railway and Hudson's Bay Co Overseas Settlement; and in 1930 chairman of the board of the *Morning Post*. In 1940 he was president of the Institute of Marine Engineers. He was a government adviser on transport during both world wars; and served as high sheriff and JP in Cheshire. He succeeded to the baronetcy on the death of his brother in 1903 and was created GBE in 1920. In 1907 he married Mary Ann Lefroy, daughter of the Dean of Norwich, and granddaughter of Charles MacIver, one of the founders of the Cunard Co. See *The Times*, 17 October 1946.

BAUMAN, Robert (Patten)
(27 March 1931 -)
Pharmaceutical company executive, born in the USA, the son of John Nevan Bauman Jr and Lucille Miller née Patten. Educated at Ohio Wesleyan University (BA) and Harvard School of Business (MBA), Bauman served in the USAF between 1955 and 1957, before joining the General Food Corporation. He was president of international operations at GFC between 1974 and 1981. He became director and chief executive of the Avco Corporation, 1981-85; and vice-chairman and director of Textron Inc, 1985-86. In 1986 he was appointed chairman and chief executive of the Beecham Group and when this UK pharmaceutical firm merged in 1989 with its US rival, SmithKline (to form SmithKline Beecham), Bauman became its chief executive. In 1991 this company, which is amongst the top three drugs companies in the world, joined the ranks of firms with profits of more than £1 billion a year. Bauman himself is one of the highest-paid UK executives with a salary of £1.2 million in 1991. He married in 1961 Patricia Hughes Jones: they have a son and a daughter. See Bob Bauman, *Plants and Pets* (1982); Corinne Simcock, *A Head for Business* (1992).

BAXENDALE, Joseph William
(1848 - 23 June 1915)
Road haulage industry entrepreneur, only son of Joseph Hornby and Mary Baxendale, he was educated at Harrow and Pembroke College, Oxford, before joining the family firm of Pickfords, taken over by his grandfather in 1850. Though he was the senior partner by 1894 and senior shareholder after the firm became a limited company in 1901, he withdrew when his cousin Lloyd Henry Baxendale (qv), the active manager, decided to break an agency agreement with the London & North Western Railway. Disillusioned, Joseph William quit the firm and withdrew his capital. Thereafter his main business interest was as director of the Phoenix Assurance Co. The pleasures of sport, which captured him at Oxford, stayed with him throughout his life. On the family estates he rode and hunted, serving as Master of the Hursley Hounds, 1892-1902. He was high sheriff of Hampshire, 1893. He married, in 1874, Frances Margaret Julia, daughter of the Hon Francis Scott and sole heiress and representative of George, last Earl of Egremont, leaving one son and two daughters. See Gerard Turnbull, *Traffic and Transport: An Economic History of Pickfords* (1979).

BAXENDALE, Lloyd Henry
(3 February 1858 - 21 May 1937)

Road haulage industry entrepreneur, born at Totteridge near Barnet, elder son of Lloyd Baxendale, 'gentleman', and his wife Ellen née Turner, he was educated at Eton and Christ Church College, Oxford. In 1879 he became a junior partner in Pickfords, the firm acquired by his grandfather in 1850. He was made a full partner, with his brother Francis Hugh, in 1894. After the business was converted into a limited company he served as chairman, 1901-12, employing 8,500 in 1907. His decision (supported by his brother) in 1901 to break an agency agreement with the London & North Western Railway led to his cousin Joseph William Baxendale (qv) withdrawing from the business. The shift from horse to motor transport further depleted the firm's resources and led Baxendale into an alliance with Carter Paterson, the main rival. Baxendale was chairman of the joint firm 1912-33, though power lay with the Carter Patersons. After it was taken over by the Proprietors of Hay's Wharf in 1920, he stayed on as ordinary director. He resigned when the four mainline railway companies acquired the business in 1933. Conservative, Anglican and a promoter of Newbury Racecourse, Lloyd Henry ('Harry') married Constance Louisa, daughter of Charles Raymond Pelly. They had one daughter. See DBB; Gerard Turnbull, *Traffic and Transport: An Economic History of Pickfords* (1979).

BAXTER, James
(1888 (?) - 1962 (?))

Sewing machine company executive, born in Lancashire, Baxter was a long-time employee of Singer Manufacturing Co, subsidiary of the American multinational, at Clydebank, Scotland. By the 1930s he was company manager in Italy. During the Second World War he returned to Clydebank as works manager. By the early 1950s he was managing director and in 1955 became chairman, when nearly 13,000 worked at Singer's at Clydebank. This was a remarkable achievement since the American parent firm usually nominated an American manager to run their Clydebank operation. Baxter was married, with daughters. He predeceased his wife, dying in the Bournemouth area c.1962. See *Red S Review* 25 (December 1955).

BAYER, Charles
(1846 - 1930)

Corset manufacturer, born probably in one of the German states, he came to Britain in 1860 and ten years later opened his ladies' outfitters business at 61 Wigmore Street, London. By 1875 he was described as a crinoline manufacturer and over the next twenty years had various addresses in the wholesale clothing and drapery area of London. In the 1890s he was at 31 London Wall and also had a large building in Golden Lane, Victoria Buildings. By 1910 he employed nearly 5,000 in his factories in London, Bath, Bristol, Gloucester, Portsmouth, Preston, Londonderry and elsewhere. The firm became a limited company in 1917 and still employed 5,000 in the 1920s. After Bayer's death it was reconstructed and in the 1950s was absorbed into Carrington Viyella. Bayer married in 1869 and had seven children by 1910. Information from Michael F Bywater and Sarah Levitt.

BEALE, Sir John Field
(15 January 1874 - 9 December 1935)

Industrialist, born at St Pancras, London, the son of James Samuel Beale, a senior partner in the firm of solicitors employed by the Midland Railway, and Margaret née Field. Educated at Harrow and Trinity College, Cambridge, he joined the family firm, Beale & Co, as solicitor in 1899. After succeeding his father as partner and deputy chairman, he became a director and later deputy chairman of the Midland Railway. He was recruited to the boards of the firms in the Guest, Keen & Nettlefolds group in 1925 (the Field family owned the Birmingham Screw Co) and became chairman and managing director four years later. Beale was also chairman of the Legal Insurance Co, a director of the Midland Bank, and during the First World War chairman of the Wheat Executive and First Secretary in the Ministry of Food. He was knighted in 1918. Beale married in 1901 Daisy Emma Game: they had two sons and two daughters. He left £35,726. See Charlotte J. Erickson, *British Industrialists: Steel and Hosiery 1850-1950* (1959); Edgar Jones, *A History of GKN: The Growth of a Business, 1918-1945* (1990).

BEARDMORE, William
Baron Invernairn
(6 October 1856 - 9 April 1936)

Shipbuilder, born in Greenwich, the eldest son of William Beardmore, engineer and then assistant manager of the Deptford Works of the General Steam Navigation Co, and Sophia Louisa Holfman; his father moved to Glasgow as partner in the Parkhead Forge, but died in 1877. William attended Glasgow High School and Ayr Academy, evening classes at Anderson's College and, at the end of his apprenticeship with the Parkhead Forge, the Royal School of Mines in South Kensington. On returning to Glasgow he persuaded his uncle to invest in open-hearth steel plant. Now in sole control of the firm, William expanded the business to meet new demands for steel from shipbuilders and railways during the mid-1880s and 1890s. He decided to venture into shipbuilding in 1899, and built a large new shipyard at Dalmuir on the lower Clyde. Lack of capital forced him to form a limited company which, in exchange for finance, gave control of the firm to Vickers, Son & Maxim. Beardmore remained chairman and managing director, though in 1907 (when he employed 4,500) had to share executive power with a Vickers nominee, until 1913, on account of shrinking profits. The First World War drastically altered the market situation: Beardmores produced 69 vessels (including a battleship and an aircraft carrier), 3,500 field guns, 650 planes and two airships. In the early war years the company's plants were the focus of labour unrest on the Clyde, with massive confrontations between the totally autocratic Sir William (he was made a baronet in 1914) and his workforce. The collapse of shipping and shipbuilding markets in the 1920s exposed Sir William's strategic weaknesses. He relied on bank borrowing and cost cutting to save his business. Neither could staunch his losses. Vickers sold the business to him in 1926 but the banks and the Treasury refused to extend their credit. Invernairn (he was raised to the peerage in 1921) was ousted from executive control and the company was reconstructed under the guidance of Montagu Norman (qv) Governor of the Bank of England. Beardmore married, in 1902, Elspeth, daughter of David Tullis, a leather merchant; there were no children. See *DSBB*; John R Hume and Michael S Moss, *Beardmore: The History of a Scottish Industrial Giant* (1979).

BEASLEY, Ammon
(25 November 1837 - 27 March 1924)

Railway manager, born at Bilton near Rugby, the son of Thomas Beasley, a shoe maker, and his wife Ann née Heritage. At an early age Beasley began work on the Great Western Railway at Wolverhampton, in the goods department under J Grierson. When Grierson was promoted to Paddington as chief of the goods department, Beasley moved with him as an assistant and succeeded his boss in 1863 when Grierson became general manager of the GWR. Beasley remained in charge of goods at Paddington for nearly thirty years, a valued executive frequently consulted by the GWR directors. In 1892 he accepted the post of general manager of the Taff Vale Railway, which ran between Cardiff and Merthyr Tydfil, servicing the Glamorgan coal and iron and steel industries. Beasley stayed until 1917 when he was elected deputy-chairman. By 1907 the company was employing just over 4,000 people. Dedicated to efficiency and an upholder of the Victorian rail-

way ethos, Beasley within six years made appreciable reductions in the TVR's overhead costs and by 1917 had almost doubled net revenue, although capital was increased by under 20 per cent. Under his regime the TVR's ordinary stock once more paid a 10 per cent dividend. Beasley achieved fame (or notoriety) in 1900 when he sued the Amalgamated Society of Railway Servants for damages incurred on the TVR by an eleven-day strike. The case went to the House of Lords which held the union responsible, leading to a fine of £23,000. In 1905 Beasley founded the Bristol Dockowners' Association in an attempt to cut down competition from the newly-opened port of Barry. He was married and had at least one son (later Judge Horace Owen Compton Beasley of the High Court of Burma) and three daughters. See *Contemporary Portraits and Biographies, Cardiff Section* (1898); *Western Mail*, 28 March, 1 April 1924.

BEATON, Neil Scobie
(18 August 1880 - 23 August 1960)

Scottish Co-operative Wholesale Society executive, born at Assynt, Sutherland, the son of a shepherd. Educated by a travelling schoolmaster, by 1897 he was working in the grocery trade in Edinburgh and was soon involved in his lifelong commitment to the co-operative movement. In 1919 he became propaganda agent for the SCWS and in five years established eight new retail societies. He was elected to the board in 1924 and devoted much effort to establishing co-operative branches in his native Highlands. From 1932 to 1946 he was president of the SCWS, a period which saw annual sales almost treble from £16 million to £44 million, and combined capital increase from £9 million to £24 million. While he greatly expanded the SCWS, both in geographical area and manufacturing/trading activity, he neglected opportunities to develop stores of the variety goods or wide-range departmental kind in the 1930s. Beaton married Martha Miller Hay: they had one son and two daughters. See *DSBB*.

BECK, Sir (Edgar) Philip
(9 August 1934 -)

Builder and construction company executive, the son of (Sir) Edgar Charles Beck (b 1911), an engineer and later chairman at John Mowlem & Co, and Mary Agnes Sorapure. The Beck's family links with Mowlem date from the 1920s when Philip's merchant banking grandfather was involved in persuading Mowlem, then nearly a hundred years old, to support an emerging scaffolding company, which was to become SGB. After Ampleforth College and Jesus College, Cambridge (MA in history), and National Service in the Life Guards,

Philip Beck worked on various Mowlem schemes around the world. He became a director of Mowlem in 1964 and succeeded his father as chairman in 1979. Recently Mowlem's projects have been widely spread and include: the building of private prisons, a turnkey project for the Docklands Light Railway, and a short take-off and landing airport in London's dockands (which has brought financial problems to the group). Mowlem's turnover in 1991 was £1,386 million (with a £1.5 million loss after tax) and the group employs 15,800. Beck was knighted in 1988. His brother is deputy chairman of Mowlem, having previously run SGB, which was brought into the group in 1986. In 1991 Beck married Bridget Cockerell née Heathcoat-Amory. He has two sons from a previous marriage to Thomasina Joanna Jeal.

BECKETT, Rupert Evelyn
(2 November 1870 - 25 April 1955)
Clearing banker, was born in Leeds, the third and youngest son of William Beckett (Denison) and Hon Helen Duncombe. Educated at Eton and Cambridge, at 19 he joined and gradually assumed control of the family's banking business, whose interests extended into transport and newspapers. In 1921 Beckett's was absorbed by the Westminster Bank, one of the Big Five, which was keen to expand in the North. In 1931 Beckett became chairman of the Westminster Bank, a post he held for twenty years: in that period the Bank's assets grew from £300 million to over £800 million. In 1947 he became chairman of the Committee of London Clearing Banks and of the British Bankers' Association. A Conservative, he eschewed a Parliamentary career, but served as a JP and DL of the West Riding. In 1896 he married Muriel Helen Florence (d 1941), daughter of Lord Berkeley Paget. He left £1,202,000 gross. See Theodore E. Gregory, *Westminster Bank through a Century* (1936); *DBB*.

BECKWITH, John (Lionel)
(19 March 1947 -)

BECKWITH, Peter (Michael)
(20 January 1945 -)
Property developers, the sons of Colonel Harold Beckwith, a Hong Kong army officer and a former Professor of Economics at Stanford, and Agnes née Duncan, from a prosperous Scottish family. John was born in Chelsea, London; Peter at Barsilly, near Delhi, India. Both were educated at Harrow. John was articled to accountants; Peter attended Emmanuel College, Cambridge, and then trained as a solicitor. In 1969 they set up Second London Wall, a property company, which in 1975 (after a

successful Scottish project) was renamed London & Edinburgh Trust. LET was floated in 1983 and shortly afterwards was one of the top five UK property companies. By mid-1989 LET was capitalised at £260 million and profits had soared from £1 million in 1982 to £50 million in 1988. The Beckwiths became disillusioned with the Stock Market in 1990 and sold their joint 29 per cent shareholding in LET to a Swedish company for £80 million - though both stayed on as jointchairmen to run it for the new owners. In 1990, in the midst of the property slump, LET's pre-tax profits fell by half. John married in 1975 Heather Marie Robbins, by whom he had two sons and one daughter; Peter married in 1968 Paula Gay Bateman: they have two daughters. See Judi Bevan and John Jay, *The New Tycoons* (1989).

BEDFORD, John
(16 January 1903 - 11 November 1980)
Head of department chain store, born in Birmingham, the son of John Bedford, a journeyman brass caster, and his wife Rosalind née Nicholls, he started work in a Birmingham department store, first as assistant, later as buyer. He joined Debenhams in 1932 as manager of a shop taken over in Stratford-upon-Avon. With the firm he moved to Yarmouth and, in 1938, Plymouth, to restore the finances of Spooners, a Debenham subsidiary. Wartime bombing, which destroyed Debenhams' premises, tested his organisational abilities and brought him to prominence in the city and in planning its reconstruction. He was promoted to Debenhams' main board in 1948 and moved to London. He quickly became joint managing director, deputy chairman (1954) and then chairman and managing director, 1956-70. By 1955 Debenhams employed 11,000. Under Bedford's direction the firm expanded massively, raising over £20 million capital to fund acquisitions (three or four firms a year) and the remodelling of stores to capture the popular end of the market. His attempts to introduce uniform branding and centralised buying took effect after his retirement in 1971. His main interest outside business was the Methodist Church. He married in 1927 Florence Mary, daughter of Aaron Illingworth Oddy; they had one daughter. See *DBB*.

BEECHING, Richard
Baron Beeching
(21 April 1913 - 23 March 1985)
Industrialist, born at Sheerness, Kent, the son of Hubert Josiah Beeching, a journalist, and his wife, Annie Twigg, a schoolmistress. Educated at Maidstone Grammar School and the Imperial College of Science & Technology, London (BSc,

physics, 1934; PhD, 1937), his early experience was with the Fuel Research Station at Greenwich and Mond Nickel. Beeching achieved prominence as deputy chief engineer of armaments at the Ministry of Supply's Fort Halstead. In 1948 he joined ICI, managing its fibres and metals divisions, before becoming an ICI technical director in 1957. Beeching's greatest renown (and notoriety) came with his next appointment as chairman of British Railways in 1963, when his report, 'The Re-shaping of British Railways', presented a reasoned and detailed account of rationalising the system with the proposed closure of 2,000 stations and the shedding of 70,000 jobs. The report caused a furore, though many of the changes were not implemented in full. But the Report, with Beeching's cost-conscious management style, succeeded in his aim of polarising the economic and social arguments about running 'British Rail' (the new name, coined in 1964) in an increasingly roads-dominated society. In 1965 he returned briefly to ICI as deputy chairman and was also in 1966 appointed chairman of the Royal Commission on Assizes and Quarter Sessions. After leaving ICI in 1970, he became chairman of Redland Ltd, remaining in an executive capacity until 1977; and was also chairman of Furness Withy, 1972-3. In 1938 he married Ella Margaret née Tiley: they had no children. Beeching was made a life peer in 1965. See Terry Gourvish, *British Railways, 1948-73: A Business History* (1986); *DNB*.

BEHARRELL, Sir George Edward
(26 May 1899 - 6 June 1972)

Rubber manufacturer, born in York, eldest son of John George Beharrell (qv), railway manager, and his wife Kate Ripley, he was educated at Wellingborough and briefly served in the Royal Engineers at the end of the First World War. His early career was spent in the shipping business, at home and in South Africa. In 1928 he joined Dunlop Rubber Co (of which his father was managing director) in the buying department, as assistant to the chief purchasing agent. After moving through all departments he was made director of equipment sales, responsible for dealing with car, cycle and aircraft manufacturers, in 1932. He moved to the firm's main board in 1942, becoming joint managing director in 1943, managing director in 1945, deputy chairman in 1949, and chairman in 1957, retiring in 1967. Under his leadership Dunlop Rubber reached a workforce in excess of 100,000 and 110 factories worldwide (including 51 in the UK) in 1961. Prominent in trade associations, he was knighted in 1961. His private interests included golf, art, economics, literature and gar-

dening. In 1921 he married Barbara, daughter of Walter Waddington; they had two sons and two daughters. See *The Times*, 7 June 1972.

BEHARRELL, Sir (John) George
(11 March 1873 - 20 February 1959)

Industrialist, born at Almondbury, near Huddersfield, the son of George Beharrell, a schoolmaster, and Elizabeth née Dalby. Educated at King James's School, Aldmondbury, then privately and at Leeds University, he joined the North Eastern Railway at York and by 1914 was assistant goods manager. Lloyd George appointed him to the Ministry of Munitions, where he worked in transportation with Sir Eric Geddes (qv). In 1919 he was Director-General of Finance & Statistics in the Ministry of Transport; and two years later he advised the Geddes 'axe' committee on public expenditure. In 1922 he joined the board of the Dunlop Rubber Co as managing director, after Geddes had been appointed chairman, and together they restructured and diversifield the group. After Geddes' death in 1937, Beharrell became Dunlop chairman, 1937-49, and then president, 1949-57. He was acknowledged as a spokesman for the rubber industry and held numerous posts, such as the presidency of the Institute of the Rubber Industry, 1933-6. He was also president of the FBI, 1932-33. He succeeded Geddes as chairman of Imperial Airways. Beharrell was knighted in 1919. He married in 1898 Kate née Ripley, by whom he had a daughter and three sons - one of whom, George (qv), succeeded him as managing director of Dunlop. See Keith Grieves, *Sir Eric Geddes: Business and Government in War and Peace* (1989).

BELLMAN, Sir Charles Harold
(19 March 1886 - 1 June 1963)

Building society manager, born in Paddington, one of three sons and four children of Charles Henry Bellman, a coachbuilder who had moved to London from Penzance, and his wife Ellen née Clemens, he attended a London Board school at Kilburn. Leaving at fourteen he was coached into passing the Railway Clearing House exams and worked there for the next fourteen years. During the First World War a medical condition kept him from active service and he worked in the Ministry of Munitions, rising to be an assistant commissioner. Meantime, like his father, he became an investing member of the Abbey Road & St John's Wood Building Society. He joined its board in 1918, became assistant secretary in 1920 and secretary in 1921. The Abbey Road, founded in 1875 by deacons and traders belonging to the Abbey Road Baptist Church, was fifteenth largest building society in the UK with assets of £1 million in 1921.

The interwar years favoured building societies, offering falling interest rates, strong demand for houses, rent restrictions on letting. Between 1919 and 1939 the assets of British building societies increased eleven times: the Abbey Road's increased sixty-seven times and by 1939 it was the second largest society in Britain. This achievement was largely due to Bellman. He vigorously advertised the society, bringing distinguished speakers like fellow Methodist Sir Josiah Stamp (qv) to AGMs, and wrote several books explaining and promoting the social benefits of property ownership. He built up a branch and agency network. He made it easier to buy a house by offering borrowers ways of meeting much of the 20 per cent of a house price that building societies would not normally fund, by means of an insurance policy or by a builders' pool. Further he worked to regulate the activities of building societies, of which there were nearly 900 in the early 1940s, and of builders. He was active in the National Association of Building Societies and its successor, the Building Societies Association; in setting up a Building Societies Status Enquiry Bureau, giving records on builders; in creating the Building Societies Institute; and in forming the National House Builders' Registration Council, in 1936. At the Abbey Road, Bellman became general manager in 1927, managing director in 1930 and chairman in 1937. He was responsible for moving headquarters from Finchley Road to new premises in Baker Street, in 1927. During the Second World War he decided that the future lay with big building societies and in 1944 he negotiated a merger with the National Building Society managed by Bruce Wycherley. Bellman became first chairman of the Abbey National and joint managing director, with Wycherley. He continued as chairman until his death but resigned as managing director in 1948. In 1944 the Abbey National had assets of £82 million (£49 million from the Abbey Road). Sir Harold Bellman (he was knighted in 1932) gave voluntary service to many causes, education and medicine most prominently. A strong Methodist (a lay preacher and a member of the Methodist conference), he met his wife, Kate Peacock, a fellow Sunday School teacher, at his Wesleyan chapel in Paddington. They married in 1911 and had two sons and a daughter. See Sir Harold Bellman, *Cornish Cockney: Reminiscences and Reflections* (1947); *DBB*.

BENNETT, Peter Frederick Blaker
Baron Bennett of Edgbaston
(16 April 1880 - 27 September 1957)
Industrialist, born at Dartford, Kent, the son of Frederick Charles Bennett, a carpenter, and his wife Annie Eliza née Blaker, he was educated at Five Ways Grammar School (part of the Edward VI Foundation), Birmingham, leaving to train in the Austin Motor Co. He joined the Electrical Ignition Co at Sparkbrook in 1903 and four years later formed his own company, Thomson-Bennett, backed by James Albert Thomson, a Scottish motor factor, making magnetos. Having survived against a virtual monopoly in the motor car market exercised by the German manufacturer Robert Bosch AG, Thomson-Bennett were the only British company making magnetos at the outbreak of war in 1914. In December that year they were acquired by Joseph Lucas Ltd, the large vehicle accessory manufacturer. Bennett became a Lucas director in 1916 and in 1919 joint managing director with Harry Lucas, son of Joseph Lucas, the firm's founder. Harry's son Oliver was joint managing director with Bennett from 1923 until his death in 1948, making a formidable partnership, with day-to-day management in the hands of Bertram Waring (qv), an accountant. Bennett was both joint managing director and chairman of Lucas from the early 1940s until 1951, returning in 1953 as joint managing director. Under the rearmament programme Lucas, a major supplier of electrical components, expanded rapidly, its workforce increasing from 20,000 in 1935 to 50,000 in 1939, easing back to 45,000 in 1955. Between the wars Bennett was an important, if low-profile, figure in British industry: president of Birmingham Chamber of Commerce, 1931-2; a British delegate to the Ottawa Conference on imperial tariffs in 1932; president of the Society of Motor Manufacturers and Traders, 1935-6; president of the Federation of British Industries, 1938-40 (and member of its Grand Council for thirty-seven years from 1917). During the Second World War he was Industrial Adviser to the Ministry of Supply, 1938-39; Director General of Tanks and Transport, 1939-40; and chairman of the Automatic Gun Board, 1941-44. Later he served on the Anglo-American Productivity Council and on several delegations sent to study American production methods. In addition, he was a director of ICI and of Lloyds Bank. Bennett succeeded Neville Chamberlain as MP (Conservative) for Edgbaston in 1940, retiring due to ill-health in 1953. He was Parliamentary Secretary at the Ministry of Labour, 1952-53. Knighted in 1941, Bennett was made a peer in 1953. A Methodist by upbringing and choice, he also gave much of his time to the Scouts and the YMCA. He married in 1905, Agnes, daughter of Joseph Palmer; there were no children. See Harold Nockolds, *Lucas: The First Hundred Years* (2 vols, 1976-78); *The Times*, 30 September 1957.

BENSON, Air Commodore Constantine Edward

(1895 - 20 September 1960)

Clothing company chairman and merchant banker, youngest son of Robert Henry Benson, merchant banker of Buckhurst, Sussex, he was educated at Eton and Balliol College, Oxford. During the First World War he served in the Grenadier Guards at Gallipoli and in France, winning the DSO. Afterwards he became a partner in the family firm of Robert Benson & Co (later Robert Benson, Lonsdale & Co; and then Kleinwort Benson) and then director of Lonsdale Investment Trust (the parent company), Lloyds Bank and Montague Burton Ltd. He succeeded Sir Montague Burton (qv) as chairman of Burtons, the clothing manufacturer and retailer, in 1952, coincidentally following a sudden collapse in wool prices. This forced the firm to write down its stock by 1.6 million and Benson to find new management talent by taking over Jackson the Tailor Ltd and gaining its two joint managing directors, Sidney and Lionel Jacobson (qv). They sold off the cloth manufacturing operations and concentrated on clothing manufacture and retailing. By 1958 Lionel Jacobson was chairman, running the firm until the Ralph Halpern (qv) era of the 1970s-1980s. Benson joined the Auxiliary Air Force prior to 1939 and during the Second World War attained his highest military rank, commanding the Eighth Army's branch of the Allied Military Government. He married in 1921 Lady Morvyth Lillian Ward, daughter of the 2nd Earl of Dudley; they had one daughter. See Eric M Sigsworth, *Montague Burton the Tailor of Taste* (1990); *The Times*, 22, 27, 28 September, 19 October 1960.

BERNARD, Sir Dallas Gerald Mercer

(22 March 1888 - 26 November 1975)

Merchant banker and industrialist, son of Edmund Bowen Bernard, JP of Snakemoor, Botley, Hampshire, he entered HMS *Britannia* but was invalided out of the Navy while still a midshipman and went into commerce. Moving up the ranks of Jardine, Matheson & Co, leading Asian merchants, he became managing director in 1922 and then chairman of the Hong Kong & Shanghai Banking Corporation in 1924. Two years later he was elected to the Executive Council of Hong Kong. He returned to England in the mid-1930s. He was director of the Bank of England, 1936-49, and the Bank's Deputy Governor, 1949-54. Bernard was chairman of the British Bank of the Middle East, 1954-65, director of the Commonwealth Development Finance Co and chairman of the Jordan Currency Board. Sir John Hanbury

Williams in 1954 recruited him to Courtaulds board on which he served as deputy chairman, 1954-62, and chairman, 1962-4. He was 'caretaker' at the helm of Courtaulds during difficult years: when a takeover bid from ICI was successfully repulsed and a new generation of technically-skilled directors led by the 'tempestuous and ambitious' Frank Kearton (qv) succeeded to power. Bernard was made a baronet in 1954. A Christian Scientist, Bernard strongly supported the YWCA. He married, in 1922, Betty, eldest daughter of Sir Charles Addis; they had one son and two daughters. See D C Coleman, *Courtaulds: An Economic and Social History* vol 3 (1980); *The Times*, 27 November, 3, 6 December 1975.

BERNSTEIN, Sidney Lewis

Baron Bernstein of Leigh

(30 January 1899 - 5 February 1993)

Television entrepreneur, born in Ilford, Essex, into a large Jewish family headed by Alexander Bernstein, quarry and cinema chain owner and property dealer from Sweden, and his wife Jane, daughter of Russian immigrants. He grew up in Ilford and then Cricklewood, leaving school at fifteen to enter his father's cinema business. At twenty-two he inherited the family's four cinemas, just as 'talkie' technology arrived. Tall, elegant, forceful and energetic, Bernstein during the interwar years expanded his cinema business, went into theatre management and film making, and found his political bearings. He merged his chain (named Granada in fond memory of walking holidays in Spain) with Gaumont British, becoming managing director. Then, starting in 1930 at Dover, he opened a number of giant Granada cinemas seating thousands. He carried out market research on his audiences, pioneered Saturday morning shows for children, and campaigned for Sunday opening. In 1927 he put on a season of plays at the Court Theatre and in 1930 built the Phoenix Theatre in the West End, opening with the first production of Noel Coward's *Private Lives*. He was a founder in 1924 of the Film Society, which gave British audiences a chance to see the work of Soviet film directors. During the Second World War Bernstein was film adviser to the Ministry of Information and from 1944 head of the psychological warfare division attached to Supreme Headquarters Allied Expeditionary Force, bringing over his friend Alfred Hitchcock to make several films. In the late 1940s Bernstein and Hitchcock formed a production company, Transatlantic Pictures, which made a number of Hitchcock films. After the setting up of the Independent Television Authority in 1954, Bernstein overcame his original opposition to commercial television and formed a company, Granada

(TV Network) Ltd (a wholly owned subsidiary of his Granada Theatres Ltd), which was awarded one of the first television franchises. Bernstein chose the north of England as his region after looking at two maps, he claimed, one showing population density, the other, rainfall. Based in Manchester, Granada began transmitting on 3 May 1956, its output strongly shaped by Bernstein. He advocated quality but eschewed the over-academic; he approved social documentaries but detested the sensationalising or vulgarising of issues; though not a northerner, he sought programmes reflecting the culture and talent of the region. Two programmes achieving large audiences and most reflecting his influence were the enormously successful *Coronation Street*, a soap opera set in Salford which was first shown in 1960 and still runs; and *World in Action*, a trenchant current affairs series. Although Granada TV had some difficult early months, it was soon highly profitable. Bernstein retired from the chairmanship of Granada TV in 1969. He remained chairman of the Granada Group Ltd until 1979. Television made less than 20 per cent of the group's profits, the rest coming from the activities into which Bernstein had diversified since the early 1930s: theatres, publishing, television rental, bingo, bowling alleys and motorway services. A member of the Labour Party since his teens, Bernstein was made a life peer in 1969 under the Wilson government. Bernstein's first marriage to a *Daily Express* journalist, Zoe Farmer, was dissolved; in 1954 he married Sandra Malone, a Canadian, by whom he had a son and two daughters. See Bernard Sendall, *Independent Television in Britain* (2 vols, 1982-83); *The Times*, 6 February 1993.

BERRY, James Gomer
1st Viscount Kemsley of Dropmore
(7 May 1883 - 6 February 1968)
Newspaper proprietor, born in Merthyr Tydfil, third son of John Mathias Berry, an estate agent, and his wife Mary Ann née Rowe, he was educated at Merthyr and in 1901 joined his elder brother William Ewart Berry (qv) in London. For 35 years they built up an integrated printing and publishing empire, including the network of provincial newspapers being run by Allied Newspapers Ltd formed in 1924. When the Berry-Iliffe (Sir Edward Iliffe had joined in 1920) partnership amicably dissolved in 1937, Lord Kemsley (Gomer Berry was made a baronet in 1928, a baron in 1936 and a viscount in 1945) took Allied Newspapers and the *Sunday Times*. Allied Newspapers was one of the two largest chains of provincial newspapers in Britain, the other belonging to Harold Harmsworth, Lord Rothermere (qv). Strongest in Manchester, Glasgow, Cardiff, Tyneside and Sheffield, Allied

Newspapers by 1947 had a combined morning circulation of 2.1 million, an evening circulation of 1.36 million and a Sunday circulation of 5.67 million. Kemsley was attacked by witnesses before the Royal Commission on the Press in 1947-48 but no proof emerged that he was ever issuing political directives to his editors. Kemsley was most passionately devoted to the *Sunday Times* but by the 1950s other parts of his group were showing signs of the proprietor's neglect. He began selling his holdings in 1952, disposing of the bulk (including the *Sunday Times*) to Roy Thomson (qv) for about £5 million in 1959. An arriviste, Kemsley had an exaggerated respect for the elements and inhabitants of upper class culture. He married twice: in 1907, to Mary Lilian née Holmes (d 1928), by whom he had six sons and a daughter; and, in 1931, to Edith née du Plessis. Though his four surviving sons worked under Kemsley, all preferred to be rentiers rather than entrepreneurial newspaper proprietors ruling a problematic empire and facing heavy death duties. Kemsley regretted having sold his newspapers and retired to Monte Carlo where he died. See *DBB*.

BERRY, William Ewart
1st Viscount Camrose of Hackwood Park
(23 June 1879 - 15 June 1954)
Newspaper proprietor, second of the three sons of John Mathias Berry, a Merthyr Tydfil estate agent, and his wife Mary Ann née Rowe, he left school at fourteen and became a junior reporter on the *Merthyr Times*. After five years working on newspapers in South Wales he moved to London in 1898, again as a newspaper reporter. There he spotted a market opportunity and in 1901, with a £100 loan from his elder brother Henry Seymour Berry (1877-1928; from 1926, Baron Buckland of Bwlch), he launched the *Advertising World*, a weekly designed to promote advertising as a subject. So successful was it that Bill Berry summoned his younger brother, James Gomer Berry (qv), to London to help him. Thus began a thirty-five year partnership, with Bill working on the editorial, Gomer on the commercial side. They acquired the *Sunday Times*, their first newspaper, for £80,000 in 1915; the *Financial Times* in 1919; Kelly's Directories in 1920 (a deal which brought Sir Edward Iliffe into their partnership); the Hulton papers, for £5.5 million from Harold Harmsworth, Lord Rothermere, in 1924, a business which they formed Allied Newspapers Ltd to run; the Amalgamated Press (including the Imperial Paper Mills), for £8 million, again from Rothermere, in 1926; the Lloyd paper mills in Kent, for £3.2 million, in 1927; and, later that year, the *Daily*

Telegraph, a serious daily with a dwindling circulation of 84,000, for £1.2 million. With such a powerful vertically-integrated group of national and provincial newspapers and magazines, the two Berry brothers ranked alongside Max Aitken (qv) and the Harmsworths (qv). However, the partnership broke up amicably in 1937. Camrose (Bill Berry was knighted in 1921, made a peer in 1929 and elevated to viscount in 1941) took the Daily Telegraph, the Financial Times and the Amalgamated Press. He invested much effort in building up the Daily Telegraph, the circulation figures of which reached 750,000 in 1939 and one million in 1947. Aiming to make his paper one that presented facts rather than party propaganda, he personally earned Churchill's admiration and Hitler's enmity. Camrose daily attended his fifth floor offices in the paper's Fleet Street building (constructed in 1930) until shortly before his death. Camrose wrote two studies of British newspapers, London Newspapers: Their Owners and Controllers (1939) and British Newspapers and Their Controllers (1947). Tall, handsome, elegant, he avoided abuses of editorial power but allowed a stifling paternalism to develop which contributed to the family's loss of the Daily Telegraph proprietorship under his son Michael (qv). Long mindful of his Welsh and Nonconformist roots, Camrose gave generously to causes in Merthyr and the National Museum of Wales; and later to Eton College (which educated his sons) and Chartwell (Churchill's home). William Berry married, in 1905, Mary Agnes née Corns; they had four sons and four daughters. See Duff Hart-Davis, The House the Berrys Built: Inside the Daily Telegraph, 1928-1986 (1990); Lord Hartwell, William Camrose: Giant of Fleet Street (1992).

BERRY, The Honourable (William) Michael
Baron Hartwell of Peterborough Court in the City of London
(18 May 1911 -)
Newspaper proprietor, second son of William Ewart Berry (qv), 1st Viscount Camrose, and Mary Agnes, eldest daughter of Thomas Corns, he was educated at Eton and Christ Church, Oxford, and began work on one of his father's provincial newspapers, the Aberdeen Evening Express. After reporting and sub-editing on two other Scottish provincial papers Michael Berry edited the Sunday Mail, Glasgow, 1934-35, and was managing editor of the Financial Times, 1937-39. After the Second World War, in which he reached the rank of lieutenant colonel and assistant economic adviser to the Fifth Corps, he returned to the family newspaper business, and wrote a book, Party Choice (1948). On

the death of his father in 1954 he succeeded as chairman of Amalgamated Press Ltd, a firm then employing 10,500, and editor-in-chief of the Daily Telegraph which with a circulation figure of over a million was the largest serious daily in the UK. As editor-in-chief, Lord Hartwell (he was created a life peer in 1968) preserved his inheritance all too faithfully: the old paternalistic structure induced sycophancy and isolated him from realities below his fifth floor office. Here management structures were subordinated to editorial priorities and disconnected from prudent commercial policies and practices. Further, the Daily Telegraph, like the rest of Fleet Street, was riddled by the extortionate behaviour of the print unions. The situation was exacerbated by Hartwell's personality and predilections. A very shy man, he found communication difficult and, despite his PPE degree under Roy Harrod, he neglected commercial controls, much preferring his editorial role. 'I was always terribly shocked when other people ran their newspapers like biscuit factories, just to make money,' he once said. When, in 1983, it was decided to move to new printing plants at Trafford Park, Manchester, and West Ferry Road in the East End of London, the need for new capital exposed the Daily Telegraph's true position. From this predicament Hartwell was rescued in 1985-86 by the Canadian businessman Conrad Black, but it cost him and his family their proprietorship of the Daily Telegraph. Michael Berry married in 1936, Lady Pamela Margaret Elizabeth Smith (d 1982), younger daughter of the 1st Earl of Birkenhead, by whom he had two sons; in her time she was a very active society hostess. See Duff Hart-Davis, The House the Berrys Built: Inside the Telegraph, 1928-1986 (1990).

BIGGAM, Sir Robin Adair
(8 July 1938 -)
Industrialist, born in Lanark, the son of Thomas Biggam, who worked for the British Linen Bank, and his wife Eileen. Educated at Lanark Grammar School, he trained as a chartered accountant with Peat, Marwick Mitchell, 1960-63. He worked for ICI between 1964 and 1981 in the fibres division and was soon made a director, working alongside Sir John Harvey-Jones (qv). He then joined the ailing ICL, the largest indigenous UK computer manufacturer, as finance director. Alongside the managing director, Robb Wilmot, and Peter Bonfield (qv), Biggam helped restore ICL's profitability by 1982. After a spell at Dunlop, 1984-85, and Trafalgar House, he joined BICC Ltd as managing director in 1986. He was appointed chief executive in 1987 and succeeded Sir William Barlow as chairman in January 1992. The group included the leading cable maker in the UK (BICC Cables), a major

cables division in America, the Balfour Beatty construction division, and one of Australia's leading industrial groups (Metals Manufactures). In 1991 BICC's turnover was £3,790 million (pre-tax profit £81 million). Biggam is also a non-executive director of Redland. He was a founder member of the SDP and was knighted in 1993. He married in 1962 Elizabeth McArthur McDougall: they have a son and two daughters. See Martin Campbell-Kelly, *ICL: A Business and Technical History* (1989).

BIRCH, Peter (Gibbs)
(4 December 1937 -)
Building society executive, the son of a West Country chemist, who rose to prominence in the Robertson jam company. Educated at Allhallows School, Devon, he did his National Service in Jamaica and then joined Nestlé in 1958 on the marketing side. In 1965 he joined the safety-razor firm, Gillette, eventually becoming managing director of Gillette UK in 1981. In 1984 he became chief executive of the Abbey National Building Society. He is also a director of Hoskyns, Argos and Scottish Mutual Assurance and served as chairman of the Council of Mortgage Lenders, 1991-92. He married in 1962 Gillian née Benge: they have three sons and one daughter. See Barry Ritchie, *A Key to the Door: The Abbey National Story* (1990).

BIRKIN, Sir (John) Derek
(30 September 1929 -)
Metals and minerals mining executive, the son of Noah and Rebecca Birkin. Educated at Hemsworth Grammar School he held a string of managing directorships between 1966 and 1975 at Velmar, Nairn Williamson and Tunnel Holdings, becoming chairman of the latter, 1975-82. He joined the Rio Tinto Zinc Corporation in 1982, becoming chief executive and deputy chairman between 1985 and 1991. Birkin pursued RTZ's proven and successful policy of expansion into large-scale, capital intensive natural resource projects - most notably in RTZ's acquisition in 1989 of BP minerals for £2.6 billion. Under Birkin RTZ became one of the largest producers of gold outside South Africa; besides producing over half the world's borates, nearly a third of its titanium dioxide feedstock, and a substantial share of its zircon, diamonds and uranium. Birkin was appointed chairman of RTZ in 1991. In that year turnover was £4,885 million, with pre-tax profits of £562 million (a fall from 1989, when the figures were £6,156 and £1,104, respectively); and the RTZ Group employed over 73,000 workers (14,000 in the UK). Birkin is also a director of George Wimpey, Rio Algom Ltd (Canada), The

Merchants Trust, British Steel and Barclays. He was a member of the Review Body on Top Salaries, 1986-9. Birkin was knighted in 1990. In 1952 he married Sadie Smith: they have a son and daughter.

BIRRELL, Sir (James Drake) 'Jim'
(18 August 1933 -)
Building society executive, born and brought up in Yorkshire, the second of three children of James Russell Birrell and Edith Marion Birrell, both of whom were schoolteachers. Educated at Belle Vue Grammar School, Bradford, he declined the chance to go up to university and instead followed the example of an uncle, who was an accountant. In 1949 he was articled to Boyce Welch & Co and qualified as a chartered accountant in 1955. After RAF service between 1955 and 1957, he joined Price, Waterhouse in the first of several accountancy jobs. In 1968 he joined the Halifax Building Society as a chartered accountant. He gradually worked his way up - via an advanced management training programme at Harvard in 1986 - to become chief executive at the Halifax in 1988. He headed the biggest building society in the world, with an asset base of about £60 billion (when Birrell joined it was £1.3 billion), holding the savings of 15 million customers, catering for 1.8 million borrowers, and providing 20 per cent of mortgages. He retired in 1993, when he was knighted. He married in 1958 Margaret Anne Pattison: they have two daughters.

BIRTWISTLE, Albert
(10 June 1849 - after 1917)
Cotton spinner and manufacturer, born at Great Harwood, Blackburn, son of William Birtwistle JP, cotton spinner, and his wife Rachel, he was educated at Rotherham, Whalley Grammar School and Frankfurt am Main before entering the family firm and succeeding his father. By 1907 Birtwistle & Fielding were the largest millowners and manufacturers in Blackburn, employing 5,000. An Anglican and a JP, Albert Birtwistle belonged to the Reform Club in Manchester, the Union in Blackburn and Pleasington Golf Club. He married in 1881 Annie Mary, niece of the late James Astley JP of Beardwood Hall, Blackburn. They had at least four sons. See W Ralph Hall Caine, *Lancashire Biographies Rolls of Honour* (1917); W B Tracy and W T Pike, *Lancashire at the Opening of the Twentieth Century* (1903).

BIRTWISTLE, Brigadier-General Arthur
(29 May 1877 - 12 May 1937)
Cotton manufacturer, eldest son of William Birtwistle JP, founder of William Birtwistle Allied

Mills, he entered the family firm and before the First World War succeeded his father in charge of a group of cotton mills in Blackburn, Preston and outlying districts, with 5,000 looms and over 150,000 spindles in Blackburn alone. After the First World War (in which he served with the 1st East Lancashire Brigade of the Royal Field Artillery) he sat on the council of the British Cotton Growing Association and took titular offices with the local branches of the British Legion, the YMCA and the Playing Fields Association. He and his father were benefactors of Blackburn Cathedral. A founder member of the Council of Social Service, Arthur Birtwistle promoted the allotments movement as a remedy for unemployment. He married, in 1906, Alice, daughter of W Hillmen, by whom he had a son and a daughter. See *Northern Daily Telegraph*, 13 May 1937.

BISHOP, Sir Michael (David)
(10 February 1942 -)
Airline operator, born at Bowdon, Cheshire, the son of Clyde Leonard Bishop and Lilian née Frost. After attending Mill Hill School, he declined the chance to run his father's Manchester engineering company and joined the airline industry in 1963, when he set up an aircraft handling business at Manchester Airport for Mercury Airlines (which was taken over in 1964 by British Midland). At 27 he was effectively running British Midland Airways for the City firm Minster Assets. In 1978, with the help of a rich American dentist, he bought them out for £1.8 million in one of the first management buy-outs. Bishop became chairman and the biggest shareholder. In 1988 the Scandinavian airline, SAS, bought a 25 per cent stake in British Midland for £25 million, valuing the company at £100 million, and leaving Bishop very wealthy. The following year he had to deal with the Kegworth air crash, which killed 47 British Midland passengers. By 1991 Bishop's blend of conservatism and opportunism had made British Midland the UK's second largest domestic airline, with more take-off and landing slots at Heathrow than any other airline except British Airways. BM carries 6 million passengers yearly, with annual sales of £400 million, and 4,000 staff. Bishop is also chairman of Channel 4 TV. A bachelor, he supports the D'Oyly Carte Opera and inner-city projects in Birmingham. His 58 per cent stake in BM was worth an estimated £96 million in 1992. Created CBE in 1986, he was knighted in 1991. See Bill Gunston, *Diamond Flight* (1988).

BLAKENHAM, Michael John Hare
2nd Viscount Blakenham of Little Blakenham
(25 January 1938 -)
Industrialist, the son of the first Viscount Blakenham (1911-82) and Hon Beryl Nancy Pearson, the daughter of the Second Viscount Cowdray (whose father, Weetman Dickinson Pearson (qv), had built up the building and contracting group of the same name). Educated at Eton, Blakenham took an engineering apprenticeship, then read economics at Harvard University. After experience with Lazards and the Standard Industrial Group (which in the late 1960s was acquired by Pearson's), he worked in different parts of the Pearson group, such as Royal Doulton and Longman, before becoming a director in 1971. In 1983 he became chairman of Pearson - in which the family own a large, but not controlling equity - and was also managing director after 1986. Pearson's most profitable activities are in publishing (for example, it owns the *Financial Times* and Longman), but it also has interests in oil services, investment banking (Lazards) and fine china (Doulton). Blakenham followed the third Lord Cowdray in concentrating on well-defined sectors. In 1984 he reduced the Pearson holding in Lazards from 79 per cent to 50 per cent, sold off the group's minor engineering interests in 1986, ended its oil exploration activities in 1989, and instead in 1987 bought the US publisher Addison-Wesley and expanded into entertainment (Chessington Zoo, Tussaud's and B Sky B). In 1991 turnover was £1,600 million (pre-tax profit £173 million) and the workforce was 28,000 (17,927 in the UK). Blakenham is a director of Sotheby's, Elsevier NV and MEPC; and was chairman of the Royal Society for the Protection of Birds, 1981-6. In 1965 he married Marcia Persephone, the daughter of the Hon Alan Hare: they have one son and two daughters.

BLANK, (Maurice) Victor
(9 November 1942 -)
Banking executive, born in Stockport, the son of Joseph Blank, a gentleman's outfitter, and Ruth née Levey. Educated at Stockport Grammar School, he read history at St Catherine's College, Oxford. His earliest business venture in his twenties was Operation Match, the UK's first computer dating agency, launched with a friend, Andrew Balcombe. In 1964 Blank was articled to the London law firm Clifford-Turner (now Clifford Chance) and was a partner at twenty-six. As a solicitor to the likes of Jim Slater (qv), Blank gained experience very quickly (he co-authored a book on take-overs with his friend, (Sir) Mark Weinberg

(qv)). In 1981 he joined Charterhouse Bank as head of corporate finance and was appointed chief executive in 1985, when Charterhouse was bought by the Royal Bank of Scotland for £150 million. Blank enhanced the standing of Charterhouse, bringing it into prominence with its funding of the buyout of Woolworth from its US parent (a deal which brought him £8 million from a personal stake in the venture, now known as Kingfisher). Blank became chairman of Charterhouse in 1991 and two years later he concluded the deal which saw the controlling interest of the Bank pass to a group of French and German bankers for £25 million (with the Royal Bank of Scotland retaining a 10 per cent stake). He married in 1977 Sylvia Helen née Richford: they have two sons and one daughter. See M V Blank and Mark Wienberg, *Take-Overs and Mergers* (1962, 4th edition, 1980).

BLYTH, Sir James
(8 May 1940 -)
Industrialist, the son of Daniel Blyth and Jane Power Carlton. Educated at Spiers School and Glasgow University, he worked for the Mobil Oil Co, General Foods and Mars between 1963 and 1974. In 1974 he joined Lucas as a director and general manager, working in its batteries and aerospace divisions. Between 1981 and 1985, he was head of defence sales for the Ministry of Defence, before becoming managing director of Plessey's in 1986. In 1987 he became director and chief executive of Boots. Since Blyth took over, Boots' turnover has increased from £2,351 million to £3,565 million, pre-tax profits from £242 million to £358 million, and the workforce has reached over 83,000. Although it is a pharmaceutical manufacturer and has high hopes with a new heart drug Manoplax, most of Boots' success comes from its famous Chemists' stores. By 1992 it had over 1000 stores, generating (with the aid of the latest checkout information technology) £228 million in pre-tax profits (a compound annual growth rate of 25 per cent over the preceding four years). Blyth's £900 million purchase in 1989 of the Ward White businesses (Payless, Halford and A. G. Stanley), however, has proved less happy: by 1992 it was making losses. Blyth is also non-executive director of Imperial Group, Cadbury-Schweppes, and British Aerospace. Knighted in 1985, he became a governor of the London Business School in 1987. In 1967 he married Pamela Anne Campbell Dixon: they have one daughter (one son deceased).

BONFIELD, Peter (Leahy)
(3 June 1944 -)
Computer company executive, born in Baldock, Hertfordshire, the son of George and Patricia Bonfield. His father was an engineer for the computer firm ICL; his Welsh mother was a nurse. Educated at Hitchin Boys Grammar School, he studied engineering at Loughborough University (BTech Hons) and joined Texas Instruments in 1981. He transferred to the Dallas headquarters and then became a director of their European marketing operations. In 1981 he was invited by Robb Wilmot - an old colleague from Texas Instruments and managing director of the UK computer firm, ICL - to join the latter as a director of marketing. Bonfield assisted Wilmot and Robin Biggam (qv) in rescuing ICL from the doldrums (it was virtually bankrupt by 1981 and dependent on government support) and by 1984 they had restored its profitability. In 1984 the STC Group took over ICL and Bonfield became chairman and managing director in the following year (and deputy chief executive in 1987) of the resulting STC International Computers. STC ICL boosted the profits and turnover of its parent (usually contributing about 60 per cent): in 1990 pre-tax profits of the computer division were down 26 per cent to £110 million on a static turnover of £1.6 billion - an excellent performance in a poor economic climate. But the parent company was in poorer shape and in 1990 the Japanese computer manufacturer, Fujitsu, bought an 80 per cent stake in ICL for £748 million. Bonfield, who with Wilmot, had negotiated an important technology exchange deal in 1981, backed the takeover and in 1990 he became chairman and chief executive of ICL. In 1991 ICL's turnover was £1,875 million (pre-tax profit £62 million) and it employed nearly 23,000, making it the fourth biggest computer company in Europe. Bonfield was made a CBE in 1989. In 1968 he married Josephine Houghton. See Martin Campbell-Kelly, *ICL: A Business and Technical History* (1989).

BONSOR, Sir Henry Cosmo Orme
(2 September 1848 - 4 December 1929)
Brewer, born at Great Bookham, near Dorking, son of Joseph Bonsor 'gentleman' and Eliza Denne née Orme, he was educated at Eton, and joined Combe & Co, brewers, in 1867. Within a decade he was running the firm. Twenty years later he took it to a position of dominance alongside Bass and Guinness when in 1898 he forged the merged business of Watney, Combe & Reid Co Ltd. Bonsor was its chairman 1898-1928. Like some other mergers of the day the constituent firms over-valued themselves (to the benefit of their family owners) and saddled the new business with an inflated capital, of £15 million in Watney, Combe & Reid's case. This, together with a relative decline in the alcoholic drinks market until the

1940s, produced disappointing profits. As chairman and treasurer of the National Trade Defence Association, 1888-95, Bonsor moulded extra-parliamentary agitation on behalf of the drink trade against government interference. He was a leading figure in the formation of the Brewers' Society in 1904 and president of the Institute of Brewing from 1904. His wider business commitments included directorships of the Bank of England and the South Eastern Railway Co. A Conservative, he was MP for Wimbledon, 1885-1900, and was made a baronet in 1925. He married twice: first, in 1872, to Emily Gertrude, daughter of James Fellowes, by whom he had three sons and four daughters; and secondly, in 1886, to Mabel, daughter of James Brand. See *DBB*.

BOOT, Jesse
1st Baron Trent of Nottingham
(2 June 1850 - 13 June 1931)

Manufacturing and retail chemist, born at Nottingham, only son of John Boot, a medical herbalist and Wesleyan lay preacher, and his second wife Mary née Wills, he attended a local school but had to leave when he was ten following the death of his father. He helped his mother and sister working in a small herbalist shop. In 1874 he began selling proprietary medicines at cut prices, advertising in local newspapers from 1877. New premises were built in Goosegate, Nottingham in 1883 and branches were formed in Lincoln, Sheffield and other large places within a short train journey away. Opposition to general retailers like Boot dispensing medicines came from the Pharmaceutical Society. Their unsuccessful case, heard in the Lords, brought the ruling that limited companies could employ qualified pharmacists: a decision that prompted Boot in 1883 to turn his business into a limited liability company. Boot formed a manufacturing department (starting production in 1885) in Nottingham; by 1898 it employed 542 people. Simultaneously he extended his retail network, up to 33 shops in 1893 and 126 in 1897. He went into partnership with James Duckworth of Rochdale, a Methodist tea dealer, which gave Boot a chain of shops in Lancashire. He acquired William Day's drug store chains in London and the south of England, 65 shops, which gave Boot 251 branches in 1901. By 1914 Jesse Boot had 560 retail branches owned by the several companies he established and controlled. From his late forties rheumatoid arthritis progressively paralysed Jesse Boot. Carried everywhere, he retired at the end of the First World War to Jersey, where he had met and married his wife, Florence Anne née Rowe, in 1886 (on a recuperative holiday following his nervous breakdown). While his wife played a major role in

developing the fancy goods, books and stationery side of the retail stores, she, their son, John Campbell Boot (qv), and two daughters did not share the asceticism that illness induced in Jesse Boot. He feared that when he died they would get control of his business and fritter it away in riotous living. In 1920, therefore, he sold his interest to the American Louis Kroh Liggett, founder of the Rexall drug business, for £2.275 million. Most of this money he gave to his native city to provide parks, boulevards and hospital wards, but chiefly to establish a university college housed in impressive buildings on parkland outside Nottingham. When this was opened by King George V in 1928, Jesse Boot was created a baron (he was knighted in 1909 and made a baronet in 1916, for gifts to the Liberal party). See Stanley Chapman, *Jesse Boot of Boots the Chemist* (1974); *DBB*.

BOOT, John Campbell
2nd Baron Trent
(19 January 1889 - 8 March 1956)

Manufacturing and retail chemist, the only son of Jesse Boot (1850-1931) - 1st Lord Trent and founder of the famous Boots Pure Drug Co - and Florence Ann née Rowe. Educated at the Leys School and Jesus College, Cambridge (for a year only, since he ran away to Vancouver), he was a playboy before the First World War, during which he served as an army captain in France. The new American owners made him a director in 1920 (much to his father's chagrin) along with J E Greenwood and sent him to the USA to learn the Liggett system of merchandise control. On returning to Nottingham he chaired the retail executive of the company. J C Boot was chairman from 1926 to 1954: he expanded Boots, while maintaining its reputation for quality, and the firm's ownership was eventually repatriated in 1933 from Liggett's. Aided by Greenwood (from whom he became estranged) and increasingly by John Savage (qv), Boots under the 2nd Lord Trent largely followed the policies laid down by his father. A Liberal in politics, Boot was a paternalist (he was chairman of the Council of the Industrial Welfare Society, 1945-52) and a member of the Church of England (though he was initially a Nonconformist). Created a baronet in 1916, a KBE in 1954, Boot succeeded to his father's title in 1931. In lifestyle, Trent was a complete contrast to his father. He relished enormously the riches and distinction of heading a hugely successful firm. On the 45,000-acre estate his mother had bought him soon after his father's death he played the Scottish laird: hunting, shooting, fishing and farming and reading romantic tales of Scotland. And he enjoyed being a public figure. He was first Chancellor of the University of Nottingham, 1948-

54. He married in 1914 Margaret Joyce Pyman: they had four daughters. See Stanley D Chapman, *Jesse Boot of Boots the Chemist* (1974); *DBB* (Jesse Boot).

BOWATER, Sir Eric (Frederic) Vansittart
(16 January 1895 - 30 August 1962)

Paper manufacturer, born at Beckenham, Kent, the second of five children of (Sir) Frederick Bowater (1867-1924) and Alice née Sharp. Educated at Charterhouse, he was invalided out of the army during the First World War, but began to prove himself in the family paper business, founded by his grandfather. After 1924 he helped bring the firm's new production facilities on-line at Northfleet and emerged as head of the company in 1927. He then embarked on an unprecedented expansion before 1940: in partnership with Lords Rothermere and Beaverbrook (qqv), he doubled Northfleet's capacity; took over from the Berry brothers (qv) the largest newsprint business in Europe, Edward Lloyd Ltd; and gained control of a mill at Corner Brook in Newfoundland. The expansion was based on the risky strategies of allowing control of Bowater's to pass (temporarily) to Rothermere and by heavy borrowing. In the 1950s Bowater benefited from the massive demand for newsprint, taking the opportunity this offered to diversify into packaging, paper towels and tissues, to expand further overseas with an American mill, and even to set up the firm's own steamship company. Between 1951 and 1960 sales increased from £54 million to £142 million and pre-tax profits from £8.8 million to £15.7 million. But by 1960 (when the firm employed over 23,000) a more depressed market brought a cash crisis at Bowater's at the end of Sir Eric's career. He was knighted in 1944. Bowater married first, in 1915, Blanche Currie née de Ville, by whom he had a daughter; and secondly in 1937 after a divorce, Margaret Perkins, by whom he had a son. Eric Bowater left £495,181 gross. See William J. Reader, *Bowater: A History* (1981); *DBB*; *DNB*.

BOWMAN, Sir James
(8 March 1898 - 25 September 1978)

Nationalised coal industry chairman, born at Great Corby near Carlisle, third of five sons of Robert James Bowman, a blacksmith, and Mary née Murray, he served with the Royal Marines in the First World War. Afterwards he became a coal-miner at Ashington, Northumberland, rising in the 1920s to the position of inspector and first full-time trade union official at Ashington. In July 1939 he was elected vice-president of the Miners' Federation of Great Britain and was re-elected unchallenged of it and of its successor from 1945, the National Union of Mineworkers, until 1949. In the trade union and labour movement he had enormous influence outside the mining industry. Sitting on the Coal Production Council during the Second world War, he was a fierce proponent of coal-mine nationalisation. This was secured in 1946 but labour unrest continued, stirred by postwar coal shortages, a severe winter in 1947 and the upheavals following nationalisation. When the NCB was reorganised in 1949 Bowman (a member of the TUC General Council 1945-49) was appointed chairman of its Northern Division. He became chairman of the NCB in 1956, boss of 700,000 employees: making Bowman with Citrine (qv) one of the few individuals in modern times in Britain to cross from union leadership to the chairmanship of a major employer. During his five years in office Bowman successfully reversed the NCB's policy from raising production and manpower to reducing production without damaging the mining community or losing efficiency. This was achieved by improvements in marketing, coal-mining technology and industrial relations. A skilled, patient and firm union leader, Bowman proved invaluable when, on the management side, he personally led negotiations with the trade unions, calling them to greater reasonableness with his plain speaking and weight of reputation. Reconciling commercial and social objectives, however, eluded him (and most other nationalised industry heads in the 1950s). Knighted in 1957, Bowman was created a baronet when he retired in 1961. He married in 1923 Jean, daughter of Henry Brooks of Ashington; they had a son and a daughter. See William Ashworth, *The History of the British Coal Industry vol 5 1946-1982: The Nationalised Industry*(1986); *DBB*.

BRADMAN, Godfrey (Michael)
(9 September 1936 -)

Property developer, born in Willesden, north London, the son of William Isadore Bradman - a poor Jewish shopkeeper - and Anne Brenda née Goldsweig. He left secondary modern school at fifteen and qualified as an accountant in 1961, taking his examinations by correspondence. He set up his own accountancy firm, specialising in tax avoidance. In 1978 he bought Rosehaugh, a former tea company, as his quoted shell, and switched his attention to property. In 1981 he initiated the deal which saw Charterhouse Bank buy out Woolworth UK's assets (Bradman had noticed that Woolworth UK's property holdings were worth four times its share price): Rosehaugh made more than £20 million in share options after the buy-out. In the 1980s Rosehaugh Stanhope Developments (Bradman had teamed up with Stuart Lipton (qv) of the property and building firm Stanhope) emerged as Britain's foremost developer. Broadgate, at London's Liverpool Street Station, and the regeneration of the King's Cross area, were amongst its most prestigious projects. Bradman was also involved in several high-profile social causes, concerning housing for the poor, anti-abortion, AIDS, air pollution and freedom of information. But in 1992 RSD collapsed with debts of £350 million, the receivers finding a company with more subsidiaries than employees and a host of poorly-conceived and inadequately-controlled projects. Bradman married in 1975 Susan Clayton Bennett: they have three sons and three daughters.

BRANSON, Richard (Charles Nicholas)
(18 July 1950 -)
Music, communications and transport entrepreneur, born at Blackheath, south London, the son of Edward James Branson, a lawyer and later financial consultant, and Evette Huntley née Flindt. After a private education at Stowe, he left at sixteen with three 'O' levels and founded *Student* magazine, 1968-69. The Virgin Mail Order business for gramophone records was his first success in 1969 and this led directly to his nationwide chain of Virgin record shops, the first founded in 1971. By 1973 the group had its own record label and had an immediate bestseller (5 million copies), with Mike Oldfield's album *Tubular Bells*. In 1984 he started the cut-price Virgin Atlantic airline; and the group also acquired interests in travel, hotels and nightclubs. In 1986 the Virgin group went public, though Branson then made it private again (allowing Japanese investors a substantial stake). With a flair for publicity (he has crossed the Atlantic by balloon and power-boat), he is Britain's youngest billionaire, with a personal fortune estimated at £900 million in 1992. Virgin's turnover was about £1 billion. In 1992 he sold Virgin's music interests to Colin Southgate's (qv) Thorn EMI for over £500 million. It was thought that this will finance the expansion of Virgin Atlantic, which in 1992 had 2,400 global employees, eight Boeing 747's and a turnover in 1991 of £383 million (which resulted in a £3 million loss). In 1993 Branson's Virgin Atlantic won £610,000 and an apology from British Airways, under Lord King and Sir Colin Marshall (qqv), after Branson had taken them to court for an alleged 'dirty tricks' campaign. Branson has also dabbled with the former breakfast television operator, TV-am, and is exploring ways of running his own train service after the British Rail privatisation. In 1989 he married Joan Templeman (an earlier marriage was dissolved in 1969). See Mick Brown, *Richard Branson: The Inside Story* (1988, revised edition, 1992).

BROACKES, Sir Nigel
(21 July 1934 -)
Property developer and industrialist, born in Wakefield, the son of Donald Broackes, a country solicitor, and his wife Nan Alford. Educated at Stowe, his first job (interrupted by National Service) was in a Lloyds underwriter's office in London, 1952-55. In 1956 he founded Trafalgar House and entered the London property market. In the boom of the late 1950s and 1960s, Broackes specialised in office redevelopment, cleverly exploiting loopholes in local government regulations limiting City building. Broackes's company became one of the fastest growing London real estate firms: by 1963 (when it was publicly floated) it owned property valued at over £10 million. Broackes became chairman of Trafalgar House in 1969 and then broadened and internationalised its interests to include construction, engineering, passenger shipping (through the Cunard Steam-Ship Co) and hotels. In 1991 turnover was £3.4 billion, with a pre-tax profit of £122 million. But many of Broackes's acquisitions performed poorly (for example, his purchase of the engineering firm Davy embroiled Trafalgar in problems with North Sea oil contracts) and in October 1992 he was forced to step down and become honorary president. A director of Distillers Co, 1985-86, he has also served on the boards of various property and housing trusts, including a spell as chairman of the London Docklands Development Corporation. He was knighted in 1984. Broackes married in 1956 Joyce Edith Horne: they have two sons and one daughter. See N Broackes, *A Growing Concern* (1979); Oliver Marriott, *The Property Boom* (1967).

BROCK, John
(1834 - 1916)
Chemical manufacturer, born in Manchester, son of William Brock of Nantwich, he was educated privately and at Chorlton Hall School. By the early 1880s he headed Sullivan & Co Ltd, chemical manufacturers of Widnes, one of a number using the Leblanc method to produce chlorine and bleaching powder. When the Leblanc manufacturers of Widnes and St Helens formed the Lancashire Bleaching Powder Manufacturers' Association in 1883, Brock was chosen chairman. He held that position (under a president and four vice-presidents) when the Leblanc manufacturers of Lancashire, Tyne-Tees and Glasgow merged in 1890 to form the United Alkali Co. Under Brock this large (12,000 employees in 1907) unwieldy conglomerate of family firms survived chiefly by price and output agreements with Brunner, Mond and smaller rivals, most utilising the more modern Solvay technology. He married Sarah, daughter of

James Mowle of Chester. See W J Reader, *Imperial Chemical Industries: A History vol 1 The Forerunners, 1870-1926* (1970); W B Tracy and W T Pike, *Lancashire at the Opening of the Twentieth Century* (1903).

BROCKLEHURST, Robert Walter Douglas Phillips
(31 May 1861 - 22 December 1948)
Textile manufacturer, the son of C D F Phillips FRS and Martha née Brocklehurst. Educated at Eton and Trinity College, Cambridge (BA 1882), in 1905 he succeeded his uncle, F D Brocklehurst, when he assumed the additional name. He became vice-chairman of the Fine Cotton Spinners & Doublers Association Ltd, which employed 30,000 in 1935. In 1902 he married Isabel Edith CBE, daughter of Sir Patrick Watson MD. Brocklehurst was appointed JP in 1906, DL in 1914, and served in the African and European wars.

BRODRICK, Sir Thomas
(31 March 1856 - 26 October 1925)
Co-operative Wholesale Society executive, born in Scarborough, the son of Patrick Brodrick, a bricklayer's labourer, and his wife Bessie née Donion, he was educated privately locally and worked for the town's CWS while a boy. At sixteen he became a junior clerk in the CWS headquarters in Manchester. After qualifying in both the administrative and the trading sides he was appointed CWS accountant in 1884. Scores of CWS retail societies elected him as their auditor and in this position he won their confidence and political support. When in 1899 the CWS chaired by John Shillito (qv) decided that the company secretaryship should be transferred from the national committee to a responsible official, Brodrick was selected. Patient, quiet, earnest, with ample good sense, he oversaw the growth of the CWS from nearly 17,000 employees in 1907 to over 31,000 in 1923 when he retired. From 1913 until 1923 he was also secretary of the Co-operative Insurance Society. He was knighted in 1922, having sat on several government commissions and the Royal Commission on the Civil Service. He belonged to and was buried from St Mary's Catholic Church, Eccles. Brodrick, in 1884, married Margaret Kelly. See *The Producer* (November 1925); Percy Redfern, *The New History of the CWS* (1938); *The Times*, 28 October 1925.

BROOKES, Raymond Percival
Baron Brookes of West Bromwich
(10 April 1909 -)
Industrialist, born in West Bromwich, the son of William Percival Brookes, a wholesale grocer's representative, and Ursula Rosina née Butler.

Educated at West Bromwich Lodge Estate School, he became an apprentice at the local drop forging and engineering firm Charles Bunn Ltd, while attending evening classes at Kenrick Technical College. He became managing director of Bunn's in 1939, but in 1941 left to join Guest, Keen & Nettlefolds to manage its subsidiary Garrington's. In 1944 he was appointed to the Garrington board, became its managing director in 1951, and chairman four years later. Brookes's influence within GKN was shown by its emergence as an automotive engineering group, rather than as primarily a steelmaker with engineering adjuncts. In 1964 he was appointed GKN managing director: the next year he became chairman, a post he held until his retirement in 1974 (when he became the firm's first life president). GKN turnover and profits climbed steadily: in 1965 pre-tax profits stood at £30 million on a turnover of £353 million; by 1974 they increased to £90 million on £1,137 million turnover. Major organisational changes included arranging GKN's subsidiaries into product-oriented divisions with overseas sub-groups. Outside GKN Brookes was a part-time member of the British Steel Corporation, vice-president of the Engineering Employers Federation, president of the Society of Motor Manufacturers and Traders and president of the Motor Industry Research Association. He served on the Industrial Development Advisory Board and was a member of the Wilberforce Committee of Inquiry into the electricity supply industry dispute. He was knighted in 1971 and awarded a life peerage in 1975. Brookes married in 1937 Florence Edna née Sharman: they had one son. See *DBB*.

BROWN, James
(1862 - 13 January 1941)
Shipyard manager, born in Kirkcudbright, he studied engineering at Glasgow University, 1877-78, and crowned his five years' apprenticeship at the Provanside Works of A & P Stevens with a Whitworth Scholarship in 1886. After a spell in the drawing office of J & G Thomson (later John Brown & Co) of Clydebank he went to Spain in 1889 as assistant manager to Astilleros de Nervion, Bilbao, rising to engineering manager. Eleven years later he returned to Emgland as works manager of Palmers Shipbuilding & Iron Co at Jarrow. He moved back to the Clyde in 1903 as engineering manager at Scott's Shipbuilding & Engineering Co, a firm employing 5,000 in 1907 and a major builder of marine propulsion units and battleships. Brown became a director of Scott's in 1905 and managing director and deputy chairman in 1914, holding these positions until his death. He served on the council of the Institution of Mechanical

Engineers and was a vice-president of the Institution of Naval Architects, governor of the Royal Technical College, Glasgow, and a member of the management committee of Lloyd's Register of Shipping. He was created a CBE in 1918. Brown was married with four sons, two of whom were killed in the First World War. He lived at Greenock where he was a member of the Finnart Church of Scotland. See *Proceedings of the Institution of Mechanical Engineers* (1941).

BROWNE, Sir Benjamin Chapman
(26 August 1839 - 1 March 1917)
Marine engineer and shipbuilder, born at Stouts Hill, Uley, Gloucestershire, youngest son of Colonel B C Browne of the 9th Lancers and later of the Gloucestershire Yeomanry, and of Mary Anne née Baker. After Westminster School and a year in the Applied Science Department of King's College, London, Browne trained as a mechanical engineer in the Elswick Works of William Armstrong. Following experience on several engineering contracts he returned to the Tyne and with several partners bought the Forth Bank Engine Works of R & W Hawthorn c. 1870. Browne specialised in marine engines and relocated the business on a riverside site. He became chairman of a new company R & W Hawthorn, Leslie & Co Ltd, formed in 1885 when his firm merged with Andrew Leslie's Hebburn shipyard. By the time Browne retired in 1915 annual turnover had increased tenfold, to £1.5 million; the workforce exceeded 5,250; and the firm was the leading supplier of marine engines, steam turbines and destroyers to the Admiralty. Professionally he was a member of the Institutions of Civil Engineers, Mechanical Engineers and Naval Architects. In Newcastle Browne assumed entrepreneurial and cultural leadership roles, promoting a public electricity supply, engineering education and literary pursuits. He took a conciliatory line in the engineering workers' dispute of 1897-98. Conservative and Anglican, he sat on Newcastle Council and was knighted in 1887. Browne married Annie, the daughter of R T Atkinson, in 1861; they had nine children of whom seven survived their father. See *DBB*.

BROWNE, Sir Edward Humphrey
(7 April 1911 - 20 February 1987)
National Coal Board manager, born in the Warwickshire coalfield at Astley, son of James T Browne, a mining engineer, and his wife Ethel Mary née Hills, he was educated at Repton School and Magdalene College, Cambridge, where he was a choral scholar, and Birmingham University, where he took a joint mining degree. He joined Manchester Collieries, one of the best-run large firms in the coal industry, as a mining agent in 1932 and four years later became manager of Chanters Colliery. He was chief mining engineer of Manchester Collieries, 1943-46. Following nationalisation in 1946 Browne became Production Director of the North Western Division of the National Coal Board, with the mammoth task of reinvigorating the country's most rapidly declining coalfield. His most ambitious scheme was at Bradford Colliery, Manchester, where an underground tunnel beneath the city centre took coal directly from coal face to power station. While Director-General of Production for the NCB, 1947-55, he made a detailed survey of the condition and potential of every coal field and NCB colliery which became the basis of a fifteen-year plan, the *Plan for Coal* (1950). As chairman of the West Midlands Division of the NCB, 1955-60, he employed 57,400 in one of the three regularly profitable divisions in the NCB's complement of nine. As deputy chairman of the NCB, 1960-67, under Lord Robens (qv), he chaired the working party which in 1965 sought ways of making the South Western Division a viable coalfield. It recommended closure of half the 91 collieries by 1970; in the event 35 were closed and for a short while (1967-68) South Wales was brought into profit. Sir Humphrey Browne (he was knighted in 1964) resigned in 1967 to enter private industry, as chairman of the John Thompson Group. In three years he reorganised this engineering holding company into a divisionalised corporation with greater profitability. Simultaneously he was chairman of the Woodall Duckham Group. He returned to nationalised industry management in 1971 as chairman of the British Transport Docks Board, retiring in 1982. A vigorous exponent of 'enterprise' and a 'true blue Tory' he welcomed the privatisation schemes of the Thatcher government. Browne married in 1934 Barbara Stone (d 1970); they had two sons. See William Ashworth, *The History of the British Coal Industry vol 5 1946-1982: The Nationalised Industry* (1986); *The Times,* 25 February 1987.

BRYANT, Frederick
(1878 - 27 April 1942)
Deputy-Director of Naval Construction at the Naval Dockyards, the son of Edward Bryant. He was educated at the Royal Naval College, Greenwich. In 1935 the Naval Dockyards were amongst the top dozen UK employees, with over 30,000 workers. Bryant married in 1901 Edith Maud Quinton: they had a son and a daughter. Bryant was awarded a CB in 1936 and an OBE.

BUCKLEY, Harold
(1900 - 5 June 1977)

Co-operative Wholesale Society manager. He joined the personal staff of the Secretary (chief executive officer) of the CWS, then Sir Thomas Brodrick (qv), at CWS headquarters in Manchester in 1917. After many years of servicing CWS committees he was appointed deputy secretary and executive officer of the English and Scottish joint CWS in 1938, within months becoming its secretary. In 1945 he was elected deputy secretary and executive officer of the CWS and then secretary in 1952, holding this post until 1965. Buckley was the fourth secretary or full time executive officer in the history of the CWS. The CWS employed 52,000 in 1955. The far more numerous shareholders in the CWS retail societies displayed a worrying apathy about the principle of co-operation as living standards rose and rival retail chains attracted consumer loyalty. Reorganisation within the CWS, and the application of market-oriented policies, were badly needed. They tarried until Buckley had left office, though he was secretary of the Joint Reorganisation Committee of 1964-65 which recommended 'constitutional changes' and 'a new trading relationship [between the CWS and the CWS retail societies] based on interdependence'. See *Co-operative News* 15 June 1977; Sir William Richardson, *The CWS in War and Peace, 1938-1976* (1977).

BULLOCK, William Edward
(14 March 1877 - 17 March 1968)

Motor car manufacturer, born at Handsworth, Birmingham, the son of William Bullock, a smith, and Beatrice Caroline née Barnett. Educated at Smethwick Technical School, in 1909 he became works manager at Singer & Co, one Coventry's pioneer car manufacturers. Bullock helped the firm move towards the emerging mass market with the production of light cars, such as the Singer Ten, and then after 1919 (when he became managing director) he launched an extensive programme of expansion. In 1929 Singer produced about 28,000 cars (15 per cent of UK output) and was the third largest British motor manufacturer. Singer's market share fell rapidly in the 1930s, however, and in 1936 Bullock left the company. He was a vice-president of the Society of Motor Manufacturers and Traders. Bullock married three times: the first in 1902 to Nellie Elizabeth Parsons (d 1934) produced a son and a daughter. See Kenneth Richardson, *The British Motor Industry, 1896-1939* (1977); *DBB*.

BULLOUGH, Sir George
(28 February 1870 - 26 July 1939)

Textile machinery manufacturer, born at Accrington, the eldest child of John Bullough who controlled Howard & Bullough, textile machinery makers of Accrington, and Alice née Schmidlin. From Harrow School he entered the family firm, the third generation of family ownership. On his father's death in 1891 the firm became a private limited company with a capital of £500,000, of which George Bullough owned half. He became chairman, retaining this position until his death. The firm employed 5,000 in 1907 and 5,250 in 1927 shortly before it merged with Platt Bros and four other firms to form Textile Machinery Makers Ltd. It was the largest English manufacturer of ring spinning frames. After the First World War Bullough had less to do with the day-to-day management of the business than earlier. For services to the government he was knighted during the Boer War (when his luxury yacht was converted to a floating military hospital) and created a baronet in the First World War (when he publicly loaned £50,000 to the government interest free). A Conservative and an Anglican, he was a leading member of both the Jockey Club and the National Hunt Committee. Bullough married in 1903 Monica Lilly, the eldest daughter of the 4th Marquis de la Pasture; they had one daughter. See *DBB*.

BURBIDGE, Sir Richard Woodman
(7 December 1872 - 3 June 1945)

Department stores manager, the elder son of Sir Richard Burbidge (1847-1917), a shop assistant, and Emily née Woodman. In 1893 he joined Harrods, where his father as general manager and then managing director had begun making it one of the most famous department stores in the country. In 1901 he became general manager in succession to his father; and when the latter died suddenly in 1917, Woodman Burbidge succeeded him as second baronet and managing director. When the first chairman, Sir Alfred Newton, died in 1921, Burbidge filled that position too until his death. He made numerous trips abroad, especially to the firm's subsidiary in Buenos Aires. He was also a member of the Empire Marketing Board and the Board of Trade Advisory Council, and the president in 1928 of the Incorporated Association of Retail Distributors. He became a CBE in 1919. In 1896 he married Catherine Jemima née Grant: they had three daughters and a son, Richard, who took over as managing director in 1935 (when Harrods employed 6,292). He left £146,988. See Sean Callery, *Harrods: The Story of Society's Favourite Store* (1991); Tim Dale, *Harrods: The Store and the Legend* (1981); *DBB* (Sir Richard Burbidge).

BURN, Sir Joseph
(6 March 1871 - 12 October 1950)
Insurance company executive, who joined the Prudential Assurance Co aged fifteen and trained as an actuary. Elected Fellow of the Institute of Actuaries in 1894, in 1908 he was appointed joint assistant actuary of the Prudential, and four years later became the company's sole actuary. From 1920 to 1941 he was general manager of the Prudential, and was then appointed director and president (the latter being an honorary position he held until his death). Burn was an early proselytizer for office mechanisation, which led to the Prudential's involvement with Powers Accounting Machines Ltd, on which Burn had a seat on the board from 1919 to 1945. He was president of the Institute of Actuaries and of the Insurance Institute of London. He was made a CBE in 1918 and promoted KBE two years later. In 1894 he married Emily Harriet, daughter of Richard Smith: they had three sons and two daughters. See Joseph Burn, *Vital Statistics Explained* (1914), *Stock Exchange Investments in Theory and Practice* (1904); R W Barnard, *A Century of Service: The Story of the Prudential 1848-1948* (1948); *The Times*, 13 October 1950.

BURROWS, Sir Robert Abraham
(17 March 1884 - 14 August 1964)
Mining and insurance executive, the son of Miles F Burrows, a Lancashire magistrate, and Gertrude née Dawbarn. Educated at The Leys School, Cambridge, in 1904 he joined Fletcher, Burrows & Co, with which his family was connected. He continued in joint control of this business, after it became part of Manchester Collieries Ltd in 1929. The latter employed 14,193 workers in 1935. He succeeded Joseph Ramsden (qv) as chairman of Manchester Collieries in 1943, a well-run business in a generally poorly-run industry. When the mines were nationalised he became a part-time member of the National Coal Board and later investigated its management organisation. He was a co-founder in 1918 of the Lancashire & Cheshire Coal Research Association and was for a decade its first president. He was a member of the Fuel Research Board, 1923-27, and had also been deputy chairman of the District Bank Ltd, chairman of the National Boiler & General Insurance Co and deputy chairman of the Alliance Assurance Co. For six years he served as chairman of Remploy, until he retired in 1955 through ill-health. He was also a chairman of the old LMS Railway from 1946-48. He was a JP and former high sheriff. Knighted in 1937, he was made a KBE in 1952 for his work for the disabled. In 1911 he married Eleanor Doris née Bainbridge: they had two sons and two daughters. See *The Times*, 15 August 1964.

BURTON, Sir Montague Maurice
(15 August 1885 - 21 September 1952)
Clothing manufacturer and retailer, born in Kurkel, Lithuania, the only son of Jewish parents - Hyman Judah Ossinsky, a bookseller, and his wife Rachel Edith née Ashe. After attending a Jewish parochial school, in 1900 he migrated alone to England, adopted his English name, and in 1909 began his wholesale bespoke men's tailoring business in Sheffield. By 1913 he was based in Leeds and from there launched his national retailing organisation of Burton's high street shops. The business - which became a public company in 1929 as Montague Burton, Tailor of Taste Ltd - began with £100 but by 1950 had a working capital of £15 million and 20,000 workers. Burton shops numbered 40 in 1919, 333 in 1929, 595 in 1939 and 635 in 1952. A paternalist, widely travelled and well read, Burton (who was knighted in 1939) endowed several chairs in English universities and also supported Zionist causes. In 1909 he married Sophia Amelia Marks, the daughter of a furniture dealer. He left £687,495. See Eric M Sigsworth, *Montague Burton: The Tailor of Taste* (1990); *DBB*; *DNB*.

BURY, Oliver Robert Hawke
(3 November 1861 - 21 March 1946)
Railway manager, born in Paddington, London, the son of Edward Bury, a barrister, and his wife Mary Elizabeth née Dowker, he trained as a railway engineer on the London & South Western Railway and then worked in the engineering department of the Coleford & Monmouth Railway. In his thirties he commenced a series of appointments with South American railway companies: the Great Western Railway of Brazil; the Entre Rios in Argentina Railway (general manager and chief engineer); the Buenos Aires & Rosario Railway (general manager). He returned to England in 1902 to become general manager of the Great Northern Railway, at Kings Cross. Under his leadership, in 1906 a rapprochement was achieved between the GNR and the Great Central Railway under Sam Fay (qv), fierce competitors since the opening of the Great Central in London in 1899. After retiring in 1912 Bury became a director of the GNR and of the London & North Eastern Railway (after it absorbed the GNR in 1923) until 1945. He was also chairman of the London Electricity Supply Corporation and of London Power Co. He served in 1904 as a Commissioner in the inquiry into the management of the Egyptian State Railways. Bury was a member of the Institution of Civil Engineers. See *Railway Gazette*, 11 October 1912; *Railway Year Book* (1908).

BUTLIN, Sir William ('Billy') Heygate Edmund Colbourne

(27 December 1899 - 12 June 1980)

Leisure industry pioneer, born in Cape Town, the son of William Butlin, an engineer and son of an Anglican clergyman, and Bertha née Hill, daughter of a travelling baker and showman. Educated at St Mary Redcliffe school in Engand, he completed his schooling in Toronto (where his mother resided after divorce and remarriage). His first job in Canada was in a department store, but by 1921 he had returned to England to run his own fairground stall. Noticing the increasing popularity of seaside recreation, in 1927 he opened an amusement park at Skegness followed by others on the east and south coasts. Butlin's Dodgem cars, Big Dipper and Wall of Death - attractions he had mostly imported from abroad - were a sensation. In 1935 he opened his first holiday camp at Skegness and his business - now floated as a public company, Butlin's Ltd - expanded rapidly. By the late 1940s about 1.6 million people a year holidayed in Butlin's five camps. In 1965 Butlin's camps had assets of £27.75 million and profits were a healthy £4.7 million. He survived a disastrous attempt to expand in Bermuda, but cheap air travel and package deal holidays sent his business into decline. Butlin retired in 1958 to a Jersey tax haven and the business was sold in 1972 to the Rank Organisation for £43 million. Awarded the MBE for his war work in providing accommodation for the troops, he was knighted for his charity work, particularly on behalf of underprivileged children. He married three times: first in 1927 to Dorothy Mabel Cheriton (one daughter); second in 1959 to Norah, sister of Dorothy (one son, two daughters); and third in 1976 to Sheila Devine (one son, one daughter). See Billy Butlin (with Peter Dacre), *The Billy Butlin Story* (1982); *DBB*.

BUTTERWORTH, Sir Alexander Kaye

(4 December 1854 - 23 January 1946)

Railway manager, born at Clifton, Bristol, the son of George Butterworth, curate of Henbury, Clifton, and his wife, Frances Maria née Kaye, younger daughter of a bishop of Lincoln. He was educated at Marlborough College and then the University of London, securing an LLB before being called to the Bar in 1878. He joined the legal staff of the Great Western Railway in 1883 and became an acknowledged expert on railway rates. After a short time as Clerk to Bedfordshire County Council he was appointed solicitor to the North Eastern Railway in 1891 at a salary of £1,500 per annum. In 1906 he succeeded Sir George Gibb as the NER's general manager (at £5,000 per annum), remaining in post until 1922. During his tenure he dealt with the problems of growing labour unrest, state control of railways during the First World War, and post-war railway reorganisation. Through his efforts the mergers which created the London & North Eastern Railway were successfully negotiated. In 1926 he became a director of Armstrong, Whitworth. For many years he was chairman of the London Chest Hospital and a director of Welwyn Garden City. In the 1930s he was chairman of the Pedestrian Association. Butterworth married twice: first, in 1884, to Julia (d 1911), daughter of George Wigan MD; second, in 1916, to Dorothea Mavor, daughter of Luke Ionides, a stockbroker, and widow of Ebenezer Mavor. See *DBB*.

BUXTON, Andrew (Robert Fowell)

(5 April 1939 -)

Banker, the eldest of three children, born into an old and wealthy Quaker brewing family in London (his father was chairman of Truman Hanbury Buxton), which was also connected to the Barclays banking clan. Buxton's father died when he was four and his mother remarried a banker, who also happened to work for Barclays. Educated at Winchester and Pembroke College, Oxford, where he read politics, philosophy and economics (and by his own admission emerged with an undistinguished degree), he joined Barclays in 1963 as a graduate trainee. After spells in the USA and in Ipswich as a regional director, he joined the Lombard Street head office at 33. By 1979 he had responsibility for the corporate division and was appointed chief executive of Barclays in succession to Sir John Quinton (qv) in 1992. His appointment was seen as an echo of the feudal system, which had served Barclays so well in the past when British banking was class-ridden and insulated from competition. Buxton also planned to take over from Quinton as chairman in January 1993. But the problems Barclays faced in restructuring in the 1990s as branch banking contracted and Buxton's own past record (he was involved in many of the property deals that had landed the Bank with massive bad debts) meant that the institutional shareholders blocked this time-honoured dual office. In 1993 Buxton announced the roles would be split. Barclay's profits plunged 30 per cent in 1991 as it set aside £1.8 billion against bad debts, owed by such borrowers as the Canary Wharf developers Olympia & York and Gerald Ronson's (qv) Heron Corporation. In December 1992 Barclays wrote off £240 million of the £440 million loan to Imry (which was the biggest ever property loan made by a single British bank). In March 1993 Barclays reported a pre-tax loss for the previous year of

£242 million after writing off £2.6 billion of bad debts: it was the first loss the Bank had made in its 96-year history and the worst in British banking history. Buxton holds a non-executive directorship of the drugs company SmithKline Beecham. He married in 1965 Jane Margery Grant: they have two daughters.

BYTHELL, John Kenworthy
(20 April 1840 - 18 August 1916)
Canal company chairman, born in Hulme, Manchester, son of James Bythell, a calenderer and maker-up, he joined the Manchester merchant firm of Gaddum & Co, serving as their resident partner in Bombay, 1864-75. Elected chairman of the Bombay Chamber of Commerce in 1872, he was instrumental in effecting harbour extensions before returning to England in 1875. The Manchester Ship Canal Act was secured in 1885 and the following year Bythell became a founder member of the Manchester Ship Canal Consultative Committee. After Daniel Adamson, the leading but abrasive promoter, stepped down in 1887, Bythell joined the Manchester Ship Canal Co board. He acted as deputy chairman in 1891 and was elected chairman and full-time chief executive at £3,000 a year in 1894, retiring in 1916. The Ship Canal opened for traffic in January 1894. Under Bythell Manchester rose from sixteenth to fourth port in the UK. His achievement rested on an alliance with Manchester Corporation which (in 1904) gave the Corporation a perpetual majority on the MSC board of directors in return for financial support: especially needed in view of the rate war being waged by Liverpool merchants and shipowners. Bythell increased Canal usage by developing warehouses and grain elevators, funded and run by related companies; by setting up a shipping line, Manchester Liners Ltd, with the support of Sir Christopher Furness, North East shipowner, industrialist and fellow Nonconformist, and the Canadian government; and by building a railway link between Manchester docks and the new industrial estate at Trafford Park. In 1907 the MSC was employing about 9,000 people. A Liberal and a devout Presbyterian (at Higher Broughton), Bythell shunned personal publicity and declined national honours. See *DBB*; D A Farnie, *The Manchester Ship Canal and the Rise of the Port of Manchester* (1980).

C

CADBURY, Edward
(20 March 1873 - 21 November 1948)
Confectionery manufacturer, born at Edgbaston, Birmingham, the eldest son of George Cadbury

and Mary née Tylor. Educated at a Friends' school, Oliver's Mount, Scarborough, and in London and abroad, in 1894 he joined the famous confectionery firm of Cadbury Bros founded by his father. On the death of his uncle, Richard Cadbury, in 1899, the business was converted into a limited company and Edward became managing director, with particular responsibility for exports and the female workforce. He was especially responsible for developing personnel management within the firm. He was chairman of British Cocoa & Chocolate Co (the merged Cadbury and Fry firm formed in 1918) from 1932 until 1943, and chairman of Cadbury Bros (of which Fry's became a subsidiary in 1935) from 1937 until 1943. In the family tradition he was keenly interested in welfare and social reform: a Fabian, he was chairman of the liberal *Daily News*, campaigned against 'sweated industries', and supported Birmingham University. He married in 1896, Dorothy, daughter of Dr Francis Howitt: they had no children. See Edward Cadbury, *Experiments in Industrial Organisation* (1912); Gillian Wagner, *The Chocolate Conscience* (1987).

CADBURY, George
(19 September 1839 - 24 October 1922)
Chocolate manufacturer, born in Birmingham, the third son of John Cadbury, founder of the family business, and his second wife, Candia, daughter of George Barrow, a merchant and shipowner from Lancaster. George was educated at a local Quaker day school. At fifteen he joined his elder brother Richard in their father's firm, manufacturing and retailing cocoa and chocolate. Ill-health forced John to hand over his business, then declining, to his two sons in 1861. Long hours and the launch of Cadbury's Cocoa Essence, an unadulterated cocoa, in 1866 rescued the firm. Between 1861 and 1879 turnover rose from nearly £28,000 to £103,000 and employees from 20 to 200. Expansion required new premises. George implemented his belief that a healthy environment benefited both employees and firm and in 1879 the business was moved from Bridge Street to a greenfield site south west of the city, dubbed Bournville after a local stream. Sales soared to £1 million in 1900 and employees to 4,683 in 1907. After Richard Cadbury's death in 1899 the firm became a private limited company, Cadbury Brothers Ltd, with George as chairman and two sons and two nephews as managing directors. George Cadbury's reputation rested on his Quaker principles; his enlightened treatment of employees; his model village at Bournville; and his support of the Liberal Party in whose interest he bought the *Daily News*. In a Quaker tradition he declined all public honours. George Cadbury married Mary Tylor (d 1887) in 1873; and secondly

Elizabeth Mary Taylor (later Dame Elizabeth Cadbury) in 1888. There were three sons and two daughters of the first marriage and three sons and three daughters by the second. See *DBB*; A G Gardiner, *The Life of George Cadbury* (1923).

CADBURY, Sir (George) Adrian (Hayhurst)
(15 April 1929 -)

Confectionery manufacturer, the son of Laurence John Cadbury (qv) and Joyce née Mathews. Educated at Eton, he read economics at King's College, Cambridge, before a spell of National Service with the Coldstream Guards. He was a managing director of Cadbury Schweppes Ltd between 1969 and 1973; a director of the Cadbury Group in 1962; and chairman of Cadbury Schweppes in 1975. Despite some difficult years, when the firm became a potential takeover target, Cadbury achieved solid success with its strong portfolio of brands, a strategy of concentrating on two income streams (chocolate and drinks), and the recognised growth potential on the beverage side. Sir Adrian (he was knighted in 1977) retired in 1989 and, though his brother Dominic (qv) remained as chief executive, for the first time in four generations the chairmanship passed to an outsider, Sir Graham Day (qv). Cadbury has also served as a director of IBM (UK) Ltd and of the Bank of England. He is chancellor of the University of Aston and was president of Birmingham Chamber of Commerce, 1988-89. A Quaker like his forebears, Cadbury has a particular interest in business ethics: during the 1980s he campaigned to promote the use and powers of non-executive directors. He also chaired the Committee on the Financial Aspects of Corporate Governance, which reported in 1992 and recommended *inter alia* the need for splitting the chairman and chief executive roles. He married in 1956 Gillian Mary née Skepper (d 1992), by whom he had two sons and one daughter. See Adrian Cadbury, *The Company Chairman* (1990).

CADBURY, Laurence John
(30 March 1889 - 5 November 1982)

Chocolate manufacturer, born in Birmingham, the fourth son of George Cadbury (qv), chairman of Cadbury Brothers Ltd, and the first child of George's second wife, Elizabeth Mary née Taylor. Educated at Leighton Park School and Trinity College, Cambridge, where he read economics, Laurence Cadbury joined the family firm in 1911, the first graduate member of the family to do so. He visited the USA to study business methods in 1913. After the First World War in which he served in France in the Friends' Ambulance Unit

(receiving the Croix de Guerre and the OBE), he returned to Cadbury Bros and was made a director. He played a leading role in coordinating the financial interests of the Cadbury and Fry businesses after they were merged in the British Cocoa & Chocolate Co Ltd in 1919. He was also responsible for the extension of the Bournville works and the installation of mass production machinery. He sat on the committee which set up overseas subsidiaries in the dominions between the wars. He succeeded his elder brother Edward as chairman of Cadbury Bros and of BC & CC in 1944, retiring from the former in 1959 and from the latter in 1964. Employees (worldwide) rose from 16,000 in 1939 to 28,000 in 1962. His main contribution was to lead in the transformation of a home-based family firm into a professionally-managed international company. He married in 1925 Joyce Mathews. Their eldest son is Sir Adrian Cadbury (qv). See *DBB*.

CADBURY, (Nicholas) Dominic
(12 May 1940 -)

Confectionery manufacturer, born in Birmingham into the famous chocolate manufacturing dynasty: he was the son of Laurence John Cadbury (qv) and Joyce née Mathews and a direct descendant of the Cadbury who had founded the firm in 1831. Educated at Eton and Trinity College, Cambridge, he was awarded an MBA at Stanford University. He joined Cadburys as a management trainee in 1964 (his brother, (Sir) Adrian Cadbury (qv), was eleven years older and already *en route* for the chairmanship) and then worked in the firm's South African operation. In 1969 Cadbury's merged with Schweppes, ending the family's control of the business. However, Dominic Cadbury took charge of marketing chocolate in the UK. Under his guidance Milk Tray introduced a Man in Black, Frank Muir was signed up for a Fruit 'n Nut campaign, and Creme Eggs were launched as a seasonal speciality. Since 1984 Dominic Cadbury has been chief executive and the business has prospered (a threatened takeover by the US group, General Cinema, was successfully avoided). In 1991 Cadbury's turnover was £3.2 billion, with pre-tax profits of £316 million (confectionery sales totalled £1.4 billion, soft drinks £1.8 billion): it employed 35,000. He is also a director of Guinness and the *Economist* Newspaper Group. In 1972 Cadbury married Cecilia Sarah Symes: they have three daughters. Gillian Wagner, *The Chocolate Conscience* (1987).

CADBURY, Paul Strangman
(3 November 1895 - 24 October 1984)

Chocolate manufacturer, born in Birmingham, only son of Barrow (son of Richard and nephew of

George Cadbury qv) and Geraldine Cadbury, he
was educated at Leighton Park School, Reading,
and (briefly) at St John's College, Cambridge,
before the First World War broke out. After the
war, in which he served in the Friends' Ambulance
Unit, Paul Cadbury joined Cadbury Bros and
within a year became a managing director in charge
of sales and marketing. In 1921 he joined the
British Cocoa & Chocolate Co board (which jointly ran Cadburys and Frys). He was elécted chairman of Cadbury Bros and of J S Fry & Sons in
1959, retiring in 1965. During the Second World
War he served on Birmingham City Council and
was secretary of the West Midland Group on post-
war Reconstruction and Planning. He sat on the
Royal Commission on Local Government in the
Greater London Area, 1957-60. He married
Rachel Wilson, also a Quaker, in 1919; they had
six children. See J F Crosfield, A History of the
Cadbury Family (2 vols, privately printed, 1985).

CADBURY, William Adlington
(17 February 1867 - 8 July 1957)
Confectionery manufacturer, born at Edgbaston,
Birmingham, the son of Richard Cadbury (1835-
1899) and Elizabeth née Adlington. After education
at Friends' schools at Southport and Hitchin and
engineering experience in England and Germany,
he joined the family firm at Bournville in 1887. On
the death of his father, when Cadbury Bros became
a private limited company, he was appointed one
of the five managing directors. William Cadbury
had an important influence on the sales and buying
side: for example, he developed important new
cocoa production areas in British West Africa. In
1909 he and Cadburys were involved in a famous
court case, when a newspaper accused the firm of
profiting from slave labour in the Portuguese
cocoa-growing islands, a libel which did not stick.
In 1922 he became chairman of the board of
Cadbury Bros, an office he held until his retirement
in 1937. A Birmingham City councillor, he also
became mayor and alderman, and was given the
freedom of the City in 1938. He married in 1902
Emmeline Hannah, elder daughter of Dr William
Wilson: they had four sons and two daughters. See
W A Cadbury, Labour in Portuguese West Africa
(1910); David J Jeremy, Capitalists and Christians
(1990).

CADMAN, John
1st Baron Cadman of Silverdale
(7 September 1877 - 31 May 1941)
Petroleum company executive, born in Silverdale,
Staffordshire, the second and eldest son of James
Cope Cadman, a colliery manager, and Betty née
Kelling. He attended Durham College of Science

and began a varied career in mining engineering,
before becoming from 1908-20 the Professor of
Mining at Birmingham University and a government adviser on petroleum. In 1921 he joined the
Anglo-Persian Oil Co (later a part of British
Petroleum), becoming chairman in 1927. Under
Cadman APOC extensively negotiated with the
Persian government the concessionary relationship,
1928-33. Respected for his scientific acumen and
technological understanding, Cadman served on
numerous government committees. He became a
peer in 1937 and FRS in 1940. In 1907 Cadman
married Lilina Harrigan, daughter of the Magistrate
of the Port of Spain. He left £234,748. See John
Rowland and Basil, Second Baron Cadman,
Ambassador for Oil: The Life of John, First Baron
Cadman (1960); R W Ferrier, The History of the
British Petroleum Company. Vol 1: The Developing
Years 1901-1932 (1982); DBB; DNB.

CADOGAN, The Right Honourable Sir Alexander George Montagu
(25 November 1884 - 9 July 1968)
Diplomat and chairman of the governors of the
British Broadcasting Corporation, youngest son of
the 5th Earl Cadogan, then Lord Lieutenant of
Ireland, and his wife, Lady Beatrix, daughter of the
2nd Earl of Craven, he was educated at Eton and
Balliol College, Oxford, where he gained a second-
class degree in modern history. He was nominated
an attaché in the Diplomatic Service in 1908, moving up through the ranks to First Secretary in 1919,
Counsellor in 1928, Minister Plenipotentiary at
Peking, 1933-35, Ambassador at Peking, 1935-36,
Deputy Under-Secretary at the Foreign Office,
1936-38, Under-Secretary, 1938-46 (accompany-
ing Churchill to Yalta and Potsdam), and, finally in
his diplomatic career, Permanent Representative of
HM Government in the UK to the United
Nations, 1946-50. He was government director of
the Suez Canal Co, 1951-57, and chairman of the
BBC, 1952-57. While Sir Ian Jacob (qv) as
Director-General had a much larger part in policy-
making at the BBC than Cadogan, the Suez crisis
brought Cadogan to the fore. With Jacob he took
responsibility in late October 1956 for giving the
Leader of the Opposition, Hugh Gaitskell, the
immediate right to make a (dissenting) reply to the
decision broadcast by Prime Minister Sir Anthony
Eden to invade Egypt. Though threatened with a
reduction of £1 million in the government subsidy
to Bush House, they stood their ground, believing
that opposing views reflected the divisions in the
country and therefore were in the national interest.
Outside the BBC, Cadogan was a director of the
National Provincial Bank and of the Phoenix
Assurance Co. He gained numerous honours, his

first knighthood coming in 1934; he was sworn of the PC in 1946 and received the OM in 1951. Cadogan married, in 1912, Lady Theodosia Acheson, daughter of the 4th Earl of Gosford; they had a son and three daughters. See Asa Briggs, *The BBC: The First Fifty Years* (1985); *The Times*, 10 July 1976.

CAHILL, John Conway
(8 January 1930 -)
Industrialist, born in Ruislip, Northwood, the son of Francis Conway Cahill, a company secretary, and Dorothy Winifred née Mills. Cahill joined BTR (founded as British Tyre & Rubber in 1934) in 1955, shortly before the arrival of (Sir) Owen Green (qv). The latter as head of BTR helped transform it into a wide-ranging but highly successful conglomerate. Cahill became BTR's deputy overseas general manager in 1963, joined the board of directors in 1968 and was appointed deputy managing director in 1976. He was chairman of BTR's Pan-American operations between 1979 and 1987. In 1992 he became chairman of British Aerospace, succeeding Sir Graham Day (qv). In his first year BAe posted a £1.2 billion loss - the biggest in UK corporate history. Despite the go-ahead for the Eurofighter 2000 project and a £4 billion order for Tornado aircraft, heavy losses in its commercial aircraft business and its Rover car subsidiary led Cahill to plan a cost reduction programme aimed at reducing employee numbers to 90,000 in 1993 (BAe employed 123,000 in 1991). Cahill married in 1956, Giovanni Caterina née Lenardon: they have three daughters.

CAINE, Sir Michael (Harris)
(17 June 1927 -)
International food and agricultural group executive, the son of (Sir) Sydney Caine (b 1902), a civil servant and later director of the London School of Economics, and Muriel Anne née Harris. Educated at Bedales, Lincoln College, Oxford, and George Washington University in the USA, Caine joined Booker McConnell Ltd in 1952. He was appointed to the board in 1964, serving as chief executive between 1975 and 1984. He has been chairman of the group (now named Booker) since 1979. The company operates in food distribution, agribusiness, and fish and prepared products. Turnover in 1991 was £3,298 million (pre-tax profits £104 million), with a workforce of about 24,000 world-wide. Food distribution now accounts for over half the profits. The group sponsors the well-known annual Booker literary prize for fiction. Caine is governer of the Institute of Development Studies; deputy chairman of the Commonwealth Development Corporation; director of the Commonwealth

Equity Fund; and chairman of Channel Five. Caine was knighted in 1988. He married in 1952 Janice Denise née Mercer: they had one son and one daughter. The marriage was dissolved in 1987, when he married Emma Harriet Nicholson, a Conservative MP.

CAIRD, Patrick Tennant
(1848 - 7 January 1933)
Shipbuilder and railway company chairman, born in Greenock, son of James T Caird, a shipbuilder, and his wife Elizabeth née McArthur, he was educated in Scotland and Germany and after a five-year engineering apprenticeship in his father's firm was appointed its engineering manager, in 1870. Nearly twenty years later, on his father's death, he succeeded as chairman of Caird & Co, eventually selling out to Harland & Wolff in 1916. He became a director of the Glasgow & South Western Railway in 1891, deputy chairman in 1897 and chairman in 1900, retiring in 1915. In this period the GSWR expanded by acquisition and new construction, gaining access to Stranraer and building up a steamer fleet. Caird was a Unionist in politics. He married Jane Neilson by whom he had a son and three daughters. See *The Bailie*, 20 August 1902; *DSBB*.

CALLENDER, Sir Thomas Octavius
(9 April 1855 - 2 December 1938)
Electrical cable manufacturer, born in Glasgow, the eldest son of William Ormiston Callender and Jean née Marshall, who were in the leather trade. The family formed an asphalt and bitumen business in London in 1877, which as Callender's Cable & Construction Co became a leading cable manufacturer. Educated in Greenwich and in France, Tom Callender was managing director from 1896-1938, a period which which saw annual sales grow from under £100,000 to over £1 million. In 1907 the firm employed 5,000. A president of the Electrical Trades Benevolent Association, he also served as vice-president of the FBI. A JP for Kent, he was knighted in 1918. In 1884 he married Bessie Emmeline Pinnock of Erith, by whom he had one son, Thomas Ormiston (d 1941). He left £383,276. See Robert M Morgan, *Callender's, 1882-1945* (1982); *DBB*.

CAMDEN, John
(18 November 1925 -)
Construction materials company executive, the son of Joseph Reginald Richard John Camden and Lilian Kate McCann. Educated at Royal Worcester Grammar School and Birmingham University (BSc), he served in the Tank and Intelligence Corps during the Second World War, before

becoming a civil engineer for Ready Mixed Concrete in 1952. RMC (the name changed in 1981) originated in Bedford in 1926, but was taken over by Australians and registered in 1952. Camden first set up a plant in Birmingham, then directed the firm's Dusseldorf activities. Appointed in 1962 to head European operations, in 1966 he was brought home to become RMC's managing director (a post he held until 1985). He conducted business more formally than his previous boss, giving more power to regional managers. By 1974, when Camden became chairman, RMC was the world's biggest ready-mixer and highly profitable. In the depressed early 1970s, he expanded into the US and into DIY (acquiring the Great Mills stores). In 1982 profits reached £55 million and, despite some problems, RMC had a prosperous German business, expanding UK road-building, and thriving new Scottish subsidiaries. Camden became executive chairman in 1986. By 1992 RMC's turnover was £2,589 million (pre-tax profit £216 million), its workforce 25,000: though it had attracted adverse publicity over its *Bowbelle* Thames dredger that was involved in the sinking of the *Marchioness* pleasure boat in 1989, and also over environmental issues. In 1972 Camden married Daine Mae Friese: the have two daughters (and Camden had one son and two daughters by a former marriage). See Michael Cassell, *The Readymixers* (1986).

CAMPBELL, Colin Frederick
1st Baron Colgrain
(13 June 1866 - 3 November 1954)

Clearing banker, born in Scotland, the son of George W Campbell, a member of a distinguished banking family. His mother was the second daughter of Sir James Weir Hogg, Bt. After Eton and experience in the family business of Finlay, Campbell & Co, he joined the board of the National Provincial Bank in 1903, the beginning of a fifty-year association. In that period (during which he was chairman 1933-46), the NPB became one of the Big Five banks: its branches grew from 300 to some 1,500, and its deposits from £50 million to £800 million. His wartime services as chairman of the British Bankers' Association and the Clearing House brought him a peerage in 1946. In 1890 he married Lady Angela Mary Alice Ryder (d 1939), second daughter of the Fourth Earl of Harrrowby. He left £95,648. See Sir Theodore E G Gregory, *The Westminster Bank through a Century* (2 vols, 1936); *DBB*.

CAREY, Sir Peter (Willoughby)
(26 July 1923 -)

Industrialist, born in Stockwell, south-east London, the son of John Delves Carey, a schoolmaster, and his wife Sophie, a nurse at Westminster Hospital. Educated at Portsmouth Grammar School, Oriel College, Oxford (where he studied classics), and the School of Slavonic Studies, he served in the Second World War and became an information officer for the British Embassy in Belgrade, 1945-6. He worked for the Foreign Office (German Section) between 1948 and 1951, and then held a succession of top posts in the Board of Trade, the Ministry of Technology and the Department of Trade & Industry, where he was permanent secretary, 1976-83. During 1983-90 he was a director (chairman 1987-89) of Morgan & Grenfell Holdings, the securities wing of the renowned merchant bank, which involved him in the financial boom and bust of the 1980s and the DTI investigation of the Guinness takeover (involving Ernest Saunders and Gerald Ronson (qqv)). He was also on the boards of Westland, BPB Industries, Cable & Wireless and NV Philips. In 1983 he became a director of Dalgety, the food and agribusiness group, and was chairman between 1986 to 1992. During this period Dalgety's, which had been founded in Australia in 1846, underwent vigorous rationalisation. In 1987 £150 million was raised by selling non-core businesses to move more strongly into snack food (Golden Wonder, Continental Savouries and Hunters' Foods) and supplying supermarkets. Between 1986 and 1992 turnover fell from £4,910 million to £3,659 million, but pre-tax profits rose from £75 million to £111 million). Dalgety had over 16,000 workers in 1992. Carey was made a CB in 1972, KCB in 1976 and a GCB in 1982. In 1946 he married Thelma Young: they had three daughters. See Wynford Vaughan-Thomas, *Dalgety: The Romance of Business* (1984).

CARLISLE, Alexander Montgomery
(8 July 1854 - 5 March 1926)

Shipbuilder, born at Ballymena, Co Antrim, son of John Carlisle, an inspector of National Schools, and his wife Catherine née Montgomery, he was educated at the Royal Academical Institution, Belfast, where his father had moved to teach English. At sixteen he was apprenticed with Harland & Wolff, the Belfast shipbuilders, with whom his cousin William James Pirrie (qv) was doing so well. After completing his apprenticeship he very shortly became chief draughtsman and in 1878 shipyard manager. Subsequently he was general manager and chairman of the managing directors of Harland & Wolff. He worked on the designs of a number of White Star liners including the ill-fated *Titanic*, and for the Cunard Line, the *Lusitania*. Carlisle resigned from Harland & Wolff at the relatively early age of 56, probably because he clashed with Pirrie, his brother-in-law as well as his cousin, the company chairman. Carlisle remained a consultant to the company but moved to London. An independent Unionist, he was sworn of the Irish Privy Council in 1907. He married Edith Wooster, an American. See Herbert Jefferson, *Viscount Pirrie of Belfast* (Belfast, 1948); Michael Moss and John R Hume, *Shipbuilders to the World: 125 Years of Harland & Wolff, Belfast, 1861-1986* (1986); *The Times*, 6 March 1926.

CARLOW, Charles
(1849 - 27 January 1923)
Coal manager, born at Methilhill, Fife, son of Charles Augustus Carlow, a colliery manager, and Catherine Euphemia née Dryburgh, Carlow attended Dunfermline Grammar School and then worked with his father before studying mining engineering at Edinburgh and Glasgow. After four years as an assistant colliery manager, in 1872 he was appointed at the early age of 23 manager of the newly-formed Fife Coal Co. Carlow responded quickly to vicissitudes of trade, investing in new pits and new technology. By the late 1880s dividends of 15 per cent and more were attained. Carlow joined the board in 1893, became managing director in 1895 and chairman in 1907; he chaired the company until his death. By 1914 the Fife Coal Co was Scotland's premier colliery combine, employing 15,000 and producing 4.5 million tons of coal a year. Carlow closely identified with the adjacent mining communities of Methilhill and Leven, living at the latter and serving as an elder in its United Free Church of Scotland church. He married Mary, daughter of William Lindsay, a landed proprietor and first chairman of Fife Coal Co. They had at least one son, Charles Augustus Carlow (qv), who became joint managing director of the company, with his father, in 1917. See *DSBB*.

CARLOW, Charles Augustus
(30 November 1878 - 13 August 1954)
Mining engineer and coal company executive, born in Scotland, the son of Charles Carlow (qv) and grandson of ex-Provost William Lindsay of Leith. After technical education at Heriot-Watt College, Edinburgh, and the Scottish Mining School (where he was a medallist), he gained experience in the coalfields of the north of England and qualified to work in both English and Scottish coal mines. In 1917 he became managing director of the Fife Coal Co, where his father and grandfather had worked. He was elected chairman and managing director in 1939, a post he held until coal nationalisation in 1952. He held office as chairman or vice-chairman of most of the coal trade organisations in Scotland. He was also past-president of the Mining

Institute of Scotland, of the Association of Mining Electrical Engineers, and of the Institution of Mining Engineers. Carlow left £250,000. See *The Times*, 14 August 1954.

CARNELLEY, William
(7 May 1823 - 8 October 1919)
Cotton manufacturer, born at Barnsley, son of Thomas Carnelley, he trained as a linen handloom weaver before 1840 when he went to Manchester in pursuit of better work. He joined John Rylands & Sons which then had mills at Wigan and Ainsworth as well as finishing works and collieries at Wigan and a Manchester warehouse. As the firm expanded Carnelly was sent to different mills to assist and to learn supervisory roles. When John Rylands established a fustian department in his consolidated Manchester warehouse in 1847 Carnelly was put in charge. The untimely deaths of John Rylands' sons caused a succession problem which Rylands solved in 1873 by incorporating the business. With a capital of £2 million and properties valued at well over £1 million, it was the largest vertically integrated cotton manufacturer in Lancashire. By 1907 it employed 8,000. Carnelly was made a director, becoming managing director in 1896. After John Rylands died in 1888 Carnelly became an alternate chairman, with Reuben Spencer (1830-1901). From 1901 he was continuously chairman until he retired just before his death at the age of 94. In 50 years he never took a full week's holiday from work. A Wesleyan, he wrote two books about the Bible. Carnelly was married and had at least one son. See *DBB* (John Rylands); *Manchester Guardian*, 27 July 1916;

CAYZER, William Nicholas
Baron Cayzer of St Mary Axe in the City of London
(21 January 1910 -)
Shipowner and financier, the son of Sir Augustus Cayzer (1876-1943) 1st Bt, and his wife Ina Frances née Stancombe. He was the grandson of Charles Cayzer, who founded the family shipping firm in 1878. Educated at Eton and Corpus Christi College, Cambridge, he inherited the baronetcy in 1943 and succeeded his father as chairman. He rose to prominence in the mid-1950s, when Cayzer's Clan Line took over Union Castle and emerged at the head of the industry with a fleet of over 100 ships and a firm named British & Commonwealth Shipping. In 1951 Cayzer set up Caledonia Investments, which he floated in 1960, and used as the vehicle for the family's 49 per cent B & C stake. In the 1960s and 1970s Cayzer diversified into finance and for a time backed John Gunn (qv), who became chief executive of B & C. Under

Cayzer's chairmanship, Gunn's wheeler-dealing in property and banking made B & C into one of the fastest-growing glamour stocks of the 1980s. But in the summer of 1987 Cayzer tired of Gunn's flamboyance and sold out of B & C for £427 million - only weeks before the October 1987 stockmarket crash! - even taking care to secure a banker's guarantee on the money owed. Some of the proceeds have been invested in a 45 per cent stake in Bristow Helicopters, once owned by B & C (which collapsed in debt in 1990). Caledonia has also invested in a glass company, a brewery, a Swiss industrial group and Harry Ramsden, the fish and chip chain. Cayzer, worth an estimated £350 million, remains as chairman, with his nephew, Peter Buckley, as chief executive. Described as the epitome of white-gloved power and an ardent supporter of the Conservative Party, he was created a life peer in 1982. He married in 1935 Elizabeth Catherine née Williams: they have two daughters, but no heir. See Augustus Muir and M Davies, *A Victorian Shipowner: A Portrait of Sir Charles Cayzer, Baronet of Gartmore* (1978).

CHAMBERLAIN, Arthur
(11 April 1842 - 19 October 1913)
Metal goods and ammunition manufacturer, born at Camberwell, Surrey, the third son of Joseph Chamberlain, a shoe manufacturer, and his wife Caroline née Harben, he attended University College School, leaving at 16 to join Nettlefold & Chamberlain, Birmingham screw manufacturers in which his father had invested. In the 1860s Arthur partnered his brothers Richard and Joseph (later Colonial Secretary and tariff reformer) in running Smith & Chamberlain, Birmingham brass founders. However, the bulk of his business career was spent with Kynoch Ltd, a cartridge and ammunition business employing 2,500 in the 1880s when it was imperilled by bad management. A shareholders' revolt ejected George Kynoch in 1888 and installed a new board under Arthur Chamberlain. He remained very much in charge until his death. Kynochs' employment in nine works around the country reached 6,000 in 1894 and 8,000 in 1907. Like his illustrious brother Joseph, Arthur was a Unitarian; unlike him he was a Liberal and a freetrader. Arthur in 1870 married Louisa, daughter of Timothy Kenrick, member of another Birmingham Unitarian cousinhood; they had two sons and seven daughters. See *DBB*.

CHAMBERLAIN, Arthur
(1880 - 7 August 1941)
Engineering company chairman, elder son of Arthur Chamberlain (qv) and his wife Louisa née Kenrick, he succeeded his father as chairman of Kynoch Ltd and as director of several other companies. One of these was Tubes Ltd which in 1919 became a constituent of Tube Investments, a merger of five Birmingham firms. Arthur Chamberlain was its chairman until his death and played an important part in 1929 when he commenced discussions with Allan Macdiarmid (qv) of Stewarts & Lloyds which led to a market-sharing arrangement and a guaranteed supply of 100,000 tons of iron and steel a year for TI when Stewarts & Lloyds' new plant opened at Corby (in 1934). Under Chamberlain at TI Ivan Stedeford (qv) became a managing director. By the mid-1920s Chamberlain had left the Kynoch board and was chairman of Charles Churchill & Co Ltd and of the Churchill Machine Tool Co Ltd, with which he stayed. To his major directorships of TI and Churchill he added Roneo Ltd, again as chairman, in the mid-1930s. His ordinary directorships included the General Electric Co and the Midland Bank. Living at Edgbaston in 1920, Chamberlain had moved to Chelsea by 1925 and by 1931 had moved again to Rackenford Manor, Crediton, Devon where he took up hunting. Clearly valued as an industrial board member, he was overshadowed by his cousins, Austin and Neville. See *The Times*, 11, 23 August 1941.

CHAMBERS, Sir Stanley Paul
(2 April 1904 - 23 December 1981)
Chemical manufacturing company chairman, born at Southgate, Middlesex, the son of Philip Joseph Chambers, a commercial clerk and later a City wine merchant, and Catherine née Abbott, Paul Chambers attended the City of London School and, as an evening student, the LSE where he took a BCom in 1928 and an MSc in 1934. He joined the Inland Revenue and rose rapidly, making his name as a member of the Indian Income Tax Inquiry Committee (1935) and later Taxation Adviser to the Indian Government. Returning to the UK in 1940 he was appointed Assistant Secretary to the Board of Inland Revenue, and then Secretary 1942-47. After a subordinate A G T Shingler devised the cumulative principle, Chambers introduced the PAYE (Pay As You Earn) system of taxation. He left the Civil Service and joined ICI as director in 1947. Within a year he was finance director, in 1952 one of three deputy chairmen and in 1960 chairman of ICI, holding the post for eight years. Sir Paul Chambers (he was knighted in 1965) injected financial targets and constraints into ICI's hitherto predominantly scientific ethos. Reorganisation at the top of ICI allowed senior executives more time to develop strategic corporate planning and investment policies. Chambers' abortive attempt to take over

Courtaulds in 1961-62 was a distinct failure. On the positive side, under his chairmanship ICI's exports doubled in value and as a proportion of total sales rose from 17 to 24 per cent. On retiring from ICI Chambers became chairman of three insurance companies. He was married twice: first, in 1926, to Dorothy Copp (marriage dissolved 1955); second, in 1955, to Mrs Edith Pollack, by whom he had two daughters. See *DBB*.

CHANDLER, Sir Colin (Michael)
(7 October 1939 -)

Industrialist, born in Greenwich, south-east London, the son of Henry John Chandler and Mary Martha née Bowles. His father was a toolmaker; his mother a shirtmaker. Educated at St Joseph's Academy, a Catholic grammar school in Blackheath, he left at sixteen and became one of the first commercial apprentices at the De Havilland aircraft factory at Hatfield (his parents had discouraged him from attending university). After a day-release course at Hatfield Polytechnic, he qualified as a chartered management accountant. At De Havilland he was a contracts officer, and then in 1966 became assistant to the commercial manager of Hawker Siddeley at Kingston. A decade later he was running the Kingston operation. In 1978, when Hawker became part of the newly-formed British Aerospace, he became head of the giant company's 12,000-strong Kingston-Brough division. But after joining the board as marketing director, he decided that he did not like the direction BAe was moving under Ray Lygo and in 1985 was seconded as head of defence sales at the Ministry of Defence. In 1988 he negotiated Britain's largest ever defence contract, the Al Yamamah air defence project with Saudi Arabia. He was rewarded with a knighthood in 1988, though the £20 billion contract has since been dogged by controversy over back-handers. He did not return to BAe, but instead joined Vickers as heir apparent to Sir David Plastow (qv): Chandler became managing director in 1990, chief executive in 1991 and chairman in 1992. His arrival coincided with a loss at Vickers in 1992 of £25.9 million (before tax) and a reduced dividend and he had to announce the cutting of 950 jobs at Vickers' subsidiary Rolls Royce, which lost £15.8 million (before interest) in 1992. He is also a non-executive director of Siemens Plessey Electronic Systems. In 1964 he married Jennifer Mary Crawford: they have one son and two daughters.

CHESTERFIELD, Arthur Desborough
(21 August 1905 -)

Banker, son of Arthur William Chesterfield, a Hastings businessman, and Ellen née Harvey, he attended Hastings Grammar School, leaving at 18 to join the Westminster Bank's Eastbourne branch. After seven years in branch offices he moved to the department of the London area general manager. Following the outbreak of war in 1939 he was transferred to the office of the chief general manager, Sir Charles Lidbury (qv). After four years he had a short spell as a branch manager and then returned to the Westminster Bank's central administration: assistant general manager, 1945; joint general manager, 1947; deputy chief general manager, 1949; chief general manager, 1950 until his retirement in 1966. Two major achievements came under Chesterfield: the creation of a residential staff college, a very significant contribution to management training and corporate ethos; and the computerisation of data processing. On leaving the Westminster Bank Chesterfield took on a number of company directorships. He was made a CBE in 1962. He married Betty (d 1980) daughter of John Henry Downey; they had two sons and three daughters. See *The Westminster*, February 1966.

CHETWOOD, Sir Clifford (Jack)
(2 November 1928 -)

Construction company executive, born in Fulham, west London, the son of Stanley Jack Chetwood, a lorry driver, and Doris May née Palmer. In 1951 he joined the first management trainee intake of the construction firm, George Wimpey & Co Ltd. By the age of thirty he was regional manager of Wimpey Birmingham and in 1969 he became a full director of Wimpey, which at the time was the UK's biggest housebuilder. Chetwood became chairman of the board of management, 1975-9; and headed Wimpey Construction UK, 1979-83. In 1984 he became chairman of Wimpey and was chief executive, 1982-90. Chetwood took over at the helm of Wimpey when it was being crippled by a recession and by poor management, which resulted in overseas losses of £41.7 million for 1983, when Wimpey's turnover was £1,393 million. He launched a stringent and wide-ranging restructuring programme, which cost 9,500 jobs, and gave him the reputation of being a tough and demanding workaholic. By 1988 Wimpey had broken the £100 million pre-tax profits barrier, but profits dipped thereafter and by 1991 Wimpey was feeling the effects of the worst recession in the UK building industry since the 1930s. Wimpey made a loss of £16 million in 1991 (from a turnover of £1,752 million) and in the following year

Chetwood retired from the Wimpey chairmanship. He became president of the Building Employers' Federation in 1989, and chairman of Construction ITB in 1990. He was knighted in 1987. In 1953 he married Pamela Phyllis Sherlock: they have one son and three daughters. See *New Civil Engineer*, 5 April 1990; Valerie White, *Wimpey: The First Hundred Years* (1980).

CHRISTIE, John Hyde
(1836 - 24 June 1926)
Turkey red dyer, born at Barrhead, eight miles south-west of Glasgow, son of William Henry McLean Christie, joiner and farmer, and his wife Helen née Hyde, he was educated at the Andersonian College and the Glasgow laboratory of Dr William Wallace. In 1856 he joined John Hyde & Co, silk manufacturers and dyers of Port Dundas, run by his cousin John Hyde. After three years he moved to the Vale of Leven to the newly-reconstituted firm of John Orr Ewing & Co, turkey red dyers, as chief chemist at its Alexandria Works. The pursuit of quality and fastness of colour occupied his attention initially. The search for artificial dyes followed in the late 1860s. However, German competitors first manufactured synthetic alizarine, substituting for the madder root in making the red pigment essential to turkey red dyeing. British failure to pursue these alizarine experiments gave the Germans a monopoly in 1882 whereupon they raised prices, bringing the Dunbartonshire trade to a standstill. Scottish and English manufacturers formed the British Alizarine Co Ltd to negotiate quotas with the German manufacturers and gained membership of the Alizarine Convention. Christie was a director of the BAC, 1882-1922, and its chairman, 1904-22. The episode convinced Christie of the merits of combination. When overseas tariffs began to hurt exports of British-dyed yarns in the 1890s Christie, his son Henry and Henry Brock, another partner in Orr Ewing, organised the merger of three firms in 1898 to form the United Turkey Red Co Ltd. A fourth joined in 1900, bringing 5,000 employees in the Vale of Leven under the UTR. John Hyde Christie was its chairman, 1898-1922, a period which saw the trade suffer from post-war boom and collapse and difficult labour relations. Christie was prominent in local government in Dumbarton. He married Jessie née Fulton, a farmer's daughter, by whom he had three sons and three daughters. See *DSBB*.

CITRINE, Walter McLennan
1st Baron Citrine of Wembley
(22 August 1887 - 22 January 1983)
Nationalised electricity industry chairman, born in Liverpool, the son of Alfred Citrine, a seafarer and

Isabella née McLennan, he attended elementary school until twelve and a half and then worked in a flour mill before securing an apprenticeship with a firm of electrical contractors. In 1911 he joined the Liverpool branch of the Electrical Trades Union and three years later became full time district secretary. He moved to Manchester as assistant general secretary of the ETU but in 1924 transferred to a wider sphere as assistant secretary of the Trades Union Congress, becoming secretary in 1926. He held this post until 1946 when he was appointed to the National Coal Board as manpower and welfare member. A year later he was chosen to be the first chairman of the British Electricity Authority, remaining in post until 1957. At the Electricity Authority, as he had at TUC headquarters, Citrine created a strong central administration. It merged 600 former independent and municipal undertakings into 12 new area boards for the distribution of electricity and the Central Electricity Generating Board for its production and transmission. Citrine built bridges between the unions and the nationalised industry. He was criticised for failing to adopt the latest technology. He was knighted in 1935, was sworn of the Privy Council in 1940, and created a baron in 1946. Quiet, patient, moderate and honest, Citrine was a rare example of successful top leadership on both sides of British industry. He married Doris Slade (d 1973) in 1913; they had two sons. See *DBB*; Leslie Hannah, *Engineers, Managers and Politicians: The First Fifteen Years of Nationalised Electricity Supply in Britain* (1982).

CLARK, Alfred Corning
(19 December 1873 - 16 June 1950)
Gramophone company executive, born in New York City, the eldest son of Walter Lowrie Clark, a confectionery manufacturer, and Marie née Rowe. After attending Felsted and acquiring experience in the international phonograph and gramophone industry, Clark became managing director of the Gramophone Co Ltd, the Middlesex-based company, which after a period of American control in 1931 emerged as Electric & Musical Industries Ltd (EMI). Capitalised at £6.2 million, EMI was a holding company, controlling the Gramophone Co (popularly known as His Master's Voice or HMV), the Columbia Gramophone Co and the Parlophone Co. Corning was chairman until 1945 and briefly also became managing director and then president. A British subject after 1928, Clark married twice: firstly to Florence Beecher née Crouse (they later divorced); secondly in 1921 to writer Gertrude Ivy Sanders. He left £73,758. See G Jones, 'The Gramophone Company: An Anglo-American Multinational, 1898-1931', *Business History Review* (1985); *DBB*.

CLARK, Sir Allen George
(24 August 1898 - 30 June 1962)

Electrical equipment manufacturer, he was born at Brookline near Boston, USA, elder child of Byron George Clark, a United Shoe Machinery Corporation executive, and his wife Helen née Peirce. When his father was posted to Europe the family settled in England and Allen Clark was educated at Felsted School. After the First World War (in which he was commissioned in the RFC) Allen in 1920 joined the Plessey Co Ltd, a small tool making firm in Ilford, his father buying him a share in the business. With the proceeds of a contract to design and make radio receivers for Marconi, the firm built a new factory at Ilford and in 1925 formed a private company, Plessey Co (1925) Ltd. Clark became joint managing director with W O Heyne, a talented mechanical engineer. Deliberately pursuing the latest electrical technologies, confining their business to the capital goods market and restricting sales to financially sound companies, the firm grew to 500 employees in 1931, a wartime peak of 11,500 and 5,250 in 1945. Demand for electrical and electronic equipment with military applications continued with the Cold War. By 1955 Plessey employed over 15,000 and at Clark's death, over 50,000, located in 16 manufacturing plants and three research laboratories and organised in six groups. Profits rose from £600,000 in 1951 to £4.3 million in 1960. During this expansive last decade Clark continued his search for new technology (which included silicon research from 1952) first by licencing agreements with foreign firms, then by joint ventures abroad and latterly by takeovers. Clark was a big man, six feet tall and heavily built with a penchant for stetsons and cigars. A slave-driver, he worked his employees as hard as himself. He married in 1925 Jocelyn, daughter of Percy Culverhouse, chief architect of the Great Western Railway; they had two sons (who succeeded him in the business) and a daughter; subsequently they divorced. See *DBB*.

CLARK, Sir George Smith
(8 November 1861 - 23 March 1935)

Shipbuilder, he was born at Paisley, Scotland, son of James Clark, a partner in the firm of J & J Clark, thread manufacturers, and his first wife Jane Smith, daughter of a Glasgow shipowner. From Merchiston Castle School, Edinburgh, he moved to Belfast and trained in the Harland & Wolff shipyard where he met Frank Workman (qv) who had established a small shipyard on the Lagan. They went into partnership in 1880, employing 150 men on four acres. By 1907 they employed 8,000 and by 1920 10,000 with 100 acres of yards. The firm pioneered the Parsons gas turbine engine, the

Victorian built for the Allan Line in 1904 being the first turbine-propelled ocean steamer. Specialising in building medium-sized cargo boats, rarely over 10,000 tons, they also led in the construction of insulated and refrigerated fruit carriers. From being a world-class shipyard before the First World War, Workman, Clark & Co became a spectacular casualty of the post-war trade stagnation and over-supply of shipping capacity, and fraud. In 1920 the firm was taken over by the Northumberland Shipping Co but instead of investing a £3 million debenture loan (raised at the point of takeover) in Workman, Clark, it was used to pay off one of the Northumberland's old debts. Clark resigned from the board, becoming (unwillingly) a very rich man in selling out. A huge burden of fixed interest debt further pulled down the firm. In 1927 the directors, including Clark, were sued for issuing a false prospectus in 1920. They won the original trial but lost on appeal. The firm went into temporary liquidation and, though reorganised, did not survive the depression. Clark, a Presbyterian, Unionist MP for Belfast 1907-10 and created a baronet in 1917, remained active in politics as a Unionist Senator in the Northern Ireland Parliament 1925-35. In 1881 he married Frances Elizabeth Matier; they had two sons. See *DBB*.

CLARK, James Oscar Max
(26 September 1877 - 2 January 1958)

Thread manufacturer, the son of Robert M Clark of Paisley. Educated at Uppingham and King's College, Cambridge, he joined the thread manufacturers J & P Coats in 1898, taking charge of Anchor Mills, Paisley, founded in 1812 by his great grandfather, James Clark. He was appointed director of Coats in 1905, elected chairman in 1928, and held the post until his retirement in 1946. The firm employed 10,000 in 1935. He was a director of the Union Bank of Scotland, the Reinsurance Corporation, and a number of other trust companies; and a member of the Prime Minister's Panel of Industrialists in 1938-39. He married in 1902 Winifred Mary, daughter of James Halsall: they had two sons and a daughter. See J O M Clark and E B Noel, *A History of Tennis* (1924).

CLARKE, (John) Neil
(7 August 1934 -)

Mining executive, born in Lincoln, the son of George Philip Clarke, a foundry engineer who helped develop the Spitfire and Whittle's jet engine, and Norah Marie née Bailey. Educated at Rugby and King's College, London (LLB), he qualified as an accountant and spent the 1960s as partner in the accountancy firm of Rowley, Pemberton, Roberts & Co. In 1969 he joined the

0

mining group Charter Consolidated as head of taxation, becoming chief executive in 1982. He was appointed chairman of the troubled precious metal company Johnson Matthey in 1984 (in which Charter was the biggest shareholder) and helped formulate a rescue plan. He left Charter in 1988 and worked for the engineering firm Molins, before succeeding Lord Haslam (qv) as chairman of the British Coal Corporation in 1991. Against a backdrop of a rapidly shrinking coal industry and management squabbles (one of his first jobs was to organise the departure of the commercial director, Malcolm Edwards, a staunch defender of the industry), Clarke led the negotiations for the renewal in March 1993 of British Coal's contract with the privatised national generators, Power-Gen and National Power. Under that contract, these companies were forced to take much of their output from British Coal (accounting for 80 per cent of the latter's output), but were under little obligation to do so after March 1993. Partly as a result of the impending collapse of this market, in October 1992 Clarke announced that British Coal was to close 31 pits and make 30,000 miners redundant. A public outcry and union opposition led to a Parliamentary inquiry, which criticised Clarke for his handling of the affair. But if the original decision goes ahead, the period between 1984 and 1993 will have seen the number of British Coal's pits dwindle from 170 to 18, its workforce from 170,000 to 25,000. Neil Clarke in 1959 married Sonia Heather Beckett: they have three sons.

CLARKE, Sir Robert (Cyril)
(28 March 1929 -)
Food manufacturer, the son of Robert Henry Clarke and Rose née Bratton. He was educated at Dulwich College and Pembroke College, Oxford, where he read history. After a spell of National Service with the Royal West Kent Regiment, he joined the chocolate manufacturers, Cadbury Bros, as a trainee in 1952. He was attracted by that company's ethical approach to business and has remained a believer in corporate responsibility to employees and the environment. By 1957 he was marketing director for Cadbury Confectionery and five years later became managing director of Cadbury Cakes. In 1971 Cadbury and Hector Laing's (qv) United Biscuits launched a joint endeavour marketing cakes and Clarke was appointed managing director. It was not a great success and United Biscuits later took over the whole business, allowing Clarke to switch companies. With the demise of the cake business, Clarke soon moved up the ranks at United Biscuits, joining the board of United Biscuits (UK) Ltd in 1974. By 1977 he was managing director of UB Biscuits,

group chief executive of United Biscuits Holdings in 1986, deputy chairman in 1989, and finally chairman in succession to Laing in 1990. In 1991 United Biscuits' turnover was £2,979 million with pre-tax profits of £211 million, and it employed over 40,000. Since 1988 Clarke has been a non-executive director of Thames Water. He was knighted in 1993. He married in 1952 Evelyn (Lynne) Mary née Harper: they have three sons and one daughter.

CLEAVER, Sir Anthony (Brian)
(10 April 1938 -)
Computer manufacturer, the son of William Brian Cleaver and Dorothea née Peeks. Educated at Berkhamsted School and Trinity College, Oxford, he joined IBM UK Ltd in 1962. The British subsidiary of the American multinational computer firm, IBM UK was established in 1949 with a capital of £2 million, and by the 1960s had emerged as Britain's leading computer manufacturer. Cleaver after a succession of senior posts became general manager of IBM UK in 1984 and succeeded Sir Edwin Nixon as chief executive in 1986, becoming chairman in 1990 (when the chief executive's post was filled by Nick Temple (qv)). In the early 1990s he has been involved in restructuring IBM UK in the face of a recession and increasing Japanese competition, at a time when IBM's world-wide lead was being challenged. In 1991 IBM UK's turnover was about £4 billion and it employed about 15,000. In 1962 he married Mary Teresa Cotter; they have one son. Cleaver was knighted in 1992.

CLEGG, Ronald (Anthony)
(8 April 1937 -)
Property developer, born in the Lancashire cotton town of Littleborough, the only child of Stanley and Cicely Clegg, who ran a restaurant business. After National Service, in 1961 he became a salesman with a Glossop textile manufacturer. Two years later it was taken over by Mountain Mills, a Bradford worsted suit-maker, which later Tony Clegg was to manage in partnership with its boss, Ernest Hall. As textiles declined, Clegg went into property and by the time he amicably parted from Hall in 1983 he headed his own development company - Mountleigh. With Clegg's (and his new partner, Paul Bloomfield's) skills for spotting the hidden assets in properties (for example, in 1986 they bought the United Real Property Trust for £117 million and had soon dismembered and sold it for £140 million), Mountleigh's rise was spectacular. But in 1988 Clegg needed an operation for a brain tumour and in 1989 he sold his shares for £70 million and retired to his Yorkshire estate to breed Highland cattle. The other shareholders must

have wished they had done the same when the property boom collapsed, for in early 1992 Mountleigh (once described as a company that illustrated the worst financial excesses of the 1980s) went into receivership. Clegg is involved with various charities and trusts (he is deputy chairman of the Prince's Youth Business Trust). In 1963 he married Dorothy Eve Glaze: they have three daughters. See Philip Beresford, *The Sunday Times Book of the Rich* (1990).

CLORE, Sir Charles
(24 December 1904 - 26 July 1979)

Property developer and industrialist, born in Mile End, East London, the son of Israel Clore, a clothing manufacturer, and his wife Yetta née Abrahams, both Russian Jewish immigrants, he attended an elementary school before joining his father's firm. In 1924 Clore emigrated to South Africa to live with a cousin engaged in large scale fruit farming. He became interested in agriculture and in films. He returned to England in 1927 and started speculating in property, not always successfully. Capital from South African investments enabled him to expand during the Second World War when property prices were low. After the war his opportunities exploded. Many companies were inefficiently run, with assets underworked and dividends kept low. Share prices in the late 1940s and 1950s undervalued companies, not least because investor expectations were low. However, the Companies Act of 1948 required public companies to publish more information about their true assets and profits. Clore and others, like Isaac Wolfson and Hugh Fraser (qqv), saw and seized the chance to appeal to shareholders over the heads of directors, giving a good price for shares and making a killing for themselves by asset-stripping. He deployed the takeover bid (as it was called) to acquire a number of firms, primarily Furness Shipbuilding in 1951, Bentley Engineering in 1952, and J Sears (True-Form Boot) Co in 1953. Sears was turned into a holding company in 1955 when the group employed 20,000 workers. His most ambitious bid, for the brewery group of Watney Mann in 1959, failed. In 1960 he merged his property company, City & Central Investments, with Jack Cotton's City Centre Properties. It was an uncomfortable alliance and Clore, a 'cautious and thoughtful introvert', in contrast to Cotton, withdrew from it in 1968. Clore became immensely rich (he left £123 million, by a 1985 reckoning) but was enormously generous (not least to Israeli institutions), in recognition of which he was knighted in 1971. In 1977 he decided to emigrate but died in a London clinic. He married in 1943, Francine Rachel Halphen, a heroine of the French resistance; they had a son and a daughter but divorced in 1957. See David Clutterbuck and Marion Devine, *Clore: The Man and His Millions* (1987); *DBB*; Charles Gordon, *The Two Tycoons: A Personal Memoir of Charles Clore and Jack Cotton* (1984).

CLOWES, Peter
(8 December 1942 -)

Financier, born in Flixton, Manchester, where his parents, Eric and Mary Clowes, ran a hardware store. Educated at Chorlton Grammar School, he left at sixteen and joined his father selling paraffin and hardware. He graduated to selling insurance and developed his investment ideas at Cannon Assurance, where he met his future lover Elizabeth Barlow. Together in 1973 they founded Barlow Clowes & Partners to deal in gilts for private investors. Clowes told the 18,000, mainly elderly, investors that his business was 'as safe as the Bank of England'. But instead of investing in gilts, Clowes spent the money on dubious investments and a luxury lifestyle (which included, for example, the purchase of ocean-going yachts previously owned by Christina Onassis). Using a mixture of lies, the manipulation of offshore trusts and 'bond-washing' techniques, Clowes hoodwinked investors and the Department of Trade and Industry and stole nearly £100 million before the firm collapsed in 1988. Clowes was jailed for ten years and an embarrassed Conservative Government paid investors £150 million compensation. Clowes married his first wife, Patricia Slann, a shopkeeper's daughter, when he was twenty-one; his second wife, Pamela, became his business partner after Elizabeth Barlow left in 1978. See Lawrence Lever, *The Barlow Clowes Affair* (1992).

COATS, Archibald
(23 March 1840 - 11 May 1912)

Textile manufacturer, born in Paisley, Scotland, second son of Peter Coats, sewing thread manufacturer, and his wife Glorianna née Mackenzie, he attended Merchiston Castle School in Edinburgh and then entered the family firm of J & P Coats in 1864-65 as a junior partner. He soon became the leader of the family's third generation then based at Ferguslie Mills, Paisley. In the 1870s production for the USA market was transferred to Pawtucket, Rhode Island; consequently new markets had to be found for Paisley output. While his cousin Thomas Glen Coats took charge of production, Archibald developed selling and finance. With the assistance of Otto Ernst Philippi (qv), a brilliant marketing specialist, as foreign sales manager, he overhauled the firm's selling system in the 1880s and in 1889-90 negotiated a remarkable joint selling arrangement with two rival companies. Archibald's support was critical in the decision to convert the firm into a limited liability company (with a capital of £5.75 million) in 1890. In 1896 Archibald Coats achieved a merger with three competitors, including Clark & Co of Anchor Mills, Paisley, and thereby created one of the largest late-Victorian multinationals: J & P Coats Ltd, with 60 branch houses, 150 selling depots, 21,000 employees worldwide (11,000 in the UK), a market value of £22 million and profits just under £1 million. Of a shy disposition, Archibald Coats played a smaller public role than his father but was known as a staunch Unionist, a benefactor of Paisley institutions and a manager of St James United Free Church. He married Elizabeth née Hodge; they had three sons and three daughters. See *DSBB*.

COATS, Ernest Symington
(1873 - 4 August 1938)
Thread manufacturer, the younger son of George Coats, of Staneley. He joined the board of J & P Coats, the famous sewing thread company founded by his family, in 1900 and had long been an expert in central manufacturing processes and yarn-buying. He spent much of his time at the Ferguslie Mill, but was also a director of several Coats companies in Europe. A traditional paternalistic family director, he was married with six sons and a daughter, and left £29,515 gross. See *Paisley and Renfrewshire Gazette*, 6 August 1938.

COCKBURN, William
(28 February 1943 -)
Postal services executive, born in Edinburgh, into a Catholic family, the eldest of eight children. His father was a hospital porter. Educated at Holy Cross Academy, a Catholic grammar school, he eschewed a university education because of the need to begin earning a living. He joined the Post Office in 1951. After holding various junior and middle management positions, he became a personal assistant to the chairman, Sir William Ryland, between 1971 and 1973 (and was succeeded in that post by Iain Vallance (qv)). He was appointed to the board when he was thirty-eight and became managing director of Royal Mail, the biggest job in the Post Office with the most people. In October 1992, he took over from Sir Bryan Nicholson (qv) as the Post Office's chief executive, taking charge of an organisation with an annual turnover of over £5 billion and nearly 200,000 employees. One of his first jobs will be to deal with the Government's decision (expected in 1993) determining whether the PO will be the next nationalised industry for privatisation. He was made a CBE in 1989. He is married with two daughters.

COCKSHAW, Sir Alan
(14 July 1937 -)
Engineering and construction company executive, born at Walkden, near Swinton, the son of John Cockshaw, a pottery tile placer, and Maud née Simpson. He attended Farnworth Grammar School and Leeds University, where he took a BSc. He became chief executive of Fairclough Civil Engineering, 1978-85; Fairclough-Parkinson Mining, 1982-85; and Fairclough Engineering, 1983-84. He became chief executive of AMEC between 1984 and 1988, and was appointed chairman of AMEC in 1988. The group is a comprehensive, engineering, construction and development company. AMEC's turnover rose from £793 million in 1988 to £2,338 million in 1991, but pre-tax profits fell from £34.5 million to a £9.9 million loss. In 1992 the group reported an £87.5 million loss, which Cockshaw blamed on a 'deplorable' performance from the Australian business; problems with cladding on its Brighton property developments; and 'bad luck and bad judgement' in its investment in an Irish property group. In 1991 the group employed about 30,000. Cockshaw married in 1960 Brenda Payne: they have a son and three daughters. He was knighted in 1992.

COHEN, Sir (John Edward) 'Jack'
(6 October 1898 - 24 March 1979)
Retailer, born Jacob Kohen (a name he changed in 1937) at St George-in-the-East, London, the second son of Avroam Kohen and Sime née Garinda. His father, a Polish immigrant Jew, was an East End journeyman tailor. Educated at the local elementary school, Jack (as he was known) left at fourteen and after war service began street trading in the 1920s, coining the brand-name 'Tesco' from the initials of his partner, T E Stockwell, and his own name. He opened his first store in 1931 and within eight years had a hundred stores in the London area. In 1947 'Jack the Slasher' introduced self-service ideas he had seen in America and his stores began to spread nationwide. Expansion in the 1960s was boosted by the abolition of Retail Price Maintenance, which Cohen helped demolish by using Richard Tompkins' (qv) Green Shield stamps. When Cohen retired as chairman in 1970 Tesco had 834 self-service stores, placing it fourth in size behind Co-op, Fine Fare and Allied Suppliers. Tesco's turnover mushroomed from £21 million to £238 million between 1961 and 1970, while net profits mounted from £607,000 to £6.6 million. Tesco was valued at £120 million, with Cohen and his family holding a £22 million interest. Cohen was knighted in 1969. In 1924 he married Sarah ('Cissie') Fox, who provided capital and

support during his career. A Zionist and a freemason, Cohen left £1,957,640. See Maurice Corina, *Pile It High, Sell It Cheap; The Authorised Biography of Jack Cohen, Founder of Tesco* (2nd edition, 1978); DBB.

COHEN, Sir Rex Arthur Louis
(27 November 1906 - 26 February 1988)

Retailer, grandson of Louis Samuel Cohen, the nephew of David Lewis (founder of Lewis's the Liverpool department store), Rex Arthur Louis Cohen was the son of Rex David Cohen and his wife Florence Rahel née Isaacs. Educated at Rugby and Trinity College, Cambridge, he joined the family firm, Lewis's Investment Trust, in 1928, working his way up through the business. By the late 1930s Lewis's had stores in Manchester, Birmingham, Glasgow, Leeds, Hanley and Leicester, as well as Liverpool where it was headquartered, employing over 12,000 in all. During the Second World War Rex Cohen rose to be Assistant Quarter Master General of the 2nd Army and was appointed OBE. He returned to the family firm in 1945 as joint managing director. Under the chairmanship of Frederick James Marquis, Lord Woolton (qv), Lewis's in 1951 acquired Selfridge's, in London's West End. Cohen became chairman in 1958, succeeding Sidney Leake (qv). For his work as chairman of the NAAFI he was knighted in 1964. The following autumn the family firm, a public company since 1924, was snatched from his grasp by Charles Clore (qv) in a month-long takeover battle. Cohen found new business opportunities as chairman of the Meat and Livestock Commission (1967-72), director of United Racecourses, and a member of the Racing Committee of Enquiry. He was chairman of Higgs & Hill, the building contractors, 1966-72, during a property boom. He married in 1932 Nina Costello; they had one daughter. See Asa Briggs, *Friends of the People: The Centenary History of Lewis's* (1956); *The Times*, 2 March 1988.

COHEN, Sir Robert Waley
(8 September 1877 - November 1952)

Oil company executive, born in London, the second son of Nathaniel Louis Cohen, a member of the leading Ashkenazi family. His mother was a daughter of Professor Jacob Waley of University College, London. Educated at Clifton and Emmanuel College, Cambridge (where he was a Scholar), in 1901 he joined the Shell Transport & Trading Co. Expecting to work abroad, instead he stayed at the firm's London offices and eventually became managing director. He was an advocate of the recruitment of graduates for business. Cohen took an active part in the management of other trading firms, including the Eastern & African Corporation, Baldwins, and the United Africa Co. As president of the Central Synagogue in London, he was virtually the head of Anglo-Jewry, and he always took a close interest in the development of Palestine. Cohen was made a KBE in 1920. He married in 1904 Alice (d 1935), daughter of Henry Edward Beddington: they had two sons and one daughter. See *The Times*, 29 November 1952.

COLERIDGE, David (Ean)
(7 June 1932 -)

Insurance company executive, the son of Guy Cecil Richard Coleridge MC and Katherine Cicely Stewart Smith. A distant relative of the poet Samuel Taylor Coleridge, he was born in Bombay, where his father was a partner in a firm of cotton brokers. The family returned to England in the 1930s and after Eton, aged 19 he joined Glanvill Enthoven - a broker for the insurance firm of Lloyd's. Elected an underwriting member of Lloyd's in 1955, two years later he joined R W Sturge & Co (later Sturge Holdings), the publicly-quoted company which is the largest agency within Lloyd's. As such, Sturge's runs syndicates of Names - the outside investors whose wealth provides Lloyd's capital. He became chairman of Sturge in 1978. Under Coleridge (who by 1992 was both chairman and largest single shareholder), Sturge's prospered: between 1980 and 1990 pre-tax profits rose from £684,000 to £31.5 million, though this fell in 1991 to £8.9 million. Coleridge was one of the few people who earned more than £1 million in 1991. His chairmanship of Lloyd's after 1990 (he was deputy chairman in 1985, 1988, 1989) coincided with a difficult period in the company's history, as a series of massive insurance claims in the 1980s caused losses of £1.5 billion. With many Names facing ruin, it was alleged that working Names were found in the more successful syndicates, while outside Names were forced into poor performers. David Rowland (qv), head of Sedgwick Insurance, succeeded him in January 1993. In 1955 Coleridge married Susan Senior, who was connected with two wealthy families - the Seniors, prosperous City stockbrokers, and the Joiceys (qv) of Northumberland coal fame: they have three sons. See Cathy Gunn, *Nightmare on Lime Street: Whatever Happened to Lloyd's of London?* (1992); Jonathan Mantle, *For Whom the Bell Tolls: The Lesson of Lloyd's of London* (1992).

COLLIER, Joseph
(c 1898 - 27 August 1967)

Drapery manufacturer and retailer who kept a low profile even after emerging on the board of the United Drapery Stores. This had been formed in

1927 to acquire five department stores and a credit drapery business. Collier became a UDS director in 1945 and managing director in 1946; he was chairman from 1959 until 1966 when he was made company president. The firm grew chiefly by acquisition in the expansive trading years of the 1950s and 1960s. Under the UDS banner were retail chains like John Collier (formed by merging two acquisitions, the Fifty Shilling Tailors and Prices Tailors) and Alexandre Ltd, all supported by extensive manufacturing facilities. By 1955 UDS employed about 17,000 in its various high street chains and factories. Partly to inject new management into the business a merger was being negotiated between UDS and Burtons at the time of Joseph Collier's death. It was halted by the Monopolies Commission. At this point UDS owned 584 shops, compared to Burtons' 593. Collier was a supporter of cardiovascular research at Hammersmith Hospital and a freeman of the Metropolitan Borough of Southwark. See Monopolies Commission, *United Drapery Stores Ltd and Montague Burton Ltd. A Report on the Proposed Merger* (1966-67, Cmnd 3397); Eric M Sigsworth, *Montague Burton: The Tailor of Taste* (1990); *The Times*, 26 August 1967.

COLMAN, Sir Michael (Jeremiah)
(7 July 1928 -)

Branded consumer products manufacturer, the son of Sir Jeremiah Colman 2nd Bt (1886-1961) and Edith Gwendolyn Tritton. The Colman family's manufacture of mustard and starch in the nineteenth century had made its name a household word. Educated at Eton, in 1949 he joined the family firm and in 1970 he was appointed to the board of Reckitt & Colman. He became finance director, 1980-6, and chairman after 1986. Under Colman R & C has continued to grow in a low-growth industry, marketing its famous brands such as Jif, Steradent, Robin, Robinson, Lemsip, Dettol and Harpic. (Household and toiletries accounted for £1,247 million of turnover in 1991, easily surpassing food, drugs and other sales.) Since 1986 R & C has sold its unprofitable US leisure interests and potato processing industries, but expanded in the personal care field by buying in 1989 the Spanish babycare company, Nenuco. Under Colman, R & C was one of the first British companies to prepare for the single European market by announcing in 1989 that the responsibility for certain products and marketing would be divided between various facilities in Spain, Germany and France. R & C's sales rose from £1,493 million (trading profit £180 million) in 1987 to £1,986 million (trading profit £292 million) in 1991. Its workforce in 1991 was about 23,000. In 1955

Colman married Judith Jean Wallop, the daughter of Vice-Admiral Sir Peveril William-Powlett: they have two sons and three daughters. See *Reckitt & Colman: A Brief History* (1988); *DBB* (Jeremiah James Colman).

CONRAN, Sir Terence (Orby)
(4 October 1931 -)

Home-furnishings retailer, designer and restaurateur, born in Esher, Surrey, the son of a gum importer. Educated at Bryanston public school and London's Central School of Art, in 1950 he became a window dresser in Simpson's. His first business venture was a small chain of bistros in Chelsea called the Soup Kitchens, but in 1964 he opened his first Habitat store in London's Fulham Road. The store reflected Conran's interest in modern design, his love of French styles, and his idea of selling kitchenware alongside furniture in a range of bright, attractive designs. His ideas caught the mood of the 1960s and Habitat stores became ubiquitous. In 1982 Conran expanded by acquiring the Mothercare group and then in a £1.5 billion merger in 1986 he linked Habitat with the giant British Home Stores to create Storehouse. The combine was not successful and became a victim of the decline in retail spending and management feuding. Conran resigned from an ailing Storehouse in 1990 to concentrate on design. Besides his chairmanships of Habitat (1971-88), Habitat Mothercare (1982-88), and Storehouse (1986-90), he was chairman of J. Hepworth & Son (1981-83). By 1992 he had bought the Conran Shop and was involved in running a small number of London and Paris restaurants. He was said to be down to his last £30 million (from about £200 million five years before). In 1963 he married his second wife, Caroline, a cookery writer: they have two sons and one daughter. His former wife, Shirley, is a best-selling novelist. He was knighted in 1982. See Terence Conran, *The House Book* (1974); Barty Phillips, *Conran and the Habitat Story* (1984).

COOPER, David
(3 July 1855 - 28 October 1940)

Railway manager, born at Waterside, Ayrshire, son of John Cooper, iron miner, and Margaret Alexander, at twelve he became a parcels clerk with the Glasgow & South Western Railway. Two years later he became a booking clerk at Maybole beginning a self-education which continued when in 1872 he transferred to the superintendent's office in Glasgow. He was upgraded from clerk to assistant to the general manager in 1885 and then to superintendent of the line in 1889. At the early age of thirty-nine he became general manager of the Glasgow & South Western Railway, remaining in post until 1922 when the company was absorbed in the London, Midland & Scottish Railway Co. He was director of the LMS 1922-32. His long career spanned changing fortunes for railways: late nineteenth-century expansion, labour problems before the First World War, wartime state control, public ownership and rationalisation after the war. Cooper married in 1885 Lizzie Mathieson; they had at least three sons. See *DSBB*; William S Murphy, *Captains of Industry* (1901).

COOPER, Francis D'Arcy
(17 November 1882 - 18 December 1941)
Accountant and industrial manager, born in London, the son of Francis Cooper, of the accountancy firm of Cooper Bros, and Ada Frances née Power. Educated at Wellington College, in 1899 he joined the family firm, which brought him into close contact with William Lever (Lord Leverhulme) (qv), one of its clients. D'Arcy Cooper became (in his own words) Leverhulme's 'blue-eyed boy'. Lever Bros' financial problems after 1920 brought D'Arcy Cooper onto the company board and he became chairman in 1925. He rationalised the company's structure and product line and oversaw the negotiations with Dutch margarine manufacturers that in 1929 resulted in the formation of Unilever, which with a nominal capital of £100 million was one of the largest companies in Europe. He was made a baronet in 1941. He married Evelyn, daughter of Arthur Radford, in 1939; and left £648,012. See Charles Wilson, *The History of Unilever: A Study in Economic Growth and Social Change* (2 vols, 1954); *DBB*; *DNB*.

COPE, Sir Alfred
(c 1877- 13 May 1954)
Coal mining executive, began his career in the Customs and Excise Department in 1896 aged 19. After some 25 years' service, he became Second Secretary in the Ministry of Pensions during 1919-20, and then served for two years as Assistant Under-Secretary for Ireland, acting as an intermediary between Lloyd George's government and the Sinn Fein leaders before and after the establishment of the Irish Free State. After a period as general secretary to the Liberal Party, in 1925 he was asked by Sir Alfred Mond (qv) to become managing director of the newly-formed Amalgamated Anthracite Collieries Ltd. Until he left the post in 1935, when the AAC employed 12,558, Cope was charged with the task of unifying a large number of relatively small and competing coal mines at a time of difficult labour troubles. He was knighted in 1922. See *The Times*, 14 May 1954.

CORBY, Sir (Frederick) Brian
(10 May 1929 -)
Assurance company executive, the son of Charles Walter and Millicent Corby. Educated at Kimbolton School and St John's College, Cambridge, he joined the Prudential Assurance Co Ltd in 1952. He worked his way up to become group general manager by 1979, then chief executive in 1982. Quiet, mild-mannered and a qualified actuary, Corby fitted the classic man-from-the-Pru mould. But under Corby the Prudential took on board some of the changes that affected the financial services sector in the 1980s, moving into more profitable areas such as unit trusts, personal pensions, investment management and estate agencies. In 1983, 90 per cent of profits came from life assurance; five years later, thanks in part to a highly profitable investment department under Mick Newmarch (qv), the figure was below 60 per cent. Corby also gave the company a new logo and pushed it towards a more streamlined, decentralised structure. In 1990 he handed over as chief executive to Newmarch and became chairman. He was vice-president of the Institute of Actuaries, 1979-82; and president of the CBI, 1990-92. He was knighted in 1989. Corby married in 1952 Elizabeth Mairi McInnes: they have one son and two daughters.

CORNESS, Sir Colin (Ross)
(9 October 1931 -)
Building materials company executive, the son of Thomas and Mary Evelyn Corness. His Scots father owned a whisky company that now resides within Guinness. Educated at Uppingham School and Magdalen College, Oxford (where he read law), he studied business administration at Harvard, before being called to the Bar at the Inner Temple in 1956. He joined Taylor Woodrow as a legal eagle, where his ability caught the eye of Lord Frank Taylor. A director of Taylor Woodrow Construction Ltd between 1961 and 1964, he joined the Redland group (to Taylor's annoyance) in 1965 and became chairman in 1977. Redland had started life in 1920 as the Redhill Tile Co, Reigate, Surrey, to provide jobs for unemployed servicemen. By 1990 it was one of the four leading building materials firms in the UK. Corness's major contribution has been to make Redland into a more international company, so that its business now spans 31 countries. He has continued the company's profitable strategy of expansion in Germany, begun in 1954. In 1991 Redland absorbed Steetley, making it one of the world's leading building materials companies. Profits were £5 million when Corness joined. In 1991 it had 30,000 workers world-wide (8,500 in the UK),

sales of £1.5 billion and pre-tax profits of £186 million. Knighted in 1986, Corness sits on the Court of the Bank of England, and holds non-executive posts at S G Warburg, Nationwide Building Society and Unitech. He retired as non-executive director of Courtaulds in 1991.

CORNWALL, Ernest
(28 January 1875 - 30 April 1966)
Banker, the son of Andrew Cornwall, of Lapford, Devon. He joined the Whitchurch branch of the National Provincial Bank aged 17, and after seven years left to gain further experience at branches in Manchester, Leeds, Hull and Sunderland. In 1913 he became deputy head of the advance department at the Bank's London head office and after steady promotion was appointed chief general manager in 1934 (by which time the National Provincial Bank employed 8,000). In 1945 he became a director and by 1962 had completed 70 years' service with the Bank. He was also a chairman of Finney's Seeds Ltd. He married Florence Emily (d 1955), daughter of J W Read, of Whitchurch, Hislop. See *The Times*, 3 May 1966.

CORNWALLIS, Wykenham Stanley
2nd Baron Cornwallis of Linton
(14 March 1892 - 4 January 1982)
Paper manufacturer and publisher, the second and elder surviving son of Colonel Fiennes Stanley Wykeham Cornwallis, a landowner and local government leader in Kent who in 1927 was raised to the peerage, and his wife Mabel née Leigh. Educated at Eton and the Royal Military College, Sandhurst, he served with the Royal Scots Greys and General Staff during the First World War, gaining an MC. Like his father (whom he succeeded in the title in 1935) he was chairman of Kent County Council and from 1944 until 1972 was Lord Lieutenant and Custos Rotulorum of the county, highest among many other local offices; he was also a prominent Freemason. In business he was a local director of Royal Insurance Co and of Barclays Bank; and president of Whitbread Fremlins Ltd. In 1945 he became a director of Albert E Reed & Co which had a number of paper mills in Kent. He succeeded Ralph Reed as chairman in 1954, but remained non-executive, dividing his time between his several business interests and public offices. Patrick Gordon Walker (qv) ran Reeds but neither Cornwallis nor Walker was a match for Cecil Harmsworth King (qv), head of the Daily Mirror Group, which took a controlling interest in Reeds in 1960 and then integrated it into the International Publishing Corporation two years later. Cornwallis married twice: first, in 1917, to Cecily Etha Mary (d 1943), daughter of Sir

James Walker; second, in 1948, to Esme Ethel Alice, widow of Sir Robert Walker; there was a son and a daughter by the first marriage. See *The Times*, 7 January 1982.

COURTAULD IV, Samuel
(7 May 1876 - 1 December 1947)
Rayon manufacturer and patron of the arts, born at Bocking, Essex, the second son of Sydney Courtauld and his wife Sarah Lucy née Sharp. Schooled at Rugby, he joined the family's famous silk business in 1898 and became chairman in 1921, by which time Courtaulds, with a plant at Coventry and a profitable American subsidiary, was a pioneering rayon manufacturer. Under Courtauld the company became a respected, if conservative, industrial giant. Popularly described as a 'shy, arty, philanthropic rayon millionaire', he declined a barony in 1937, but was a friend of leading artists and created and endowed the Courtauld Institute of Art in the University of London. In 1901 he married Elizabeth Theresa Frances Kelsey. He left £1,030,126. See Donald C Coleman, *Courtaulds: An Economic and Social History* (3 vols, 1969-80); *DBB*; *DNB*.

COZENS-HARDY, Edward Herbert
3rd Baron Cozens-Hardy of Letheringsett
(28 June 1873 - 22 October 1956)
Glass company executive, the second son of 1st Baron Cozens-Hardy, sometime Master of the Rolls. Educated at Rugby and the Royal Technical College, he served a pupillage with the Brush Co, and then in 1898 set up an electrical consulting firm with Colonel O'Gorman. This brought him into contact with the St Helens' glassmakers, Pilkington's, and (after his sister married R A Pilkington in 1903) he joined the board in 1908. He was especially active in Pilkington's between the wars and was responsible for an internal reorganisation in 1931, which replaced the old partnership structure with a new board structure, a key element of which was an executive committee on which Cozens-Hardy and Ronald Weeks (qv) were key figures. The firm employed 10,000 in 1935. He was chairman of the executive committee from its formation until 1939, when he temporarily retired, but returned to serve Pilkington's until his death. A JP and DL in Lancashire (he also became a JP for Norfolk), he had an interest in Liverpool University and in local hospitals. He succeeded to the family title on the death of his elder brother in 1924. In 1906 he married Gladys Lily, daughter of Arthur Wrigley Cozens-Hardy: they had one son and two daughters. See Theodore C Barker, *The*

Glassmakers: Pilkington: The Rise of an International Company, 1826-1976 (1977).

CRAIG, Sir John
(11 December 1874 - 1 February 1957)

Steel manufacturer, born at Clydesdale, New Stevenson, Scotland, son of Thomas Craig, a puddler at David Colville's Dalzell Ironworks, and Elizabeth Wilson, he attended Dalziel Public School, Motherwell, until he was 14 when he became an office boy at Colville's. After 15 months in the general office he became an order clerk. His diligence marked him out and in 1895 when John Colville, eldest of the founder's sons, entered parliament, Craig was given his post at the Royal Exchange in Glasgow. After John Colville's sudden death in 1901 Craig's career accelerated and by 1910 he was a company director. Prior to the First World War Colville's acquired a number of firms to secure their supplies of coal and pig iron. When Archibald and David Colville died suddenly in 1916 John Craig was elected chairman. With singleness of purpose Craig led the firm to pre-eminence in the Scottish steel industry. The firm's ownership passed to Harland & Wolff in 1920 but almost immediately the post-war boom collapsed and swept the shipping, shipbuilding and steel industries into depression. Craig and James Lithgow (qv) rescued the Scottish steel industry between 1930 and 1936 by using Colville's to acquire and then modernise and integrate steel businesses. The Second World War postponed full implementation of Colville's schemes. Craig's last major initiative was the fully integrated steelworks opened in 1957 on a greenfield site at Motherwell: the Ravenscraig project. That year Sir John Craig (he was knighted in 1944) retired. From early manhood the Dalziel Free Church and the YMCA engrossed his spare time. Craig married, in 1901, Jessie Sommerville, a school teacher and daughter of John Sommerville a master shovel maker; they had two sons and three daughters. See *DSBB*; Peter L Payne, *Colvilles and the Scottish Steel Industry* (1979).

CRAWFORD, Sir William
(1840 - 12 May 1922)

Linen manufacturer, son of the Reverend Alexander Crawford, Presbyterian minister of Randalstown, Ulster, and his wife Anna née Gardiner, he was apprenticed at sixteen to the York Street Flax Spinning Co, Belfast. In 1862 he was sent to reorganise the firm's Paris branch and afterwards became the York Street Co's representative there, staying until 1887. He was then appointed managing director and returned to Belfast. By the 1880s the company was the largest vertically integrated flax spinning and weaving firm in the world with 55,000 spindles, 1,000 power-looms and 4,000 operatives. Crawford defended the company (a limited liability one since 1864) against depression and competition from cotton by attention to foreign markets and seeking novel applications for linen. Crawford was active in the business, charitable and religious (Presbyterian) life of Belfast and was knighted in 1906 for his services in the building of the Royal Victoria Hospital, Belfast. He married in 1866 Annie Coulson, daughter of the Reverend James Glasgow, a missionary in India; they had four sons and a daughter. See *DBB*.

CROMPTON, John Gilbert
(29 December 1819 - 29 November 1913)

Banker and iron manufacturer, born at Chesterfield the son of Gilbert Crompton, one of the fourth generation of Derby and Chesterfield bankers, he was educated at Rugby and Trinity College, Cambridge, and then entered the family bank, Crompton, Newton & Co. After the bank merged with another in 1877 he became chairman of the new firm, Crompton & Evans's Union Bank Ltd, remaining in office until a few months before his death. In partnership with his brother George (1823-97) he controlled the Stanton Iron Works Co (Ltd from 1878) from 1857 until his death, maintaining an autocratic paternalism. The works grew from three small furnaces, making 750 tons of pig iron a week, with the addition of new works producing 2,000 tons a week in the early 1870s. By 1907 the business employed 6,000. Crompton was a director of the Midland Railway. He was mayor of Chesterfield in 1848 and of Derby in 1855, and was High Sheriff of Derbyshire in 1873. He left the Liberal party over Home Rule. Though his forebears were Nonconformist he was an Anglican. See *The Times*, 1 December 1913; Stanley D Chapman, *Stanton and Staveley: A Business History* (1981).

CROSS, Herbert Shepherd
(1 January 1847 - 9 January 1916)

Bleacher, the third son of Thomas Cross (1805-79), a bleacher, cotton spinner and banker of Bolton, and his wife Ellen Thompson née Mann of Liverpool, he was educated at Worksop School, Harrow and Exeter College, Oxford. Diverted by ill-health from a legal career, he and two brothers on the death of their father formed a partnership to manage the family bleaching concern. When in 1900 this joined the newly-formed Bleachers' Association, a defensive merger of 53 firms employing 10,780, Thomas Cross & Co was valued at £206,615, the fourth largest firm in the amalgamation. Herbert Shepherd-Cross (he took his father-in-law's name in 1884) chaired the

DANNATT

Bleachers' Association from its formation until his death, being chosen not least because he was an MP (Conservative) for Bolton from 1885 until he retired in 1906. The original proprietors provided a board of 48 directors and branch rather than company interests prevailed at first, with the chairman showing partiality towards his Mortfield Bleachworks, despite the efforts of two managing directors. When one of these died in 1904 a series of changes produced four managing directors whose capital spending was overseen by a finance committee. Shepherd-Cross played a diminishing role partly because he was drawn to his Hertfordshire estate (purchased in 1884) by the life of the country gentleman. He married twice: first, in 1870, Lucy (d 1891), only daughter of Reverend Shepherd Birley; second, in 1895, Patty Penelope, daughter of James Hortor of Edinburgh. See DBB; David J Jeremy, 'Survival Strategies in Lancashire Textiles: Bleachers' Association Ltd to Whitecroft PLC, 1900-1970s' Textile History 24 (1993).

CRUDDAS, William Donaldson
(26 September 1831 - 8 February 1912)
Engineer, he was the second son of George Cruddas, a Tyneside industrialist, financier and, from 1846, partner of William George Armstrong later 1st Baron Armstrong of Cragside (1810-1900) the Tyneside armaments manufacturer and shipbuilder. William Cruddas was placed in the firm and trained to succeed his father on the financial side. In 1861 he became a partner and controlled the financial activities for three decades. When the firm merged with Charles Mitchell & Co and was converted to a limited liability company in 1882 Cruddas became financial director. On Tyneside he was prominent in business, social and political life: director of several local firms; a benefactor of the Church of England; MP (Conservative) for Newcastle, 1895-1900; High Sheriff of Northumberland in 1903. Cruddas married Margaret Octavia, the daughter of William Nesham, in 1861; they had three daughters. See DBB.

CUNLIFFE-LISTER, Samuel
2nd Baron Masham
(2 August 1857 - 24 January 1917)
Worsted and silk manufacturer, he was born in Manningham, the elder son of Samuel Cunliffe Lister (1815-1906), worsted manufacturer and inventor of a mechanical wool comb (for which in 1891 he was raised to the peerage), and his wife Anne née Dearden. He was educated at Harrow and St John's College, Oxford. The family firm, converted to a public company Manningham Mills in 1889, failed to interest him. He succeeded to his

father's title, fortune and 24,000 acres in 1906 but 'preferred a private life to that of business and public works ... his activities lay in the direction of art'. Unmarried, he was succeeded by his brother. See Complete Peerage.

D

DALRYMPLE, James
(1860 - 1 July 1934)
Transport manager, born of a farming family in Galloway (other sources say Manchester), he grew up on a farm at Boreland near Gatehouse-of-Fleet, Kirkcudbrightshire where he was educated. He joined the Union Bank of Scotland at Gatehouse and after a few years was transferred in 1880 to Glasgow. He left the bank the following year and joined the office of the City Chamberlain; in 1884 he moved to the department of the City Accountant and Registrar where he spent ten years, qualifying as a chartered accountant. In 1894, when the Corporation took over the tramways from the Glasgow Tramway & Omnibus Co, Dalrymple was appointed accountant of the new department. Some time after he was made deputy to the manager, John Young, succeeding Young who left in 1904 to become general manager of the Metropolitan District Railway in London. Dalrymple ran Glasgow's tramways until 1926 seeing track mileage increase from 79 to over 270 and passengers able to ride from Lanarkshire coalfields to the banks of Loch Lomond, to the chagrin of the railway companies. In 1907 he was employing 5,000, in 1922 8,700. A strict disciplinarian, Dalrymple refused to reinstate a hundred men after the General Strike of May 1926. When he was overruled by the Corporation he resigned. In retirement, he made the last of his overseas visits to advise urban authorities on their transport problems: departing in 1927 for Brazil to analyse Sao Paulo's traffic situation. He was an elder in Berkeley Street Free Church of Scotland and he helped to found the Tramway Men's Friendly Society. He married Elizabeth Gardner née McGowan; they had at least one son and one daughter. See George Eyre-Todd, A Biographical Dictionary of ... Glasgow Citizens (1907); Glasgow Herald 2, 5 July 1934; Mitchell Library, Glasgow, Calendars of Confirmations; C A Oakley, The Last Tram (1962).

DANNATT, Sir Cecil
(21 September 1896 - 18 December 1981)
Managing director of a leading electrical engineering company, the son of Mark and Hannah Dannat, he was educated at Burton-on-Trent

Grammar School and Armstrong College, Newcastle-upon-Tyne. Graduating in electrical engineering in 1921 (his studies having been interrupted by the First World War in which he served in the York and Lancaster Regiment and received the MC at Messines Ridge in 1917), he joined Metropolitan-Vickers at Trafford Park, Manchester, and shortly took charge of the electrical and magnet section of the research department. He gained the DSc from Durham University in 1936 and four years later was appointed professor of electrical engineering at Birmingham University, making contributions to naval gunnery for the Admiralty. He returned to Metrovick full time in 1944, becoming deputy chief engineer in 1945, chief electrical engineer and director in 1947, assistant managing director in 1951, and serving as managing director, 1954-60. He sat on the board of the parent company, Associated Electrical Industries, 1954-63, and was vice-chairman, 1960-62. He was knighted in 1961. Dannat's career typified that of the majority of senior managers at Metrovick: focusing on engineering excellence to the exclusion of market and commercial realities. Unlike many of his colleagues he was on good terms with the senior managers of British Thomson-Houston of Rugby, the other main component of AEI. These problems faced and foiled the AEI chairman of the postwar era, Oliver Lyttelton (qv). Dannat married, in 1925, Winifred Ethel Flear; they had two sons. See Robert Jones and Oliver Marriott, *Anatomy of a Merger: A History of GEC, AEI and English Electric* (1970); *The Times*, 22 December 1981.

DAVIDSON, John Martin
(7 December 1890 - 7 July 1965)

Scottish Co-operative Wholesale Society executive, born in Cathcart Street, Glasgow, to John Davidson, journeyman woodcarver, and his wife Isabella née Callender. He trained as a brass moulder and was minute secretary and executive member of the Scottish Brassworkers' Society 1913-1917. As a trade union administrator he was appointed a director of the Kinning Park Co-op Society in 1921 and its president in 1926. Kinning Park under his leadership became the second largest Society in Scotland and eventually the largest in Glasgow. Davidson became president of the United Baking Society and in 1932 was elected a director of the Scottish CWS. He was elected president in 1946 and served until 1965. On the SCWS board he sat on a number of committees of the English and Scottish Joint CWS, the British Luma Electric Lamp Society, the Co-operative Insurance Society and the International Co-operative Alliance. At some time he was also a director of the Scottish

Textile Manufacturing Co and the Ettrick Mill Spinning Co. In 1955 he was elected President of the Co-operative Congress, held in Edinburgh. He was survived by his wife, May; they had no children. See *Co-op News*, 4 December 1954; *Co-operative Review*, January 1955; *Scottish Co-operator*, 10 July 1965.

DAVIES, David
1st Baron Davies of Llandinam
(11 May 1880 - 16 June 1944)

Industrialist, born in Llandinam, Wales, the son of Edward Davies and Mary née Jones. His grandfather, David Davies (1818-90), was a prominent Welsh industrialist, builder of railways, founder of the Ocean Coal Co, coal magnate, and creator of Barry Docks. He was educated at Merchiston Castle School, Edinburgh, and King's College, Cambridge (where he studied history). His extensive business interests included: the chairmanship of Ocean Coal & Wilson's; United National Collieries Ltd; Burnyeat, Brown & Co; Cambrian & General Securities Ltd; director of the Great Western Railway; and director of the Midland Bank. He was also Liberal MP for Montgomeryshire from 1906 to 1926 and was appointed Lloyd George's Parliamentary Secretary in 1916. He became an advocate of international peace through the League of Nations. He was created a peer in 1932. He married twice: in 1910, May née Penman (d 1918), by whom he had one son; in 1922, Henrietta Margaret (Rita) née Fergusson, producing two sons and two daughters. See David Davies, *The Problem of the Twentieth Century* (1930); *The Times*, 17 June 1944.

DAVIES, George (William)
(29 October 1941 -)

Clothing chain store retailer, born in Netherton, Lancashire, the son of George Davies, a manager in a pie and sausage factory, and his wife Mary. Educated at Bootle Grammar School and the Faculty of Dentistry, Birmingham University (which he left before completing his first year), his first job was as a stock controller at Littlewoods. In 1972 he set up School Care, a mail order school clothes company, which foundered in 1975. In 1980 he joined J Hepworth & Son, chaired by (Sir) Terence Conran (qv), as merchandise director and assistant managing-director of a new ladies' venture. In 1981 he used Hepworth's as a vehicle to launch his Next concept in niche fashion and mail order marketing: a chain of women's fashion shops, selling good-quality, well-coordinated middle fashion clothes for working women aged twenty-five to forty. When Conran left Hepworth in 1985, Davies became chief executive and changed its name to Next. He was chairman between 1987 and 1988. Profits rose from £4 million in 1981 to over £90 million in 1988. But Davies' policy of rapid expansion and heavy borrowing led to disagreements with the board and he was fired in 1988. He married twice: in 1965 to Anne Margaret Allen (three daughters); and in 1985 to Elzbieta Krystyna Szabdey (two daughters), with whom he set up the George Davies Partnership in 1988. After showing a net profit of a £1 million in 1992 (making, amongst other things, clothes for Asda), Davies announced the launch of a £10 million mail order venture called Xtend. See George Davies, *What Next?* (1989); Judi Bevan and John Jay, *The New Tycoons* (1989).

DAVIES, Howard John
(12 February 1951 -)
Director of the Confederation of British Industry, the son of Leslie Powell Davies, an architect who worked for Whitbread designing pub interiors, and his wife Marjorie. Raised in north Manchester, he was educated at Manchester Grammar School, the Memorial University of Newfoundland, and Merton College, Oxford University (where he read history and modern languages), before taking a master's degree at Stanford Graduate School of Business. He joined the Foreign Office, which took him to the British Embassy in Paris, 1974-6, and then to the Treasury, 1976-82. He then worked for the management consultants McKinsey (where he acted as special adviser to the Chancellor of the Exchequer), before his appointment as controller of the Audit Commission at the age of thirty-five. In 1992 he became director of the CBI, succeeding Sir John Banham (qv) (who had also come into the job via the Audit Commission). Davies has been a director of GKN since 1990. He writes articles for magazines including the *Spectator* and *The Economist*, especially on economics and the public sector. He married in 1984 Prudence Mary Keely: they have two sons.

DAVIS, Sir Herbert
(12 March 1891 - 20 February 1972)
Food and detergent manufacturer, born in Stoke Newington, the son of James Davis, an ivory turner, and his wife Ann née Studdeard, he was educated at the Grocers' School, Hackney and at St John's College, Cambridge, reading natural sciences and history. He joined Crosfields, the Warrington soap makers, in 1912, remaining until Lever Brothers bought it from Brunner, Mond in 1919. During the First World War he was seconded to Government to handle edible oil supplies. Afterwards he joined Jurgens, again specialising in buying raw materials. Anton Jurgens moved him to

a (rudimentary) policy-making function in 1926. Excess capacity throughout Europe in the 1920s created fierce competition between the margarine manufacturers. Davis, who favoured rationalisation, was closely involved in the litigations between Jurgens and Van den Berghs and then the negotiations which merged them in 1927 as the Margarine Union. Davis became secretary of the Margarine Union. In 1929 the Union and Lever Brothers merged to form Unilever, with Davis again at the centre of negotiations. During the 1930s he rationalised and consolidated Unilever's oil milling activities in the UK and in 1937 was appointed to the board. During the Second World War he was again seconded to Government, to the Food Ministry as Director of Oils and Fats. Not only were oils and fats smoothly distributed but supplies of the essential vitamins A and D were procured for Britain and her allies: achievements for which Davis was knighted in 1943. In 1942 he became a vice-chairman of Unilever, retiring in 1956 by which time the Anglo-Dutch multinational employed over 50,000 in the UK and 240,000 worldwide. Davis married Eva Fitzgerald Radford in 1912; they had two daughters. See *The Times*, 22 February 1972.

DAVIS, Sir John Henry Harris
(10 November 1906 - 27 May 1993)
Cinema and film executive, born in Hereford, the son of Sidney Myering Davis, a school master, he was educated at the City of London School which he left at 18 to become a junior accountant for the Welsh Coal & Steel Combine. Three years later he joined British Thomson-Houston which, supplied with technology by its American parent, General Electric of America, in 1929 produced a sound-film apparatus. A subsidiary, Sound Equipment Ltd, was set up as a joint venture with Oscar Deutsch, founder of the Odeon chain of cinemas, and Davis managed the account. In January 1938 he became chief accountant of Odeon Theatres Ltd and, a few months later, secretary and financial controller. When, on Deutsch's death in December 1941, J Arthur Rank (qv) took over, Davis became joint managing director and in 1948, still as Rank's right-hand man, chief executive of the Gaumont and Odeon film production and distribution empire, Odeon Theatres. A ruthless autocrat, he pruned the unprofitable production side, closing studios at Shepherds Bush, Denham, Islington and Highbury, and concentrating film making at Pinewood. This and the profits of 600 cinemas brought the business back into profitablity. By 1955 the Rank empire employed 26,000. In the face of a decline in cinema-going, Davis merged the Odeon and Gaumont circuits in 1958, reducing

the chain to 380 cinemas and converting others for bowling, bingo and dancing. His most momentous diversification decision came in 1956 when he decided to support Chester Carlson in developing the Xerography principle (already rejected by IBM and RCA). Davis succeeded Lord Rank as chairman in 1962 and watched his Anglo-American subsidiary, Rank Xerox, achieve post-tax profits of £30 million or three quarters of the Rank Organisation's total profits in 1968. Sir John Davis (he was knighted in 1971) retired in 1977. He married four times: first to Joan née Buckingham in 1926; secondly to Marion Louise Davis in April 1947; thirdly to Dinah Sheridan in 1954; fourthly to Felicity Mary Rutland, a company director, in 1976. See *The Times*, 29 May 1993.

DAVIS, Peter John

(23 December 1941 -)

Publishing company executive, the son of John Stephen Davis and Adriaantje Baat. Educated at Shrewsbury School and the Graduate Institute of Marketing, he went into marketing with various food companies. He worked at Sainsbury's, 1976-86, where he was appointed assistant managing director in 1979, before joining Reed International in 1986. He became chief executive in 1986 and chairman in January 1990. Reed is one of the world's largest publishing and information companies, selling both regional newspapers and national magazines, such as *New Scientist* and *Computer Weekly*. It publishes Butterworth's law books and other standard bibliographic tools; has been an innovator in own-brand books; and is a leading publisher of childrens' books. Under Davis, Reed has expanded further in the bibliographic market, acquiring the German firm K G Saur in 1987 and the Australian D W Thorpe in 1988. In the following year Martindale-Hubbell, publisher of US law books, was bought; and in 1990 Reed acquired Verlag Francke in Germany. In January 1993 Davis became (while remaining chairman of Reed International) joint-chief of Reed Elsevier, after Reed's merger with the Dutch group. Reed Elsevier has a stock market value of £6.8 billion, sales of £2,461 million and a workforce of 25,600. A director of Satellite Broadcasting Ltd, Davis is a non-executive director of the Granada Group and chairman of the Adult Literacy and Basic Skills Unit. He married in 1968 Susan Hillman: they have two sons and a daughter.

DAWSON, Frank Harold

(14 February 1896 - 29 June 1972)

Shipping company executive, born at Tranmere near Birkenhead, the son of Frank Dawson, a schoolmaster, and his wife Margaret Hannah née Harrison, he was educated at the Liverpool Institute High School and at 16 started work in the head office of the Cunard Steam-Ship Co Ltd in Liverpool. From 1914 until 1920 he served with the King's (Liverpool) Regiment, receiving the MC, being thrice mentioned in despatches and attaining the rank of captain. He returned to Cunard's head office in 1920 but was transferred to Southampton after the inauguration of the Cunard Express Service from Southampton to New York in 1922. He became responsible for the company's Southampton activities including the operation of the 81,000 ton *Queen Mary*, experience which was invaluable after the outbreak of war in 1939. Dawson was then sent to Australia where he was involved in the conversion of the two *Queens* and the *Mauretania* as transports and the operation of the *Queens* when based in Sydney during service between Australia and the Middle East. He later returned to the UK and was Assistant Director of Sea Transport at the Ministry of Transport in London, work for which he was made a CBE in 1948. Dawson was appointed an assistant manager of Cunard in 1945, deputy general manager in 1947, director of the Cunard Steam-Ship Co Ltd and of Cunard White Star in 1949, and general manager in 1950, retiring in 1959. His tenure in Cunard's top executive post saw a boom in passenger shipping, for which Cunard developed dual-purpose ships, with scheduled services during spring and summer and cruising during winter months. However, bad labour relations, the problem of replacement (of the *Queens*), rising costs, penal taxation, and looming competition from jet aircraft, increasingly threatened Cunard's classic transatlantic and imperial shipping services. Dawson was president of the Institute of Shipping and Forwarding Agents in 1951, chairman of the Liverpool Steam Ship Owners' Association in 1955-56 and of the Employers' Association of the Port of Liverpool in 1954-57, and was made an honorary RNR captain in 1953. He married in 1924 Florence Kathleen, daughter of Captain James C Barr; they had two daughters. See Francis E Hyde, *Cunard and the North Atlantic, 1840-1973* (1975); Liverpool University Archives, Cunard papers.

DAY, Sir (Judson) Graham

(3 May 1933 -)

Industrialist, the son of Frank Charles Day and Edythe Grace née Baker. He was born and educated in Halifax, Nova Scotia, first at Queen Elizabeth High School and then Dalhousie University, where he read law (LLB). He ran a private law practice in Windsor, Nova Scotia, during 1956-64 and then joined Canadian Pacific Ltd of Montreal and

Toronto, 1964-71. His industrial career began in the UK with Cammell Laird Shipbuilders Ltd, which led to the deputy chairmanship of British Shipbuilders during 1975-76. He returned briefly to Canada as Professor of Business Administration and director of the Canadian Marine Transportation Centre, Dalhousie University, 1977-81. He was chairman of British Shipbuilders, 1983-86, and then held a trio of top chairmanships: at the Rover Group, 1986-91 (chief executive, 1986-88); British Aerospace between 1991 and 1992, when a boardroom coup ousted Professor Sir Roland Smith (qv); Cadbury Schweppes since 1989; and Powergen since 1990. Graham Day was knighted in 1989. In 1958 he married Leda Ann née Creighton: they have one son and two daughters. See Corinne Simcock, *A Head for Business* (1992).

DE FERRANTI, Sir (Gerard) Vincent (Sebastian)
(16 February 1893 - 20 May 1980)
Electrical and electronic equipment manufacturer, born in Chelsea, London, the second son of Sebastian Ziani de Ferranti (1864-1930), founder of the family electrical business, and his wife Gertrude Ruth née Ince, he was educated at Repton and then apprenticed to Yarrows, the Clyde shipbuilders. His brother's death in the First World War made Vincent (as he was known) heir apparent and after the War (in which he served in the Middle East, winning the MC) he joined the firm at Hollinwood near Oldham, expanding the transformer department. When the National Grid was built in 1928-33 Ferranti's won almost a third of the transformer contracts. Vincent became a director of the family firm in 1924 and on the death of his father in 1930 he bought enough shares to secure control of the company. During the 1930s he developed the production of radios (a loss maker) and special electronics, including X-ray tubes, valves and radar equipment. The Second World War saw the company expand from two to six factories. After 1945 Vincent focused on transformers (at Chadderton, Lancs) and airborne radar equipment (at Edinburgh). Links with Manchester University took the firm into the pioneering production of computers while defence contracts (particularly the Bloodhound guided missile) in the 1950s led to the converging technology of semiconductors and microelectronics. Between 1935 and 1955 the firm grew from 7,000 to over 11,000 employees. When Sir Vincent (he was knighted in 1948) retired in 1963 Ferrantis employed 20,000 and was one of the top three firms in its industry. Vincent de Ferranti married in 1919 Dorothy Hettie Campbell Wilson, daughter of Reginald Page Wilson an engineer; they had two sons and

three daughters. He left £377,612. See John F Wilson, *Ferranti and the British Electrical Industry, 1864-1930* (1988); *DBB*.

DE SAVARY, Peter (John)
(11 July 1944 -)
International entrepreneur, born at Southminster, Essex, the son of John de Savary, a timber merchant, and Vera Helen née Wright. He was educated at Charterhouse, where he was awarded one O-level in religious instruction. At sixteen he went to Canada, where he worked as a salesman, before returning home at twenty-one to work in his father's business. By the mid-1970s he was making his fortune (estimated by himself at £100 million by 1990) in the Middle East oil industry. Subsequently, as a self-styled 'land-value enhancement specialist', he has acquired a diverse range of interests in the property and leisure fields - especially in the south-west of England. His millionaire and ostentatious lifestyle made him a public figure in the 1980s, which was enhanced by his chairmanship of a syndicate that challenged for the America's Cup in 1983. In 1988 he was voted Tourism Personality of the Year by the English Tourist Board. He married in 1986 (Lucille) Lana Paton: he has two sons and two daughters by a former marriage. See Philip Beresford, *Sunday Times Book of the Rich* (1990).

DENT, Charles Hastings
(1863 - 28 October 1956)
Railway manager, the son of Captain Charles Bayley Calmady Dent RN (1832-94), the London & North Western Railway Co's marine superintendent at Holyhead, 1867-93, and his wife Corrina née Coureaumelli, he became a premium apprentice with the LNWR at Crewe. He later joined the train running department and then managed the locomotive department sheds and shops at Preston. In 1892 he became an assistant to the district superintendent at Liverpool, transferring to Wigan before returning to Liverpool as chief assistant to the superintendent of the northern division of the LNWR whom he succeeded in 1899. In 1903 he was appointed general manager of the Great Southern & Western Railway Co. Headquartered in Dublin and chaired by Sir William Goulding (qv), the GSWR was Ireland's largest railway system, extending from Dublin to Queenstown, from Rosslare to Kenmare on the south coast and, on the west coast, from Valentia to Collooney near Sligo Bay, a total of 1,100 miles out of Ireland's 3,100 miles of railway. In 1907 the GWSR employed just over 8,000 people. Dent moved back to mainland Britain in 1913 on becoming general manager of the Great Northern

Railway Co, retiring in 1923 when Britain's 130 railway companies were merged into four groups. He was chairman of the general managers conference of the Railway Clearing House for 1920 and, earlier, member of the Railway Executive Committee and a similarly-named committee associated with the Ministry of Transport. Dent was recalled as 'A man of few words, disdaining all unnecessary formalities'. See W J Gordon, *Our Home Railways* (2 vols, 1910); *Railway Gazette*, 9 November 1956; Joseph Tatlow, *Fifty Years of Railway Life* (1923).

DEWRANCE, Sir John
(13 March 1858 - 7 October 1937)
Chairman of engineering and coal-mining companies, born in London, the third child and only son of John Dewrance and Elizabeth née Curtis. After attending Charterhouse and King's College, London, in 1879 he took over his father's private engineering company, which manufactured steam engine parts. From 1899 until 1937 he was chairman of Babcock & Wilcox Ltd, the water-tube steam boiler manufacturers. With the help of the managing director, Sir James Kemnal (1864-1927), Babcock & Wilcox was exceptionally profitable: issued capital increased from £320,000 in 1899 to £4.6 million in 1929. Dewrance's other interest was in the Kent coalfield as chairman of the Kent Coal Concessions in 1914. Active in several professional societies, he served as president of the Institution of Mechanical Engineers in 1923 and of the Institute of Metals 1926-8. He was created a KBE in 1920 and raised to GBE in 1928. In 1882 he married Isabella, granddaughter of the inventor Richard Trevithick. He left £589,171. See *DBB*.

DICK, Alick Sydney
(20 June 1916 - 8 March 1986)
Motor car manufacturer, born at Massingham, Norfolk, the younger son of Walter Dick, a medical practitioner, and his wife Mabel Ernestine née Buckell, he was educated at Chichester High School and Dean Close School, Cheltenham, leaving at 16 to attend the College of Aeronautical and Automobile Engineering in Chelsea. In 1933 he went to Coventry where his uncle (Major Sydney Dick) introduced him to the flamboyant John Black (1895-1965), managing director of Standard Motors (the uncle and Black being brothers-in-law). Black secured a student apprenticeship in the toolroom for Alick Dick and six years later Dick was moving up the management hierarchy in the shadow aero engine factory system. In 1943 he was in sole charge of Standard's Mosquito aircraft production programme. He became personal assistant to Sir John Black in 1945, assistant managing direc-

tor of Standard in 1947, and managing director of Standard in 1954 when it employed 11,000. Standard-Triumph (formed in 1945 when Standard bought the Triumph Motor Co) was the smallest of the big five British motor manufacturers and met difficulties in the volume car market. With proceeds of the sale in 1959 of £17.6 million of tractor production interests Dick invested in a new saloon model, the Herald. Due to government regional policy its components were made in different parts of the country (eg bodies at Speke on Merseyside) and sales were hit by the 1960-61 recession. After merger talks with Rover and Rootes failed, in 1960 Standard-Triumph merged with Leyland, but Alick Dick clashed with Henry Spurrier (qv) and resigned, never again to hold a top job in the British motor industry. He married, in 1940, Betty Melinda Eileen née Hill, the daughter of Benjamin Alan Hill, an engineer; they had three sons. See *DBB*; *The Times*, 11 March 1986; David Toms and Tom Donnelly, *The Motor Car Industry in Coventry since the 1890s* (1985).

DIXON, Alfred Herbert
(22 February 1857 - 10 December 1920)
Cotton manufacturer, born in London, the son of Henry Hall Dixon, a well-known racing journalist, and his wife Caroline, he was educated at Kensington Grammar School and at Brighton and then apprenticed with the Reddish Spinning Co, near Stockport, of which his uncle was a director. On the recommendation of William Houldsworth (qv), head of the Reddish Co, Dixon in 1876 joined A & G Murray, one of the oldest fine spinning firms in Manchester then needing new managerial talent. This Dixon supplied, as managing director of Murrays 1881-97. To counter excessive competition in fine cotton spinning, Houldsworth, Scott Lings, the Reddish managing director, and Dixon between them in 1898 created the Fine Cotton Spinners' & Doublers' Association, an amalgamation of 31 firms in which finance and raw cotton purchasing were centralised. Dixon was managing director of the Fine Spinners 1898-1917, and chairman 1917-20, making the business more vertically integrated. By 1909 50 firms employing four million spindles and over 30,000 workers had joined, by labour ranking the largest manufacturing business of its day. Dixon was active in the Federation of Master Cotton Spinners (established 1905), the International Cotton Federation, the Federation of British Industries (established 1916). He was also a director of the Manchester Royal Exchange (1909-20) and president of the Textile Institute (1920). In 1880 Dixon married Caroline, daughter of Henry Sandford, manufacturer; they had two children of whom only the daughter survived. See *DBB*.

DOBSON, Benjamin A Palin
(1904 - 4 July 1962)

Textile machinery manufacturer, of an old Bolton family, who gained his early business experience with the family firm Dobson & Barlow Ltd. He later became a foreign representative for the textile engineering enterprises controlled by Howard & Bullough Ltd, of Accrington, and then worked as sales director for Platt Bros, the Oldham firm of textile machinery makers. He had a distinguished career in the Royal Artillery during the Second World War and attained the rank of lieutenant-colonel. He won the Smithills ward in Bolton for the Conservatives in 1929, becoming Bolton Town Council's youngest member at the age of 25. He also served as a JP. He and his wife, Mrs B A P Dobson, had three sons. See *Bolton Journal*, 6 July 1962.

DOBSON, Benjamin Palin
(1878 - 26 November 1936)

Textile machinery manufacturer, born at Doffcockers, Heaton, the eldest son of (Sir) Benjamin Dobson (1847-98), head of Dobson & Barlow the Bolton textile machinery makers, and his wife Coralie née Palin, he was educated at Rossall School (1891-95) and then entered the family firm. On the death of his father he became a director of the firm and was active in management until the 1930s. Dobson & Barlow merged with five other machine builders to form Textile Machinery Makers Ltd in 1931 and two years later the Kay Street, Bolton, works were closed. Benjamin Dobson, who had managed it, then retired but continued as chairman of Dobson & Barlow Securities Ltd, a holding company within the TMM combine. A member of the school Cadet Corps, Dobson joined the Territorial Army and saw service on the Suez Canal and in France during the First World War reaching the rank of lieutenant-colonel. He was a member of the Institutions of Mechanical Engineers and of Mining Engineers and a fellow and past president of the Textile Institute. Benjamin Dobson lived at Whitestock Hall, Haverthwaite, Ulverston. He married the eldest daughter of A T Holden and was survived by his wife, two sons and a daughter. See *Bolton Evening News*, 27 November 1936.

DOCKER, Sir Bernard Dudley Frank
(9 August 1896 - 22 May 1978)

Industrialist, born in Edgbaston, Birmingham, the only son of Frank Dudley Docker (qv), he went to Harrow and then worked in his father's firm, Metropolitan Carriage, Wagon & Finance Co, during the First World War. He became a director of

MCWF in 1920 and deputy chairman in 1924. By 1925-26 he was a professional non-executive director, and was one of his father's nominees on the Vickers board. He was chairman of the Birmingham Railway Carriage & Wagon Co, 1934-60 and, more importantly, chairman of the Birmingham Small Arms group, 1940-56. In tandem with James Leek, his managing director, Docker managed 67 BSA factories and 28,000 workers during the Second World War. After 1945 BSA sought to recapture its world markets in motor cycles, cycles, machine tools, cars, taxis and steel. They acquired the motorcycle firms Ariel and Triumph. By 1956, when BSA employed over 18,000, Docker and Leek had achieved a five-fold increase in profits since 1940, largely due to wartime contracts. Appearances were deceiving. On the motor cycle side obsolete production methods, stagnant design and failure to capture scale economies exposed the firm to French and German competition in the 1950s and Japanese competition in the 1960s. However, Docker's downfall came from his second wife, the flamboyant and extravagant Lady Docker, born Norah Turner, raised in a public house and by profession a dance hostess (Bernard Docker, her third husband, was knighted in 1939; he was married to Jeanne Stuart an actress for a few months in 1933-34). She sought control of Daimler, a BSA subsidiary, with the aim of diverting it from the royalty trade into the mass market, lending the firm a plutocratic image with her party-going gold-plated Daimler. A boardroom coup ejected the Dockers from BSA in 1956. See *DBB*.

DOCKER, Frank Dudley
(26 August 1862 - 8 July 1944)

Industrialist and financier, born at Smethwick, the fifth and youngest son of Ralph Docker, a solicitor, and Sarah Maria née Sankey, DD (as he was known) was educated privately and at King Edward VI Grammar School, Birmingham. He started in his father's law firm but with his brother William in 1881 founded the firm of Docker Bros, dealers in stoving black varnish. By 1887 they made their own varnish, supplying railways and shipping lines. Docker Bros Ltd, with a capital of £150,000, was registered in 1899. DD won industrial eminence in Birmingham by masterminding the merger of five of his rolling stock customers in 1902 to form the well-structured Metropolitan Amalgamated Railway Carriage & Wagon Co (name changed in 1912 to Metropolitan Carriage, Wagon & Finance Co), with himself as chairman. MARCW employed 14,000, most in the Birmingham area, in 1907, the year it took over Docker Bros. DD became a director of Birmingham Small Arms in

1906 and of the Midland Bank in 1912. Advocating a strong role for businessmen in government, he launched the Business League in 1910, the Midland Employers' Federation in 1913, and was foremost in forming the Federation of British Industries in 1916. In the second merger wave (1918-20s) he devised deals by which MCWF and Vickers, the steel and armaments giant, bought the British Westinghouse Electrical Co, based at Trafford Park, Manchester, and subsequently known as Metrovick. The following year, 1919, he persuaded Vickers to buy MCWF for the inflated price of £12.1 million and himself joined the Vickers board. When his hopes of post-war industrial reconstruction faded he became embittered with the FBI (which rejected his Protectionism) and when the Vickers board pursued a strategy of sprawling diversification he resigned from it, in 1920. However, through nominees on the board he remained crucial to Vickers, sharing in the reconstruction of the firm in 1925-26, selling off Metrovick to General Electric of America in 1928, and arranging the merger between MCWF and Cammell Laird the same year. Thereafter he was active in rescuing BSA in 1932-34 and in shadowy dealings through his private financial vehicle, the Electric & Railway Finance Corporation (Elrafin) which he formed in 1921. DD had his hand in many other pies. Essentially he was a backstairs fixer and a prime figure in Britain's merger movement. Docker married Lucy Constance née Hebbert, daughter of a solicitor, in 1895; their only child was Bernard (qv). See R P T Davenport-Hines, *Dudley Docker: The Life and Times of a Trade Warrior* (1984).

DODD, John
(1838 - 17 February 1912)

Textile machine maker, John Dodd spent his working life in the Oldham firm of Platt Bros, the largest textile machinery builders of the late nineteenth century. Founded in 1822, its original name of Hibbert & Platt was changed to Platt Bros & Co in 1854 when John Platt (1817-72), the dynamic head of his family, bought out the Hibbert interest and made five of his most talented managers his partners. John Dodd was one of them. Dodd started as a pattern maker, became a fitter and in due course went through the works on the technical side. With a strong grasp of detail, he and his fellow managers supported Platt in perfecting the carding machine, the roving frame and the self-acting mule. Dodd's role lay not least in 'watching the patent world and securing new inventions likely to be of service'. The firm became a limited company in 1868 and Dodd one of the directors. On the death of Samuel Radcliffe Platt (1845-1902), son of

John, Dodd became chairman. Under his leadership the firm's turnover peaked in 1906, with the workforce at 12,000, down three thousand from the 1890s. Outside business Dodd was a magistrate, a Liberal Unionist and a Low Churchman (active in All Saints Church and the Protestant Churchmen's Alliance), a trustee of the Infirmary, a council member of the Chamber of Commerce (opposing decimalisation) and a supporter of Oldham Lyceum and the Territorial Force. Dodd was twice married and left two married daughters. See *Oldham Chronicle*, 20 February 1912.

DONALDSON, Sir Hay Frederick
(7 July 1856 - 5 June 1916)

Ordnance manufacturer, born at Sydney, Australia, the second son of Sir Stuart Alexander Donaldson, first Premier of New South Wales, and his wife Amelia née Cowper. He was educated at Eton, Trinity College, Cambridge, Edinburgh and Zurich, finishing his engineering training at the London & North Western Railway Works, Crewe. Qualifying as both a civil and a mechanical engineer, he worked on projects in Goa (1884-87), railway and harbour construction (1887-91) and the Manchester Ship Canal (1891-97). He was chief engineer of the London India Docks Joint Committee, 1898-99, before moving into military engineering. Between 1899 and 1903 he was Deputy Director General of Ordnance Factories and Chief Mechanical Engineer of Ordnance Factories. From 1903 until his death he was Chief Superintendent of Ordnance Factories, employing over 15,000 (about 14,000 at Woolwich) in 1907. The function of the Ordnance Factories was 'to provide a reserve of productive power capable of rapid expansion when emergency threatened', but not to compete against the private armaments manufacturers, and to preserve low production costs in peacetime. Donaldson addressed this last requirement by introducing a system of cost accounting. When the Ministry of Munitions was established in 1915 Sir Frederick Donaldson (he was knighted in 1911) became technical adviser to the Minister. Donaldson married Selina, younger daughter of Colonel F M Beresford MP; they had a son and two daughters. See Oliver F G Hogg, *The Royal Arsenal: Its Background, Origin and Subsequent History* (2 vols, 1963).

DORMAN, Sir Arthur John
(8 August 1848 - 12 February 1931)

Steel manufacturer, born at Ashford, Kent, the son of Charles Dorman, a currier and later a coal and timber merchant, he was educated at Christ's Hospital and, after a short time in Paris, was apprenticed to a Stockton-on-Tees iron manufacturer. In 1876 he formed a partnership with Albert de Lande Long to make iron bars for shipbuilding. They moved into steel girder production using imported haematite in open-hearth furnaces in the 1880s and local (phosphoric) ores in basic process furnaces in the 1890s. During the 1900s Dorman sought growth via verical integration and merger, Bell Bros being his largest acquisition (in 1902). By 1907 he employed 9,500. The First World War brought further expansion but contracting markets in the 1920s damaged the firm. An old man flanked by old men, Dorman failed to rationalise. Thus, although the firm built the Sydney Harbour Bridge, the contract produced a loss. Merger in 1929 with Bolckow Vaughan, a large and more ailing neighbour failed to solve Dorman Long's problems in Sir Arthur Dorman's lifetime (he was knighted in 1918 and made a baronet in 1923). Dorman married Clara, daughter of George Lockwood, a Stockton merchant and shipbuilder; they had four sons and three daughters. See Jonathan S Boswell, *Business Policies in the Making: Three Steel Companies Compared* (1983); *DBB*.

DOUGLAS, George
(1858 - 26 November 1947)
Woollen and worsted dyer, son of David Maitland Douglas, a manager and later a partner in the Bradford stuff merchanting firm of A & S Henry, and his wife Margaret née McConnell, Douglas was educated at Bradford Grammar School before joining his father's firm. He spent a year at the Yorkshire College and in 1878 moved to the famous firm of Edward Ripley & Son, dyers of Bowling near Bradford. He became responsible for some internal reorganisation and was promoted to general manager and junior partner. Intense competition in the 1890s convinced him of the need to reorganise piece dyeing in Bradford and district. On his initiative the Bradford Dyers' Association, an amalgam of 22 firms with 90 per cent market share, was formed in 1898. By 1907 the BDA employed 7,500. Douglas became a joint managing director and, in 1909, sole managing director, until his retirement in 1945. From 1924 he was also chairman. Until the depression of the 1930s the BDA was one of the more efficient textile mergers created in the 1890s-1900s merger wave. Douglas was married and had a son and a daughter. See *DBB*.

DOULTON, Henry Lewis
(12 February 1853 - 3 December 1930)
Pottery manufacturer; only son of Sir Henry Doulton (1820-97), inheritor of a small Lambeth pottery which he built up into the Doulton empire with 4,000 employed in seven works in the 1890s,

and his wife Sarah née Kennaby. Henry was educated at Harrow and entered the family business in 1872, progressing through all the departments including the manufacture of china, earthenware, stoneware, electrical porcelain, sanitary and chemical ware. He became a partner in 1880 and took sole control on the death of his father. In 1898 he converted the firm into a joint stock company with a capital of £1.1 million (the value, almost, of its tangible assets). Henry became chairman, retiring in 1925 when he handed over to a nephew, Lewis John Eric Hooper. The accolade of 'Royal' was conferred by King Edward VII on the products of the firm in 1901 when Henry was granted a Royal Warrant. In the decade before 1914 competition in sanitary ware was keen though Doultons won contracts for several large liners like the *Mauretania, Aquitania* and *Titanic*. With a keen interest in innovation the firm developed new types of electrical insulator for London's underground railway system. Demand for most of the company's products was stifled by the First World War, however. At the end of 1918 Henry handed the managing directorship to Eric Hooper. A paternalist, Henry was especially interested in Lambeth Parish Church and Archbishop Temple's Boys' School. He married Jessie Maria née White in 1885; they had no surviving children. See Desmond Eyles, *Royal Doulton, 1815-1965* (1965); *Pottery Gazette and Glass Trade Review*, 1 January 1931.

DRAYTON, (Harold Charles Gilbert) 'Harley'
(19 November 1901 - 7 April 1966)
Transport financier, born at Streatham, London, the elder son of Gilbert Drayton, a gardener with the London County Council, and his wife Annie née Keep, on the early death of his mother he and his brother were brought up in the Croydon home of Alexander Low a Scottish sanitary inspector. 'Harley', as he was known, left school at 14 and became an office boy at Government Stocks & Other Securities Investment Co, one of a dozen investment companies run by Viscount St Davids (John Wynford Philipps). Here he was noticed by J S Austen, a solicitor, confidante of St Davids and chairman of British Electric Traction Co, 1921-42. Austen and Drayton managed the St Davids investment group from 117 Old Broad Street. By 1933 Drayton was a director of Government Stocks and in 1938 succeeded Austen as manager. A shadowy figure, Drayton became director of about 40 companies including BET whose board he joined in 1933. After the death of St Davids in 1938 and Austen in 1942, he headed the St Davids group and in 1946 succeeded as chairman of BET, remaining so until his death. BET was a holding company in

road passenger transport of national significance. Harley Drayton successfully applied two major policies. He resisted nationalisation of buses in 1948. With John Spencer Wills (qv), he took BET into British film and television, chairing the British Lion Film Corporation and in 1954 forming Associated Rediffusion, one of the first television programme companies. His marriage in 1926 to Christine Collie Low was childless but happy. See *DBB*; Roger Fulford, *The Sixth Decade: 1946-1956* (1956); G E Mingay, *Fifteen Years On: The BET Group, 1956-1971* (1973).

DUCAT, David
(1 June 1904 - 13 February 1989)
Packaging manufacturer, born at Stoke Newington, London, son of William John Ducat, a bank clerk, and his wife Amy née Smith, he was educated at Merchant Taylors' School and Gonville and Caius College, Cambridge, reading mathematics and distinguishing himself as a Wrangler. From college he went straight into a management traineeship with the Metal Box Co headed by Robert Barlow (qv). Ducat moved up the managerial hierarchy, qualifying as an Associate of the Chartered Institute of Secretaries in 1935. During the Second World War he served in the Ministry of Production. Towards the end of the war the Metal Box organisation was developed into a more centralised and functionally defined structure and a younger generation of managers brought forward. Ducat's appointment in 1945 to the board of Barringer, Wallis & Manners, one of the subsidiaries, was part of the centralisation policy. Growth (in 1948 Metal Box had 16,000 in the UK) defeated Barlow's autocratic rule. In 1947 he resigned the managing directorship but within months sacked his successor. Ducat, an organisation man, and G S Samways, formerly director in charge of manufacturing, were appointed joint managing directors. Samways resigned in 1954, Ducat continued until 1966. He was vice-chairman 1952-66, deputy chairman 1966-67 and chairman 1967-70. At his retirement Metal Box employed 30,000 in the UK and 20,000 overseas (chiefly South Africa, India and Italy). During the 1950s and 1960s the business was transformed from a metal container manufacturer into a packaging manufacturer producing a range of products from plastic film to aerosols. Ducat married in 1933 Hiliary Mildred Stokes; they had three sons and one daughter. See W J Reader, *Metal Box: A History* (1976).

DUDLEY, Sir William Edward
(1868 - 7 May 1938)
President of the Co-operative Wholesale Society, born in Runcorn, and started work aged 12 in the office of the Bridgwater Canal Co (later part of the Manchester Ship Canal), and eventually became head of the engineer's office. He joined the Co-operative Movement in the Cheshire and North Wales area and was elected to the CWS board in 1911. A member of the Consumers' Council and of fourteen departmental committees during the First World War, he served on the Royal Commission on Food Prices (1924) and National Food Council. He was elected president of the CWS from 1933 until his retirement in 1936, when the CWS employed nearly 50,000 (making it amongst the top ten UK employers). He also held CWS-nominated directorships on the Manchester Ship Canal and Manchester Collieries Ltd. A member of the Church of England, Dudley was awarded an OBE in 1920, and was knighted in 1926. See Percy Redfern, *The New History of the CWS* (1938).

DUMBLE, Colonel Wilfrid Chatterton
(1871 - 1962)
Transport manager, born at Coburg, Ontario, he was the eldest child and only son of the second marriage of John Henry Dumble, an English engineer who went to Canada to survey the disputed Quebec-Maine boundary, with Sarah Georgina Chatterton. Educated at Trinity College School, Port Hope, and the Royal Military College, Kingston, he graduated in 1892 to a commission with the Royal Engineers. After training at Chatham in England he served during the Boer War mainly in Bermuda and retired with the rank of captain in 1907. Around 1906 he worked with Sir Charles Parsons at Newcastle-upon-Tyne, gaining experience in electrical engineering. Possibly this helped when in July 1907 he was appointed joint general manager of the London General Omnibus Co at a salary of £1,500. The LGOC had been formed by a merger of numerous smaller companies in 1855 and by 1907 employed over 4,000. At Dumble's instigation the original liveries were abandoned in 1907 and all omnibuses painted a distinctive red. He shared in talks with the Underground Electric Railway Co Ltd in 1911 to work out a system of interchangeable and through tickets, which were available by 1914. The major change in his time was the switch from horse-drawn to motor buses which gathered pace after 1910. By April 1912 Dumble was the sole general manager of the LGOC but for reasons unknown resigned in May 1913. The following year he returned to the army, reputedly was involved in the development of the tank and reached the rank of colonel. Late in life he married a wealthy American divorcee, Mary Spur, whom he met on one of his

many return visits to his birthplace. There were no children. See Theodore C Barker and Michael Robbins, *A History of London Transport* (2 vols, 1963-74).

E

EARLE, Sir George Foster
(8 February 1890 - 11 December 1965)

Cement manufacturer, son of John Hudson Earle, of G & T Earle, a firm of cement manufacturers in Hull founded in 1809, and his wife Alice née Bainbridge, he was educated at Harrow and St John's College, Cambridge. Entering the family firm, George Earle became secretary and a director in 1914, and then served in the army in the First World War. Meantime the firm and the industry changed rapidly. Situated on the Humber the company had cement works at Wilmington near Hull, at Stoneferry and at Barton-on-Humber by 1914. Rotary kilns, which greatly improved methods of Portland cement manufacture, were installed from 1906. More widely, the rise of indigenous cement industries abroad in the 1890s, and the consequent loss of foreign markets, led to intensified competition at home. To check falling prices 24 firms in the London area (which produced 80 per cent of the UK's cement) merged in 1900 to form the Associated Portland Cement Manufacturers Ltd, a combine promoted by Osborne O'Hagan (qv). To bring most of the rest of the industry within the amalgamation, the British Portland Cement Manufacturers Ltd was formed in 1911 as a subsidiary of APCM. Earles was one of the 32 companies taken over by BPCM. In 1907 the APCM had a weekly capacity of 24,000 tons while 28 of the BPCM firms had a weekly capacity of 31,000 tons, together equal to 82 per cent of the industry. Between the wars demand for cement increased, with the housing boom in the South. When a joint selling organisation was formed in 1925, with the Blue Circle trademark, Earles retained its own selling organisation and Pelican trademark. The APCM Group rationalised, modernised and effectively imposed price agreements between the wars. A strong sellers' market remained into the 1950s when the APCM Group employed 11,000. George Earle became a director of APCM in 1921 and of BPCM in 1922, and managing director of both in 1937. He was chairman of the APCM Group, 1946-56, and managing director, 1946-55. He was knighted in 1954. Earle was twice married. See P Lesley Cook and Ruth Cohen, *Effects of Mergers: Six Studies* (1958); *The Times*, 13 December 1965.

ECCLES, Sir Josiah
(29 July 1897 - 14 October 1967)

Electricity supply industry executive, son of Johnston Eccles and his wife Mary Anne, he served in the army during the First World War (winning the Military Medal) before going to Queen's University, Belfast, where he took a first in engineering in 1922. He served an engineering apprenticeship with Metropolitan-Vickers Electrical Co, 1922-28, and then joined Edinburgh Corporation electricity department, heading it by 1940. In 1944 he was appointed City Electrical Engineer of Liverpool and after nationalisation in 1948 became chairman of the Merseyside and North Wales Board. Promoted to deputy chairman of the British Electricity Authority in 1954, he opposed pressure to expand the nuclear power generation programme but was overruled by the Macmillan (Conservative) government. The result was overcommitment to an over-large construction programme of Magnox power stations from 1957. Eccles retired in 1961 (with a consolation knighthood in 1957), promotion blocked by his political masters. He married Katherine Lillie Gillah Summerson, daughter of a solicitor, in 1930; they had a son and two daughters. See *DBB*; Leslie Hannah, *Engineers, Managers and Politicians: The First Fifteen Years of Nationalised Electricity Supply in Britain* (1982).

EDINGTON, William Gerald
(2 February 1895 - 28 June 1968)

Clearing banker, born in Liverpool the son of Harold Snape Edington and his wife Florence, he was educated at Holt High School, Liverpool, and entered the Dale Street, Liverpool, branch of the London City & Midland Bank in 1911 as a junior. He served with the 9th King's Liverpool Regiment throughout the First World War, returning with the handicap of an artificial leg. Promoted to manager of the Oldham branch of the Midland in 1934, he gained experience in dealing with the financial repercussions of the cotton industry's collapse (and wrote a paper on the subject). He went to London in 1937 as the Midland general manager's assistant and quickly progressed to become chief general manager in 1946, remaining in office until March 1956. His tenure, shared with Harold L Rouse until 1951, was not a happy one. The Midland lost its position as the largest clearing bank; post-war reconstruction of the branch network fell behind; and deteriorating labour relations led to the dissolution of the Staff Association. Edington was heavily to blame. The dominant but cautious force in senior management, he imposed unimaginative central controls over his branch managers, with predictable effects. On retiring he became a director of the Midland. He married Anne née Harrison (d 1957); they had one son and one daughter. See A R Holmes and Edwin Green, *Midland: 150 Years of Banking Business* (1986); *Midland Chronicle*, August 1968.

EDWARDES, Sir Michael (Owen)

(11 October 1930 -)

Industrialist, born in South Africa, the son of Denys Owen Edwardes and Audrey Noel née Copeland. Educated in Grahamstown at St Andrew's College and Rhodes University, where he studied law (BA), his early business experience was in his father's Cape Battery Co, which led to him joining the Chloride Co in the UK in 1951. In 1963 he was appointed head of Chloride's Central African operations; and then asked to restructure the Group's UK business. Aged 39 he joined the board and helped rationalise the Group's Exide battery division. He was chairman of Chloride (with 20,000 employees) between 1974 and 1977, when profits took off: in 1971-77 pre-tax profits increased from £3.5 million to £26 million. He was appointed to the National Enterprise Board 1975-77. Edwardes was chairman and chief executive of the UK car giant British Leyland between 1977 and 1982, where his changes in management and labour relations were much publicised. He trimmed BL's workforce from 200,000 to 110,000, introduced new technology and drastically cut losses. This led to a string of appointments: in 1984-5 he was chairman and chief executive of Dunlop Holdings and also joined the boards of Mercury Communications, ICL, Minorca SA, Charter Consolidated and RK Carvill International Holdings. He has married twice: first in 1958 to Mary née Finlay, the daughter of the founder of the South African shipping line, Safmarine (they had three daughters); second in 1988 to Sheila Ann née Guy. He was knighted in 1979. See Michael Edwardes, *Back from the Brink* (1983).

EGAN, Sir John (Leopold)

(7 November 1939 -)

Motor car manufacturer, born at Rawtenstall in Lancashire, the son of James E Egan, who owned a Rootes dealership. Educated at the local grammar school and Bablake School, Coventry, Egan took a degree in petroleum engineering at Imperial College, London, 1958-61, before joining Shell International. In 1966 he took a London Business School MSc degree on one of the first UK business studies courses. In 1968 he joined General Motors operations in the UK and then three years later moved to British Leyland, where he headed Unipart. After a spell at Massey-Ferguson, in 1980 he was appointed chairman of BL's loss-making

Jaguar Cars Ltd. Egan directed Jaguar's £297 million privatisation in 1984 and tranformed its fortunes: in 1980 it made less than 14,000 cars and lost £52 million after tax; by 1986 car production was 41,437 with £83 million profit. Jaguar was especially successful in the US in the early 1980s, helped by marketing and a favourable exchange rate. Egan was chairman and chief executive until 1990, when he left to become chief executive of BAA, the owner of Heathrow, Gatwick, Stansted and four other airports. (Jaguar's profits meanwhile collapsed at the end of the 1980s.) Egan is now intent on making BAA (which has a stock market value of £3.8 billion and 8,500 workers) a more customer driven and commercially-oriented company by (his critics say) making its airports as much a place to shop in as to fly from. In 1963 he married Julia Emily Treble: they have two daughters. He was knighted in 1986. See Michael Donne, *Above Us the Skies: The Story of BAA* (1991); John Underwood, *The Will to Win* (1989).

ELLERMAN, Sir John (Reeves)

(1862 - 16 July 1933)

Shipping magnate and financier, born at Hull, the son of Johann Herman Ellerman and Anne Elisabeth Reeves. Johann Ellerman was a Hamburg corn merchant and shipbroker; his mother was the daughter of a local solicitor. Brought up in France, he briefly attended King Edward VI School in Birmingham, and then articled himself to an accountant in that city. He had soon moved to London and became a partner with Quilter, Ball & Co. Aged 24 he founded his own accountancy firm and entered the world of shipping. In the 1890s he successfully reorganised the Leyland Co in the 1890s, which demonstrated his *modus operandi* - purchasing old declining merchant shipping firms and then using his formidable financial skills to make them profitable again. Leyland, later sold to the American financier J P Morgan for between £1 million and £2 million, made Ellerman a multi-millionaire. He rapidly expanded his shipping empire between 1900 and 1904, entering the South African, Indian and Far East trade, and forming Ellerman Lines from the ships he had retained from Leyland. Ellerman also had a wide portfolio of non-shipping interests: for example, by 1918 he owned shares in over 70 breweries and was chairman of J W Cameron and Hoare & Co; and also held shares in 22 collieries by the 1920s, which supplied fuel for his fleet. He was also for a time the largest shareholder in the *Financial Times*, a major shareholder in the *Daily Mail* and with Lord Northcliffe (qv) bought into *The Times* in 1912. In the 1920s he became one of the largest London landowners, through the Ellerman Property Trust.

By 1916 Ellerman was the richest man in the UK and possibly the richest in British history, with a fortune estimated at £55 million - an estate which appears to have diminished little in the more difficult 1920s and 1930s. He left the largest sum in British history to that date - £36,685,000 - about 30 per cent of all wealth passed by probate in that year! Yet he has not been regarded as a major historical figure: the fact that he shunned publicity, cared little for high society, had no interest in charitable works and seems to have been a relatively colourless individual may be responsible. He was made a Companion of Honour in 1921 and received a baronecy when he was 43. He married Hannah née Glover sometime between 1898 and 1908 and had two children: a daughter, Annie Winifrid, who later wrote novels under the pseudonym 'Bryher'; and a son, John (1909-1973), who assumed control of his business. See James Taylor, *Ellermans: A Wealth of Shipping* (1976); *DBB*; *DNB*.

ELLIOT, Sir John
(6 May 1898 - 18 September 1988)
Railway manager, born in East Battersea, London, the younger son of Ralph David Blumenfeld, editor of the *Daily Express* (1904-32), and his cousin and wife Theresa 'Daisy' née Blumfield, Elliot (he dropped his surname in 1923) was educated at Marlborough and Sandhurst and served on the Western Front, resigning from the army in 1921 to become a journalist. After a year with the New York Times he joined the *London Evening Standard* but left in 1924 following a disagreement with Max Aitken, Lord Beaverbrook (qv). He joined the Southern Railway in 1925 as a public relations assistant reporting directly to Sir Herbert Walker (qv). In charge of advertising, he projected a new image for the rapidly modernising and and electrifying Southern. He became development assistant to the traffic manager in 1930, assistant traffic manager in 1933, assistant general manager in 1937, deputy general manager in 1939 and general manager in 1947. After nationalisation he was re-titled as 'chief regional officer' of the Southern Region of British Railways. Three years later he transferred from Waterloo to Euston to run the London Midland Region, chiefly to improve maintenance and morale. In 1951 he was promoted to chairman of the Railway Executive, head of British Railways under the British Transport Commission, a tenure overshadowed by organisational debates. When this post was abolished in 1953 Eliot became chairman of London Transport, increasing investment (especially in the Victoria Line). Knighted in 1954, he retired in 1959. He married in 1924 Elizabeth Marjorie, daughter of Dr A S Cobbledick; they had a son and a daughter. See *DBB*; Sir John Elliot, *On*

and *off the Rails* (1982); T R Gourvish, *British Railways, 1948-73: A Business History* (1986); *The Times*, 20 September 1988.

ELLIOTT, Albert George
(3 December 1889 - 13 November 1975)
Engineer, born in Upper Holloway, London, the son of Charles Henry Elliott, a grocer, and his wife Adelaide née Powell, he trained at Northampton Engineering College and also London University. Elliott was responsible for engine design at the Napier Co before joining Rolls-Royce in 1912 to take charge of the engine drawing office. For 20 years he was attached to Sir Henry Royce's (qv) personal staff at West Wittering near Chichester, assisting Royce in designing the Eagle, the company's first aero engine (1914-15); the Kestrel, an aluminium alloy aero engine (1925-31), and the Merlin aero engine (1929-35) which powered the Spitfire aircraft in the Second World War. Elliott succeeded Royce as chief engineer in 1933; he became a director in 1945 and joint managing director in 1951, retiring from these posts in 1955. He married first, in 1921, Cecilia, daughter of Rennie Gray of Aberdeen, and second, in 1962, Ann, daughter of George Wrightson of Kirk Ireton Derbyshire. See Ian Lloyd, *Rolls-Royce* (3 vols, 1978).

ELLIS, Sir Charles Edward
(12 September 1852 - 19 February 1937)
Iron and steel manufacturer, second son of John Devonshire Ellis (1824-1906), partner of John Brown (1816-96) the Sheffield steel and armour plate manufacturer, and his wife Elizabeth Bourne a Shropshire farmer's daughter, he was educated at Lancing College and Trinity College, Cambridge, gaining a second-class degree in history. He was called to the Bar in 1878 and practised on the North Eastern Circuit. In 1890 he became a director of John Brown & Co, his father having been chairman and managing director since John Brown retired in 1872. In 1899 the firm bought control of the Clydebank Engineering & Shipbuilding Co, Glasgow, to secure an outlet for the firm's Atlas Works (Sheffield) steel output. By 1907 John Brown & Co employed 20,000 in Sheffield, the North East and on Clydebank, building Cunard liners and Royal Navy battleships. C E Ellis served as managing director, 1892-1915 and 1919-1928. The wartime interlude was spent in the Ministry of Munitions (Council member and Director General of Ordnance Supply). Ellis was made a KCB in 1917 and a GBE in 1919. He married, in 1881, Inez Blanche née Faviell; there were no surviving children. See *The Times*, 20 February 1937.

ENGELBACH, Charles Richard Fox
(20 May 1876 - 19 February 1943)

Motor vehicle manufacturer, born in London, the son of Lewis Engelbach, a War Office clerk of Huguenot origins, and Jessie née Bryan. He attended Sandringham School, Stockport. Experience in car production at Armstrong, Whitworth and in wartime munitions work, led to his selection in 1921 as works director at the Austin Motor Co's plant at Longbridge, near Birmingham. Regarded as one of the finest production engineers in the UK (attested by his presidency of the Institute of Automobile Engineers), Engelbach reorganised Austin in the mid-1920s: car production rising from 16,429 in 1925 to 37,520 in 1927. A Freemason, he married in 1902 Florence née Neumegan, a renowned Spanish portraitist, and had two sons. He left £110,733 gross. See R A Church, *Herbert Austin: The British Motor Car Industry to 1941* (1979); *DBB*.

ENNIS, Lawrence
(31 August 1871 - 5 May 1938)

Steel manufacturer, born at West Calder, Scotland, the son of Arthur Ennis and Katherine née Weir. As a child he went with his family to America, where he worked as a engineer on various bridge and structural projects, but in 1903 he returned to England to join Dorman, Long in Middlesbrough as a superintendent of bridge and constructional works. In 1905 he became works manager and in 1915 general manager, when he was also involved with labour relations as president of the Iron & Steel Trades Association. In 1924 he was appointed director of Dorman, Long and became the resident engineer in charge of the Sydney Harbour Bridge project during 1924-32. He was managing director of the Middlesbrough firm from 1932 to 1937, when it employed about 27,000. In 1893 he married Margaret, daughter of American engineer Peter Phillips. Ennis was awarded the OBE in 1913 and was made CMG in 1933. Ennnis was a Catholic. He left £37,457 gross. See *The Times*, 7 May 1938.

ERIKS, Sierd Sint
(26 September 1900 - 27 September 1966)

Electronics industrialist, born at Oosterzee in Holland, the son of Jan Eriks, manager of an agricultural co-operative, and his wife Janna née Klijnsna, he was educated at Rotterdam Commercial High School. He joined the sales organisation of NV Philips Gloeilampenfabrieken at Eindhoven in 1924 and moved from selling Christmas tree lights to radio valves and X-ray tubes in a few months. He spent 1925-29 in Australia and New Zealand building up a market share for Philips. In 1929 he was made general manager of Mullard Wireless Service Co, a UK radio maker recently acquired by Philips. Eriks transformed it into an advanced electronics manufacturer. He moved the plant from London to Blackburn, to escape from the wartime hazards he foresaw and to help relieve the unemployment he deplored, and set up a vertically-integrated operation which became the most important source of radio valves for allied forces throughout the war. He set up a major research laboratory in Surrey. After the war the Mullard company sponsored research labs at the universities of Oxford, Cambridge and London. TV gave a new impetus to electronics and Mullard captured 70 per cent of the radio and TV receiver manufacturers' market. By 1955 Mullard employed 16,000. Eriks received an honorary KBE in 1961 and was honoured in the Netherlands. He married, in 1942, Margaret Isabel Duncanson, daughter of Robert Duncanson a master builder; the marriage failed and there were no children. See *DBB*.

EVANS, Robert
(28 May 1927 -)

Gas utilities executive, the son of Gwilym and Florence May Evans. Educated at Old Swan College, Blackburn College, the City of Liverpool Technical College and Liverpool University, in 1943 he joined the aero-engineering firm of D Napier & Sons Ltd. He has worked for British Gas ever since 1950 (apart from a spell with Burmah Oil between 1956 and 1962), holding posts with the North Western, Southern, North Thames and East Midlands regions. He became chief executive in 1983, in time for the huge sale of British Gas to the public for £5,434 million in December 1986. Evans was appointed chairman and chief executive of British Gas in 1989. The turnover of British Gas has risen from £7,364 million in 1988 to £10,254 million in 1991; while operating profits rose from £1,063 million to £1,666 million. In 1991 Evans directed a corporation with 84,500 employees. He was president of the Institution of Gas Engineers in 1981-82 and was appointed CBE in 1987. In 1950 he married Lilian May née Ward: they have one son and one daughter.

EZRA, Derek
Baron Ezra of Horsham
(23 February 1919 -)

Nationalised coal company chairman, the son of David and Lillie Ezra. Educated at Monmouth School and Magdalene College, Cambridge, he served in the army between 1939 and 1947 and then joined the National Coal Board. He was to spend his career within the industry, working in

FAYED

sales and marketing in the 1950s and 1960s, and
becoming NCB chairman between 1971 and 1982.
He produced a Plan for Coal, endorsed by the
Government, to replace obsolescent plant by new
capacity to stave off prospective decline in employment, in the hope - which proved in vain - of pro-
ceeding to renewed expansion ten years later. The
trend of his tenure at the NCB was slightly downward. Ezra also served as chairman of J H Sankey &
Son, Petrolex, British Fuel, Solvay and Redland.
Awarded the MBE in 1945, he was knighted in
1974 and created a life peer in 1983. He married in
1950 Julia Elizabeth Wilkins. See Derek Ezra, *Coal
and Energy* (1978), *The Energy Debate* (1983);
William Ashworth, *History of the British Coal
Industry: Vol 5, 1946-1982* (1986).

F

FAIRFAX, Albert Kirby
12th Baron Fairfax of Cameron
(28 June 1870 - 4 October 1939)
Banker and industrialist, born in Maryland, USA,
the eldest son of John Contee Fairfax, MD, *de jure*
11th earl of Fairfax, and Mary née Kirby. He
worked as a clerk for the New York bankers
Brown Bros, then moved to England to take up his
peerage, and in 1900 joined the London branch of
the International Banking Corporation. In 1906 he
became associated with William P Bonbright &
Co, eventually becoming senior partner. In 1925
he established Fairfax & Co, a discount house at 16
George St, Mansion House. He was also chairman
of the Amalgamated Cotton Mills Trust, which
employed 8,000 in 1935. He married in 1922
Maud Wishart née McKelvie: they had two sons.
See *The Times*, 5 October 1939.

FAY, Sir Samuel
(20 December 1856 - 30 May 1953)
Railway manager, born at Hamble, Hampshire, the
son of Joshua Fay, a gardener, and his wife Ann née
Philpot, at 16 he joined the London & South
Western Railway as a clerk and by 1891 was assistant storekeeper. His chance came in 1892 when
he was appointed manager of the bankrupt
Midland & South Western Junction Railway. With
energy and resourcefulness Fay brought it back to
solvency in 1897. In 1899 he returned to the
London & South Western as superintendent of the
line. With proven abilities in 1902 he became general manager of the Great Central Railway at a
salary of £3,000 a year. The Great Central was
struggling, having overspent on its London extension. Fay developed it by exploiting its command
of routes between the North and the South and

South West, not least by a variety of public relations exercises. In 1907 the Great Central
employed over 25,000. During the First World
War Sir Sam Fay (he was knighted in 1912) went
to the War Office as Director of Movements and
later had a seat on the Army Council. When in
1923 the Great Central was absorbed by the
London & North Eastern Railway (as part of the
scheme which reduced the 130 independent railways to four groups), Fay retired. He was chairman
of Beyer Peacock & Co the Manchester locomotive builders, 1923-33. Fay married in 1883 Ann
née Farebrother; they had six children. See *DBB*.

FAYED, Mohamed Al-
(January 1933 -)
Entrepreneur and department store owner, born
(according to one source in 1929) in one of the
poorest districts of Alexandria, Egypt, the eldest of
three sons of Ali Ali Fayed, a primary school
teacher. According to his brief *Who's Who* entry,
he was educated at Alexandria University. Later
Mohamed worked as a sewing machine salesman,
but he was soon befriended by Adnan Kashoggi (of
later arms-dealing fame), who recruited him to
head his furniture import business in Saudi Arabia.
In 1954 he married Kashoggi's sister, Samira: they
later had a son, Emad ('Dodi'). By 1957 Mohamed
had parted from both his boss and wife and began
his own business career, taking advantage of the
upheavals in the Nasser years and finding a lucrative role as a middleman between Middle East sul-
tans and British contractors. In 1975 (now adding
Al to his name) Fayed briefly joined the board of
Tiny Rowland's (qv) Lonrho, but left after a disagreement. In 1979 he bought the Hotel Ritz,
Paris, and at about the same time married his
Finnish second wife, Heini, by whom he had four
children. In 1985 Mohamed and his two younger
brothers, Salah and Ali, paid £615 million for the
House of Fraser, the store group that owns
Harrods, much to the fury of Tiny Rowland,
whose earlier bid for the group had been blocked
by the Government. Rowland and Lonrho pursued
a campaign of vilification against the Fayeds, which
was partly vindicated when a Department of Trade
report concluded in 1990 that the brothers had lied
about their origins and the true source of their
wealth (rumoured to have come from the Sultan of
Brunei). While the war with Rowland continues,
the Fayeds have retained control of Harrods and are
spending lavishly on it, hoping to enhance its reputation as a shopping paradise for the rich and
famous. A private company, Harrods was making
profits of £28 million a year when they took over:
the most recent available total in November 1990
showed profits of £26 million when most other

retailers were booming. See Sean Callery, *Harrods: The Story of Society's Favourite Store* (1991); Michael Moss and Alison Turton, *A Legend of Retailing: The House of Fraser* (1989); Tiny Rowland, *A Hero From Zero: The Story of Kleinwort Benson and Mohamed Fayed* (1988).

FINNISTON, Sir (Harold) Montague (Monty)
(15 August 1912 - 2 February 1991)

Nationalised steel company chairman, born in Glasgow into a Jewish working class family, the son of Robert and Esther Finniston. Educated at Allan Glen's School, Glasgow, and Glasgow University, he became a lecturer at the College of Science & Technology in the city, where he was awarded a PhD on the behaviour of coke. This brought him into the steel industry, where he was to have a glittering career as a metallurgist. From 1948 to 1958 he was chief metallurgist at the UK Atomic Energy Authority at Harwell at an important stage in the development of nuclear power. After a period with the International Research & Development Co in Newcastle, he returned to the steel industry in 1967 as the technical board member to Lord Melchett (qv) at the British Steel Corporation. He assumed the chairmanship of BSC after Melchett's premature death in 1973 and - sharing the latter's optimistic belief in increasing world steel demand - continued with the BSC's expansion. He was to be frustrated by the collapse of the world steel market due to an oil-driven recession in 1973-75 and cutbacks in public expenditure. The new Labour Government was unwilling to sanction the job losses that were required if costs were to be contained. BSC's cash needs escalated as its sales fell, its capital spending plans were all but aborted, and Finniston to his disappointment was not re-appointed for a second term in 1976. But he chaired the Government enquiry into the engineering profession in 1979, producing *Engineering our Future* (the Finniston Report), which resulted in the founding of the Engineering Council in 1981. He had the rare distinction of being elected both FRS and FEng, besides similar recognition - FRSE - across the border. He took a particular interest in the links between industry and the universities, receiving some fifteen honorary degrees. He was knighted in 1975. In 1936 he married Miriam Singer: they had one son and one daughter. See H M Finniston, *Structural Characteristics of Materials* (1971); Geoffrey F Dudley and Jeremy J Richardson, *Politics and Steel in Britain, 1967-88: The Life and Times of the British Steel Corporation* (1990).

FIRTH, Sir William John
(21 July 1881 - 11 November 1957)

Steel and tinplate manufacturer, born in London, the son of Richard Firth. He entered the tinplate trade aged 20 and within ten years was directing the Grovesend group of works, which later amalgamated with Richard Thomas & Co. He built up the tinplate output of Richard Thomas after his appointment as managing director and chairman in 1931 and recognised the importance of the latest technological developments, such as the wide strip mill. But he was to lose control of the company (which employed 10,000 by 1935) when outside finance from the Bank of England was needed for a new strip mill at Ebbw Vale. After disagreements with the board he retired from Richard Thomas in 1940: his attempts to regain control and prevent the merger with Baldwins in 1944 were unsuccessful. Firth, who was knighted in 1932, was chairman of the International Tinplate Cartel, president of the Swansea Metal Exchange, and a member of the International Tin Committee. He married in 1909 Helena Adelaide née Garrett, by whom he had two sons. See *The Times*, 12 November 1957.

FLECK, Alexander Baron Fleck of Saltcoats
(11 November 1889 - 6 August 1968)

Chemical company chairman, born in Glasgow, the son of Robert Fleck, a coal merchant, and Agnes Hendry née Duncan, he was educated at Saltcoats Public School and Hillhead High School, leaving at 14 to become a laboratory assistant at Glasgow University. He gained an honours degree in chemistry, joined the staff in 1913 and under Professor Frederick Soddy's supervision worked on the chemistry of radio elements, securing a DSc in 1916. Fleck entered industry in 1917 as chief chemist of the Castner Kellner Co at Wallsend-on-Tyne, becoming works manager in 1919. Castner Kellner was taken over by Brunner, Mond in 1920 and when the latter became a component of Imperial Chemical Industries in 1926 Fleck found himself responsible for planning the ICI sodium cyanide works at Billingham. Over the next two decades he moved up the ICI hierarchy: manager of the Alkali Division, 1927-31; managing director of the General Chemicals Division, 1931-37; chairman of the Billingham Division, 1937-45, during which time he kept the plant going, despite enemy air raids, producing ammonia, hydrogen, methanol, chlorine and other chemicals indispensable to the war effort. He reached the ICI main board in 1944, being given responsibility for a new plastics plant at Wilton on Teesside. He was elected deputy chairman in 1951 and then chairman in 1953, retiring in 1960. By 1954 ICI sales reached £352 million with a trading profit of £72 million and UK employees numbered 112,000 in over 100 plants. During his first year he introduced profit sharing in order to promote an understanding of the company. In contrast to his predecessor Lord Harry McGowan (qv), an authoritarian paternalistic figure, Fleck was very much a modern professional manager, both in his technical background and his liberal attitude to labour relations. He was knighted and made an FRS in 1955 and created a baron in 1961. Fleck married Isabel Mitchell née Kelly (d 1955) in 1917; they had no children. See *DBB*; William J Reader, *Imperial Chemical Industries: A History* vol 2 (1975).

FLETCHER, Eric George Molyneux
Baron Fletcher of Islington
(26 March 1903 - 9 June 1990)
Politician and film company chairman, the son of Clarence George Eugene Fletcher, Islington Town Clerk, he was educated at Hackney Downs School, Radley College and the University of London, qualifying as a solicitor in 1924. He began his political career when elected to London County Council as a member for South Islington in 1934, sitting until 1949. He was elected a Labour MP in the Labour landslide of 1945 and sat until he retired in 1970 when he was made a life peer. An active layman in the Church of England, he was a delegate to the World Council of Churches in Amsterdam in 1948 and later was a member of the Church Assembly. He held many company directorships, especially in the entertainment industry and was deputy chairman of the Associated British Picture Corporation, 1946-64. Originally opposing the creation of commercial television, he almost succeeded in persuading Sir Philip Warter (qv) from forming a programme company, ABC TV. As deputy chairman of ABC Television, Fletcher criticised extravagance in TV programme making. He married Bessie Winifred Butt in 1929; they had two sons and a daughter. See Bernard Sendall, *Independent Television in Britain* (2 vols, 1982-83); *The Times*, 12 June 1990.

FORBES, Sir William de Guise
(21 June 1856 - 14 February 1936)
Railway manager, born in Dublin, the son of William Forbes, general manager of the Midland Great Western Railway, he was educated at Dulwich College and on the Continent. In 1873 he joined the London, Chatham & Dover Railway, whose chairman and general manager was his uncle James Staats Forbes (1823-1904), starting in the goods department and moving to the accountant's office. In 1889 he became Continental manager and made Victoria Station the chief gateway to the Continent, displacing the South Eastern Railway's

Charing Cross. The posts of traffic manager and then assistant general manager followed but his chance to escape his uncle's shadow came in 1899 when he moved to the London, Brighton & South Coast Railway. In charge of the LBSCR until grouping in 1923 he rebuilt its section of Victoria Station, introduced Pullman services to Brighton, offered a faster cross-Channel steamer service, ran through-services from Liverpool and Manchester to Brighton, and in 1903 started an electrification progamme. He was knighted in 1915. In 1923 Sir William Forbes became one of the three general managers of the Southern Railway but retired after six months. He married, in 1902, Louise Tronche of Souillac, France, and had one son. See *DBB*.

FORD, Sir Leslie Ewart
(27 July 1897 - 22 March 1981)
Port manager, son of Elias Ford, a Great Western Railway manager, he was educated at Cardiff High School and in 1912 joined the GWR, later serving with the Welch and Monmouthshire Regiments during the First World War. Returning to the GWR he held several middle management posts and became a Brunel Medallist at the LSE in 1924. In 1928 he was moved into dock management: at Penarth (assistant in charge, 1928), Swansea (assistant docks manager, 1929), Port Talbot (docks nanager, 1933), Cardiff and Penarth (docks manager, 1938), assistant chief docks manager (1939), chief docks manager and manager of the GWR's steamers (1944). He was appointed general manager of the Port of London Authority in 1948, serving until 1964. Here he had to manage a major world port 'amid the conflicting currents of post-war reconstruction, technological changes in maritime transport and a consistently delicate labour situation'. He began the long shift of activity out of the East End of London and further down the Thames to the Erith-Tilbury section. He was knighted in 1956. Ford married, in 1925, Mary Mabel née Powles; they had one daughter. See *The PLA Monthly*, September 1948; *The Times*, 30 March 1981.

FORMAN, Harry Buxton
(1842 - 15 June 1917)
Post Office manager, born in London, he was educated at Teignmouth and entered the Civil Service in 1860. Like a more famous employee of the General Post Office, Anthony Trollope, he found time to generate a literary output, chiefly editions of the works of Shelley, Keats and William Morris. He retired from the Post Office in 1907 with the rank of Second Secretary and Controller of Packet Services. That year the business was the largest commercial employer in the UK, with 212,000

employees. He married, in 1869, Laura née Selle; they had two sons and a daughter.

FORRESTER-PATON, Alexander
(2 December 1880 - 8 April 1954)

Woollen yarn manufacturer, born in Alloa, the son of Alexander P Forrester-Paton (d 1915), a member of the textile firm of J Paton, founded in the early nineteenth century. Educated at Craigmount School, Edinburgh, and The Leys School, Cambridge, he joined the family firm and became a director in 1906 when the business became a private limited company as John Paton, Son & Co. In 1920 Patons merged with J & J Baldwin to form Paton & Baldwins (paid up capital £3.2 million): Forrester became vice-chairman in 1933 and chairman from 1938 (when the firm employed about 7,000) until his retirement in 1951. His business policy of enlightened paternalism strongly reflected his Free Church upbringing. In public life he was a Liberal, temperance advocate, and keen supporter of the YMCA. A JP, he was active on the Alloa Council, and was an honorary Sheriff Substitute. In 1910 he married Mary Emma Louise Shaw, whose father Thomas Shaw became 1st Baron Craigmyle: they had five sons. See *Alloa Record*, 14 April 1954; private information.

FORSTER, Sir Archibald (William)
(11 February 1928 -)

Oil company executive, the son of William Henry and Matilda Forster. Educated at Tottenham Grammar School, he took a degree in chemical engineering at Birmingham University, where he was a Cadman medallist. Following National Service with the RAF, he joined the Esso Petroleum Co in 1951. After a series of senior posts in refinery management, by the mid-1970s he was assistant to the chairman and involved with corporate planning at the Exxon Corporation (the holding company of Esso). Since 1983 he has been chairman and chief executive of Esso UK (and thus of its two arms, Esso Petroleum and Esso, Exploration & Production), which by the early 1990s was producing about 13 per cent of total UK oil and gas output and supplying about one-fifth of the country's petroleum products. In 1991 Esso UK's turnover was £6,233 million (with pre-tax profits of £497 million) and it employed 4,226 workers. Forster is also on the board of Lloyd's Register of Shipping and was president of the Oil Industries Club, 1982-83, and of the Institute of Petroleum, 1988-90. He was knighted in 1987. He married in 1954 Betty Margaret Channing: they have three daughters.

FORTE, Charles
Baron Forte of Ripley
(26 November 1908 -)

Hotel and catering chain operator, born at Monforte, Italy, the son of Rocco Forte and his wife Maria Luiga. His father came to Scotland in 1911 and opened a cafe in Alloa; Charles and his mother followed in 1913. He was educated at Alloa Academy and Dumfries College. In 1935 he opened his first milk bar in Regent Street, London, and after the War (when he was briefly interned) he expanded into hotels. Pre-tax profits of the business rose from £20,900 in 1955 to £5.5 million in 1970, when Forte merged with Trust Houses: with assets of £120 million and 215 hotels, Forte's combine overtook Maxwell Joseph's (qv) Grand Metropolitan as the UK's biggest hotelier. He became chief executive of Trusthouse Forte in 1971 and chairman in 1978. In 1990 THF employed over 70,000 staff in 800 hotels. Until 1989, when a five-year truce was signed, Forte engaged in annual battles for control of the Savoy Group, headed by Sir Hugh Wontner (qv). A paternalist, preaching the virtues of hard work, Forte was an admirer of Margaret Thatcher. His personal fortune was estimated at £160 million in 1992. He was made a life peer in 1982. In 1943 he married Irene May Chierico: his son and heir Rocco Forte (b 1945) - an Oxford graduate and trained accountant - took over as both chairman and chief executive in 1992, though his father remains on the board. See Charles Forte, *Forte: The Autobiography of Charles Forte* (1986).

FORTESCUE-FLANNERY, Sir James
(16 December 1851 - 5 October 1943)

Cable manufacturer, born at Liverpool, the eldest son of Captain John Flannery Seacombe. He was educated at the Liverpool School of Science, while serving an apprenticeship as an engineer at the Britannia Engine Works, Birkenhead. He entered the London office of Sir Edward Reed, chief constructor of the Navy, spending five years designing and inspecting machinery, varied by some seagoing experience. Starting business on his own account as a consulting engineer and naval architect, he eventually founded the firm of Flannery, Baggallay & Johnson Ltd. He became chairman of Callender's Cable & Construction Co and a director of Barclays Bank. A founder member and first president of the Society of Consulting Marine Engineers & Ship Surveyors, he was a former president of the Institution of Marine Engineers, and an ex-president of the Liverpool Shipbuilders' Guild and the Junior Engineers' Institution. He served as a Unionist MP for Shipley, Yorkshire, between 1895 and 1906, and for Malden, Essex, between 1910 and 1922. Knighted in 1899, he was created a baronet in 1904. In 1882 he married Edith Mary Emma (d 1936), daughter of Osborn Jenkyn: they had two daughters and a son. See *The Times*, 6 October 1943.

FOULDS, (Hugh) Jon
(2 May 1932 -)
Building society executive, born in Bury, Lancashire, the son of E J Foulds, a Quaker family doctor, and Helen Shirley née Smith. Educated at Bootham School, he was groomed to take over the family cotton business, Thomas Foulds & Son, and was sent to study textiles at Salford University. After National Service, he joined the business, but soon recommended its closure. In 1959 he moved to the Industrial & Commercial Finance Corporation (later 3i), which had been set up by Lord Piercy after the war at the behest of the Bank of England and the clearing banks to provide venture capital for British business. Between 1976 and 1988 Foulds was a director and the chief executive of 3i; after 1988 he became deputy chairman. In 1986 he joined the board of the Halifax Building Society and was appointed chairman in 1990. The Halifax is the world's biggest mortgage provider, with assets of £61 billion and pre-tax profits of more than £600 million a year. Foulds, like the other building society executives, is much vexed with the problems of the collapse of the property market and the number of households with negative equity. The Halifax called on the Government to slash interest rates and intervene directly in the housing market to avoid a crisis in 1993. In 1992 the Halifax raised pre-tax profits by 8 per cent to £680 million. Foulds has also been a non-executive director of Eurotunnel since 1988, and holds similar positions with a number of other investment and management groups. He married first in 1960 Berry Cusack-Smith, by whom he had two sons: and after that marriage was dissolved in 1970, he married in 1977 Helene Senn. See Corinne Simcock, *A Head for Business* (1992).

FRAME, Sir Alistair (Gilchrist)
(3 April 1929 -)
Industrialist, born in Dalmuir, Dumbartonshire, the son of Alexander Frame and Mary née Fraser. Educated at Glasgow and Cambridge Universities (MA, BSc), he was director of the reactor and research groups of the UK Atomic Energy Authority, 1964-68. He joined the Rio Tinto Zinc Corporation in 1968, was appointed to the main board in 1973 and was chief executive and chairman between 1978 and 1985. He was chairman of RTZ between 1985 and 1991, when J D Birkin (qv)

became chief executive. He followed the expansionist strategy devised by the creators of RTZ's postwar fortunes, Mark Turner and Val Duncan. By 1986 RTZ's turnover was £4,345 million, with pre-tax profits of £595 million. In 1990 he became chairman of the pharmaceutical firm, Wellcome. Together with his chief executive, John Robb (qv), Frame is successfully improving Wellcome's commercial and marketing focus. In 1992 Wellcome announced a massive share sale, designed to reduce the Trust's holding in the firm from about 74 per cent to 50 per cent. Formerly a director of Plessey and Britoil, he was chairman of the troubled Davy Corporation, 1990-91, and has been a director of Eurotunnel since 1990 and a non-executive chairman of British Steel since 1992 (retiring from the latter post through ill-health in April 1993). Frame was knighted in 1981. In 1953 he married Sheila née Mathieson; they have one daughter.

FRANKS, Oliver Shewell
Baron Franks of Headington
(16 February 1905 - 15 October 1992)
Academic, diplomat and banker, he was born in Bristol, the son of the Reverend Robert Sleightholme Franks, who from 1910 was principal of the Congregationalists' Western Theological College, and his wife Katherine née Shewell. Educated at Bristol Grammar School and The Queen's College, Oxford, he became professor of moral philosophy at Glasgow University in 1937. After another meteoric career in the Ministry of Supply and Aircraft Production during the Second World War he returned to his old college as provost but within two years was back in the world of action as British Ambassador at Washington, 1948-52. Returning to England he accepted a directorship of Lloyds Bank (held 1953-75), serving as deputy chairman in 1953 and chairman 1954-62. To Lloyds, with 18,000 employees the second largest clearing bank (behind Barclays), and the City he brought a new dynamism with his 'ability and determination to reason matters out on their merits, within the framework of tradition, rather than accept them on the grounds of tradition alone'. He was a member of the Committee of London Clearing Bankers (1960-62), of the Radcliffe Committee (Report, 1959), and of the National Economic Development Council (1962-64); a director of Schroders (1969-84); and chairman of Friends' Provident & Century Life Office (1955-62). In 1962 he returned to Oxford but participated on many public bodies. He was knighted in 1946, made a life peer in 1962 and awarded the OM in 1977. He married, in 1931, Barbara Mary Tanner; they had two daughters. See *The Times*, 17 October 1992.

FRASER, Hugh
1st Baron Fraser of Allander
(15 January 1903 - 6 November 1966)

Retailer, born in Glasgow, the son of Hugh Fraser and Emily Florence née McGowan; his father headed the department store in Buchanan Street founded by his grandfather in 1851. Educated at Warriston School and Glasgow Academy, Hugh Fraser entered the family firm, Fraser Sons, and mastered the whole business. He was appointed managing director in 1924 and chairman, on the death of his father, in 1927. More ambitious than his father, he expanded carefully, adding two stores in 1936 and 15 more in the 1940s, driven in part by his determination to keep English retail groups out of Scotland. In 1947 the firm was floated as a public company, House of Fraser Ltd, with a capital of £1 million. Armed with fresh capital Hugh Fraser carried his acquisition offensive over the Border, buying Binns Ltd of Sunderland in 1953, John Barker & Co the Kensington group in 1957, and Harrods Ltd in 1959 (after a battle with United Drapery Stores and Debenhams). At his death House of Fraser had 75 department stores in the UK. A generous philanthropist (his Hugh Fraser Foundation for Charity was endowed in 1960 with £2.5 million) he was made a baronet in 1960 and a baron in 1964. Fraser married in 1931, Kathleen Lewis, daughter of Sir Andrew Lewis, Aberdeen shipbuilder; they had one son and one daughter. See *DSBB*; Michael Moss and Alison Turton, *A Legend of Retailing: House of Fraser* (1989).

FRASER, Sir Robert Brown
(26 September 1904 - 20 January 1985)

Director-General of the Independent Television Authority, born in Adelaide, Australia, of Scottish stock, son of Robert and Thusnelda Fraser, he was educated at St Peter's School, Adelaide, Trinity College, University of Melbourne, and the London School of Economics (BSc Econ). On the advice of the LSE's Harold Laski, he became a leader writer for the *Daily Herald* in 1930, unsuccessfully contested York as Labour candidate in the 1935 general election, and during the Second World War headed the publications division of the Ministry of Information, 1941-45. Briefly Controller of Production in the Ministry of Information, 1945-46, Fraser was Director-General of the Central Office of Information, 1946-54, for which he was knighted in 1949. His major contribution came while he was the first Director-General of the ITA (selected for the post by open competition in 1954). Under the ITA's first chairman, Sir Kenneth (later Lord) Clark, Sir Robert Fraser, though a socialist by conviction, devised the plan for a highly competitive system of regional companies selling

programmes to one another. In fact his goal of intense competition was precluded by the success of the two-tiered system (public authority and public companies) but the regional structure has remained. Fraser and Clark also decided that in the sensitive area of news, bulletins would come from a special organisation created by the programme contractors, rather than Associated Press/Reuters. Hence in 1955 Independent Television News Ltd was established, funded jointly, but not controlled by, the four original programme companies: Associated-Rediffusion, launched by John Spencer Wills (qv); Granada, by Sidney Bernstein (qv); Associated Broadcasting Development Co Ltd, later ATV, by Norman Collins, Val Parnell and Lew Grade (qv); and ABC Television, by Sir Philip Warter (qv). When the Committee of Enquiry in Broadcasting under Sir Harry Pilkington (qv) reported in 1962, the ITA was criticised for fronting greedy tycoons instead of regulating and controlling their operations. The imperious Lord Hill, appointed as the third ITA chairman to change all this, found that Fraser and the ITA were by no means the media magnates' poodles; rather more public control was, however, thereafter exerted. During Fraser's tenure the television companies' financial problems were accentuated by the government's advertising levy and the need to invest heavily in colour (introduced in 1969). On retiring from the ITA in 1970, Sir Robert Fraser was chairman of ITN, 1970-74. Warm-hearted and unassuming, Fraser exercised more authority and wisdom than the public posturings of Bernstein, Grade or Hill might have implied. Surprisingly, he received no public honour for his role as the architect of commercial television in Britain beyond an honorary fellowship of the LSE (1965) and the gold medal of the Royal Television Society (1970). Fraser married, in 1931, Betty Harris; they had one daughter. See *The Times*, 21 January 1985; Bernard Sendall, *Independent Television in Britain* vols 1-2 (1982-83); Jeremy Potter, *Independent Television in Britain* vols 3-4 (1989-90).

FRASER, William Lionel
(15 June 1895 - 3 January 1965)

Merchant banker and industrialist, born in Kensington, London, the son of Harry Fraser, a butler, and his wife Alice née Barnard, he attended St Mary Abbots Church School, Kensington, a Cambridgeshire village school and (on a scholarship) Pitman's School in London. At Pitman's he learned French, German, Spanish, shorthand, typing and commercial subjects: of much use when he started work with Bonn & Co, a small banking firm, in 1911. After the First World War, in which Fraser served in France and in Naval Intelligence,

Bonn in 1921 merged with Helbert Wagg, merchant bankers, and Fraser managed the new foreign exchange department in a period of currency instability. In 1925 he transferred to the (share) dealing department, again displaying prudence and skill. Duties unchanged, he was appointed a director of Helbert Wagg in 1934. During the Second World War he served in the Treasury, acting as a liaison officer with Allied Governments. He also began accepting directorships: Spicers (1940-50), Thomas Tilling (1942-65), Atlas Assurance (and then its successor Royal Exchange Assurance), Tube Investments and Babcock & Wilcox (1950-60). Tilling sold its bus and garage interests to the British Transport Commission in 1949 for £25 million, £5 million of which Fraser (chairman 1949-65) used to build the business into a diversified industrial holding company - taking it from eight subsidiaries and 2,000 employees in 1949 to 100 subsidiary companies and 18,000 employees in 1962. Babcock & Wilcox, engineers and contractors, Fraser (chairman 1950-60) took into atomic power station construction: in 1954 they won the contract for the first atomic power station in the country at Calder Hall, Cumberland. A Christian Scientist and an optimist, Fraser married, in 1931, Cynthia Elizabeth, daughter of Francis Walter; they had a daughter and two sons. See *DBB*; W Lionel Fraser, *All to the Good* (1963).

FRASER, William Milligan
1st Baron Strathalmond of Pumpherston
(3 November 1888 - 1 April 1970)
Petroleum entrepreneur, born in Glasgow, the son of William Milligan Fraser and Janet née Loch, he was named after his father, founder and managing director of the Pumpherston Oil Co, the leading Scottish shale-oil company. Educated at Glasgow Academy and the Royal Technical College, Glasgow, he joined his father's company in 1909, became a director in 1913 and on the death of his father in 1915 became company chairman. After the First World War he formed Scottish Oils Ltd, to produce, refine and market both shale and crude oil in Scotland. Within months it was absorbed by the Anglo-Persian Oil Co. Founded in 1909 to work a rich oil concession in Persia, APOC was majority-owned by the Admiralty, for strategic reasons, from 1914. Fraser and Sir John Cadman (qv) were appointed joint managing directors of APOC in 1923, with the former becoming deputy chairman to Cadman in 1928. He helped produce the agreement (1928-34) with Royal Dutch Shell setting up joint marketing arrangements (Shell Mex & BP). He was a key figure behind the secret Achancarry agreement (1928) to reduce oil supply in the face of the depressed international oil

demand. And he went to Persia in 1933 to negotiate a new oil concession. Succeeding Cadman's in 1941, Fraser's chairmanship (until 1956) spanned the wartime negotiations culminating in the Anglo-American Oil Treaty of 1944 and the concessionary crisis with Persia of 1947-51. After the Shah nationalised the Persian oil industry in 1951 Fraser played a leading part in creating a consortium (in which his company, named Anglo-Iranian Oil after 1935 and British Petroleum after 1955, had a 40 per cent share) to produce oil and buy it from the National Iranian Co. Fraser was knighted in 1939 and created a baron in 1955. He married, in 1913, Mary, daughter of Thomas McLintock, an internationally-known Scottish chartered accountant; they had one son and one daughter. See *DBB*; Ronald W Ferrier, *The History of the British Petroleum Company: The Developing Years, 1901-32* (1982).

FRY, Joseph Storrs
(6 August 1826 - 7 July 1913)
Chocolate manufacturer, born in Bristol, eldest of the three sons of Joseph Storrs Fry I (1767-1835), of the third generation in the family firm of Bristol chocolate makers, and his wife Mary Ann née Swain, he was educated at home in the Quaker tradition and at Bristol College. He entered the family firm in 1846 having earlier spent a year with a public accountant. He became a partner in 1855, joining his father, uncles and cousin Francis James Fry. The famous chocolate cream bar was introduced in 1866 and the firm expanded as Victorian population and standards of living rose in the second half of the nineteenth century. In 1869 the firm had 250 employees and one factory; in 1907 it employed 4,600 in eight factories, all in Bristol city centre. Joseph Storrs Fry II took full control of the firm in 1886. Despite growth there is evidence that opportunities were missed such as in marketing a high grade British milk chocolate. A devout Quaker in the evangelical tradition, Joseph Storrs Fry II was especially concerned about the welfare side of his family business and, outside the firm, was involved in many Christian, charitable and educational activities. Unmarried, he died old, blind and a millionaire, leaving his business in such a weak state that within a few years it was taken over by Cadbury Bros. See *DBB*.

G

GALPIN, Rodney Desmond
(5 February 1932 -)
Banker, the son of Sir Albert James Galpin (1903-84) KCVO CBE, a Secretary in the Lord Chamberlain's Office and Serjeant-At-Arms to the

Queen. Educated at Haileybury and the Imperial Service College, his father helped Galpin get into the Bank of England in 1952, through a friend and former director. Via a spell at Johnson Matthey, Galpin worked his way up to executive director at the Bank of England, 1984-88. He became chairman and chief executive of Standard Life in 1988. Since 1979 (when John Major left the company's public relations department for politics) Standard, whose banking roots lay in turn-of-the century branches in Asia and Africa, had lurched from crisis to crisis. Galpin was charged with reversing an image battered by takeover talks with the Royal Bank of Scotland and Lloyds, Third World bad debts, and corporate collapses such as Brent Walker and Asil Nadir's (qv) Polly Peck. Pre-tax profits of £150 million for 1990, the reduction of problem countries' bad debts from £4.46 billion in 1987 to £2.7 billion in 1990, and the installation of new management showed Galpin's intent to change the culture at Standard. Galpin retired in Spring 1993, when Standard planned to split the chairman and chief executive role. In 1956 he married Sylvia Craven: they have one son and one daughter. Galpin became a freeman of the City of London in 1981.

GAMAGE, Sir Leslie
(5 May 1887 - 17 October 1972)
Electrical manufacturer, second son of Albert Walter Gamage, the London department store entrepreneur, and Jane Murdoch (married 1888), he was educated at Marlborough and Exeter College, Oxford (senior scholar) and then qualified as a solicitor in 1914. After the First World War (reaching a captaincy in the 24th London Regiment, was wounded, won the MC and was held prisoner) he became company secretary of the General Electric Co, the industry's giant then growing via electrical product diversification under the dynamic leadership of Hugo Hirst (qv). His legal knowledge, and his marriage in 1919 to Hirst's elder daughter Muriel Elsie, gave him a strong position within the company. Hirst, whose only son died of Spanish 'flu in 1919, regarded Gamage as the family's representative of the next generation. Within a few years Gamage was appointed a director. With Harry Railing (qv), he was appointed joint general manager in 1941, by which time the company had grown from 14,000 in 1919 to over 40,000 in 1939 and was expanding further during the Second World War. After Hirst's death in 1943, Gamage became vice-chairman to Railing, succeeding Railing in 1957, when GEC employed over 60,000 in the UK. He proved to be the wrong man for the job. Under the influence of his wife Gamage initially preserved GEC's structure

as Hirst left it. Markets and technologies soon exposed this mistake. The Prudential refused to subscribe more loan capital in 1959, forced Gamage to call in management consultants (Urwick Orr), and led to the adoption of a divisional structure. Failing to implement change fast enough (he was aged seventy) Sir Leslie Gamage (he was knighted in 1959) was forced by GEC's merchant bankers (Morgan Grenfell) to resign, in 1960. For some years Gamage was president of the Institute of Export and in 1941 president of the Chartered Institute of Secretaries. He and his wife had no children. See Robert Jones and Oliver Marriott, *Anatomy of a Merger: A History of GEC, AEI and English Electric* (1970); *The Times*, 18 October 1972.

GARDINER, Sir Thomas Robert
(8 March 1883 - 1 January 1964)
Post Office executive, born at Cork, the son of Matthew John Gardiner, a Post Office surveyor, and Elizabeth Granger. Educated at Lurgan College, County Armagh, the Edinburgh Royal High School and Edinburgh University, he joined the Post Office in 1906. From 1913 to 1917 he was private secretary to the Secretary of the Post Office; Controller of the London Postal Service, 1926-34; Deputy Director-General in 1934; and Director-General in 1936 (when the Post Office was the largest employer in the UK with 232,000 workers), a post he held until his retirement in 1945. He was responsible for the reorganisation of the Post Office on the basis of the Bridgeman Report and the setting up an integrated regional organisation. He was also Secretary of the Ministry of Home Security, 1939-40; chairman of Stevenage New Town Development Corporation, 1947-48; vice-chairman and acting chairman of the National Dock Labour Board, 1949-51; a government director of the Anglo-Iranian Oil Co, 1950-53; and a member of the Royal Commission on Scottish Affairs, 1952-54. He was awarded the GBE in 1941 and made GCB in 1954. He married Christina Stenhouse in 1919. See *The Times*, 2 January 1964.

GARDNER, Walter Frank
(6 November 1900 - 16 July 1983)
Insurance company general manager, born in Streatham, son of Walter Gardner, a grocer's manager, and his wife Emma Mabel née Holter, he was educated at Dulwich College and joined the staff of the Prudential at the age of 19. He was posted immediately to the actuarial department and spent his early career there. In five years he passed all the examinations to become a Fellow of the Institute of Actuaries. After a few more years' experience he was promoted to principal clerk in 1931, deputy controller in 1932, controller in 1934 and an assis-

tant actuary (the lowest general managerial rank) in 1939. He became joint actuary in 1943 and in 1945 actuary to The Prudential Assurance Co Ltd. In 1947 Gardner, concerned at the losses on old policies due to the government's low interest rate policy (reaching 2.5 per cent in 1947), and the prospect of excessive profits when interest rates rose (as well they might in the long term), withdrew the Prudential from the group (mostly occupational) pensions market where it was the leader. He took it back into that market in 1951 when he introduced 'with profit' options on group pension contracts. On the retirement of Sir Frank Morgan (qv) in 1950 Gardner became chief general manager of the Prudential, remaining in office until 1960, by which date the company employed well over 20,000. Afterwards he was a director of the Prudential, 1961-71 and deputy chairman, 1965-69. President of the Instititute of Actuaries, 1952-54, Gardner was created a CBE in 1953. Speaking German as the result of secondment to a Berlin office when young, he was well-known in Europe and jointly authored a German-English dictionary of life assurance. He married twice: first, in 1925, to Constance Gladys née Haydon (d 1945), by whom he had a daughter; second, in 1949, to Kathleen Lilian née Smith, widow of Dr Frederick Lishman of Bexhill. See Leslie Hannah, *Inventing Retirement* (1986); *Prudential Bulletin* 32 (1950), 42 (1960); *The Times*, 23 July 1983.

GAVEY, Sir John
(11 August 1842 - 1 January 1923)

Engineer and Post Office manager, born in Jersey, the son of John Gavey of St Heliers, he attended Victoria College there and on leaving school in 1860 trained as an engineer under (Sir) William Henry Preece, the telegraph pioneer, in the Electric & International Telegraph Co. On the nationalisation of telegraphs in 1870 Gavey followed Preece (who became Divisional Engineer) into the Post Office, being appointed Superintendent of the South Eastern Subdivision and in 1872 of the Great Western Subdivision. He became Superintending Engineer of the South Wales District in 1878; Chief Technical Officer at headquarters in 1892; Second Assistant Engineer-in-Chief in 1897; Assistant Engineer-in-Chief and Electrician in 1899; and Engineer-in-Chief and Electrician (the post Preece held 1892-99) in 1902; consulting engineer to the Post Office in 1908, retiring in 1913. Gavey was responsible for numerous technical developments, not least the organisation and development of the trunk telephone line system. He was president of the Institution of Electrical Engineers in 1905 and was knighted in 1907. He married, in 1870, Mary de Gruchy of

Jersey; they had two sons and three daughters. See *The Times*, 4 January 1923; Charles Welch, *London at the Opening of the Twentieth Century* (1905).

GEDDES, Sir Eric Campbell
(26 September 1875 - 22 June 1937)

Transport company executive and industrialist, born in India, at Agra, the son of Acland Campbell Geddes, a Scottish civil engineer, and Christina Helena Macleod née Anderson. His early education at a string of reputable schools had been interrupted by his rebelliousness, but his energy proved of greater use to the North Eastern Railway and to Lloyd George, who made Geddes Deputy Director-General of Munitions Supply and then Inspector General of Transportation and Controller to the Admiralty during the First World War. In 1917 he joined the Cabinet as First Lord of the Admiralty and Unionist MP for Cambridge. In 1919 he became Minister of Transport and then in 1922 advised Lloyd George on reductions in national expenditure (the 'Geddes Axe'). After resigning as MP in 1922, Geddes became chairman until his death of both Dunlop Rubber, which he helped rescue from previous financial chicanery, and of Imperial Airways. Knighted in 1916, he married Alice Gwendolen Stokes in 1900. He left £112,894 gross. See Keith Grieves, *Sir Eric Geddes: Business and Government in War and Peace* (1989); *DBB*; *DNB*.

GEORGE, (Edward Alan John) 'Eddie'
(11 September 1938 -)

Banker, born in Dulwich, south London, the son of Alan George, a postman, and his wife Elizabeth Olive. Eddie George won a county council scholarship to Dulwich College, after which he took a second-class degree in economics at Emmanuel College, Cambridge. He spent his National Service with military intelligence in Berlin. In 1962 he became a Bank of England trainee, entering its overseas division, where he specialised in East European affairs. He hoped that this would serve as an apprenticeship for a post at the World Bank in Washington. He had two important spells on secondment to international institutions: one at the Bank for International Settlements in Basle; the other to the International Monetary Fund in Washington. He was the Bank of England's adviser on international monetary questions between 1974 and 1977. He then entered the Bank's money markets division, becoming deputy chief cashier and assistant director of the gilt-edged division. In 1982 he became executive director of the Bank, eventually becoming deputy governor to Robin Leigh-Pemberton (qv) in 1990. In 1993 he was appointed

Governor of the Bank, assuming control of an organisation that employs about 4,500, is very profitable (paying over £67 million to the Treasury in 1992), but the purpose of which is not well defined. He has the reputation of an arch anti-inflationist, who supported Margaret Thatcher's monetarism in the 1980s, was critical of Britain's entry into the ERM, and sympathises with the idea of an independent Bank of England with powers to curb inflation. But he takes charge during a critical period for the Bank, when its power is being eroded on all sides: it has failed to win the independence to fix monetary policy and has also been weakened by the European Community's banking directives. He married in 1962 Clarice Vanessa Williams: they have one son and two daughters.

GEORGE, Sir Edward James
(1886 - 25 October 1950)
Iron and steel manufacturer, born in Oswestry, Shropshire. He became secretary of Richard Evan & Co, of Haydock, Lancashire, and in 1905 joined the Consett Iron Co as secretary and commercial manager. Subsequently, he became manager, managing director, and then deputy chairman from about 1936 until his retirement in 1940. In the late 1930s Consett was second only to Dorman Long in North-East England as an iron and steel combine, employing nearly 7,000 workers in 1935. George also held the chairmanship of the Orconara Iron Ore Co. A founder member and honorary vice-president of the Iron and Steel Institute, he was president of the British Iron and Steel Federation in 1933. He was also a member of the council of the FBI and was once chairman of the British Sulphate of Ammonia Association. George was a Methodist local preacher and had been chairman of the Consett Urban District Council. He was knighted in 1939. See *The Times*, 26 October 1950; Kenneth Warren, *Consett Iron 1840 to 1980* (1990).

GIBBS, Walter Durant
4th Baron Aldenham and 2nd Baron Hunsdon
(11 August 1888 - 30 May 1969)
Banker, eldest son of Herbert Cokayne Gibbs, 1st Baron Hunsdon (1854-1935) and his wife Anna Maria née Durant, he was educated at Eton and Trinity College, Cambridge, and then entered the family merchant bank, Antony Gibbs & Sons. He served in the First World War in the Middle East. He joined the board of the Westminster Bank in 1924, became deputy chairman in 1931 and in 1950 succeeded Rupert Beckett (qv) as chairman. He retired at the end of 1961 but kept his seat on the board. His business interests were confined to banking and merchanting and, in a period of heavy bank regulation, he had the task often of representing the industry as chairman of the Committee of London Bankers, 1954-56, and president of the British Bankers' Association. He was director of a half a dozen minor banks. His style was refreshingly informal, his manner modest, his mind incisive. He succeeded his father in 1935 and his cousin, Baron Aldenham, in 1939. He married, in 1919, Beatrix Elinor, daughter of Herbert Paul and widow of Algernon Villiers; they had two sons. See *The Times*, 2 June 1969; *The Westminster*, April 1957.

GILL, Sir Anthony (Keith)
(1 April 1930 -)
Executive of electrical engineering components manufacturer, the son of Frederick William and Ellen Gill. His father was a clerk in a solicitor's office in Colchester. Educated at the High School, Colchester, he left school at 14 and became an engineering apprentice, later winning a state scholarship to Imperial College, London (where he took a degree in engineering). After National Service, in 1956 he joined a diesel fuel injection equipment maker (Bryce Berger Ltd) - later taken over by the engineering group, Lucas. In 1972 he joined the board of Lucas CAV and became a joint-managing director of Lucas Industries in 1980. He was appointed chairman and chief executive of Lucas in 1987. Since 1981, when it recorded its first loss, Lucas under the successive chairmanships of (Sir) Godfrey Messervy (qv) and Gill has moved into more advanced and international activities, such as aerospace, to offset the decline of its traditional car parts business. By the early 1990s these restructuring plans had been hit by the recession, with Lucas barely able to maintain its dividend despite cutbacks (since the 1980s the UK workforce has declined from 64,000 to 24,000). Gill's plan to maintain investment during the recession proved controversial, especially since the City had stumped up £260 million for two rights issues since the mid-1980s. In 1992 Lucas and Gill hit trouble: there was a £8.8 million net loss on £2.25 billion sales and two directors left. Gill has a reputation for ruffling feathers: he holds scathing views on civil servants, the tax system, and the CBI, and believes high-technology companies should be run by engineers. Gill, who was knighted in 1991, is a non-executive director of National Power and the Post Office. In 1953 Gill married Phyllis Cook: they have one son and two daughters.

GILL, Sir Frank
(4 October 1866 - 25 October 1950)
Telecommunications entrepreneur and pioneer, born at Castletown in the Isle of Man, the younger son of Henry Corlett Gill, an advocate, and his

wife G H Claxton. Educated privately, he gained his technical education under W E Ayrton at the Finsbury Technical College and under such luminaries as Sir Oliver Lodge and Sir Ambrose Fleming. He joined the United Telephone Co in London in 1882, the start of a career in which he became a leading figure in telephony, both in the UK and abroad. He became director and vice-president of the International Standard Electric Corporation; and chairman of Standard Telephones & Cables Ltd, Creed & Co Ltd, International Marine Radio Co Ltd, and Standard Telecommunication Laboratories Ltd. He was also associated with the National Telephone Co of Spain and the Shanghai Telephone Co. He was past-president of the Association of Supervising Electrical Engineers and of the Institution of Electrical Engineers. In 1895 he married Caroline Maude née Beckwith: they had a son and a daughter. He was knighted in 1941. See F Gill (with W W Cook), *Principles Involved in Computing the Depreciation of Plant* (1917); *The Times*, 27 October 1950; Peter Young, *Power of Speech: A History of Standard Telephones and Cables, 1883-1983* (1983).

GILLESPIE, James John
(1873 - 1942)
Accountant and industrialist, the son of J J Gillespie, an accountant (FCA, 1881). He was admitted to the Institute of Chartered Accountantss in 1895 and became an FCA in 1911. His firm, Gillespie Bros, based in Newcastle-upon-Tyne, specialised in theatrical finance, especially in London. Colonel Gillespie (in the Second World War, he served as a Territorial officer with the Northumberland Fusiliers) later became associated with Sir Edward Moss and Richard Thornton, whose interests were merged into Moss Emprires in 1898. Gillespie became a director of Moss Empires in 1920 and later its chairman, and was on the boards of a number of other cinema theatres. He was also a director of British Ropes Ltd from 1924 until 1937, when it employed 8,000 workers. See *The Accountant*, 31 January 1942.

GIORDANO, Richard Vincent
(24 March 1934 -)
International gases and healthcare company executive, born in the USA, the son of Italian immigrants Vincent and Cynthia Giordano. Brought up in a comfortable middle-class home, his father was in business as a clothing manufacturer. Educated at Harvard College, Cambridge (BA) and Columbia University Law School (LLB), he practised law on Wall Street before joining Airco, the American healthcare company, of which he subsequently became president and chief executive in 1971. The

British Oxygen Co bought Airco in 1978 and in the following year Giordano moved to London to become chief executive of the combined group. He is credited with reorganising the BOC Group into a global performer, turning the transatlantic business into one company and opening up the Far East. But he became best known in the 1980s for being for a few years the UK's highest paid executive (in 1991 his £1.02 million annual salary was the fifth highest). He became the first US born industrialist to receive an honorary KBE in 1989. He stepped down as chief executive in 1991, relinquishing the chairmanship of BOC (a post he has held since 1985) in January 1992, though he remained a non-executive director. In 1992 BOC's turnover was £2,862 million (pre-tax profits £332 million) and the group employed about 37,000 workers. In 1991 he was also appointed a non-executive deputy chairman of Grand Metropolitan. He was also a director of National Power, Georgia-Pacific Corporation and Reuters. He married in 1956 Barbara Claire Beckett (from whom he separated in about 1987): they have one son and two daughters. See BOC, *Around the Group in 100 Years* (1986).

GIROLAMI, Sir Paul
(25 January 1926 -)
Pharmaceutical company executive, born in Venice, the son of a mosaics artist who migrated to England in 1928. Educated at the London School of Economics and trained as an accountant, his early business experience was with Chantrey & Button and Coopers & Lybrand. He joined the pharmaceutical firm Glaxo in 1968 as finance director, becoming managing director in 1980, chief executive 1980-86, and chairman in 1985. (His chief executives have been Bernard Taylor, Dr Ernest Mario and Dr Richard Sykes (qv)). Glaxo, originally famous for its dried milk, had become a front-ranking UK drug company under a previous chairman Sir Harry Jephcott (qv). But under Girolami it joined the world league, second only to Merck, its growth powered by a highly successful research effort under Sir David Jack coupled with Girolami's successful international marketing initiatives, especially in the USA. Glaxo's 'Zantac', an ulcer drug, emerged during the 1980s as the world's best-selling medicine. Measured by its market capitalisation (£323 billion), Glaxo briefly became the UK's biggest company in 1991. Since 1980 the company's turnover has mushroomed from about £400,000 to over £4 billion in 1992, but Glaxo's ability to maintain this momentum will depend on its success in finding a successor to Zantac, which generates nearly half the company's profits. The resignation of chief executive Mario in

1993 demonstrated Girolami's rejection of one route to further expansion - a move into the 'over the counter' drugs market. It seems that Glaxo will remain committed to its traditional strength - the prescription drugs market - until Girolami retires, which will probably not be until he is 70. Sir Paul (he was knighted in 1988) concentrates entirely on Glaxo's business, has no liking for publicity or outside directorships and spends much of his time travelling. Girolami in 1952 married Christabel Lewis: they have two sons and one daughter. See Geoffrey Tweedale, *At the Sign of the Plough* (1990); Matthew Lynn, *The Billion Dollar Battle: Merck v Glaxo* (1991).

GLADSTONE, Robert
(1833 - 12 July 1919)

Port company chairman, born in Liverpool, eldest son of Thomas Steuart Gladstone of Capenoch, Dumfriesshire, he was educated at Eton and Edinburgh University and then engaged in the India and China trade, becoming a partner in Ogilvy, Gillanders & Co. He was elected a member of the Mersey Docks & Harbour Board in 1881, chaired its finance committee in the 1890s and the Board itself, 1899-1911. To the extent that it licensed and monitored the porters, lumpers and stevedores manning the port of Liverpool, the MDBH was their employer. By 1907, 16,000 worked under its aegis. Cautious in his decision-making, Gladstone was nevertheless responsible for two developments which transformed the port of Liverpool at the beginning of the twentieth century. One was the construction of an imposing new Dock Office, built at the Pier Head, 1901-7. The other was the so-called Gladstone system, a plan for the development of the port as a totality, rather than adding dock to dock in piecemeal fashion. Gladstone was a JP for Liverpool for thirty-two years, treasurer of University College, Liverpool for twenty-two years and prominently associated with the project to build an Anglican cathedral. A classical scholar, he regularly read Greek and Latin to the end of his life. He married, in 1860, a second cousin, Mary Ellen (d 1905), daughter of Robertson Gladstone, a brother of the Prime Minister, W E Gladstone. They had four sons and six daughters. See *Lancashire: Biographies, Rolls of Honour* (1917); Stuart Mountfield, *Western Gateway. A History of the Mersey Docks and Harbour Board* (1965); *The Times*, 15 July 1919; P J Waller, *Democracy and Sectarianism: A Political and Social History of Liverpool, 1868-1939* (1981).

GLUCKSTEIN, Isidore Montague
(2 November 1890 - 16 January 1975)

Caterer and food manufacturer, son of Montague Gluckstein (1854-1922), one of the Gluckstein and Salmon clan of Jewish cigar dealers who in 1894 formed the catering firm of J Lyons & Co Ltd, and his wife Matilda Franks, Isidore was educated at St Paul's School and Sidney Sussex College, Cambridge. After the First World War (in which he reached the rank of captain with the London Regiment) he was called to the Bar (Inner Temple). He became one of about 20 family members (headed by the three Salmon brothers Harry, Maurice and Julius) who, between the wars, managed a workforce of 30,000 manufacturing food at Cadby Hall, selling it in white-and-gold teashops or London Corner Houses, and serving it in a chain of hotels. Tea, ice cream, bread and cakes: these were the Lyons staples. However, post-1945 top management comprised 20 less able kinsmen. The end of wartime restrictions in 1953-54 encouraged the rise of rivals in all Lyons's markets: Brooke Bond, Typhoo, Schweppes, Walls (Unilever). Consumers had access to self-service supermarkets. Isidore Gluckstein, a managing director in the 1950s, chairman, 1956-60, and president, 1961-68, proved unequal to the task of revitalising the family business. He married Rosalind Sophie (d 1973), daughter of the Reverend Michael Adler; they had two sons. See *DBB*.

GODBER, Frederick
Baron Godber of Mayfield
(6 November 1888 - 10 April 1976)

Petroleum executive, born in Camberwell, South London, only son of Edward Godber, a carpenter, and his wife Marion née Peach, he left school at 16 and joined the Asiatic Petroleum Co as clerk in its secretarial department. Asiatic Petroleum (later Shell Petroleum Co) was the marketing company for Shell Transport & Trading Co and Royal Dutch Petroleum Co prior to their merger in 1907. Godber moved up within Shell Petroleum until 1919 when he was sent to the USA to learn about exploration and production, the 'upstream' side. He stayed until 1928 as president of an upstream subsidiary. Recalled to London in 1928 he became a director of Shell Transport & Trading Co, a managing director in 1934, and from 1937 until 1946 chairman of Shell Union Oil Corporation, USA. During the Second World War he served on a committee of the government's Petroleum Board. In 1946 he was appointed chairman of Shell Transport & Trading, retiring in 1961. During his chairmanship refining was progressively switched from the oilfields to Europe (for strategic reasons), a move facilitated by the advent of supertankers; and Shell Centre was built on the South Bank, London, from which to oversee an expanding UK workforce (25,000 in 1955) and some multinational operations. Godber was knighted in 1942 and created a baron in 1956. He married, in 1914, Violet Ethel Beatrice, daughter of George Lovesy of Cheltenham; they had two daughters. See *DBB*.

GOLDSMITH, Sir James (Michael)
(26 February 1933 -)

Financier and industrialist, born in Paris, a descendant of the German Jewish Goldschmidt family. His father was Frank Goldsmith MP (1878-1967), a barrister who left Britain in the anti-German hysteria of the First World War and became a famous French hotelier; his mother was a French woman, Marcelle Mouiller. He left Eton at 17, having already won £8,000 betting on horses. In the 1960s he amassed an empire of small companies in the UK and France, first in foods (through a holding company, Cavenham), and then in banking and investment. By the early 1970s he was the UK's biggest grocer and by the end of the decade the third largest retailer in the world. In the 1980s he switched his attentions to America, where he became a corporate raider. In 1982, for example, he bought Diamond Corporation for £246 million and sold it for three times as much two years later. He shrewdly anticipated the 1987 stock market crash by selling all his major holdings when the market peaked; but in 1989 he returned to the British scene with a £13 billion projected takeover of the British American Tobacco Group. Abandoning this in 1990, he swapped his large American forestry interests for a 49 per cent stake in a mining company owned by Lord Hanson (qv). This marked Goldsmith's retirement, but he has plans to use his vast fortune (estimated at over £700 million) in an ecological crusade directed from his large Mexican estate. His business career and taste for gambling have regularly featured in the gossip columns: so, too, has his private life. At twenty he eloped to Scotland with Maria Isable Patino, daughter of a Bolivian tin magnate, who died in 1954 giving birth to a daughter. He has since married twice: to Ginette Lery and Lady Annabel Vane Tempest Stewart. He has had seven children by four women. Knighted in 1976, he was made Chevalier Legion d'Honneur in 1978. See James Goldsmith, *Counterculture* (3 vols, 1985-90); Ivan Fallon, *Billionaire* (1991).

GOLLANCZ, Sir Victor
(9 April 1893 - 8 February 1967)

Publisher, born in London, the only son of Alexander Gollancz and Helene (Nellie) née Michaelson, a Polish family with a long rabbinical heritage. Educated at St Paul's School and at New College, Oxford, where he read classics, he entered the publishing firm of Benn Bros in 1921. After personality clashes with Sir Ernest Benn, he left and founded Victor Gollancz Ltd in 1927. Gollancz was soon recognised as the most exciting general publisher in London, with bestselling authors that included A J Cronin and Dorothy Sayers, and a socialist stance that led him to set up the Left Book Club in 1936. A pacifist and supporter of many humanitarian causes, he was himself a prolific writer on the moral issues of the day. He was knighted in 1965. In 1919 he married Ruth Lowy, daughter of a stockbroker: they had five daughters. He left £28,603. See Victor Gollancz, *Reminiscences of Affection* (1968); Sheila Hodges, *Gollancz: The Story of a Publishing House 1928-1978* (1978); *DBB*; *DNB*.

GOODAY, John Francis Sykes
(25 February 1847 - 16 January 1915)

Railway manager, born at Sudbury, Suffolk, the son of John Francis Sikes Gooday, a solicitor, and his wife Anna late Addison née Brown, he was educated at Sir Anthony Brown's School, Brentwood, Essex. He entered the service of the Great Eastern Railway in 1863 and for some time was the company's agent at Leeds. In 1877 he became Continental traffic manager, building up the Great Eastern's fine steamer fleet, serving notably Harwich to the Hook of Holland and to Antwerp. In January 1898 he was appointed general manager of the London, Brighton & South Coast Railway, only to resign the following year in order to return to the Great Eastern as general manager. On retiring in 1910 he was appointed a director of the company; he also became a director of the London, Brighton & South Coast Railway. He was unmarried. See *Railway Year Book* (1908); *The Times*, 18 January 1915.

GOODISON, Sir Nicholas (Proctor)
(16 May 1934 -)

Stockbroker, born in Hertfordshire, the son of Edmund Harold Goodison and Eileen Mary Carrington Proctor. Educated at Marlborough College and King's College, Cambridge, where he read classics, in 1958 he joined the family stockbroking firm of Quilter Goodison & Co. He became a partner in 1962 and was elected to the Stock Exchange Council in 1968. In 1976 he became chairman of the Stock Exchange and assumed the task of ensuring that London became a fully international market, retaining its place as a world financial market despite the UK's relative industrial decline. From 1986 to 1988 Goodison was chairman of the International Stock Exchange, after the transformation in the City had culminated in the so-called Big Bang. In 1989 he was appointed chairman of the Trustees Saving Bank, after its 1980s strategy of rapid growth had turned sour because of the bad property debts (totalling nearly £600 million in 1992) of its subsidiary Hill Samuel. Goodison is a director of General Accident, Ottoman Bank and British Steel and has served on several banking and stockbroking groups: for example, he is president of the British Bankers' Association. He is also an authority on antique clocks, barometers and furniture: besides publishing standard reference works on these subjects, he is also president of the Antiquarian Horological Society, chairman of the Courtauld Institute of Art, has been editorial director of the *Burlington Magazine*, and a trustee and member of many other arts bodies. He is chairman of the National Art-Collections Fund and Honorary Keeper of Furniture at the Fitzwilliam Museum. He was knighted in 1982 and awarded the Chevalier Legion d'Honneur in 1990. He married in 1960 Judith Abel Smith: they have one son and two daughters. See Sir Nicholas Goodison, *English Barometers 1680-1860* (1968, 2nd edition 1977); *Ormolu: The Work of Matthew Boulton* (1974).

GORDON-SMITH, Ralph
(22 May 1905 - 29 March 1993)
Scientific and electronic instrument manufacturer, only son (there were three daughters) of Allan Gordon-Smith, grandson of the founder of a London clockmaking business and the man who took the firm into motorcar and aircraft instrument manufacture, and his wife Hilda Beatrice née Cave. Educated at Bradfield College, Ralph gained early commercial experience in accountancy and motor mechanics in the UK and France before joining the family firm in August 1927. He spent two years on the sales and service side and in 1930 took charge of exports. The company extended its production of aviation instruments in the 1930s when its workforce grew from 1,700 to 8,000. On the death of his grandfather, Samuel Smith II, Ralph became a director in January 1933; and in 1939, assistant managing director. In October 1947 he succeeded his father, by then Sir Allan Gordon-Smith (who was chairman), as group managing director, standing down in 1967. Ralph became chairman in 1951 when his father died. He remained in office until 1973 (when he became life president) and was a non-executive director until 1978. During these decades he pursued the twin policies of decentralisation and diversification. S Smith & Sons was renamed Smiths Industries in 1965, reflecting the wider market in which the company operated. Products ranging from car radios to advanced aircraft systems and instruments were manufactured. One of these was the world's first automatic landing system for aircraft (first demonstrated on 4 November 1966). The company began supplying

Boeing with machmeters in 1961. Smiths' workforce grew from 16,800 in 1955 to 24,500 in 1965. Ralph Gordon-Smith married, in 1932, Beryl Mavis Cundy; there were no children. See *The Times*, 17 April 1993.

GOULDING, Edward Alfred
1st Baron Wargrave
(5 November 1862 - 17 July 1936)
Industrialist, the son of William Goulding, MP for Cork. Educated at Clifton College and St John's College, Cambridge, he was called to the Bar at the Inner Temple in 1887. He then pursued a career in politics. He was a member of London County Council, 1895-1901, and a prominent Unionist member of the House of Commons for Devizes (1895-1906) and Worcester (1908-22). A supporter of Joseph Chamberlain's tariff reform movement, he chaired the Tariff Reform League Organisation Department from 1904-1912. He was rewarded with a baronetcy in 1915. He became chairman of Rolls Royce Ltd (which employed 6,900 workers in 1935) and of the Central London Electricity Distribution Committee (1934) Ltd. He was unmarried and his title, awarded in 1922, became extinct. See *The Times*, 18 July 1936.

GOULDING, Sir William Joshua
(7 March 1856 - 12 July 1925)
Railway company chairman, born at Cork, the eldest son of William Goulding MP, a Dublin fertiliser manufacturer, and his wife Maria Heath née Manders, he was educated at St John's College, Cambridge, where he excelled in athletics, cricket and rugby union, and played rugby for Ireland. He entered the family firm, W & H M Goulding Ltd of North Wall, Dublin, eventually succeeding his father as chairman. In the 1890s and 1900s he became prominent in developing railways and transport facilities in Ireland. He was chairman of the Great Southern & Western Railway of Ireland by 1907, when it employed over 8,000; deputy chairman of the Fishguard & Rosslare Harbour & Railway Co; and chairman of the Irish Railway Clearing House. A prominent Unionist and tariff reformer, he was a pillar of the Irish establishment, sitting in the General Synod of the Church of Ireland and serving as Deputy Lieutenant for County Cork, as high sheriff of County Dublin (1906) and County Kildare (1907). He was both prominent and active in Ireland's highest masonic orders. He sat in the Irish Convention, 1917-18, and after Irish independence in 1922 became a Senator for Southern Ireland under the short-lived Government of Ireland Act of 1920. Goulding was created a baronet in 1904. He married, in 1881, Ada née Stokes; they had one son. See E F

Cosgrave and W T Pike, *Dublin and County Dublin in the Twentieth Century* (1909); *Representative British Freemasons* (1915).

GRACIE, Sir Alexander
(14 November 1860 – 2 March 1930)

Engineer and shipbuilder, son of John Gracie of Landrick, Dunblane, Perthshire, he trained as an engineer on the Clyde, gaining experience with Thomson's of Clydebank and Denny's of Dumbarton. At Clydebank he rose to be principal engineer and 'a foremost engineer in a district where great engineers are common'. In 1893 he moved up the Clyde to the Fairfield Shipbuilding & Engineering Co Ltd as engineering manager under Sir William George Pearce (qv). On Pearce's death in 1907 he became a director and when the new chairman Dr Francis Elgar died in 1909 Gracie became managing director and chairman. By this time Fairfields was one of the largest shipyards on the Clyde employing 6,000 on the construction of vessels as large as battle-cruisers and battleships. Gracie enlarged the Fairfield Dock, continued to adopt new innovations (eg in turbine development, for which the firm won a world-wide reputation), and, like other firms, made agreements (sealed by board seats for Gracie) to secure vertical integration (eg with Cammell, Laird & Co of Sheffield for armour plate, and with Coventry Ordnance Works for guns). He sat on various government committees, notably the Admiralty Committee on Design of 1904 (which laid down principles for warship construction) and the Royal Commission on Fuel Oil and Engines (1912) which urged the use of oil instead of coal in warships. Fairfields which had such a strong reputation before the First World War lost it during hostilities. Labour disputes and poor timekeeping were attributed by an Admiralty observer to poor management. Despite this record Gracie was knighted in 1918. In the 1920s he added directorships of English Electric Co and Leeds Forge Co to his membership of the Scottish Committee of the London, Midland & Scottish Railway. In 1904 Gracie married Catherine Fullerton Rutherford; they had three daughters. See *The Bailie*, 7 August 1912, 13 March 1918; *The Times*, 3 March 1930.

GRADE, Lew
Baron Grade of Elstree
(25 December 1906 –)

Theatrical agent and television entrepreneur, he was born at Tokmak, a village near Odessa, Russia, eldest of the four children and three sons (the third, Leslie, and a daughter were born in England) of Isaac Winogradsky, a storekeeper, and his wife Golda née Eisenstadt who emigrated to London in 1912 to escape anti-Jewish attacks. Louis, or Lew as he became known, was educated at Rochelle Street School in Bethnal Green, in London's East End. Leaving school at 14, he worked in a clothing business but at 17, discovering the usefulness of an excellent memory and a head for figures, he set up a small embroidery firm with his father. Meantime he took up dancing, carried off the World Charleston Championship in 1926 and in the 1920s and early-1930s had a career as a performer, much of it on the Continent. In 1934 he moved into agency work, drawing on his European contacts. He teamed up with Joe Collins and by 1936 Collins & Grade (he changed his name in the 1920s) had a hundred acts on their books. During the Second World War he organised variety shows for the troops. When his brother Leslie, also a theatre agent, was called for active service abroad in 1943, Lew Grade left Collins and established the firm of Lew & Leslie Grade Ltd. In the late-1940s they expanded their agency work to the USA and by the early 1950s Lew & Leslie Grade were the largest theatrical agency in Europe, producers and presenters of plays, musicals, revues, pantomimes. In 1954, when the Independent Television Authority was set up, the Grades joined Prince Littler, Val Parnell and others in forming Incorporated Television Co. Its application for a network contractor's licence was rejected on the grounds that they were too powerful. However, they were allowed to join a financially weaker group (the Associated Broadcasting Development Co) and so ATV (Associated Television Ltd) arrived. From 1954 until 1968 ATV had the contract for London weekend and Midlands weekday programmes. Lew Grade became deputy managing director of ATV in 1956 (when he left his agency business), managing director in 1962 (when Littler retired), and chairman in 1973. He retired in 1977, when he was given the honorary role of president of ATV Network, but remained chairman of the parent company ATV Corporation, renamed Associated Communications Corporation, until 1982 when he sold out to Robert Holmes à Court, an Australian entrepreneur. During its first 15 years or so ITV was 'principally an entertainment culture, created by men who came from show-business backgrounds, understood what audiences wanted and made sure that they got it'. *Crossroads* (which ran 1964-80 and gave employment to 15,000 actors) and *Sunday Night at the London Palladium* epitomised Grade's kind of entertainment. Yet Grade also televised Shakespearian productions and other serious works. If some found him too lowbrow, Grade was also criticised for getting a disproportionately high return on his investment in commercial television. Others thought that

Parnell and Grade got too many concessions out of the ITA Director-General, Sir Robert Fraser (qv). Their opportunities certainly diminished after 1968 when they chose and were awarded the Midland region ITV contract with its seven-day service. Though a restless and wily wheeler-dealer, Grade found his attempts to return to the London scene by investing in London Weekend Television firmly blocked by Fraser. The danger of disturbing the balance of competition and co-operation between the four central companies and the ten regional ones was unacceptable to the ITA. Grade's image, of the portly, cigar-smoking plutocrat, seemingly personified commercial television. In the collective councils of the programme companies, however, he was an untypical, sometimes isolated, figure. Lew Grade was knighted in 1969 and made a life peer in 1976. He married, in 1942, Kathleen Sheila Moody; they had no children of their own but adopted a son. Neither he nor his cousin, Michael Grade, the son of Lew's brother Leslie (1916-79), worked for ATV. See Lew Grade, *Still Dancing: My Story* (1987); Jeremy Potter, *Independent Television in Britain* vols 3-4 (1989-90); Bernard Sendall, *Independent Televison in Britain* vols 1-2 (1982-83).

GRAND, Keith Walter Chamberlain
(3 July 1900 - 17 September 1983)
Transport manager, born in Wavertree, Liverpool, son of Douglas Henry Grand, a commission merchant, and his wife Emma Gertrude née Chamberlain, he was educated at Rugby and then joined the Great Western Railway in 1919 at Park Royal goods station. After further experience at Ealing Broadway and in the divisional superintendent's office at Paddington, he was transferred to the general manager's office in 1922. Over the next fourteen years he had a succession of posts: three years in the USA as the GWR's agent; working in publicity at Paddington, 1929-34; general assistant to the superintendent of the line in 1934; and divisional superintendent at Swansea in 1936. He was particularly interested in developing railway-operated air services in the 1930s and sat on the boards of several small airlines and bus companies in the GWR region. After two assistantships at Paddington he was made assistant general manager of the GWR in 1941. Upon nationalisation on 1 January 1948 he became chief regional officer, Western Region, British Railways, remaining in post until 1959. He strongly disliked the overly-centralised British Transport Commission and notoriously resisted co-operation with the BTC's Railway Executive, blocking staff transfers to Executive headquarters and making unauthorised statements to the Press. As full-time member of the British Transport Commission, 1959-62, he was

'better remembered for his conviviality and love of the turf than for his managerial contribution'. Grand married twice: first, in 1925, to Alice née Gates (d 1969) of Ontario; second, in 1971, to Enid Wheatley; there were two children by the first marriage. See T R Gourvish, *British Railways, 1948-73: A Business History* (1986); *Journal of the Institute of Transport* 29 (1960).

GRANET, Sir William Guy
(13 October 1867 - 11 October 1943)
Railway manager, born at Genoa, the son of William Augustus Granet, merchant and banker of Genoa, and his wife Adelaide Julia née Le Mesurier, he was educated at Rugby and Balliol College, Oxford. After four years in his father's firm he was called to the Bar at Lincoln's Inn and practised on the Northern Circuit. He moved into the railway world in 1900 when he was appointed the first salaried secretary to the Railway Companies Association. This led to his appointment in 1905 as assistant general manager of the Midland Railway. As general manager of the Midland Railway (which employed over 66,000 in 1907), 1906-18, he took the company out of a stagnant position, successfully negoiated with the unions in a decade of rising militancy, and in the latter half of the First World War ran the government-controlled railway system as Director General of Movements and Railways. In 1918 he became chairman of the Midland and, after 1923, chairman of the London, Midland & Scottish Railway (one of the groupings established by Government). Before retiring from the LMS in 1927 he brought in Sir Josiah Stamp (qv) as his successor. Granet served on several government bodies, notably the Royal Commission on the Civil Service (1911-14), the Geddes Committee (1921-22) and the South African Railways Commission (1933). His membership of the board of Lee, Higginson, merchant bankers, who lent huge sums to Ivar Krueger the Swedish match 'king', cast a cloud over Granet's later years after Krueger committed suicide in 1932. The boards of Lloyds Bank and The Times Publishing Co would not accept his resignation, however. In 1892 Granet married Florence Julia Gully, daughter of William C Gully, later Speaker of the House of Commons and 1st Viscount Selby; they had one daughter. See *DBB*.

GRANT, Sir (Matthew) Alistair
(6 March 1937 -)
Food retailer, the son of John Grant, an East Lothian plasterer, and his wife Jessie. Educated at Woodhouse Grove School, Yorkshire, he was commissioned in the Royal Signals, 1955-57. He eschewed Edinburgh University for a sales job at

Batchelor Foods in Sheffield; and then became a product manager at Lyons, 1963-65. After a spell in advertising and finance, in 1968 he joined Fine Fare (part of Garfield Weston's (qv) empire), under James Gulliver (qv). Together they founded Oriel Foods in 1973. Four years later they established Argyll, which between 1977 and 1983 became one of the UK's largest retailing combines. After an attempted takeover of Distillers in 1986, when Argyll was beaten by Guinness and its chairman Ernest Saunders (qv), Gulliver left and Grant became chief executive. He immediately completed a £681 million takeover of Safeway supermarkets. Grant became chairman in 1988. By 1990 Argyll was valued at more than £2 billion and had 64,000 employees. Two years later Grant's pay had reached £973,000 a year. His outside activities have included a visiting professorship (in retailing) at Stirling University, the presidency of the Advertising Association and chairmanship of the Agricultural & Food Research Council. In 1963 he married Judith Mary Dent: they have two sons and a daughter. Grant was knighted in 1992.

GREEN, Michael (Philip)

(2 December 1947 -)
Television and video company entrepreneur, born in London, into a wealthy middle class Jewish family. His father, Cyril, ran the Tern shirt company; his mother, Irene, was a child psychologist. Educated at Haberdashers' Aske's, a London public school, he left halfway through his A-level economics course and became a printing compositor with David, Osler & Frank. He made his first £1 million through the growth of a private company, Tangent Industries: he produced mail order catalogues using Carlton photographic studio, which he bought in 1970. Lord Wolfson's (qv) Great Universal Stores was a major customer (in 1972 Green had married Wolfson's daughter, Janet: they had two daughters before the marriage was dissolved in 1989). Green moved into the growing video market and formed Carlton Communications. When he floated it in 1983, it was making profits of £1.5 million and was valued at £10 million; by 1993 it was valued at £15 billion (with Green owning a stake of over £41 million). The group has taken over UEI, the electronics combine, and Technicolor in California; and by the early 1990s it had a commanding position in the British TV sector through winning the London weekday ITV franchise and having 20 per cent stakes in both Central TV and the breakfast TV group GMTV. Since 1991 Green has been a director of Central Independent Television. His second marriage in 1990 was to Theresa Buckmaster: they have one son. See Judi Bevan and John Jay, *The*

New Tycoons (1989); Andrew Davidson, *Under the Hammer: The ITV Franchise Battle* (1992).

GREEN, Sir Owen (Whitley)

(14 May 1925 -)
Multinational conglomerate executive, born in Stockton-on-Tees, the son of John Paddings Green, a chief marine engineer, and Mabel Ida née Parry. Educated at Stockton on Tees Grammar School, he served in the Royal Navy during the Second World War and then trained as an accountant (ACA 1950), joining Charles Wakeling & Co, 1947-56. In 1956 he became financial director at BTR, a nondescript manufacturer of rubber products founded as the UK offshoot of the American tyre giant Goodrich and renamed the British Tyre & Rubber Co in 1934. Under the chairmanship of Sir David Nicolson, Green (who became managing director in 1967) was one of the key individuals who transformed the group. By 1972 he had helped develop its famous system of financial controls and planning, with a lean (and secretive) head office team which left operating management largely to its own devices. Green's self-professed key to business was the 'bottom line' and he scorned many of business's social objectives, such as good labour relations (not surprisingly his company have been involved with a number of acrimonious disputes with workers). But since 1972 Green has increased BTR's profits and earnings every year, despite three major economic recessions. BTR entered the 1980s as a medium-sized company with sales of £43 million; by the 1990s its profits topped £1 billion on sales of over £7 billion. BTR's manufacturing activities range widely from beer bottles, to motor components to women's tights and its world-wide takeovers have included Thomas Tilling, Dunlop, and Nylex; though its bids in the late 1980s for Pilkington Bros and the American group Norton proved unsuccessful. Green became chairman of BTR in 1984 (when he was knighted) and will remain so until 1993 (when he plans to hand over to finance director Norman Ireland), though in 1990 he handed over as chief executive to Australian-born Alan Jackson. In 1992 BTR's pre-tax profits reached £1.09 billion and the group employed 131,000. Green and his wife Doreen have one son and two daughters. See Corinne Simcock, *A Head for Business* (1992).

GREENBURY, Sir Richard

(31 July 1936 -)
Food and clothes retailing chain executive, the son of Richard Oswald Greenbury and Dorothy née Lewis. Educated at Ealing County Grammar School, in 1953 he joined Marks & Spencer as a junior management trainee (salary £3.50 per week)

at their Ealing branch. Following nine years in stores, he was brought to the Marble Arch headquarters as a trainee merchandizer by Simon Marks (qv), who instilled in him the company's commitment to quality and value. Greenbury became a full director of Marks & Spencer in 1972 and joint managing director in 1978, when he was responsible for all clothing procurement and, later, the food, homewear, footwear, gifts and exports buying operations. In 1986 he became chief operating officer, chief executive in 1988 and succeeded Lord Rayner (qv) as chairman in April 1991 (salary £500,000 per annum). In 1991 the company announced pre-tax profits of £616 million, up 2 per cent on 1990 results. Marks & Spencer is worth £6 billion and employs world-wide 74,000 staff. Greenbury's strategy is to continue exploiting opportunities for growth in the UK, especially in new products in clothing and foods, and treble the size of the company's European operations (where it owns 17 stores). Meanwhile he is focusing on the Canadian business, where the company owns 270 stores, but does not make a profit; and also on the US, where the Brooks Bros and Kings Supermarkets businesses are underperforming. Greenbury holds non-executive directorships at ICI and Lloyds Bank; and was non-executive director of British Gas Corporation, 1976-87, and MB (Metal Box), 1985-89. He married twice: first in 1959 to Sian Eames Hughes, by whom he had two sons and two daughters; second in 1985 to Gabrielle Mary McManus. He was knighted in 1992.

GREENER, Anthony (Armitage)
(26 May 1940 -)
Drinks company executive, the son of William and Diana Marianne Greener. Educated at Marlborough (one A-level), he shunned university and for six months worked in the family cotton waste business in Lancashire. In 1962 he joined Thames Board Mills (a Unilever cardboard box subsidiary) and spent a decade working his way up from trainee to marketing manager. In the early 1970s Greener joined Dunhill, then a small tobacco company, making upmarket cigarettes. Before he left in 1987, Greener transformed it into a diversified group, with 90 per cent of its products in luxury items that had no connection with cigarettes. Dunhill Holding's stock market value soared from £15 million to more than £350 million. He became a non-executive director of Guinness in 1986 on the eve of its involvement in the controversial takeover of Distillers, masterminded by Ernest Saunders (qv). Within months he was one of the executive troika at Guinness and set about transforming Distillers: with Sir Anthony Tennant (qv) he reorganised its marketing and distribution

and made it a much more profitable business. Greener became chief executive of Guinness in 1992 and succeeded Tennant as chairman in 1993. He directs the UK's fifth biggest company by market value. Ironically, one of his first actions was to cut 700 jobs at Guinness's Distillers subsidiary. He married in 1974 Audrey Ogilvie: they have a son and a daughter.

GREENWOOD, Hamar
1st Viscount Greenwood of Holbourne
(7 February 1870 - 10 September 1948)
Industrialist, born in Whitby, near Toronto, Canada, the son of John Hamar Greenwood, a barrister. Educated at Whitby public school and Toronto University (BA Law), he settled in England in 1875 and was called to the Bar in 1917, becoming a KC in 1919. He also followed a successful political career: as Liberal MP for York, 1906-10, and Sunderland, 1910-22, and Conservative MP for East Walthamstow, 1924-29. Before 1914 he acted as Parliamentary private secretary to Winston Churchill and was Chief Secretary for Ireland, 1920-22. An influential figure in Anglo-American relations, he was closely associated with the Pilgrims' Society. His administrative and executive talents proved useful in business and from 1934 to 1947 he was chairman of the Middlesbrough iron and steel firm of Dorman Long, being appointed when it was in financial difficulties. Greenwood was a figurehead chairman, with little understanding of steel, and most of the restructuring at Dorman Long in the 1930s was initiated by (Sir) Ellis Hunter (qv). The firm employed 27,452 in 1935. He was president of the British Iron and Steel Federation in 1938. Created a baronet in 1915, he was awarded a peerage in 1929. He married in 1911 Margery née Spencer: they had two sons and two daughters. He left £44,823 gross. See The Times, 1 September 1948.

GREIG, Sir Alexander
(1878 - 5 May 1950)
Food retailer, who was connected with the trade for over 50 years. The printed sources on his career are mute. Until his retirement in 1946, he was the managing director of the Allied Suppliers Group of companies (formerly Home & Colonial Stores, which employed 10,000 in 1935). A member of the London Provision Exchange and a fellow of the Institute of Certificated Grocers, he was a Director of Retail Coordination and Retail Trade Adviser to the Ministry of Food. He was knighted in 1947. He married in 1904 Jeanie Duncan McNab (d 1949): they had a son and a daughter. See The Times, 4 May 1950; Peter Mathias, Retailing Revolution (1967).

GRESLEY, Sir Herbert Nigel
(19 June 1876 - 5 April 1941)
Locomotive designer and builder, born in Edinburgh, the son of the Reverend Nigel Gresley, an Anglican clergyman. He was educated at Marlborough College. From 1923 until his death Gresley was chief mechanical engineer of the London & North Eastern Railway, working cordially under its chief general manager, Sir Ralph Wedgwood (qv). Gresley was one of the great steam locomotive designers, famous for his express passenger 'Pacifics', such as *Mallard*. He was knighted in 1936. He married in 1901 Ethel Francis Fullagar, daughter of a solicitor, and they had two sons and two daughters. He left £27,962. See F A S Brown, *Nigel Gresley: Locomotive Engineer* (1966); *DBB*.

GROSVENOR, Richard de Aquila
1st Baron Stalbridge
(28 January 1837 - 18 May 1912)
Railway company chairman, born in Dorset, fourth son of the 2nd Marquess of Westminster and his wife, Elizabeth Mary, daughter of the 1st Duke of Sutherland, he was educated at Westminster School and Trinity College, Cambridge. For three decades he pursued a political career: as Liberal MP for Flintshire, 1861-86, he rose to become Chief Whip in 1880. Sworn of the Privy Council in 1872, he was created Baron Stalbridge in 1886. Elected a director of the London & North Western Railway in 1870, Stalbridge was appointed chairman in 1891, continuing in office until 1911. By 1907 the LNWR was the largest railway company of its day, employing nearly 78,000. Under his administration the company's mileage was edged up from 1,890 to 1,966; the servicing of loan capital was reduced from 4 to 3 per cent debenture stock; net receipts rose from £5.3 million to £5.98 million; passengers carried lifted from 62.1 million to 83.7 million; and goods from 37.7 million tons to 53.9 million (per annum figures). Stalbridge promoted cooperation between railway companies and welfare schemes within the LNWR. In particular, he established a company savings bank (1895); an extension to the superannuation fund to cover widows (1900); and the adoption of the St John Ambulance Association throughout the LNWR. Over a century ahead of its time, he was a staunch supporter of the Channel Tunnel (heading a promotional committee suggested by Napoleon III in 1867). Stalbridge married twice: first, in 1874, to the Honourable Beatrix Charlotte Elizabeth (d 1876), youngest daughter of the 3rd Viscount de Vesci; secondly, in 1879, to Eleanor Frances Beatrice, younger daughter of Robert Hamilton Stubber of Moyne. There was a daughter by the first marriage,

and three sons and two daughters by the second. See *Complete Peerage*; *The Times*, 20 May 1912.

GROSVENOR, Robert Wellesley
2nd Baron Ebury
25 January 1834 - 13 November 1918)
Politician and retail company chairman, son of the 1st Baron Ebury (a son of the 1st Marquess of Westminster) and his wife Charlotte, daughter of the 1st Baron Cowley, he was educated at Harrow and King's College, London. After serving in the 1st Life Guards, 1853-66, he retired as captain in order to enter politics. He sat as Liberal MP for Westminster, 1865-74, and succeeded to the title on the death of his father in 1893. Thereafter he became one of many peers who accepted, no doubt for useful fees, directorships of public companies. He was chairman of the Army & Navy Co-operative Society Ltd. Formed in 1871 to supply army and navy officers with consumer goods (groceries, stationery, drapery, perfumery, fancy goods and tailoring; banking and refreshment rooms were added later) at the lowest possible prices, in 1907 it employed 6,275 in its workshops, warehouses and stores, mostly in London. It also had an agency in Plymouth and depots in India. In addition Ebury was chairman of the Army & Navy Auxiliary Cooperative Society Ltd, formed in 1882 to supply fresh provisions, boots, furniture and estate agency services. His other directorships included the Havana Cigar & Tobacco Factories Ltd, Webley & Scott Ltd, Van Den Berghs Ltd, and the National Mortgage & Agency Co of New Zealand Ltd. He married, in 1867, the Honourable Emilie Beaujolais White, daughter of the 1st Baron Annaly; they had two sons and two daughters. See *Complete Peerage*; Michael Moss and Alison Turton, *A Legend of Retailing: House of Fraser* (1989); *The Times*, 14 November 1918.

GUINNESS, (Arthur Francis) Benjamin
3rd Earl of Iveagh
(20 May 1937 - 18 June 1992)
Brewer, the only son of Viscount Elveden and Lady Elizabeth Hare, younger daughter of the Earl of Listowel. When his father was killed in action at Arnhem in 1945, Benjamin Guinness became heir to the Guinness brewing dynasty. Educated at Eton, Trinity College, Cambridge, and the University of Grenoble, he joined the Guinness board as Viscount Elveden in 1958. Between 1960 and 1962 he was assistant managing director of Guinness, working in both Dublin and Park Royal, London. Appointed chairman aged 25, he launched an unsuccessful strategy of unbridled diversification from the core brewing business, which precipitated

a decline only arrested when Guinness (who had now inherited the title of Earl of Iveagh, after the death of his grandfather in 1967) recruited Ernest Saunders (qv) as chief executive in 1981. Called for interview at Farmleigh, Iveagh's house near Dublin, Saunders found a scene of aristocratic decay - lunch at a tiny table in the middle of a huge draughty dining room served by a butler padding down forgotten corridors. Iveagh abdicated all responsibility to Saunders - handing over the chairmanship in 1986 - a move he regretted after the scandal involving the Guinness takeover of Distillers. Iveagh fired Saunders in 1987, though the takeover proved to be the making of Guinness. By 1991 the company was worth £10 billion and pre-tax profits were almost £1 billion - boosting the value of the family's holdings (some 2 per cent) to nearly £200 million. Iveagh was Guinness president between 1986 and 1992, retiring from the board three weeks before his death and leaving it for the first time without a descendant of Arthur Guinness, who founded the Dublin stout brewery in 1759. He married in 1963 Miranda née Smiley, by whom he had two sons and two daughters, before their divorce in 1984. Iveagh left an estate in England and Wales of £13,670,268 million. See Nick Kochan and Hugh Pym, *The Guinness Affair: Anatomy of a Scandal* (1987); James Saunders, *Nightmare: The Ernest Saunders Story* (1989);

GULLIVER, James Gerald
(17 August 1930 -)
Food retailer, the son of William Frederick Gulliver, a Campbeltown grocer, and his wife Mary. Educated at Campbeltown Grammar School, he attended Glasgow University (first-class honours degree in engineering) and Georgia Institute of Technology, USA, before briefly joining the Royal Navy, 1956-59. He then became a management consultant with Urwick, Orr & Partners before entering the grocery trade at Fine Fare, part of Garfield Weston's (qv) group, in 1965. Here he met his future business partner, Alistair Grant (qv), and together they founded the Argyll Group in 1977. Under Gulliver's chairmanship, Argyll became one of the UK's largest supermarket combines: it owns 326 Safeway stores. After the abortive Distiller's takeover in 1986, Gulliver left Argyll (reputedly with £55 million) and was succeeded by Grant. Gulliver then tried to resuscitate Sir Phil Harris's (qv) Queensway carpets group, renaming it Lowndes Queensway. But high interest rates and the fall in consumer spending foiled his plans and he resigned in 1990. He still had interests in hotels, the Waverley Cameron paper and packaging business, and a public relations firm. He has been a visiting professor at Glasgow University; a

member of the Prime Minister's Enquiry into Beef Prices, 1973; and a director of Manchester United Football Club. He has been married three times: after his first two marriages were dissolved, he married Marjorie Moncrieff in 1985. He has three sons and two daughters from his first marriage to Margaret Joan née Cormack. William Kay, *Tycoons: Where They Came From and How They Made It* (1985).

GUNN, John (Humphrey)
(15 January 1942 -)
Financier, the son of Francis (Bob) Gunn and his wife Doris. Educated at Sir John Deane's Grammar School, Northwich, and Nottingham University (BA), he joined Barclays Bank in 1964. His phenomenal rise began after 1979 when he headed the broking firm, Exco. In the early 1980s, the value of Exco soared: floated on the market at £56 million in 1981, by 1985 it was worth £500 million. Besides Gunn, one man who benefited was Lord Cayzer (qv), whom fast-talking Gunn had persuaded in 1979 to contribute to a £5.2 million buyout of Exco for a 30 per cent stake. When Gunn left Exco after a disagreement in 1985, Cayzer appointed him chief executive of his subsidiary British & Commonwealth Holdings. Gunn began to work his familiar magic on B & C, turning it into a leading financial combine, aided by heavy borrowing. In 1987, with immaculate timing, Cayzer sold his B & C shares for £427 million, and three years later B & C collapsed with debts of £1 billion after writing off £550 million in its ill-fated acquisition, Atlantic Computers Leasing. Gunn then joined forces with Howard Hodgson (qv) to form a consultancy, but this disintegrated and by 1992 Gunn had moved to Lloyd's insurance broker Edgar Hamilton as a 'corporate development adviser'. In 1965 he married Renate Sigrid née Boehme: they have three daughters.

H

HADFIELD, Sir Robert (Abbott)
(28 November 1858 - 30 September 1940)
Steel manufacturer and metallurgist, born in Sheffield, the son of Robert Hadfield (1831-88) and Marianne née Abbott. He declined to go up to Oxford or Cambridge and instead joined his father's steelmaking firm in 1879, becoming chairman of Hadfields in 1888 until his death. His discovery of manganese and silicon steels in the 1880s established his reputation and enabled Hadfields to become a world-ranking alloy steel and armaments manufacturer. Under Hadfield turnover grew from £73,000 in 1888 to £5 million in 1940; the work-

force from 400 to 9,200 - though, like other arms manufacturers such as Vickers (qv), Hadfields performed poorly between wars. Hadfield was knighted in 1908, elected FRS in 1909, and made a baronet in 1917. He married Frances Belt née Wickersham, an American heiress, in 1894. He left £420,690. See R A Hadfield, *Metallurgy and Its Influence on Modern Progress* (1925); G Tweedale, "The Metallurgist as Entrepreneur: The Career of Sir Robert Hadfield" *Historical Metallurgy* (1993); *DBB; DNB.*

HAGUE, Sir Charles Kenneth Felix
(17 September 1901 - 4 February 1974)

Engineering company executive, son of Albert Hague and Florence Muriel née Flux, he was educated at New College School, Oxford, and Leeds University. He joined Babcock & Wilcox Ltd, water tube boiler makers and engineers (originally in 1881 a branch of an American parent, but from 1891 a wholly independent company), in 1924. At first he headed half-a-dozen people in the testing department, later he moved to the calculating department and then in 1930 he was sent to New York to open an American office for the company. Building up useful contacts, after four years he returned to London to take charge of the sales department. By 1935 he was sales manager, at which time Babcock & Wilcox employed 8,700 in the UK, in works in Renfrew, Dumbarton and Oldbury. Hague was made a director in 1940, deputy managing director in 1942 and managing director in 1945. He held this last position until 1958, meantime serving as deputy chairman, 1950-60. He was chairman from 1960 until 1968. While at the helm Hague oversaw dramatic technological changes, chiefly a move into nuclear engineering. From 1947 Babcock & Wilcox was involved by Sir Claude Gibb of Reyrolle Parsons, heavy electrical equipment manufacturers, in the design of boilers for electric power generation from pressurised gascooled reactors. When the government in 1955 announced a ten-year programme for building twelve nuclear power stations, four consortia, each with a wide range of technical competencies and sharing the great financial risks involved, were formed to bid for the contracts. Babcock & Wilcox, the leading firm of boiler makers, joined British Nuclear Design & Construction Ltd, with English Electric (heavy electric equipment) and Taylor Woodrow (contractors who had worked on Calder Hall where the reactor opened in 1956 to produce both plutonium and electricity). In 1955 Babcock & Wilcox employed nearly 16,000. Sir Kenneth Hague (he was knighted in 1953) was deputy chairman of the Royal Ordnance Factories Board, 1951-58; member of the Iron and Steel Board, 1959-64; president of the Engineering Employers' Federation, 1958-60; and president of the Institution of Mechanical Engineers, 1961-62. Hague married twice: first, in 1926, to Marjorie née Thornton by whom he had a son and a daughter; second, in 1960, to Mrs Helen Wallace Sutherland. See *The Circulator* (Christmas 1968); Margaret Gowing, *Independence and Deterrence* (2 vols, 1974).

HALPERN, Sir Ralph (Mark)
(26 October 1938 -)

Clothing retailer, born in north London the son of Jewish refugees from Nazi Austria, who arrived in Britain in 1938. His father, Bernard, had been a successful retailer and banker, but did not prosper in the UK. Educated at St Christopher School, Letchworth, Halpern began his career as a shopfloor trainee at Selfridge's department store. In 1961 he moved to Leeds and became a manager of a store of Burton's, the menswear chain founded by Sir Montague Burton (qv) that was then close to collapse. He became chairman in 1981 and in the 1980s consumer boom made the Burton Group second only to Marks & Spencer in Britain's fashion market (with a share of more than 12 per cent), revolutionising its dowdy image with a string of famous names - Debenhams, Top Shop, Dorothy Perkin. From a company making an annual loss of £100 million in 1977, within ten years he transformed Burton into a holding company worth £1.6 billion, controlling about 1,900 shops and stores (in the 1960s it had 600) with 35,000 staff. But Halpern's high salary (he was the first British businessman to earn £1 million annually); a Department of Trade & Industry investigation into the Debenham's takeover; and his extra-marital love-life - all generated adverse publicity. After a slump in high street sales and a disastrous flirtation with the property market, Halpern left Burton in November 1990 with an annual pension of £456,000 as part of a severance package of £2 million - one of the biggest payoffs ever given to a UK businessman. He was knighted in 1986. He has a daughter from his marriage to former wife Joan.

HAMILTON, Lord Claud John
(20 February 1843 - 26 January 1925)

Railway company chairman, he was born at Harrow, the second son of James, 1st Duke of Abercorn and Lady Louisa Russell, second daughter of John, 6th Duke of Bedford. He served in the Grenadier Guards, 1862-67, and was then colonel of the 5th Battalion, the Royal Inniskilling Fusiliers, 1867-92: a background which shaped his authoritarian and paternalist style in business. On Lord Salisbury's recommendation he was appointed a director of the Great Eastern Railway in 1872 and became vice-chairman in 1874. He worked closely with the chairman, Charles Henry Parkes, and succeeded him in 1893, remaining in post until 1923 when the GER was absorbed in the London & North Eastern Railway. Serving a sparsely populated agricultural region, the GER was never very prosperous. Hamilton, however, much improved its performance. From the 1880s he developed Continental traffic through Harwich, obtained a share of coal traffic by acquiring running powers over North Eastern Railway track, and expanded hotel, restaurant and restaurant car services by subcontracting catering. He was hostile to interference from unions and government alike. A Conservative, he was MP for Londonderry, 1864-68; King's Lynn, 1869-80; Liverpool, 1880-88; and South Kensington, 1910-18. He married, in 1873, Caroline, daughter of Edward Chandos Pole; they had a son and a daughter. See *DBB*.

HAMPSON, Stuart
(7 January 1947 -)

Department store executive, the son of Kenneth and Mary Hampson. His father was an Oldham policeman and freemason, who died when he was four. The masons secured Hampson's education at the Royal Masonic School, Bushey, and from there he went up to St John's College, Oxford, to read modern languages. In 1969 he joined the Board of Trade and began a career as a 'high-flyer' within the civil service. He eventually became principal private secretary, but in 1982 decision-making in the business world proved more attractive and he joined the John Lewis Partnership, the famous cooperative department store group based in London. Hampson became a department store manager and by 1986 was in charge of the development programme. Three new stores were opened under his stewardship. In 1989 he was nominated deputy chairman and became chairman in February 1993 - only the fifth chairman since John Lewis founded the business in 1864. He took over a group with 22 department stores and the Waitrose chain of supermarkets in the south-east: pre-tax profits were £71.4 million in 1992 on sales of £32.36 billion and the company employed about 40,000. Hampson married in 1973 Angela McLaren: they have one son and one daughter.

HANBURY-WILLIAMS, Sir John Coldbrook
(28 May 1892 - 10 August 1965)

Textile manufacturer, born at Henley-on-Thames, the son of Major-General Sir John Hanbury Williams, who became Marshal of the Diplomatic Corps, and Annie Emily née Reiss, he was educat-

ed at Wellington College. He then entered his maternal grandfather's firm, Reiss Brothers, merchants of Manchester and London trading in the East: a career broken by the First World War in which he served in the Hussars. In 1926 he joined Courtaulds, the rayon manufacturers, on the yarn export side. He became a director in 1930, deputy chairman in 1943 and then chairman, 1946-62. As director he was responsible for the company's foreign affairs, but was powerless in 1941 to prevent the sale of Courtaulds' highly-profitable subsidiary the American Viscose Corporation as part of American Lend-Lease. Courteous, dignified, handsome, autocratic and capricious, Hanbury-Williams had no interest in, or understanding of, new trends in industrial organisation or production technology. Courtaulds' expansion into paint, chemicals and packaging in the 1950s derived from the initiatives of younger directors like Alan Wilson and Frank Kearton (qv). When in 1960-61 Paul Chambers (qv), chairman of ICI, suggested a merger between ICI and Courtaulds, Sir John Hanbury-Williams (he was knighted in 1950) proved receptive. However, any surrender to ICI was rejected by a majority of Courtaulds' directors. They won the merger battle with ICI which ended in March 1962, a few months before Hanbury-Williams departed. In 1928 he married Princess Zenaida Cantacuzene, daughter of the Russian Prince Michael Cantacuzene; they had a son and two daughters. See D C Coleman, *Courtaulds: An Economic and Social History* (3 vols, 1969-80) vol 3; *DBB*.

HANN, Edmund Lawrence
(19 August 1881 - 10 August 1968)

Coal magnate, the son of Edmund Mills Hann (qv) and Mary Brown. Educated at Haileybury, he was a gold medallist at the South Wales Institute of Engineers. He became chairman of Powell Duffryn Ltd. From 1941 to 1942 he was Regional Fuel Controller for Wales. He married in 1907, Mary Alice Redwood: they had four daughters.

HANN, Edmund Mills
(1850 - 4 October 1931)

Coal company manager, son of William Hann, 'a prominent figure in the industrial life of Durham', he was apprenticed at the Hetton Collieries where he qualified as a colliery manager. In 1879, after managerial experience in Yorkshire collieries, he moved to South Wales and joined the Powell Duffryn Co as manager of the New Tredegar and White Rose Collieries in the Rhymney Valley. Formed in 1864, the Powell Duffryn Co participated in the late nineteenth-century South Wales boom in coalmining which pushed the region level with the North East by 1913. The boom exploited steam coal, suitable for railway locomotives and steamships: in 1876 'PD' coal was rated in the highest class by the Admiralty. Hann demonstrated an unusual combination of technical skill and business acumen and in 1883 was appointed manager of all the company's pits in the Rhymney and Aberdare valleys. Unprofitable pits were abandoned and new pits sunk with the aid of the latest pumping technology. Between 1880 and 1910 Powell Duffryn's annual output rose from 750,000 to four million tons of coal. With employment at 6,000 in 1907, PD was the largest coal company in South Wales. Reading rooms and hospitals were provided for employees. E M Hann retired in 1919 but remained a director (he joined the board in 1916). His son George had acted as his assistant since 1904 but died, following an operation, before he could succeed his father. E M Hann's wife predeceased him and he was survived by six sons and one daughter. See A P Barnett and D Willson-Lloyd (ed), *The South Wales Coalfield* (1923); *The Powell Duffryn Steam Coal Company Limited, 1864-1914* (1914); *Western Mail and South Wales News*, 5 October 1931.

HANSON, James Edward
Baron Hanson of Edgerton
(20 January 1922 -)

Multinational corporate entrepreneur, brought up in Huddersfield, the son of Robert Hanson CBE and Louisa Ann (Cis) née Rodgers. A product of the Yorkshire gentry, he left school early and started running his father's haulage business. He inherited much of the £3 million when the business was nationalised in 1948 and went to Canada to form his own road-haulage business. He then partnered Gordon White (qv) in a greetings card business - Hanson White - before they joined forces in running a commercial vehicle and sales distribution business, Oswald Tillotson Ltd (taken over by the Wiles Group in 1964). Hanson became chairman of Wiles in 1965, having taken control backed by a £300,000 capitalisation, and in 1969 it was renamed Hanson Trust, of which Hanson has since been chairman. Hanson's speciality is buying and rationalising companies, so that a leaner, fitter and more profitable organisation results. Hanson's reputation as a corporate raider came into its own when White help him lay the foundation of the Trust's transatlantic success (its emblem is a knotted Union Jack and Stars and Stripes). Their activities - with Hanson reputedly the dealmaker and White the administrator - soon spawned a conglomerate with dozens of (mainly Anglo-American) businesses: including John Player cigarettes, Ever Ready batteries, house bricks and hot dogs. His takeover in 1989 of Consolidated Goldfields for £3.5 billion

was then the biggest takeover in British industrial history. By the end of the 1980s Hanson Trust was amongst the top ten British companies with a stock market value of over £8 billion and it was out-performing every other British company except Polly Peck and Glaxo. In 1992 Hanson Trust's turnover was £7.6 billion (pre-tax profit £545 million) and it employed 93,000. In the early 1990s Hanson's sights were briefly trained on Imperial Chemical Industries and on Rank Hovis McDougall: eventually he dropped his interest in ICI and his bid for RHM was topped by his former protégé, Greg Hutchings (qv). In his early years Hanson had a playboy image, fostered by romances with film stars (he was briefly engaged to the actress Audrey Hepburn in 1954). He married in 1959 Geraldine née Kaelin, a New York office worker: they have two sons and one daughter. Knighted in 1976 by his friend Harold Wilson, Hanson supports the Conservative Party and was made a life peer in 1983. See Ivan Fallon and James Strodes, *Takeovers* (1987).

HARBEN, Sir Henry
(24 August 1823 - 2 December 1911)

Assurance company executive and chairman, born in Bloomsbury, London, the eldest son of Henry Harben, a City wholesaler, and his wife, Sarah née Andrade, he was educated privately, worked in an uncle's stores and was then articled to a surveyor. He published a ready reckoner, *The Weight Calculator* in 1849. In 1852 he was appointed accountant to The Prudential Mutual Assurance, Investment, & Loan Association (renamed The Prudential Assurance Co in 1867) and four years later became secretary (in effect, chief executive officer). The Prudential started to transact industrial life assurance in 1854: business relying on agents (salesmen-collectors) who obtained small life assurances by door-to-door solicitation and collected premiums weekly or monthly (originally aimed at the industrial working class market, hence the name). Harben proved to be a brilliant 'man manager', especially in selecting and motivating his agents and their superintendents. A growing UK population and rising real incomes in the second half of the nineteenth century offered an expanding market of which Harben and the Prudential rapidly took advantage. His numbers of agents rose from 11,704 in 1891 to 14,996 in 1901 and 17,832 in 1911 (some being part-time employees). Supervisory staff increased from 2,190 in 1901 to 2,740 in 1911 In 1898 the Holborn Bars headquarters of the 'Pru', opened in 1879, had to be extended to accommodate the 2,000 head office staff. By 1887 the company had a 75 per cent share of the industrial assurance market, with seven million policies in force and a premium income of £3 million, rising to 20 million policies in force and a premium income of £60 million in 1911. Harben relinquished the secretaryship in 1874 and became resident director. He was deputy chairman, 1878-1905, and chairman, 1905-7, and president from 1907 until his death. Harben was an innovator, forming estate and statistical departments in 1864, discontinuing medical examinations in 1866, and publishing the company's mortality experience in 1871. In terms of office technology the record was more mixed, with the Pru being an early adopter of the arithmometer but long delaying the use of typewriter and telephone. Outside business Harben was active in local government in Hampstead (being its first mayor in 1900) and Sussex (where he had a country estate, was a DL and, in 1898, high sheriff). He was knighted in 1897. Harben married twice: first, in 1846, to Ann née Such (d 1883), by whom he had one son, Henry Andrade Harben (d 1910); second, in 1890, to Mary Jane née Cole, by whom he had at least one daughter. See R W Barnard, *A Century of Service: The Story of the Prudential, 1848-1948* (1948); *DBB*.

HARMSWORTH, Alfred Charles William
Viscount Northcliffe
(15 July 1865 - 14 August 1922)

Newspaper and periodical proprietor, born at Chapelizod, near Dublin, the son of Alfred Harmsworth, a former schoolteacher then reading for the Bar, and Geraldine Mary. Educated at Stamford Grammar School and a day school at St John's Wood, at 16 he set out on a career in journalism. In 1888 he launched *Answers to Correspondents*, a popular weekly filled with useless information and competitions: sales of this and other Harmsworth publications soon reached a million a week. Alfred provided journalistic flair; his brother Harold (qv) financial acumen. Between 1894 and 1896 the Harmsworths moved into newspapers, buying the *Evening News* and the *Daily Mail*, aiming at the mass market of those who could read but not think. In 1905, two years after Harmsworth had launched the *Daily Mirror*, Associated Newspapers Ltd was incorporated with a share capital of £1.6 million. In 1907 he also bought and attempted to revive the fortunes of *The Times*. He regarded himself primarily as a journalist, but he nevertheless transformed the popular magazine and newspaper market and raised the status and pay of journalists. In 1917 Lloyd George appointed him director of the British War Mission to the United States. In 1888 he married Mary Molly Milner, daughter of a failing sugar merchant: they had no children, but he fathered three children by a mistress, Kathleen Wrohan. Alfred was awarded a baronetcy in 1904 and a barony in 1905. He left £5,248,937. See Paul Ferris, *The House of Northcliffe: The Harmsworths of Fleet Street* (1971); Reginald Pound and Geoffrey Harmsworth, *Northcliffe* (1959); *DBB*; *DNB*.

HARMSWORTH, Harold Sidney
1st Viscount Rothermere of Hemsted
(26 April 1868 - 26 November 1940)

Newspaper and periodicals proprietor and paper manufacturer, born in St John's Wood, London, the son of Alfred Harmsworth and Geraldine Mary née Maffett. Educated at Henley House, a private school, and Marylebone Philological School, he became a clerk with the Board of Trade. In 1889 he became his brother Alfred's (qv) business manager and remained so until the latter's death, exercising close financial control with a penchant for cost-cutting. Alfred kept the *Daily Mail* and *The Times* out of his hands, but he was given responsibility for the firm's papermaking operations in Newfoundland. Harold also launched a newspaper of his own in Scotland, the *Daily Record*, bought Northcliffe's shares in the *Daily Mail* and also successfully founded the *Sunday Pictorial*. After Northcliffe's death Harold set up the Daily Mail Trust: he briefly bought the Hulton group of newspapers from Beaverbrook (qv), before selling them to the Berry brothers (qv) at a profit. He and Beaverbrook also in 1922 exchanged shares in each other's companies and had joint interests in the Mersey Paper Mills of Bowater (qv). As a newspaper proprietor, Harold was not a success: in 1933 the *Express* replaced the *Daily Mail* as the largest selling daily newspaper; and the *Daily Mirror* also lost impetus. The Liberal Party gave him a barony in 1914; and he was awarded a viscountcy in 1919 after serving as director-general of the Royal Army Clothing Department and Air Minister during the war. In 1893 he married Lilian née Share: they had three sons (two of whom died in the war) before she left him. Not widely liked and politically naive (his support for Mussolini and Hitler became notorious), his chief interest in later life was making money. Though reputed in 1926 to be worth £26 million, his UK estate was proved at £281,000. See Harold Harmsworth, *Solvency or Downfall? Squandermania and Its Story* (1921); Paul Ferris, *The House of Northcliffe: The Harmsworths of Fleet Street* (1971); *DBB*; *DNB*.

HARRIS, Brigadier (Hon) Sir Lionel Herbert
(15 April 1897 - 18 March 1971)

Post Office executive and engineer, younger son of Thomas Harris of London, he was educated at Sir

Walter St John's School, London, and then sent when nearly 17 to Australia by his widowed father who persuaded him to accept an agricultural apprenticeship on offer from the federal government. In 1915 Harris joined the Australian Imperial Forces, serving with the 5th Australian Divisional Signal Company in France, and reaching the rank of corporal. After the Armistice he stayed in England, passed his intermediate BSc in engineering and won a Kitchener Scholarship to the City and Guilds Engineering College (later part of the Imperial College of Science) where, in two years, he gained a first class in electrical engineering. Working in the research branch of the Post Office Engineering Department at Dollis Hill, 1922-39, he gained an MSc, acquired experience of ordinary Post Office engineering, and in 1926 was commissioned in the Royal Signals (Territorial Army). During the Second World War Harris served with the British Expeditionary Force, 1939-40; commanded GHQ Signals; was chief staff officer, Lines of Communication, 1942-43; and chief of telecommunications at the Supreme Headquarters of the Allied Expeditionary Force, 1943-45. Afterwards he ascended some of the highest rungs in the Post Office: as Regional Director of the GPO in Scotland, 1945-49; Controller of Research at the GPO, 1949-54; and Engineer-in-Chief of the GPO, 1954-60. Knighted in 1957, Harris held American and French as well as British military decorations. He wrote an account of his early career, *Signal Venture* (1951). He was colonel of his old regiment, the 44th (Home Counties) Signal Regiment (TA). In 1920 Harris married Daisy Edith Barkel; they had one son. See *The Times*, 19 March 1971.

HARRIS, Sir Philip (Charles)
(15 September 1942 -)
Carpet chain store owner, the son of Charles William Harris and Ruth Ellen née Ward. Educated at Streatham Grammar School, at 16 he took over the family's three lino and carpet shops in south London when his father died. By the 1980s he had built the business, named Harris Queensway, into a nationwide chain. Harris was regarded as one of Britain's brightest businessmen and was knighted in 1985. But in 1987 profits began to slide and in the following year he sold the business to James Gulliver (qv). Harris collected some £70 million from the deal and shrewdly declined to support a rival management buyout bid for the renamed Lowndes Queensway group, which soon went spectacularly bankrupt. Instead, he founded the Carpetright chain, which in 1992 had about 80 shops: the group made £3 million profits in 1991. Harris also has substantial property

interests. Harris married in 1960 Pauline Norma née Chumley: they have three sons and one daughter. See Philip Beresford, *The Sunday Times Book of the Rich* (1990).

HARRISON, Sir Ernest (Thomas)
(11 May 1926 -)
Electronics company executive, the son of Ernest Horace Harrison and his wife Gertrude Rebecca Gibbons. Educated at Trinity Grammar School, Wood Green, London, he qualified as an accountant in 1950. He joined Racal Electronics, the company founded by Sir Raymond Brown (1920-91) and Jock Cunningham, as secretary and chief accoutant in 1951. In 1958 he was a Racal director and in 1966 became both chairman and chief executive. Under Harrison Racal achieved its greatest growth. In 1989 he merged Racal and the British Communications Corporation, thus strengthening Racal's tactical communications business: the result was that pre-tax profits exceeded £1 million for the first time. American acquisitions, such as Milgo Electronics Corp in 1977, increased US sales from $5 million to about $355 million between 1976 and 1982. After Racal acquired Decca for its radar expertise in 1980, beating Arnold Weinstock (qv) to the deal, its profits began growing at 25 per cent a year. In the electronics industry's shake-out in the mid-1980s Harrison launched Racal Telcom (the cellular telephone network), which was phenomenally successful and was soon generating a third of Racal's profits. By 1992 Harrison's vigorous management style and capacity to exploit niches had lifted Racal's turnover to £1,606 million (pre-tax profit £55 million) and the workforce to over 34,000. It was involved in telecommunications, defence and specialised electronics: while the success of Racal Telecom had led to its demerger and listing as a separate company, Vodafone; and its security business Chubb had also been demerged. Awarded an OBE for his work in the National Savings movement, Harrison was knighted in 1981. In 1960 he married Phyllis Brenda Knight née Janie: they have three sons and two daughters.

HARRISON, Sir Frederick
(1844 - 31 December 1914)
Railway manager, the son of George Harrison of Newport, Monmouthshire, he was educated at the Royal Naval School, New Cross. In 1864 he joined the London & North Western Railway, working as a clerk for George Findlay, then district superintendent for Shrewsbury and South Wales. A few months later he accompanied Findlay to Euston when Findlay was appointed LNWR chief goods manager. In 1871 Harrison was moved to Liverpool as assistant district superintendent. Three

years later he took charge of the Chester and Holyhead section, but briefly: in 1875 he went back to Euston as assistant superintendent of the line. After ten years he was made chief goods manager and then in 1893 succeeded his old chief, now Sir George Findlay, as LNWR general manager. Harrison held the post until 1909. By this time the LNWR was the largest railway in Britain, employing nearly 78,000 in 1907. Harrison served under Lord Stalbridge, Richard Grosvernor (qv). On retirement Sir Frederick Harrison (he was knighted in 1902) was made a director of the LNWR; he also became a director and deputy-chairman of the South Eastern Railway; a member of the South Eastern & Chatham Railway Company's managing committee; and a director of Ocean Accident & Guarantee Corporation. Harrison served on the Royal Commission of 1900 which enquired into the working of military hospitals in South Africa. He married twice: Fanny Louisa née Thomas in 1868; Jessie Margaret née Goldie in 1888. See *The Times*, 2 January 1915.

HARTLEY, Sir Harold Brewer

(3 September 1878 - 9 September 1972)
Transport executive, born in London, the only son of Harold T Hartley, a mineral water manufacturer and publisher, and Kate née Brewer. After reading chemistry at Oxford (where he became honorary fellow at Balliol), Hartley entered business in 1930 as vice-president of the London, Midland & Scottish Railway, which eventually led to a chairmanship of the LMSR's Railway Air Services. In 1946 he became chairman of British European Airways and then during 1947-9 of the larger British Overseas Airways Corporation. An important Government scientific adviser on energy matters, he was first chairman of the Electricity Supply Research Council 1949-52, and president of the World Power Conference 1950. In 1906 he married Gertrude (d 1971), eldest daughter of a future Master of Balliol: they had a son, later Air Marshall Sir Christopher Hartley, and a daughter. He was elected FRS in 1926 and knighted in 1928. He left £48,406 gross. See *DBB*.

HARVEY, Sir Robert James Paterson

(28 July 1904 - 8 July 1965)
Post Office executive and Civil Servant, born in Edinburgh, the son of the Reverend Thomas Harvey, he was educated at Daniel Stewart's College and Edinburgh University where he gained a first class in history in 1926. He immediately joined the General Post Office as an assistant principal and after rapid promotion became in 1934 Chief Superintendent of the London Postal

Service. In 1936, after a year at the Imperial Defence College, he went to the Treasury as principal. During the Second World War he was private secretary to the Minister of Food but returned to the Treasury in 1941 as assistant secretary, being promoted to under secretary in 1946. Harvey went back to the Post Office in 1947 as regional director of the Home Counties, responsible for all Post Office services in the area (postal, telephonic and telegraphic). Two years later he was promoted to director of inland telecommunications. In 1954-55 he was director of radio and accommodation and in 1955 became Deputy Director-General (at a salary of £5,800 by 1962). Before retiring in 1964 he signed for the UK the international agreement on satellite communications which led to the establishment of a committee to create and control a global system of satellite communications. Harvey was knighted in 1960. He married, in 1934, Margaret née Mitchell; they had two sons and one daughter. See *The Times*, 10 July 1965.

HARVEY-JONES, Sir John (Henry)

(16 April 1924 -)
Chemical manufacturer and industrial pundit, born in Hackney, London, the son of Mervyn Harvey-Jones and his wife Eileen Wilson. He was brought up in India, where his father was a civil servant. Educated at Tormore School, Deal, and the Royal Naval College, Dartmouth, from 1937 to 1956 he worked for the Royal Navy, specialising in submarines, interpreting and intelligence. He joined Imperial Chemical Industries in 1956 as a work study officer at Wilton. He became chairman of ICI Petrochemicals Division in 1970; joined the main board in 1973; and was appointed chairman in 1982. He transformed ICI's traumatic losses in 1980-81 to £1 billion profit in 1984-5 and by 1987, when he retired, he had radically restructured the company into two distinct arms: the traditional bulk commodity chemicals and the speciality growth sectors. His floral ties, unruly hair, and outspoken views - expounded in best-sellers such as *Making it Happen* (1987) and TV appearances as a business 'troubleshooter' - have made Harvey-Jones one of the best known British industrialists. He is a non-executive director of Grand Metropolitan. He married in 1947 Mary Evelyn Atcheson: they have one daughter. Harvey-Jones was awarded an MBE in 1952 and knighted in 1985. See John Harvey-Jones, *Getting it Together: Memoirs of a Troubleshooter* (1991); Andrew Pettigrew, *The Awakening Giant: Continuity and Change at ICI* (1985)

HASLAM, Sir Robert
Baron Haslam of Bolton
(4 February 1923 -)

Industrialist, the son of Percy and Mary Haslam. Educated at Bolton School and Birmingham University, where he took a first-class BSc in coal mining, he joined Manchester Collieries Ltd in 1944. In 1947 he joined ICI's Nobel Division and worked his way up through the ranks: after holding a number of senior posts in its Plastics and Fibres Divisions, Haslam was deputy chairman of ICI between 1980 and 1983. He then headed two troubled state-owned industries, serving as chairman of the British Steel Corporation between 1983 and 1986 (a part-time appointment, since Haslam was also chairman of the sugar giant Tate & Lyle over the same period) and chairman of the National Coal Board between 1986 and 1990. Under Haslam, who succeeded Ian MacGregor (qv), the BSC became a politically less prominent organisation and was able to achieve planned cutbacks in manpower and production. When Haslam left the BSC in 1986, the Corporation had recorded its first profit in a decade. Haslam also succeeded MacGregor at the Coal Board, where he joined in the aftermath of the year-long miners' strike. Despite the high profile of his predecessor, it was Haslam who instituted some of the major changes in the coal industry. He cut the number of mines from 169 to 86 and the workforce from 221,000 to 105,000. But he improved productivity and attempted to give the NCB a new image in 1987 with a change of name - to the British Coal Corporation. Though deficits were incurred under Haslam to the tune of £1,000 million, operating profits had recovered by 1985-86. Haslam also held directorships at the Bank of England, Imperial Metal Industries and Carrington, Viyella and several other firms. Haslam was knighted in 1985 and made a life peer in 1990. He married in 1947 Joyce Quin: they have two sons. See Geoffrey F Dudley and Jeremy J Richardson, *Politics and Steel in Britain 1967-1988: The Life and Times of the British Steel Corporation* (1990).

HATRY, Clarence Charles
(16 December 1888 - 10 June 1965)

Company promoter and financier, born at Belsize Park, London, the son of Julius Hatry, a prosperous silk merchant, and Henriette née Katzenstein. Educated at St Paul's School, aged 18 he took over the family business on the death of his father. Stricken with illness, he was soon declared bankrupt, though he paid most of his liabilities within two years. In 1911 he began insurance broking and soon found his métier as a company promoter, one of the first of the twentieth-century breed of financiers who recognised the advantages of large industrial combinations. Hatry was particularly active in the inter-war period when his property and finance companies - notably the Austin Friars Trust and Corporation & General Securities Ltd - were involved in the shipbuilding, cotton and glass industries. In 1929 he took over the United Steel Companies, but his grand designs - based partly on fraud - did not survive the stock market crash and in the same year his companies had debts of £14 million. Hatry was jailed until 1939. The affair was a significant factor in the subsequent tightening and regulation of the British capital market. After the war Hatry could still be found wheeler-dealing in industries as diverse as coffee bars and industrial cleaning. In 1909 he married Violet ('Dolly') Marguerite née Ferguson. He left just £828. See *DBB*; *DNB*.

HAYMAN, Sir (Cecil George) Graham
(1 April 1893 - 10 March 1966)

Petroleum industry executive, born in London, the son of Charles Henry Hayman, an engineer, and his wife, Clara Annie Cuthbert, he left school at 15 and worked for two years for a manufacturing chemist, another two years for a firm of solicitors, and then another two years for a financial house in the City. After the First World War, in which he served throughout with the 7th London Regiment, he became manager of F A Hughes & Co Ltd, chemical manufacturers and merchants. He moved in 1922 to be secretary of Herbert Green & Co, who had an industrial distillery at Hull; to his disappointment this was sold in 1925 to the Distillers Co Ltd (DCL). Hayman drifted for a while and then in 1927 formed Solvent Products Ltd, based at Dagenham, to produce ethyl alcohol from molasses. DCL, moving into industrial chemical and solvents and away from its staple interests in whisky and fermentation, bought him out and gave him a seat on their board in 1936. Hayman proceeded to master DCL's widespread interests and took the company into plastics and polystyrene production in the late 1930s. Though he knew little advanced chemistry, he proved to be a talented co-ordinator. By 1955 (when the firm employed about 20,000 in the UK) Sir Graham Hayman (he was knighted in 1954) was chairman of DCL's main board management committee and in 1958 became its first non-whisky chairman. He preferred licensing agreements to setting up plants abroad, and he chose to make primary products for smaller plastics firms to make-up, mix or mould for final consumers. In 1918 he married Elsie Lilian née Leggett; they had a son and a daughter. See *DBB*.

HEATH, Cuthbert Eden
(23 March 1859 - 8 March 1939)

Insurance underwriter and broker, he was born at Forest Lodge near Southampton, the third son of Captain (later Admiral Sir) Leopold George Heath, RN, and his wife Mary Emma née March. Prevented by deafness from following the family tradition, a career in the Navy, he attended Brighton College, spent two years abroad in France and Germany and at 18 was found a place with the insurance brokers, Henry Head & Co. Elected a member of Lloyd's in 1880, with a £7,000 loan from his father, he began underwriting marine risks in 1881. Heath, distinguished on the floor of Lloyd's by his height and the black-box deaf aid he carried, led the way in adding non-marine insurance to the staple marine insurance work of Lloyd's. He began by reinsuring fire business for a company of which his father was a director, in 1885. Later he moved into a variety of new risks: against smallpox (for those who had been vaccinated); workmen's compensation (following the Employers' Liability Act of 1880); motor insurance at Lloyd's (from 1904); aviation insurance, commenced in 1919 with Sir Edward Mountain (qv), but initially unsuccessful; and a new form of reinsurance, copied from America, the 'burning cost' system of self-rated reinsurance. From the start he offered broking as well as underwriting services and for this he formed a partnership, C E Heath & Co, in 1890, which fed his underwriting syndicate. In 1910 the partnership was registered as a private company. Heath's success rested on his great skill in estimating risk, deriving partly from his well-kept records. Measures of his success were his income (about £60,000 a year by the 1930s) and the value of his estate at death (£1,052,008). He married, in 1891, Sarah Caroline Gore Gambier, daughter of a clergyman. The had one daughter. See Antony Brown, *Cuthbert Heath: Maker of the Modern Lloyd's of London* (1980); *DBB*.

HENDERSON, Sir Alexander
1st Baron Faringdon
(28 September 1850 - 17 March 1934)

Financier and railway company chairman, born in London, the second son of George Henderson, a printer's reader, and Eliza née Cockshutt, he was educated privately and then joined Deloittes the railway accountants before moving into stockbroking with the firm of Thomas Greenwood. Henderson became a member of the London Stock Exchange in 1873 and, as Greenwood's partner, specialised in large, long term investments. In less than 20 years he made a fortune and bought the Buscot Park estate in Berkshire, enlisting Sir Edward Burne-Jones to decorate the saloon. In 1894 he became chairman of the Manchester, Sheffield & Lincolnshire Railway, then impoverished by the imprudent and diffuse initiatives of his predecessor Sir Edward Watkin. Henderson revived it by means of a rolling stock trust company which sold equipment to the MSLR on hire purchase terms. This allowed the company to expand from a provincial to a trunk railway, signified by its name change to the Great Central in 1897. Sam Fay (qv) proved an able chief executive under Henderson's chairmanship which lasted until 1922 when Henderson became deputy chairman of the London & North Eastern Railway. Simultaneously Henderson had a host of investments, particularly in South America. A Tariff Reformer, Henderson was MP (Liberal Unionist) for West Staffordshire, 1898-1906, and MP (Unionist) for St George's, Hanover Square, 1913-16. He was created a baron in 1916. Henderson married, in 1874, Jane Ellen née Davis (d 1920); they had six sons (four of whom died between 1922 and 1933) and a daughter. See *DBB*; David Wainwright, *Henderson* (1985).

HENDERSON, Sir Denys (Hartley)
(11 October 1932 -)

Chemical manufacturer, born in Colombo, Sri Lanka, the son of John Hartley Henderson, a tea planter, and Nellie née Gordon. Educated at Aberdeen Grammar School and the University of Aberdeen (MA, LLB), he joined Imperial Chemical Industries Ltd as a lawyer in the secretary's department, London, in 1957. Steady promotion followed: by 1977 he was chairman of the Paints Division, joining the board in 1980. He became ICI's youngest chairman in 1987, succeeding Sir John Harvey-Jones (qv). In contrast to his predecessor's emphasis on cost effectiveness, Henderson's aims to foster marketing skills within ICI. He heads an operation which employs 130,000, produces 15,000 different products and has sales of £11.5 billion spread across 150 countries. In 1991 ICI, its profits hit by a recession, was threatened by a hostile takeover from Lord Hanson (qv) - a move strongly resisted by Henderson. But in 1993 - in a move that his critics say was triggered by Hanson - Henderson and his board split ICI into two parts: one a bioscience and pharmaceuticals division (named Zeneca); the other, a paints and industrial chemicals division still called ICI. The demerger was accompanied by a £949 million restructuring programme and plans to axe 9,000 jobs. Henderson was knighted in 1989. He is chairman of Henley Management College and in 1993 was appointed chancellor of Bath University. He married in 1957 Doreen Mathewson Glashan: they have two daughters.

HENNESSY, Sir Patrick
(18 April 1898 - 13 March 1981)

Motor car manufacturer, born at Middleton, County Cork, Ireland, the son of Patrick Hennessy, an estate foreman and a Roman Catholic, and his wife Mary née Benn (a Protestant who had been disowned by her family on her marriage), he was educated at Christ Church School before running away to join the Royal Inniskilling Fusiliers, under age in 1914. He was commissioned, captured by the Germans, and after the war took a government-funded agricultural course at Cork University. In 1920 he secured a job in the foundry of the new Ford tractor plant in Cork. Gaining experience in the blacksmith's forge, the machine shop, the assembly line, testing and demonstrating, he was transferred to Ford's British plant at Trafford Park, Manchester, to learn about sales techniques. Back at Cork in 1923 he became Ford sales representative for Ireland and then service manager in 1924. His big chance came in 1928 when, following the collapse of the world tractor market, Henry Ford decided to concentrate his world tractor plant at Cork. When Hennessy so organised production in Cork that he was able to meet a huge order for spares for 25,000 tractors from the USSR - an order which could not be met at Dearborn - he was marked for promotion. He became purchase manager for Ford of Britain in 1931 and efficiently co-ordinated parts supply for the Model Y car being built at the new Ford plant at Dagenham. In 1939 Hennessy was appointed general manager, one of three who ruled Ford of Britain under the chairmanship of Percival Perry (qv). During the Second World War Hennessy's work at the Ministry of Aircraft Production, 1940-41 earned him a knighthood; he spent the rest of the war at Dagenham and in 1945 was made a director of Ford of Britain. When Perry retired in 1948 Sir Patrick Hennessy became managing director, remaining until 1963. Meantime he became deputy chairman in 1950 and chairman in 1956, retiring in 1968. Under Hennessy, with markets buoyant, growth was rapid. Production at Dagenham was doubled; a greenfield site at Halewood near Liverpool was acquired for a new plant (opened in 1963); and new models, most notably the Cortina, appeared. Employment rose from nearly 25,000 in 1955 to 40,000 in 1960. Hennessy married, in 1923, Dorothy Margaret née Davis; they had two sons and a daughter. See *DBB*; Mira Wilkins and Frank E Hill, *American Business Abroad: Ford on Six Continents* (1964).

HERON, Michael (Gilbert)
(22 October 1934 -)

Chairman of the Post Office, whose father worked all his life behind a Post Office counter. He has described himself as an absolute product of the welfare state: he won a scholarship to St Joseph's Academy, Blackheath, and then went into the army and up to New College, Oxford. He became a management trainee at BOCM Silcock Ltd, working as managing director of Feeds. Between 1976 and 1982 he was chairman of Batchelors Food, subsequently joining Unilever as a deputy co-ordinator of its world-wide food and drinks interests. In 1986 he became a director at Unilever, working as head of personnel. In 1992 he competed with Michael Perry (qv) for the top job at Unilever and when he was disappointed in that quest he accepted the chairmanship of the Post Office in succession to Sir Bryan Nicholson (qv). Heron and his chief executive, William Cockburn (qv), took charge of an organisation with some 200,000 workers and an uncertain future, with the Government about to decide whether to go ahead with the Post Office's privatisation. He has refused to be drawn on whether he himself favours privatisation - though he has stated that if it does happen the Post Office should be kept together. Heron shunned outside commercial directorships at Unilever, but is involved with various CBI committees and projects. In 1958 he married Celia née Hunter: they have one son and two daughters.

HEWLETT, Alfred
(1830 - 14 September 1918)

Mining engineer, colliery viewer and colliery owner, born at Oxford, eldest son of Alfred Hewlett, a schoolmaster and later curate of the Church of England, and his wife Catherine née Gibson, at the age of 14 he was articled to Mr Piggott, the Earl of Bradford's agent and manager of his collieries near Bolton. On qualifying he became manager of Charnock Richard Collieries at Chorley belonging to Joseph Darlington, whose daughter he married c. 1852/53. In 1853 he went to Ince near Wigan to assist his brother-in-law, James Darlington, in managing the Ince Hall Coal & Canal Co, becoming mine manager in 1854. Hewlett secured the coveted post of mining agent and manager of the 24th Earl of Crawford and Balcarres' collieries near Wigan in 1860. For the next five years he negotiated the formation of the Wigan Coal & Iron Co, a merger of the Earl's 16 collieries with Kirkless Hall Coal & Iron Co, Standish & Shevington Cannel Co and Broomfield Colliery. When the Wigan Coal & Iron Co was registered in 1865 Hewlett became managing director. He held this post until 1912. The business in 1865 produced 2.2 million tons of coal; in 1907, 5 million tons. In the latter year it employed 10,000. Hewlett married Elizabeth née Darlington; they had two daughters. See *DBB*.

HEYWORTH, Geoffrey
Baron Heyworth of Oxton
(18 October 1894 - 16 June 1974)

Food and detergent manufacturer, born at Oxton, near Birkenhead, the son of Thomas Blackwell Heyworth, a Liverpool corn merchant, and his wife Florence née Myers, he was educated at Dollar Academy in Scotland. In 1912 he joined Lever Bros at Port Sunlight at 15s a week, moving to the accounts department and then to Canada, 1913-24, interrupted by war service with the Canadian Highlanders, 1915-18. Back in England he took charge of exports and the campaign to sell Lux toilet soap. He was appointed chairman of Crosfields and in 1931 became one of the three men assigned to rationalise Lever's soap trade (there were 49 manufacturing and 48 selling companies and it took until 1960 to reduce them to one). Between 1941 and 1959 he was chairman of Unilever Ltd and vice-chairman of Unilever NV, the Dutch side of the business, and a member of the committee of three who ran both sides. With the support of senior executives like Sir Herbert Davis (qv), Heyworth transformed Unilever. Members of the old founding families were removed from top management and replaced by professional managers. The company, a large multinational business, was taken into new markets, notably frozen foods. One of Heyworth's great concerns was to improve links between industry and higher education, and he was a prime mover in establishing the Administrative Staff College. Heyworth was knighted in 1948 and created a baron in 1955. He married, in 1924, Lois née Dunlop of Ontario. See *DBB*; Charles Wilson, *The History of Unilever* (3 vols, 1954-68).

HILL, Edward John
(27 October 1897 - 2 January 1965)

Clearing banker, second son of J W Hill, he joined the Romford branch of Lloyds Bank in 1915, became a branch manager in 1929 (at Willesden Green) and after a series of London appointments went to head office as an assistant general manager in 1945. From joint general manager in 1948 he was promoted to deputy chief general manager in 1951 and then chief general manager in 1953, retiring in 1960, a period in which the chairman throughout was Sir Oliver Franks (qv). 'Elegant and intellectual, Hill was a very proficient banker, decisive and far-seeing', realising the need for medium-term lending to finance the export of capital goods in the postwar world, and keen to take the bank into the hire-purchase market (which he did in 1958). On his retirement he joined the board of Lloyds Bank. He was also a director of the National Bank of New Zealand and of Bowmaker Ltd. Leisurely walking was his main pastime. Hill married twice: first, in 1924, to Joyce Mary Owen (d 1951), by whom he had two sons and a daughter; second, in 1953, to Gertrude Sylvia Frank. See *The Times*, 4 January 1965; J R Winton, *Lloyds Bank, 1918-1969* (1982).

HILL, Sir Enoch
(10 September 1865 - 13 May 1942)

Building society manager, born at Ball Haye Green, Leek, Staffordshire, eldest of the four sons and three daughters of Henry Hill and Elizabeth née Taylor, both manual workers in the local silk spinning industry, he became a 'half-timer' in the silk industry when 8 years old, and a full-timer at 13. In his teens he had numerous casual jobs and was apprenticed as a printer. Hill's life opportunities came through the local parish church where he was an energetic Sunday School teacher, Band of Hope secretary and lay reader. The vicar and the local grammar school headmaster rectified deficiencies in his education; the vicar gave him a hand printing press, allowing Hill to set up on his own; and he met his first wife, the orphaned neice of an accountant who, though blind, was secretary to the Leek United Building Society. While developing his printing business, Hill read for the Leek United secretary, which led to his appointment as clerk in 1886 and secretary in 1896 (after which he transferred his printing business to his brothers). Succeeding in doubling the Leek United's assets to £100,000 by 1902, Hill was chosen, out of 300 candidates, as secretary for the Halifax Permanent Building Society. A strong believer in home ownership, he vigorously promoted the Halifax in a range of ways, from varying share options to high profile publicity. Assets rose from £1.4 million in 1902 to £2.8 million in 1910, £5.9 million in 1918 and £33 million in 1928. By 1906 it was the largest building society in the UK, and held this place under Hill's leadership. After 1918 the housing shortage, coupled with the Rent Restriction Acts and low interest rates, increased the demand for owner-occupation which Hill met by expanding the Halifax network, moving to London in 1924 (though headquarters remained at Halifax where a new head office was opened in 1921 and again in 1931) and merging in 1928 with the Halifax Equitable Building Society. The new Halifax Building Society had assets of £47 million, or 17.5 per cent of all building society assets, increasing to £123 million, or 16.2 per cent of the building society total in 1938. Hill, general manager 1902-38, became managing director in 1916 and president and managing director of the Halifax in 1928, stepping down in 1938 but remaining a director until his death. Sir Enoch Hill (he was knighted in 1928) was also chairman of the National Association of Building Societies, 1921-33, supporting his successor Harold Bellman (qv) in seeking a code of practice for the industry. A Conservative and a Freemason, Hill was an unsuccessful candidate in four general elections. He married twice: first, in 1887, to Esther Haynes (d 1904), by whom he had a son; second, in 1906, to Bertha H B Gee. See *DBB*; O R Hobson, *A Hundred Years of the Halifax* (1953).

HILTON, Sir Robert Stuart
(28 December 1870 - 10 October 1943)
Electrical equipment and steel manufacturer, born in Wigan, the son of Thomas Hilton, a cotton spinner and later an agent, and Rose Elizabeth Hawkins née Hawthorne. After attending Sedbergh School and Wigan School of Mines and wartime work organising munitions in Birmingham, Hilton became managing director of Metropolitan-Vickers Electrical Co in 1919. During 1927-39 he was managing director at United Steel Companies and helped Sir Walter Benton Jones (qv) in its financial reconstruction in the early 1930s. An advocate of industry-wide rationalisation and cooperation, Hilton became president of the British Iron & Steel Federation in 1938. He was knighted in 1942. In 1899 he married Julia Ethel, daughter of James McBryde: they had one son and one daughter. He left £24,250. See Jonathan S. Boswell, *Business Policies in the Making: Three Steel Companies Compared* (1983); *DBB*.

HILTON, William
(1833 - 17 December 1909)
Textile machinery manufacturer, born at Royton, in his late teens he went to work for the Oldham textile machine makers who from 1854 were known as Platt Bros & Co. He ascended the engineering works hierarchy, from foreman in the speeds department to general works manager, director (1895), and vice-chairman (from 1902), serving under John Dodd (qv). Raised in the Church of England, in adulthood Hilton was a Primitive Methodist and a Liberal. He was appointed a JP in 1907. Hilton was married twice and left a widow, a son and three daughters. See *Oldham Chronicle*, 25 December 1909.

HINTON, Christopher
Baron Hinton of Bankside
(12 May 1901 - 22 June 1983)
Nuclear engineer, born at Tisbury, Wiltshire, the son of Frederick Henry Hinton, a schoolmaster, and Kate née Christopher. Educated at Chippenham Secondary School, he was apprenticed with the Great Western Railway at Swindon (taking evening classes at Swindon Technical College), and then took a first class degree at Trinity College, Cambridge, in mechanical sciences. Aged 25, he joined Brunner Mond (later part of ICI) and four years later became chief engineer. The Second World War brought him into public service as deputy-director general of the explosive-filling factories. In 1945 he took charge of what was to become the Industrial Group of the UK's atomic energy project, which soon provided Britain with its first atomic bomb and then in 1956 (when Calder Hall was opened) a world lead in civil nuclear power. Between 1956 and 1964 Hinton was first chairman of the Central Electricity Generating Board (a vast enterprise with an annual income of £600 million and annual capital expenditure of £400 million), where he continued to influence the size and structure of the British nuclear power programme. Hinton was chairman of the international executive committee of the World Energy Conference, 1962-68, adviser to the World Bank, president of the Institution of Mechanical Engineers 1966-67, president of both the Council of the Engineering Institutions and of the new Fellowship of Engineering, and was active in various House of Lords Select Committees. He was awarded a string of honours rare for an engineer, including a knighthood in 1951, KBE 1957, FRS 1954, a life peerage in 1964 and the Order of Merit 1976. In 1931 he married Lillian Boyer: they had one daughter. See Christopher Hinton, *The Future of Nuclear Power* (1957); Margaret Gowing, *Independence and Deterrence* (1974); *DBB*; *DNB*.

HIRST, Hugo
Baron Hirst of Witton
(26 November 1863 - 22 January 1943)
Electrical engineering entrepreneur, born at Altenstadt, near Munich, the son of Emanuel Hirsch, a distiller. Hirst came to England in 1880 to escape Prussian militarism, and in 1886 joined Gustav Byng in selling electrical accessories. In 1900 the business became the General Electric Co capitalised at £85,000. After the War, Hirst launched GEC on an ambitious and successful programme to dominate electrical engineering: profits exceeded £1 million in 1925; and the workforce grew from 14,000 in 1919 to 40,000 in 1939. A protectionist, business nationalist and imperialist,

Hirst was involved in numerous trade, technical and political societies: for example, he was president of the FBI in 1936 and 1937. He was created a baronet in 1935 and received a baronetcy in 1934. In 1892 he married his cousin, Leontine, by whom he had one son and two daughters. He left £498,651. See Robert Jones and Oliver J D Marriott, *Anatomy of a Merger: A History of GEC, AEI and English Electric* (1970); *DBB*; *DNB*.

HIVES, Ernest Walter
1st Baron Hives of Duffield
(21 April 1886 - 24 April 1965)

Aircraft manufacturer, born at Reading, the son of John Hives, a factory clerk, and Mary née Washbourn, he was educated locally at Redlands School, worked in garages for five years and then in 1908 joined Rolls-Royce where he remained. By 1911 he was testing cars at Brooklands. Henry Royce (qv) liked him and from 1912 Hives was involved in engine production. Royce died in 1933 and Hives in 1936 became general works manager at Derby and oversaw the development of the Merlin engine which powered the Spitfire and Hurricane fighter planes of the Second World War. From 1942 Hives directed the development of the jet engine, discarding Whittle's design in favour of the axial flow jet. He became managing director of Rolls-Royce in 1946 and served as chairman, 1950-57, heading a workforce which had grown from nearly 7,000 in 1935 to nearly 38,000 in 1955. Under his leadership the firm developed both the pure jet (eg the Avon engine) and the turboprop engine (eg the Dart); and motorcar manufacture was moved to Crewe the war. Hives was made a Companion of Hon. in 1943 and raised to the peerage in 1950. He married Gertrude Ethel née Warwick in 1913; they had four sons and three daughters. See *DBB*; Ian Lloyd, *Rolls-Royce* (3 vols, 1978).

HODGSON, Howard (Osmond Paul)
(22 February 1950 -)

Funeral director and entrepreneur, born in Birmingham, the son of Osmond Paul Charles Hodgson and Sheila Mary née Ward. Educated at Aiglon College, Villars, Switzerland, and Birmingham Tutorial College, he joined the family funeral business, Hodgson & Sons (founded in 1850), in 1969. In 1975 he bought out his father for £14,000. By a process of managerial reform and merger, he transformed his father's almost moribund (!) business into an international funeral conglomerate, which when it was floated as a public company in 1990 was worth £90 million. Shortly afterwards, Hodgson retired and sold his shares for £9 million, ostensibly to concentrate on writing and broadcasting. But he continued his interest in business and launched a consultancy with John Gunn (qv), which ended in November 1992. He also ran Hodgson Securities, which by 1993 was in receivership, and was involved in a controversial computer accounting franchise business named Prontac. In 1972 he married Marianne née Katibien: they have two sons and one daughter (one son is deceased). See Howard Hodgson, *How to Become Dead Rich* (1992).

HOGG, Sir Christoper
(2 August 1936 -)

Synthetic textiles company executive, the son of Anthony Wentworth Hogg and Monica Mary née Gladwell. Educated at Marlborough College and Trinity College, Oxford (MA, Honorary Fellow 1982), he studied business at Harvard University (MBA) and in Lausanne at IMEDA (Institute ... for Enterprise). He joined the bankers Hill Samuel in 1963 and then moved to the Industrial Reorganisation Corporation (IRC) in 1966. In 1968 he joined Courtaulds, became a director in 1973, and was chief executive between 1979 and 1991 and chairman, 1980-93. Faced by imports and shrinking overseas markets, Hogg began reversing the expansionist strategy in cotton and hosiery industries of his predecessor, Lord Kearton (qv). But Hogg expanded other parts of Courtaulds' old empire - in paints, chemicals and packaging - so that the result in 1990 was a demerger of Courtauld's into two main categories: those concerned with polymer science; and the older fibres, chemicals and films division. In 1992 turnover was £1,943 million with pre-tax profits of £201 million. Courtaulds employs some 23,000 workers, with about 11,000 in the UK (in 1975 the firm had employed a UK workforce of 100,000). Hogg is also chairman of Courtaulds Textiles and Reuters Holdings, and a director of the Bank of England and a trustee of the Ford Foundation. He married in 1961 Anne Patricia née Cathie: they have two daughters. He was knighted in 1985. See Christopher Hogg, *Masers and Lasers* (1963); Corinne Simcock, *A Head for Business* (1992).

HOLDEN, Sir Edward Hopkinson
(11 May 1848 - 23 July 1919)

Clearing banker, born at the *Bull's Head*, Tottington near Bury, Lancashire, the son of Henry Holden, a calico bleacher and later a beerseller, and his wife Ann née Hopkinson, he attended the Wesleyan elementary school in nearby Summerseat. An introduction from a fellow member of Summerseat Wesleyan chapel gained him an apprenticeship with the Bolton branch of the

Manchester & County Bank in 1866, starting at £30 annually. Promoted to a Manchester head office clerkship in 1873, Holden took evening classes at Owen's College and tuition in law. His ascent to the heights began when he moved to the Birmingham & Midland Bank as accountant at £300 a year in 1881. Though having less than a dozen branches its directors had determined to expand by acquisition, rather than succumb to more aggressive rivals. Holden became the instrument and then the architect of this policy. His duties included the appraisal of premises and selection of staff for new branches and (with J A Christie, the bank's sub-manager) supervision of amalgamations with other banks. Starting with the Union Bank of Birmingham in 1883, a string of other local banks were acquired. By 1890 the B&M had total deposits of £5.6 million and 45 branches. In 1891 Holden negotiated the B&M's first acquisition of a London bank (the Central Bank of London) after which the bank was renamed the London & Midland Bank and Holden and Christie were made joint general managers at £2,000 a year. In the 1890s Holden was the energetic exponent of banking amalgamations. By 1898 the Midland (as it became known) had deposits of £32 million and 250 branches in England and Wales. Holden's acquisition of the City Bank in 1898 gave the Midland a prestigious presence on Threadneedle Street, London, and earned Holden promotion to managing director and a salary of £5,000. He was forced to delegate administration to three joint general managers in order to secure another wave of amalgamations and to develop links with overseas banks. He pursued several innovations including a foreign exchange department (set up in 1905), new technological systems (eg telephones) and improved bank staff training. In 1908 Holden became chairman of the Midland emerging as leader of the whole banking community. He continued to engineer amalgamations, believing scale would allow British banks to remain internationally competitive, and dealt personally only with the largest or most powerful customers. At the time of his death the Midland had over £349 million of deposits and a network of 1,300 branches, making it the largest bank in the world. During the First World War Sir Edward Holden (he was made a baronet in 1909 and twice declined a peerage) was very influential, being credited with the idea of issuing currency notes and in 1915 went to New York with Lord Reading to negotiate stabilisation of exchange rates. In his last years he trained Reginald McKenna (qv) as his successor. A Liberal and a free-trader Holden was MP for Heywood, Manchester, 1906-10; he combined Wesleyan Methodism with service as a churchwar-

den and active freemasonry. He married, in 1877, Annie Cassie (d 1905) from Aberdeen; they had two sons and a daughter. See *DBB*; A R Holmes and Edwin Green, *Midland: 150 Years of Banking Business* (1986).

HOLDEN, Sir George
(16 April 1890 - 26 September 1937)

Cotton manufacturer, the son of Sir Edward Thomas Holden (1831-1926) and his wife Helen Sarah Yates. He was the managing director of Combined Egyptian Mills Ltd, which at his death controlled 35 mills in Lancashire, with a total spindleage of over 3 million, and a workforce of over 10,000. He was also vice-president of the Master Cotton Spinners' Federation and a member of the Manchester Chamber of Commerce. A magistrate, he was mayor of Leigh between 1920 and 1922. He succeeded to the baronetcy in 1926. He married Margaret Adamson née Smith in 1913: they had three sons and one daughter.

HOLDEN-BROWN, Sir Derrick
(14 February 1923 -)

Beverage conglomerate executive, the son of Harold Walter Holden-Brown and Beatrice Florence née Walker. Educated at Westcliff, he served in the Royal Navy during the Second World War, before taking the advice of his father (a director of United Drapery Stores) to train as an accountant. He qualified in 1948. He held a number of posts in drinks and brewing companies - Hiram Walker & Sons, Cairnes Ltd, Grant's of St James's, Ind Coope - becoming chairman of the Victoria Wine Co in 1964. This eventually brought him onto the board of Allied-Lyons, succeeding Sir Keith Showering (qv) as chairman and chief executive in 1982. Holden-Brown made Allied-Lyons more aggressive and efficient and also expanded overseas. In the mid-1980s he successfully resisted a bid by the Australian drinks giant Elders IXL and by 1987 had established an important presence in North America by purchasing Hiram Walker-Gooderham & Worts in Canada. Operating in three main divisions - brewing, wines and spirits and food - sales of Allied-Lyons' famous brands (Skol, Harvey's Bristol Cream, Teachers, Tetley tea and Lyons coffee) have made it the largest beverage company outside the US and the fourth largest in the world. Holden-Brown retired as chairman in 1991 - a year after the company had lost £147 million on foreign exchange dealing - and was succeeded by Michael Jackaman (qv). A director of Sun Alliance & London Insurance and the Midland Bank, Holden-Brown has also served as chairman of the Brewers' Society, 1978-80. He was knighted in 1979. He married in 1950 Patricia Mary Ross

Mackenzie: they have one son and one daughter. See Asa Briggs, *Wine for Sale: Victoria Wine and the Liquor Trade 1860-1984* (1985).

HOLDSWORTH, Sir (George) Trevor
(29 May 1927 -)

Industrialist, the son of William Albert Holdsworth and Winifred née Bottomley. Educated at Hanson Grammar School, Bradford, and Keighley Grammar School, he trained as a chartered accountant with Rawlinson, Greaves & Mitchell in Bradford, 1944-51. After a spell at Bowater Paper Corporation, he joined Guest, Keen & Nettlefolds in 1963. In 1970 he joined the board and was appointed chairman of GKN in 1980, the year the steel and engineering company announced a loss of £1 million - the first since it was incorporated in 1902. Holdsworth immdediately began restructuring the group: he reduced the workforce from 93,000 in 1980 to 38,000 in 1988; moved out of steel; fostered the development of automotive and industrial-service businesses; and began to spread overseas. In 1989, the year after he handed over the chairmanship to (Sir) David Lees (qv), GKN reported pre-tax profits of £215 million - a dramatic improvement from 1980. Besides a number of outside directorships, Holdsworth was also chairman of Allied Colloids Group since 1983; chairman of British Satellite Broadcasting, 1987-90; and deputy chairman of the Prudential, 1988-92. In 1990 he became chairman of National Power, the newly-privatised electricity generator, which in 1991 had a turnover of £4,378 million (pre-tax profit £479 million) and a workforce of over 15,000. Holdsworth was knighted in 1982. In 1951 he married Patricia June Ridler: they have three sons.

HOLE, Francis George
(29 November 1904 - 22 September 1973)

Railway hotel company executive, eldest son of Francis Hole, he was educated at King's College School, London, and then trained with Thompson McLintock & Co, qualifying as a chartered accountant in 1929. He became assistant to Arthur Towle, Controller of Hotel Services on the London, Midland & Scottish Railway in 1934. Towle's father, Sir William Towle, had promoted hotel-keeping with the expansion of railways in the nineteenth century so that the LMS chain included hotels of distinction like Gleneagles and Turnberry. Hole succeeded Towle in 1945 and became a member of the Hotels Executive of the British Transport Commission when the railways were nationalised in 1948. With dedication and attention to detail Hole skillfully assimilated all the hotels of the four former railway groups into a single structure and, simultaneously, achieved high standards of service throughout the ensuing hotel network. Hole became chief of British Transport Hotels and Catering Services, 1954-55; general manager, 1955-58; chairman and general manager, 1959-62; then, following the abolition of the British Transport Commission, director and general manager of British Transport Hotels Ltd, 1963-68. He chaired the British Hotels and Restaurants Association, 1963-65. Hole married, in 1934, Jean Mary née Thomas; they had a son and a daughter. See *The Times*, 10 October 1973.

HOLLAND-MARTIN, Robert Martin
(10 October 1872 - 27 January 1944)

Railway transport executive, born at Overbury Court, Tewkesbury, the son of the Reverend Frederick Whitmore Holland and Penelope née Martin (he took the additional surname of Martin by Royal licence in 1917). Educated at Eton and Trinity College, Oxford, he joined the board of the London & South Western Railway in 1910. He became a director of the Southern Railway Co on its formation, and was made deputy chairman in 1932 and chairman from 1935 (when it employed 65,000) until his death. He also served as chairman of the Railway Companies' Association. He was deputy chairman of Martins Bank, with which his family had long been associated, and chairman of the London board of the bank. He was president of the Institute of Bankers, 1929-31, and served for thirty years as honorary secretary of the Bankers' Clearing House. He was on the boards of the Gas Light & Coke Co, a governor of Guy's Hospital, and a fellow (and for many years treasurer) of the Society of Antiquaries. Chairman from 1925 to 1932 of the County of London Territorial Army & Air Force Association, and a sheriff of Worcestershire in 1938, he was active in the Home Guard from 1940. He married in 1897 Eleanor Mary née Martin: they had six sons. See *Southern Railway Magazine*, March-April 1944.

HOLLINS, Sir Frank
(16 April 1843 - 27 January 1924)

Cotton manufacturer, born in Stockport, fourth son of Edward Hollins, a cotton manufacturer, and his wife Margaret Harding née Woody, he was educated at Bridgnorth Grammar School and Rossall School and then entered his father's firm in Preston. After his father's retirement in 1872 a bitter fraternal quarrel, finally resolved in the Notttinghamshire Assizes in 1879, left Frank in charge of Hollins Bros. He boldly merged in 1885 with the ailing Preston giant Horrockses, Miller &

Co, of which he became managing director, and two years later merged with the Bolton firm of Crewdson, Cross & Co. The business was rationalised, economies of scale effected and by 1913 Horrockses, Crewdson was employing 6,500 workers, 300,000 spindles (including 94,000 rings) and 7,500 looms. Sir Frank Hollins (he was made a baronet in 1907) sold Horrockses for £5.25 million to the Amalgamated Cotton Mills Trust in 1919. Hollins, a Liberal and a free trader, was chairman of the Master Spinners' Association, 1894-1917, and was largely responsible for the industrial peace which then prevailed in northern Lancashire. He married, in 1875, Dora Emily Susan Cox; they had four sons. See DBB.

HOLMES, Major-General Sir Noel Galway
(25 December 1891 - 24 December 1982)

Coal Board divisional chairman, born in Galway, Ireland, the fourth son of Captain H W Holmes, he was educated at Bedford School and then pursued a distinguished military career, serving in both World Wars and reaching the rank of major general in 1943 and Deputy Quartermaster-General at the War Office, 1943-46. He retired in 1946, the year he was knighted, and became chairman of the North Eastern Division (which covered Yorkshire), one of nine, of the National Coal Board. Early on, Galway was criticised by both NUM union leaders and NCB central management for the high-handed manner in which he responded to the unjustified Grimethorpe strike of August 1947. More positively, area managers in his division were given more scope to settle practical issues than were the Scottish area managers, for example. Under the NCB chairman, Sir Hubert Houldsworth (qv), Holmes's division by 1955 was the largest in employment (139,400) but second in terms of output and productivity (in each case, behind the East Midlands), and it was slipping compared to its previous record. Holmes retired in 1957. He married twice: first, in 1920, Mary née Clifford (d 1978) by whom he had a son and a daughter; second, in 1979, Irene Tennant. See William Ashworth, The History of the British Coal Industry vol 5 1946-1982: The Nationalised Industry (1986).

HOLMES, Sir Peter (Fenwick)
(27 September 1932 -)

Oil company executive, born in Athens, the son of Gerald Hugh Holmes and his wife Caroline Elizabeth. His family had roots in the consular service and he lived in Budapest until he was 8, before moving with his British father and American mother to the US during the Second World War. He read history at Trinity College, Cambridge (MA), where he met and married in 1955 Judith Millicent née Walker (they have three daughters). After graduation they trekked the Himalayas, which resulted in his first travel book. Holmes was awarded the Military Cross during service with the British Army in Korea. He joined Shell in 1956, and after steady promotion headed its operations in Libya and Nigeria. He became managing director of Shell Transport & Trading (one of the two holding companies operating Shell) in 1982, and was appointed chairman in 1985. Under Holmes's co-chairmanship, Shell became the world's most profitable company at the end of the 1980s and succeeded Esso as the world's leading oil company. Shell handles about a tenth of the world's oil and natural gas outside the former centrally planned economies. In 1991 the net proceeds of Shell companies were £58 billion and the company had a workforce of 133,000. In 1992 Holmes became chairman of Shell's committee of managerial directors. He was knighted in 1988. See Peter Holmes, Mountains and a Monastery (1958).

HOLT, Sir Richard Durning
(1868 - 22 March 1941)

Shipowner and dock company chairman, the son of Robert Durning Holt (1832-1908) of Sefton Park, Liverpool, senior partner in George Holt & Co, cotton brokers, he was educated at Winchester and New College, Oxford. He joined his uncles Alfred and Philip in Alfred Holt & Co, shipowners in the China trade, becoming a partner of what in the interwar years was one of the largest private shipowning companies in the world. By the late 1930s his firm managed the Blue Funnel Line which included the Ocean Steam Ship Co and the China Mutual Steam Navigation Co. He was chairman of the Elder Dempster Lines Ltd from 1932 and of Glen Line Ltd. Holt became a member of the Mersey Docks & Harbour Board in 1896 after a prolonged business tour in the Far East. Thereafter he played an increasingly important role in the counsels of the Board and served as chairman, 1927-29 and 1930-41, when it employed about 16,000, as before the First World War under Robert Gladstone (qv). Under Holt's leadership the Gladstone system of docks was completed in 1927. In the Board's negotiations with the Merseyside Co-ordination Committee Holt supported the construction of the Birkenhead tunnel, but not a Wallasey branch, which led to the Mersey Tunnel Act of 1925 and the opening of the Mersey Tunnel in 1934. Holt was chairman of the Liverpool Steam Ship Owners' Association in 1923 and president of the Chamber of Shipping of the United Kingdom in 1937. He was a director of Martins Bank Ltd, 1928-41, acting as deputy chairman, 1934-37 and

1938-41, and as chairman, 1937-38. Outside business, Holt was MP (a staunch Liberal like his father) for the Hexham Division of Northumberland, 1907-18. He was created a baronet in 1935. He married, in 1897, Eliza Lawrence, eldest daughter of John Wells of New Brunswick, NJ, USA; they had three daughters. See Stuart Mountfield, *Western Gateway: A History of the Mersey Docks and Harbour Board* (1965); *The Times*, 24 March 1941; P J Waller, *Democracy and Sectarianism: A Political and Social History of Liverpool, 1868-1939* (1981).

HORNBY, Charles Harry St John
(25 June 1867 - 26 April 1946)

Book and newspaper distributor and printer, born at Much Dewchurch, Herefordshire, the eldest son of Charles Edward Hornby, a curate, and Harriet Catherine née Turton. Educated at Harrow, he read classics and literature at New College, Oxford. Called to the Bar in 1892, he gave up law in that year to join W H Smith & Son at the invitation of W F D Smith (later Viscount Hambledon) (qv). He became a partner in 1894. Largely under his direction Smith's, which had been established in 1792 in London, was transformed from a business consisting of railway bookstalls into a national chain of distinctive shops. In the words of the firm's historian: 'Hornby was the last of the great Victorians who had given W H Smith a national reputation and made its history read rather like a Victorian novel'. Under Hornby turnover increased from about £1.5 million to over £17 million from 1894 to 1946; annual net profits from £157,000 to about £1.5 million. Deeply interested in the art of printing, he extended Smith's activities in this direction and also founded the Ashendene Press as a vehicle for his private designs. A collector of medieval and Renaissance manuscripts, he was a trustee of the Wallace Collection and the British Museum. He married in 1898 Cicely née Barclay: they had three sons and two daughters. See Charles Wilson, *First With the News: The History of W H Smith, 1792-1972* (1985).

HORNBY, Michael Charles St John
(2 January 1899 - 7 December 1987)

Newsagent and bookshop company executive, eldest son of Charles Harry St John Hornby (qv), partner of W H Smith & Son, and his wife Cicely née Barclay, he was educated at Winchester and Sandhurst (where he won the sword of honour) before serving as a lieutenant with the Grenadier Guards in France in 1917-18. He then went to New College, Oxford, 1919-21, before joining W H Smith & Son in 1921. He became a partner in 1924, a director of W H Smith & Son Ltd from 1929 and, after joining his old regiment and holding staff appointments during the Second World War, its vice-chairman, 1944-65; he was also a director of the holding company, W H Smith & Son (Holdings) Ltd, 1949-69. In the tightly-knit family firm of Smiths, Hornbys and Aclands of the 1930s, Michael Hornby became the expert on the wholesale side of the business. After the partnership was turned into a public company in 1949 (to pay off the death duties of Lord Hambleden), Michael Hornby became one of four managing directors. He was especially good at picking and encouraging subordinates. In the 1960s he resisted the tendency to spread selling lines. Outside business his many interests included music (he was a fine pianist), poetry, gardening and foxhunting. He married Nicolette Joan née Ward in 1928 and had two sons and a daughter, the eldest son being Sir Simon Hornby (qv). See *The Times*, 11 December 1987; Charles Wilson, *First with the News* (1985).

HORNBY, Sir Simon (Michael)
(29 December 1934 -)

Newspaper and book retailer and distributor, the son of Michael Hornby (qv) and Nicolette Joan née Ward. His father was vice-chairman of the W H Smith & Son Ltd, 1944-65; his grandfather had helped transform the business after joining in 1893. Educated at Eton and New College, Oxford (where he read law), he spent six months at Harvard Business School and six months at J C Penney, the American retailer. After service in the Grenadier Guards between 1953 and 1955, Hornby joined W H Smith & Son in 1958, was appointed to the board in 1974 and has been chairman since 1982. He has continued Smith's strategy of retaining its long-standing qualities of dependability, despite charges that this has made the company a shade predictable and of having unfulfilled potential. But he has moved the group into more modern areas of marketing. Besides its famous book and newspaper shops, Smith's now operates W H Smith Retail, Our Price and has also bought the book chain founded by Tim Waterstone (qv), with a view to expansion in the US. In 1992 Hornby began a joint-venture with Virgin Retail, founded by Richard Branson (qv), to operate 14 megastores and 12 computer games centres. In 1992 Smith's turnover was £2,127 million (pre-tax profit £112 million), with a workforce of 29,318 (including 26,162 in the UK). Hornby is a non-executive director of Lloyds Bank and Pearson and a non-executive director and chairman of Lloyds Abbey Life. He is also chairman of the Design Council. Hornby was knighted in 1988. A friend of the Royal Family, he married in 1968 Sheran Cazalet, the daughter of the Queen Mother's racehorse trainer. See Charles Wilson, *First With the News: The History of W H Smith & Son 1792-1872* (1985).

HORNE, Robert Stevenson
Viscount Horne of Slamannan
(28 February 1871- 3 September 1940)

Railway executive and industrialist, born in Slamannan, Stirlingshire, the youngest son of the Reverend Robert Stevenson Horne and Mary née Lockhead. He achieved a first class degree in mental philosophy at Glasgow University, briefly joined the Scottish Bar, and then under Eric Geddes (qv) became involved in First World War railway reorganisation, eventually becoming Third Civil Lord at the Admiralty. In Lloyd George's Coalition Government he was successively Minister of Labour and Chancellor of the Exchequer. After leaving the Exchequer at the age of 51 his wider experience led him to join the board of several companies (in 1940 he was on the board of ten), chief among which was the National Smelting Co (which he chaired from 1923) and the Great Western Railway (elected chairman in 1934). Under Horne the GWR's ordinary dividend fell below 3 per cent for the first time, not least due to the decline of the mining and metals industries in South Wales. A Unionist MP for Hillhead, Glasgow, 1918-37, he was created KBE in 1918, CBE in 1920, and became a peer in 1937. As he was unmarried, the peerage became extinct. He left £64,923 gross. *DBB; DNB.*

HORNE, Sir William Edgar
(21 January 1856 - 26 September 1941)

Insurance company executive, born in London, the son of Edgar Horne (d 1904). Educated at Westminster School, he joined the family firm of Horne & Co, surveyors, headed by his father. The latter was also one of the founders and chairman (1877-1904) of the Prudential Insurance Co. Horne became a Prudential director in 1904, vice-chairman in 1917, and chairman from 1928 until his death. From 1910-22 he sat as Unionist MP for Guildford; he served as alderman and mayor of the City of Westminster; and was a president of the Surveyors' Institution. He married in 1886 Mary née Anderson: they had two sons and one daughter. Horne was knighted in 1929. See *The Times*, 29 September 1941.

HORTON, Robert (Baynes)
(18 August 1939 -)

Oil entrepreneur, the son of William Harold Horton and Dorothy Joan née Baynes. After attending King's School, Canterbury, he studied engineering at the University of St Andrews (BSc) and was Sloan Fellow at the Massachusetts Institute of Technology, 1970-71 (MSc). He joined British Petroleum in 1957 and earned a reputation as a troubleshooter. In the 1970s he dealt with BP's tanker fleet at a time of falling petrol consumption; and by the early 1980s had charge of rationalising BP's chemical division. In 1986 BP chairman, Sir Peter Walters (qv), made Horton chairman of Standard Oil in Cleveland, Ohio. Between 1986-88 Horton swung this BP subsidiary from a $250 million a year loss to $560 million profit. In 1990 he succeeded Walters as BP chairman, heading the third biggest oil company in the world (after Shell and Esso). BP was the leading British-based company in turnover, though underlying profitability had been in decline since 1988, when net profit was £1.43 billion. On his appointment Horton immediately instituted cutbacks, though he insisted on maintaining the dividend even in 1991 when profits slumped from £1.6 billion to £415 million. Having gambled on a price rise that never came and having made enemies with his abrasive style (in an American magazine he boasted: 'Because I am blessed with a good brain, I tend to get the right answer rather quicker and more often than most people'), he was replaced after a boardroom coup in June 1992 by rival David Simon (qv). A Conservative and member of the Bow Group, after his sacking by BP (for which he is believed to have been paid over £1 million compensation), he was appointed vice-chairman of British Rail to help pave the way for the Conservative Government's controversial privatisation. Horton himself was destined to become head of Railtrack, the new track authority. In 1962 he married Sally Doreen née Wells: they have one son and one daughter.

HOULDSWORTH, Sir Hubert Stanley
(20 April 1889 - 1 February 1956)

Chairman of the nationalised coal industry, born at Heckmondwike, Yorkshire, the son of Albert Houldsworth, a manufacturing chemist and his wife Susannah née Buckley, he was educated at Heckmondwike Grammar School and Leeds University whose staff he joined after a spell school teaching. He gained a DSc (1925) and then qualified as a barrister, taking silk in 1937, becoming a bencher in 1943 and recorder of Doncaster 1946-48. He specialised in the legal problems of the coal industry and during the Second World War rose to be Controller General in the Ministry of Fuel and Power (1944). After the coal mines were nationalised in 1946 Sir Hubert Houldsworth (he was knighted in 1944) was appointed chairman of the East Midlands Division. The East Midlands was dramatically more successful than the other eight divisions of the National Coal Board, producing in

1947 19 per cent of British coal from 10 per cent of the collieries. In 1951 Houldsworth was made chairman of the NCB. With new sources of energy on the horizon in the mid-1950s Houldsworth placed an emphasis on the search for new sources of coal. However, at the management level, heading a workforce of 700,000, he lacked the necessary administrative skills. His attempt in 1953 to devolve power downwards to the divisional and area managers, his presidential style and his distrust of NCB colleagues brought so much dissatisfaction that a committee of inquiry into NCB organisation under Dr Alexander Fleck (qv), ICI chairman, was appointed to investigate. Reporting in 1955, it judged the basic structure of the NCB sound but wanted the national board urgently reformed, with members offering experience of the industry and assuming specific responsibilities. All full-time NCB members put their resignations in the hands of the Minister. Sir Hubert Houldsworth died a few months before he planned to retire, just after being made a baronet. Houldsworth married, in 1919, Hilda Frances, daughter of Joseph Clegg; they had one son. See William Ashworth, *The History of British Coal vol 5 1946-1982: The Nationalised Industry* (1986); *DBB*.

HOULDSWORTH, Sir William Henry
(24 August 1834 - 18 April 1917)

Cotton and iron manufacturer, born in Manchester, fourth son of Henry Houldsworth, manager of his uncle Thomas's fine-spinning mills in Manchester, and his wife Helen née Hamilton, he was educated at Mr Jackson's school at Broughton, Manchester, and St Andrew's University. He joined his father and uncle in managing Thomas Houldsworth & Co and in the 1850s took over. In 1865 he moved the business to Reddish near Stockport and in 1870 set up a second company, the Reddish Spinning Co Ltd. These were absorbed into the Fine Cotton Spinners' & Doublers' Association, a merger of 31 firms, in 1898 chaired by Sir William Houldsworth (he was made a baronet in 1887, recognition for winning many Lancashire workers to the Conservative Party - he himself was MP for Manchester, 1883-1906). Its managing director was Alfred Dixon (qv). Houldsworth also inherited the Coltness Iron Works in Lanarkshire, the second largest in Scotland, which he actively headed from the late 1890s until his death. Both at Reddish and Coltness he demonstrated a concern for his employees' welfare. A tariff reformer, currency reformer (advocating bimetallism), promoter of the Manchester Ship Canal, and High Churchman, Sir William Houldsworth retired to his Scottish estate

in 1906. Houldsworth married Elisabeth née Crum in 1862; two sons survived. See *DBB*.

HOYLE, Joshua Craven
(c. 1866 - 16 March 1942)

Cotton spinner, the son of Edward Hoyle, of Moorlands, Bacup, Lancashire. He joined the family firm of Joshua Hoyle & Sons, cotton spinners and manufacturers, and was actively associated with it for over 50 years until he retired from the chairmanship for health reasons in 1935. At this date the firm employed 7,500. He served as alderman and mayor of Bacup and as a JP and DL, being made a freemen of the borough in 1920. He contested the Rossendale Division for the Conservatives in 1910. A prominent Freemason, Hoyle was also active in organising the local Volunteers. He married in 1893 Mary Beatrice née Law-Schofield (d 1937): he was survived by a daughter. See *Bacup Times*, 21 March 1942.

HUNTER, Sir Ellis
(18 February 1892 - 21 September 1961)

Steel company chairman, born at Great Ayton, Yorkshire, younger son of William Hunter, headmaster of the village school and his wife Alice née Davison, he was educated at Middlesbrough High School and then qualified with a local firm of accountants. After spending the First World War as a temporary civil servant in the Ministry of Munitions, he returned to the North East. He became a local partner with the accountants W B Peat & Co in 1922 and in 1928 a general partner in the newly-formed partnership of Peat, Marwick, Mitchell & Co. Among their clients was Dorman, Long & Co, the dominant steelmaker of the North East, employing 27,000 in 1935 but facing shrinking markets and led by a geriatric management. That year Hunter became secretary of Dormans' Debenture Holders' Association. In 1938 he became deputy chairman of Dorman, Long and managing director soon after. In the 1930s he got rid of the old guard, restructured the commercial side of the business and pruned corporate office administration. He was the power behind the figurehead chairmanship of Hamar Greenwood (qv). Despite Hunter's reforms, Dorman, Long's capital equipment and the firm's location were outdated. Hunter became chairman in 1948, remaining in charge until 1961. As chairman of the British Iron and Steel Federation, 1945-53, he presided over the blistering political debate over the control and ownership of the iron and steel industry. In 1945 he set up a committee to form a seven-year plan for the renovation and expansion of a nationalised steel industry. Eventually he came to oppose nationalisation and Churchill in 1951 denationalised steel on Hunter's advice. After 1953 Hunter confined himself to Dorman, Long, which in 1955 employed 31,000, again striving to put it on its feet. Hunter was knighted in 1948 and received the GBE in 1961. He married Winifred Grace née Steed in 1918; they had two daughters. See *DBB*; Steven Tolliday, *Business, Banking and Politics: The Case of British Steel, 1918-1939* (1987).

HUNTER, Sir George Burton
(19 December 1845 - 21 January 1937)
Shipbuilder, born at Sunderland, third son of Thomas Hunter, a shipwright, and Elizabeth née Rowntree, he had little schooling but had apprenticeships in engineering and shipbuilding (with W Pile, Hay & Co on the Wear). After further experience on the Clyde he returned to manage Pile's yard in 1871. After Pile's death in 1873 Hunter partnered S P Austin until 1879/80 when he moved to the Tyne to become partner with the widow of Charles S Swan, as C S Swan & Hunter, at Wallsend-on-Tyne, employing 700 men and boys on the seven-acre site. Hunter expanded the yards, adopted new technology (eg travelling cranes), and re-financed the business in 1903 with the formation of Swan, Hunter & Wigham Richardson Ltd. In 1906, when they built the 33,000 ton *Mauretania* for Cunard, the firm employed nearly 6,000. After the First World War Sir George Hunter (he was knighted in 1918) bolstered his firm's position by purchasing controlling interests in steel and diesel engine firms on the Clyde. Conservative investment policies enabled Swan, Hunter to survive the vastly reduced demand for shipping tonnage in the 1920s. Hunter resigned as chairman in 1928 but remained active to the last. A paternalist with little sympathy for unions, Hunter was a leader in his industry. He married, in 1873, Ann née Hudson; they had two sons and three daughters. See *DBB*.

HUTCHINGS, Gregory (Frederick)
(22 January 1947 -)
Industrialist, born in Venezuela, the son of a port captain with Gulf Oil. Educated at Uppingham, he became a management trainee with the construction group, Costain. For seven years he worked as a freelance consultant for the construction industry and also ran a holiday company for American tourists visiting Britain. He then attended Aston University to study for an MBA (he also has a BSc degree). In the late 1970s, a turning point in his career was a successful interview with Lord Hanson (qv), who invited him to join the Hanson Trust. Here he discovered how to get low-technology industries to perform better for their shareholders by better management and cutting bureaucracy -

techniques he was to use to good effect when in July 1983 he borrowed £1 million and bought F H Tomkins, an industrial fasteners company valued at £5 million. Hutchings - who differs from Hanson in rarely selling off companies if they perform well - built up one of the UK's fastest growing conglomerates, which included companies manufacturing bicycles, valves, lawnmowers and revolvers (Smith & Wesson). In 1992 he stymied his old boss, Lord Hanson, by successfully bidding £926 million for Rank Hovis McDougall, which gave Tomkins a market value of nearly £2 billion. The group has a workforce of 46,000. Hutchings is one of the highest paid UK executives, with a salary in 1992 approaching £1 million. His wife, Caroline, runs a film and television casting company.

HUTCHISON, James Seller
(15 October 1904 - 1 April 1986)
Chemical manufacturer, born in Glasgow, the son of R F Hutchison, he was educated at Greenock Academy and Glasgow University and qualified as a Scottish chartered accountant in 1928. His boss in the accountancy firm, Steven J L Hardie and an associate Robert Watson McCrone (a civil engineer), in 1922 formed Alloa Shipbreaking Co (renamed Metal Industries Ltd in the late 1920s) to buy and break up the German fleet at Scapa Flow and raise the ships one at a time and sell them for scrap. Using oxyacetylene cutters, they found it cheaper to make their own oxygen. They bought a new process for liquefying and storing liquid oxygen and Metal Industries' offshoot, Oxygen Industries Ltd, was soon in a patent battle with the market leader, the British Oxygen Co. Founded in 1886, but little more than a collection of producing centres in the late 1920s, BOC took over Oxygen Industries in an out-of-court settlement. Hardie joined the BOC board in the late 1930s and Hutchison followed, becoming a director in 1940. By the Second World War both gas and electric welding were used in ship construction, instead of riveting, and BOC expanded to meet demand in this and other areas. Hutchison was elected vice-chairman in 1947 and chairman in 1950, retiring in 1972. During his tenure it was the growth of the steel industry in the 1950s which undergirded the expansion of BOC and its 'tonnage' plants each making 10,000 million cubic feet of oxygen and 3,000 million cubic feet of nitrogen annually in the late 1950s. BOC's workforce rose from 7,000 in 1946 to 30,000 (worldwide) in 1966. Hutchison was especially responsible for directing BOC overseas after 1945. By 1955 BOC, based at Edmonton, north London, had 17 subsidiary companies in the UK and 12 abroad, employing 13,000 and 7,000 respectively. Hutchison married Kathleen née

Maude of Leeds; they had two daughters. See BOC, *Around the Group in 100 Years* (1986); *Times Prospectuses* 119 (1956).

HUTTON, Lucius Octavius
(1835 - 22 April 1911)

Railway company chairman, born at Elm Park, County Dublin, the son of Thomas Hutton, JP, DL, he was educated in Dublin and Germany and as a member by inheritance of the Irish ruling classes he took his place on the boards of public charities and companies alike. In 1900 he was a director of the Great Northern Railway Co of Ireland, the Royal Bank of Ireland, the Patriotic Assurance Co of Ireland, and the Waterford, Limerick & Western Railway Co. By 1907 he was chairman of the GNRCI (then employing 5,500 and the second largest railway in Ireland) and governor of the Royal Bank of Ireland, a JP for the County of Dublin, and a governor of the City of Dublin Hospital and the Stewart Institute for Imbeciles and Mental Diseases. He married, in 1858, Margaret, daughter of the Reverend William Bruce, by whom he had two daughters and a son. See Herbert H Bassett, *Men of Note in Finance and Commerce* (1900); E S Cosgrave and W T Pike, *Dublin and County Dublin in the Twentieth Century* (1908).

HUXHAM, Frank

Ammunition manufacturer, whose career has been misted over. In 1907 he was managing director of Kynoch Ltd, ammunition manufacturers of Birmingham, then employing 8,000 and very much directed by the elder Arthur Chamberlain (qv). Huxham was a chartered accountant by training, qualifying in 1892. The records of the Institute of Chartered Accountants of England and Wales show him to have been at Oakfield, Perry Bar in 1896, in Birmingham 1907-12 and in Glasgow 1913-16. He was no longer listed after 1920 so was possibly dead by then. See *Under Five Flags: The Story of Kynoch Works, Witton, Birmingham, 1862-1962* (1962).

HYDE, Frederick
(18 March 1870 - 24 January 1939)

Banker, born at Manchester, the son of the Reverend John Hyde. Educated privately, he became a junior clerk in the Derby Commercial Bank in 1885, later to be absorbed by the Midland Bank (then known as the Birmingham & Midland Bank). When the latter absorbed the Central Bank of London in 1891, Hyde moved to the City, where he came to the attention of the Midland's chairman, Sir Edward Holden (qv). In 1909 Holden appointed Hyde as general manager of the Midland. Hyde became one of Holden's trusted lieutenants, rivalling him in energy, and helping the chairman's expansionist plans (the Midland's total deposits rose from £94 million in 1913 to £349 million at the end of 1918). Hyde became a joint-managing director on Holden's death in 1919 and sole managing director in 1929 - a position he held until 1938 (by which time the Bank employed over 13,000). Under McKenna (qv) and Hyde the Midland in the difficult 1930s developed more cautiously than in the expansive pre-1914 world under Holden. Hyde was also managing director of the Midland Bank Executor & Trustee Co, a director of the Clydesdale Bank and of the North of Scotland Bank. He was president of the Institute of Bankers, 1927-29. He married Maud, third daughter of Richard Mountford Deeley: they had one son and two daughters. See A R Holmes and Edwin Green, *Midland: 150 Years of Banking History* (1986); *The Times*, 25 January 1939.

I

INGLIS, Sir James Charles
(9 September 1851 - 19 December 1911)

Railway manager, born in Aberdeen, the son of James Inglis, a baker, and his wife Jane née Smith, he was educated at Aberdeen Grammar School and Aberdeen University. Here he gained prizes in natural sciences and mathematics but left before taking a degree in order to train as an engineer, first with millwrights in Glasgow and then with a civil engineering practice in London. Between 1875 and 1892 he moved between salaried appointments and consultancy, in projects constructing docks, harbours and railways. In 1892 he joined the Great Western Railway as assistant engineer and then chief engineer, 1893-1903. In 1903 he became GWR chairman at a salary of £3,000 a year but was also retained as the company's consulting engineer at £1,000 a year. During his tenure he was responsible for improving the operating ratio (working expenditure as a percentage of gross revenue), increasing opportunities for staff training, the promotion of express and long distance trains, improved advertising, the introduction of road and rail motor services, and pooling agreements to reduce inter-company competition. However, he was unable to restrain his chief locomotive engineer, G J Churchward, from building faster but heavier trains which increased depreciation of the permanent way. Inglis was knighted in 1910. He never married. See *DBB*.

J

JACKAMAN, Michael Clifford John
(7 November 1935 -)

Beverage conglomerate executive, the only child of Air Commander Clifford Thomas Jackaman OBE and his wife Lily Margaret. Educated at Felsted School and Jesus College, Cambridge (where he read languages), from 1976 to 1978 he was a departmental manager at Harveys of Bristol Ltd, the renowned sherry firm, which was part of Allied Breweries (after 1979 known as Allied Lyons) under (Sir) Keith Showering (qv). Jackaman became a marketing director at Allied Lyons in 1978, until 1983; then served as chairman of Hiram Walker, Allied Lyons' North American drinks business, during 1983-91. In 1988 he was appointed vice-chairman at Allied Lyons, succeeding Sir Derrick Holden-Brown (qv) to the chairmanship in July 1991. He heads a world leader in food, drink and hospitality: with brands such as Beefeater, Courvoisier, Tetley Bitter and Tetley Tea, and with 6,000 pubs and Victoria Wine Stores. At the start of 1991-92 Jackaman and his board restructured the business (into spirits and wine, retailing, brewing and wholesaling, and food manufacturing divisions); sold off some of its older businesses (such as Showerings and Lyons Maid) to give Allied a tighter focus; and invested in various joint ventures overseas with Domecq, Suntory and Carlsberg. Jackaman aims to shake off Allied's image as the most sluggish earnings generator of the UK's big three foods and drinks combines. Allied Lyons's turnover rose from £5,133 million in 1991 to £5,360 million in 1992 (with pre-tax profits of £623 million and £610 million, respectively), with around 73,000 staff. In 1960 Jackaman married Valerie Jane Pankhurst: they have one son and one daughter.

JACKSON, William Fulton
(12 November 1855 - 30 November 1932)

Railway manager, born in Glasgow, the son of John Jackson, he was educated at St Enoch's Parish School, leaving at 16 with the Dux medal. For six years he worked for Messrs Westlands, Laidlaw & Co, first as clerk then as cashier and bookkeeper. In 1877 he moved to Edinburgh for a post in the office of the secretary of the North British Railway. Soon after he was put in charge of the Rates and Taxes Department, proving such a master of the subject that in 1898 he was chosen by the five Scottish railway companies to give evidence on their behalf before the Royal Commission on Local Taxation. The key to his success as a rating agent stemmed from his knowledge of his territory,

derived from walking over every section of the North British line, a distance of 1,250 miles. In July 1899 he was appointed manager of the North British Railway, holding the post until 1918. In 1907 the North British was, with 24,000 employees, the largest railway in Scotland. During Jackson's tenure the NBR expanded its domination of the railway network in Fife, against the opposition of Randolph Wemyss (qv), though as a concession to Wemyss built a third dock at Methil. The NBR also constructed a goods warehouse in High Street, Glasgow, and mineral lines in Lothian. Experienced in preparing and defending his company's parliamentary bills, Jackson was a skilled advocate. In 1908 he chaired the Railway Clearing House general managers' conference. See *The Bailie*, 9 January 1901; A Eddington and W T Pike, *Edinburgh and the Lothians at the Opening of the Twentieth Century* (1904); *London & North Eastern Railway Magazine* (January 1932).

JACKSON, William Lawies
1st Baron Allerton of Chapel-Allerton
(16 February 1840 - 4 April 1917)

Tanner and railway company chairman, born at Otley, near Leeds, eldest son of William Jackson, a tanner, he was educated at a private school at Adel and at the Moravian School at Fulneck and then joined the family firm in Leeds. In the 20 years after his father's death in 1858 he built this up into one of the largest tanneries in England, employing 200 and producing 300,000 hides a year. Jackson in 1869 embarked on a political career, commencing with a seat on Leeds Town Council, continuing as MP (Conservative) for Leeds, 1880-85, and for the Northern Division of Leeds, 1885-1902, and culminating as Chief Secretary for Ireland, 1891-92. He chaired the Jameson Raid inquiry of 1896-97. He was sworn of the Privy Council in 1890 and created a baron in 1902. In the 1890s he was a director of the East Lincolnshire Railway, the Forth Bridge Railway, and the Eastern Telegraph Co, and was a trustee of the Submarine Cables Trust. From 1895 he chaired the Great Northern Railway (32,000 employees in 1907) and was responsible for a modernisation programme. By 1907 he was also chairman of the Cheshire Lines Committee (4,700 employees in 1907). His tannery business declined and the firm closed in 1912 following Jackson's retirement. He was a leading Freemason and a devout member of the Church of England. He married, in 1860, Grace née Tempest, daughter of an Otley butcher; they had two sons and five daughters. See *DBB*.

JACOB, Lieutenant-General Sir Edward Ian Claud

(27 September 1899 – 24 April 1993)

Director General of the BBC, son of Captain (later Field Marshal Sir Claud) Claud William Jacob (1863-1948) and his wife Clara Pauline née Wyatt, he was educated at Wellington College, the Royal Military Academy, Woolwich, and King's College Cambridge. He was commissioned into the Royal Engineers in 1918 and reached the rank of brevet lieutenant-colonel in 1939. During the Second World War he served as Military Assistant Secretary to the War Cabinet, 1939-46. In 1946 Sir Ian Jacob (he was knighted in 1946) retired from the army and joined the BBC, commencing as Controller of European Services and then Director of Overseas Services, 1947-52. On leave of absence from the BBC in 1952, acting as Chief Staff Officer to the Minister of Defence and Deputy Secretary (Military) to the Cabinet, he returned to the BBC as Director-General in 1952, retiring in 1960. His tenure as chief executive was marked by the trans-formation of the BBC from a sound broadcasting organisation into one broadcasting sound and vision (by which time ITV had begun). The coun-try had a million television sets in 1951, 5 million in 1955 and 11 million in 1961. In the mid-1950s the BBC employed 16,000. On the sound broad-casting side Jacob took the decisions to introduce the VHF system, to cut back on the Third Programme, and to occupy the Light Programme almost wholly with entertainment. He was intoler-ant of attacks on established institutions (excluding Malcolm Muggeridge from broadcasting because he had published an article critical of the monarchy). On the other hand, he and his chairman, Sir Alexander Cadogan (qv), courageously defied the government in giving the Leader of the Opposition, Hugh Gaitskell, the immediate right of reply to the broadcast of the Prime Minister, Sir Anthony Eden, announcing the Anglo-French invasion of Egypt during the Suez Crisis of 1956. Jacob was awarded the GBE in 1960. After he left the BBC he became a director of Fisons, 1960-70; of EMI, 1960-73; chairman of Covent Garden Market Authority, 1961-66; and a trustee of the Imperial War Museum, 1966-73. In the 1970s he served in local government in Suffolk, as county councillor, JP and DL. Jacob married in 1924 Cecil Bisset Treherne; they had two sons. See Asa Briggs, *The BBC: The First Fifty Years* (1985); *The Times*, 26 April 1993.

JACOBSON, Lionel

(1 July 1905 –)

Clothing retailer, born at Newcastle-upon-Tyne, the son of Moses Jacobson, a merchant tailor, and his wife Annie née Lehrman, he was educated at St John's College, Oxford (where he took a third in jurisprudence in 1926). Lionel Jacobson and his brother Sidney became very successful in the cloth-ing trade. By 1946 Lionel was chairman of Donegal Tweed and by 1951 was chairman and joint man-aging director (with Sidney) of Jackson The Tailor Ltd of Newcastle-upon-Tyne. In the early 1950s Jacksons had five factories and 48 shops. Compared to Montague Burton Ltd, with its 635 shops, 11 factories and 20,000 employees just before Sir Montague Burton (qv) died in 1952, this looked puny. But Burtons lacked managerial talent. The chairman, C E Benson (qv), lost no time in bring-ing the Jacobsons onto the Burton team by acquir-ing a controlling interest in Jackson The Tailor in July 1953. By 1955-56 Lionel Jacobson was chair-man of Burtons, retiring in 1970, when he was made president. Under Jacobson Montague Burton Ltd was restructured. Cloth manufacturing at Leeds was abandoned and the factories demolished or turned into distribution centres. The shops were modernised. Some attention was given to fashion and style of garment, especially in female clothing sold through the Peter Robinson subsidiary (39 shops in 1967) during the 'swinging sixties'. However, Burtons catered predominantly for the male side of the market and until the 1970s the arrival of Ralph Halpern (qv) did not shake off a dowdy image and a loss-making record. See T W Cynog-Jones, 'Retail Giants: No 13, Montague Burton Ltd' *New Dawn* (1963); Eric M Sigsworth, *Montague Burton: The Tailor of Taste* (1990).

JAMES, Sir John Ernest

(1874 – 3 June 1963)

Steel company executive, born at Stockton-on-Tees, the son of John James. He became an apprentice roll turner at the Stockton Malleable Iron Works, where his father and a number of his uncles were employed. The company became part of the South Durham Steel & Iron Co Ltd in the Furness group, and when the Cargo Fleet Iron Co Ltd was started as an extension of the group's activ-ities, James was transferred to take charge of the rolling mills. Later he became general works man-ager and was on the board of all the steel compa-nies in the group. When the Lancashire Steel Corporation was established in 1930, James became the first chairman. It employed 19,450 in 1935. In 1934 he also became chairman of the Whitecross Co when it was taken over and three years later he accepted another chairmanship when the Lancashire & Corby Steel Manufacturing Co was formed. He also served as chairman of the Lancashire Steel Manufacturing Co, Pearson & Knowles Engineering Co, and Rylands Bros. James was knighted in 1949 and retired as chairman of Lancashire Steel in 1962, when he became president. In 1900 he married Grace Laura née Sowler (d 1960): they had one daughter. See *The Times*, 4 June 1963.

JEPHCOTT, Sir Harry
(15 January 1891 - 29 May 1978)

Pharmaceutical manufacturer, born at Redditch, Worcestershire, the third and youngest son of John Josiah Jephcott (1853-1929), a train driver, and Helen née Matthews. Educated at King Edward VI Grammar School, Birmimgham, and at West Ham Technical College, he trained as a pharmacist, taking a first-class honours degree in chemistry at London University in 1915. In 1919, after a spell in the civil service, he joined the milk-food company Glaxo as an analyst. Austere, hard-working and ambitious, Jephcott helped transform the company into a science-based pharmaceutical company, first by introducing vitamin D into its milk products in the 1920s and then by ensuring that Glaxo was in the vanguard of post-war scientific advances in antibiotics, vaccines and steroids. He became managing director of Glaxo Laboratories in 1935 and chairman in 1945, two years before Glaxo became a public company. Between 1947 and 1963, when Jephcott retired from the chairmanship, Glaxo's issued capital had increased from about £800,000 to over £13 million and net profits from £1.1 million to £3.3 million. He had numerous interests outside Glaxo: he was a director of Metal Box and friend of Sir Robert Barlow (qv); chaired Government committees, such as the Council for Scientific & Industrial Research; and held many professional offices and honours, such as the presidency of the Association of British Chemical Manufacturers. He was knighted in 1946. He married in 1919 Doris née Gregory: they had two sons. Jephcott left £2,011,589 gross. See Richard Davenport-Hines and Judy Slinn, *Glaxo: A History to 1962* (1992); *DBB*; *DNB*.

JOB, Peter
(13 July 1941 -)

News and information company executive, the son of Frederick Job and Marion née Pickard. Educated at Clifton College and Exeter College, Oxford, he joined Reuters as a journalist in 1963 and from 1971 was involved with the firm's business developments in Latin America, Asia, Africa and the Middle East. From 1978 he was charged with Reuter's Asia operations. A chairman of Visnews, a Reuters subsidiary, he was appointed to the Reuters' board in 1988 and became chief executive in March 1991. Founded in London in 1851 by a German Jew, Paul Julius Reuter, the company had moved into supplying information for the growing financial and services sector in the 1960s. Expanding on the back of the financial deregulation of the Thatcher years, Reuters' profit grew from £3.7 million in 1980 to £340 million in 1991 (from a turnover of £1,466 million). In 1991 it employed 10,640 workers. Job maried in 1966 Christine Cobley: they have one son and one daughter. See Donald Reed, *The Power of News* (1992).

JOHNS, Sir Arthur William
(1873 - 13 January 1937)

Engineer and naval designer, educated at the Devonport Dockyard, which he entered as an apprentice in 1887. Four years later he won a scholarship to the Royal Naval Engineering College, Keyham, and in 1892 moved on to the Royal Naval College at Greenwich, where he studied for three years. In 1898 he returned to Greenwich as instructor in naval architecture, and in 1901 joined the staff of the Constructive Department of the Admiralty, when he was engaged, among other duties, upon the designs of the King Edward VII class of battleship. In 1910-12 he was principal overseer of the Admiralty at the Thames Ironworks, Blackwall, during the construction of the battleship *Thunderer*, the last big man-of-war to be built on the Thames. On her completion he was placed in charge of British submarine design, work he continued during the war, when he was also concerned with the design of rigid airships and was chairman of the joint technical committee on aviation arrangements in His Majesty's ships. In 1930 he succeeded Sir William Berry as Director of Naval Construction, having served as deputy for some time, though he had to retire through ill-health in 1936 (by which time his organisation employed over 31,000). He was made a CBE in 1920, a CB in 1929, and was promoted to KCB in 1933. In 1930 he became vice-president of the Institution of Naval Architects. See *The Times*, 14 January 1937.

JOHNSON, Henry
(20 March 1866 - 11 June 1938)

Textile manufacturer, born in Macclesfield, the son of William Jackson, a silk throwster, and Elizabeth née Martin. Leaving school aged 12, he later joined Samuel Courtauld & Co in 1895 and in 1907 became manager of the firm's new rayon plant at Coventry. He joined the board of newly-formed Courtaulds Ltd in 1914, becoming managing director and a dominant figure over the company's rayon mills until 1938. Harry (as he was known) was an old-style mill boss: knowledgeable, but hard-driving and bullying, and - unlike his chairman Samuel Courtauld (qv) - hostile to labour. He left £558,889. See D C Coleman, *Courtaulds: An Economic and Social History* (3 vols, Oxford, 1969-80) 2; *DBB*.

JOHNSON-FERGUSON, Sir Jabez Edward
(27 November 1849 - 10 December 1929)
Politician and steelmaster, born near Manchester, only son of Jabez Johnson JP of Kenyon Hall, cotton manufacturer, and Mary née Johnson, he was educated privately and at St John's College, Cambridge (a maths scholar who became 32nd wrangler in 1872) and was called to the Bar at the Inner Temple in 1877. He joined the family firm of Jabez Johnson, Hodgkinson & Pearson, cotton and quilting manufacturers, and became its chairman when it was registered as a limited company in 1892. He assumed the name of Johnson-Ferguson in 1881. A political career accelerated his business prominence. He sat in parliament as a Liberal for Loughborough, 1885-86, 1892-1900, and was made a baronet in 1906, the year he became chairman of Bolckow, Vaughan & Co, iron and steel manufacturers and colliery owners of Middlesbrough on Teesside. By the 1920s Bolckow, Vaughan was ailing badly. The onset of depression, misjudged acquisitions, high gearing, non-recovery of large sums from the government, and general mismanagement led in 1924 to a shareholders' revolt and a critical report by outside accountants. Sir Edward Johnson-Ferguson was forced to resign as chairman but remained as director until 1927. He was also sometime chairman of Bacares Iron Ore Mines and director of Dorman, Long which in 1929 took over Bolckow, Vaughan. During the First World War Sir Edward was on the Staff at Gallipoli and in France. He married in 1874 Williamina, the daughter of W A Cunningham; he left a widow, a son and four daughters. See Jonathan Boswell, *Business Policies in the Making: Three Steel Companies Compared* (1983); *The Times*, 11 December 1929.

JOICEY, James
1st Baron Joicey of Chester-Le-Street, County Durham
(4 April 1846 - 21 November 1936)
Coal mine owner, born in Tanfield in County Durham, the younger son of George Joicey, an engineer, and Dorothy née Gowland. After attending Gainford School near Darlington, he joined his uncle's private coal firm, Joicey & Co, in 1863 and gained control in 1881. He consolidated and then expanded this firm, which in 1924 merged with Lambton & Hetton Collieries to form Lambton, Hetton & Joicey Collieries Ltd. In the interwar

period the company became a leading European coal producer, with the board of directors drawn entirely from the Joicey family and their connections. As a leading north-east businessman he was involved in the North Eastern Railway Co; was president of the Mining Association of Great Britain; and owned three newspapers. A Liberal MP for Chester-le-Street in 1885 (though after 1931 he joined the Conservatives), he was created a baronet in 1893 and a peer in 1906. He married twice: firstly in 1879 to Elizabeth Amy née Robinson (d 1881); secondly, in 1884 to Margaret Smyles Drever. The elder son of the first marriage succeeded to the title. He left £1,519,717 gross. See *DBB*; *DNB*; Barry Supple, *The History of the British Coal Industry: Vol 4, 1913-1946* (1987).

JOICEY, James Arthur
2nd Baron Joicey of Chester le Street, County Durham
(1 May 1880 - 24 July 1940)
Colliery owner, the son of Sir James (1st Baron) Joicey (qv) and Elizabeth Amy née Robinson. Educated at Harrow and Jesus College, Cambridge, he succeeded to the barony and the leadership of the family coal empire - centred around the Lambton, Hetton & Joicey Collieries Ltd - in 1936, when the group employed over 13,000 workers. He married in 1904 Georgina Wharton, second daughter of Augustus D. Burdon, by whom he had three daughters. He was found shot dead in the grounds of his home, Ford Castle, Northumberland, after a rabbit shoot and was succeeded to the barony by his brother Hugh Edward Joicey (1881-1966).

JONES, Sir Henry Frank Harding
(13 July 1906 - 9 October 1987)
Gas company engineer and director and Gas Council chairman, born in Paddington, London, the only son of Frank Harding Jones, a third generation civil and gas engineer, and his wife Gertrude Octavia née Kimber, he was educated at Harrow and Pembroke College, Cambridge, where he took a first in mechanical sciences. He trained with George Evetts, consulting gas engineer and a driving force in the firm of H E Jones & Son. He designed and constructed gas plants; worked on parliamentary, rating and valuation matters; and was involved in the integration of gas grids. During the Second World War he was an infantry officer with the Essex Regiment at Dunkirk and the Far East, and then held Staff appointments, attaining the rank of brigadier. By 1948 Jones was deputy chairman of the Wandsworth & District and the Watford & St Albans Gas Cos and director of many other gas companies. After the nationalisation of the gas

industry in 1948 he was appointed chairman of the East Midlands Gas Board in 1949. In 1952 he became deputy chairman of the Gas Council and then chairman, 1960-72. By 1960 the industry's dependence on coal was ending. Imports of natural gas from the Gulf of Mexico had just begun and Jones negotiated for more from Algeria. The discovery in 1965-66 of huge reserves under the North Sea transformed prospects for the gas industry. Sir Henry Jones (he was knighted in 1963) decided not to convert North Sea gas to low pressure town gas (thereby losing half its calorific value) but to build an entirely new gas grid and to convert all domestic and industrial appliances, covering 14 million consumers, to the higher pressure. This took ten years, 1967-77, and cost £1,000 million (including writing off £400 million for old gas plant): a better record than that of the Japanese. At the organisational level Jones took the advice of the management consultants McKinsey & Co and strengthened the central powers of the Gas Council, by replacing the powerful Area Board chairmen with regional managers. This paved the way for the creation of a new central authority, the British Gas Corporation, in 1973. Jones was made a KBE in 1965 and a GBE in 1972 and received many professional honours. He married, in 1934, Elizabeth née Langton; they had three sons and a daughter. See DBB; *The Times*, 13 October 1987; Trevor I Williams, *A History of the BritishGas Industry* (1981).

JONES, Sir Walter Benton
(26 September 1880 - 5 December 1967)
Steel manufacturer, born at Cannock, Staffordshire, the son of (Sir) Frederick John Jones, chief executive of the Rother Vale Collieries, and Annie Elizabeth née Benton. After reading history at Cambridge University, Benton Jones joined his father, firstly as managing director of the Rother Vale Collieries, and then as executive director after the Collieries' takeover in 1918 by the United Steel Companies. In 1927 he became chairman of United Steel (a position he retained until 1962), and alongside his managing director, Robert S. Hilton (qv), successfully reorganised this troubled industrial giant. He was a devotee of industrial cooperation. In 1941 he also took on the managing directorship of United Steel, handing over to Gerald Steel (qv) in 1947. Benton Jones married in 1907 Lily née Fawcett: their son, Peter Benton Jones, also joined the management of United Steel. He left £36,631. See Walter Benton Jones, 'The History and Organisation of the United Steel Companies Ltd', in Ronald S Edwards and Harry Townsend (eds), *Business Growth* (1966); Jonathan Boswell, *Business Policies in the Making: Three Steel Companies Compared* (1983); DBB.

JOSEPH, Sir Maxwell
(31 May 1910 - 22 September 1982)
Hotel, brewing and entertainments company chairman, born in Whitechapel, London, the son of Jack Joseph, a tailor, and Sarah née Orler. Max (later changed to Maxwell) Joseph attended Pitman's Business School, joined an estate agents and in 1928 founded his own agency with a few hundred pounds lent by his father. His property dealings were interrupted by the Second World War (when he was in the Royal Engineers), but by 1948 he was concentrating on small hotels. He foresaw the enormous growth in travel and leisure and by 1962 had established his famous Grand Metropolitan Hotels Group. An able and ambitious financier, with no great liking for the City or the establishment, Joseph expanded GM with a series of takeovers: Truman's brewery (1971); Liggett's drinks and tobacco (1980); and Pan Am's Intercontinental Hotels (1981). By 1981 GM's turnover was £1,827 million (making it the 12th biggest UK company by that measure) and its takeover of Intercontinental had made it the ninth largest hotel group in the world. Joseph resigned as chairman of GM in 1982, having appointed Stanley Grinstead as successor. He was knighted in 1981. He left £17,313,831 gross, most of which he left to his second wife Eileen Olive née Warrell (he had divorced his first wife, Sybil Neda née Samuel, in 1981). See Grand Metropolitan, *Facts and Figures 1988: 25 Dynamic and Successful Years* (1988); DBB; DNB.

K

KALMS, Stanley
(21 November 1931 -)
Electronic products chain store retailer, born Harold Stanley Kalms in west London, the son of Charles Kalms, a company director of Hendon, and Sarah née Schlagman. Educated at Christ's College, Finchley, in 1948 he joined his father's photographic studio in Edgware, west London. (Charles Kalms had started his business in Southend in 1937.) He persuaded his father to expand into photographic products, such as cameras and accessories, thus launching the Dixons' group. In the 1950s, Dixons emerged as a leading photographic dealer, based in Edgware, with six retail branches and an extensive mail order business. Kalms, who became a director in 1951, gave Dixons a competitive edge at this time by forging direct links with Japanese manufacturers, who often made products to Dixons' specification to be sold under the brand-name 'Prinz'. In 1962 Dixons went public: it had 16 branches and a flagship store at Marble Arch,

London. In 1967 Kalms became chairman and chief executive of Dixons, which was now expanding steadily, acquiring competitors such as Ascotts (1962), Bennetts (1964) and Wallace Heaton (1972) and diversifying into developing and printing. With a more upmarket high-technology image (by the 1980s it was selling audio, TV and video), Dixons was poised to become the Sainsbury's of consumer electronics retailing. In 1984, after a bitter battle, Kalms added the Currys Group and greatly boosted the number of Dixon's retail outlets. By 1993 the Group's store portfolio was: Dixons 358, Currys 371, Currys' Superstores 128; and it also operated 352 photo-processing stores (Supasnaps) and 187 Silo outlets (the US power retailer). Turnover in 1991-92 was £1,862 million, compared to £1.4 million in 1962 when Dixons went public. Kalms is also a non-executive director of British Gas, Camberwell Health Authority and the Centre for Policy Studies. He married in 1953 Pamela Jimack: they have three sons.

KEARTON, Christopher Frank
Baron Kearton of Whitchurch, Buckinghamshire
(17 February 1911 - 2 July 1992)
Industrialist, born at Tunstall, Stoke-on Trent, the son of Christopher John Kearton, a bricklayer, and Lilian née Hancock. From Hanley High School he went to St John's College, Oxford, where he graduated with first class honours in natural science. In 1933 he joined ICI's Billingham division and was seconded for a time to the Atomic Energy Project. In 1946 he joined Courtaulds Ltd, becoming a director in 1952, a managing director in 1957, deputy chairman in 1961 and chairman from 1964 to 1975. He transformed and expanded Courtaulds man-made fibres business with an aggressive policy of expansion: under Kearton, Courtaulds net assets rose from about £90 million to nearly £760 million and its profits from about £10 million to £120 million (the highest in the firm's history). From 1966-68 he was chairman of the Industrial Reorganisation Corporation, a government body charged with fostering company mergers in British industry. He was also chairman and chief executive from 1976 to 1979 of the British National Oil Corporation, the Labour-inspired attempt at a nationally-controlled North Sea oil industry. Tireless in working both for the improvement and rationalisation of his own company and other sectors of British industry, he also served as part-time adviser to the UK Atomic Energy Authority and other government energy bodies. In 1980 he became chancellor of Bath University. He was awarded an OBE in 1945, elected FRS in 1961, knighted in 1966, and made a life peer in 1970. In

1936 he married Agnes Kathleen Brander: they had two sons and two daughters. See Donald Coleman, *Courtaulds: An Economic and Social History* (3 vols, 1969, 1980); *DBB*.

KEEN, Arthur
(23 January 1835 - 8 February 1915)
Nut, bolt and steel manufacturer, born in Cheshire, the son of Thomas Keen, a yeoman farmer and innkeeper, he had a brief education and then joined the London & North Western Railway Co, becoming LNWR agent at Smethwick. Through his (then future) father-in-law Thomas Astbury, a wealthy ironfounder, he was introduced to Francis Watkins, an American who had come to England to market a patent nut-making machine. Keen and Watkins formed a partnership ca 1856 and operated works in Smethwick. They formed a limited company in 1864. Keen bought out Watkins and in 1865 merged with the Stour Valley Works, West Bromwich, and the Cwmbran Iron Works near Newport. The new firm, called the Patent Nut & Bolt Co, was chaired by Joseph (later Sir Joseph) Dodge Weston with Keen as managing director. In 1895, on the death of Weston, Keen became chairman of Patent Nut & Bolt. In the pursuit of the independence of vertical integration (and growth), he rapidly negotiated a series of acquisitions. He took over the Dowlais Iron Co, steelmakers (with a new integrated plant at East Moors, Cardiff) which had belonged to the Guest family since the eighteenth century, in 1899, valuing the Guest properties at £1.53 million and Patent Bolt & Nut at £1 million. The new company, Guest, Keen & Co, chaired by Keen (until his death), was then used in 1902 to buy up Nettlefolds, neighbouring screw manufacturers at Smethwick, and Crawshay Bros, Cyfarthfa, Ltd a rival steelmaker at Merthyr Tydfil. Guest, Keen & Nettlefolds in 1907 employed over 21,000. Outside GKN Keen supported Sir Edward Holden (qv) in his expansion of the Birmingham & Midland Bank. Politically he was a Liberal Unionist and a tariff reformer. Keen married, in 1858, Hannah Astbury by whom he had ten children. See *DBB*; Edgar Jones, *A History of GKN vol 1 Innovation and Enterprise, 1759-1918* (1987).

KEEN, Arthur Thomas
(1861 - 27 June 1918)
Nut, bolt and steel manufacturer; a son of Arthur Keen (qv), the founder of Guest, Keen & Nettlefolds, he trained for the legal profession and was called to the Bar, though never practiced. For some years he was private secretary to his father and succeeded him as chairman of GKN in 1915. The First World War saw the company grow massively, with a capital of £5 million and 50,000

employees in 1918, compared to 22,000 in 1907. Arthur Keen found the responsibility too much. He had a nervous collapse and in May 1918 went into a Surrey nursing home suffering from depression. A few weeks later he committed suicide by cutting his throat. He left a widow and four children. GKN archives.

KESWICK, Sir John Henry
(13 July 1906 - 5 July 1982)

Merchant and trader, born at Cowhill, Dumfries, the son of Henry Keswick, a merchant, and his wife Wynefride Johnstone. After attending Eton, he read history at Trinity College, Cambridge. A relative of the Jardine family that had founded the Far Eastern traders Jardine Matheson, in 1929 he followed the family line into the business, moving to Shanghai in 1931. After wartime work with the Ministry of Economic Warfare, he returned to the Far East and was chairman of Jardine Matheson in Hong Kong between 1952 and 1956. Back in the UK, he became a leader in fostering better commercial relations with China, becoming president of the China Association and president of the Sino-British Trade Council, 1963-73. Keswick was highly influential in mounting the exhibition of British technology in Beijing in 1964 and in other trade missions. According to John Swire (qv), Keswick's remarkably pronounced back of the head, which so resembled the Chinese god of happiness, led to the country Chinese often touching him. He was appointed CMG in 1950, and KCMG in 1972. He married in 1940 Clare née Elwes: they had one daughter. See *DNB*.

KESWICK, Henry Neville Lindley
(29 September 1938 -)

KESWICK, Simon Lindley
(20 May 1942 -)

Finance and trading company executives, born into the Scottish Dumfries family of Sir William Keswick (1903-90) and Mary née Lindley. In the nineteenth century the Keswicks had married into the Jardine family, founders of the powerful Hong Kong trader, Jardine Matheson. Henry attended Eton and Trinity College, Cambridge (where he read economics and law), and then did National Service in the Scots Guards and worked in the City. He arrived in Hong Kong in 1972 to take up his family inheritance as chairman of Jardine Matheson at 32. The results of his chairmanship before he left the colony in 1975 were uneven: he failed to take advantage of Hong Kong's rapid expansion into the New Territories, then invested in UK property before the early 1970s crash. The group began to decline in wealth and power, but in

1983, after a bitter family struggle to regain control of the business, he brought in his youngest brother Simon as chairman. The latter had also attended Eton and Trinity College and had been chairman of Jardine Matheson Insurance Brokers, 1978-82. Under Simon, the group more than recovered its fortunes in the 1980s economic boom in Hong Kong. Although the Keswicks only control about 15 per cent of the shares in Jardine Matheson (and friendly interests another 15 per cent or so), they direct its fortunes. Unable to countenance the takeover of Hong Kong by the Chinese communists in 1997, the Keswicks have begun moving their investments abroad. In 1992 Jardine Matheson began buying their way into the troubled property conglomerate, Trafalgar House; floated the insurance arm in the City; and Simon joined the board of Hanson Trust. Henry married in 1985 Tessa (Lady Reay) née Lovat, his former fiancee from his twenties. Simon married in 1971 Emma née Chetwode: they have two sons and two daughters.

KING, Cecil Harmsworth
(20 February 1901 - 17 April 1987)

Newspaper proprietor, was born at Totteridge, north London, fifth of the seven children of Lucas (later Sir Lucas) White King, a deputy commissioner in the Indian Civil Service (later professor of oriental languages at Trinity College, Dublin), and his wife Geraldine, sister of Alfred and Harold Harmsworth (qqv). Raised in Dublin, King was educated at Winchester and Christ Church, Oxford, where he took a second-class honours degree in history. Both his brothers died in the First World War. Under the patronage of his uncles he worked on the *Glasgow Record*, the *Daily Mail* and the *Daily Mirror* (which he joined in 1926). That year he received his first directorship, of Rothermere's Empire Paper Mills. In 1929 he became advertising director of Daily Mirror Newspapers. With Harry Guy Bartholomew, in 1933 he transformed the *Daily Mirror* from a middle-class picture paper into a brash tabloid, but still supporting Labour. King revived the *Sunday Pictorial*, another ailing member of the Harmsworth stable, by appointing Hugh (later Lord) Cudlipp to be editor at the age of 24. With Bartholomew's departure in 1951, King became chairman of the Mirror Group, then a spectacular success. The acquisition of the Amalgamated Press, and its numerous publications, from the Berry family (qv) for £18 million in 1958, and then the Odham's group for £37 million in 1961 gave King the opportunity to create an enormous integrated paper-to-publishing empire, the International Publishing Corporation in 1962-63. Its pillars were the Reed paper group, the *Daily Mirror* and the string of magazines and periodicals gained with the Amalgamated Press and Odham's. IPC became the largest publishing company in Britain, with 30,000 employees and a turnover of £124 million in 1965. With Odham's had come an interest in the loss-making *Daily Herald*. King unsuccessfully tried to revive it with a relaunch in 1964 when it was renamed the *Sun*; eventually it was sold to Rupert Murdoch (qv) in 1969. Withdrawn, scholarly, arrogant, Cecil King came to believe in the 1960s that British society was in danger and that he was destined to come to its aid. Foolishly, he overplayed his roles as citizen (he tried unsuccessfully to get Lord Mountbatten to head a new administration), as proprietor (he owned only 1 per cent of IPC's equity) and as editor. When, in May 1968, he signed a *Daily Mirror* editorial demanding that prime minister Harold Wilson should go, he was ousted from the IPC board by his fellow directors. King was chairman of the Newspaper Proprietors' Association, 1961-68; a director of the Bank of England, 1965-68; member of the National Coal Board and of the National Parks Commission (later the Countryside Commission) from 1966. By 1969 he had resigned from his public offices and retired to Dublin, where he wrote his multi-volumed diary and memoirs and opinionated pieces in *The Times*. Besides grouse-shooting, King was interested in the paranormal. King married twice: first, in 1923, to Agnes Margaret Cooke (d 1985), daughter of the Regius Professor of Hebrew at Oxford, by whom he had two sons and a daughter; second, in 1962 (after divorcing his first wife), to Dame Ruth Railton, founder of the National Youth Orchestra. He also adopted the three orphaned children of his nephew. See *The Times*, 20 April 1987.

KING, Sir James
Laird of Campsie and Carstairs
(13 July 1830 - 1 October 1911)
Banker and railway company chairman, born in Glasgow the son of John King of Levernholme and Campsie, a merchant, and his wife Christina McNie, he was educated at Glasgow High School and Glasgow University and then joined his father in the Hurlet & Campsie Alum Co. He inherited interests in this and a second modest chemical firm but rather than become an entrepreneur he preferred to be an investor, building up a large and complex portfolio worth £676,000 when he died. He became prominent in the public life of late nineteenth-century Glasgow: member of Glasgow Town Council, 1874-76; Lord Provost of Glasgow, 1886-89; Lord Dean of Guild; president of the Chamber of Commerce; Dean of the Faculties of Glasgow University; Chancellor's Assessor to the University; chairman of the execu-tive council of the Glasgow Exhibition of 1888; member of the Royal Commission on the Western Highlands and Islands, 1889; member of the Crofters' Colonisation Board. He was knighted in 1887 and created a baronet in 1888. Outside his private business he was a director of the Clydesdale Bank, 1868-1911, and chairman, 1881-1911. Though it is not clear how far he determined bank policy, under him the Clydesdale's market share in terms of deposits rose from 9.2 to 11.2 per cent. He became deputy chairman of the Caledonian Railway Co in 1888, and chairman in 1906, until his death. The Caledonian, employing 21,000 in 1907, was the second largest of Scotland's ten railways and covered territory between Carlisle, Glasgow and Edinburgh but also extended to Aberdeen on the east coast and Oban on the west coast. Under Sir James King and his general manager, Robert Millar (qv), the Caledonian confirmed its high reputation for the speed and comfort of its passenger services. Sir James King sat on a number of other company boards, almost all focused on Glasgow: he was essentially a Glasgow man. He married, in 1861, Marian, daughter of William Westall of Streatham Common, Surrey; they had four sons and a daughter. See *DSBB*; W J Gordon, *Our Home Railways* (2 vols, 1910).

KING, John (Leonard)
Baron King of Wartnaby
(29 August 1917 -)
Airline and engineering executive, born in Brentwood, Essex, the son of Albert John King, an army sergeant, and Kathleen née Buggy. His early education and upbringing was in Dunsfold, Surrey. After experience in motor car engineering, King established a group of industries in Ferrybridge, Yorkshire, which became the Pollard Ball & Roller Bearing Co. In 1969 - when it had become the third biggest UK ball bearing manufacturer - Pollard's was taken over by the Government-sponsored Industrial Re-organisation Corporation (IRC) and King sold out (reputedly for about £10 million). In 1970 he joined Babcock & Wilcox and was appointed chairman two years later, dividing his time between that and running Dennis Bros, a company that specialised in making fire engines. In 1981 Margaret Thatcher appointed him chairman of British Airways, with the remit of transforming it from a £150 million a year loss-maker into an effective world airline. King axed 23,000 jobs, ordered American aircraft, dropped several routes and successfully resisted Government proposals to dismember the company's valuable network of routes. He also saw off the challenge of Sir Freddie Laker (qv), oversaw privatisation, absorbed Adam Thompson's (qv) British Caledonian, put paid to

the expansionist plans of SAS, and guided a new, slicker BA on an aggressive expansionist course. By 1993 BA had 48,453 employees, carried 25 million passengers in 227 aircraft, and earned pre-tax profits of £302 million on a turnover of £5.3 billion - making it the world's most profitable airline. In February 1993 his chief executive Sir Colin Marshall (qv) became BA chairman, when King retired five months early in the aftermath of an alleged BA 'dirty tricks' campaign against Richard Branson's (qv) Virgin Atlantic. He became BA's first president. One of the UK's highest paid executives (by 1993 his posts at BA and Babcock netted nearly £1 million a year), King enjoys the life of a country squire, likes riding to hounds and supports the Conservative Party. Knighted in 1979, he was made a life peer in 1983. He married twice: first in 1941 to Lorna Kathleen Sykes (d 1969), by whom he had three sons and one daughter; second in 1970 to Hon Isabel Monckton. See Duncan Campbell-Smith, *Take-Off: The British Airways Story* (1986); John Dodd, 'The Clamping Stay King', *Independent*, 15 July 1990; Arthur Reed, *Airline: The Inside Story of British Airways* (1990).

L

LAING, Hector
Baron Laing of Dunphail
(12 May 1923 -)
Food manufacturer, born into a wealthy family in Edinburgh, the eldest of the three sons of Hector Laing and Margaret Norris née Grant. His grandfather had made his name with the 'Digestive' biscuit and was the first chairman of McVitie & Price. Educated at Loretto School, Musselburgh, Scotland, he attended Jesus College, Cambridge, for a year and then served in the war as a tank commander with the Scots Guards, winning the American bronze star. He joined McVitie's Harlseden factory in west London in 1947, where he started making cakes with his hands. A year later McVitie merged with Macfarlane to form United Biscuits, of which Laing became a director in 1953, managing director in 1964, and was chairman between 1972 and 1990. Under his leadership UB grew, largely by acquisitions, to gain a 50 per cent share of the biscuit market (with its Digestives still a brand leader) and a 40 per cent share of the snack market (with brands such as KP Nuts). However, in 1986 he lost a bruising battle with Lord Hanson (qv) for ownership of the Imperial Group, the tobacco and drinks company. Laing was a director of the Bank of England, 1973-91. A paternalist, he was chairman of Business in the Community and with Sir Mark Weinberg (qv) created The Per

Cent Club to encourage businesses to give at least a half of one per cent of their profits to the community. A personal friend of Margaret Thatcher, he became a joint-treasurer of the Conservative Party in 1988. Laing was knighted in 1978 and created a life peer in 1991. He married in 1950 Marian Clare, daughter of Major General Sir John Laurie.

LAING, Sir (John) Maurice
(1 February 1918 -)
Contractor, born in Carlisle, the second son of John William Laing (qv), builder and contractor, and his wife, Beatrice née Harland, he was educated at St Lawrence College, Ramsgate, and then joined the family firm as a trainee manager and like his elder brother (William) Kirby was made a director in 1939. During the Second World War Maurice (as he was known) served in the RAF as a glider pilot, Kirby in the Royal Engineers. When they returned to the firm in 1945 their father was 70 and members of his generation of managers and directors had died or retired. In 1946 the two brothers became managing directors under the governing directorship of their father; three employee directors made up the board. In a period of post-war austerity they faced the choice of retrenchment or expansion. Expansion it was. An excellent pre-war reputation, large-scale wartime engineering contracts, a skilled and loyal staff, and strong capital reserves in Laing's Properties Ltd: all allowed them to diversify away from house building. By 1950 they were employing 15,000 men and were still expanding. The business was converted into a public company, John Laing & Sons (Holdings) Ltd, in 1952, Kirby and Maurice remaining managing directors under the chairmanship of their father. Perhaps their major triumphs were the rebuilding of Coventry Cathedral (all profits on which the Laing family returned to the Cathedral), sections of the M1 Motorway, participation in the construction of nuclear power stations, and in the engineering work for the extraction of oil and gas from the North Sea. When their father retired in 1957, Kirby took over the chairmanship until 1976. Maurice Laing, less retiring than his brother, participated in numerous public bodies, starting with a UK Trade Mission to the Middle East in 1953. He was first president of the Confederation of British Industry in 1965-66, a director of the Bank of England, and a member of the National Economic Development Council, 1962-66. Sir Maurice Laing (he was knighted in 1965, three years before his elder brother) became chairman of John Laing Ltd in 1976. Like their father Maurice and Kirby Laing were strong evangelical Christians. Maurice, in 1940, married Hilda Violet Richards; they had one son. See Roy Coad,

Laing: The Biography of Sir John W Laing, CBE (1879-1978) (1979).

LAING, Sir John William

(24 September 1879 - 11 January 1978)

Builder and civil engineering contractor, born in Carlisle, third but only surviving son of the seven children of John Laing (1842-1924), third generation head of a small firm of builders, and his wife Sarah née Wood, he was educated at Sedbergh School and Carlisle Grammar School and at 15 entered the family firm to serve a three-year apprenticeship as bricklayer-stonemason. In 1908 he took over the firm's management and in 1910 became sole proprietor. The First World War gave him the chance to move into civil engineering contracts, including a munitions factory at Gretna Green and an aerodrome in Fife. From 50 employees in the 1890s the firm grew to 4,000 in 1917 and turnover from £11,000 in 1912 to £0.5 million in 1920. Between the wars Laing made his name as a quality housebuilder. In the face of pent-up housing demand and government building subsidies, Laing converted his business into a private company, John Laing & Son Ltd, and in 1926 moved his headquarters from Carlisle to Mill Hill in north London, to get a share of the fastest-growing house building market, the South East. He built up his assets by forming a second company, Laing's Properties Ltd, to acquire and manage houses, shops, flats and factories. With others in 1937 he promoted the National House Builders' Registration Council to guarantee the quality of speculative house building; and to increase house ownership, he and other builders set up the builders' pool system, an arrangement with the building societies led by Harold Bellman (qv), which reduced cash deposits required for house mortgages. Laings' turnover topped £1 million in 1930, £2 million in 1936 and £3 million in 1938. During the Second World War the firm returned to civil engineering on a large scale. They built 54 airfields, the underground headquarters of RAF Bomber Command, munitions factories and sections of the D-Day Mulberry Harbour and, at their wartime maximum, employed over 10,000. The Minister of Works heavily relied on Laing and Godfrey Mitchell (qv) of Wimpey for professional advice. Another post-war housing shortage saw Laings building 10,000 houses, utilising concrete technology, between 1945 and 1949. John Laing handed management over to his two sons William Kirby and John Maurice (qv) well before 1952 when the company went public. Sir John Laing (he was knighted in 1959) retired in 1957 when he was employing over 15,000. A Conservative and a paternalist, Laing from his childhood was a devout

and enormously active Christian in the Brethren tradition. His wife, Beatrice née Harland, whom he married in 1910, came from the same tradition. See Roy Coad, *Laing: The Biography of Sir John W Laing, CBE (1879-1978)* (1979); *DBB*.

LAKER, Sir (Frederick) Freddie (Alfred)

(6 August 1922 -)

Airline operator, born into a working-class family and educated at Simon Langton School, Canterbury. His father was a merchant seaman, who left his mother when Freddie was 5; she remarried three years later. At 16 he began work on the shopfloor of Short Bros aircraft factory in Rochester. After war service with the Air Transport Auxiliary, he founded Aviation Traders to deal in war-surplus aircraft. While this business thrived - it received a timely boost during the Berlin airlift in 1948 - Laker ran a freight company, Air Charter, which by 1954 was operating car and passenger services between Southend and Calais. In 1958 his business was acquired by British United Airways, where Laker remained as managing director until 1965. But in 1966 he set up his own airline, Laker Airways, a charter company for the emerging package holiday industry. In the early 1970s he battled successfully against the international airline cartel for the right to fly cut-price transatlantic charters, introducing his famous Skytrain service in 1977. But the oil crisis, exchange rate fluctuations, and intense competition ended the adventure in 1982 when Laker went bankrupt. He later won several million dollars from his competitors for unfair competition, but he was never able to re-establish himself. His cut-price ethos, however, finds its echo in the 1990s in the Virgin Atlantic Airline of Richard Branson (qv). Laker was knighted in 1978. He has married four times. Befriended by Tiny Rowland (qv), in 1991 he works for a Lonrho travel company in Florida and in 1992 announced the founding of Laker Airways (Bahamas) Ltd operating charters to the US. See Howard Banks, *The Rise and Fall of Freddie Laker* (1982); Roger Eglin and Barry Ritchie, *Fly Me, I'm Freddie!* (1980).

LANCASTER, Sir Robert Fisher

(5 September 1885 - 4 December 1945)

Co-operative Wholesale Society executive, born at Kendal, the son of Thomas and Mary Lancaster. Educated at Kendal grammar school, he served articles and was admitted as a solicitor in 1908. He was managing clerk with the Newcastle firm, Botterell, Roche & Temperley, and took charge of the solicitor's office at the CWS in 1917. In 1923 he succeeded Sir Thomas Brodrick as Secretary of the

CWS. By 1935 the firm employed nearly 50,000 and ranked amongst the top companies in the UK. Lancaster was knighted in 1945. He married in 1918 Dora Mary Watson: they had two daughters.

LANDAU, Sir Dennis (Marcus)
(18 June 1927 -)
Co-operative Society executive, the son of Michael Landau, a metallurgist. Educated at Haberdashers' Aske's School, he joined the drinks company Schweppes in 1952. By 1970 he was managing director of the foods division of Cadbury Schweppes, but left in the following year to become a food controller for the Co-operative Wholesale Society. In 1980 he became chief executive and, believing that the Co-op could be a wealth creator as well as a distributor, began streamlining and integrating its organisation. He began shedding its downmarket corner shop image, introduced Co-op superstores, sold off its rag-bag collection of overseas subsidiaries, and encouraged merger of the numerous societies (reducing the number from 200 to 69). When he retired from the chairmanship in 1992, Landau headed what was still one of the largest businesses in the UK. The CWS had a total turnover of £3.02 billion (with a trading profit of £44 million - a ratio of 1.45 per cent) and employed 31,000. It was the UK's biggest farmer, biggest undertaker, and was amongst the leading firms in travel and dairy farming. It had 11 per cent of the packaged grocery market (compared to about 16 per cent for Sainsbury and Tesco). Landau was knighted in 1987.

LANE, Sir Allen
(21 September 1902 - 7 July 1970)
Publisher, born in Bristol, the son of Samuel Allen Williams, a municipal architect, and Camilla née Lane. Educated at Bristol Grammar School, aged 16 he was taken under the wing of a distant cousin, John Lane (d 1925), who made him heir apparent to his Bodley Head publishing business. (Allen underlined his status by changing his name in 1919.) In 1926 Allen Lane became managing director of the Bodley Head, but in 1935 dismayed at the conservatism of the board (they were reluctant, for example, to publish James Joyce's *Ulysses*) he founded Penguin Books. With its paperback format, cheerful covers, original authors and low price, the imprint became a phenomenal success across the English-speaking world. Between 1951 and 1960 - Penguin's golden era - annual sales increased from 9.8 million books to over 17 million and in the following year Lane made Penguin a public company. An autocrat, who groomed no successor and had no son, Lane sold Penguin short-

ly before his death to S Pearson & Co for £15 million. Lane was knighted in 1952 and made a Companion of Honour in 1969. In 1941 he married Lettice, the daughter of Sir Charles Orr: they had three daughters. He left £1,216,474 gross. See *Fifty Penguin Years* (1985); J E Morpurgo, *Allen Lane: King Penguin* (1979); *DBB*; *DNB*.

LAW, Robert Urquhart
(23 April 1899 - 6 February 1984)
Builder and civil engineer, born at Saltcoats, near Ardrossan, Scotland, son of James Law, a bookkeeper, and his wife Catherine née Brown, he was apprenticed to a civil engineering firm, training interrupted by military service during the First World War. Law afterwards resumed his apprenticeship, qualifying as an associate member of the Institution of Civil Engineers in 1923. Over the next seven years he gained a broad and varied experience in civil engineering and public works especially after he joined the staff of the Divisional Road Engineer of the Ministry of Transport in Edinburgh. He moved to George Wimpey & Co, headed by Godfrey Mitchell (qv) in 1931. Mitchell recruited him to establish a branch in Scotland, not least to threaten the road surfacing firms who, with access to cheaper supplies of asphalt, had moved into the South East of England undercutting Wimpey. Law built up Department 8 (as the Scottish region was known in Wimpey) so well that he was made first chairman of the firm's Board of Management when that was formed in 1937: while Mitchell was familiar with the commercial side of building and contracting, he was not a trained engineer or builder. Law was one of the subordinates he wisely chose to manage the growing business. Made a director in 1938, Law soon after was moved to London. In 1945 he was appointed managing director of Wimpey, under Mitchell's dominating chairmanship. After 30 years with the firm Law retired in 1961. He was married. See Valerie White, *Wimpey: The First Hundred Years* (1980); *Wimpey News* (May 1961).

LAWRENCE, Sir Herbert Alexander
(8 August 1861 - 17 January 1943)
Banker and industrialist, born at Southgate, Middlesex, the fourth son of Sir John Lawrence, Viceroy of India, and Harriette Katherine née Hamilton. Educated at Harrow and Sandhurst, Lawrence in 1903 went into the City of London, where his wealthy connections (in 1892 he had married Isabel Mary née Mills, the daughter of Lord Hillingdon, head of the banking firm of Glyn Mills Currie) allowed him to collect a string of directorships in South African mines and in various banks. In 1914 he resumed his Army career and by

1918 was chief of general staff to Haig's army in France. In 1919 he returned to banking as manager of Glyn Mills, of which he later became chairman. This led to his appointment in 1926 as chairman of Vickers, an armaments conglomerate whose activities he helped restructure. A close friend of leading bankers and politicans, Lawrence held many other City directorships and appointments. He retired from the helm at Vickers in 1937. He was appointed CB in 1916, KCB in 1917 and GCB in 1926. He left £107,207. See *DBB*; *DNB*.

LAWRIE, John
(October 1861 - 30 July 1935)
Department store manager, son of John and Jane Lawrie, of Ayton, Berwickshire, he was educated at Ayton High School and then served a four year apprenticeship with a local draper. After two years in Newcastle-upon-Tyne and a year in Paris, he moved to London and became a salesman with Swan & Edgar. In the course of 15 years with them he was promoted to assistant manager. He left to manage John Barnes & Co's shop in the Finchley Road. In 1901 William Whiteley (qv) invited him to join the firm of William Whiteley Ltd as managing director. Lawrie held this post until 1927 when Whiteleys was taken over by Gordon Selfridge (qv). 'Finding it impossible permanently to give up business life, he bought Parnells Limited, in Victoria Street, S W. He was at his office until the end of his last week'. In 1922 he was elected chairman of the Royal Commercial Travellers' Schools, Pinner, for whom he raised over £24,000. He married, in 1885, Elizabeth née Elliott; they had four sons and a daughter. See *The Times*, 31 July 1935.

LAWSON, Sir Arthur Tredgold
(8 February 1844 - 1 June 1915)
Engineering company chairman, eldest son of John Lawson (d 1883) of Bramhope Manor near Leeds, and his wife Sarah née Baker, he was educated at St Peter's School, York, Winchester and Cambridge and then entered the Leeds engineering business established by his grandfather, Samuel Lawson. His father built up the firm which specialised in textile machinery. The three firms of Samuel Lawson & Sons of Mabgate Foundry, Leeds, Fairbairn, Naylor & Macpherson & Co Ltd of the Wellington Foundry, Leeds, and Combe, Barbour & Combe of the Falls Foundry, Belfast, merged in 1900 to form the public company of Fairbairn Lawson Combe Barbour Ltd. The value of the constituent firms was £1.1 million, over £733,000 paid in cash. Employing over 5,000 in 1907 the amalgamated company had a near monopoly on the manufacture of flax spinning machinery. Sir Andrew Fairbairn

(1828-1901) was the first chairman and was succeeded by Sir Arthur Lawson (created a baronet in 1900). Lawson was also a director of the Great Eastern Railway Co, Sheffield District Railway Co and the Yorkshire Conservative Newspaper Co. Leader of the Conservative party in Leeds, 1886-1904, Lawson was a strong Churchman. He married, in 1879, Louise Frederica Edith Augusta née O'Brien, daughter of John Stackpoole O'Brien JP of Ennis, Co Clare and Tanderagee, Co Armagh; they had two sons and a daughter. See *Who's Who: Yorkshire, 1912* (1912); *Yorkshire Post* 2 June 1915.

LAZELL, (Henry George) Leslie
23 May 1903 - 17 November 1982)
Pharmaceutical entrepreneur, born in London, the elder son of Henry William Lazell, a wine merchant's manager, and Ada Louise née King. He left elementary school before he was 14 to become an office boy for the Inland Revenue at Somerset House. Later he worked as a ledger-keeper at the pharmaceutical firm of Allen & Hanburys and qualified as both an accountant and secretary. He moved to Macleans the toothpaste firm in 1930 and became a director six years later. In 1938 Macleans was bought by Beechams Pills Ltd and this brought Lazell on to the Beecham board. After 1951, when he became managing director of Beecham (he was chairman between 1958 and 1968), it was Lazell's achievement to transform the group - a sprawling badly co-ordinated company tied to older proprietary products - into an international science-based pharmaceutical manufacturer. Lazell launched the firm's own research effort after 1945 and achieved brilliant success with synthetic penicillins. Beecham's turnover rose from £25 million in 1952 to £134 million in 1969; profits from £2.6 million to over £25 million. Self-taught, competitive and an advocate of the highest ethical standards, he had an unsurprising distaste for the British Establishment, which never honoured him. From 1966 to 1968 he was also a non-executive director of ICI. In 1938 he married Doris Beatrice Try: they had one son. See Leslie Lazell, *From Pills to Penicillin: The Beecham Story* (1975); *DBB*.

LEAKE, Sidney Henry
(31 May 1892 - 28 January 1973)
Retailer, son of Henry and Elizabeth Leake, he was educated at the Model School, York, and then trained for a career in education with the Teachers' Training College in York. The outbreak of the First World War took him into the Ministry of Munitions, 1915-19 (including service with the Military Mission in Russia in 1917), work for which he received the OBE in 1918. He worked for the War Office in 1919 and the Colonial Office

in 1920. Leake moved into business in 1921 when he joined Crosse & Blackwell, the food manufacturers, but moved again in 1923 when he was recruited by Frederick Marquis (qv) to become a general manager with Lewis's, the large Liverpool, Manchester and Birmingham department store. Leake became a director of Lewis's Investment Trust (as the holding company was named in 1929) in 1934, a joint managing director in 1939, deputy chairman in 1945, and chairman in succession to Marquis (now Lord Woolton) in 1951. During his tenure the West End rival of Selfridges Ltd, acquired by Woolton in 1951, was absorbed into the Lewis's organisation and a major Lewis store was built in Bristol. He retired in 1958 and settled in Bromley, Rhodesia. Leake married, in 1924, Gertrude Elizabeth née Burnell; they had two sons and a daughter. See Asa Briggs, *Friends of the People: The Centenary History of Lewis's* (1956); *The Times*, 30 January 1973.

LECKIE, Robert Walker
(4 November 1885 - 25 July 1949)

Scottish Co-operative Wholesale Society executive, born at Armadale, West Lothian, to John Leckie, a coalminer, and Isobella née Wallace. After a short spell in a local moulding foundry he entered the grocery trade with a private firm but soon joined the Armadale Society. Augmenting his experience with part-time study he became branch manager with the Hillwood Society; after three years he took charge of the Penicuik Association's central grocery and 8 years later became general manager. Similar positions with the Brechin, Pathhead and Sinclairtown societies followed until 1923 when he took charge of the ailing Leith Provident Society. Within 8 years he increased membership from 10,600 to 17,250 and doubled the total dividend paid to them. He succeeded John Pearson as secretary of the SCWS in 1931, when Leckie became the first permanent official in the post. He died in office. A forceful personality, Leckie played an important role in guiding and advising many of the retail units in Scotland while he was SCWS secretary. He was also secretary of the British Luma Co-operative Electric Lamp Society, a joint Scottish and Swedish venture whose factory opened at Shieldhall, Glasgow, in 1939. Leckie was an active member of the Church of Scotland, serving as elder of Cramond Church near Barnton, Edinburgh, where he lived. Awarded the OBE in 1948, he was survived by his wife. See *Scottish Co-operator*, 8 August 1931, 30 July 1949.

LEE, Lennox Bartram
(18 August 1864 - 14 December 1949)

Calico printer, born at Broughton, Salford, the son of Sir Joseph Cocksey Lee (1832-94), cotton manufacturer and co-founder of the firm of Tootal Broadhurst Lee & Co Ltd (in 1888), and his wife Henrietta née Hill, he was educated at Thorpe Mandeville and Eton before serving for two years with the Sherwood Foresters, 1883-85. He then travelled widely, particularly in North West Africa (where the Lees were involved in commerce and Christian missions). In 1889 he commenced training in his father's calico-printing firm, the Rossendale Printing Co, one of the best of its kind, and became a first-class practical printer. Encountering the problems of undercutting in a highly competitive industry, heavy dependence on merchants, high investment costs, large price fluctuations and long term market decline, he sought solutions first in cartels and then in merger. When the Calico Printers' Association was formed in 1899 Lee took the Rossendale Printing Co into the amalgamation of 46 printing and 13 marketing firms, representing 85 per cent of the industry's capacity. Lee became a leading member of the CPA executive, 1899-1908, cutting the 84 directors down to six, reducing excess capacity, and emerging as CPA chairman in 1908. He retired nearly 40 years later. His major strategy was market-led: this determined his preference for vertical integration, for rationalisation (CPA employment fell from 20,500 in 1903 to 12,000 in 1930 to 6,000 in 1946), and for overseas expansion (in the 1930s). His encouragement of research and development produced the discovery of terylene in the CPA's Broad Oak laboratory in 1941 (by J R Whinfield and J T Dickson) which a shortage of capital forced the CPA to let ICI develop under licence (royalties from which supported the CPA in the post-war years). Outside business Lennox Lee, a devout Anglican, became a country gentleman in Herefordshire: from c. 1900 he regularly retreated to How Caple Court from Wednesday night to Sunday evening. Lee married, in 1892, Edith McLellan; they had two sons and a daughter. His second son, Roger Malcolm Lee, succeeded him as CPA chairman in 1947 (the elder son having died in the First World War). See *DBB*.

LEES, Sir David (Bryan)
(23 November 1936 -)

Engineering and automotive products company executive, the son of Rear-Admiral D M Lees and his wife C D M Lees. Educated at Charterhouse, he qualified as a chartered accountant in 1962. He was chief accountant at Handley Page Ltd, 1964-69, and then joined GKN (formerly Guest, Keen &

Nettlefolds) in 1970. Appointed to the board as finance director in 1982, he became group managing director of GKN in 1987, and was appointed chairman and chief executive in 1988. In the 1980s GKN was undergoing major restructuring, initially under Lees's predecessor, Sir Trevor Holdsworth (qv). Lees continued to reorient GKN: the group continued to expand its overseas operations, especially on the automotive side, which accounts for over half the sales and has Ford, Toyota and Honda among its customers. Sales to Japan increased under Lees and GKN was granted a listing on the Japanese Stock Exchange in 1989. Industrial services now account for over a third of GKN's turnover. Between 1987 and 1989 profit before tax rose from £140 million to over £200 million, but fell by £95 million in 1991, as a world-wide economic recession hit GKN. After severe cost cuts, profits recovered in the following year. The group employed 30,000 (12,000 in the UK) by 1992. Since 1991, when he was knighted, Lees has been a director of the Bank of England and a non-executive director of Courtaulds. He is also chairman of the Economic and Financial Policy Committee of the CBI. In 1961 he married Edith Mary Bernard: they have two sons and a daughter.

LEES, Sir William Clare
(9 December 1874 - 26 May 1951)

Chairman of textile finishing conglomerate, born in Ashton-under-Lyne, the son of William Lees, director of a cotton finishing firm, and Emma née Clare. After briefly joining his father, in 1906 Lees became a director of the Bleachers' Association: composed of 53 firms engaged in the trade, it was the UK's ninth largest company by capital. In 1933 he was appointed chairman of the managing directors and was closely involved in the rationalisation of the Association by stabilising foreign competition and by supporting a policy of diversification. In its jubilee year, 1950, Lees became chairman: from 1933 to his death the Association's profits had doubled from £535,851 to £1,244,211, though assets had shrunk. He was a director of a number of other companies and had a wide administrative experience (he was a member of the Balfour Committee, 1924-9). Lees was knighted in 1924 and received a baronetcy in 1937. He married Kathleen née Nickson in 1901; they had a son and daughter. He left £129,822. See DBB; David J Jeremy, 'Survival Strategies in Lancashire Textiles: Bleachers' Association Ltd to Whitecroft PLC, 1900-1970s' Textile History 24 (1993).

LEIGH-PEMBERTON, (Robert) Robin
Baron Leigh-Pemberton
(5 January 1927 -)

Banker, born into one of the great landowning families of Kent, the son of Robert Douglas Leigh-Pemberton. Educated at Eton and Trinity College, Oxford, Robin Leigh-Pemberton served in the Grenadier Guards before becoming a practising barrister in 1954. He left the Bar in 1960 to run his estate and farm, but in 1966 he was invited onto the board of the foundry company Birmid Qualcast, a client of the National Westminster Bank, which appointed him to its south-west regional board. He joined Natwest's main board in 1972 and became chairman in 1977. In 1983 he was appointed by Margaret Thatcher as the Governor of the Bank of England. A blatant political appointee (besides his background he shared the Conservative Party's commitment to monetarism and combatting inflation), Leigh-Pemberton was criticised for his lack of banking experience. He was described as a man who looks and sounds like a film director's idea of someone who is big in the City, but who does not actually hold real power. Much of the detailed running of the Bank was said to have been left to Eddie George (qv), while Leigh-Pemberton limited most of his activities to a semi-ambassadorial role. He won friends for his open manner, but his period at the Bank brought it into unprecedented dispute over the Johnson Matthey and BCCI scandals and the loss of up to £5 billion of taxpayers' money in the foreign exchange markets on Black Wednesday. He retired as Governor at the end of 1992 and was succeeded by Eddie George. He has been Lord-Lieutenant of Kent since 1982, a former chairman of Kent County Council and pro-chancellor of Kent University. In 1953 he married Rosemary Davina, daughter of Col D Forbes and the Dowager Marchioness of Exeter: they have five sons. He became a life peer in 1993.

LEMON, Sir Ernest John Hutchings
(1884 - 15 December 1954)

Railway executive, who gained his theoretical education at Heriot-Watt College, Edinburgh, and his practical training at the Hyde Park Works of the North British Locomotive Co and the Highland Railway, Inverness. He joined the Midland Railway in 1911 as chief wagon inspector and became works manager at Derby in 1917. After the formation of the London Midland & Scottish Railway, in 1923 he was appointed a divisional manager and after a succession of senior posts became vice-president of the LMSR between 1932 and 1943. At the LMSR, which was the second largest UK employer in 1935 with 222,220 workers, Lemon introduced continuous locomotive production methods and reorganised motive power depots. He was Director-General of Aircraft Production between 1938 and 1940. Awarded the OBE in 1918, he was knighted in 1941. See *The Times*, 17 December 1954.

LETCH, Sir Robert
(10 January 1899 - 9 July 1962)

Dock and port manager, born at Bromley, Poplar, London, elder son of Robert John Letch, a railway guard, and his wife Ellen Rebecca May Dooel, he joined the Port of London Authority in 1915 and worked his way up the administrative side to become assistant general manager in January 1940. For twelve months, when German bombing was heaviest and the Royal Navy was extensively using the docks, he was responsible for the defence of the port. He was then charged with inaugurating the Clyde Anchorages Emergency Port (utilising overside discharge at small local piers). In January 1942 he was detached from the PLA to serve as regional port director for the Clyde and then Scotland, 1941-42, and for the North Western Area, 1942-45. He was knighted in 1945. While in Glasgow he was struck by a cargo block, an accident which led to total blindness. This did not prevent him from continuing his career. In 1947 he became a full time member of the Docks and Inland Waterways Executive (under the British Transport Commission, in charge of the nationalised transport industry), and later its deputy chairman. When in 1954 the Executive was split up Letch became general manager of the British Transport Docks Division and chairman of the Docks Management Board, employing 20,000 in 1955. Despite his blindness he had a remarkable memory, a grasp of detail and an imagination which allowed him to visualise not only dock facilities he once saw but also improvements he had never seen but had authorised. See *The Times*, 10, 13, 18 July 1962.

LEVER, Sir Ernest Harry
(22 November 1890 - 4 September 1970)

Steel company chairman, born in Islington, London, the son of Thomas Bains Lever, a master builder, he was educated at the William Ellis Endowed School and then entered the Prudential Assurance Co as a clerk in 1907. An exceptional mathematical ability enabled him to qualify as a Fellow of the Institute of Actuaries when he was 22. After the First World War, in which he served throughout in the Royal Artillery (reaching the rank of captain), his knowledge of foreign exchange technicalities led to his involvement in negotiations over German reparations. He was appointed joint secretary of the Prudential in 1931. He sat on the Board of Trade Departmental Committee on Fixed Trusts in 1936; was chairman of the British Insurance Association's Investment Protection Committee, 1938-40; and in 1940 was appointed by the Control Committee (acting for the Securities Management Trust chaired by Montagu Norman (qv) governor of the Bank of England) chairman and finance director of Richard Thomas & Co, the South Wales steel makers, then in financial difficulties. At a salary of £12,500 a year plus expenses of £2,500, Lever reorganised the firm. Having seen the old guard, notably Sir William Firth (qv), retire, he brought the firm into profitability during wartime and forged links with Baldwins Ltd. In November 1944 Richard Thomas bought Baldwins for £5.6 million. Lever then outlined proposals for modernising the South Wales steel and tinplate industries, to be centred on a new wide strip mill at Port Talbot. Out of these came the Steel Co of Wales formed in 1947. The Steel Co of Wales in 1955 was separated from Richard Thomas & Baldwins which then was based on a fully integrated steelworks and continuous strip mill and tinplate works at Ebbw Vale, together with a large number of old style tinplate works. Sir Ernest Lever (he was knighted in 1954) was chairman of Richard Thomas and then RTB, 1940-59, and chairman of the Steel Co of Wales, 1947-55 (each of which employed over 20,000 in 1955). He was president of the British Iron and Steel Federation in 1956 and also a director of Lloyds Bank, 1953-61. Lever married first, in 1913, Florence née Millington, by whom he had two sons. The marriage was dissolved in 1939 and he married secondly in 1940 Mrs Phyllis Irene Blok. See *The Times*, 5 September 1970; John Vaizey, *The History of British Steel* (1974).

LEVER, William Hesketh
1st Viscount Leverhulme
(19 September 1851 - 7 May 1925)

Soap and food manufacturer, born in Bolton, Lancashire, the elder son of James Lever, a Congregationalist retail grocer and his wife, Eliza née Hesketh. A brilliant marketing man, Lever made his name and fortune selling and manufacturing 'Sunlight' soap. Lever Bros, which went public in 1894 (capital £1.5 million), soon became the leading soap manufacturer in the UK. Spurred by Lever's aggressive marketing techniques and policy of buying out rivals, the firm by 1906 was capitalised at £4.7 million (with Lever holding all the ordinary shares - value £1.8 million) and employed 3,000 UK employees. Besides its domestic dominance, the firm became an early British multinational with seven overseas factories, and later had extensive interests in Africa and its own fleet of steamers. Lever's wealth allowed him to indulge his taste for paternalism, notably in his spacious model company town of Port Sunlight. But in business his control of the firm outlasted his commercial judgement, which became distorted by megalomania. A disastrous speculative investment in the Niger Co in 1920 effectively ended his control of the firm, when the board insisted on the appointment of a professional accountant, Francis D'Arcy Cooper (qv). Lever sat as MP (Liberal) for the Wirral 1906-9. He was created a baronet in 1911, a baron in 1917 and a viscount in 1922. Lever married, in 1874, Elizabeth Allen (d 1913), the daughter of a Bolton linen draper, in whose memory he built the Lady Lever Art Gallery at Port Sunlight. Lever left £1.6 million and a business which employed capital of £64.5 million and over 20,000 employees world-wide. See William Hulme Lever (2nd Viscount Lever), *Viscount Leverhulme* (1927); Charles Wilson, *The History of Unilever* (2 vols, 1954); *DBB*; *DNB*.

LEWINTON, Sir Christopher

(6 January 1932 -)

Engineering and metals company executive, the son of Joseph and Elizabeth Lewinton. He became a chartered engineer after attending Acton Technical College and the University of London. After Army service he became disillusioned with the UK, which he felt treated engineers as second-class citizens and did not do enough to encourage the creation of wealth, and emigrated to the US. From 1960 to 1970 he was president of Wilkinson Sword USA, returning to the UK in 1970 to become chief executive of Wilkinson Sword Group. In 1978, when Wilkinson Sword was acquired by Allegheny International, he joined the main board of the company and was the London-based chairman of the international operations of Allegheny International, a $3 billion US public company, headquartered in Pittsburgh. In 1986 he became chief executive at the TI Group, which had been founded in 1919 as a Birmingham-based engineering company (known as Tube Investments). Lewinton's remit was to transform what was perceived as a largely dull Midlands metal basher into an internationally-focussed seals, tube and aerospace engineer. Lewinton (who became chairman and chief executive in May 1989) sold off non-core businesses, such as Croda, Russell Hobbs and Raleigh bicycles, and bought John Crane (seals), Bundy (tubes) and Dowty (aerospace). By 1993 TI had a market capitalisation of about £1.3 billion and had rejoined the FTSE 100 Index. Lewinton is also a director of Reed International. He was knighted in 1993. He married in 1979

Louise Head, after a previous marriage to Jennifer Alcock was dissolved: he has two sons and two stepchilden. See Corinne Simcock, *A Head for Business* (1992).

LEWIS, John Spedan

(22 September 1885 - 21 February 1963)

Department store owner, born in Marylebone, London, the son of John Lewis, the founder and proprietor of the John Lewis department store in Oxford Street, London, and his wife Eliza née Baker, John Spedan Lewis was educated at Westminster School (a Queen's scholar). Shunning a university education, he joined his father's firm in 1906, as his younger brother Oswald (1887-1966) did soon after. On reaching their majorities their father gave them each a quarter of the capital of the business (£50,000). Horrified to discover inefficiency and exploitation of staff, John Spedan, in defiance of his father, devised the business Partnership. He was able to test some ideas when in 1914 he was given the management of the Peter Jones store in Sloane Square. He improved wages, catering and hostelling arrangements and separated sales from buying. By 1919 turnover had increased five-fold to £½ million. On the death of his father in 1928 he raised fresh capital by converting the store to a public company, John Lewis & Co Ltd, which provided £1.5 million. Soon after he formed the John Lewis Partnership Ltd with a capital of £312,000. Under the First Trust Settlement he and his wife assigned to the trustees all their shares in John Lewis & Co Ltd and Peter Jones Ltd, with the condition that profits he and his wife would otherwise have had be distributed to employees who then became shareholders (for the duration of their employment) in the Partnership. In return Spedan Lewis took interest-free deferred bonds totalling £1 million repayable out of profits over 30 years. In case the experiment misfired he also retained the ordinary shares in John Lewis & Co Ltd. His optimism was rewarded and in 1950 under the Second Trust Settlement he transferred all his remaining shares and ultimate control to the trustees. Expansion of the business was marked by the extension of West End premises, the opening of department stores in the provinces, acquisition of the Waitrose food shop group (1937), and purchase of a large part of Selfridges in 1940. Spedan Lewis retired in 1955. At this point there were over 12,000 employees. In 1962 £1.5 million was distributed to 16,000 Partners. Spedan Lewis married, in 1922, Sarah Beatrice Mary Hunter; they had two boys (the elder died in childhood) and a girl. See *DBB*; John Lewis PLC, *John Spedan Lewis, 1885-1963* (1985).

LIDBURY, Sir Charles
(30 June 1880 - 25 July 1978)
Clearing banker, born in Middlewich, Cheshire, the son of Frank Albert Lidbury, a school teacher, and Emily née Harding. He left school at 13 and joined a local branch of Parr's Bank, where his steady promotion resulted in his eventual appointment from 1930-47 as chief general manager at the Westminster Bank (which had absorbed Parr's). A specialist in foreign banking, he was also general manager of the Westminster Foreign Bank Ltd, 1928-47. He was a director of the Westminster Bank, 1936-62, while still chief general manager, and during this period emerged as the most powerful figure in the Bank. He was president of the Institute of Bankers and chairman of the Chief Executive's Committee of the Clearing Banks. He married in 1909 Mary née Moreton (d 1939); they had two daughters. He left £246,522 gross. See Theodore E Gregory, *The Westminster Bank Through A Century* (2 vols, Oxford, 1936); DBB.

LINDSAY, David Alexander Edward
27th Earl of Crawford and Balcarres
(10 October 1871 - 8 March 1940)
Coal mine proprietor, born at Denecht, Aberdeenshire, the eldest son of the 26th Earl of Crawford (qv) and Emily Florence née Bootle-Wilbraham. After Eton and Oxford University, Lindsay succeeded his father in 1913 as chairman of the family-owned Wigan Coal & Iron Co. After 1930 Lord Crawford merged a number of companies to form the Wigan Coal Corporation and the Lancashire Steel Corporation: he was actively engaged as chairman of the former, which employed over 11,000 men at 12 collieries, at his death; and also a director of the latter, which owned large works at Irlam and Warrington. Unionist MP for Chorley, he held a number of Government and Cabinet posts, such as Minister of Transport and President of the Board of Agriculture and Fisheries. Deeply interested in the arts, he held a multitude of public appointments and headed numerous historical and artistic societies. He was elected FRS in 1924 and was a KT. In 1900 he married Constance Lilian, daughter of Sir Henry Carstairs Pelly; they had two sons and five daughters. He left £514,799, of which £125,734 was in settled land. See DBB; DNB.

LINDSAY, James Ludovic
26th Earl of Crawford and Balcarres
(28 July 1847 - 31 January 1913)
Iron and coal proprietor, born at St Germain-en-Laye, France, the son of the 25th Earl, whom he succeeded in 1880, and his wife Margaret, daughter of Lieutenant-General James Lindsay of Balcarres, he was educated at Eton and Trinity College, Cambridge. Astronomy (for studies in which he was elected FRS in 1878), sport (yachting and throwing the hammer), exploring (for ornithological purposes) and stamp collecting occupied much of his life. His 14,500 acres, many in Scotland, also included tracts around Wigan where his seat was Haigh Hall (the location of his magnificent library). Politically a Conservative, he was MP for Wigan, 1874-80. His Wigan estates lay on the Lancashire coal field which his father had developed through the Wigan Coal & Iron Co, formed in 1865 and run by Alfred Hewlett (qv). The 26th Earl succeeded his father as chairman of the company which by 1907 employed 10,000. He was also president of the Wigan and District Chamber of Commerce. Lindsay married, in 1869, Emily Florence née Bootle-Wilbraham; they had five sons and a daughter. The eldest son, David Lindsay (qv), succeeded his father. See *The Times*, 1 February 1913.

LIPTON, Stuart
(9 November 1942 -)
Property developer, born into a Jewish household in north London, the son of Bertram Green and Jeanette Lipton. His mother co-founded the Chinacraft chain. His parents divorced when he was 12 and he lost sight of his father after the 1970s. Educated at Rockhurst boarding school, near Newbury, and Berkhamsted School, Hertfordshire, he joined an estate agency as an office boy. In the 1960s he launched himself in the property market as an estate agent and was a millionaire when he was 30. He sold his company, Sterling Land, for £28 million a month before the crash in 1973. In 1983 he founded Stanhope Properties for the development of City office buildings in the post-Big Bang era. In the boom of the 1980s Lipton teamed up with Godfrey Bradman (qv), to form Rosehaugh Stanhope Developments. With such prestigious projects as the Broadgate office development in London, RSD became one of the glamour companies. By 1989 Stanhope's profits were over £15 million. Lipton owned a third of the equity in Stanhope, and the Reichmann brothers of Canary Wharf fame owned another third. But Lipton and Bradman failed to foresee the end of the property boom: in 1992 Rosehaugh collapsed with massive debts; and Stanhope struggled for survival. In 1993 Lipton's Stanhope may survive, but only as a much smaller entity. His stake in the company, valued at about £100 million in 1989, was worth about £10 million three years later. Lipton has been a member of the Royal Fine Art Commission since 1988. He married in 1966 Ruth Kathryn Marks: they have two sons and a daughter.

LIPTON, Sir Thomas Johnstone
(10 May 1850 – 2 October 1931)

General provisions merchant, was born in a Glasgow tenement, the only surviving son of Thomas Lipton, a Presbyterian and labourer from County Monaghan, Ireland, and his wife Frances née Johnstone who fled from the potato famine and set up a tiny shop in Crown Street, Glasgow. Young Thomas, educated at St Andrew's Parish School, worked successively as an errand boy, shirt-maker's assistant and Burns Line cabin boy before saving enough to take a steerage passage to New York. After five years in the USA he returned to Glasgow with savings of $500 and in 1871 opened his first shop, 'Lipton Market' in Stobcross Street, Anderston, Glasgow. Over the next 20 years he opened similar grocery stores all over Britain, meeting the demand for foodstuffs from the middle and working classes concentrated in the country's spreading cities. Handpicking staff and sites; stan-dardising the presentation of goods; explicit pricing and no credit; and integrating backwards to suppli-ers (his major coup being the purchase of tea plan-tations when he visited Ceylon in 1890): these were the techniques behind his business growth. By 1898 he had 243 branches in the UK, 12 plan-tations in Ceylon and a large headquarters in the City Road, London (opened 1894). That year, 1898, he sold the business to the public for £2.5 million, but remained chairman. By his seventies he was losing his old skills and was ousted by a share-holders' revolt in 1927 (when Lipton Ltd had 615 shops). Thereafter Liptons was acquired by Van den Berghs who installed managers from their Meadow Dairy Co to revive Liptons which went into the Home & Colonial (later Allied Suppliers) group. After the death of his mother, to whom he was singularly attached (he never married) in 1889, Thomas Lipton purchased Osidge Park, Southgate, Middlesex, where, attended by his Singalese ser-vants, he lived until his death. A lavish host and a generous benefactor to charitable causes (for which he was knighted in 1898), he entered the Prince of Wales's circle in the late 1890s and took up yacht-ing, one of the sports of kings. Five times he chal-lenged for the America's Cup (1889, 1901, 1904, 1920 and 1930), each without success. Pioneering the sale of wholesome, safe food (and not just tea), sold cheaply and efficiently: this was Sir Thomas Lipton's major contribution to British society. See *DSBB*; Sir Thomas Lipton (with William Blackwood), *Leaves from the Lipton Logs* (1931); Peter Mathias, *Retailing Revolution* (1967).

LISTER, Sidney John
(1 November 1877 – 12 September 1959)

Shipping company executive, born at Plympton, Devon, to William Henry Lister, master of the Union Workhouse, and Elizabeth Ann née Woolcock, he joined the Cunard Steam-Ship Co at its head office in Liverpool c. 1895. He worked in many departments before being promoted to general passenger manager in 1909 and later, assis-tant manager. He was made joint general manager (with F Litchfield) in 1921, sole manager in 1933 and a director in 1929. When Cunard and White Star Line merged in 1934, Lister was elected a director of the new company, Cunard White Star, and became joint managing director with A B Cauty of the White Star Line. Cauty retired in 1936 leaving Lister in supreme managerial control. Lister's period as Cunard's managing director, 1934-45, saw major changes in Cunard's markets. American restrictions on immigration, from the 1920s, led to a massive reduction in emigrant traf-fic. Conversely, cabin and tourist class passengers were a growth area in the 1930s. In response, Cunard fought within the North Atlantic Conference (the shipping companies' cartel) for advantageous classifications for their ships. Equally importantly, from 1929 the Cunard board, under Sir Thomas Royden and then Sir Percy Bates (qv), moved to a 'big ship' replacement policy which saw the construction of the 81,000 ton *Queen Mary* (built 1930-34 at a cost of £3.277 million) and her sister ship *Queen Elizabeth* (1937-38), financed in part by the government (in exchange for taking over the White Star Line, a casualty of the Royal Mail debacle, of which the government was a major creditor). The Second World War saw much of the Cunard fleet of 18 ships requisitioned for military service. Cunard staff headed by Lister were put under Admiralty orders to manage and operate the ships. After his retirement as managing director Lister, who was remembered as a benevolent auto-crat, kept his seat on the boards of Cunard and Cunard White Star until 1950. He was also a direc-tor of Cunard House Ltd and a past chairman of the Liverpool Steam Ship Owners' Association. He was married and had two sons, the younger being killed in the Second World War and the elder being sometime a Lancashire County cricket cap-tain. See *Journal of Commerce*, 22 March 1945, 4 January 1951; Francis E Hyde, *Cunard and the North Atlantic, 1840-1973* (1975); *Liverpool Daily Post*,17 March 1945, 4 January 1951; Liverpool University Archives, Cunard papers.

LITHGOW, Sir James
(27 January 1883 - 23 February 1952)
Shipbuilder, born at Port Glasgow, the son of William Todd Lithgow, shipbuilder, and Agnes Birkmyre. Educated at the Glasgow Academy and privately in Paris, he became apprentice in the family firm of Lithgows Ltd in 1901, and then assumed control alongside his brother, Henry (d 1948), in 1908. They expanded into coal, iron and steel, and though there was some contraction in the 1930s (when Lithgow was a key figure in the Scottish steel industry, in the rationalising activities of National Shipbuilders Security Ltd, became a director of the Bank of England, and took over the Fairfield yard), by 1952 Lithgows was the world's largest private shipyard. He was also concerned with labour relations as president of the Shipbuilders Employers Federation in 1920 and vice-president of the National Confederation of Employers Organisation in 1922. He also undertook a wide range of public service during two world wars. He was president of the FBI, 1931-32, and president of the Iron and Steel Federation, 1943-45. He married in 1924 Gwendolyn Amy, daughter of the shipowner John Harrison: they had one son and two daughters. Created a baronet in 1925, he was made an honorary citizen in Port Glasgow in 1951, a recognition of both his industrial and social work and his gifts to the Church of Scotland. He left £443,961 gross. See *DSBB*.

LIVESEY, Sir George Thomas
(8 April 1834 - 4 October 1908)
Gas company manager and chairman, born in Islington, London, the son of Thomas Livesey (d 1878), a clerk with the Gas Light & Coke Co but later manager of the South Metropolitan Gas Co, and his wife Ellen née Hewes, he left school at 14 and joined the South Metropolitan Gas Co. He was appointed assistant manager in 1857, engineer in 1862, and on his father's death became engineer and company secretary. To keep pace with the spread of suburban London south of the Thames and the adoption of gas lighting, new gasworks had to be built at East Greenwich (designed by George Livesey and large enough to contain the Albert Hall). When, in the 1870s, the Gas Light & Coke Co took over seven gas companies north of the Thames and then in 1878 proposed swallowing up the South Metropolitan, Livesey quickly acquired the Phoenix Co and the Surrey Consumers Co to make his own company the dominant gas supplier south of the Thames. Livesey became chairman of the South Metropolitan in 1885 and died in office. Between 1871 and 1908 the price of South Metropolitan gas was reduced from 3s 2d to 2s 3d per 1,000 cubic feet. When his stokers were unionised in the late 1880s and the Gas Workers Union demanded a closed shop, Livesey rejected the idea and introduced a co-partnership scheme for non-union men. A bitter strike followed in 1889-90 and unions were excluded from the company, marking the emergence of 'new unionism' among the country's unskilled workforce. Although Livesey (a devout Anglican) preached the merits of co-partnership, in 1907 the 5,000 co-partners (out of 6,000 employees) did not have the freedom of shareholders to buy and sell shares or even withdraw all their dividends. Despite a lack of formal training, Sir George Livesey (he was knighted in 1902) was a practical gas engineer with a world-wide reputation. In 1874 he was president of the Institution of Gas Engineers. Livesey married Harriet née Howard in 1859; there were no children. See *DBB*.

LLEWELLYN, Sir David Richard
(9 March 1879 - 15 December 1940)
Coalmine owner, born at Aberdare, the eldest of five sons of Alderman Rees Llewellyn, a former colliery manager, and Elizabeth née Llewellyn. Educated at Llandovery College, he qualified as a mining engineer, before rising rapidly to prominence as a coalowner when he linked his fortunes to the Welsh industrialist Henry Seymour Berry and the 'Cambrian Combine', which was involved in the exploitation of Welsh coal, especially anthracite. This connection also brought Llewellyn onto the board of John Lysaght Ltd (integrated makers of galvanised sheets), and thence Guest Keen & Nettlefolds (GKN), when it absorbed Lysaghts. As one of the more enlightened coalowners, he was a long-serving member of the regional Coalowners' Association. A Liberal, he became chairman of Aberdare District Council in 1920. He was awarded a baronetcy in 1922. In 1905 he married Magdalene née Harries; they had four sons. He left £714,131. See *DBB*.

LLEWELLYN, William Morgan
(1887 - 1943)
Coalmine owner, the third and eldest surviving son of Rees Llewellyn. He became a mining pupil at his father's colliery at Bwllfa and gained his manager's certificate aged 20. He succeeded his father as general manager of the Bwllfa Dare Collieries and afterwards became managing director of the Welsh Associated Collieries. He was chairman of the North's Navigation Collieries (1899) Ltd, of the Graigola Merthyr Co, and of C L Clay Ltd and a director of the Powell Duffryn Steam Coal Co, Welsh Associated Collieries Ltd and the Ynisarwed Colieries Co. By 1935 Powell Duffryn employed 13,512. He was chairman of the Monmouthshire

and South Wales Coalowners' Association in 1936. See *Iron and Coal Trades Review*, 24 September 1943.

LORD, Cyril
(12 July 1911 - 29 May 1984)

Textile and carpet manufacturer, born in the Droylsdon district of Manchester, the son of Richard Lund Lord, a Co-operative Society stores clerk, and Kate née Hackney. Educated at the Central School, Manchester, he briefly became a clerk with the CWS Bank, before becoming an apprentice with Ashworth Hadwen, a local spinning and weaving firm (he also attended evening classes in textile technology at Manchester College of Technology). In 1939 he set up his own converting firm, then joined the Cotton Board during the war, which brought him into contact with his future partner, William McMillan, a Belfast solicitor. Together they founded a textile merchant firm, Cyril Lord Ltd, in Belfast in 1945. Profits grew from £15,443 in 1946 to £566,174 in 1952 as the textile trade boomed, but foreign imports (which Lord was active in lobbying against) led to his move into carpet manufacture. He founded Cyril Lord Carpets Ltd in 1955 and was a pioneer in tufted carpets made from man-made fibres. A great showman and publicist (he once appeared in a Batman film as the Holy Matman), Lord's empire crashed in 1968 after the collapse of his Northern Ireland spinning and weaving business and a disastrous foray into UK carpet retailing at the time of falling consumer demand. Lord married three times: first in 1936 to Bessie Greenwood, by whom he had two sons and two daughters; second in 1960 to Shirley Hussey; and finally in 1974 to Aileen, widow of Val Parnell. See *DBB*.

LORD, Leonard Percy
1st Baron Lambury of Northfield
(15 November 1896 - 13 September 1967)

Motor vehicle manufacturer, born in Coventry, the son of William Lord, a baths superintendent, and Emma née Swain. Lord attended Bablake School, Coventry. He came to the attention of William Morris (qv) as production engineer at the Wolseley Co. In 1933 Morris appointed him managing director at his Cowley works and Lord successfully restructured production. In 1938 he joined the Austin Group, becoming managing director and chairman in 1945, and in the face of growing foreign competition masterminded the merger of Austin and Morris to form the British Motor Corporation (BMC) in 1951. Lord was chairman of the BMC from 1952-61. The Corporation's performance was uneven - net profits in 1952-3 were £3.8 million, in 1962-3 £9.4 million - but there

was a steady growth in output from 278,840 vehicles in 1952-3 to 748,470 in 1962-3 - a reflection of Lord's emphasis on innovation and organisation. He was made a KBE in 1954, when he was also elected president of the Institution of Production Engineers. He was made a peer in 1962. In 1921 he married Ethel Lily née Horton; they had three daughters. See Jonathan Wood, *Wheels of Misfortune: The Rise and Fall of the British Motor Industry* (1988); *DBB*.

LORIMER, Sir William
(4 November 1844 - 9 April 1922)

Locomotive engineer and steel manufacturer, born at Sanquhar, Dumfriesshire, the son of William Lorimer, a mining engineer, and Margaret Kirkhope Whigam, he was educated at the local parish school and then at 15 joined the Glasgow & Edinburgh Railway Co, possibly as an apprentice. In 1864 he moved into locomotive engineering, joining Henry Dubs of Dubs & Co on the south side of Glasgow. Three years later he became principal assistant to Dubs and in 1875 became a partner of Dubs and his two sons. Dubs died in 1876 and Lorimer became managing partner. In 1903 Dubs & Co merged with Neilson, Reid & Co and Sharp, Stewart & Co to form the North British Locomotive Co Ltd, the largest locomotive engineering company in Europe, employing nearly 8,000 in 1907. Lorimer was elected chairman. By 1920 the constituent firms in the NBL had built 22,000 locomotives. Through Henry Dubs, a founder and the manager of the Steel Co of Scotland from 1874, Lorimer also became a director of this firm, retiring in 1920, and serving as chairman from 1896 until retirement. The firm employed almost 6,000 in 1907. In his businesses Lorimer exerted a sound and conservative judgement. He was knighted in 1917. Lorimer married twice: first, in 1869, to Jane née Smith (d 1902); second, in 1913, to Mary Elizabeth née Sieber, by whom he had four sons and four daughters. See *DSBB*.

LUSK, William Clardy
(10 September 1875 - 25 February 1944)

Electrical engineering company executive, born in Nashville, Tennessee, of Scottish descent, the son of Alfred Hume and Elisabeth Clardy Husk. He graduated from Yale University as a BSc. In 1897 he joined the General Electric Co of America, where he made his mark as the firm's foreign representative in India, 1901-4. He joined that firm's London office in 1904, becoming manager of British-Thomson Houston's export department in 1910, and eventually managing director in 1922. He became chairman of BTH in 1929, the year after it had merged with British Westinghouse into Associated Electrical Industries. As deputy chairman of AEI, Lusk soon became the dominating presence, serving as managing director in 1932 (when the firm employed approaching 30,000) until his death in 1944. Cold and authoritarian, he proved deeply unpopular, if effective. He married Louise Casler of New York in 1926: they had no children. Lusk was naturalised in 1938. See Robert Jones and Oliver Marriott, *Anatomy of a Merger: A History of GEC, AEI and English Electric* (1970).

LYLE, Charles Ernest Leonard
1st Baron Lyle of Westbourne
(22 July 1882 - 6 March 1954)

Sugar refiner, born in Edmonton, Middlesex, the son of Charles Lyle, a partner in a London sugar refinery famous for 'Lyle's Golden Syrup', and Margaret née Brown. After Harrow and Cambridge, Leonard Lyle joined the family firm and when in 1921 it merged with the other great British refiner, Henry Tate & Sons, he became a director of the new company. He was chairman of Tate & Lyle during the period 1928-38, when it emerged as the main UK sugar refiner, with 75 per cent of the country's refining capacity. In 1918-22 and again in 1923-4, he was elected Unionist MP for the Stratford division of West Ham and served as Parliamentary Private Secretary to the Food Controller in 1920-1. He was knighted in 1923 and made a baronet in 1932. He returned to Parliament in 1940-45 as Conservative MP for Bournemouth, and vehemently opposed Labour plans to nationalise sugar refining. Churchill gave Lyle his hereditary peerage in his resignation honours' list. In 1904 he married Edith Louise née Levy (d 1942); they had a son and two daughters. He left £664,910. See Philippe Chalmin, *The Making of a Sugar Giant: Tate & Lyle, 1859-1989* (1990).

LYONS, Sir William
(4 September 1901 - 8 February 1985)

Motor-cycle side-car and motorcar manufacturer, born at Blackpool, the second son of an Irish musician, William Lyons, and Minnie née Barcroft. Educated at Arnold House School, Blackpool, at 17 he became a trainee at Crossley Motors Ltd in Manchester. In 1922 he began a partnership in Blackpool manufacturing Swallow motor-cycle side-cars and, later, car bodies for Austin and Morris (qqv). The business moved to Coventry in 1929, where Swallow Side-Car & Coachbuilding Co was started. The firm went public in 1935 as SS Cars Ltd, with Lyons as head, and soon after the first Jaguar car was produced. In 1945 the firm became Jaguar Cars Ltd (dropping the unfortunate

SS letters), which Lyons established as a unique and stylish marque. Particular attention was paid to the American market and to advertising, with Jaguar's sports car credentials soon underlined by regular victories in the Le Mans 24-hours race. In the 1960s Jaguar absorbed other Coventry car makers, such as Daimler and Guy Motors, but was in turn merged with the British Motor Corporation (the possibility of Jaguar remaining a family firm ended in 1955 when Lyons's son was killed driving a Jaguar). Lyons remained chairman of Jaguar and became a deputy chairman of BMC, but retired when the latter merged with Leyland in 1972. He was pleased to see Jaguar returned to private ownership under (Sir) John Egan (qv). He held no other directorships, but was president of the Society of British Motor Manufacturers and Traders and other similar bodies. Lyons was knighted in 1957. He married in 1924 Greta née Brown: they had two daughters and one son. See Andrew Whyte, *Jaguar: The History of a Great British Car* (1980); *DBB*; *DNB*.

LYTTELTON, Oliver
1st Viscount Chandos
(15 March 1893 - 21 January 1972)

Metal dealer and electrical manufacturer, he was born in London, the son of Alfred Lyttelton, seventh brother of the 8th Viscount Cobham and a barrister (who became a Conservative MP from 1895 and Colonial Secretary, 1903-5), by his second wife Edith Sophy née Balfour. Lyttelton was educated at Eton and Trinity College, Cambridge, leaving without taking a degree. After the First World War (in which he was an officer in the Grenadier Guards) he spent a year with the merchant bank, Brown, Shipley, and then in 1920 was recruited by Sir Cecil Budd to the British Metal Corporation, established in 1918 to secure British supplies of non-ferrous metals around the British Empire and to direct them into Empire smelters and refineries for obvious strategic reasons. Budd and Lyttelton, unable to control a widespread imperial industry in entirety, concentrated on finance, shipping and sales and successfully federated major interests. In 1939 Lyttelton was made Controller of Non-Ferrous Metals at the Ministry of Supply. Churchill appointed him President of the Board of Trade in 1940 (he became an MP soon after), and in 1942 he became Minister of Production, with a seat in the Cabinet, succeeding Max Aitken, Lord Beaverbrook (qv). After the war he served as chairman of Associated Electrical Industries, 1945-51, and again 1954-63, giving up his parliamentary seat in 1954. In his first administration at AEI he failed to integrate the constituent companies of the group (Metropolitan-Vickers and

British Thomson-Houston) while in the second he succeeded in raising large sums of money in the City only to see them spent recklessly by engineers whose science and technology he did not understand. AEI's giant organisation (87,000 employees in 1955) needed a ruthless, market-oriented chairman who arrived in the shape of Arnold Weinstock (qv) in 1967. Lyttelton was sworn of the Privy Council in 1940, made a viscount in 1954 and created a Knight of the Garter in 1970. He married in 1920 Lady Moira Godolphin Osborne, youngest daughter of the 10th Duke of Leeds; they had three sons and a daughter. See DBB; Robert Jones and Oliver Marriott, *Anatomy of a Merger: A History of GEC, AEI and English Electric* (1970).

M

McALLISTER, Ian (Gerald)
(17 August 1943 -)

Motor car company executive, born in Scotland, the son of Ian Thomas McAllister, a tax officer, and Margaret Mary née McNally. Educated at Thornleigh College, Bolton, and University College, London (BSc Econ), he joined the Ford Motor Co in 1964. After a number of posts in analysis, operations and marketing, he became general field manager in 1979. He joined the board in 1980, working on the sales and marketing side of the company in Germany and the USA. In 1991 he became managing director of Ford Motor Co and chairman in the following year, at a difficult time for the firm. In the late 1980s the UK was Ford's most profitable and important market, but in 1991 Ford plunged to an operating loss of £523 million and at the end of 1992 its leadership of the UK market was usurped by Rover. McAllister has placed Dagenham, its biggest UK factory on a two-and-a-half-day week. Nevertheless, with a workforce of over 50,000 and a turnover in 1991 of £6,191 million, Ford was still amongst the top 20 companies in the UK. McAllister married in 1968 Susan Margaret Frances Mitchell, by whom he had three sons and one daughter.

McALPINE, Alfred James
(15 June 1908 - 6 November 1991)

Contractor, eldest of three children and only son of Alfred David McAlpine, fourth of the seven sons of Robert McAlpine (qv), and his wife Ethel May née Williams, he was educated at Repton and, briefly, Cambridge. He joined his grandfather's company, Sir Robert McAlpine & Sons Ltd as a timekeeper in 1928, staying until 1935 when he and his father, Sir Alfred McAlpine (he was knighted in 1931), took the firm's Midlands, North Wales and North

West subsidiary into an independent position, completing the separation in 1940 when it was renamed Sir Alfred McAlpine & Son Ltd. Confined to the North Midlands and the North West, Sir Alfred and his son 'Jimmie' (to distinguish him from his father) kept to the agreed market division. Their early work included the Birkenhead section of the Mersey Tunnel, work on the Manchester Ship Canal and on Bowaters' paper mills at Ellesmere Port. Rearmament brought more contracts including the Rootes airframe factory at Speke. On Sir Alfred's death in 1944 Jimmie became chairman, holding office until 1985 when he became company president. Like his father he depended on a core team of practical managers, including his brother-in-law Peter Bell. After 1945 the firm was responsible for all manner of factories, civic and industrial buildings, including power stations. It won motorway construction contracts worth £1,745 million (1985 values) between 1959 and 1986, the first being the Warrington-to-Preston stretch of the M6. By the early 1970s the firm was constructing a fifth of Britain's new roads. Jimmie, a colourful character who preferred visiting large and complex construction sites to sitting in board meetings, developed loyalty and skill by insisting that control of the labour force and plant remain in the hands of those who worked up from labour themselves (in contrast to competitors who employed qualified engineers), and by giving a special prominence to quantity surveyors. Besides fast and vintage cars, Jimmie McAlpine's other passion was his South African company which he started in 1948 and ran until 1985, not least for access to long spells of sunshine each year. Market sharing between the two main McAlpine companies ended in 1983. Hating publicity (he refused to have a *Who's Who* entry and reputedly took 11 valium before first meeting the Queen) and shunning all trade and employers' associations, Jimmie McAlpine was late in reacting to the 1980s shift away from public sector to private work, leaving his son and successor, Bobbie, to implement the appropriate managerial changes in the late 1980s. Jimmie McAlpine married five times and was survived by his wife Cynthia, two daughters and a son. See Tony Gray, *The Road to Success: Alfred McAlpine, 1935-1985* (1987); *Independent*, 4 January 1992; *The Times*, 13 November 1991.

McALPINE, Sir Robert
(13 February 1847 - 3 November 1934)

Contractor, born at Newarthill, Lanarkshire, the son of Robert McAlpine, an underground manager who died when Robert was six years of age, and Ann née Paterson, he left the local school at the age of 10 to work as a pit trapper. Between the ages of 15 and 21 he served a bricklayer's apprenticeship, returning to coalmining when building work was scarce. He then set up as a jobbing builder, moving into larger contracts after 1872 when he built 100 miners' cottages, financed with a loan from the City of Glasgow Bank. By the late 1870s he regularly employed several hundred men and was investing in property in the expanding area around Hamilton, his base and where he was town councillor, 1878-81. Although he was bankrupted in 1880 by a nationwide depression, his firm continued, headed by his cashier William Richmond. Robert, discharged from bankruptcy, returned in 1881 and the following year won the major contract, worth £300,000, for building a new sewing machine factory for the Singer Manufacturing Co at Kilbowie, Clydebank. This was a watershed. Completion in 1885 led to series of railway contracts in central Scotland and the West Highlands. His success derived partly from a readiness to use new technology, like concrete in the 1870s, reinforced concrete from 1904, and the latest labour-saving machinery for construction (steam excavators and cranes). His two eldest sons became partners in 1893 and the firm became known as Robert McAlpine & Sons. By 1907, when five sons partnered their father, the firm employed 7,500. They moved into England in 1904, shifted their head office from Clydebank to London in 1916 and in the First World War completed £5 million worth of war contracts. In recognition Robert McAlpine was created a baronet in 1918. During the 1920s the firm built the Wembley Stadium and the British Empire Exhibition buildings and the Dorchester Hotel in Park Lane (opened 1931). McAlpine married twice: first in 1868 to Agnes Hepburn (d 1888), by whom he had six sons and four daughters; secondly in 1889 to Florence Christina Palmer (d 1909), by whom he had a son and two daughters. See *DSBB*; Iain Russell, *Sir Robert McAlpine & Sons: The Early Years* (1988).

McALPINE, William Hepburn

(31 October 1871 - 20 February 1951)
Contractor, born in Hamilton, Lanarkshire, the second son of Sir Robert McAlpine (qv), the founder of the construction firm of that name, and his wife Agnes, he left Ayr Academy at 16 in order to assist his father. Working in all the main departments of the contracting business, at the age of 18 he was put in charge of his first contract. During the First World War he was responsible for maintaining tight control over expenditure. His elder brother, Robert Jr, suffering from health problems, retired after 1918 leaving William as the most senior of the second generation, now headquartered in London. A construction contract for the

British Sugar Manufacturers Ltd, producers of beet sugar, led William to direct McAlpines into substantial portfolio investments in this new industry. In the 1920s also he personally supervised the company's largest projects, the construction of docks at Tilbury and Southampton. After the death of his father and elder brother in 1934, William headed the firm. However, management was very much a collective family affair, with about 40 of the McAlpines and their relatives working in the company. One branch, who managed the firm's business in the Midlands, North Wales and the North West, and led by Alfred David McAlpine (1881-1944), formed a new construction company, Sir Alfred McAlpine & Son Ltd in 1940. Both parent and offspring firms were major contractors in Britain throughout the rest of the twentieth century. William married in 1898 Margaret Donnison Bishop; they had three sons and two daughters. See *DSBB*.

McCANCE, Sir Andrew

(30 March 1889 - 11 June 1983)
Steel manufacturer, born at Cadder near Glasgow, the son of John McCance, a cloth buyer and merchant, he was educated at Morrison's Academy, Crieff, Allan Glen's School, Glasgow, and the Royal School of Mines in London. He returned to Glasgow in 1910 and worked for Beardmore's, the shipbuilder, mostly in the armour shop, and gained a London DSc in 1916. With the backing of Colville's, the steel maker, he and a fellow metallurgist in 1919 formed Clyde Alloy Steel Co which struggled for five years and then showed profits. Meantime John Craig (qv), the Colville chairman increasingly relied on McCance for technical expertise and when in 1930 Colvilles Ltd was formed from the merger of David Colville & Sons and James Dunlop & Co, McCance was given a seat on the board. Over the next 25 years he was responsible for pushing forward new innovations, and remodelling and integrating steel making plants, his virtuosity being recognised by election to FRS in 1943, appointment as deputy chairman and joint managing director of Colvilles in 1944, and a knighthood in 1947. Despite outside opposition, after the Second World War he and Craig revived their 1936 development plan which involved the creation of a new integrated iron and steel complex at Motherwell, the Ravenscraig Works (in operation 1957-92). McCance succeeded Craig as chairman of Colvilles in 1957, retiring in 1968. He sat on numerous professional bodies, holding the presidencey of the British Iron and Steel Federation in 1957-58. He married, in 1936, Joya Harriett Gladys Burford; they had two daughters. See *DSBB*; Peter L Payne, *Colvilles and the Scottish Steel Industry* (1979).

MACDIARMID, Sir Allan Campbell
(18 August 1880 - 14 August 1945)
Iron and steel manufacturer, born in Glasgow, third son of Allan Macdiarmid, a merchant, and his wife Elizabeth née Tulloch, he was educated at Kelvinside Academy and Uppingham and then trained as a chartered accountant with McClelland, Ker & Co in Glasgow. In 1909 he became secretary of Stewarts & Lloyds, to whom he devoted the rest of his career, joining the board in 1918, becoming deputy chairman in 1925, and chairman in 1926, dying in office. Under Macdiarmid, Stewarts & Lloyds, whose plants were in the West of Scotland and Birmingham, developed a more professional, rationalised and centralised organisation. Further, aiming at supremacy in steel tube production he developed an ambitious strategy which included the acquisition of small tube firms, the negotiation of important agreements with competitors (like Tube Investments) and customers, and the construction of a massive integrated iron, steel and tube works at Corby, Northamptonshire (opened in 1934). Close to ironstone reserves and incorporating the latest technology, the Corby plant produced some of the cheapest steel in Europe. In the difficult capital and product markets of the late 1920s and 1930s, Macdiarmid was a pastmaster of skilful negotiation, bringing guile, nerve and persistence whether dealing with Whitehall or manoeuvring to stay outside the industry's cartels. A shy man, often shabbily dressed, Macdiarmid was knighted in 1945. He married, in 1910, Grace Buchanan, daughter of J H McClure, a rope manufacturer; they had three sons and two daughters. See Jonathan S Boswell, *Business Policies in the Making: Three Steel Companies Compared* (1983); *DSBB*; Frederick Scopes, *The Development of Corby Works* (1968).

McFADZEAN, Francis Scott
Baron McFadzean of Kelvinside
(26 November 1915 - 23 May 1992)
Industrialist, born in Troon, Scotland, the son of a solicitor. He ran off to sea at 14, but returned to study at Glasgow University and at the London School of Economics, where he took a degree in business administration. He was recruited into the civil service, joined the Board of Trade in 1938, later moved to the Treasury and then (after serving in the army during the war) in 1949 he worked for the Colonial Development Corporation. At the CDC he fell out with his boss Lord Reith (qv) and went to Shell, where he eventually became chairman of Shell Transport & Trading (the UK part of the Anglo-Dutch combine) between 1972 and 1976. This period was marked by a dramatic rise in the cost of oil, after the OPEC decision in 1973 to

cut production and raise prices. Knighted by Harold Wilson in 1975, he was appointed chairman of British Airways the following year, where he showed his ability to cut staff and follow unpopular policies (such as the decision to buy American rather than British aircraft) that were to impress Margaret Thatcher. She made him a peer in 1980 and appointed him chairman of Rolls Royce, the aero-engine firm that had been rescued from bankruptcy in 1971. In his three years there, McFadzean greatly improved productivity, shedding many thousands of jobs, and prepared the way for Rolls-Royce's privatisation. He was visiting professor of economics at Strathclyde University in 1967, where he worked to improve business education. In 1971 he became chairman of the Trade Policy Research Centre. His books elucidated an austere monetarist view of economics and business. In 1938 he married Isabel Beattie (d 1987): they had one daughter, Felicity, who married Lord Marsh, the Labour minister. In 1988 he married Sonja Khung, who survived him. See F C McFadzean, *Galbraith and the Planners* (1968), *The Operation of a Multi-national Enterprise* (1971).

McFADZEAN, William Hunter
Baron McFadzean of Woldingham
(17 December 1903 -)
Cable manufacturer, born in Stranraer, Wigtownshire, the second son of Henry McFadzean, a farmer and later a grain merchant, and his wife Agnes Wylie, he was educated at Stranraer Academy and High School and Glasgow University, and then qualified as a chartered accountant in 1927. He joined the accountants, Chalmers, Wade & Co, where he was responsible for auditing the accounts of British Insulated Cables Ltd at Prescot, Lancashire. In 1932 he became their accountant and formed a friendship with the chairman, Sir Alexander Roger (qv), another Scot. McFadzean played an important part in the negotiations of 1942-45 which led to the merger of the two dominant firms in the industry, BIC and Callender's Cable & Construction Co, which produced British Insulated Callender's Cables Ltd, a business with 40,000 employees. Roger became chairman and McFadzean an executive director. In 1947 the latter became deputy chairman and in 1950 chief executive. McFadzean became chairman and managing director in 1954, retiring from the managing directorship in 1960 and from the chairmanship in 1973. Between 1945 and 1973 BICC became a significant multinational, with a global workforce of over 50,000 in 17 countries and annual sales of £500 million. McFadzean was, inter alia president of the Federation of British Industries, 1959-61, founder-chairman of the Export Council

of Europe, 1960-64, and of the British National Export Council, 1964-66. For services to industry he was knighted in 1960 and created a life peer in 1966. McFadzean married, in 1933, Eileen, née Gordon; they had a son and two daughters (one adopted). See *DBB*.

McGOWAN, Harry Duncan
1st Baron McGowan of Ardeer
(3 June 1874 – 13 July 1961)

Chemical manufacturer, born in Glasgow, the son of Henry McGowan, a master flesher and brass finisher, and Agnes née Wilson. He joined Nobel's Explosive Co as office boy in 1894 and became its boss by 1918. In 1926 he and Alfred Mond (qv) conceived the merger of the UK's leading chemical firms into Imperial Chemical Industries Ltd. McGowan was chairman of ICI, 1930-50 and a long-serving managing director. His diplomatic activity was to the fore in the 1930s when he masterminded ICI's cartel system and its overseas subsidiaries; and after 1940 he led the company into plastics and synthetic fibres. He was a director of numerous industrial and financial companies and served on several professional and Government committees: he chaired, for example, the committee on electrical distribution in 1935-36. A ruthless autocrat, he was described as a 'twentieth century industrial Tory'. He was created KBE in 1918 and a baron in 1937. In 1903 he married Jean Boyle Young (d 1952): they had two sons and two daughters. He left £207,453. See William J Reader, *Imperial Chemical Industries* (2 vols, 1970-75); *DBB*; *DNB*.

MacGREGOR, Sir Ian (Kinloch)
(21 September 1912-)

Industrialist, born in Kinlochleven, Scotland, the son of a works accountant and a schoolteacher. He was brought up in the strict traditions of the United Free Church. Educated at George Watson's College, Edinburgh, Glasgow Hillhead School, and Glasgow University, where he took a degree in metallurgy, MacGregor began his career as a metallurgist at Beardmores in 1935. After the war his main career was in America (where he became naturalised) with Amax, a small molybdenum producer, which he helped build into an industrial giant. In the 1980s, the British Government, attracted by his stance as a union basher and cost-cutter, appointed him chairman of the British Steel Corporation, 1980-83. The potential transfer fee of over £1 million to be paid to MacGregor's former employers, the New York merchant bankers Lazard Frères, immediately created political controversy (the actual sum paid in 1985 was £875,000). MacGregor's dour image, funereal style and ruth-

less reputation (which he himself appeared to cultivate) seemed to be perfectly attuned to the objectives of the Prime Minister, Margaret Thatcher. He cut the BSC workforce by nearly a half (from 166,000 to about 80,000), though the policy had already been set out by Sir Charles Villiers (qv). MacGregor then left to head the National Coal Board between 1983 and 1986 (at one stage he had proposed doing both jobs). At the NCB he dealt with the year-long miners' strike after March 1984, though he had little long-term impact on the coal industry, most of the major subsequent changes being carried out by his successor, Sir Robert Haslam (qv). MacGregor was knighted in 1986 by a Conservative Government well pleased with the results of his efforts – halting the decline of steel and defeating the coal unions – but was less popular with the thousands who lost their jobs. In the early 1990s MacGregor was still finding employment as a company doctor – with Mountleigh, HunterPrint and Holmes Protection – though with far less success. See Ian MacGregor (with Rodney Tyler), *The Enemies Within* (1986); Martin Adeney and John Lloyd, *The Miners' Strike* (1986).

MACKAY, James Lyle
1st Earl of Inchcape
(11 September 1852 – 23 May 1932)

Shipowner, he was born at Arbroath, Scotland, the second son and fourth child of James Mackay, a master mariner who was drowned when James Lyle Mackay was 10, and his wife Deborah Lyle, daughter of a Nova Scotia shipbuilder. Educated at Arbroath Academy and Elgin Academy, he spent a year as a lawyer's clerk and trained with a rope and canvas maker before breaking away from Arbroath to work for a London shipping agent. In 1874 he became an assistant in the Calcutta firm of Mackinnon, Mackenzie & Co, managers of the British India Steam Navigation Co. Bounding in energy and ability, he retrieved the BI's interests from its Bombay agents who were damaged by the collapse of the City of Glasgow Bank in 1878 and that year was made a partner in Mackinnon, Mackenzie. For the next twenty years, Mackay not only shared in the management of BI, and other ship agencies, but also in that of a range of businesses in jute, tea and coal in Bengal, cotton and wool in Madras, banking, railways and river steamers. He was rewarded with mounting personal wealth and social recognition: as president of the Bengal Chamber of Commerce, 1889-93; member of the Calcutta Port Commission, 1885-94; and member of the Viceroy's Legislative Council. The death of Sir William Mackinnon in 1894 took Mackay back to England. Within months he became a senior partner in Mackinnon, Mackenzie and managing direc-

McKENNA

tor of BI, eventually in 1913 succeeding as chairman of BI. His main achievement was to merge the shipping interests of BI and the Peninsular & Oriental Steam Navigation Co (in 1914) under the P&O name, with himself as chairman (remaining so until his death) at a salary of £5,000 a year and 2.5 per cent of net profits (a commission he declined in the mid-1920s when excess world shipping capacity hit P&O's profitablility). In 1917 the group accounted for 1.5 million tons, or 7.7 per cent of the national tonnage; in 1919, for 427 ships totalling 2.25 million tons; and in 1928, for 324 steamers, with ship and shore employees totalling 9,591. Lord Inchcape (Mackay was knighted in 1894, made a KCSI in 1910, a baron in 1911, a viscount in 1924 and an earl in 1929) augmented his reputation by selling off surplus shipping for the government after the First World War; by sitting on the Committee on National Expenditure chaired by Sir Eric Geddes (qv) in 1922; and by declining the crown of Albania, offered to him in 1921. Mackay married, in 1883, Jean Shanks, daughter of an Arbroath engineering company owner; they had a son and three daughters (one of whom tragically disappeared in 1928 in an attempt to be the first woman to fly across the Atlantic). Inchape left £2,124,707. See DBB; Stephanie Jones, Trade and Shipping: Lord Inchcape, 1852-1932 (1989).

McKENNA, Reginald
(6 July 1863 - 6 September 1943)
Banker, born in Kensington, Middlesex, son of William Columban McKenna, a Crown surveyor, and Emma née Hanby. After a mathematics degree at Cambridge, he was called to the Bar in 1887, and then became Liberal MP for Monmouthshire 1895-18. His distinguished political career included spells as First Lord of the Admiralty 1908-11 and Chancellor of the Exchequer 1915-16. He was groomed by Sir Edward Holden (qv) for the chairmanship of the Midland Bank, which he assumed in 1919 and held until his death. He maintained the Midland's position as the largest UK clearing bank: deposits which had exceeded £380 million in 1919, rose to £566 million by 1939; and over 700 new branches were opened. McKenna was probably the most intelligent and ambitious of the clearing bank chairmen between the wars. He was a supporter of Keynes and did not hesitate to oppose Bank of England financial policy (for example, he publicly criticised the return to the Gold Standard in 1925). On the other hand, the Midland under McKenna co-operated with the Bank of England in restructuring major industrial firms that were victims of trade depression or mismanagement, like Kylsant's (qv) Royal Mail Co. In 1908 he married Pamela (d 1943), daughter of Sir Herbert Jekyll:

they had two sons. He left £89,448. See A R Holmes and Edwin Green, Midland: 150 Years of Banking Business (1986); DBB; DNB.

MacKINNON, Lachlan
(1871 - ?)
Transport executive, born at Montrose, into a Highland family: his father was in business as a lath splitter. Educated at the Highland Society School, he joined Glasgow Corporation Cleansing Department as a clerk. In 1892 he transferred to the tramways department and gradually worked his way up through a succession of posts until in 1927 he was appointed general manager of Glasgow Corporation Tramways. In 1935 it employed about 5,000. In about 1903 Mackinnon married Mabel Campbell Tait: they had one son and three daughters. He was a member of St Columba's Church, Glasgow. See Glasgow Weekly Herald, 21 January 1933.

McKINSTRY, Sir Archibald
(1877 - 6 October 1952)
Industrialist, the son of Robert McKinstry, of County Antrim. Educated at Queen's College, Belfast, and the Royal University of Ireland, in 1902 he joined the British Westinghouse Co as a junior engineer. He was connected with that company and Metropolitan-Vickers until 1930, serving as a director and export chairman of the latter. He visited Australasia in 1911 and was director of munitions in Australia during the First World War. He was a director of the British Broadcasting Co during 1922-27; a managing director and deputy chairman of Babcock & Wilcox, 1931-51; and a vice-chairman at Metal Box, the packaging company founded by Robert Barlow (qv). He visited Spain in 1929 as a member of an FBI trade mission; was on the industrial panel of the Ministry of Production in 1902; and a member of the Royal Commission on Awards to Inventors, 1947. He was knighted in 1943. In 1914 he married Sarah Ogden Taylor, daughter of John Bark: they had one son. See Archibald McKinstry, 'Notes on Electrical Calculations of High Voltage Transmission Lines', Journal of the Institution of Electrical Engineers (1920); The Times, 11 October 1952.

McLAREN, Charles Benjamin Bright
1st Baron Aberconway of Bodnant
(12 May 1850 - 23 January 1934)
Industrialist, born in Edinburgh, the third son of Duncan McLaren (1800-86), merchant and later MP for Edinburgh, and Priscilla née Bright, sister of John Bright, MP the Anti-Corn Law leader, he was educated at Edinburgh University, Bonn and

Heidelberg. After a spell in journalism, he was called to the Bar at Lincoln's Inn in 1874 and practised as a Chancery lawyer specialising in company and mercantile law. He became a QC in 1897, the year he retired from law to devote himself to industrial affairs. Entry to industry was facilitated by his marriage in 1877 to Laura the only daughter of Henry Davis Pochin, a chemical manufacturer who died in 1895 leaving Laura heir to his fortune (a son being cut out of the will). A business career was also assisted by his parliamentary seats: MP (Liberal) for Stafford, 1880-86, and for Bosworth, 1892-1910. Among the directorships inherited from his father-in-law were the Tredegar Iron & Coal Co, Sheepbridge Coal & Iron Co, Palmer's Shipbuilding & Iron Co, Staveley Coal & Iron and Bolckow Vaughan. His most important directorships were John Brown & Co, the Sheffield steelmakers who moved into shipbuilding at Clydebank in 1899, and the Metropolitan Railway Co. McLaren was director of John Brown from 1882, deputy chairman from 1897, and chairman, 1906-34. Before 1914 John Brown (which employed 20,000 in 1907) built passenger liners like the *Lusitania* and *Aquitania* and warships like the *Repulse* and *Hood*. During the depressed inter-war years the firm built the 81,200 ton *Queen Mary* (1930-34), a contract worth £3.27 million. McLaren's role at John Brown was supervisory and financial, as it was at the Metropolitan Railway which he chaired, 1904-33. McLaren was made a baronet in 1902, a PC in 1908 and a baron in 1911. By his wife, a passionate advocate of womans' rights, he had two sons and two daughters. See *DBB*.

McLAREN, Henry Duncan
2nd Baron Aberconway of Bodnant
(16 April 1879 - 23 May 1953)

Industrialist, born at Barnes, Surrey, the son of Charles Benjamin Bright McLaren (qv) and Laura Elizabeth née Pochin. His background and early education (history at Oxford and then the Bar) provided an entrée into politics as Liberal MP for West Staffordshire 1906-10, parliamentary private secretary to Lloyd George, and Liberal MP for Bosworth 1910-22. Thereafter his business interests were paramount. He was chairman of English Clays Lovering Pochin & Co Ltd and also of a string of engineering and steelmaking companies connected with his father - notably Firth Brown, John Brown, Sheepbridge, Cottonwood, Yorkshire Amalgamated Collieries and Tredegar - though some doubted how effectively he could manage all these concerns. An expert on rhododendrons, he gave his gardens at Bodnant to the National Trust. He was made CBE in 1918. In 1910 he married

Christabel Mary Melville, daughter of Sir Melville Macnaghten, chief of the CID. He left an estate of £242,252 gross and £23,525 in settled land. See Eric Mensforth, *Family Engineers* (1981); *DBB*; *DNB*.

MacLAURIN, Sir Ian (Charter)
(30 March 1937 -)

Food retailing chain operator, born in Blackheath, London, the son of Arthur George and Evelina Florence Maclaurin. Educated at Malvern College, he did National Service with the RAF until 1958, when he joined the domestic appliance company Vactric. In 1959 he became a management trainee at Tesco, the supermarket chain that had been built up by Sir John E Cohen (qv). He joined the board in 1970, became managing director in 1973, and chairman in 1985. Maclaurin was responsible for replacing Tesco's traditional policies and image (with their emphasis on Green Shield Stamps) with a new centralised administration based on superstores - a strategy that by 1990 had made Tesco a close second to Sainsbury as the UK's leading food retailer. In 1992 - the year Tesco opened its 200th superstore - group profits (before property profits) exceeded £500 million for the first time. At £545 million, this figure had more than doubled in five years. Tesco employs over 87,000 workers. Meanwhile, Maclaurin became the second highest paid executive with a salary of £1.48 million in 1990 (he still earned over £1 million in 1992). In 1992 he was president of the Institute of Grocery Distribution and a non-executive director of Guinness and the National Westminster Bank. Awarded the Freedom of the City of London in 1981, he was elected a Fellow of the Royal Society of Arts in 1986, and knighted in 1989. He married in 1961 Ann Margaret née Collar: they have one son and two daughters. See David Powell, *Counter Revolution: The Tesco Story* (1991).

McMAHON, Sir Christopher
William (Kit)
(10 July 1927 -)

Banker, born in Melbourne, the son of Dr John Joseph McMahon and Margaret Kate née Brown. Educated at Melbourne Grammar School, he read history and English at the University of Melbourne, then took a first in politics, philosophy and economics at Magdalen College, Oxford. He subsequently pursued a dual career as an economics tutor (at Oxford University and the Treasury) and government adviser (with the British Embassy and the Treasury). In 1964 he joined the Bank of England as adviser, serving as deputy governor in 1985. In 1986 he became the Midland Bank's chief executive, inheriting poor management and heavy debts, partly due to Midland's ailing US subsidiary, the Crocker Bank. As chairman in April 1987, he was faced with announcing the first full-year loss by a British clearing bank this century. Besides Third World debts, McMahon also faced an informal takeover approach from the Saatchi brothers (qv) and, more seriously, the effects of recession. He invested heavily in modernisation and laid the groundwork for the subsequent takeover of Midland by the Hong Kong & Shanghai Banking Corp in 1992. But by then McMahon had left, handing over the chairmanship to Brian Pearse (qv) in 1990, convinced that the projected merger with HSBC had failed. McMahon was a member of the Plowden Committee on the Aircraft Industry, 1964-65; and a director of Eurotunnel between 1987 and 1991. He was knighted in 1986. He married first in 1956 Marion Kelso, by whom he had two sons; and second in 1982 Alison Barbara Braimbridge. See C W McMahon, *Sterling in the Sixties* (1964).

MAGGS, Leonard
(27 May 1890 - 23 August 1959)

Dairy company chairman, born at Melksham, Wiltshire, the youngest of the eleven children of Charles Maggs, a hemp manufacturer, and his wife Charlotte Elizabeth Stratton, he was educated at Wycliffe College, Stonehouse, Gloucestershire, and the British Dairy Institute at University College, Reading. After a year in Normandy learning French and French cheesemaking he worked for, and then owned, a retail milk business before joining his brother Joseph in 1912 in the wholesale business his father had helped to found in 1896, the Wilts United Dairies. In 1915 this became the core of a new combine, United Dairies Ltd. After the First World War, in which Leonard Maggs served as a lorry driver with the RASC, he became an inspector for United Dairies, assistant to the managing director of its subsidiary the Wilts United Dairies in 1920, managing director of Wilts United in 1923, director of United Dairies in 1925 and chairman, 1942-59. His main achievement was the acquisition in 1959 by United Dairies Ltd of Cow & Gate Ltd, manufacturers and exporters of infant and invalid foods and dairy products. United Dairies (which employed about 11,000 in 1955) then had about 600 retail shops and 40 creameries and condenseries while Cow & Gate had nine factories and a distribution network. The resultant firm changed its name to Unigate Ltd. Maggs died within months of the completion of the merger. See *DBB*.

MAITLAND SMITH, Geoffrey
(27 February 1933 -)

Footwear, clothing and sportswear retailing executive, the son of Philip John Maitland Smith and Kathleen née Goff. Educated at University College School, London, he trained as a chartered accountant and became a partner in Thornton Baker & Co between 1960 and 1970. In 1971 he became a director of Sears Holdings, the large retailing conglomerate built up by Sir Charles Clore (qv), which owns such famous names as Dolcis, Selfridges and Olympus. He became chief executive in 1978, succeeding Leonard Sainer (qv) as chairman in 1985 (three years later he relinquished the post of chief executive). Maitland Smith continued the rationalisation of Clore's empire that had begun under Sainer. In particular, he focused the company on retailing. In 1978 he bought Olympus Sportswear, soon established as a highly successful chain within the group. Then Wallis, Foster Bros Clothing, Adams and Millet's were acquired. Two other important strategies were expansion in Europe and the purchase of Freeman's in 1988, which gave Sears an important share of the mail order market. Under Maitland Smith, Sears had become a wide-ranging, but integrated group: in 1992 it employed 45,000 workers at over 3,750 locations and had a turnover of £1,979 million (pre-tax profit £81 million). Maitland Smith holds non-executive directorships at Asprey, Midland Bank and Hammerson Property. See Corinne Simcock, *A Head for Business* (1992).

MARKHAM, Charles Paxton
(14 April 1865 - 29 June 1926)

Iron manufacturer, born at Brimington Hall near Chesterfield, his father was Charles Markham, managing director of the nearby Staveley Coal & Iron Works, and his mother, Rosa, the daughter of Sir Joseph Paxton, celebrated designer of the 1851 Crystal Palace. Trained by his father, he became a director of the Staveley Co in 1888, soon after his father's death; chaired shareholders' meetings from 1894; and chaired the board from 1903 until his death. He, more than anyone else, was responsible for the policies which saw the company grow from 6,500 employees in 1907 to 37,500 (including 14,000 at Staveley) in 1925. During the 1890s the market for cast iron pipes, which the firm had met since the 1860s, was hit by American, German and French competition. Iron making was modernised with a large investment in new plant, the Devonshire Works, in 1905-12. At the same time Markham increasingly moved into coalmining and ironstone quarrying, so that by 1925 only 3,000 of his employees were employed in ironmaking and chemicals. Untypically for his day, Markham in the 1900s and perhaps earlier, favoured unions for coalminers. He married Margaret Hermine Jackson, daughter of T H Jackson, the wealthy chairman of the Clay Cross Co; they had no children. See

Stanley D Chapman, *Stanton & Staveley: A Business History* (1981); *DBB*.

MARKLAND, Stanley
(3 July 1903 - 24 May 1986)

Motor vehicle manufacturer, born at Macclesfield, the son of Fred Markland, a laundry proprietor's assistant, and his wife Elizabeth née Hodgkinson, he was educated at Chorley Grammar School. At 17 he was apprenticed to Leyland Motors Ltd where in 1921 he gained the company's first engineering scholarship. He moved to the research department, becoming chief of research in 1936, assistant chief engineer in 1941, and chief engineer in 1945. He joined the Leyland board in 1946 and in 1953 was made works managing director. He also became managing director of Albion Motors (a Leyland subsidiary in Glasgow) in 1957 and then moved to Coventry in 1961 to be managing director of Standard Triumph International, which had just been acquired by Leyland. As an engineer Markland was a brilliant exponent of the large diesel engine in trucks and buses; as a production engineer he impressively brought Albion and Standard into profitability. For reasons that are unclear he was, however, passed over when the Leyland chairman Sir Henry Spurrier (qv) sought a successor, in favour of Donald Stokes (qv), head of Leyland sales. Consequently Markland left the Leyland goup in 1964. For the next four years he was a main board director of Guest, Keen & Nettlefolds, then increasingly moving into the supply of motor industry components. He then retired. Markland was married and had a son. See *DBB*.

MARKS, Simon
1st Baron Marks of Broughton
(9 July 1888 - 8 December 1964)

Chain store chairman, born in Leeds, the son of Michael Marks and Hannah née Cohen. He joined his father's chain of penny bazaars, Marks & Spencer, in about 1907 and by the end of the First World War was chairman. Marks and his collaborator Israel Sieff (qv) made Marks & Spencer perhaps the most consistently successful of all British companies: registered as a public company in 1926 (capital under £1 million), by 1958 capital was over £53 million, with a turnover from 237 stores of £130 million. A family-run concern, Marks & Spencers reflected Marks's personal obsession with quality, value for money, and good working conditions. He was knighted in 1944 and awarded a barony in 1961. A committed Zionist, he also donated heavily to educational and charitable foundations. He married in 1915 Miriam, daughter of Ephraim Sieff and sister of Israel Sieff. He left

£1,830,935. See Goronwy Rees, *St Michael: A History of Marks & Spencer* (1969); *DBB*; *DNB*.

MARQUIS, Frederick James
1st Earl of Woolton
(23 August 1883 - 14 December 1964)

Department store manager, born in Salford, the son of Thomas Robert Marquis, a saddler, and Margaret Ormerod. Fabian in outlook, Marquis obtained an MA at Manchester University, before working at a Liverpool charitable settlement. In 1920 he joined Lewis's, the retailing organisation, becoming chairman in 1934. He brought to this Jewish family-run concern managerial drive and a social conscience, launching its expansion after conversion into a public company in 1924 (issued capital £1.7 million). Growth culminated in 1951 in the acquisition of the famous London store, Selfridges. A business statesman, he was active on a number of national committees and company boards: he was, for example, chairman of the Retail Distributors' Association in 1934. He also became Minister of Food in 1940 and later a member of the War Cabinet. In 1945 he joined the Conservative party and ended his political career as Minister of Supply. Knighted in 1934, he was given a barony in 1939, made a CH in 1942, became a viscount in 1953 and an earl in 1956. He married twice: in 1912 to Maud (d 1961), daughter of Thomas Smith; and then in 1962 to Dr Margaret Eluned Thomas. See Asa Briggs, *Friends of the People: The Centenary History of Lewis's* (1956); *DBB*; *DNB*.

MARSHALL, Sir Colin (Marsh)
(16 November 1933 -)

Airline executive, born at Edgware, Middlesex, the son of Marsh Edward Leslie and Florence Mary Marshall. Educated at University College School, Hampstead, he was a purser for seven years with the Oriental Steam Navigation Co. In 1958 he joined the Chicago office of the car rental firm Hertz as a management trainee, after his father (a managing director of the Daimler Hire Co) had introduced him to a Hertz vice-president. In 1964 he switched to Avis, where by 1976 he had become president and chief executive - the only Englishman at that time to head a large US corporation. After a hostile takeover bid from Norton Simon, in 1981 he joined Sears Holdings as a director and deputy chief executive, before being recruited by Lord King (qv) in 1983 as chief executive of British Airways. By 1992 (when King announced he was relinquishing the chairmanship to Marshall) they had made BA the world's most profitable airline, with pre-tax profits of £285 million from annual revenues of over £5 billion, with a 48,000 workforce. Marshall was less flamboyant than King, but both were committed to transforming BA into a global airline. Marshall believes that as air competition intensifies in the 1990s only a dozen or so of the major airlines will survive: hence BA has formed partnerships with Australian, Russian and German airlines and has penetrated the American market with a deal with USAir. In February 1993 Marshall became BA chairman five months early, when King decided to step down after the company had to pay £600,000 in damages and make a public apology to Richard Branson's (qv) Virgin Atlantic, after an alleged 'dirty tricks' campaign. Knighted in 1987, Marshall is also on the boards of Grand Metropolitan, the HSBC Holdings and IBM (UK). In 1958 he married Janet Winifred née Cracknell: they have one daughter. See Arthur Reed, *Airline: The Inside Story of British Airways* (1990); Corinne Simcock, *A Head for Business* (1992).

MARSHALL, Sir James Brown
(25 February 1853 - 22 July 1922)
Director of Dockyards, the son of Samuel Marshall, of Berwick, he started as an apprentice in the Royal Dockyard, Portsmouth in 1867 and subsequently passed through the Royal School of Naval Architecture and the Royal Naval College, Greenwich. He rose to become Director of Dockyards at the Admiralty in 1906, a post he held until 1917. By 1907 the Royal Dockyards employed nearly 26,000. On retiring from the Admiralty he joined the board of Messrs John Samuel White & Co, first as deputy chairman and later chairman. Marshall was knighted in 1911. He married Alice née Pharaoh. See *The Times*, 24 July 1922.

MARTIN, Sir James
(21 September 1861 - 21 August 1935)
Food company executive, the son of William Butts Martin, of the City of London. Educated at Christ's Hospital, he became a Fellow of the Society of Incorporated Accountants & Auditors (of which he was later president) and helped organise accountancy as a profession in South Africa in 1894. He was chairman of Allied Suppliers, Lipton, the Ely & King's Lynn Beet Sugar Factories, the Home & Colonial Stores, the Maypole Dairy Co and Maypole Margarine Works; government financial representative on Home Grown Sugar Ltd; and a director of the Ipswich Beet Sugar Factory and the London board of the Scottish Union & National Insurance Co. Martin was a frequent government adviser on company law, accountancy and taxation; and he was one of the commissioners of the London Passenger Transport Arbitration Tribunal. A JP, he was knighted in 1919. Martin married in

1888 Sara née Firminger: they had two daughters. See *The Times*, 22 August 1935.

MASEFIELD, Sir Peter (Gordon)
(19 March 1914 -)
Airline executive, born at Trentham, North Staffordshire, the son of Dr William Gordon Masefield, a surgeon and physician, and Marian née Lloyd-Owen. He was educated at Westminster School, Chillon College (Switzerland), and Jesus College, Cambridge, where he read engineering. A successful journalist, he edited *The Aeroplane* magazine, but gave this up in 1943 to become adviser on air transport to Lord Beaverbrook (qv). After the war, he was air attaché to the British Embassy in Washington, which involved him in international negotiations over airline regulation. In 1949 he joined the state-owned British European Airways as chief executive under Lord (William Sholto) Douglas: they established it as Europe's dominant airline. He left in 1955 and during the following 25 years or so managed Bristol Aircraft Ltd, attempted to launch a range of British light aircraft while chairman of Beagle Aircraft, became chairman of the British Airports Authority, served as deputy chairman of British Caledonian, and was appointed chairman and chief executive of London Transport. He was unusually active in professional and learned societies (for example, he was president of the Royal Aeronautical Society, 1959-60) and was a member of several important committees, such as the Aeronautical Research Council, 1958-61. He was knighted in 1972. In 1936 he married Patricia Doreen née Ronney: they have a daughter and three sons. See Peter Masefield, *To Ride the Storm - The Story of the Airship R101* (1982); *DBB*.

MATTHEWS, Bernard
(24 January 1930 -)
Poultry farmer and food manufacturer, began his working life as an auctioneer's clerk earning 35 shillings a week. To supplement this income he invested in 20 turkey eggs and an incubator, but his first attempt to raise them failed - he had not allowed for the cost of the feed. He then worked as an insurance clerk and tried the turkey business again: this time their shelter blew down! Third time lucky, he borrowed £3,000 in 1955 and bought a decayed Jacobean mansion, Great Witchingham Hall near Norwich, and used it as a turkey farm. He soon established himself as the leading turkey farmer, expanding into the surrounding 35-acre estate and then buying disused airfields. Matthews was particularly successful in marketing turkey meat as an all-year-round non-luxury product, dreaming up novel ways to sell it (such as in chopped and processed supermarket

packs of turkey burgers, balls and steaks). His advertising agency, Ogilvy & Mather, also packaged Matthews himself for TV, where he appeared as a ruddy-cheeked, tweedy farmer, extolling the virtues of his 'bootiful' birds in East Anglan burr. Now a national figure, he has also drawn less favourable publicity for polluting East Anglian rivers and the poor working conditions of his 2,600 local employees. Profits of his business (which he has protected by heavy patenting of his processes) hit over £15 million by 1990; while Matthews himself had a personal fortune estimated at £50 million. His family own 40 per cent of the business. By 1992 he provided over a third of the 9 million turkeys consumed on the British Christmas dinner table. Matthews made £3.3 million before tax in 1992, against £13.2 million the previous year, a 75 per cent drop - partly due to increased competition from American and Continental producers. He is separated from his wife, Joyce: they have three adopted children. He also has a son by a Dutch woman. He was awarded a CBE in 1992.

MAXWELL, (Ian) Robert
(10 June 1923 - 5 November 1991)
Publisher and communications entrepreneur, born Kan Ludvik Hoch, the third child of poor Jewish peasants (Michael and Ann Hoch) in a remote village in Czechoslovakia. He escaped death by the Nazis (the fate of his parents), by leaving for Budapest in 1939. He arrived in Britain the following year, changed his name, joined the army and was awarded the MC. In 1949 he founded Pergamon Press to publish science journals, which fulfilled his ambition to become a millionaire - though he was branded by Board of Trade inspectors in 1971 as 'not a person who can be relied on to exercise proper stewardship of a publicly quoted company'. However, in 1981 he founded Maxwell Communication Corporation as a vehicle for larger, global ambitions. In 1984 he took over Mirror Group Newspapers, which he revived, before switching his attention across the Atlantic to buy Macmillan Inc. By the 1990s Maxwell Communications Corporation employed nearly 20,000 in 28 countries. Lauded as a brilliant communications mogul and the saviour of the *Daily Mirror* newspaper, a more considered assessment of his abilities prevailed after he had been found drowned off his yacht in obscure circumstances near Tenerife: his empire promptly collapsed amid massive debts and pension fund chicanery. A committed Zionist, Maxwell was given a state funeral in Israel. Maxwell was Labour MP for Buckingham, 1964-70. He married in 1945 Elisabeth Maynard: they had four sons and five daughters. His two sons and business partners,

Kevin (Britain's biggest bankrupt) and Ian, face criminal charges for assisting their father in plundering the *Daily Mirror*'s pension funds. See Robert Maxwell, *The Economics of Nuclear Power* (1965); Tom Bower, *Maxwell: The Outsider* (1988).

MAXWELL, Sir William
(30 November 1841 - 9 February 1929)
Chairman of the Scottish Co-operative Wholesale Society, born in Glasgow, the son of George Maxwell, a coachbuilder, he was educated at Paisley and at twelve was apprenticed to a Glasgow coachbuilder. He improved his education by studying at evening classes and spent four years at the Glasgow School of Design. At the age of 20 he went on a sketching tour of England and in Manchester became imbued with the ideas of co-operation. He returned to Glasgow and became an active trade unionist, serving as treasurer to his trade society in Glasgow. In 1864 he moved to Edinburgh, joined the St Cuthbert's Co-operative Association, became its secretary and in 1880 was chosen by St Cuthbert's as their representative on the board of directors of the Scottish CWS. He was elected interim chairman of the Scottish CWS in 1881 and then chairman in 1882, holding the post until 1907. Turnover of the Society rose from £800,000 in 1881 to £2.2 million in 1889 and £7.5 million in 1907. Credit for this performance must go to Maxwell. First, he took the Scottish CWS into manufacturing, in addition to distribution. In 1886 12 acres of ground were purchased at Shieldhall, Glasgow, and £50,000 was invested in plant to manufacture boots and shoes, ready-made clothing, furniture, brushes, and preserves, and also a printworks. The Shieldhall factory made an annual average profit of 19.1 per cent under Maxwell. Second, he expanded the Society's buying system, establishing purchasing centres in Ireland, the USA and Europe (all of which he toured for this purpose) and making purchasing agreements with the English CWS. By 1907 the Scottish CWS employed over 7,000. Maxwell failed to get into parliament in 1900. He left the Scottish CWS in 1908, having been elected president of the International Co-operative Alliance, a post he held until 1921 when ill-health forced him to retire. He was knighted in 1919. Maxwell married three times: first to Ann née Forrest (d 1892); second, in 1894, to Agnes Sutherland (d 1923); third, in 1924, to Mary Emily Bowers. See *DSBB*; James Kinloch and John Butt, *History of the Scottish Co-operative Wholesale Society Limited* (1981).

MAY, George Ernest
1st Baron May of Weybridge
(20 June 1871 - 10 April 1946)

Insurance company executive, born at Cheshunt, Hertfordshire, the son of William May, a grocer and wine merchant, and Julia Ann née Mole. Educated at Cranleigh School, he joined the Prudential Assurance Co in 1887, qualifying eight years later as an actuary. After success in the investment department, he was company secretary, 1915-31. During the war, he instigated the move which placed the Prudential's American securities at the Treasury's disposal. Under May, the Prudential's assets increased from £95 million to £256 million, while income rose from £3.6 million to £12.7 million. In 1931 he retired from the Prudential and joined the Government's Economy Committee, which was charged with examining public expenditure. The resulting May Report was highly critical of Labour Government spending in the depression, which prompted J M Keynes's comment that it was 'the most foolish document I have ever had the misfortune to read'. In 1932 May was made chairman of the newly-appointed Import Duties Advisory Committee (a position he retained until his death). May was awarded a KBE in 1918, a baronetcy in 1931, and a barony in 1935. In 1903 he married Lily Julia née Strauss: they had two sons and one daughter. He left £195,902 gross. See DBB; DNB.

MEANEY, Sir Patrick (Michael)
(6 May 1925 - 16 July 1992)

Industrialist, born Patrick Henry Meaney, in Wandsworth, south London, the son of Joseph Meaney, a tram driver, and Ethel Clara née Martin. He was educated at Wimbledon College and the Northern Polytechnic. After the Second World War, he joined Thomas Tilling Ltd, a haulage group, which had been built up into a wide-ranging conglomerate by William Lionel Fraser (qv). Meaney became a director of Tilling in 1961, then managing director in 1973, and was therefore involved in engineering its rapid growth. He came to the fore in 1983 when he defended a recession-hit Tilling against a takeover bid by BTR under (Sir) Owen Green (qv). It was then the largest takeover battle seen in the City and the first to use full-page advertisements attacking the opponent. Meaney traded insults with Green (complimenting him on doing 'a fantastic job with a scruffy-looking lot of companies') and though Tilling eventually succumbed to BTR, Meaney exacted a substantial price for the shareholders. In 1983 he accepted the chairmanship of the Rank Organisation after a downturn in its results: with the chief executive Michael Gifford he raised profits from £62 million in 1982 to £252 million before tax in 1991.

Meaney was also deputy chairman of the Midland Bank between 1984 and 1992, arguing the Bank's case in favour of merging with the Hong Kong & Shanghai Bank and against a possible takeover by Lloyds. He was also a director of ICI, Tarmac and MEPC; and chairman of the Horserace Betting Levy Board, 1985-92, and of the Mecca Leisure Group, 1990-92. Meaney was knighted in 1981 for services to exports. He married Mary June Kearney: they had one son, Adam. See Times, 20 July 1992.

MESSERVY, Sir (Roney) Godfrey (Collumbell)
(17 November 1924 -)

Industrialist, the son of Roney Forshaw Messervy and Bertha Crosby née Collumbell. Educated at Oundle and Cambridge University, he served in the Royal Engineers during the Second World War and then in 1949 became a trainee at the electrical engineering components firm of Lucas. After managing various Lucas subsidiaries at home and abroad, he became chief executive and chairman of Lucas Industries in 1980. Messervy's main task was to restructure the company as its traditional UK car parts business contracted. In 1981 Lucas recorded a loss as the car industry declined, but it swung back into profit in 1983, as the company expanded abroad. Between 1979 and 1988 the proportion of UK sales to total group turnover fell from 51 to 38 per cent, and thereafter foreign subsidiaries accounted for a greater proportion of sales than those in the UK (where Lucas cut its labour force by 35,000). Shortly after Godfrey Messervy handed over to Anthony Gill (qv) in 1987, Lucas was ready to be split into automotive, aerospace, applied technology and industrial divisions. Messervy has also been chairman of the Costain Group, 1987-90, and of Asda, the supermarket chain, in 1991. Knighted in 1986, he was president of the Birmingham Chamber of Industry & Commerce, 1982-83, and deputy president of the Society of Motor Manufacturers and Traders, 1988-90. In 1952 he married Susan Patricia Gertrude née Nunn: they have a son and two daughters.

MICHAEL, Sir Peter (Colin)
(17 June 1938 -)

Electronics entrepreneur, born in Croydon, the only child of Albert 'Mick' Michael, the stamps tycoon of Stanley Gibbons, and his wife Enid. Educated at Whitgift School, Croydon, he read engineering at Queen Mary College, London University, and did postgraduate work in nuclear physics. In the 1960s he worked for Rolls Royce, Smiths Industries and Plessey, but depressed by the lack of vision in British industry in 1968 he founded his own computer firm, Micro Consultants. It led eventually to his development of pioneering digital special effects for television through a company named Quantel. In 1981 Quantel merged with United Engineering Industries (UEI), of which Michael was chairman after 1986. Michael netted £60 million when he sold UEI to Michael Green's (qv) Carlton Communications in 1988 for £526 million, though he bought back the old UEI office in Newbury, Berkshire, and began looking for new ventures. In 1989 he began what looked like a repeat of his UEI success when he was brought in to rescue the troubled Cray Electronics group and rapidly reversed its fortunes. He also has a £4 million (37 per cent) stake in Classic FM, the consortium which launched Britain's first national commercial radio station for classical music; chairs the Pilot Investment Trust he launched in 1993; and owns a Californian vineyard. A former member of Margaret Thatcher's think-tank, he served as a non-executive director at British Coal during its strike-ridden years. Appointed CBE in 1983, he was knighted in 1989. He married in 1962 Margaret Baldwin: they have two sons. See Philip Beresford, *The Sunday Times Book of the Rich* (1990).

MILLAR, Robert

(1850 - 18 September 1908)

Railway company manager, born in Stirling, the son of Robert Millar, a schoolmaster, he was educated at his father's school at Bannockburn and in 1864 started training in the Stirling office of Robert Campbell, procurator fiscal. After four years he switched from law to a commercial career, working for Lawes Chemical Manure Co in Dublin, Messrs Arthur & Co of Glasgow, and then, in 1874, the Caledonian Railway Co, as clerk at the Buchanan Street goods station. From assistant canvasser in the office of the general goods manager, he moved in 1879 to Ireland as traffic agent. He returned to Glasgow in 1889 as chief traffic agent and in 1895 joined the general manager's office where he became an expert on the company's mineral traffic. Appointed an assistant district superintendent in 1898, he was promoted to superintendent of the western district in 1901 but did not assume the office because the general manager, William Patrick, suddenly died and Millar was appointed in his place. Over the next seven years Millar was responsible for the building of the Station Hotel in Princes Street, Edinburgh, the massive extension of Glasgow Central Station and its hotel, and the extension of Grangemouth Docks. By 1907 the Caledonian Railway was the second largest of the ten railway companies in Scotland, employing over 21,000. Millar married, in 1879, Jeanie Forgie, daughter of a farmer; they had one son. See George Eyre-Todd, *Who's Who In Glasgow in 1909* (1909).

MILNE, Sir James

(4 May 1843 - 1 April 1958)

Railway manager, born in Dublin, son of Joseph Milne JP, a director of a fertiliser manufacturer. James ('Jimmy') took a BSc at Manchester University and then joined the Great Western Railway as an engineer. After an interlude in Whitehall - where he worked with Sir Eric Geddes (qv), providing statistical support for the Ministry of Transport and the Committee on National Expenditure - Milne was general manager of the GWR, a giant concern with an issued capital of £147 million and 106,429 workers, 1929-47. During the 1930s the GWR's profits suffered from the decline of the coal and steel industries of South Wales. In 1941, in an unprecedented move requiring legislative sanction, Milne was appointed a director of GWR (whilst still serving as a company official). He was also deputy chairman of the Railway Executive Committee, 1941-7; and in 1948 reported for the Eire Government on transport in Ireland. He was made a Companion of the Order of the Star of India in 1923 for his work for the Indian Retrenchment Committee; and was knighted in 1932 and created KCVO in 1936. He married in 1912 Norah Rebecca, the daughter of a Liberal MP: they had two sons. His estate was valued at £80,858. See Terence R Gourvish, *British Railways, 1948-73* (1986); *DBB*.

MILNE-WATSON, Sir David

(10 March 1869 - 3 October 1945)

Gas company executive, born in Edinburgh, the son of wealthy parents, David Watson and Anne Carnegie née Milne. After an abortive career as a barrister, he joined the Gas Light & Coke Co in 1897, and by 1919 had become governer and managing director of the company in succession to Sir Corbet Woodall (qv). Under Milne-Watson Gas Light & Coke became the largest gas company in the UK (and also in the world), producing by 1938 one eighth of the country's gas. He also helped establish and was chairman of the National Gas Council, 1919-43. He was knighted in 1927 and received a baronetcy in 1937. He married in 1899 Olga Cicely (d 1952), daughter of the Reverend George Herbert: they had two sons, the younger of whom, Michael (qv), became governor of Gas Light & Coke after Milne-Watson's retirement in 1945. He left £84,740 gross. See Stirling Everard, *The History of the Gas Light & Coke Company 1812-1949* (1949); *DBB; DNB*.

MILNE-WATSON, Sir Michael

(16 February 1910 -)

Gas company executive, younger son of David Milne-Watson (qv), general manager of the Gas

Light & Coke Co, and his wife Olga Cecily née Herbert, he was educated at Eton and Balliol College, Oxford, and then joined the Gas Light & Coke Co as a trainee in 1933, when his father was the company's governor (chairman). The company was the largest gasworks undertaking in the world, covering London north of the Thames, and was technically one of the most efficient. Michael Milne-Watson was promoted to commercial manager by 1939. After war service in the navy, which he joined as an ordinary seaman and then qualified as a navigating officer, he returned to the GLCC as joint managing director in 1945 and then governor, 1946-49. On nationalisation of the gas industry in 1948-9, he was appointed chairman of the newly-formed North Thames Gas Board (larger than the GLCC) at the relatively young age of 37. Within the gas industry the NTGB, now one of twelve equal boards, lost the dominant position enjoyed by the GLCC. While Sir David had worked to develop national structures for the industry, Michael was more inward-looking and seemed less interested in the Gas Council than in the fortunes of the NTGB. Nevertheless, he was visionary in his support of the importation of liquified methane by sea and the conversion of Canvey Island to use this methane or natural gas instead of manufactured gas. This experience provided a sound basis for the later adoption of natural gas from the North Sea by the whole industry (conversion occurring, 1967-77). Michael Milne-Watson resigned from the NTGB in 1964 to become deputy chairman and then chairman of the state-owned steel makers Richard Thomas & Baldwin, 1964-67. Afterwards he was chairman of the William Press group, 1969-74; a deputy chairman of the British Steel Corporation, 1967-69; and director of the Industrial & Commercial Finance Corporation Ltd, 1963-80; Commercial Union Assurance, 1968-81; Finance for Industry, 1974-80; Rose Thomson Young (Underwriting) Ltd, 1982-. He was chairman of BUPA, 1976-81. Knighted in 1969, he succeeded his brother as third baronet in 1982. Michael Milne-Watson married, in 1940, Mary Lisette née Bagnall; they had one son. See Malcolm Falkus, *Always under Pressure: A History of North Thames Gas since 1949* (1988); W K Hutchison, *High Speed Gas: An Autobiography* (1987).

MIRMAN, Sophie
(28 October 1956 -)
Clothing retail chain operator, born in London, the only child of Serge and Simone Mirman: her father was vice-president of Christian Dior UK; her mother, a well-known milliner. Educated at the French Lycee in London (Baccalaureat), she worked for Marks & Spencer between 1974 and 1981 and became a secretary to (Lord) Marcus Sieff

(qv) (later non-executive chairman of her company). After helping to set up the Tie Rack shop chain, in 1983 she opened her first Sock Shop in Knightsbridge Underground Station, London, selling a range of high-fashion stockings, tights and socks. In 1984 she married Richard Ross, who was a financial controller for the Tie Rack, and who became her business partner (they have one son and a daughter). By 1987, when the company was floated as Sock Shop International, it was valued at £27.5 million. By 1989 there were 103 shops in the UK and 33 in France and America; and sales had increased from £613,000 in 1985 to £25.8 million in 1988. But Mirman made a disastrous attempt to expand in the US and this combined with Sock Shop's heavy debt burden of £17 million (interest charges rose between 1987 and 1989), its administrative problems and UK transport strikes brought her management of the company to an end. Mirman and her husband received nothing from their 80 per cent stake in Sock Shop - once worth nearly £60 million - when the debt-laden company was sold by administrators in August 1990 for £3 million. Subsequently, she became joint-managing director of Trotters Childrenswear Accessories in the King's Road, London. See Judi Bevan and John Jay, *The New Tycoons* (1989).

MITCHELL, Sir Godfrey Way
(31 October 1891 - 9 December 1982)
Builder and civil engineering contractor, born at Peckham, London, the younger son of Christopher Mitchell, a London County Council clerk of the works who later part-owned granite quarries in Alderney, and Margaret née Way, he was educated at Haberdashers' Aske's School at Hatcham, leaving at 16 to enter the London office of his father's firm. Following a bout of TB, he served in the Royal Engineers during the First World War attaining the rank of captain. In 1919 he bought the Hammersmith firm of building contractors, George Wimpey, for £3,000. To road building and the like he added speculative housebuilding in 1928, civil engineering work in the 1930s and major contracts during the Second World War, like 93 out of 577 airfields built for the RAF and USAAF. For a time Mitchell was Controller of Building Materials at the Ministry of Works and was knighted in 1948 for his war services. The postwar demand for housing led to further growth for Wimpey who built 18,000 out of 200,000 local authority houses a year in the early 1950s. On the civil engineering side the firm built Heathrow Airport and a new steelworks at Port Talbot. By 1950 turnover stood at £27 million, making Wimpey the largest construction company in the UK. It became a multinational in 1947 when it won construction contracts in the

newly discovered Kuwaiti oil field. Before Sir Godfrey Mitchell retired in 1973 the discovery of oil in the North Sea (in 1969) took Wimpey into the large scale and complex work of designing, building and servicing drilling rigs. The firm's turnover in 1973 stood at £240 million. Mitchell disliked publicity, confined his public offices to the building industry, and in 1955 set up a charitable trust which in 25 years gave away £10 million. He married, in 1929, Doreen Lilian Mitchell (1902-53); they had two daughters. See *DBB*; Valerie White, *Wimpey: The First Hundred Years, 1880-1980* (1980).

MOND, Alfred Moritz
1st Baron Melchett of Landford
(23 October 1868 - 27 December 1930)

Chemical manufacturer and industrialist, born at Farnworth, near Widnes, the second son of Ludwig Mond (1839-1909) and Frederike (Frida) née Lowenthal. His father was a chemicals manufacturer and one of the founders of Brunner, Mond. Educated at Cheltenham College and St John's College, Cambridge (where he failed his degree in natural sciences), he studied law at Edinburgh University and was called to the Bar at the Inner Temple in 1894. He joined the board of the chemical firm Brunner, Mond in 1895 and was soon made managing director, though he was also heavily involved with the Mond Nickel Co. Between 1906 and 1928 he followed a political career as a Liberal MP for Chester, Swansea and Carmarthen and was a supporter of Lloyd George. He was the first Commissioner of Works, 1916-21, and Minister of Health, 1921-22. By 1923 he was back at Mond Nickel as chairman and two years later was chairman of Brunner Mond. Along with Harry McGowan (qv), Mond masterminded the formation of Imperial Chemical Industries (Brunner, Mond; Nobel; United Alkali; and British Dyestuffs) in 1926, of which he became chairman. In the 1920s he became an advocate of pure research, rationalisation, Empire union and industrial co-operation (in 1928 he instituted the Mond Turner conference with the TUC). He was also closely associated with the Zionist movement. He was made a baronet in 1910, sworn of the Privy Council in 1913, made a peer in 1928, and elected FRS in 1930. In 1894 he married Violet née Goetze: they had one son, Henry Ludwig, and three daughters. He left £1,044,174 gross. See Alfred Mond, *Industry and Politics* (1927); William J Reader, *Imperial Chemical Industries: A History* (2 vols, 1970-75); *DBB*; *DNB*.

MOND, Julian (Edward Alfred)
3rd Baron Melchett of Landford
(9 January 1925 - 16 April 1973)

Banker and nationalised industry executive, born in London, the second son of Henry Ludwig Mond (1898-1949), and grandson of Alfred Mond (qv), the chemical industrialist of ICI fame. His mother was Amy Gwen née Wilson of Klerksdorp, Transvaal. Educated at Eton, he was a pilot in the Royal Navy during the Second World War, before beginning a career in merchant banking in the City of London as a director of Hill, Samuel. In 1967 the Labour Government appointed him chairman of the newly-nationalised steel industry. As head of the British Steel Corporation - a combine which had a total capital of £1,400 million and a labour force of 270,000 - Melchett had the task of merging 14 manufacturing companies and over 200 of their subsidiaries. He proved a respected and well-liked leader, but the keystone of his strategy (which he forced through in spite of an unsympathetic Conservative Government after 1970) - a dramatic expansion on the Japanese model - proved misguided. After his premature death from a heart attack, the world steel industry was hit by the worst slump since the 1930s and his grandiose plans (also pursued by his successor, Monty Finniston (qv)) foundered. In 1947 he married Sonia née Graham: they had one son and two daughters. He left £310,500 gross. See Geoffrey F Dudley and Jeremy J Richardson, *Politics and Steel in Britain, 1967-88: The Life and Times of the British Steel Corporation* (1990); *DBB*.

MONEY-COUTTS, Sir David Burdett
(19 July 1931 -)

Banker, born in Somerset, the son of Hon Alexander B Money-Coutts and Mary née Hobhouse. He is a direct descendant of Thomas Coutts, who presided over the bank of the same name in the late eighteenth century. His cousin is the 8th Baron Latymer; his father (a director of Imperial Tobacco before he joined the Coutts bank) was the second son of the 6th baron; and his mother was the daughter of Sir Reginald Hobhouse from an old Wilstshire-Somerset family. After Eton, where he was an Oppidan Scholar, and National Service with the Royal Dragoons, he read philosophy and economics at New College, Oxford. In 1954 he joined Coutts & Co, which has been a wholly-owned subsidiary of the National Westminster Bank since the 1920s, while retaining its separate identity. He became a director of Coutts in 1958, managing director between 1970 and 1986 and has been chairman since 1976. Like his ancestor, his wears his frock coat to work every day at what is still the most exclusive private bank: customers must earn a minimum of £50,000 per annum or have liquid assets of £150,000. He once remarked: 'we are not snobs but some of our customers are'. He has also served as director of several financial and insurance companies - for example, he was deputy chairman of Phoenix Assurance, 1984-85, and has been chairman of M & G, the investment group since 1990. He was knighted in 1991. He married in 1958 Penelope Utten Todd: they have one son and two daughters. See Edna Healey, *Coutts & Co 1692-1992* (1992).

MOORES, Sir John
(25 January 1896 - 25 September 1993)
Football pool promoter and retailer, born in Eccles, Lancashire, the son of John William Moores and Louise née Fethney. He left elementary school at 14 to become a messenger boy and then studied telegraphy, joining the Commercial Cable Co. In 1923 he began Littlewoods football pool (the first dividend was £2 12s) and within ten years was a millionaire. By the Second World War he had also founded Littlewoods Mail Order Stores in Liverpool and established a well-known retailing chain. By 1990 the Liverpool-based Littlewoods Organisation was Britain's richest family business, worth over £1.6 billion with 30,000 staff, completely owned by the 32 offspring of the Moores' dynasty. The pools part of Littlewoods is highly secretive and with a virtual monopoly of the market (over 75 per cent) is almost recession-proof. However, the transfer of control within the family did not run smoothly and after a fall in profits - they fell from £49 million in 1978 to £11.5 million two years later - Moores returned as chairman in 1980-82 (having retired in 1977). Professional managers were then introduced: (Sir) Desmond Picher (qv) became chief executive in 1983 and another outsider, Leonard van Geest, was appointed non-executive chairman in 1990. By 1991 the company's mail order business was up for sale for £400 million. Moores was knighted in 1980. He became life president of the company and still lived in Merseyside, where he was a keen Everton football club supporter all his life. He married in 1923 Ruby Knowles (d 1965), daughter of a Liverpool shipping clerk: they had two sons and two daughters. See *DBB*.

MORGAN, Sir Frank William
(23 June 1887 - 21 April 1974)
Insurance company executive, born at Clapton, Middlesex, eldest son of Alfred Morgan, a telegraph clerk (later assistant superintendent at the Central Telegraph Office), and his wife Mary Anne née Hitch, he was educated at Parmiter's School and at fifteen started work with the Prudential Assurance

Co Ltd in the postal department. By 1914, still a junior clerk, he was in the Ordinary Branch Policy department. During the First World War Morgan served with the Honourable Artillery Company (A Battery) and the Royal Field Artillery, being commissioned from the ranks and winning the MC. He returned to the Prudential in 1918 and, having proven leadership qualities, was one of half a dozen younger men selected in 1922 to promote in provincial centres the fire, accident and other classes of insurance which the Prudential had begun to write in 1919. As General Branch controller at Nottingham for six years he made a reputation as a pioneer in organising and motivating insurance salesmen. On this basis in 1928 he was promoted to manager for India, Burma and Ceylon and set up an autonomous head office, replacing old agencies with a new body of inspectors and organising agents. The Indian business, in sums assured, passed £1 million in 1932. Searching for new markets, Morgan made prospecting visits to East Africa and Malaya. He was moved in 1933 to Egypt as manager for the Near East but the following year was recalled to London to be an assistant manager in charge of life business overseas. He became deputy general manager in 1939 and succeeded Sir Joseph Burn (qv) as general manager in 1941. The 1940s and 1950s saw him at the top of the Prudential, as general manager until 1950; director, 1950-53; and chairman, 1953-65. The Prudential, now diversifying away from the industrial insurance with which it had long been associated, was the largest insurance company as measured by employment, with 17,000 employees in 1935 and 20,000 in 1955. Morgan fulfilled his role as an insurance industry leader. He advised the government on the implications of the Beveridge Report and the subsequent introduction of the National Insurance Scheme (for which he was knighted in 1948) and in 1949 he strenuously opposed the government's proposal to nationalise the industrial life offices and many friendly societies. On his retirement in 1965 Sir Frank Morgan received the honourary title of company president. Morgan married, in 1926, Beatrice Agnes, widow of Frederick Christian Dietrichsen; there were no children. See R W Barnard, A Century of Service: The Story of the Prudential, 1848-1948 (1948); Prudential Bulletin 32 (1950), 47 (1965).

MORGAN, Peter (William) (Lloyd)
(9 May 1936 -)
Industrialist, born in the Swansea valley, Wales, the only son of Matthew Morgan, a Lloyds Bank clerk, and Margaret Gwyneth née Lloyd. He was educated at Llandovery College, served as a second lieutenant in the Royal Signals during his National

Service, and attended Trinity Hall, Cambridge, where he read history. In 1959 he joined IBM (UK) Ltd as a sales trainee, became a sales director twelve years later, and joined the IBM (UK) board in 1983. During this period IBM (UK) established itself as the leading British computer manaufacturer. In 1989 he began a five-year term as director-general of the Institute of Directors, a London based organisation (with a staff of 150) that represents some 50,000 members of the British business community. He also holds non-executive directorships with South Wales Electricity and National Provident Institution. He married in 1964 Elisabeth Susanne Davis: they have three daughters.

MORLEY, Samuel Hope
1st Baron Hollenden of Leigh
(3 July 1845 - 18 February 1929)
Hosiery merchant and manufacturer, born at Clapton, Middlesex, eldest of the five sons of Samuel Morley (1809-86), the Nottingham merchant hosier and manufacturer and philanthropist, and his wife Rebekah Maria née Hope (a banker's daughter), he was educated at Trinity College, Cambridge, and then entered his father's firm. By 1900 this comprised seven factories in Nottingham and satellite manufacturing villages, employing 3,173; outworkers numbering 3,950; and staff in a warehouse in Nottingham and another in Wood Street in the City of London totalling 1,241. Samuel Hope Morley, who became the senior partner, and his brother Howard added a shirt, tie and umbrella making factory in Golden Lane, London. He retired in 1923 leaving his elder son, Geoffrey Hope-Morley, to carry on the business. Samuel Hope Morley was a director of the Bank of England and its deputy governor 1901-2 and governor 1903-5. He was high sheriff of the County of London in 1893 and held numerous lesser offices. Like his father he was a supporter of numerous charitable causes, from the Warehousemen, Clerks, and Drapers' Schools at Purley (treasurer for 53 years), to the Nottingham City Mission. For recreation he was a keen yachtsman and held a master's certificate. A Conservative, he was created a peer in 1912. Morley married, in 1884, Laura Marianne, daughter of the Reverend G Royds Birch; they had two sons. See *Complete Peerage*; *DBB*; *The Times*, 20 February 1929.

MORRIS, William Richard
Viscount Nuffield of Nuffield
(10 October 1877 - 22 August 1963)
Motor vehicle manufacturer, born in Worcester, the son of Frederick Morris, a draper's assistant, and Emily Ann née Pether. The most successful and wealthiest British industrialist of his age began his career as a bicycle repairer, before launching the manufacture of motor cars in Oxford after 1910. His early success was based on a policy of producing a well-advertised and popularly-priced car for the mass market; on the application of American mass production techniques; and on spreading financial risks amongst a large group of components suppliers. In 1926 Morris Motors Ltd was registered as a public company (issued capital £3 million) and soon became the foremost UK producer: by 1938 Morris was producing 90,000 cars a year and profits were over £2 million. In 1951 profits were £8.7 million and Morris employed over 20,000 workers. By then Morris's close personal control of the business had ceased and other factors, such as American competition, dictated that Austin (qv) and Morris merge as the British Motor Corporation, of which Morris became the first president. Personally modest and unostentatious, he married in 1904 an Oxford schoolteacher Elizabeth née Anstey. He became a baronet in 1929, a baron in 1934 and in 1938 became Viscount Nuffield. He left £3,252,764, but had already donated £30 million to charities, ensuring by his benefactions to Nuffield College in Oxford and the Nuffield Foundation that it was not only his cars that made his name a household word. See Richard J. Overy, *William Morris, Viscount Nuffield* (1976); *DBB*; *DNB*.

MORSE, Sir Christopher Jeremy
(10 December 1928 -)
Banker, the son of Francis John Morse and Kinbarra née Armfield-Marrow and a descendant of several generations of successful brewers in Norwich. Educated at Winchester and New College, Oxford (where he took a first-class degree in literature and humanities), he trained in banking at Glyn Mills & Co and was made a director in 1964. A year later he was seconded to the Bank of England, responsible for international business, and then in 1975 went to Lloyds Bank, first as deputy-chairman and then, two years later, as chairman. Although Lloyds suffered a crisis in 1982, when Latin American debts almost ruined the company, Morse and his right-hand man, Brian Pitman (qv), recovered the situation by steering Lloyds into solid low-risk businesses such as life assurance (through Lloyds Abbey Life) and private banking. The result was that by the 1990s Lloyds was the UK's most profitable bank, ahead of both Barclays and Natwest, which are more than twice its size. But in 1992 Morse and Pitman failed in their bid to absorb the Midland Bank. Morse retired in February 1993 - the longest serving chairman of the world's top 50 banks. In 1955 he married Belinda Marianne née Mills: they have three sons

and one daughter (one daughter is deceased). He was knighted in 1975.

MORTON, Sir (Robert) Alastair (Newton)

(11 January 1938 -)

Industrialist, born in Johannesburg, South Africa, the son of Harry Newton Morton, a Scottish oil worker, who had married Elizabeth Martino from an Afrikaaner family. Educated at St John's College and Witwatersrand University, Johannesburg, he won the first de Beers scholarship and read law at Worcester College, Oxford. In 1964 he was a special graduate student at the Massachusetts Institute of Technology. Prompted by his dislike of apartheid to seek his fortune abroad, his career has spanned mining, merchant banking, oil, engineering and industrial finance. He first came to prominence between 1967 and 1970 at Harold Wilson's Industrial Reorganisation Corporation, where Lord Kearton (qv) recognised his talents. Characterised as arrogant, abrasive and ambitious, by the 1980s he was winning a reputation for crisis management. In 1982 he was called in by the Bank of England to rescue the financial services group Guinness Peat, which was close to collapse. In 1987 he was head-hunted (again by the Bank of England) to head Eurotunnel, the company floated to realise the dream of driving a cross-Channel from Britain to France - the world's largest engineering project. This proved to be one of the stormiest of all appointments, with Morton dealing with a succession of seemingly intractable problems: generating private investment (the UK Government refused to finance the project), spiralling costs (which had virtually doubled to over £8 billion by 1992), disputes with the contractors, late deliveries of rolling stock, and persuading the Government to finance infrastructure projects in time for the Tunnel's planned opening in 1993. Morton has also held non-executive directorships at Royal Ordnance and British Steel. He was knighted in 1991. He married in 1964 Sarah Bridget, daughter of Sir Edgar Stephens, once a local government officer in Warwickshire: they have a son and a daughter.

MOSLEY, Tonman

1st Baron Anslow of Iver

(16 January 1850 - 20 April 1933)

Railway company chairman, born at Anslow, Burton-on-Trent, the second son of Sir Tonman Mosley, 3rd Baronet, and Catherine née Wood, he was educated at Repton School and Corpus Christi College, Oxford, graduating with a third class in law and history in 1872. He was called to the Bar at the Inner Temple in 1874 and practised on the Midland Circuit. Mosley was clearly a county man:

a JP for Derbyshire and Buckinghamshire, a DL for Staffordshire and Buckinghamshire, chairman of the Derbyshire Quarter Sessions (1897-1902), and chairman of Buckinghamshire County Council (1904-21). His two attempts to enter parliament, as a Conservative in 1885 (when he contested the Lichfield seat) and as a Liberal in 1914 (when he stood for the southern division of Buckinghamshire), failed. As a county man of the Midlands he became deputy chairman of the North Staffordshire Railway Co and a committee member of the Grand Junction Canal. He was chairman of the North Staffordshire Railway Co, 1904-23. With 4,800 employees in 1907 the company, which served the Potteries, was just large enough to figure in the top hundred employers in the UK economy at the beginning of the twentieth century. Mosley was made a CB in 1911 and created a peer in 1916. He married, in 1881, Lady Hilda Rose Montgomerie, youngest daughter of the 13th Earl of Eglinton; they had two sons and two daughters. Since the sons predeceased their father the peerage became extinct at his death. See *Complete Peerage*; *The Times*, 22, 25 August 1933.

MOUNTAIN, Sir Brian Edward Stanley

(22 August 1899 - 17 February 1977)

Insurance underwriter and company chairman, the only son of Edward (later Sir Edward) Mountain (qv), founder of the Eagle Star & British Dominions Insurance Co, and his wife Evelyn Ellen Regina Siegle, he was educated at Charterhouse and the Royal Military College Sandhurst. He served in both World Wars, as a lieutenant with the 9th Lancers in the First and as lieutenant colonel with the same unit in the Second. He did not succeed his father as general manager of Eagle Star until 1947. Sir Brian Mountain (he succeeded to the title on his father's death) was chairman of Eagle Star, 1948-74, and president, 1974-77. He was also chairman of Bernard Sunley Investment Trust Ltd, English Property Corporation Ltd, and United Racecourses Ltd. In the 1950s he was chairman of United Drapery Stores Ltd which in 1955 employed 17,000 through its various subsidiaries. Edward Mountain married, in 1926, Doris Elsie née Lamb; they had two sons and a daughter. See *The Times*, 22 February 1977.

MOUNTAIN, Sir Edward Mortimer

(24 November 1872 - 22 June 1948)

Insurance underwriter, second son of Henry Stanford Mountain, a prosperous Southwark hop merchant, and his wife, Louisa née Eve, he was educated at Dulwich College and then started in a

Lloyd's insurance broker's office. With his elder brother, Henry Stanford Mountain and others, he founded an insurance broking firm, Hawley, Mountain & Co in about 1900. In 1904 he became the managing underwriter of the British Dominions Marine Insurance Co and by 1913 was underwriting over £300,000. At first specialising in marine insurance, Mountain moved into fire and motor insurance before the First World War. War inflated marine revenues and profits, allowing Mountain in 1916-17 to purchase three life insurance companies: the Eagle, the Sceptre and the Star. Mountain became chairman and managing director of the new firm, Eagle Star & British Dominions Insurance Co Ltd. The interwar depression in international trade motivated his switch away from the marine insurance market and into motor insurance, where Eagle Star was the sixth largest insurer in 1938. Mountain, however, spread Eagle Star across several types of insurance, securing his market shares by developing a branch office network, and by staying out of the tariff agreements in fire and accident insurance. With substantial investment funds in the early 1920s he supported Gibson Jarvie in forming United Dominions Trust, which provided credit finance for car insurance. He was also involved with the financier Philip Hill. An enormously energetic and brilliant individualist, who remained as chairman of Eagle Star until his death, Mountain was knighted in 1918 and created a baronet in 1922. He married, in 1897, Evelyn Ellen Regina, daughter of August Siegle, a bookseller; they had one child, Brian Edward Stanley (qv). See *DBB*.

MULCAHY, Sir Geoffrey (John)
(7 February 1942 -)
Department store executive, born in Sunderland, the eldest of three children of Maurice Frederick Mulcahy and his wife Kathleen Love. He was brought up in the Midlands, where his father was a civil engineer and part-owner of a business in Worcester; his mother was a schoolteacher. Educated at King's School, Worcester, and Manchester University (BSc) and Harvard University (MBA), after 1964 he held posts at Esso Petroleum, Norton Co, and British Sugar. He joined Woolworth Holdings in 1983, after the institutional shareholders (Paternoster) had decided to intervene in the running of the group in an attempt to stem its slide in the British retailing market (it had lost its number one position in UK retailing to Marks & Spencer in 1968). A team including Mulcahy began to turn the company round. Mulcahy (who became chief executive in 1986 and chairman in 1990) discarded the old management and introduced three trading divi-

sions. Mulcahy also created leadership or second place positions for the group in DIY through B & Q, in electricals through Comet, and in drugstores through Superdrug. By 1993 Mulcahy had plans to buy France's top electrical retailer, Darty. Turnover of the holding company (which changed its name to Kingfisher in 1989) rose from £1,185 million in 1982 to £3,389 million in 1992; while pre-tax profits grew from £38 million to £228 million over the same period. He earns a salary of £724,00, but has a reputation as a workaholic with an almost complete devotion to business. Mulcahy has been a director of British Telecom since 1988. Mulcahy was knighted in 1993 for services to retailing. He married his wife, Valerie Elizabeth, in 1965: they have one son and one daughter. See William Kay, *Battle for the High Street* (1989).

N

NADIR, Asil
(1 May 1941 -)
General trader, born in Lefke, Cyprus, the son of Irfan and Safiye Nadir. His father was a wealthy Cypriot businessman. Asil (christened Asilkan) came to the UK after taking an economics degree at the University of Istanbul in 1965. With his father he ran a successful clothing business, Weatherwell, which went public in 1971. Nadir soon became the best known Turkish Cypriot businessman in the UK. In 1980 he took over Polly Peck, an ailing East End of London clothing company. The business (measured by its share price) became one of the best performing British companies of the 1980s - its share price rising from 9p to £35 by 1983 - making Nadir a multi-millionaire. Polly Peck had a diverse range of activities: packaging, fruit and consumer electronics. In 1989 Nadir expanded Polly Peck further and bought the American fruit firm Del Monte for about £557 million and also took a 51 per cent stake in the Japanese Sansui electronics group. But this expansion, launched on heavy borrowing, was halted in 1990 when Polly Peck collapsed with debts of over £1 billion and Nadir was arrested on 20 counts of theft involving £30 million. Bankrupt, with a reputed personal fortune of £200 million lost, in 1993 Nadir absconded to Cyprus, protesting his innocence. Nadir and his wife Ayesha (whom he has married and divorced twice) have two children. See David Barchard, *Asil Nadir and the Rise and Fall of Polly Peck* (1992); Tom Hindle, *The Sultan of Berkeley Street: Asil Nadir and the Thatcher Years* (1991).

NEILSON, John
(1840 - 5 May 1935)

Coal, iron and steel master, grandson of the brother of James Beaumont Neilson the inventor of the hot blast process, and son of Walter Neilson, iron master of Coatbridge, Lanarkshire, and his wife Jane Fulton, he therefore belonged to a prominent family of ironmasters. The deaths of his father and two uncles in the early 1880s left the third generation in control of two plants, an iron and steel works at Mossend and an ironworks at Summerlee, Coatbridge. These were united as the Summerlee & Mossend Iron & Steel Co in 1887, with John Neilson as the senior partner. The partnership was converted to a limited liability company in 1896, with John Neilson as chairman. He disposed of the less efficient Mossend works in 1906, when the company's name was altered to Summerlee Iron Co Ltd, which left the firm concentrating on coal and pig iron production. By 1910 over 4,000 were employed in eight coal mines at Summerlee. John Neilson was primarily a consolidator, rather than an innovator. He married ca 1870 and had two sons and three daughters. See DSBB.

NELSON, George Horatio
1st Baron Nelson of Stafford
(26 October 1887 - 16 July 1962)

Heavy electrical equipment manufacturer, born in Islington, London, the son of George Nelson, a warehouseman, and his wife Emily Walsh née Lewis, he received a technical education culminating at the London City and Guilds Technical College. Here he won a postgraduate Brush Studentship which took him to the Brush Electrical Engineering Co at Loughborough for completion of his training as a mechanical and electrical engineer. He moved to British Westinghouse, Trafford Park, Manchester, becoming chief superintendent in 1914. After British Westinghouse merged with Vickers electrical interests in 1919 to form Metropolitan-Vickers Electrical Co, Nelson was promoted to manage its Sheffield works. His big chance came in 1930 when he was appointed managing director of the English Electric Co based at Stafford. English Electric was formed in 1919 by a merger between Dick, Kerr & Co with plants at Kilmarnock, Preston, Bradford and Rugby; Coventry Ordnance Works with factories at Coventry and on the Clyde; and Siemens Dynamo Works at Stafford. This hotchpotch of companies, mostly in the electrical industry, suffered from overcapacity, obsolescence as well as geographical diffusion. Nelson concentrated activities at Stafford and Rugby, cut out waste, developed R & D, and won contracts at home and abroad for railway electrification. In 1933 he succeeded Sir Holberry Mensforth

(who had recruited him) as chairman. During the Second World War English Electric built tanks and aircraft; afterwards it took over Marconi in order to enter the radio, radar, television and, ultimately, space technology markets. Employment grew from 4,000 in 1932 to 35,000 in 1945 and 80,000 in 1960. Sir George Nelson (he was knighted in 1943), a fatherly autocrat with a Christian faith, was especially concerned about employee welfare and the training of engineers. He was created a baron in 1960. Nelson married in 1913 Florence Mabel Howe; they had a son, Henry George, the 2nd Lord Nelson, and a daughter. See DBB; Robert Jones and Oliver Marriott, *Anatomy of a Merger: A History of GEC, AEI and English Electric* (1970).

NEWMARCH, (Michael George) Mick
(19 May 1938 -)

Insurance company executive, born in London, the son of George Langdon Newmarch, a musician in tea salons, and his wife, Phyllis Georgina. Both parents died when he was young and Newmarch was brought up in Tottenham, north London, by an aunt. After obtaining two A-levels from Tottenham Grammar School, at 17 he joined the Prudential Assurance Co as a statistical clerk. In the evenings he studied for an external economics degree at London University. Between 1982 and 1989 Newmarch served as chief executive of Prudential Financial Services and of Prudential Portfolio Managers (its investment arm), and chairman of Prudential Holborn. At PPM he marketed the Pru's investment capabilities with great success, bringing in significant funds from external sources (in nine years to 1992 funds under its management doubled to nearly £27 billion). In 1990 Newmarch became chief executive of the Prudential, having been selected to continue the revolution initiated by Brian Corby (qv) to lessen the company's reliance on insurance by moving it into more profitable financial services. Newmarch found himself head of the UK's biggest institutional investor with a workforce of nearly 20,000, 8 million customers and funds under management in excess of £51 billion. Pugnacious and ambitious, Newmarch immediately attracted criticism in May 1991 when he was attacked by shareholders for his 43 per cent pay rise (which took his salary to £547,000) in a year when Prudential profits fell 37 per cent due to a £340 million loss in its estate-agency chain. Newmarch had described the year as 'for me ... a rewarding one'. In 1992 the Prudential reported pre-tax profits of £406 million, more than double a restated figure of £182 million for the previous year. Newmarch married in 1959 Audrey Clarke: they have one son and two daughters.

NICHOLSON, Sir Bryan (Hubert)

(6 June 1932 -)

Postal services executive, the son of Reginald Hubert and Clara Nicholson. Educated at Palmers School in Grays, Essex, he attended Oriel College, Oxford, where he read philosophy, politics and economics. After National Service in the army, he joined Unilever as a management trainee in 1955. He worked on the sales side, first with Unilever, and then after 1964 with the multinational computer manufacturer Sperry Rand. In 1972 he became director of operations of Rank Xerox (UK), and was appointed chairman between 1979 and 1984. In 1984 he chaired the Manpower Services Commission. In 1987 he became chairman and chief executive of the Post Office. Nicholson headed an organisation which was amongst the top 20 industrial undertakings in the UK (in terms of turnover): in 1992 it reported pre-tax profits of £247 million - a five-fold increase. For 16 years it has been consistently profitable, receives no Government subsidy, and is thought to be ripe for privatisation. In 1992 Nicholson handed over as chairman to Mike Heron (qv) and as chief executive to William Cockburn (qv). He is a non-executive director of the International Post Corporation and GKN, having also served in that capacity with Rank Xerox, Baker Perkins and Evode. He has an interest in vocational education and training through the CBI; and is also a member of council of Business in the Community and the Prince's Youth Business Trust. He was knighted in 1987. He married in 1956 Mary Elizabeth née Harrison: they have one son and one daughter (one son is deceased).

NIMMO, Sir Adam

(7 December 1866 - 10 August 1939)

Coalmaster, born at Slamannan, Stirlingshire, son of James Nimmo (1840-1912), and his wife Jessie née Clarkson, he was educated at the Royal High School, Edinburgh, and Edinburgh University and entered the family colliery business, James Nimmo & Co, in 1889. He became company secretary when the firm converted to a private limited company in 1893 and also when it became a public company in 1897. He was appointed a director in 1902 and in 1908 succeeded his father as managing director. In 1912 the firm employed 3,000 and had an annual output of 880,000 tons. The previous year Nimmo joined the board of the Fife Coal Co Ltd, Scotland's largest colliery combine (over 12,000 in 1907). In 1923 Sir Adam Nimmo (he was made a KBE in 1918 for his services to the Coal Control during the First World War) succeeded Charles Carlow (qv) as chairman, in office until his death. Heading two of the large Scottish colliery firms, Nimmo was chairman of the Lanarkshire Coalowners' Association, the Scottish Coal Trade Conciliation Board (from 1912) and president and, in 1926, vice-president of the Mining Association of Great Britain. Strong, forceful, intransigent, he became a national leader among coalowners, expressing their opposition to nationalisation and their determination to hold down wages, in hopes of recovering export markets lost during the First World War. In the negotiations which preceded the General Strike and miners' lockout of 1926, Nimmo, Sir Evan Williams from South Wales and other national minowners achieved a local-to-national solidarity which matched that of the union. After 1930 Nimmo moved from laissez-faire individualism, advocating instead statutory cartelisation. Outside business Nimmo was a committed Unionist and a staunch Baptist. He married, in 1901, Isobel Mackinnon née Gardner; they had two sons. See *DSBB*; Barry Supple, *The History of the British Coal Industry vol 4 1913-1946: The Political Economy of Decline* (1987).

NISBETT, George Hinde

(1866 - 21 October 1940)

Engineer and cable manufacturer, born in Southwark, the son of a dealer in animal foodstuffs, he was educated at St Olave's Grammar School and then articled as a pupil to Paterson Cooper & Co Ltd, electrical engineers and installers of electric lighting plant. In 1889 he became chief assistant engineer to Major-General Charles Webber, electrical engineer and electricity supply company director. Through Webber, Nisbett in 1892 became second engineer to the City of London Electric Lighting Co where he encountered Sebastian Ziani de Ferranti who had just become a director of the British Insulated Wire Co at Prescot, Lancashire. The BIW directors in 1893 recruited Nisbett as their chief engineer. In his first decade at Prescot he patented 28 innovations relating to electrical cable design and manufacture. To raise demand for electricity he created wiring syndicates to instal domestic circuits. Increasingly he moved into copper buying and the commercial side of the business (renamed British Insulated & Helsby Cables Ltd in 1902, and British Insulated Cables Ltd in 1925). He was appointed a director in 1924 and managing director and deputy chairman in 1927, continuing in office until the year of his death. The company, which employed over 8,000 in 1935, had its main plants at Prescot and Helsby. Nisbett was especially interested in technical education, his work being recognised by an honorary MEng from Liverpool University in 1930. See BICC Archives.

NIXON, Wilfred Ernest
(1892 - 26 September 1970)

Aircraft manufacturer, born at Colchester, the son of Thomas Elms Nixon, a bootmaker's manager, and his wife Mary Rosina née Morley, he qualified as a company secretary. When the de Havilland Aircraft Co was formed at Edgware in 1920 Nixon became company secretary. A wide gulf existed on the board between Geoffrey de Havilland, aircraft designer and the firm's founder who was exclusively interested in the technical side and refused to be chairman or managing director, and the other directors. Under the chairmanship of Alan Butler, 1924-50, Nixon became a director in 1930 and managing director in 1944. His role lay on the commercial and organisational sides of the business. The company produced Geoffrey de Havilland's best-selling two-seater Moth (over 7,000 built, 1925-32) and, during the Second World War, the fast wood-framed Mosquito bomber (over 7,500 built after 1940). It also produced the first British jet propulsion engine in April 1942 and the world's first jet airliner, the Comet, in July 1949. A series of accidents, due to metal fatigue, led to the grounding of the Comets. Nixon's period as managing director and chairman, 1954-59 when the company employed over 26,000, was preoccupied with the struggle to restore the airworthiness, if not the reputation, of the Comet. Nixon was married and had two sons (one killed in the RAF during the Second World War) and two daughters (who died in 1958). See *The Times*, 28 September 1970; *DBB* (de Havilland).

NOBLE, Sir Andrew
(13 September 1831 - 22 October 1915)

Arms manufacturer, born at Greenock, Scotland, the third son of George Noble, at one time a Royal Navy lieutenant, and his wife Georgiana née Moore, he attended Edinburgh Academy and the Royal Military Academy at Woolwich. He served in the Royal Artillery, 1849-60, spending most of his time abroad, and was then recruited by Sir William Armstrong (1810-1900) to be joint manager of his Elswick Ordnance Works at Newcastle-upon-Tyne. Driven by great ambition and powered by tenacity and a huge capacity for work, Noble emerged as undoubted successor to Armstrong by the 1880s. His experimental work on ballistics and explosives earned election as FRS in 1870, a CB in 1881 and a KCB in 1883. Commercially he was deeply involved in the takeover of Charles Mitchell & Co, Tyneside shipbuilders (1882), the establishment of a branch arsenal in Italy, and the acquisition of Sir J Whitworth & Co, the Manchester armorers (1897). As chairman of Sir W G Armstrong, Whitworth & Co Ltd,

1900-1911, Noble attained record profit levels, seizing the growing opportunities offered by the arms race that preceded the First World War. The company was particularly renowned for its commitment to R & D. By 1911 it employed 20,000 on Tyneside alone. Relatively it was overtaken by Vickers, not least because of Sir Andrew Noble's capricious autocracy and suppression of managerial talent. Noble married, in 1854, Margery Durham née Campbell; they had four sons and two daughters. Two of the sons followed him into top management posts at Armstrongs, producing a much-criticised managerial dynasty. See *DBB*; Kenneth Warren, *Armstrongs of Elswick* (1989).

NORMAN, (Archibald John) Archie
(1 May 1954-)

Supermarket chain executive, the son of Dr Archibald Percy Norman, a physician at the Hospital for Sick Children, and Aleida Elizabeth Bisschop. Educated at Charterhouse, the University of Minnesota and Emmanuel College, Cambridge, where he read economics, he went to Harvard Business School (MBA 1979) and then worked for Citibank between 1975 and 1977. In 1979 he joined McKinsey, the renowned management consultants, where he rapidly became one of the firm's youngest partners. In the mid-1980s, he headed a McKinsey team advising the Kingfisher group on its strategy. He helped rebuff Dixon's bid for Kingfisher and soon after in 1986 he joined Kingfisher as finance director, effectively third in command behind (Sir) Geoff Mulcahy (qv) and Nigel Whittaker. In 1991 he became chief executive of Asda, where he embarked on a three-year programme to restore the group's fortunes. Britain's fourth largest supermarket chain in 1992 (after Sainsbury, Tesco and Argyll) - with a stock market value of £657 million and a workforce of 43,000 - Asda had slipped behind its competitors in the 1980s, largely because of an ill-fated merger with MFI in 1985 and expenditure on the Gateway supermarket chain. Asda reported a loss of £365 million in 1992, partly the effect of Norman's immediate restructuring, but by the end of 1992 it had recorded pre-tax profits for six months of £54.8 million. In 1993 Asda launched a £347 million rights issue. Share options have made Norman a paper millionaire in little over a year, plus a £400,000 per annum salary. In 1992 Norman became a non-executive director of British Rail: he is also a non-executive director of Geest. In the late 1980s, Norman stood unsuccessfully as Conservative candidate in council elections at Southwark in London, where he lived with his wife, Vanessa Mary Peet (whom he married in 1983), and their daughter.

NORMAN, Montagu Collet
1st Baron Norman of St Clare
(6 September 1871 - 4 February 1950)

Central banker, born at Kensington, Middlesex, the son of Frederick Henry Norman and Lina Susan Penelope née Collet. His father was a partner in the bankers, Martin & Co. Educated at Eton and King's College, Cambridge (which he left after a year), he joined Martin's Bank in 1892. Two years later he joined his grandfather Mark W Collet's bank, Brown Shipley & Co, and by 1906 dominated the firm (he also served in the Boer War and was awarded a DSO). In 1907 he was elected to the Court of the Bank of England and during the next decade became increasingly involved in its work. He was appointed deputy governor in 1918 and governor in 1920. Norman became a major figure in the world financial community as he grappled with a series of international problems over the Gold Standard, the Dawes Plan, the Wall Street Crash and depression, and the preparations for war. At home he was involved with the Royal Mail Shipping Group crisis and wielded financial policy as a tool in Britain's industrial regeneration. Through the Securities Management Trust, founded in 1929 as a subsidiary of the Bank, he organised professional advice for firms undergoing reconstruction, such as Armstrong, Whitworth. He retired through ill-health in 1944, accepting a peerage. In 1933 he married Priscilla Cecilia née Reytiens, a divorcee; he left £253,316. See Andrew Boyle, *Montagu Norman* (1967); *DBB*; *DNB*.

O

O'HAGAN, Henry Osborne
(13 March 1853 - 3 May 1930)

Company promoter and director, born at Blackburn, Lancashire, the son of Henry O'Hagan, a civil engineer from Ulster, and his wife Emily née Buckaman, he was educated at Rochester Grammar School and privately until his father died while working as a railway engineer in Honduras. At 15 he clerked for a City firm promoting parliamentary bills and by the mid-1870s set himself up as a company promoter specialising in tramways, collieries and breweries. To encourage company vendors, he popularised the technique of underwriting share capital by farming it out on a commission basis (in the event of the public not taking up the shares). O'Hagan appears to have been a less corrupt operator than Ernest Terah Hooley and Horatio Bottomley, or other prominent company promoters of Edwardian England. Among his promotions were the International Tea Co and Ilford Ltd the photographic company in the 1890s, and the Associated Portland Cement Manufacturers Ltd

in 1900. This last was a bold throw intended to provide for his retirement; instead it sucked him into long-term management. The APCM merged 24 firms in the London area, representing well over a third of the UK's cement industry capacity: a merger prompted by the loss of foreign markets in the 1890s and the consequent price war at home. However, the APCM issue occurred just as the Boxer Rebellion in China sent markets plunging and the subscription was £2.2 million short. The cement manufacturers met £1.1 million, O'Hagan undertook to find £1.25 million. His business friends took £400,000 of debentures; O'Hagan himself bought £840,000 of ordinary shares and, to watch his financial interest, joined the APCM board as one of two vice-chairman and one of 12 managing directors (the number by 1907, when the APCM employed over 6,000). In 1910 he switched to being a trustee but with some bitterness left the APCM and its subsidiary, the British Portland Cement Manufacturers Ltd (formed in 1911 and giving the APCM an 82 per cent share of the industry's capacity), during the First World War following a boardroom power struggle. He retired in 1924 and later published his memoirs, *Leaves from My Life* (2 vols, 1929). He married in 1878 a teenage bride, Elizabeth née Jones; one son survived him. See P Lesley Cook and Ruth Cohen, *Effects of Mergers: Six Studies* (1958); *DBB*.

ORMSBY-GORE, William George Arthur
4th Baron Harlech
(11 April 1885 - 14 February 1964)

Banker, the eldest son of George Ralph Charles Ormsby-Gore, 3rd Baron Harlech, and his wife Lady Margaret Ethel née Gordon, daughter of 10th Marquess of Huntly, he was educated at Eton and New College, Oxford. A Conservative, his parliamentary career, begun in 1910 when he was narrowly elected by Denbigh District, was interrupted by the First World War (when he served mostly in the Middle East) and culminated in 1936-38 when he was Secretary of State for the Colonies. Ormsby-Gore was most interested in art and architecture and in the 1930s published three specialised studies in this area. He succeeded his father as Lord Harlech in 1938 and during most of the Second World War he was the UK High Commissioner in South Africa. His business career began in 1944 when, on his return to England, he joined the board of the Midland Bank, becoming deputy chairman four years later and then chairman, 1952-57. Knowing little about banking, and caring more about scholarship than management, Harlech permitted the conservative, centralising policies of the chief general manager, W G Edington (qv), to dominate. Not surprisingly the Midland lost its position as the largest clearing bank in the decade after 1945. Ormsby-Gore married, in 1913, Lady Beatrice Edith Mildred Gascoyne-Cecil, daughter of 4th Marquess of Salisbury; they had three sons and three daughters. See A R Holmes and Edwin Green, *Midland: 150 Years of Banking Business* (1986); *The Times*, 15 February 1964.

ORR, William James
(1873 - 24 January 1963)
Cotton spinner and manufacturer, the son of James Orr. He joined the family firm of James Orr & Sons and became chairman of the Lancashire Cotton Corporation in 1932. Formed in 1929 with the backing of the Bank of England, its objective was to rationalise the cotton industry through vertical integration. However, the LCC initially created a horizontal merger in the spinning section of 10 million spindles, many of its constituent companies being heavily indebted to the clearing banks and running old equipment. A financial crisis developed in 1932 and the original management was replaced by a new executive headed by Orr, John Grey and Frank Platt (qv). The LCC employed 15,000 in 1935. Appointed CBE in 1920, Orr was a director of Royal Insurance Co and British Northrop Loom Co Ltd. He married in 1902 Kathleen Marguerite (d 1939), daughter of Sir Joseph Leigh of Stockport: they had one son and one daughter. Orr was awarded the Order of the Crown of Belgium. See J H Bamberg, 'The Rationalisation of the British Cotton Industry in the Interwar Years', *Textile History* 19 (1988).

OWEN, Sir Alfred George Beech
(8 April 1908 - 29 October 1975)
Manufacturer of engineering components, born at Streetly, Staffordshire, eldest of the two sons and daughter of Alfred Ernest Owen, part-owner of Rubery Owen & Co which operated a small ironworks at Darlaston, and his wife Florence Lucy née Beech, he was educated at Oundle and Emmanuel College, Cambridge. The death of his father in 1929 forced him to leave Cambridge without completing his engineering degree and to return home to take charge of the family firm where his strengths emerged on the commercial side. During the 1930s the business grew rapidly, supplying the building and motor industries and, after 1936, military components under the national rearmament programme. By the end of the Second World War the company employed 16,000: making it one of the largest private companies in the UK. This figure dropped back to 12,000 by 1955 but by 1969 when AGB (as he was known) retired there were 6,000 at Darlaston and about 10,000 in the 50 or so

nominally-autonomous subsidiary companies. All were engaged in the manufacture of a wide range of steel products: steelwork for buildings, motor car components (chassis frames, wheels, axle cases, fuel tanks), kitchen equipment, office furniture, aircraft landing gear, hydraulic mining equipment and fork lift trucks. Rubery Owen rightly earned a high reputation for its welfare provisions, first under A E Owen and then under AGB. In AGB's case, the clubs, apprentice hostel, nursery, subsidised housing, pension scheme, retirement preparation programme, which he instituted, sprang not simply from self-interest but from the evangelical Christian convictions he found as a Cambridge student. Beyond his firm AGB gained national prominence as a leader in the British Racing Motors project, culminating in 1962 when Graham Hill won the Formula I World Championship in a BRM, and as a promoter of Donald Campbell who in 1964 reached a new world speed record of 404 mph in *Bluebird*, a racing car built by a subsidiary of Rubery Owen. Outside business AGB assumed onerous duties in local government (eg as chairman of Staffordshire County Council, 1955-62), in social service (eg as chairman of Dr Barnardo's Homes, 1950-70), and in Christian work (eg as an Anglican lay reader, as treasurer of Birmingham Youth for Christ and of Billy Graham's London crusade of 1954). A serious stroke in 1969 ended the multi-faceted and enormously energetic career of Sir Alfred Owen (he was knighted in 1961). Alfred Owen, in 1932, married Eileen Kathleen Genevieve ('Viva') McMullan, daughter of Captain A McMullan, an army officer; they had three sons and two daughters. See *DBB*; David J Jeremy, *Capitalists and Christians: Business Leaders and the Churches in Britain, 1900-1960* (1990).

OWEN, Sir David John
(8 March 1874 - 17 May 1941)
Port manager, born in Liverpool, the son of the Reverend R Ceinwenywdd Owen and Elizabeth Jane Jones. Educated at the Liverpool Institute, he served his business apprenticeship for 13 years with the Mersey Docks & Harbour Board. After a brief spell as manager and secretary of Paul Bros, the Liverpool and Birkenhead flour millers, in 1908 he became manager of Goole Docks. In 1915 he took up a management post at the Belfast Harbour Commission. From 1922 to 1938 he was general manager of the Port of London Authority. His tenure saw the introduction of labour-saving mechanical equipment, with employment reaching 10,000 in the mid-1930s. Adviser to several government committees, he was president of the National Confederation of Employers Organisations, 1936-7; president of the Institute of

Transport, 1932-3; and chairman of the Merchant Shipping Reserve Advisory Committee, 1939. He was knighted in 1931. He married twice: in 1899 to Mary Elizabeth née Owen (d 1906); and then in 1908 to Marian Maud née Williams, widow of J H Thomas (they had no children). See David Owen, *The Origin and Development of the Ports of the United Kingdom* (1939); *The Times*, 19 May 1941.

OWEN, Ernest William Beech
(24 October 1910 - 25 February 1967)
Manufacturer of engineering components, born at Streetly, Staffordshire, the younger son of Alfred Ernest Owen, part-owner of Rubery Owen & Co, and his wife Florence Lucy née Beech, he was educated at Oundle School and Loughborough College. He worked closely with his brother Alfred (qv) in building up the family business during the 1930s. As a trained engineer he complemented his commercially-talented brother and was responsible for many developments in product design and manufacturing methods. Although he saw himself as a 'back-room' boy, as joint managing director Ernest Owen was a key figure after 1945 in developing hydraulic earthmoving equipment, some in conjunction with North American companies with whom he forged close links. A life-long farmer in his spare time, he was closely involved in Rubery Owen's agricultural machinery interests, manufacturing and retailing, and shortly before his sudden death from a stroke, became president-elect of the Agricultural Engineers Association. A popular figure known for his ready laugh and earthy humour, Ernest Owen was for many years chairman of the company's sports and social club and always acted as MC when thousands of employees and their families attended the annual gala and sports day. He married, in 1947, Patricia Mary Atkinson, adopting her daughter and subsequently a son in 1951. See family information via John E Owen; *The Times*, 27 February 1967.

P

PAGET, Sir George Ernest
(10 November 1841 - 30 December 1923)
Railway company chairman, the only son of George Byng Paget (d 1858) of Sutton Bonington, Loughborough, a director of the Midland Railway from its formation in 1844 and chairman, 1857-58, and his wife Sophia née Tebbutt, he was educated at Harrow. He joined the 7th Hussars in 1860, transferring in 1861 to the Royal Horse Guards from which he retired in 1867; later he held a commission in the Leicestershire Yeomanry, retiring as lieutenant-colonel. Ernest Paget became a director of the Midland Railway in 1870, chairman

of its traffic committee in 1881 and deputy chairman in 1884. He succeeded Sir Mathew William Thompson as Midland chairman in 1890. By 1907 the company had over 66,000 employees and was the third largest of the UK's 120 or so railway companies. The network Paget inherited formed a large X, with Bristol and St Pancras, London, at the base and Manchester and Carlisle at the top, with a central network between Derby, Nottingham and Sheffield. It was a coherent network, largely the creation of Sir James Allport (general manager, 1860-80) who also lowered fares and greatly improved services. Sir Ernest Paget (he was made a baronet in 1897) retired in 1911 but retained his seat on the Midland board until 1922. He was a JP and DL for Nottinghamshire and the county's high sheriff in 1898, and a JP for Leicestershire. Paget married, in 1866, Sophia née Holden; they had a son, Cecil Walter, who was general superintendent of the Midland Railway, 1907-19, and succeeded to the title, and a daughter. See *Railway Gazette*, 4 January 1924.

PALMER, Sir Charles Eric
(1883 - 16 December 1948)
Food manufacturer, the elder son of Charles H Palmer, JP, who was a director of the Quaker biscuit manufacturers, Huntley & Palmers. Educated at Harrow and Exeter College, Oxford, he became chairman of Huntley & Palmers at the age of 42 and remained in post until his death. Described as a paternalist with a shrewd business sense, under Palmer the firm's turnover rose from £1,626,000 in 1925 (net profit £183,000) to £2,863,000 in 1948 (net profit £227,000). Palmer was also chairman of Huntley Bourne & Stevens Ltd and of Associated Biscuit Manufacturers Ltd. He was president of the National Association of Biscuit Manufacturers and chairman of the Cake & Biscuit Wholesale Manufacturers' Wartime Alliance. At the end of the war he was knighted for his work with the Alliance. He married Gwenllian Salier née Jones: they had a son and two daughters. Palmer left £550,570. See T A B Corley, *Huntley & Palmers of Reading 1822-1972* (1972).

PALMER, William Howard
(3 November 1865 - 17 March 1923)
Biscuit manufacturer, third son of Samuel Palmer, one of the founders of Huntley & Palmers Ltd, the biscuit manufacturers of Reading, he was educated at Cholmeley School, Highgate, and then studied finance in Brussels and commerce with Messrs Joseph Travers & Sons in London. In Huntley & Palmers he took charge of manufacturing and packing. He was elected deputy chairman in 1904 and two years later became chairman, succeeding his

cousin George William Palmer (1851-1913), formerly MP (Liberal) for Reading. Howard Palmer rapidly introduced reforms in the internal reporting system and started the recording of overseas trade statistics. With 6,500 employees in 1907 Huntley & Palmers was the largest of the UK biscuit manufacturers and the largest employer in Reading. Its reputation as a benevolent Quaker employer evaporated in the prolonged trade depression beginning in 1903, when it cut labour costs by retarding wage rises, using short time and redundancies, and, in 1911, dismissed 200 union members. A social survey by the distinguished statistician A L Bowley, then a lecturer at Reading University College, found that 19 per cent of the town's population were living in primary poverty in 1912. Howard Palmer responded by moving the company from a rigid paternalism to a form of joint consultation. He set up works committees which in 1915 were boldly superseded by a general committee of 52 employees with the freedom to discuss issues unsettled by foremen or managers. Added to the firm's size and reputation, these reforms and Howard Palmer's national profile made Huntley & Palmers the undisputed industry leader. Howard Palmer's last major step was to merge Huntley & Palmers with Peek Frean of London (3,000 employees in 1907), the second largest biscuit maker. In 1921 the two firms became the operating subsidiaries of a new holding company, the Associated Biscuit Manufacturers Ltd. Howard Palmer was its first chairman. Palmer married Ada Morgan, the fourth daughter of William Reed; they had a son. See T A B Corley, *Quaker Enterprise in Biscuits: Huntley & Palmers of Reading, 1822-1972* (1972); *Reading Standard*, 24 March 1923.

PARK, Franklin Atwood
(18?? - 19??)

Manager of the Singer Manufacturing Co factory at Clydebank, 1904-12, born in the USA, he was sent over by the American parent company which opened its first Scottish factory in 1867 in Glasgow but in 1884 moved to a much larger greenfield site seven miles away on the northern bank of the Clyde at Kilbowie (known as Clydebank). Park's period in charge at Clydebank started with the opening of a cabinet factory, built by the firm of Robert McAlpine (qv), and saw very rapid expansion. From 7,000 employees in 1907 the workforce rose to over 11,000 in 1911. His term ended in months of labour unrest, widely felt in Britain and associated with a long trade depression, triggered at Clydebank by an attempt to cut piecework rates. A three week strike followed in March 1911. Park refused to deal with union representatives, instead dealing directly with employees by ballot. Small in

stature, Park was austere, aloof and precise. He seldom went onto the factory floor without his works superintendent through whom he communicated with employees. An able administrator, he was promoted to vice-president of the American parent company and recalled to New York in 1912. He was married and while living in Scotland at Helensburgh had one or more children. See A Dorman, 'A History of the Singer Co (UK) Ltd (Clydebank Factory)' (typescript, 1972; copy in Clydebank Public Library).

PARKER, Sir Peter
(30 August 1924 -)

Industrialist, born in Dunkirk, France, the son of Tom Parker, an engineer, and his wife Dorothy, a teacher. His childhood was spent in France and Shanghai. Educated at Bedford School, he attended London University and Lincoln College, Oxford, where he read history. Service in the Second World War took him to the Far East and Washington DC, where he was a major in the Intelligence Corps. He left Oxford in 1950 with a Commonwealth Fund Fellowship to study management at Cornell and Harvard. A year later he unsuccessfully contested Bedford for Labour. His first business opportunity came with responsibility for the first of the Duke of Edinburgh's Commonwealth Study Conferences on business and industry, 1954-6. In 1956 he joined Booker Bros McConnell Ltd (later Bookers Engineering) and by 1966 was chairman - the first of a string of senior executive posts, with Shipping Industrial Holdings, British Maltsters, Dawnay Day, Curtis Brown, Rockware, Mitsubishi Electric (UK), the British Institute of Management, the National Ports Authority, British Steel, and British Airways. His highest profile job was as chairman of British Rail, 1976-83, where he launched a major programme of electrification and the Channel Tunnel and began modernising BR with his Age of the Train campaign. But his attempts to improve productivity and cut staff (when he took over BR employed 243,000) provoked a national strike in 1982. He was also increasingly at loggerheads with a Conservative Government intent on privatising as much as the railways as possible (Margaret Thatcher *never* used the service) and which had little sympathy with Parker's ideas for cooperation between government, unions and industry. Besides his interest in management (he was a founder member of the Foundation for Management Education and chairman of the governors of London School of Economics), as one of the most intellectual and articulate of businessmen, Parker has served on many arts bodies, such as the Design Museum and the National Theatre. Knighted in 1978 he was appointed KBE in 1993. He married in 1951 Gillian, daughter of Sir Ernest Rowe-Dutton: they have three sons and one daughter. See Sir Peter Parker, *For Starters: The Business of Life* (1989).

PARKER, Ronald William
(21 August 1909 -)

Divisional chairman of the National Coal Board, born in Scotland, the son of Ernest Edward Parker, Accountant of Court, and Margaret Parker née Henderson, he was educated at the Royal High School, Edinburgh, and in 1933 qualified as a chartered accountant. Two years later he became secretary (and later director) of the Weston group of companies, launched in Scotland by Willard Garfield Weston (qv) the Canadian food manufacturer in 1934. During the Second World War Parker was (from 1942) an assistant director of finance at the Ministry of Fuel and Power; afterwards he became a partner in J Aikman, Smith & Wells, chartered accountants. A year later, in 1947, he became finance director of the Scottish Division of the National Coal Board, being promoted to deputy chairman of the North West Division in 1954, and then chairman of the Scottish Division in 1955. With nearly 84,000 employees in 1955, Scotland was the fifth largest division in the coal industry, but one that was characterised by high costs and losses, labour militancy (with some Communist labour leadership) and long term industrial decline (despite new investment the division never made a profit after 1949). During his time, Parker allowed his area managers relatively less initiative than in other divisions. He remained in charge of the Scottish Division until 1967 and then for a year as chairman of its successor, the Scottish Region of the NCB, 1967-68. He finished his career as chairman of the Scottish Gas Region, 1968-74. Parker was appointed CBE in 1959 and was an Edinburgh JP. He married, in 1937, Phyllis Mary née Sherren; they had two sons. See William Ashworth, *The History of the British Coal Industry vol 5 1946-1982: The Nationalised Industry* (1986); Lord Robens, *Ten Year Stint* (1972).

PASOLD, Eric Walter
(19 June 1906 - 5 January 1978)

Knitwear and clothing manufacturer, born in Fleissen (now Plesna) in Czechoslovakia, the son of Max Walter Pasold and Berta née Geipel. Educated at the textile college at Asch, in Bohemia, he joined the family textile business in Fleissen before setting up a UK factory at Langley, near Slough, in 1932. The war caused a complete break with the Fleissen operations and Eric (who was naturalised in 1936) and his brother Ralf concentrated on the English company: by the mid-1950s (when it went

public) Pasolds Ltd was the largest children's wear manufacturers in the UK (turnover had risen from £4,000 in the 1932 to £1.7 million in 1955) and its 'Ladybird' trademark was a household name. Pasold retired in 1968, having paved the way for a negotiated takeover of the firm by Coats Patons. An autocratic bachelor, Pasold played a leading part in the formation of Crawley New Town and founded the Pasold Research Fund for the study of textile history. He was awarded the OBE in 1961. See Eric Pasold, *Ladybird Ladybird: A Story of Private Enterprise* (1977); *DBB*.

PEACOCK, Sir Kenneth Swift
(19 February 1902 - 6 September 1968)

Steel engineering manufacturer, born at Walsall, Staffordshire, the only son of Tom Swift Peacock (qv), managing director of F W Cotterill Ltd, nut and bolt manufacturers, and his wife Elizabeth Amy née Richards, he was educated at Oundle School. He left in 1920 to join Guest, Keen & Nettlefolds which had taken over his father's firm in 1919, with his father becoming a joint managing director of GKN in 1920 (and later deputy chairman, 1933-41). After training in the works, Peacock specialised in sales and marketing. He was made a GKN director in 1933 and joint managing director in 1936, when the company employed 30,000, remaining a managing director until 1964, when GKN had nearly 100,000 employees worldwide. In addition he was deputy chairman of GKN, 1950-53, chairman, 1953-65, and president, 1965 until his death. His main achievements as chairman were to repurchase and modernise the firm's steelworks in South Wales following the denationalisation of steel in 1953. New investment was poured into both the steel and engineering sides of the business. Some grouping and decentralisation was imposed on GKN's 65 operating subsidiaries (as of 1964). Peacock was knighted in 1963. His outside interests lay in motor racing and horse riding. Peacock married twice: first, in 1925, to Hilaria (d 1926), daughter of Sir Geoffrey Syme, by whom he had a daughter; second, in 1934, to Norma Rigby, by whom he had two sons. See *DBB*; Edgar Jones, *A History of GKN: The Growth of a Business, 1918-1945* (1990).

PEACOCK, Thomas Swift
(1869 - 1946)

Steel engineering manufacturer, born at Huddersfield, the son of a linen draper. He entered a solicitor's office, then became a buyer for a Leeds iron merchant. In 1892 he joined F W Cotterill Ltd, manufacturers of nuts and bolts at Darlaston, as a company secretary. He became general manager in the following year and managing director in

1900. When in 1919, Guest, Keen & Nettlefolds Ltd, the Birmingham and South Wales steel engineering firm, decided to extend their fastener business and acquired Cotterils, Peacock was appointed a director of the main baord. In the following year, under the reorganisation inspired by the merger with John Lysaght Ltd, he rose to joint managing director of GKN. In July 1933 he became deputy chairman of GKN (two years later the firm employed about 30,000 workers, placing it amongst the top 15 UK firms) - a post he occupied until his retirement in 1941. His son, (Sir) Kenneth Swift (qv), was later a chairman of GKN. He left £239,476. See Charlotte J Erickson, *British Industrialists: Steel and Hosiery, 1850-1950* (1959); Edgar Jones, *A History of GKN: The Growth of a Business, 1918-1945* (1990).

PEARCE, Sir William George
(23 July 1861 - 2 November 1907)

Engineering and shipbuilding company chairman, born at Chatham, Kent, the only son of William Pearce (1833-88), a Chatham Dockyard-trained naval architect, and his wife Dinah Elizabeth née Sowter, he was educated at Blair Lodge, Rugby, Glasgow University and Trinity College, Cambridge (where he took an LLB) and was called to the Bar at the Inner Temple in 1885. His father moved to the Clyde as a Lloyds surveyor in 1863 and after management experience in another yard became partner in John Elder & Co in 1869. By his death in 1888 Sir William Pearce MP (he was made a baronet in 1887 and was MP for Govan from 1885) had made Fairfield Shipbuilding & Engineering Co (as it was renamed in 1886, on becoming a limited liability company) the leading shipyard on the Clyde, employing 5,000. Sir William George Pearce was trained to succeed his father as chairman of Fairfield but largely remained in the South, tending his 1,500-acre Berkshire estate, his duties as (Conservative) MP for Plymouth (1892-95), and his steam yacht on the Mediterranean. He left the management of the shipyard at Govan and the firm's London office (and 6,000 employees) to managers like Dr Francis Elgar and Alexander Gracie (qv), with whom he communicated almost daily. Sir William George Pearce married, in 1905, Caroline Eva née Coote but left no heir when he died of appendicitis. See *The Bailie*, 6 May 1903; *DSBB* (Sir William Pearce).

PEARSE, Brian (Gerald)
(23 August 1933 -)

Banker, born in Liverpool, the son of Francis and Eileen Pearse. His family were seafarers, largely with Cunard. Educated at St Edward's College in Merseyside, he planned to become a customs officer, but went into banking shortly before starting National Service. In 1950 he joined Martin's Bank, which merged with Barclays in 1968. Pearse became a Barclays troubleshooter: he had a pivotal role in the management of the UK retail bank and in the early 1980s was sent to tackle problems in the USA. On his return, Sir John Quinton (qv) appointed him finance director, until in 1991 Pearse accepted the post of chief executive of the ailing Midland Bank. He was immediately plunged into a takeover battle as Lloyds, headed by Sir Jeremy Morse and Brian Pitman (qqv), and the Hong Kong & Shanghai Banking Corporation, under (Sir) William Purves (qv), struggled for control of Midland (which employed 50,000). Better than expected results in 1991 (a profit of £36 million, when a loss was expected), enabled Pearse to decline the Lloyds' bid in 1992 and accept that of the HSBC. Under HSBC ownership, pre-tax profits improved again in 1992 to £178 million. He married in 1959 Patricia M Callaghan: they have one son and two daughters.

PEARSON, John
(9 March 1850 - 7 March 1944)

Scottish Co-operative Wholesale Society executive, born at Alloa, Clackmannanshire, to Andrew Pearson and Catherine Strang née Rintoul. He joined the local co-operative society in 1878, becoming a director in 1883 and president in 1889. He was elected as a director of the SCWS in 1888 and was appointed its first full-time secretary in 1907. He retired in 1931 when he was succeeded by Robert Leckie (qv). Pearson, by dint of longevity, became the elder statesman and father confessor to senior managers in the SCWS, which employed 7,000 in 1907 and 12,000 in 1935. At Alloa, where he spent his life, he was town councillor from 1898 to 1922, magistrate, and in 1916 provost. He was married and had at least two daughters. See *Scottish Co-operator*, 21 November 1931, 11 March 1944.

PEARSON, Sir (James) Denning
(8 August 1908 - 1 August 1992)

Engineer and aero-engine company executive, born at Bootle, in Lancashire, the son of James Pearson and Elizabeth Henderson. Educated at Canton Secondary School, Cardiff, he gained a first-class honours degree in engineering and a Whitworth Scholarship at Cardiff Technical College. In 1932 he joined Rolls-Royce Ltd from Metropolitan Vickers; then during the war he went to Glasgow to establish shadow factories for aero-engine production. In wartime RR's Merlin engine acquired a considerable reputation and Pearson persuaded (Lord) Hives (qv) to consider a commercial application for it. This was the basis for a range of RR gas-turbine engines - such as the Dart in the Viscount - which by the 1960s had made RR a world leader in civil and military markets. In 1950 Pearson became a director of RR, in 1954 managing director of its aero-engine division, then chief executive in 1957, and chairman and chief executive, 1969-70. Under Pearson RR undertook the ambitious RB211 programme to enter the international civil jet-engine business: though it was eventually a technical success, development costs of £135 million (more than double the estimated amount) bankrupted the company in 1971 and it had to be nationalised by an embarrassed Conservative Government. Pearson lost his job and he and his board were heavily criticised for their management structure and the over-dominance of engineers. He was knighted in 1963. He married in 1932 Eluned Henry, by whom he had two daughters. See James Denning Pearson, *The Development and Organisation of Rolls-Royce Ltd* (1964); Robert A S Gray, *Rolls on the Rocks* (1971).

PEARSON, Weetman Dickinson
1st Viscount Cowdray
(15 July 1856 - 1 May 1927)
Contractor and builder, born at Kirkburton, near Huddersfield, the eldest son of George Pearson and Sarah Weetman née Dickinson. Educated privately and at Pannal College, Harrogate, at 16 he joined the family contracting and building firm. By 1894 he had control of the business and soon made it one of London's leading contractors. In 1889 he won his first contracts in the USA and in Mexico (which took him into the oil industry). By the 1920s a series of large British and foreign building contracts had made Pearson the most prominent contractor of his day with a business that spanned contracting, oil, coal, electrical, newspaper and financial interests. He was a Liberal MP for Colchester 1895-1910, but preferred business to politics. He was made a baronet in 1894, a peer in 1910, promoted to a viscountcy in 1917, and created GCVO in 1925. In 1881 he married Annie, daughter of Sir John Cass, a Bradford millowner: they had three sons and a daughter. He left £4 million gross, the largest estate left by a builder and contractor, though Cowdray had given away over £1 million in benefactions. See John Alfred Spender, *Weetman Pearson: First Viscount Cowdray, 1856-1927* (1930); DBB; DNB.

PEASE, Sir Arthur Francis
(11 March 1866 - 23 November 1927)
Banker and railway company director, the son of Arthur Pease (1837-98), MP, and Mary Lecky née Pike, he was born into a Quaker dynasty with numerous tentacles concentrated in coal, iron, railway and woollen activities in south Durham and

north Yorkshire. Educated at Brighton College and Trinity College, Cambridge, he came to the leadership of the dynasty's main business vehicle, Pease & Partners, after his uncle Sir Joseph Whitwell Pease (1828-1903), 1st Baronet, was found (through an accountant's inspection of his Darlington bank, J & J W Pease in 1902) to be insolvent. Only a guarantee fund supported by Arthur Dorman (qv), Sir Christopher Furness and other North East industrialists prevented bankruptcy. Sir Joseph Pease, whose mistake had been to prop up (for benevolent reasons) a number of loss-making subsidiaries for too long, resigned, as did two of his sons. Sir David Dale succeeded them and at his death in 1906 Arthur Francis Pease became managing director and chairman of Pease & Partners, remaining in office until his own death. He immediately injected a new, more ruthless tone into the Pease management. In the coal industry, where the partnership's interests heavily lay (employing 5,300 in 1907), he became a prominent figure in the Durham Coal Owners' Association, advocating wage reductions and lock-outs and in 1919 testifying to the Sankey Commission against both merger and nationalisation. The intransigent sectionalism his uncle had so long resisted had won the day. Sir Arthur Francis Pease (he was rewarded in 1920 with a baronetcy for serving as Second Civil Lord of the Admiralty, 1918-19) became a director of Lloyds Bank in 1922 and of the London & North Eastern Railway in 1923. A civic leader in County Durham, he was a JP, a DL and in 1920 High Sheriff. Pease married, in 1889, Laura Matilda Ethelwyn née Allix; they had a son and three daughters. See M W Kirby, *Men of Business and Politics: The Rise and Fall of the Quaker Pease Dynasty of North-East England, 1700-1943* (1984).

PEASE, John William Beaumont
1st Baron Wardington of Alnmouth
(4 July 1869 - 7 August 1950)
Clearing banker, born at Westgate, Newcastle upon Tyne, the son of John William Pease (a partner in a private bank and a member of a famous Quaker industrial family) and Helen Maria née Fox. Educated at Marlborough and Oxford, he joined his father's firm in Newcastle. In 1903 this was amalgamated with Lloyds Bank Ltd (with which he already had links through his mother) bringing Pease onto the board. He was chairman of Lloyds from 1922 until 1945; and was also chairman of the Bank of London & South America during 1923-48. Pease achieved solid, but uneven, success: in real terms deposits just doubled between 1922 and 1945, though Lloyds' market share fell slightly from about 19 to 18 per cent. He was made a peer in 1936. In 1923 he married the Hon Mrs Dorothy Charlotte

Lubock, widow of the Hon Harold Lubock and elder daughter of the 1st Lord Fraser: they had two sons. Pease left £83,264 gross. See Maurice W Kirby, *Men of Business and Politics: The Rise and Fall of the Quaker Pease Dynasty of North-East England, 1700-1943* (1984); *DBB*; *DNB*.

PEDDIE, James Mortimer
Baron Peddie of the City and County of Kingston upon Hull
(4 April 1905 - 13 April 1978)
Co-operative executive, born in Hull, the son of Crofton Peddie, a colour works labourer, and Ethel née Whisker. Jim Peddie was educated at St Paul's School, Hull, and Hull Municipal Technical College, before attending the London School of Economics 1927-28. He returned to Hull to lecture in economics and joined the Labour Party and Hull Co-operative Society Ltd. After war work for the Ministries of Food and Information, in 1945 he became a director of the CWS Ltd and a leading campaigner for co-operative ideals through his chairmanship of the Co-operative Party after 1957. This was a time of growth for the CWS (sales grew from £182 million in 1946 to £488 million by 1965) and an influential period for the Co-operative Party, with Peddie becoming a national political figure. From 1965 to 1971 he was a member of the National Prices and Incomes Board under George Brown; and was often consulted on the Labour movement's financial problems. He was made a life peer in 1961. In 1931 he married Hilda Mary Alice née Bull and they had one son and two daughters. He left £183,783 gross. See Sir William Richardson, *The CWS in War and Peace 1938-1976* (1977); *DBB*.

PENNEY, William George
Baron Penney of East Hendred
(24 June 1909 - 3 March 1991)
Scientist and atomic energy executive, born in Sheerness, Kent, into an Army family, the son of W A Penney. Educated at Sheerness Technical School and the Royal College of Science, London, he spent two years at the University of Wisconsin as a Commonwealth Fund Fellow and then had three postgraduate years at Cambridge University. With a London DSc and a Cambridge PhD, he became assistant professor of mathematics at Imperial College aged 27. In 1944 he was sent with a small team of British scientists to Los Alamos to assist the Americans in the atomic bomb project. When Britain began to develop its own atomic bomb after the war, Penney as chief superintendent of Armament Research in the Ministry of Supply was brought in to supervise production. An official observer at Nagasaki, he was committed to nuclear deterrence. Penney created and led a team, which

succeeded in the 1950s in making Britain the world's third nuclear power. Drawn into wider atomic policy matters, he chaired the official inquiry into the Windscale reactor fire in 1957, became a Member for Research between 1959 and 1961, and served as deputy chairman of the UKAEA, 1961-64. He became chairman between 1964 and 1967. Under Penney the first civil nuclear programme went forward and the plans for a second programme were laid; there were also important international developments in disarmament and defence. On retirement, he became Rector of Imperial College, 1967-73. Knighted in 1952, he was created a life peer in 1967 and awarded the Order of Merit in 1969. He married in 1935 Adele Elms, by whom he had two sons; after her death he married in 1945 Eleanor Joan Quennell. See Margaret Gowing, *Independence and Deterrence* (2 vols, 1974).

PERRIN, Sir Michael Willcox
(13 September 1905 - 18 August 1988)
Pharmaceutical company executive, born in Victoria, British Columbia, Canada, the only son of the Right Reverend William Willcox Perrin, then bishop of British Columbia, and Isolene Harriet née Bailey. He came to England with his parents in 1910, attended Winchester and New College, Oxford, where he studied chemistry and physics. Interested in industrial research, he joined ICI's research centre at Winnington and in 1935 provided the impetus for the 'rediscovery' and commercialisation of polythene. Closely involved with the wartime atomic bomb project, he was Deputy Controller (Technical Policy) in the Division of Atomic Energy 1946-1951. After briefly returning to ICI, Perrin was invited to become chairman of The Wellcome Foundation Ltd in 1953. He transformed it into a research-based pharmaceutical company by supporting R & D, expanding overseas and by diversification. Sales increased from about £11 million in 1953 to over £85 million in 1970, when Perrin retired. He was awarded the OBE in 1946, the CBE in 1952 and was knighted in 1967 for his work as chairman of the Board of Governors of St Bartholomew's Hospital and as chairman of the Wellcome Foundation. In 1934 he married Nancy May, daughter of the Right Reverend Charles Edward Curzon: they had one son and one daughter. See M W Perrin, 'The Story of Polythene', *Research* 6 (March 1953); Gilbert Macdonald, *In Pursuit of Excellence: One Hundred Years Wellcome, 1880-1980* (1983); *DBB*.

PERRY, Michael (Sydney)
(26 February 1934 -)
Food and soap multinational executive, the son of Sydney Albert Perry and Jessie Kate née Brooker. Educated at King William's College, Isle of Man, and St John's College, Oxford (where he read German and Russian), he joined Unilever in 1957 as a management trainee. He worked in Holland for eight years in the toilet preparations division: as Unilever's Mr Fragrance he was responsible for such scents as Elizabeth Taylor's Passion and Calvin Klein's Obsession. He then worked for Unilever subsidiaries world-wide: a four-year spell in Thailand earned him an OBE in 1978, and he was also employed in Argentina and Japan. Perry became a Unilever director in 1985. Appointed a vice-chairman of Unilever in 1991 and a member of the Special Committee, he became chairman in 1992. He takes charge of an organisation with a turnover in 1991 of £23,163 million (making Unilever second only to BP in the UK in terms of sales) and nearly 300,000 workers. Perry is also a non-executive director of Bass. He was appointed a CBE in 1990 for services to exports as chairman of the Japan Trade Advisory Group. Perry married in 1958 Joan Mary Stallard: they have one son and two daughters.

PERRY, Percival Lee Dewhurst
1st Baron Perry of Stock Harvard
(18 March 1878 - 17 June 1956)
Motor car manufacturer, born at Bristol, the son of Alfred Thomas Perry, a clerk, and Elizabeth née Wheeler. Educated at King Edward VI's School, Birmingham, in 1904 he set up an agency for selling imported American cars. By 1909 he was Henry Ford's UK agent and helped establish the American's subsidiary at Trafford Park, Manchester. Disagreements led Perry to break with Ford after 1919, but in 1928, when Ford set up the Ford Motor Co Ltd in Dagenham, Perry accepted the chairmanship - a post he held until 1948. In 1932, when full production started, Ford UK had made 25,571 vehicles; in 1948 102,531 cars were manufactured. Knighted in 1918 for war work, Perry was made a peer in 1938. In 1902 he married Catherine née Meals, the daughter of a Hull postmaster. He left £77,699. See Mira Wilkins and Frank E Hill, *American Business Abroad: Ford on Six Continents* (1964); *DBB*.

PHELPS, Douglas Vandeleur
(29 January 1904 - 8 October 1988)
Glass manufacturer, elder son of J V Phelps and his wife Millicent Douglas née Pilkington, a granddaughter of William Pilkington (1800-1872), joint founder of the Pilkington glassmaking business at St Helens, he was educated at Harrow and Magdalene College, Oxford, where he read chemistry. He joined the family firm in 1927 and, after rigorous appraisal, was made a director in 1934, concerning himself with the manufacturing side of glass making. Mobilised with the Territorial Army in 1939, he went to the Staff College, Camberley, in 1940 and served in staff appointments throughout the Second World War. Back at St Helens he served as chairman of Pilkingtons executive committee, 1947-65, and also of the company's joint industrial council, maintenance trades council, the staff council, Chance Brothers Ltd and Fibreglass Ltd. Under the chairmanship of William Henry Pilkington (qv), Phelps took charge of the day-to-day running of the company which in 1955 employed over 20,000 (over 12,000 at St Helens). He retired as an executive director in 1965 and as a non-executive director in 1973. Outside Pilkingtons Phelps was a director of the Westminster Bank, 1955-69. He commanded the local Territorial Regiment, 1947-51, and an Anti-Aircraft Brigade, 1951-54, with the rank of brigadier, and was an ADC to King George VI and Queen Elizabeth II. He was a JP of St Helens and a DL of Lancashire, and a JP and DL of Norfolk after retiring there. Phelps married, in 1953, Helen Rosemary Cozens-Hardy. See Theodore C Barker, *The Glassmakers. Pilkington: The Rise of an International Company, 1826-1976* (1977).

PHILIPPI, Otto Ernst
(1847 - 10 February 1917)
Thread manufacturer, born at Solingen, Prussia, the son of Martin Philippi, a teacher, though other members of the family, which was of Greek descent, were engaged in banking in Hamburg. Philippi had some commercial training and in 1867 joined an uncle's cotton broking business in Liverpool and then a similar firm in New York. Not very successful, he returned to Hamburg (with British citizenship) and in 1872 joined the staff of Nicolai Wulff, agent for J & P Coats, the Paisley thread manufacturer. Here he caught the attention of Archibald Coats (qv) with his ideas for developing sales, his command of languages (German, English, French and Spanish), and his fine handwriting. Philippi was sent to South America where he organised an efficient network of sales agents. By 1879 he was running the Coats' sales organisation in all markets outside the USA. His success rested on several elements: concentration on a small range of high-quality staple articles for the household trade; the appointment of salesmen and agents with an intimate knowledge of their markets; and the operation of a detailed reporting system which kept him closely informed and in control of sales. To reduce competition in 1889 he set up the

Sewing Cotton Agency, soon renamed the Central Agency, to market jointly the thread of three firms - Coats, Clark & Co, also of Paisley, and Jonas Brook of Meltham, Yorkshire. The formation of a public company, J & P Coats Ltd, in 1890 strengthened his position with his appointment as selling director. He organised the establishment of a plant in Russia (not least to check a Russian competitor), formed a new company to manage sales in the USA, and in 1896 had a major role in the merger of Coats, Clark, Brook and Chadwick of Eagley Mills, Bolton. By 1914 Coats had mills in 14 foreign countries including Germany, Mexico and Japan, and employed 39,000 worldwide. From 1901 on medical advice Philippi lived in the south of England, at Crawley Court near Winchester, communicating with Paisley by telegram. He acted for Coats as debenture holders in the Calico Printers' Association and chaired a CPA reconstruction committee in 1902. At Crawley he created a model village but his last years were clouded by anti-German feeling during the First World War and he resigned from J & P Coats in 1916. Philippi married Magdalena Philippi by whom he had two sons and two daughters. One of the sons, E A Philippi, was appointed a Coats director in 1906 in order to liase on his father's behalf with foreign subsidiaries. See *DSBB*.

PHILIPPS, Owen Cosby
Baron Kylsant of Carmarthen
(25 March 1863 - 5 June 1937)
Shipowner, born at Warminster, third of six sons and eleven children of Canon Sir James Erasmus Philipps (1824-1912), 12th Bt, vicar of Warminster (and an enterprising Anglo-Catholic), and his wife the Honourable Margaret née Best, he was sent to Newton College, at Newton Abbot. Being a slow learner he was withdrawn in 1880 and apprenticed to Dent & Co, ship managers of Newcastle-upon-Tyne. Afterwards he moved to Glasgow, working for Allan C Gow & Co. Opportunities considerably broadened after 1888 when his eldest brother, John Wynford Philipps (1860-1938), later 1st Viscount St Davids, married a wealthy heiress, worth nearly £100,000. Educated at Oxford (attaining a third class degree in history) and a barrister, John joined Owen in forming Philipps & Co which in 1889 established the King Alfred Steamship Co Ltd (with one vessel), renamed the King Line in 1893; soon after, the brothers moved from Glasgow to London. They founded the London Maritime Investment Co in 1897 and then Owen engineered a series of manoeuvres which by 1902 saw him elected chairman of the Royal Mail Steam Packet Co. Over the next two decades he built up a huge shipping group of nearly 40 com-

panies together employing 36,000 men at sea and 23,000 ashore. He also had large shareholdings in Harland & Wolff, the Belfast shipbuilders with whose chairman Lord Pirrie (qv) Owen Philipps sometimes operated; in Colvilles, the Glasgow steelmakers; and in Thomas Hedley, the Newcastle-upon-Tyne soapmakers. He came unstuck in the 1920s when excessive world shipping capacity reduced demand for shipping services and exposed the fundamental weaknesses of Philipps's empire: a relatively new fleet of obsolete design financed by high gearing. High loan servicing charges drained profits and forced Lord Kylsant (Owen Philipps was knighted in 1910 and raised to the peerage in 1923) to sustain dividends by drawing on secret reserves. Continuing to borrow to finance new construction, Kylsant was unable to repay loans made under the Trade Facilities Act of 1921. The Treasury in 1929 appointed the accountant Sir William McLintock to investigate the Royal Mail Group. Irregularities came to light and Kylsant was charged with issuing misleading accounts (in 1926 and 1927) and a false prospectus (in 1928). He was found guilty in 1931 on the prospectus charge and served twelve months in prison. The affair led to the break-up of the Royal Mail Group with shareholders in the constituent companies losing nearly all their investments, a total net loss of between £50 million and £70 million at 1931 prices. Kylsant, formerly Liberal MP for Pembroke and Haverfordwest, 1906-16, and Unionist MP for Chester, 1916-23, emerged from Wormwood Scrubs his social standing unimpaired - his offence excused as a technical, not a moral, matter. He married, in 1902, Mai Alice Morris, heiress to a Carmarthen banking fortune; they had two daughters. His brother Laurence Richard Philipps (1874-1962), also in finance and shipowning, attained the peerage as 1st Baron Milford: thereby achieving the almost unique record of three brothers sitting in the House of Lords through business success - equalled only by the Berry brothers (qv). See *DBB*; Edwin Green and Michael Moss, *A Business of National Importance: The Royal Mail Shipping Group, 1902-1937* (1982); Anthony Vice, *Financier at Sea: Lord Kylsant and the Royal Mail* (1985).

PHILLIPPS, William Douglas
(1839 - 11 August 1932)
Railway manager, eldest son of the Reverend Thomas Phillipps, rector of Dewsall-cum-Callow, Herefordshire, he was educated at Hereford College School, and then apprenticed to John Scott Russell, the builder of Brunel's *Great Eastern*. By the time he was twenty-one he was managing a mineral railway in South Wales. After this was purchased by the Great Western and London & North Western rail-

way companies in 1871 he became manager for the latter at Swansea. A few years later he was appointed manager of the north eastern district of the LNWR with offices at Manchester. In 1882 he became general manager of the North Staffordshire Railway Co, retiring in 1919. The railway, which almost exclusively served the Potteries, employed 4,800 in 1907. After retiring, Phillipps continued with the North Staffordshire Railway as a director and consulting engineer, until it was absorbed by the London, Midland & Scottish Railway in 1922. For 40 years Phillipps was president of Stoke Conservative Club and in 1914 was made a Staffordshire magistrate. He married Alice, fourth daughter of Joseph Alcock JP, of Porthill, Staffordshire; they had a daughter. See *The Times*, 12 August 1932.

PICK, Frank
(23 November 1878 - 7 November 1941)
Transport manager, born at Spalding, Lincolnshire, the eldest child of Francis Pick, draper, and Fanny née Clarke. Educated at St Peter's School, York, he was articled to a solicitor before joining the North Eastern Railway in 1902. After 1906 he was closely involved in managing the London Underground railway and from 1933 to 1940 was vice-chairman of the London Transport Passenger Board. A Congregationalist, sensitive to economic and social objectives, Pick commissioned many of the designs - notably the bar-and-circle motif and the various station architectures - that made the Underground famous. He was chairman of the Design & Industries Association 1932-34; president of the Institute of Transport 1931-32; and was an honorary associate of the Royal Institute of British Architects (his only honour). In 1904 he married Mabel Mary Caroline, daughter of solicitor C S Woodburn: there were no children. Pick left £36,434 gross. See Theodore C Barker and Michael Robbins, *A History of London Transport* (2 vols, 1963-74); *DBB*.

PICKWORTH, Sir Frederick
(7 May 1890 - 14 July 1959)
Steel executive, born near the Manor Village, Sheffield, one of eight children of a Sheffield stonemason. Educated at Manor Council School, at 13 he got a job in a leather merchant's and then in 1904 joined the Sheffield steelmakers Cammell Laird as a clerk. In 1911 he became accountant there after attending evening classes. During the First World War he went to Nottingham as accountant for one of the first Government projectile factories, returning to Cammell Laird in 1917 as chief accountant (in that year he also studied mathematics at the Technical College - later part of Sheffield University). In 1929, when Cammell

Laird merged its steelmaking interests into the English Steel Corporation, he became assistant secretary at the ESC, then secretary. In 1936 he was appointed director of finance, administration and reorganisation. In 1944 he became general manager and was appointed ESC chairman in 1955, when it employed 16,500 and was capitalised at £13 million. Pickworth was the prime mover behind the ESC's expansion to a new Tinsley Park site, opened in Sheffield in 1963 at a cost of £26 million. He was chairman of the English Drilling Equipment Co, High Speed Steel Alloys, Steetley Co, and the American-controlled Security Rock Bits Ltd, besides serving on numerous trade associations. In 1957 he retired from the chairmanship of Darlington Forge, the ESC subsidiary, the year in which he was knighted and became Master Cutler. He died during a dinner in his honour at Darlington. See *British Steelmaker* 25 (July 1959); *Quality* 6 (June/July 1959).

PILKINGTON, Sir Antony (Richard)
(20 June 1935 -)
Glass manufacturer, a fifth generation member of the famous St Helens firm, the son of Arthur Cope Pilkington and his wife Otilia Dolores. Educated at Ampleforth and Trinity College, Cambridge (MA History), he did two years National Service before joining the family firm in 1959. He became a director in 1973 and then succeeded Alastair Pilkington (qv) as chairman in 1980. In 1992 Pilkington's was one of Britain's biggest concerns with sales of £2.6 billion and a market capitalisation of £1 billion. But Sir Antony has had to cut jobs (from 58,400 in 1989 - 13,200 of whom worked in the UK - to 37,000 by the end of 1992), decentralise management, spread production around the world (with a new headquarters in Brussels) and resist a hostile takeover bid by BTR. In June 1992 Pilkington's appointed Roger Leverton as chief executive, relieving Antony of his dual role of chairman and chief executive. At the end of 1992 Pilkington's announced the half-year losses had doubled to £29 million and that a maintained dividend would be paid from reserves. The firm's strong, paternalistic presence in St Helens since the company was founded in 1826 is weakening and there are no family successors ready when Sir Antony retires in 1995: nevertheless, the family still owns ten per cent of the shares and the Pilkington fortune is estimated at about £132 million. Antony Pilkington married in 1960 Alice Kirsty, elder daughter of Sir Thomas Dundas: they have three sons and one daughter. In 1989 he became DL of Merseyside and was knighted in 1990.

PILKINGTON, Geoffrey Langton
(23 November 1885 - 8 January 1972)

Glass manufacturer, the son of George Herbert Pilkington, a member of the famous St Helens glass-making company. Educated at Stone House, a preparatory school at Broadstairs, he went to Eton and Magdalen College, Oxford. He began work in the family firm in 1909, becoming a sub-director in 1910. A year later he joined the Lancashire Hussars and then in 1916 switched to the Royal Flying Corps. He became a director of Pilkington's in 1919 and was made chairman in 1932, after a managerial reorganisation at the company, and remained as such until 1949. He was chairman also of the Pilkington executive committee between 1939 and 1947. He was a DL for Lancashire. For many years he was an enthusiastic gardener, his main interest being irises, and he was a member of the council of the Royal Horticultural Society. He was survived by a widow and three daughters and two sons. See Theodore C Barker, *The Glassmakers. Pilkington: The Rise of an International Company, 1826-1976* (1977); *The Times*, 10 January 1972.

PILKINGTON, Sir (Lionel Alexander Bethune) 'Alastair'
(7 January 1920 -)

Glass manufacturer and technologist, born in Calcutta, the son of Lionel G Pilkington, an engineer, and Evelyn Bethune. Known as Alastair, he was educated at Sherborne and then read mechanical sciences at Trinity College, Cambridge. He joined the famous St Helens glass firm of Pilkington's as a family trainee in 1947, although he was not a relation. By 1959 he had invented float glass technology for the continous production of high-quality plate glass. It had taken seven years to perfect, but made Pilkington's the world's biggest plate glass producer. Alastair was closely involved with its licensing, the annual proceeds from which were to reach a peak of £38 million. He was chairman between 1973 and 1980, when Pilkington expanded its European links, and also took up a number of other influential appointments: director of the Bank of England and British Petroleum, and non-executive chairman of the Chloride Group. He became president of Pilkington's in 1985. Knighted in 1970, he was elected FRS in 1969. He is twice married: to Patricia Nicholls née Elliot (d 1977) in 1945 (by whom he had one son and one daughter); and to Kathleen, widow of Eldridge Haynes, in 1978. See L A B Pilkington, 'The Float Glass Process', *Proceedings of the Royal Society* 314 (December 1969); Theodore C. Barker, *The Glassmakers. Pilkington: The Rise of an International Company, 1826-1976* (1977); *DBB*.

PILKINGTON, Richard
(17 January 1841 - 12 March 1908)

Glass manufacturer, born at St Helens, Lancashire, second son of Richard Pilkington (1795-1869), co-founder of the family glassmaking business at St Helens, and his wife Ann née Evans, he was educated privately before entering the works in 1858-59. Becoming a partner in 1863, he concentrated on the sales side. The firm made sheet and rolled glass at its original Grove Street Works. When they built a second factory in St Helens, for plate glass, at Cowley Hill in 1873-76, Richard and his elder brother William Windle Pilkington (qv) resisted their cousins' suggestion that the expansion should be financed by converting the firm into a public company. Richard's visit to the USA in 1879 saw the beginnings of an overseas export trade which took the firm into a range of North American and imperial markets in the 1890s. By 1907 the firm employed over 9,000 in St Helens at Grove Street, Cowley Hill and Ravenhead (purchased from the British Plate Glass Co in 1901 to supplement Cowley's plate glass output). Richard Pilkington was also managing director of Richard Evans & Co, the Haydock coal proprietors, and chairman of St Helen's Collieries Co Ltd. Outside business he was a member of Ormskirk Street Congregational Church, a national vice-president of the YMCA, and a long-serving and enthusiastic Volunteer officer attaining the rank of colonel and receiving the CB. Active in local government he was a St Helen's town councillor from 1873 until his death, serving as mayor, alderman, JP. On the Home Rule issue he switched from the Liberals to the Conservatives and was MP for the Newton Division of Lancashire, 1899-1906. He married, in 1868, Louisa née Sinclair; they had six sons and two daughters: a strong infusion into the direction of the family firm. See Theodore C Barker, *The Glassmakers. Pilkington: The Rise of an International Company, 1826-1976* (1977).

PILKINGTON, William Henry
Baron Pilkington of St Helens
(19 April 1905 - 22 December 1983)

Glass manufacturer and industrialist, born at St Helens, Lancashire, eldest son of Richard Austin Pilkington, younger twin son of William Windle Pilkington (qv), and Hope, daughter of Sir Herbert Hardy, he belonged to the fourth generation of the glassmaking family. Entering the family firm in 1927 Harry (as he was known) soon defied his undistinguished record at Rugby and Magdalene College, Cambridge (where he took a third in history and economics) by demonstrating a powerful memory, an analytical mind, a liking for statistics and an iron self-discipline. He became a sub-director in 1930. At this point foreign (mostly Belgian) competition threatened Pilkingtons' sheet glass manufacture. Although a new window glassmaking process was secured from Pittsburgh Plate Glass Co (so rescuing Pilkingtons' market share), an unheard-of loss in 1931 precipitated a boardroom crisis which saw his father (then chairman) and an uncle (technical director) resign. A committee structure was set up to strengthen executive management. In 1935, a year after becoming a director, Harry Pilkington found himself head of sales and the senior commercial executive. Authority in the company passed to the fourth generation soon after the Second World War. Douglas Phelps (qv) became chairman of the executive committee in 1947 and Harry Pilkington company chairman in 1949; the latter remained in office until 1973. His achievements within the company included the introduction of inflation accounting, the nurturing of the revolutionary float glass process developed by Alastair Pilkington (qv), the flotation of the firm as a public company (1970), and the construction of a new company headquarters (1964). The company grew rapidly under Harry Pilkington's leadership: turnover rose from £9 million in 1946 to £58 million in 1960 to £123 million in 1970; global employees rose from nearly 16,000 in 1946 to over 31,000 in 1971. It rested on two product markets, building and the motor trade, and one main geographical one, Commonwealth countries. The next generation had the task of correcting the implied imbalances. Outside the company Lord Pilkington (he was knighted in 1953 and made a life peer in 1968) held numerous high offices in industry and technical education; undertook various special tasks for the government (like the Crichel Down Enquiry of 1954 or the Royal Commission on Doctors' and Dentists' Remuneration of 1957-60); and played a leading part in the public life of St Helens and Lancashire. A lifelong Congregationalist, he was well known for his softly-spoken voice, his twinkling eyes and his devotion to the bicycle. He married twice: first, in 1930, to Rosamund Mary Rowan (d 1953) by whom he had a son and two daughters; second, in 1961, to Mrs Mavis Wilding. See Theodore C Barker, *The Glassmakers. Pilkington: The Rise of an International Company, 1826-1976* (1977); *DBB*.

PILKINGTON, William Windle
(29 September 1839 - 15 March 1914)
Glass manufacturer, eldest of the six sons of Richard Pilkington (1795-1869), co-founder of the family glassmaking business at St Helens, Lancashire, and his wife Ann née Evans, he was educated at Bruce Castle, Tottenham, and joined the family firm in 1857. His two cousins William

Roby and Thomas, the sons of William Pilkington (1800-72), the other firm co-founder, succeeded the founders as senior partners in 1865. William Windle Pilkington and his brother Richard (qv) became partners in 1863. While William Roby superintended the Grove Street factory, Thomas directed the commercial side (and when the partnership was converted to a limited company was first chairman, 1894-98), and Richard handled sales, William Windle Pilkington was technical director and the second company chairman, 1898-1914. As technical director William Windle was responsible for installing tank furnaces (allowing round-the-clock working) in the original works; for overseeing the technical side of the new, plate glass factory built at Cowley Hill, St Helens, in 1873-76; and for registering over 50 patents. With strengths on the technical and production side William Windle Pilkington emerged as the outstanding partner of the second generation. Under his chairmanship Pilkingtons emerged as the sole British producer of plate glass and, with Chances (a much smaller concern), only British makers of window glass. The main problem the company faced was continental (especially Belgian) competition; by 1914 Pilkingtons submitted to the continentals' price agreements but increased their output by modernising their grinding machinery. The respect in which William Windle was held by his employees (numbering over 9,000 at St Helens in 1907) helped to defuse labour problems in a period when the threat of new (American) technology hung over glass blowing and gathering. Outside the business, William Windle Pilkington belonged to Ormskirk Street Congregational Church and sat on the council of the Congregational Union of England and Wales (1907). He was a supporter of the Ragged Schools, a national vice-president of the YMCA, a Volunteer (becoming colonel of the St Helens Division) and active in local government, as town councillor, 1870-90, mayor, alderman, JP, DL for Lancashire. He married, in 1867, Louise née Salter; they had four sons and three daughters. See Theodore C Barker, *The Glassmakers. Pilkington: The Rise of an International Company, 1826-1976* (1977).

PILLING, Walter
(1868 - 5 March 1940)
Cotton manufacturer, born in Rochdale, the son of John Pilling, who ran the family cotton spinning firm of John Pilling Ltd, Northwich Street Mills, Rochdale. The business traced its origins to the 1790s. When the business was taken over by Joshua Hoyle & Sons Ltd, Pilling became managing director of the firm, a post he held until 1939. He was also chairman after 1935. Prominent in the cotton

trade, he took a leading share in the foundation in the Dunlop cotton mills at Castleton, and was a director for several years of Tweedales & Smalley Ltd, the textile machinists. His other directorships included the chairmanship of the Baytree Spinning Co, Middleton, and the Spodden Manufacturing Co, Whitworth. Pilling served on the Rochdale Town Council for 13 years and was leader of the Rochdale Conservative Party, 1902-22. He left a widow, one son and three daughters. See *Bacup Times*, 9 March 1940.

PINION, James
(1852 - 25 December 1911)

Railway manager, born at Downpatrick, northern Ireland, and educated at Dundalk Educational Institution (until 1870) and, briefly, at Queen's University, Belfast, he joined the Belfast & County Down Railway in 1872 as a clerk in the secretary's office. Moving to the general manager's office in 1876, he became a traffic inspector in 1878, traffic superintendent in 1883, and general manager in 1890. He expanded his market by increasing services on the Holywood and Bangor line (acquired in 1884), by running a steamer service on Belfast Lough between Belfast and Bangor, and by building a hotel at Newcastle for tourists and golfers. The company's gross traffic receipts rose by over 55 per cent between 1890 and 1904 when Pinion was appointed general manager of the Cheshire Lines Committee. The Cheshire Lines, organised in 1865-66, was jointly owned by the Great Northern, Great Central and Midland railway companies to give them shared access to the Liverpool area via Manchester, allowing them to compete against the London & North Western and the Lancashire & Yorkshire companies. It had 4,700 employees in 1907. Pinion was dogged by ill-health after arriving in Liverpool and he resigned in March 1910. In his younger days Pinion was 'a famous Rugby football player and a great runner'. See *The Railway Gazette*, 29 December 1911; *Railway Year Book* (1908); *Transport*, 29 April 1904.

PIRRIE, William James
Viscount Pirrie of Belfast
(24 May 1847 - 7 June 1924)

Shipbuilder and shipowner, born in Quebec, the son of James Alexander Pirrie (d 1849), who had emigrated to Canada to manage a family shipping concern, and Eliza née Montgomery, he was brought to Ulster by his widowed mother and educated at the Royal Belfast Academical Institution. He entered the Belfast shipbuilding firm owned by Edward Harland and Gustav Wolff in 1862 as a premium apprentice and rapidly moved from draughtsman to assistant manager, sub-manager,

and works manager. Promoted to a partnership in 1874 he made sales his forte and after Harland and Wolff went into parliament (in 1887 and 1892 respectively) Pirrie came to prominence. On Harland's death in 1895 Pirrie became chairman, remaining in power until his own death. Under Pirrie, Harland & Wolff Ltd (as it was renamed in 1888) became a giant, ably-managed shipyard using the latest technology in big ships, particularly luxury passenger liners. The workforce rose from 3,000 in 1874 to 8,500 in 1907, 12,000 in 1914 and 15,000 in 1920. A new 2,000 acre site was developed during the First World War when Harland & Wolff was the largest shipbuilder in the UK, in 1918 accounting for 200,000 of the UK's 1.5 million tons of merchant shipping. Pirrie's managers included his brother-in-law, Alexander Carlisle (qv), and his nephew, Thomas Andrews who also worked on the design of the *Titanic* and in 1912 drowned when she sank on her maiden voyage. Harland & Wolff began building large passenger ships in 1899, culminating in 1910-14 with the *Olympic* (45,000 tons), the *Titanic* (46,000 tons) and the *Britannic* (48,000 tons) for the Oceanic Steam Navigation Co, the White Star line owned by the Ismay family. These exceeded in size the *Lusitania* and *Mauretania* built by John Brown & Co and Swan, Hunter & Wigham Richardson, respectively, for Cunard. When in 1912 Harland & Wolff secured rights to the diesel engine patented by Burmeister & Wain of Copenhagen they gained a significant technical lead in the transition from coal to oil as a source of motive power. Pirrie's interests went far beyond shipbuilding and Belfast. From the mid-1880s he moved into shipowning but his attempt to control North Atlantic routes through his International Mercantile Marine Co of 1902 failed. His alliance with Sir Owen Philipps (later Lord Kylsant) (qv) after 1912 brought Harland & Wolff close to the Royal Mail group. In 1920, before the shipping boom collapsed, Pirrie acquired David Colville & Sons, to guarantee his supplies of steel: a clutch from which John Craig (qv) rescued the Scottish firm after Pirrie's death. Pirrie, a Conservative, was elected to Belfast corporation in 1893 and served as lord mayor in 1896-97. After 1903 he switched to the Liberals (whom he funded generously), was made a baron in 1906 and a viscount in 1921. After 1918 he returned to Unionism and became a senator in the Northern Ireland parliament. Pirrie married Margaret née Carlisle in 1879; there were no children. See *DBB*; Michael Moss and John R Hume, *Shipbuilders to the World: 125 Years of Harland & Wolff, Belfast, 1861-1986* (1986).

PITCHER, Sir Desmond (Henry)
(23 March 1935 -)

Industrialist, born in Liverpool, the son of George Charles and Alice Marion Pitcher. His father was a purser in the Navy (though later he began a career in the film industry, producing the 1950s hit *Genevieve*). Educated at Liverpool College of Technology, he became an apprentice technician at A V Roe & Co. After experience as a systems engineer, in 1961 he joined Sperry, the US defence contractor. By 1974 he was the youngest and first foreign vice-president that Sperry had ever had. Eschewing the path to the Sperry chairmanship (and domicile in the USA), in 1976 he became managing director of Leyland Bus & Truck In Lancashire. In his second year in charge, the company achieved its highest ever profit - £65 million out of a group total of £100 million - but Pitcher had little taste for chairman Michael Edwardes' (qv) confrontational labour relations and he left in 1978. He went to Plessey to work under Sir John Clark and persuaded the company to build its new System X manufacturing plant in Liverpool. In 1983 he became chief executive at Littlewoods, the privately-owned group of Sir John Moores (qv). Pitcher began the reform of Littlewoods' outmoded management methods; stores were up-dated and new chains - Inside Story and Index catalogue shops - established. By 1992, despite the recession, Littlewoods was making record profits of £100 million. In 1993 Pitcher became non-executive vice-chairman of Littlewoods and also chairman of North West Water: by then he was closely involved with the regeneration of Liverpool as chairman of Merseyside Development Corporation. He has been a chairman of Everton Football Club since 1990. He was knighted in 1992 for services to Merseyside. His first marriage, which produced two sons and twin daughters, was dissolved; his second in 1991 was to Norma Barbara Niven. See Desmond Pitcher, Institution of Electrical Engineers Faraday Lectures, 1974-75.

PITMAN, Brian (Ivor)
(13 December 1931 -)

Banker, born at Cheltenham, the son of Ronald Ivor Pitman and Doris Ivy née Short. His father died when he was a baby. Educated at Cheltenham Grammar School, he took his time finding his metier, working initially for a local building society and entertaining notions of becoming a cricketer or a journalist. He joined Lloyds Bank in 1952. He became joint-general manager in 1975 and by 1983 had been appointed chief executive and director, the right-hand man of his chairman, Sir Jeremy Morse (qv). Pitman was appointed in the aftermath of Lloyds' Latin American debt crisis, which had left the bank with bad loans of £715 million, the largest ever at a British bank. Morse and Pitman recovered the situation by generating profits from personal and small company banking, its core businesses. By a mixture of luck and judgement (it avoided stockbroking and property), Lloyds emerged by the 1990s as the UK's most profitable bank. Pitman was also the architect of the failed bid for the Midland Bank in 1992. He has been described as a follower of popular culture, a jazz saxophonist with a voracity for statistics and detail. He married in 1954 Barbara Mildred Ann née Darby: they have two sons and a daughter. See Corinne Simcock, *A Head for Business* (1992).

PLASTOW, Sir David (Arnold Stuart)
(9 May 1932 -)

Industrialist, born in Grimsby, the son of James Stuart and Marie Plastow. His father became a sales director for a motor dealer, though according to Plastow the family was not wealthy. He has described his maternal grandfather as being a 'big fishing magnate'; his maternal grandfather was chairman of Grimsby Town Football Club. Educated at Culford School, Bury St Edmunds, he became an apprentice fitter at Vauxhall Motors in 1950. He moved to Rolls-Royce's motor car division at Crewe in 1958, where he became managing director in 1971, the year before its enforced nationalisation and divorce from its aero-engine sister. Plastow remained as managing director of Rolls-Royce Motors Ltd and when it was bought by Vickers in 1980, he became managing director and chief executive of the famous weapons and aircraft manufacturer. During the next decade Plastow (who was chairman after 1987) began reshaping Vickers' diversified engineering interests to form a more resilient organisation: the office furniture and printing plate businesses were sold, and instead new initiatives were added to the defence and aerospace work - Swedish water jet technology (KaMeWa), aerospace materials (Ross Catherall), cars (Cosworth) and luxury boats (Riva). These businesses in 1990 produced a profit of £41 million, but when he retired as chairman of Vickers in 1992 Vickers (which had a market value of £45 million and a workforce of 11,000) had slumped over £12 million into the red, mainly due (ironically) to mounting Rolls-Royce losses. In 1992 he became chairman of Inchcape and was also deputy chairman of Guinness and the TSB. A board member of Tenneco Inc, he was deputy chairman of BUPA and chairman of the Medical Research Council. He served on several professional bodies in industry: for example, he was twice president of the Society of Motor Manufacturers and Traders, and chairman of the council of the Industrial Society. Plastow was knighted in 1986. In 1954 he married Barbara Ann May: they have one son and one daughter.

PLATT, Sir Frank
(9 June 1890 - 8 July 1955)
Cotton spinner, born in Rochdale, the son of Thomas Platt, a mule spinner and his wife Rachel. He left school at 14 to join the local cotton spinning industry and by 1919 was a director of Higher Crompton Mills Ltd at Shaw. In the 1930s Platt emerged as an important force in the Lancashire Cotton Corporation (LCC), which aimed at rationalising the industry with Bank of England support. Platt was made managing director in 1933 and largely due to him the LCC's losses had been turned into profits that had reached about £0.5 million a year by the end of the 1930s. He became Cotton Controller during the War (he was knighted in 1943), but then returned to the LCC and was chairman, 1954-55. In 1915 he married Mary, daughter of Benjamin Lord, and they had one daughter. He left £36,591. See DBB.

PLAYER, John Dane
(29 November 1864 - 6 April 1950)
Tobacco manufacturer, born in Nottingham, the son of John Player (1839-1884) and Sophia née Clare. Educated at Nottingham High School, he joined the family tobacco manufacturing business, and alongside his brother William Goodacre Player (1866-1959) became joint managing director in 1895. By 1901 the leading UK tobacco firms had combined to form the Imperial Tobacco Co, with John Dane as one of the original directors. During the 1920s Player's share of Imperial's sales rose steadily so that by 1938 it was second only to Wills, overtaking them in 1955. The two brothers (both of whom retired in 1926) increased Player's workforce from 2,500 in 1914 to 5,000 in 1928. In 1934 John Dane was made an honorary freeman of Nottingham and a DL. He married Margaret Page in the 1890s, but they had no children. He left £2,501,621. See John Player & Sons, From Plantation to 'Players' (1953); DBB.

PLENDER, William
1st Baron Plender of Sundridge, Kent
(20 August 1861 - 19 January 1946)
Accountant, born at Felling on Tyne, the son of William Plender, a grocer and draper, and Elisabeth Agnes Smallpiece née Varday. Educated at the Royal Grammar School, Newcastle-upon-Tyne, he trained as a chartered accountant before joining the London firm of Deloitte's, of which he became partner in 1897 and senior partner in 1904. Under

his leadership Deloitte, Plender, Griffiths & Co became an international organisation. Plender was also an influential president of the Institute of Chartered Accountants in 1910, 1911 and 1929, and was also in heavy demand by the Government. Plender was at the forefront of those advocating change in the accounting profession following the Royal Mail Shipping Group case in the early 1930s. His public services were rewarded by a knighthood in 1911, the GBE in 1918, a baronetcy in 1923 and a barony in 1931. He married twice: in 1891 to Marion Elizabeth Channon (d 1930); in 1932 to Mable Agnes Stevens (née Laurie). He left £325,788 gross, but no children. See Lady Plender (ed), Lord Plender: Some Writings and Speeches (1951); Sir Russell Kettle, Deloitte & Co 1845-1956 (1958); DBB; DNB.

PLEWS, Henry
(18?? - 7 February 1918)
Railway manager, he started work at the London Road Station in Manchester of the London & North Western Railway in the office of Thomas Kay, goods manager. Later he went to Euston and under Charles Mason he organised and operated the rates department. In 1865 he succeeded George Findlay as district manager of the Shropshire and Herefordshire district of the LNWR. His opportunity to move to Ireland in 1867 resulted from arrangements between the LNWR and the Irish North Western Railway to build sea works at Greenore and to link Greenore with Dundalk and the rest of the INWR which ran to Enniskillen and Londonderry. This proved difficult because the INWR had earlier purchased the Londonderry & Enniskillen Railway on onerous terms. When the INWR merged with the Northern of Ireland Railway and the Ulster Railway to form the Great Northern Railway (Ireland) in 1876 Plews continued to manage the north west section until 1890 when he became secretary to the company. He was promoted to general manager in 1896, retiring in 1911 when he held the rank of lieutenant-colonel and was made a director of the GNRI. With 5,500 employees in 1907 the GNRI, which linked Dublin, Belfast, Londonderry and Enniskillen, was the second largest railway in Ireland. See The Railway Gazette, 30 June 1911, 15 February 1918; Railway Year Book, 1908.

PLOWDEN, Edwin Noel August
Baron Plowden of Plowden
(6 January 1907 -)
Industrialist, born into a distinguished Catholic banking and landowning family, the son of Roger Herbert Plowden (1853-1921) and Helen née Haseltine. Educated in Switzerland and Pembroke

College, Cambridge, he became a director of the merchant firm A C Tennant & Co in 1938, before joining the Ministry of Economic Warfare. In 1945 (when he was chief executive of the Ministry) he briefly returned to industry, but his political and commercial experience led to key Government appointments: as chairman of the Central Economic Board in 1947-53; and as the first chairman of the United Kingdom Atomic Energy Authority, 1953-59, where he oversaw the development of the UK's first atomic bomb, the rekindling of Anglo-US co-operation, and the growth of civilian nuclear power. In 1964 his report for the Wilson Government on the state of the British aircraft industry made his name a household word. The Report highlighted the difficulty of the UK maintaining an aircraft industry in the face of rapidly advancing technology and development costs, and recommended some form of public ownership and increasing international collaboration. He held a number of other posts: in 1963-76 he was chairmain of Tube Investments, where he began the first moves towards rationalising the TI empire assembled by Sir Ivan Stedeford (qv). He was awarded the KBE in 1946, KCB in 1951, and made a life peer in 1959. Bridget Horatia née Richmond, whom he married in 1933, is a leading figure in arts and education: they have two sons and two daughters. See Margaret Gowing, *Independence and Deterrence: Britain and Atomic Energy, 1945-1952* (2 vols, 1974); *DBB*.

PODE, Sir Edward Julian
(26 June 1902 - 11 June 1968)

Steel manufacturer, born in Sheffield, the son of Edward Pode, a schoolmaster, he was educated in HMS Conway and during the First World War served in the Royal Navy. Qualifying as a member of the Society of Incorporated Accountants (a body absorbed into the Institute of Chartered Accountants in 1957) he entered the steel industry in 1926 when he became district accountant at the Dowlais Works of Guest, Keen & Nettlefolds. When GKN's heavy steel interests were merged with those of Baldwins Ltd in 1930, to form Guest, Keen Balwins Iron & Steel Co Ltd, Pode was appointed secretary of the new company. He became secretary and joint commercial manager in 1938, assistant managing director in 1943, and managing director in 1945. When the Steel Co of Wales was created in 1947 from a preceding merger between Richard Thomas & Co and Baldwins Ltd, in order to achieve economies of scale beginning with the construction of the widest steel strip mill in the UK at Port Talbot, Pode was appointed managing director under Ernest Lever (qv). Sir Julian Pode (he was knighted in 1959) was manag-

ing director of the Steel Co of Wales, 1947-62; deputy chairman, 1961-62; and chairman, 1962-67. Under his guidance the Steel Co of Wales, effectively the steel industry in Wales, raised its ingot steel ouput from 0.5 million to 3.0 million tons a year, making it the second largest steel company in the UK, as measured by crude steel output, by 1961. Pode played a leading part on the council of the British Iron and Steel Federation, held numerous directorships, and was active in the Confederation of British Industry. In 1948 he was high sheriff of Glamorgan. He married in 1930 Jean Finlay; they had a son and a daughter. See *The Times*, 13 June 1968.

POLE, Sir Felix John Clewett
(1 February 1877 - 15 January 1956)

Railway manager, born at Little Bedwyn near Malborough, the second son of Edward Pole, a local schoolmaster and Churchman, and Emma née Clewett. He left school at 14 and joined the Great Western Railway as a telegraph lad, rising through the ranks to become general manager of the GWR between 1921 and 1928. Pole dealt with the effects of the expansion of the GWR under the Railways Act of 1921 and secured a reasonable return on its capital despite the depression. Between 1929 and 1945 he was executive chairman of Associated Electrical Industries Ltd (the second largest UK electrical group) and in the 1930s oversaw its shedding of American control (under General Electric) and steady growth (10 per cent ordinary dividends). He was knighted in 1924. Pole married Ethel Maud née Flack, the daughter of a shoemaker, in 1899: they had a son and two daughters. He left £153,305. See *Felix J C Pole: His Book* (1954, reprinted 1968); *DBB*; *DNB*

PONSONBY, Edward
8th Earl of Bessborough
(1 March 1851 - 1 December 1920)

Railway chairman and industrialist, eldest son of the 7th Earl of Bessborough (inheritor of 35,000 acres of Irish estates and one of the few nineteenth-century peers in holy orders) and his wife Lady Louisa Susan Cornwallis Eliot, he trained and served in the Royal Navy, retiring as a lieutenant in 1874. Viscount Duncannon (as he was titled before succeeding his father in 1906) was called to the Bar at the Inner Temple in 1879 and from 1884 until 1895 was secretary to Viscount Peel, Speaker of the House of Commons. His marriage in 1875 to Blanche Vere, daughter of Sir John Guest (1785-1852), who had owned the Dowlais Ironworks, and sister of the 1st Baron Wimborne, led to a variety of financial and business interests which became his main concerns in life.

Duncannon was apparently instrumental in persuading his brother-in-law to sell the Dowlais Iron Co to the Patent Bolt & Nut Co headed by Arthur Keen (qv) in 1899. Duncannon became a director of the new firm, Guest, Keen & Co, and of Guest, Keen & Nettlefolds when that was formed in 1902. As the Earl of Bessborough he chaired GKN, 1915-20, and died suddenly at a GKN directors' dinner. Earlier he was chairman of the London, Brighton & South Coast Railway Co which employed 15,000 in 1907. He was also chairman of Gordon Hotels Ltd, Ashanti Goldfields Corporation, and Apollinaris & Johannis; and he sat on the boards of the Bank of Rumania, the Imperial Ottoman Bank, and the Newhaven Harbour Co. By his marriage he had three sons and three daughters. See Edgar Jones, *A History of GKN* vols 1 and 2 (1987-1990); *The Times*, 3 December 1920.

POULSON, John Garlick Llewellyn
(14 April 1910 - 31 January 1993)
Architect, born at Knottingley, Yorkshire, one of two sons of Charles Ernest Austwick Poulson, owner of a pottery at Ferrybridge and a Methodist lay preacher, he was educated at Woodhouse Grove, Bradford, a Methodist public school, and at 17 joined an architectural firm, Garside & Pennington of Pontefract, as an articled clerk. Poor technical work led to his dismissal whilst four years of part-time study at Leeds College of Art brought no examination success. Nevertheless his father supported him in starting his own practice, at Yorkshire Penny Bank Chambers, Ropergate, Pontefract, in 1932. Driving his two 16-year old assistants hard, he cultivated contacts among local politicians, freemasons, anyone of potential usefulness, and offered low rates. Having obtained exemption from military service in 1939, he extended his practice during the war and was well-placed to profit from the post-war property boom. He did so in two ways by the early 1960s. As earlier, he spread his web of gifts and largesse but now more widely, bribing and corrupting politicians, local authority officials and public servants at all levels. A workaholic, Poulson believed everyone had a price, and became skilled at estimating it. Secondly, in the early 1960s, as a tax avoidance move, he created Ropergate Services, an all-in-one organisation incorporating architectural, surveying and engineering services. In alliance with T Dan Smith, Newcastle-upon-Tyne Labour Party chairman and council leader, as consultant, and Harry Vincent, managing director of Bovis, the building firm, Poulson offered design-to-construction packages to local authorities, chiefly in the North East of England and usually run by large-spending

Labour councils. The results were phenomenal. Poulson by 1965 headed Europe's largest architectural practice with 750 employees and a gross turnover of £1 million. Securing design-to-construction contracts for houses, flats, the Arndale Centre in Leeds, the Cannon Street Station redevelopment in London, the £3 million Aviemore tourist centre in Scotland, and much more, made Poulson a millionaire. Yet his organisation consumed contract work at a faster rate than Poulson could secure it. In 1972 he filed his own petition for bankruptcy for debts of about £250,000. Under the relentless questioning of Muir Hunter QC at the bankruptcy examination at Wakefield County Court a stream of revelations about payments and expenditures emerged which pointed to a scale of bribery and corruption unprecedented in twentieth-century Britain. Poulson was arrested in 1973, charged with conspiracy and corruption and found guilty at his trial at Leeds Crown Court in 1974. Disgraced, he was subsequently sentenced to seven years' imprisonment, but was released in 1977. His book *The Price* (1981) was almost immediately withdrawn under threat of libel proceedings. In the wake of the Poulson investigation three business associates in the House of Commons, including Reginald Maudling, the Conservative Home Secretary, were reprimanded by the House and Maudling forced to resign in 1972. Dan Smith, George Pottinger, a senior Scottish civil servant, and Andy Cunningham, Labour chairman of several North-East public authorities, got several years in prison. Eleven other public officials received lesser sentences. Worst of all, the Poulson affair undermined public confidence in the political system and especially in the Labour Party. Poulson married, in 1939, Cynthia Sykes, by whom he had two daughters; her desire for social status and wealth fuelled his corrupt behaviour. Her sister Lorna was married to John King, later Lord King of Wartnaby (qv). See Alan Doig, *Corruption and Misconduct in Contemporary British Politics* (1984); *Independent*, 4 February 1993; *The Times*, 4 February 1993.

POUND, Sir John
(27 June 1829 - 18 September 1915)
Bus company chairman, born in London the son of Henry Pound, a Leadenhall Street leather merchant, he was educated at Christ's Hospital and then entered his father's business. He extended it and became head of the firm of John Pound & Co, dressing case and trunk manufacturers. He became prominent in the civic life of the City of London: a member of Common Council in 1869, chairman of several Corporation committees, alderman in 1892, sheriff in 1895, lord mayor in 1904-5. He was created a baronet in 1905. Between 1879 and

1909 he was chairman of the London General Omnibus Co (to which he was introduced by his father-in-law, Thomas Lulham, a former chairman) and proved to be shrewd and hardy, whether dealing with the competition or his own shareholders. Recognising in 1905 that the motor bus had come to stay, he nevertheless refused to invest hastily in unreliable vehicles. Two years later, when the LGOC employed 4,000 people, he showed support for greater co-operation between London's various transport companies, a theme taken up by his general manager, Wilfrid Dumble (qv). He held numerous other directorships. Pound married, in 1856, Harriet née Lulham; they had two sons and three daughters. See Theodore C Barker and Michael Robbins, *A History of London Transport* (2 vols, 1963-74); *The Times*, 20 September 1915.

POUNTAIN, Sir Eric (John)

(5 August 1933 -)

Building materials company executive, the son of Horace and Elsie Pountain. Educated at Queen Mary Grammar School, Walsall, in 1956 he joined F Maitland Selwyn & Co, auctioneers and estate agents. He founded Midland & General Developments in 1964, which five years later was absorbed by the housebuilders, John McLean & Sons, of which Pountain became chief executive. In 1969 McLeans was in turn swallowed by Tarmac, the famous road materials manufacturer founded in 1903. Pountain became head of the housing division at Tarmac and under his policy of slow expansion and rigid controls it thrived. By 1980 a third of Tarmac's profits came from housebuilding and Pountain's division became a management model. In 1979 he became Tarmac's chief executive (he was also chairman after 1983) and implemented a policy of decentralisation and expansion that brought great success. Profits hit £393 million in 1988. But Pountain and his board failed to spot the onset and severity of the recession and, after a number of mistimed acquisitions in the US (where he invested around £600 million), profits fell to under £200 million in 1990 and had virtually disappeared two years later. In 1992 Pountain relinquished the post of chief executive (though remaining chairman) to Neville Simms. He has several non-executive directorships: at IMI, James Beattie, the Midland Bank, and United Newspapers. A supporter of Margaret Thatcher (Tarmac was one of the largest contributors to the Conservative Party), Pountain was knighted in 1985. In 1960 he married Joan Patricia Sutton: they have one son and one daughter. See J B F Earle, *Black Top* (1974).

PRESTON, Sir Walter Reuben

(20 September 1875 - 6 July 1946)

Industrialist, the son of R T Preston, an engineer, of Hayes Court, Kent. Educated at Bedford Grammar School, he served an apprenticeship at the Great Eastern Railway's works at Stratford. His engineering talents brought him the chairmanship of Platt Bros & Co (Holdings) Ltd, the presidency of Textile Machinery Makers Ltd (formed in 1931 by the merger of six textile machinery makers and employing 24,600 in 1935), a chairmanship of Henry Bessemer & Co and a directorship at the Midland Bank. He was Conservative MP for Mile End, 1918-23, and for Cheltenham, 1928-37. Preston was knighted in 1921. In 1900 he married Ella Margaret née Morris: they had three sons. See *The Times*, 9 July 1946.

PROCTER, William Thomson

(1861-1938)

Textile manufacturer, born at Alloa, the son of Robert Procter, a partner in the local sewing thread manufacturers, John Paton Son & Co. William Procter followed his father into the business and in 1917 became chairman of Patons. In 1919 Patons merged with J & J Baldwin Partners, of Halifax, to form Patons & Baldwins Ltd with a capital of £3.2 million. Procter became vice-chairman, at which date the Kilncraigs, Keilarsbrae, and Clackmannan factories employed nearly 1,700 workers. Procter later became chairman of Patons & Baldwins from 1923 until 1938, when the company employed about 7,000, and when he was succeeded by Alexander Forrester-Paton (qv). Outside the business, his main interest was as manager and benefactor of the Clackmannan County Hospital. He left a widow and a daughter and £529,054 gross. Information from Alastair Forrester-Paton; *Alloa Journal*, 29 January 1938.

PROSSER, Ian Maurice Gray

(5 July 1943 -)

Drinks and hotel company executive, born in Bath, the fourth child of Maurice Prosser, an Imperial Tobacco salesman, and his wife Freda. Educated at King Edward's School, Bath, and Watford Grammar School, he went to Birmingham University (BComm) and then in 1964 trained at Coopers & Lybrand as an accountant. He completed his articles and joined Bass Charrington in 1969, becoming financial director in 1978. At 39 he became vice-chairman and managing director, succeeding Sir Derek Palmer as chairman in 1987. Prosser extended Bass's empire by buying Holiday Inns in North America for £2 billion, so that (besides being the UK's biggest brewer) the group has 6,754 pubs, 1,383 Coral betting shops and

1,600 Holiday Inns - the largest hotel operation in the world. By 1990 Bass was worth £3.7 billion, with 115,000 employees, and with pre-tax profits of £535 million. He married in 1964 Elizabeth Herman: they have two daughters.

PURVES, Sir William
(27 December 1931 -)

Banker, born at Kelso, in Scotland's border country, the son of Andrew Purves, a farmer, and his wife Ida. Educated at Kelso High School, he left at 16 to join the National Bank of Scotland. During National Service in the Korean War he won the DSO for bravery and then returned to banking. But he decided to leave Scotland and seek a better fortune elsewhere. In 1954 he joined the Hong Kong & Shanghai Banking Corporation, working around the world, before becoming a manager in Japan and then chief accountant in Hong Kong. He succeeded Sir Michael Sandberg as chairman of the HSBC in 1986. Described as the most important figure in Hong Kong, he runs what is effectively the colony's central bank, presides over the Royal Jockey Club and is a member of Hong Kong's ruling executive council. He is also a controversial figure: he was criticised for the bank's involvement in the collapse of the conglomerate Carrian; and also for losses of £100 million after the collapse of the Australian entrepreneur Alan Bond's empire. Seeking to minimise the risks of the 1997 handover of Hong Kong to China, Purves has looked for ways for HSBC to diversify internationally and in 1987 began negotiations for a takeover of the troubled Midland Bank under Sir Kit McMahon (qv). Talks broke down in 1990 with the recession, but in 1992 HSBC launched another bid. The withdrawal of a rival offer from Lloyds led by Sir Jeremy Morse and Brian Pitman (qqv) in 1992 left the way open again for Purves, who clinched the takeover. He was knighted in 1993 for commercial and public services to Hong Kong. Purves married in 1958 Diana Troutbeck Richardson.

Q

QUIG, Alexander Johnstone
(5 January 1892 - 13 December 1962)

Chemical company executive, born in Glasgow, at the age of 15 he went straight from Glasgow High School into Nobel's Explosives Ltd as a junior clerk on the commercial side. During the First World War he served with the Glasgow Highlanders and London Scottish in France, where he was wounded, and later with the Highland Light Infantry in India. He moved quickly upwards in Nobel's, becoming managing director of Nobel Chemical Finishes Ltd (a joint Nobel and du Pont company)

in 1925, a step which gave him some American experience and contacts. Some time after Imperial Chemical Industries was formed in 1926 (from Nobel Industries Ltd, Brunner, Mond & Co Ltd, United Alkali Co Ltd and British Dyestuffs Corporation Ltd) Nobel Chemical Finishes became ICI (Paints) Ltd. Quig was appointed chairman of ICI Paint and Lacquer Group in 1936. He moved to ICI's headquarters, at Millbank, Westminster, in 1939 to be an executive manager, rising to main board commercial director in 1940 and deputy chairman, 1948-56 - second-in-command, to Sir Alexander Fleck (qv), of 115,000 employees. In executive office Quig struck a radical note. For example, when British Nylon Spinners, the joint venture between ICI and Courtaulds planned in 1939 under an agreement between ICI and du Pont (the discoverers of nylon), tarried as a result of the war, he drove forward the whole scheme on becoming a BNS director in 1944. Eventually the BNS plant at Pontypool (producing 10 million pounds of yarn a year) opened in 1949. Outside ICI Quig chaired the Industrial Management Research Association, 1946-49, and an Air Ministry committee to review the Ministry's organisation, 1948-49. He was also a founder member of the British Institute of Management. Beyond work, he kept a herd of Ayrshires on his farm in Surrey. He married, in 1952, Mrs Joan Leason, widow; there were no children. See *ICI Magazine* 1957; W J Reader, *Imperial Chemical Industries: A History* (2 vols, 1970-75) vol 2.

QUINTON, Sir John (Grand)
(21 December 1929 -)

Banker, the son of William Grand Quinton and Norah May née Nunn. Educated at Norwich School and St John's College, Cambridge, he joined Barclays Bank in 1953. Steady progress through Barclays saw him emerge as deputy chairman in 1985 and then chairman two years later. He was one of only two Barclays chairmen (the other was Frederick Macnamara Goodenough) who were not members of the founding families. In the 1980s Barclays emerged as the most profitable UK bank (in 1988 it had pre-tax profits of £1.46 billion), but when Quinton took over it was about to be overtaken by its great rival, Natwest. Under Quinton, Barclays hit back by reforming the Bank's management structure, to dilute the 'family' presence on the board. It then launched a £922 million rights issue so that the Bank could belatedly join the 1980s property boom. A huge lending binge followed, despite Barclays previous conservative stance, which nearly doubled its loan portfolio and pushed its lending to the property sector up to £8.5 billion, the largest exposure of any of the clearing banks. Quinton lent millions to the booming property companies of the 1980s: these included Tony Clegg's (qv) Mountleigh, Gerald Ronson's (qv) Heron Corporation, Speyhawk, Imry and Olympia & York, the builders of the ill-fated Canary Wharf. When the boom ended, Barclays found itself saddled with bad debts that totalled over £1 billion by 1992. Quinton, who offered a glowing testimonial for Ronson during the Guinness trial involving Ernest Saunders (qv), retired early from the chairmanship of Barclays at the end of 1992, handing over to Andrew Buxton (qv) - ironically, a descendant of one of Barclays' founding families. Quinton has held a number of other advisory posts, such as chairman of the London Committee of Clearing Bankers, 1982-83; a board member of Business in the Community since 1986; and chairman of the FA Premier League since 1992. Quinton was knighted in 1990. In 1954 he married Jean Margaret Chastney: they have one son and one daughter.

R

RADLEY, Sir William Gordon
(18 January 1898 - 16 December 1970)
Director-General of the General Post Office, born in Kings Norton, Birmingham, the only son and eldest of the five children of William Albert Radley (d 1959), a mechanical engineer (who later worked for Greenwood & Batley at Leeds and then the government Small Arms Factories at Woolwich, gaining an OBE), and his wife Lizzie Clara née Ellis, he was educated at Leeds Modern School and Faraday House Electrical Engineering College, London, where he started at the age of 16. After the First World War (in which he served in the Royal Engineers at Gallipoli), Gordon Radley (as he was known) graduated with a top first class BSc and a London University gold medal. Following a short apprenticeship with Bruce Peebles & Co of Edinburgh he joined the GPO engineering staff in 1920. Over the next 20 years he worked steadily on plasma physics research, completing a London University PhD in this area. By 1939 he was Controller of Research, managing all the GPO's research groups, with 1,000 researchers concentrated at Dollis Hill, London, during the Second World War. Out of his work on telephone switches for Colossus, the code-breaking computer at Bletchley Park, came the objective of an all-electronic telephone exchange; and development of high precision navigation systems suggested to him different ways of laying a new transatlantic telephone cable. Radley was appointed Deputy Engineer-in-Chief in 1949, Engineer-in-Chief in 1951 and Director-General in 1955, the first engi-

neer to take charge of the GPO which was then the third largest business in the UK, employing 337,000. The following year saw the opening of TAC, the first telephone cable to be laid across the Atlantic. For his achievements Radley was made a CBE in 1946, knighted in 1954, and made a KCB in 1956. Professionally he was elected president of the Institution of Electrical Engineers in 1956-57 and received the IEE's Faraday Medal in 1958. After his retirement in 1960 he accepted a number of directorships including Marconi International Marine Co, English Electric, and English Electric Computers Ltd. A devout evangelical Christian (Church of England) he wrote a small book, *Science and Faith: The Discovery of the Unknown* (1927) and contributed to the *Crusaders' Magazine*. In the 1960s he became first chairman of the Abbeyfield Society. Radley married, in 1938, Dorothy Margaret Hines; they had a son and a daughter. See David J Jeremy, *Capitalists and Christians: Business Leaders and the Churches in Britain, 1900-1960* (1990). Information from Lady Radley and Dr James H H Merriman.

RAILING, Sir Harry
(10 December 1878 - 16 October 1963)
Electrical equipment manufacturer, born in Munich, the son of Isaac Railing, a Jewish hop merchant, and his wife Hannah née Bing, Adolf Railing (he later adopted the English name of Harry) was educated at Munich University graduating in 1901 as a doctor of engineering. After experience in the USA, in 1905 he joined his elder brother, Max John (qv), an accountant who had married a cousin and sister-in-law of Hugo Hirst (qv) and was Hirst's right-hand man in building up the General Electric Co, based on Witton Park, Birmingham, and London. Harry was successively chief of the test room at Witton, technical assistant to Hirst in London, manager at Witton and, from 1911, GEC director in charge of engineering. Hirst made him joint general manager, with Leslie Gamage (qv), in 1941. On Max's death in 1942 Harry became deputy chairman of GEC and later that year, on Hirst's death, chairman. Sir Harry Railing (he was knighted in 1944) retired in 1957. Under his chairmanship GEC expanded rapidly after the war (with employment reaching 60,000 in 1955), producing a wide range of equipment from electrical appliances and parts for the domestic consumer to heavy electrical equipment for nuclear power stations (setting up an atomic energy division jointly with Simon-Carves Ltd). Only two major orders were won in the nuclear field and it became clear that GEC had overextended itself. Railing, primarily an engineer, was out of his depth when issues of commercial and financial strategy

arose. Poor middle management and boardroom tussles with Gamage exacerbated his problems. Outside GEC Sir Harry Railing was chairman of the council of the British Electrical and Allied Manufacturers' Association (the industry's cartel), 1944-45, and president of BEAMA, 1952; president of the Institution of Electrical Engineers, 1944-45; and served as advisor on engineering matters to several government departments. He married, in 1933, Clare (d 1959), daughter of Joseph Nauheim; there were no children. See *DBB*; Robert Jones and Oliver Marriott, *Anatomy of a Merger: A History of GEC, AEI, and English Electric* (1970).

RAILING, Max John
(1868 - 14 January 1942)

Electrical equipment manufacturer, born in Munich, the son of Isaac Railing, a Jewish hop merchant, and Hannah née Bing. In 1892 he arrived in England and joined the General Electric Co of (Lord) Hugo Hirst (qv). By 1906 Railing was Hirst's right-hand man, having also in 1900 married a relative of Hirst's - Amanda, daughter of Herman Hirsch. Railing was general manager until his promotion to joint managing director in 1929. Together with his brother (Sir) Harry Railing (qv), he kept a careful eye on the running of GEC and acted as a counterbalance to Hirst's ambitions and flamboyance. Although he held other directorships and was active in technical societies (he was vice-president of the Radio Manufacturers' Association), he avoided the limelight. He left £291,186 gross and was survived by his wife and two daughters. See Robert Jones and Oliver Marriot, *Anatomy of a Merger: A History of GEC, AEI and English Electric* (1970).

RAMSDEN, Joseph
(1867 - 9 September 1946)

Coalmines owner and manager, born in Shackerley, Tyldesley. Educated at Rugby, he joined his father, W H Ramsden, in his coal-mining business at Tyldesley. The firm eventually amalgamated with Manchester Collieries (formed in 1929), of which Ramsden was chairman between 1929 and 1943. The Collieries with difficulty succeeded in making the many local pits profitable again in the 1930s: by 1932 it was able to pay a small dividend to shareholders. Between 1930 and 1938 the company's output rose from 3.4 to 4.2 million, while its labour force fell from 17,256 to 15,208. Ramsden was succeeded as chairman by Sir Robert Burrows (qv). He also had interests in the Bridgewater Estates, Josiah Smale, the Macclesfield silk manufacturers, Universal Rubber Paviors of Stockport, and the National Employers'

Mutual General Insurance Association. Ramsden was closely involved in the Stockport Infirmary; and was also a renowned racehorse owner. He left two daughters, a son being killed in action in Norway. See C Grayling, *The Bridgewater Heritage* (1983); *Stockport Advertiser* 13 September 1946; Barry Supple, *The History of the British Coal Industry: Vol 4, 1913-1946* (1987).

RANK, Joseph Arthur
Baron Rank of Sutton Scotney
(22 December 1888 - 29 March 1972)

Milling and film companies chairman, born at Hull, youngest of the three sons of Joseph Rank (1854-1943), a corn miller who built up a large business by substituting steam-driven roller milling for the windmill, and his wife Emily née Voase, he was educated at The Leys School, Cambridge, and in 1905 followed his brothers into the family firm. After nearly five years' training, J Arthur Rank (as he was known) became production manager at the firm's Clarence Mills, Hull. During the First World War he served in an ambulance unit and rose to be captain in the Royal Artillery. During the war he was appointed a director of Joseph Rank Ltd; afterwards his flourmilling career was undistinguished. When the business was converted into a public company, Ranks Ltd, with a capital of £7.295 million and a 33 per cent share of the UK flour market, J Arthur became a joint managing director in charge of the animal feeds side. Greater and more exciting prospects unfolded in the 1930s when his Christian convictions (like his father he was a strong Wesleyan Methodist) took him into showing and in 1934 making religious films. From this he was drawn into forming General Film Distributors and promoted construction of Pinewood Studios (in 1935); he set up a holding company, General Cinema Finance Corporation, to handle his film industry interests (1936); and, successively, he acquired Denham Studios (1938), Elstree Studios (1939), the largest integrated film producer, distributor and exhibitor, Gaumont British Picture Corporation (1941), and the Odeon Theatre chain (1941). This last brought also the skills of John Davis (qv). During the war J Arthur Rank emerged as the most powerful capitalist in the British film industry, but he neither actively sought nor heavily wielded his power. He saw his role as mobilising finance for creative producers, like Sir Michael Balcon at Ealing Studios, and in exerting Christian influence directly through religious films. Charges of monopoly against Rank were rejected by the Palache Committee (1943-44) and between 1947 and 1951 he lost £6 million after the Labour Government reneged on its undertakings to protect the British film industry from American competition. On the death of his eldest brother in 1952, J Arthur Rank became chairman of Ranks Ltd and in 1953 surrendered his film interests to a new company, the Rank Organisation. Over the next 15 years he merged Ranks with Hovis McDougall (in 1962), creating a diversified giant with bakery, agricultural merchanting, flour milling and grocery divisions and employing 61,000 in 1966. Lord Rank (he was made a baron in 1957) retired in 1969. In the Methodist Church he was a leading layman and served as denominational treasurer. He married, in 1917, Laura Ellen, eldest daughter of Horace Marshall, later 1st Baron Marshall of Chipstead; they had two daughters. See *DBB*; Alan Wood, *Mr Rank: A Study of J Arthur Rank and British Films* (1952).

RATNER, Gerald (Irving)

(1 November 1949 -)

Jewellery chain store retailer, born in London, the son of Leslie and Rachelle Ratner. His father had opened his first jewellery shop in Hendon, north London, in 1950. Expelled from Hendon County Grammar School, Gerald Ratner went to a local private school and became managing director of the family business in 1984 after effectively ousting his father: the company was then valued at £11 million and had 130 shops, but was £350,000 in debt. He became chairman in 1986. By then he had successfully and aggressively cut Ratner's prices and shed the traditional, conservative jewellery shop mystique in favour of mass-market appeal. In the 1980s his rise was meteoric as he bought the H Samuel, Watches of Switzerland, Ernest Jones and Salisbury shop chains, and also expanded in America, where Ratners acquired a 5 per cent share of the $21 billion jewellery market. In 1991 Ratner's, now the world's largest jewellery retailer, announced record profits of £112 million, but the expansion rested on heavy borrowing (£400 million by 1991) and when sales faltered Ratner's became vulnerable. At the end of 1991 - the year when he injudiciously described the firm's products as 'total crap' - Ratner was forced to step down as chairman. The following year, he bowed to shareholders' pressure and resigned as chief executive, with a £375,000 pay-off. Ratner's lost £122 million in 1992 and its shares had fallen from 400p in 1987 to under 10p in October 1992. He has been married twice: his first marriage to Angela Trup was dissolved in 1989. See Judi Bevan and John Jay, *The New Tycoons* (1989).

RAYNER, Derek George

Baron Rayner of Crowborough
(30 March 1926 -)

Chain store retailer, the son of George William Rayner and Hilda Jane née Rant. Educated at City College, Norwich, and Selwyn College, Cambridge, after National Service he joined Marks & Spencer in 1953. After a short period in stores, he was appointed to head office and was closely involved with the Food Division and then the Export Department. He was appointed to the board in 1967, becoming joint managing-director in 1973 (when he was knighted), joint vice-chairman in 1982, chief executive in 1983 and chairman in 1984 (the first holder of that post not to be related to the founding families). By the end of 1986 the company had a turnover of £3 billion a year and accounted for 3.5 per cent of total UK retail sales. Rayner's chairmanship was marked by bold investment and vigorous expansion in the UK, including the first edge-of-town and neighbourhood stores, as well as the modernisation and computerisation of the whole chain. He also developed the Group overseas, acquiring Brooks Bros and Kings Supermarkets in the USA (Marks & Spencer already had a Canadian subsidiary). He also took time out in and around Whitehall: for example, accepting Margaret Thatcher's invitation in 1979 to advise on improving efficiency and eliminating waste in Government. He retired as chairman of Marks & Spencer in March 1991 and was succeeded by (Sir) Richard Greenbury (qv). A bachelor, Rayner was made a life peer in 1983.

READE, Robert Henry Sturrock

(May 1838 - 24 February 1913)

Textile manufacturer, born in Coleraine, the eldest son of Dr Thomas Reade, a physician, and Harriet Helena, daughter of the Reverend James T Sturrock, rector of Seapatrick, County Down, he was educated at the Royal Belfast Academical Institution and in 1854 commenced an apprenticeship with the York Street Flax Spinning Co in Belfast. Reade proved his worth when in 1856-57 he was sent to New York to set up a branch organisation. He was rewarded with one of the four managing directorships when the firm was converted into a limited liability company in 1864. By the 1880s the York Street Flax Spinning Co was the largest flax spinning concern in the world with branches in London, Manchester, Paris and New York, employing 4,000 then and 4,500 in 1907. By the 1880s Reade was chairman of the York Street Co, remaining in office until his death. He took a strong interest in the welfare of his employees, installing suction fans and providing spacious, low-cost dining facilities. For the industry he promoted many experiments in the growing and marketing of flax, in association with managing directors like Sir William Crawford (qv). He was president of the Linen Merchants' Association in 1876, the Flax Spinners' Association in 1888-94, the Flax Supply Association in 1893-1905, and the Belfast Chamber of Commerce in 1881 and 1906. Reade was a member of the northern counties committee of the Midland Railway Co. Politically a Conservative and a Unionist (but not an Orangeman), he sponsored the Ulster Convention of 1892, was a secretary of the Ulster Unionist Council, and in 1912 helped arrange meetings culminating in the solemn league and covenant. A supporter of Joseph Chamberlain, he was a member of the Tariff Commission. In the episcopalian Church of Ireland he sat on the diocesan council of Down and Connor and Dromore and for many years was a member of the Representative Body of the Church of Ireland. Reade married Dorothea Emily Florence, the youngest daughter of the Reverend George Robbins, rector of Courteenhall, Northants; they had two sons and two daughters. See *The Belfast News-Letter*, 24 February 1913; *The Times*, 27 February 1913.

REBBECK, Sir Frederick Ernest
(19 August 1877 - 27 June 1964)

Shipbuilder, born in Swindon, the son of Albert Ernest Rebbeck, a Wiltshire farmer, and Jeanette Morgan née Smith. After an engineering apprenticeship, in 1912 he became managing director of Burmeister & Wain Oil Engine Co, a supplier of diesel engines to Harland & Wolff. By 1919 Rebbeck was managing director of Harland & Wolff's Belfast engine works and after 1924, when the group's chairman Lord Pirrie (qv) died, he became a member of the board. In 1930 he was appointed chairman and, despite some criticism, restored Harland & Wolff's fortunes, aided by the rearmament programme, the War and the boom of the early 1950s. He retired in 1961, aged 84. He was on the board of several other shipbuilding and steel firms (such as Colvilles) and was president of the Institution of Marine Engineers and of the Shipbuilding Employers' Federation. Knighted in 1941, he became a KBE in 1953. In 1907 he married Amelia Letitia Glover; they had two sons (one of whom succeeded his father as managing director of Harland & Wolff) and three daughters. Rebbeck left £391 in the UK. See Michael S Moss and J R Hume, *A History of Harland and Wolff 1853-1985* (1985); *DBB*.

RECKITT, Sir Philip Bealby
(1 January 1873 - 17 November 1944)

Starch manufacturer, born at Hessle, near Hull, the son of (Sir) James Reckitt (1833-1924) and Kathleen Saunders. His father was chairman of the Reckitt & Sons Ltd, the starch manufacturers of Hull. Educated privately and at King's College, Cambridge, after an early unfulfilled ambition to become a doctor, Philip Reckitt became a director of Reckitt's and of the engineering firm of Priestman Bros, Hull. He continued the family's pioneering work in social welfare, which had been inspired by its Quaker roots. He married twice: first in 1900 to Hilda née Grotrian (d 1935); and secondly in 1939 to Margarida née Bishop. He succeeded his brother to the baronetcy in 1930. See *DBB* (Sir James Reckitt); Basil N Reckitt, *History of Reckitt & Sons Ltd* (1953).

REED, Austin (Leonard)
(6 September 1873 - 5 May 1954)

Men's outfitter, born in Reading, the son of William Bilkey Reed and Emily née Bowler. After attending Reading school, he left at 15 and joined his father's men's outfitters business in 1888. After visiting the US, he persuaded his father in 1900 to open a London branch (in Fenchurch Street) to tap the growing City commuter market with new retailing techniques. Reed's shops (such as his flagship Regent Steet store, opened in the 1920s) pioneered upper-class ready-to-wear clothing. In the inter-war period he expanded into the provinces (where there were 31 shops by 1939) and also moved into mail order. In 1920 (when it was floated as a public company) the capital of Austin Reed Ltd was £350,000; shortly after Reed's retirement in 1947 it was £1.2 million. A Congregationalist, who believed in the distribution of business wealth, Reed left £108,663 gross. He married in 1902 Emily née Wilson: they had two sons and four daughters. See B Ritchie, *A Touch of Class: The Story of Austin Reed* (1990); *DBB*.

REES, David Morgan
(29 March 1904 - 16 May 1980)

National Coal Board executive, the son of Rees Rees of Pencoed, Glamorgan, he was educated at Llandovery College, Carmarthen, and Birmingham University where he qualified as a mining engineer. After working with North's Navigation Collieries Ltd in the Maesteg valley, South Wales and then managing Caerau colliery, he became manager of the Bestwood Colliery, Nottingham in 1937 and mining agent under BA Collieries Ltd until nationalisation of the coal industry in 1946. At various times he studied mining conditions in Scotland, on the Continent and in the USA. Under the National

Coal Board he was area general manager of No 4 Area of the East Midlands Division, 1947-52, and then chairman of the South Western Division, 1952-61. Covering South Wales, Somerset and Gloucester, the South Western Division in 1955 was the second largest of the NCB's nine divisions by employment (with 107,000 employees) but the fourth by coal output (with 24.2 million tons). It was also characterised by poor industrial relations, which contributed towards relatively low productivity; uneconomic pits, despite reconstructions; and annual losses between 1947 and 1957. Radical changes recommended by a working party under Sir Humphrey Browne (qv) improved the situation in the 1960s. Rees was a council member of the Institution of Mining Engineers, a JP, and a Commander of the Order of St John of Jerusalem. He married, in 1935, Marjorie Griffith and had a son and a daughter. See William Ashworth, *The History of the British Coal Industry vol 5 1946-1982: The Nationalised Industry* (1986).

REID, Sir Hugh
(9 February 1860 - 7 July 1935)

Locomotive manufacturer, he was born in Manchester, the eldest son of James Reid, locomotive builder with Sharp, Stewart & Co until 1863 when he returned to Glasgow, and his wife Margaret A Scott. Hugh Reid was educated at the High School of Glasgow and Glasgow University. He commenced in 1878 as an apprentice at the Hyde Park Works of Neilson, Reid & Co, the Glasgow locomotive builders in which his father had become sole partner in 1876. He and his three younger brothers became partners in 1893 and when their father died in 1894 Hugh became senior partner. Faced with competition from Henry Dubs & Co and from Sharp, Stewart & Co (who moved from Manchester to Glasgow in 1888) Hugh Reid expanded and modernised the Hyde Park Works. However, observing the advantages of amalgamation in other industries, in 1903 he negotiated a merger with his rivals, to form the North British Locomotive Co Ltd. With 60 acres of works, nearly 8,000 employees and an average annual output of 447 locomotives, 1904-14, it was the largest locomotive builder in Europe. William Lorimer (qv) became chairman; Hugh Reid became deputy chairman and chief managing director. He became chairman in 1922 but neither thereafter nor earlier was he able to move the North British Locomotive Co from its almost exclusive commitment to steam, despite his own experiments with electric motors and internal combustion engines. Reid was also a director of the Clydesdale Bank, 1901-23. Outside business he was interested in his professional engineering bodies,

civic improvement, art, sport, and the Volunteer movement. He was made a CBE in 1918 and a baronet in 1922. Reid married, in 1888, Marion Maclune née Bell, daughter of a shipowner; they had three sons and a daughter. See *DSBB*; R H Campbell, 'The North British Locomotive Company between the Wars' *Business History* 20 (1978).

REID, Sir (Robert Paul) Bob
(1 May 1934 -)

Oil and transport company executive, born at Cupar, Fife, the son of a butcher (in whose shop he lost his hand in a mincer). Educated at Bell-Baxter Academy, Cupar, and St Andrews University (BA political economy and history), he joined Shell UK in 1956. After spending 22 of the next 35 years abroad (in Africa and the Far East), he was chairman and chief executive of Shell UK between 1985 and 1989. At Shell UK - the second biggest part of the world-wide Dutch/Shell empire (the biggest is Shell US) - Reid reorganised what had become a bureaucratic and inward looking group into a tight, well-run highly profitable concern. In 1990 he left Shell (whose retirement age is 55) and became chairman of British Railways Board, succeeding his namesake Sir Robert Basil Reid. Battles over Channel Tunnel rails links, commuter services and projected privatisation have ensured his high-profile, though his influence has always been strictly circumscribed by a Conservative government more committed to road rather than rail transport. He was knighted in 1990. He married his wife Joan in 1958: they have three sons.

REISS, Sir John Anthony Ewart
(8 April 1909 - 22 November 1989)

Cement manufacturer, he was born in Mayfair, London, son of James Arthur Reiss, shipping merchant of Winsford, Cheshire, and his wife Emilie Christine née Ewart. He was educated at Eton and after a year in France spent two years in Reiss Brothers, the family firm of cotton merchants in Manchester which had started with two brothers migrating from Frankfurt in 1818. He moved to an American bank in London, only to lose his job after the Wall Street crash. Spells in commodity broking and insurance followed before he joined the Associated Portland Cement Manufacturers at its Liverpool branch office in 1934 at £3 a week. He moved to Earle's (an APCM subsidiary) Manchester office and then to their head office at Hull before going to the APCM head office, Portland House, London, in 1937. He became manager of the rail sales department in 1939 and then of the transport and London merchants' sales departments. He became a director of the Cement

Marketing Co Ltd in 1944 and its chairman in 1947. He joined the boards of the APCM and its subsidiary, the British Portland Cement Manufacturers Ltd, in 1946 and became sales managing director of both in 1948. In 1955 he became vice-chairman, under Sir George Earle (qv), whom he succeeded as chairman, 1957-74. In this period of economic expansion the building and building materials industry experienced long-term growth. The APCM (which later changed its name to Blue Circle Industries) increased its workforce from 11,000 in 1955 to 13,235 in 1966). Producing 8 million tons of cement and exporting 1.25 million tons of it in 1955, APCM accounted for about two-thirds of the UK production and export markets. Outside his company Sir John Reiss (he was knighted in 1967) was chairman of the Foundation for Business Responsibilities, the British Empire Migration Council, and Aims for Freedom and Enterprise. As honorary treasurer of the British Empire Cancer Campaign he was a tireless fundraiser. Reiss was active in Moral Rearmament and helped develop the Westminster Theatre. He married twice: first, in 1938, to the actress Marie Ambrosine Phillpotts, by whom he had a son and a daughter; second, in 1951, to Elizabeth Booth-Jones née MacEwan, by whom he had two daughters. See *The Blue Circle*, April 1955; Duncan Burn (ed), *The Structure of British Industry*, (2 vols, 1961); P Pugh, *The History of Blue Circle*(1988); *The Times*, 13 December 1989.

REITH, John Charles Walsham
1st Baron Reith of Stonehaven
(20 July 1889 - 16 June 1971)
Director-General of the British Broadcasting Corporation, born at Stonehaven near Aberdeen, fifth son of the Reverend George Reith (1842-1919), minister (later Moderator) in the Free Church of Scotland, and his wife Adah Mary née Weston, he was educated at Glasgow Academy, Gresham's School, Holt, and the Royal Technical College of Glasgow. Apprenticed to the North British Locomotive Co, Glasgow, and trained as an engineer, he was commissioned in the Royal Engineers and served in France, 1914-15, until badly wounded. As a major he visited the USA in 1916-17 working on munitions supply, and gaining an MSc from Lafayette College in 1917. On returning to the UK he continued in munitions contracts, first for the Admiralty and then for the Ministry of Munitions, until 1919. Reith returned to Glasgow as general manager of the Coatbridge works of William Beardmore & Co in 1920. He joined the newly-founded British Broadcasting Co in December 1922 as general manager at a salary of £1,750 a year. The company had been formed in

the previous October by radio manufacturing interests and in January 1923 secured its monopoly licence from the General Post Office, which restricted its dividends to 7.5 per cent. Financed by listeners' licence fees rather than advertisements, the company liberated Reith from private commercial interests. He determined to make it a 'public service'. When the company was transformed into a corporation, with a new and more difficult board of governors, on 1 January 1927 the philosophy remained unchanged. Licence-holders increased in number from 2 million in 1926 to over 8.5 million in 1938, and the BBC's staff from 773 to 4,060 over the same period. Reith's name, and that of the BBC, became synonymous with high quality and moral standards. Yet with his training as a manager he was concerned about good management and appropriate organisational structures. Following a review of the BBC in 1933-34, he separated 'creative' and administrative staff and functions. As an engineer he was interested in new technical challenges. Thus, he instigated an Empire Service (from 1932) and launched a modest television service confined to the London area (from 1936). Staff were moved from Savoy Hill, off the Strand, London, to a new purpose-built Broadcasting House in Portland Place in 1932. Yet Reith in the 1930s was also seen as authoritarian. Tall, gaunt, a man of fierce hates, he had no staff association until 1939 and no listener research unit until 1936. At Nevile Chamberlain's suggestion he moved in 1938 to the chairmanship of Imperial Airways, and its successor, the British Overseas Airways Corporation, but he never settled into the job and in 1940 became Minister of Information (having been found a safe parliamentary seat at Southampton, as a National MP). Unable to work with Churchill (who moved him to the Ministry of Transport and then the Ministry of Works and Buildings) in 1942 he joined the RNVR as a lieutenant-commander, serving in the Admiralty's Combined Operations Material Department as director. After the war he had much to do with planning, chairing the New Towns Committee (1946) and Hemel Hempstead Development Corporation (1947-50). He was chairman of the State Building Society, 1960-64; director and vice-chairman of the British Oxygen Co, 1956-66; and a director of the Phoenix Assurance Co and Tube Investments. He was also Lord Rector of the University of Glasgow, 1965-68 and Lord High Commissioner of the Church of Scotland in 1967. After 1938 he increasingly felt that his exceptional talents were under-used. In later years he published his memoirs. His honours were many: knighted in 1927, created GBE in 1934, GCVO in 1939, sworn of the Privy Council in January 1940, created a baron in October 1940, made a CB in 1945 and a KT in 1969. He married, in 1921, Muriel Katherine, younger daughter of the publisher, John Lynch Odhams; they had a son and a daughter. See Ian McIntyre, *The Expense of Glory: A Life of John Reith* (1993).

RHODES, Sir Edward
(10 April 1870 - 18 December 1959)
Textile manufacturer, the elder son of John William and Charlotte Rhodes of Manchester. He was chairman of Rylands & Sons, which in 1935 employed 8,000 workers. Rhodes was also chairman to the Board of Trade and Ministry of Shipping, Textile Exports Shipping Committee, 1917-18; a member of the Board of Trade Advisory Council, 1934-37; president of the Manchester Chamber of Commerce in 1937; and a vice-president of the Associated British Chambers of Commerce, London, 1938-46. His second marriage was to Marguerite née Dodd.

RICHARDSON, Gordon (William Humphreys)
Baron Richardson of Duntisbourne
(25 November 1915 -)
Banker, the elder son of John Robert and Nellie Richardson. Educated at Nottingham High School and Gonville and Caius College, Cambridge (where he read law), he spent the war in Staff College, Camberley. He became a successful barrister and then moved into the City, holding posts with J Henry Schroder, Lloyds and Legal & General Assurance. In the 1960s he became chairman of Schroders, to which he gave a new reputation and authority. In 1973 he became the natural choice to succeed Sir Leslie O'Brien as Governor of the Bank of England. He had to deal with an immediate banking crisis in late 1973, when the Bank had to shore up many of the secondary banks that had proliferated in the days of easy credit. Eight banks collapsed and the Bank found itself lumbered with the ownership of the likes of Jim Slater's (qv) group. Richardson dealt efficiently with the crisis, but the Bank's ineffectiveness was highlighted and a new Banking Act was needed. In 1979, when Margaret Thatcher came to power, Richardson became involved in a strategy of restricting the money supply. He was succeeded by Robin Leigh-Pemberton (qv) in 1983. He was also chairman of the Industrial Development Advisory Board, 1972-73; a member of the Jenkins Committee on company law, 1959-62; and chairman of the Royal Institute of International Affairs after 1984. Richardson was created KG in 1983 and also awarded a life peerage. He married in 1941 Margaret Alison née Sheppard.

RICHARDSON, John Wigham
(7 January 1837 - 15 April 1908)
Shipbuilder, he was born at Torquay, Devon, the second son among the ten children of Edward Richardson, a Newcastle-upon-Tyne Quaker, and his wife Jane née Wigham. He attended four schools before boarding at Friends School, York, leaving at 15 to begin his engineering training. At Liverpool and then at Newcastle he was apprenticed as a shipbuilder and then studied at University College, London only briefly due to the failure of the family bank. For three years he worked in the drawing office of the Tyneside engineer, Robert Hawthorn (1796-1867) before going into partnership as a shipbuilder with C J D Christie, a Scot, in 1860, financed by £5,000 from his father. Their Neptune Yard grew, with difficulty at first. The addition of John Tweedy (1850-1916) a marine engine designer and his triple expansion engine became powerful assets, as was Richardson's investment in 1882 in the Tyne Pontoons & Dry Docks Co which brought ship repair work. By 1898 the firm employed 2,000. Richardson converted the partnership into a limited liability company in 1899 and then merged it with Swan, Hunter in 1903 to form Swan, Hunter & Wigham Richardson Ltd, chaired by George Hunter (qv) with Richardson as deputy chairman. Of the £994,000 shares initially issued, Richardson held 36 per cent. Like his friend George Livesey (qv), he adopted co-partnership. Richardson promoted Neptune Bank, the first central, large-scale electricity generating station for lighting and industrial power, opened in 1901. A bibliophile, a linguist, artist and traveller, he was an exceptionally cultured industrialist. He was active in professional engineering bodies, published numerous technical papers and founded the journal *The Shipping World* in 1882. Originally a Quaker, he became an Anglican later in life. Richardson married, in 1864, Marian Henrietta née Thol; they had five sons and two daughters. See *DBB*.

RICHMOND, Sir Frederick Henry
(30 November 1873 - 11 November 1958)
Department store manager, the son of Henry Richmond, of Marnham, in Yorkshire. He came to London as a teenager and became an apprentice to Debenhams, the drapery store (founded as Clark & Debenham in 1813). After serving in every department, he became a joint-managing director in 1919 and succeeded Ernest Ridley Debenham as chairman in 1927, when Debenham's was fused with Clarence Hatry's (qv) Drapery Trust. Following the arrest of Hatry, Richmond and his fellow director G M Wright (qv) had the task of writing down the capital from £15.1 million to £6 million. By 1937 Debenhams owned a string of provincial depart-

ment stores, totalling 77 trading units and employing probably 7,000. Richmond retired in 1950. He was also deputy governor of the Hudson's Bay Co. He married in 1921 Dorothy Agnes née Sheppard: they had a son and a daughter. He was created baronet in 1929. See Maurice Corina, *Fine Silks and Oak Counters: Debenhams 1778-1978* (1978); *The Times*, 12 November 1953.

RICKEY, Walter Josiah
(1871 - 22 May 1935)
Sewing machine company manager, born at Athol, Massachusetts, USA, and educated and trained as an engineer at the Massachusetts Institute of Technology. An expert in wood technology, he joined the Singer Sewing Machine Co's cabinet factory at South Bend, Indiana. In 1913 he was transferred to Clydebank, Scotland, to manage its subsidiary. Forceful and energetic, Rickey revitalised and reorganised Singer's factory until his death in a car crash in France in 1935. The Singer subsidiary then employed about 8,000. He was a director of the Glasgow Chamber of Commerce; a director and former chairman of the Victoria Infirmary, Helensburgh, where he lived; and a member of the local Congregational Church. He was survived by his wife, one son and five daughters. See *Clydebank Press*, 24 May 1935.

RINGHAM, Reginald
(30 April 1894 - 24 December 1973)
National Coal Board executive, the son of John Charles Ringham, proprietor of the *Swan* hotel at Mansfield, and his wife Kate Ellen née Bull, he was educated at Oundle School and in 1913 entered the mining industry as a student under Sir Arthur Markham MP, brother of Charles Paxton Markham (qv), at Oxcroft Colliery. By 1921 he was a colliery manager, at Barlborough Colliery, and the following year joined the Staveley Coal & Iron Co as manager of Warsop Main at Mansfield. In 1929 he was appointed agent of Markham Colliery at Chesterfield and in 1938 general manager of Stavelely Coal & Iron Co collieries, then employing about 5,000 men underground and producing 2.5 million tons of coal annually. Ringham became a director of the Arkwright Coal Co and when the Ministry of Fuel and Power was established in 1942 to take over the wartime but strike-prone coal industry he was made chairman of the Nottingham & Clifton Colliery Co. Following the nationalisation of the coal industry in 1946 Ringham became production director of the East Midlands Division in 1948, deputy chairman in 1949, and then chairman, 1951-60. In 1955 the East Midlands Division was the NCB's largest division by output (46 million tons) but fourth largest

by employment (102,000 employees). Politically its workforce was moderate, compared to Scotland or South Wales. Higher productivity and good labour relations derived in part from the richness, size and recency of the coalfield, stretching from South Yorkshire into Nottinghamshire, where deep, large-scale, capital-intensive mining developed. Management could also take some credit. Ringham married, in 1923, Doris Clare Fletcher; they had a daughter. See *Colliery Year Book and Coal Trades Directory* (1935, 1955); William Ashworth, *The History of the British Coal Industry vol 5 1946-1982: The Nationalised Industry* (1986).

RITCHIE, Charles
2nd Baron Ritchie of Dundee
(18 November 1866 - 19 July 1948)
Waterways and port manager, the second son of (Lord) Charles Thomson Ritchie (1838-1906) and Margaret née Ower. Educated at Westminster School and Trinity College, Oxford (BA 1888). He joined the firm of William Ritchie & Son, jute spinners and East India merchants; and also became chairman of the Santa Gertrudia Jute Mills Co. A member of a government committee on the Port of London, Ritchie eventually became vice-chairman of the Port of London Authority in 1913, serving as chairman, 1925-41, in succession to Hudson Ewbanke Kearley, 1st Lord Devonport. He was a lieutenant of the City of London and also served as mayor of Winchelsea in 1924 and 1931. In 1898 he married Sarah Ruth née Jennings, daughter of an MP: they had four sons and a daughter. See *The Times*, 20 July 1948.

ROBARTS, David John
(26 March 1906 - 26 August 1989)
Banker, eldest son of Captain Gerald Robarts, of Lillingstone House, Buckingham, and the private banking firm of Robarts, Lubbock & Co (established 1772 and absorbed into Coutts & Co in 1914), he was educated at Eton and Magdalene College, Oxford, where he read agriculture. From Oxford he went to London to the head office of the National Provincial Bank, to which Coutts & Co had become affiliated in 1920, gaining banking experience and connections of future value. He took his father's place on the board of Coutts & Co in 1930, serving as a full-time director until 1945 and an ordinary director thereafter. In 1945 Robarts became managing director of Robert Fleming & Co Ltd, a private banking company, remaining until 1953 but retaining a directorship afterwards. Meantime he had joined the board of the National Provincial Bank in 1947 and became deputy chairman in 1950. At the comparatively early age of 48 he was elected chairman of the

National Provincial Bank, holding the office from 1954 until 1968 when the National Provincial merged with the Westminster Bank to form the largest clearing bank, the National Westminster Bank, of which he was the first deputy chairman and then chairman, 1969-71, and afterwards a director. In 1976 he retired from the boards of both Fleming & Co and the National Westminster Bank. Terse and outwardly conservative, Robarts surprised his competitors in 1962 when he succeeded in eroding the long-standing governmental opposition to bank mergers and negotiated the National Provincial's takeover of the District Bank (a combination still smaller than Midland or Barclays). It was he who proposed the 1968 merger with the Westminster Bank which saw his company grow from 11,000 employees in 1955 to nearly 48,000 in 1968. Robarts was twice chairman of the Committee of London Clearing Bankers and president of the British Bankers' Association, 1956-60 and 1968-70. The former period covered the Radcliffe Committee on the Working of the Monetary System (1957-59), the Bank Rate tribunal in 1957, and the removal of post-war restrictions on lending and competition in 1958. The decision of banks to close on Saturday mornings in 1969 and the fuller disclosure of bank profits in 1970 came during his second period of leadership of the bank industry. Robarts was a director of several other companies including Union Discount Co of London Ltd, ICI, and Sun Life Assurance Society. Outside banking, though not business, Robarts was a Church Commissioner, 1957-65, and was responsible for switching many of the Commissioners' investments from gilt-edged securities to equities. He was high sheriff of Buckinghamshire in 1963. His relaxations included golf and farming. Robarts married, in 1951, Pauline Mary, daughter of Colonel Francis Follett and widow of Clive Stoddart; they had three sons and a daughter. See *The Natproban* (Spring 1954); *Signature* (June 1969); *The Times*, 31 August 1989.

ROBB, John Weddell
(27 April 1936 -)
Pharmaceutical company executive, the son of John and Isabella Robb. Educated at Daniel Stewart's College, Edinburgh, in 1952 he became a market research executive for H J Heinz. After experience with a number of other companies, in 1966 he joined the pharmaceutical firm, Beecham, as a marketing executive. By 1980 he was on the Beecham board and later became its managing director between 1985 and 1988. By 1989 he was chief executive-elect at Wellcome, taking the job in 1990 under chairman Sir Alistair Frame (qv). Robb and his team have begun transforming

Wellcome, introducing a tighter focus that the group lacked when it was floated in 1986. They have restructured the management, cut costs, redefined R & D (one of Robb's first acts was to scrap a new £45 million heart attack drug, TPA, because it was felt to be no improvement over older treatments), and sold less profitable veterinary and environmental health lines. In 1992 Wellcome Trust announced a sale of shares, which reduced its stake in the business from 73.5 to under 50 per cent. The income will fund research for new drugs to augment Wellcome's most famous money-spinners, such as the herpes treatment, Zovirax, and its AIDS drug, Retrovir. Wellcome's turnover increased from £1,469 million in 1990 to £1,606 million in 1991 (pre-tax profits from £221 million to £230 million) and the group employed over 18,000. Robb is also a deputy chairman of National Freight Corporation and a non-executive director at Allied Lyons. In 1965 he married Janet Teanby: they have two sons and a daughter.

ROBENS, Alfred
Baron Robens of Woldingam
(18 December 1910 -)
Industrialist, the son of George and Edith Robens. Educated at Manchester Secondary School, his early career until the end of the Second World War was as a trades union official and Manchester City Councillor. A Labour MP for the Wansbeck Division of Northumberland and then Byth (1945-60), he served as Private Secretary for the Ministry of Transport (1945-47) and for the Ministry of Fuel and Power (1947-51), before becoming Minister of Labour in 1951. Between 1961 and 1971 he was chairman of the National Coal Board, where he fought a public battle in the political arena on behalf of the industry. His great task was to make coal more attractive to the consumer and reduce capacity to match declining demand. Whilst modernising the coal industry, Robens cut the number of mines from 698 to 292 and the number of workers from 583,000 to 283,00. Output was cut by a quarter, so that by the time he retired from the post the NCB had made a slight surplus. Robens then took over the chairmanships of Vickers from 1971 to 1979 and of Johnson Matthey from 1971 to 1983. He was also a director of Times Newspapers, the Bank of England and several other companies. He was chairman of the Engineering Industries Council and of the Foundation and Automation and Employment, and a member of the Royal Commission on Trade Unions and Employers' Associations and several other government committees. He was created a life peer in 1961. Robens married in 1937 Eva née Powell. See Alfred Robens, *Ten Year Stint* (1972); William

Ashworth, *History of the British Coal Industry: Vol 5, The Nationalised Industry* (1986).

ROBERTSON, General Brian Hubert
1st Baron Robertson of Oakridge
(22 July 1896 - 29 April 1974)

British Transport Commission chairman, eldest son of William Robert Robertson (1860-1933), the first modern field marshal to rise from the ranks, becoming chief of the Imperial General Staff during the First World War and a baronet in 1919; not surprisingly Brian Robertson embarked on a military career. From Charterhouse he went to the Royal Military Academy, Woolwich, and was commissioned in the Royal Engineers. In the First World War he served as brigade major on the Western Front, receiving the DSO, MC and three mentions in despatches. He remained in the army until 1933, passing through the Staff College, but stopping at the rank of major. Frustrated with this situation, after his father's death he emigrated to South Africa where he became managing director of Dunlop Rubber Co. Six years later he was recalled to the army and during the Second World War rose to become chief administrative officer to the Eighth Army in North Africa and to Field Marshal Alexander in Italy. Robertson was Military Governor of the British Zone of West Germany, 1945-49, and High Commissioner to the Federal Republic of Germany, 1949-50. He returned to the army in 1950-53 as commander-in-chief, Middle East land forces, and then accepted Winston Churchill's invitation to chair the British Transport Commission, succeeding Lord Hurcomb. The BTC comprised a politically-appointed commission of 12 members (in 1954), five part-time, whose duties were to own and manage the nationalised transport systems of the UK. Under the Conservative governments of the 1950s they ruled their 801,000 employees (in 1955) through management divisions established in 1953 (for railways, road services, road passenger companies, docks, waterways and hotels and catering services). On the railways this policy of decentralisation led to the establishment of area boards overseeing full time area general managers. Road haulage services were progressively returned to private ownership. While Robertson had a genius for administration, experience of high diplomacy and a wide reputation as a man of integrity and a military leader, he was the wrong person for the job. Shy, austere, determined to lead from the top and knowing nothing about the railway industry, he had a low opinion of railway managers whom he irked by setting up a controversial, military-style general staff, between the BTC and the operating divisions. In essence, it was unclear who was running the railways: top railway executives or the BTC's general staff. Faced with imperfect economic information, changing political objectives and enormous public criticism of the railways (post-war, one of the most run-down industrial businesses in the country) Robertson and the BTC appeared to have no consistent policy. Some felt that instead of behaving like a model civil servant he should have resigned long before he retired in 1961. Lord Robertson (he was made a baron in 1961) was a director of the Dunlop Co, 1961-69, and vice-president of the International Sleeping Car Co. He held many honorary posts and titles. He married, in 1926, Edith née Macindoe; they had one son and two daughters. See T R Gourvish, *British Railways, 1948-73: A Business History* (1986); *The Times*, 30 April, 1 May, 7 May 1974.

ROBINS, Sir Ralph (Harry)
(16 June 1932 -)

Aero-engine company executive, the son of Leonard Haddon and Maud Lillian Robins. Educated at Imperial College, University of London (where he took a BSc), he joined Rolls-Royce in Derby in 1955 as a graduate apprentice. Appointed executive vice-president of Rolls-Royce in 1971, he worked his way up to become managing director of the company in 1984. He helped steer Rolls-Royce into the private sector in 1987 and became deputy chairman two years later. In 1990 he became chief executive and two years later succeeded Lord Tombs (qv) as chairman (relinquishing the chief executive's post to Terry Harrison). His appointment comes at a difficult time for Rolls (which had a turnover in 1991 of £3,515 million, pre-tax profits of £51 million, and a workforce of over 50,000), with the post-1989 decline in military and civil aircraft orders and with the company engaged in its biggest and most costly engine programme (the Trent) since the RB211. In March 1993, hit by £10 billion in combined losses in 1992, he announced that RR would shut four plants and cut 5,000 jobs (bringing the number of jobs axed at the company since 1991 to 17,400). Robins, who was knighted in 1988, is also a director of Standard Chartered Bank, Schroders and the steel company ASW Holdings. He has served as chairman of the Defence Industries Council. In 1962 he married Patricia Maureen Grimes: they have two daughters.

ROBINSON, Sir Montague Arnet
(24 April 1898 - 4 May 1975)

Port executive, born at Stanmore, Middlesex, the second son of Francis Edward Robinson, 'an MA', and his wife Amy Eliz née Hargreaves, he was educated at Westminster School and then served in the 60th Rifles during the First World War. He went into the shipping industry and by 1951 was managing director of Coast Lines Ltd and director of a number of small dock and steamer companies around the country. He became a board member of the Mersey Docks & Harbour Board in 1941, serving as deputy chairman, 1953-54, and as chairman, 1954-62. In 1947 the National Dock Labour Scheme created a National Dock Labour Board which became the holding employer, controlling the register of dock workers, with shipping and stevedoring firms being the operating employers. In effect the NDLB displaced the MDHB with regard to Liverpool dock labour, who totalled 16,304 people in 1955. The MDHB continued to own and manage Mersey docks and warehouses. However, as the Rochdale Committee found in 1962, the MDHB invested relatively little in port capital after 1945, on average £3 million a year. As a result Liverpool's dock facilities fell behind those being developed in the post-war reconstruction of continental Europe. Reasons for this situation included a lack of coordination between the nation's ports, consequent wasteful competition between ports, poor accounting systems, and the unhealthy presence of users (such as shipowners, stevedoring firms) on the boards of major ports, including Liverpool. Arnet Robinson was chairman of the Liverpool Steam Ship Owners' Association and vice-chairman of the General Council of British Shipping in 1946, and chairman of the coasting liner section of the Chamber of Shipping, 1948-50. He was knighted in 1963. Arnet Robinson married, in 1928, Beatrice E Baber, by whom he had two sons and a daughter. See Richard Lawton and Catherine M Cunningham (eds), *Merseyside Social and Economic Studies* (1970); Stuart Mountfield, *Western Gateway: A History of the Mersey Docks and Harbour Board* (1965).

ROBINSON, Sir Thomas
(2 January 1864 - 30 December 1953)
Textile manager, the son of Peter Robinson, of Stretford, near Manchester. He followed a career in politics, serving on the local council in 1894 and becoming Liberal MP for Stretford, Lancashire, 1918-24: then standing as an Independent until 1931. A JP for Lancashire, he was charter mayor of Stretford on two occasions. Deputy chairman of the Bradford Dyers' Association Ltd (employing over 8,000 in the mid-1930s), he was knighted in 1920. Robinson married twice: first in 1887 to Emma née Lowe (d 1928); second in 1936 to Emmeline Mary Standring, a member of Stretford borough council.

RODDICK, Anita (Lucia)
(23 November 1942 -)
Toiletries and cosmetics manufacturer and retailer, born at Littlehampton, Sussex, of Italian immigrants Henry and Gilda Perella. Her mother ran a café. After training and working as a teacher, Roddick's business career began in earnest with the launch of the first Body Shop in Brighton in 1976. With a £4,000 bank loan and the help of her husband (like Laura Ashley's (qv), the Body Shop is a wife-husband team), it sold a small range of hand-labelled cosmetics in refillable bottles. The popularity of the Body Shop's marketing philosophy - it uses natural, environment-friendly products and shows concern for animal rights and the Third World - allied with a successful franchising policy (her husband's idea), has led to one of the great success stories of British business. In 1992 the group had over 750 branches in 41 countries and retail sales of £147 million (pre-tax profits £25 million). She married Gordon Roddick in 1971: they have two daughters. See Anita Roddick, *Body and Soul* (1991).

ROGER, Sir Alexander Forbes Proctor
(30 January 1878 - 4 April 1961)
Financier and industrialist, born at Rhynie, Aberdeenshire, the third and posthumous son of James Paterson Roger. The family was well connected in government and banking circles. Educated at Robert Gordon's College, Aberdeen, he worked in the City of London as partner in the St Davids (Broad Street) investment group. After war work in the Ministry of Munitions (he was knighted in 1916), he returned to various City posts, including: director of the Midland Bank (1932-58); chairman of British Insulated Cables (1930-54); and chairman of Birmingham Small Arms (1932-40). Regarded by contemporaries as a 'great driving force', his involvement with these companies was largely beneficial (after BIC's merger with Callender's, profits hit record levels in the early 1950s). He was created KCIE in 1941. Roger married Helen Stuart, youngest daughter of James Campbell Clark, in 1908: they had three sons. He left £221,644 gross. See *DBB*.

ROGERS, Sir Hallewell
(25 February 1864 - 16 November 1931)
Small arms, vehicles and machine tool company chairman, born in Hampstead, London, the son of George Rogers, a bank manager, and his wife Maria née Robinson, he was educated at Stanfield's private school, Hampstead, and then at 17 moved to Birmingham becoming a factor with Jesse Collings & Wallis. In the late 1880s he purchased several small businesses and became director of a

few more. Ideologically Rogers moved from Liberalism and Nonconformity to Conservatism and Anglicanism. A supporter of Joseph Chamberlain, he was drawn into politics and in 1893 as a Conservative was elected to Birmingham City council, proving to be a sharp committee man with a keen business sense. A magistrate from 1901, alderman from 1902 and lord mayor in 1902-4, he was knighted in 1904, all of which facilitated his progress on to the boards of two prominent Birmingham companies. Through his brother-in-law, Sir James Smith, its chairman, he became a director of Birmingham District & Counties Banking Co, remaining on the board until 1916 when it was bought by Barclays Bank. In 1919 he joined Barclays main board, remaining until 1929. More significantly, he became a director of Birmingham Small Arms and its chairman, 1906-28. Formed in 1861, from the 1880s BSA faced a lack of orders for their small-arms factory at Small Heath. They diversified into the manufacture of cycles and, in the 1890s, motorcycles. By 1906 the firm employed over 4,000. Under Rogers and his deputy Dudley Docker (qv) BSA expanded by takeovers confined to its small arms and vehicles interests (it bought Daimler Motors of Coventry in 1910). During the First World War it had government orders for the production of small-arms, rifles, machine guns and shells, ambulances and tractors. After 1918 it diversified into air services (a mistake) and machine tool manufacture (poorly managed) and radios. Only motorcycles made a profit and Rogers was eventually forced to resign. He married twice: in 1885, to Lydia Watton née Smith (1855-1908), daughter of a Birmingham stationer and printer, by whom he had a son (killed in action in 1916); in 1927, to Phyllis Daisy Reeve née Burton, a widow. See *DBB*.

ROLLS, The Honourable Charles Stewart
(27 August 1877 - 12 July 1910)

Motor car promoter and manufacturer, born in London's West End into an aristocratic family, the son of John Allan Rolls (1837-1912) and Georgiana Marcia née Maclean. Educated at Eton and at Trinity College, Cambridge (BA science), his wealthy connections allowed him to indulge in one of the era's new passions - the motor car. In 1902 he set up a successful car agency and four years later joined forces with the Manchester designer and engineer Henry Royce (qv) to found Rolls Royce Ltd. Rolls gave their cars magnificent publicity by his driving exploits, but by 1908 (when the factory was moved from Manchester to Derby) he had found another interest - aeroplanes. The Rolls Royce board, however, declined his suggestion to

manufacture them and in 1910 Rolls resigned. Later in the year he became the first Englishman to be killed in an aeroplane crash. A keep-fit enthusiast, vegetarian and anti-vivisectionist, Rolls was unmarried. He left £30,936 gross. See C S Rolls, *Roadside Experiences: A Paper Read at the Automobile Club of Great Britain and Ireland* (1904); Edward J B D S Montagu, *Rolls of Rolls Royce* (1966); *DBB*; *DNB*.

RONSON, Gerald
(26 May 1929 -)

Property and petrol station owner, born in Paddington, west London, the son of Henry and Sarah Ronson, Russian Jewish refugees, who had fled tsarist pogroms. After leaving Clark's College, Cricklewood, at 15, he joined his father's furniture business. In 1957 with about £200,000 of his family's capital he set out on his own, first in property and later petrol. He founded Heron International (the name comes from his father's) in about 1960, becoming chief executive in 1976 and chairman three years later. By the end of the 1980s, Ronson - working a six-day week from his Marylebone headquarters - had built Heron into the UK's second largest private company with a turnover of £1 billion a year, embracing petrol stations, property and car sales. Ronson's policy of avoiding publicity (his *Who's Who* entry is only six lines) was shattered after Guinness's takeover of Distillers in 1986 when he was accused (and later convicted) with Ernest Saunders (qv) and others of illegal share dealing. After serving half a one-year sentence at Ford Open Prison and paying a £5 million fine, he was released in February 1991, only to be hit hard by the recession, the effects of a disastrous expansion in the US, and bad investments in such companies as Nazmu Virani's (qv) Control Securities. By 1992 Ronson owed his bankers £1.5 billion and he had lost 95 per cent of his empire. He and his wife Gail were married in 1967 and have four daughters. See William Kay, *Tycoons: Where They Came From and How They Made It* (1985); Jeffrey Robinson, *The Risk Takers: Portraits of Money, Ego and Power* (1985).

ROOTES, Sir Reginald Claud
(20 October 1896 - 20 December 1977)

Motor vehicle manufacturer and distributor, born at Goudhurst, Kent, the younger son of William Roots, a cycle and motor engineer, and his wife Jane née Catt, he attended Cranbrook School and then entered the civil service, working in the Admiralty, 1915-19. After the First World War he joined his brother, William Edward Rootes (qv), as joint managing director of the family motor distributorship, Rootes Ltd. Reginald's strength lay on the administrative side and, after the takeover of

Humber in 1932, integrating the manufacturing organisation. After the Second World War, in which he managed the firm and over 6,000 employees single-handed, his organisational skills were taxed to the limit. Though they were the twelfth largest car maker in the world (by volume of output) by 1960, Rootes Motors Ltd (formed in 1949) had its factories spread over an awkward geographical area from Coventry to Swindon, Luton and Folkestone, employing 20,000 (as well as 1,000 dealers). The problem intensified after 1961 when, responding to government regional policy, Rootes built an assembly plant for the Hillman Imp at Linwood, Renfrewshire, Scotland, but were obliged to supply 80 per cent of the materials from the Midlands, 300 miles away (and conversely to move finished vehicles that distance or further south). Sir Reginald Rootes (he was knighted in 1946) gave up his managing directorship after the American firm Chrysler bought a controlling interest in Rootes Motors Ltd in 1964; he continued as a director until 1966. Of a quieter temperament than his brother, he confined his interests to the motor trade and to farming in Kent. He married twice: first, in 1922, to Ruth Joyce née Bensted, daughter of a stone merchant, by whom he had a son and whom he divorced in 1938; second, in 1938, to Nancy Norris Beadle. See *DBB*.

ROOTES, William Edward
1st Baron Rootes of Ramsbury
(17 August 1894 - 12 December 1964)

Motor vehicle manufacturer and distributor, born at Hawkhurst, Kent, the elder son of William Rootes, a cycle and motor engineer, and his wife Jane née Catt, he was educated at Cranbrooke School and apprenticed with Singer Motors Ltd of Coventry in 1913. In 1915 he volunteered as a pupil engineer in the Royal Naval Volunteer Reserve (making lieutenant's rank) transferring to the Royal Naval Air Service in 1917. After the war he persuaded his brother Reginald (qv) to join him as joint managing director of the family motor distributorship, Rootes Ltd. By the late 1920s they were the largest motor vehicle distributors in the UK, 'Billy', as he was called, being a brilliant salesman. From 1925 they moved into manufacturing. With an investment of £1 million from the Prudential Assurance Co in 1929 they took over Humber Ltd of Coventry and its two subsidiaries, Hillman of Coventry and Commer of Luton. They made further acquisitions, including Clement Talbot Ltd and Sunbeam Motor Car Co Ltd in 1935, and by the late 1930s were one of the 'Big Six' British vehicle makers. Whereas Reginald concentrated on administration, Billy gave the firm a high public profile. He served on various motor

industry bodies (especially concerning himself with exports) and during the Second World War headed the supply council at the Ministry of Supply. After the war he built up a strong market in the USA. By 1950 Rootes were meeting strong competition from foreign car makers. Billy Rootes eschewed the possibility of going up market with a limited range of models. Instead he opted for expansion in the highly competitive mass market with a new design, the rear-engined Hillman Imp. The organisation of production, which commenced in 1963, proved a nightmare as Reginald discovered. Export problems and poor industrial relations led to losses in 1962 and 1963. Lord Rootes (he was knighted in 1942, made a GBE in 1955 and a baron in 1959) therefore persuaded Chrysler in 1964 to take a £12.3 million interest in his company, equivalent to 30 per cent of the voting shares and 50 per cent of the non-voting ones, with transfer to Chrysler to be complete by 1970. He did not live to see this. Outside business Billy Rootes, one of Coventry's last entrepreneurs (though he never lived there), was prominent in fund raising to establish the University of Warwick and found his relaxation in farming on the Berkshire-Wiltshire border. He married twice: first, in 1916, to Nora Press, a miller's daughter, by whom he had two sons; second, after their divorce in 1951, he married Ruby Joy Ann née Duff, formerly wife of Sir Francis Henry Grenville Peek, 4th Bart and previously widow of Sir Charles Thomas Hewitt Mappin, 4th Bart. See *DBB*.

ROSS, Sir Henry James
(14 March 1893 - 4 April 1973)

Drink and chemicals company chairman, the son of William Henry Ross (1862-1944) accountant, secretary, general manager (from 1900) and chairman (1925-35) of the Distillers Co Ltd (DCL), and Annie Gilmour Pollok née Dalgleish, he was educated at George Watson's College, Edinburgh, The Leys School, Cambridge, and the Institut Tilly, Berlin. He joined DCL as a trainee in 1910, gained practical experience in the Glenochil, Carsebridge and Caledonian Distilleries and took a brewing course at Heriot-Watt College, Edinburgh, before entering the Royal Naval Volunteer Reserve in 1914 as a sub-lieutenant and being invalided out in 1916. He then became assistant to the DCL general manager, his father, until 1924 when he and two others were made deputy general managers. He became a director in 1925, serving on the technical, research and executive committees, and a director of several DCL whisky companies, of Scottish Malt Distillers Ltd, and of the United Yeast Co Ltd. He joined the DCL management committee in 1939, became its chairman in 1946 and then deputy chairman of DCL in 1947 and chairman, 1948-58. He was DCL president from 1958 but retired from the board in 1963. Under the chairmanship of Sir Henry Ross (he was knighted in 1952) DCL continued to grow in size and to diversify. Begun in the late 1930s, the move into industrial chemicals and plastics was vigorously promoted after 1945 by Graham Hayman (qv), chairman of the management committee. Ross married, in 1917, Blanche Alix Jowett Newbould; they had two sons. See *DCL Gazette*, October 1926; *The Times*, 6 April 1973.

ROTHSCHILD, Sir Evelyn (Robert Adrian) de
(29 August 1931 -)

ROTHSCHILD, (Nathaniel Charles) Jacob
4th Baron Rothschild
(29 April 1936 -)

Bankers and descendants of the famous Rothschild banking dynasty, Evelyn was the son of Anthony Gustav de Rothschild (1887-1961) and a great-great-grandson of the founder of the famous City bank, N M Rothschild & Sons; his mother was Yvonne Cahen d'Anvers. Jacob was the son of (Nathaniel Mayer) Victor (3rd Baron) Rothschild (1910-90), a polymath of military intelligence and Think Tank renown, and Barbara Hutchinson. Evelyn was educated at Harrow and Trinity College, Cambridge; Jacob at Eton and Christ Church College, Oxford, where he took a first-class honours degree in history. Both cousins joined N M Rothschild: by the 1970s Jacob was the most dynamic member of the bank, but Evelyn held the majority shareholding. Tensions developed, which according to the Rothschild's historian were due to the fact that: 'Jacob wanted to transform and enlarge NMR, using public money, into a major concern capable of competing with the giants. Evelyn wanted to maintain the bank as a private business, achieving growth cautiously and remaining competitive within a more restricted field'. In 1980 Jacob left NMR, leaving Evelyn as chairman. Both have been successful since the breach. NMR has stayed a private bank, expanding steadily, with Evelyn as second only to the Governor of the Bank of England in the unofficial hierarchy of the City. Jacob took over the management of Rothschild Investment Trust, a small investment business, and made it into a major financial institution, later partnering Sir James Goldsmith (qv) in an ambitious takeover bid for BAT. In 1990 he founded J Rothschild Assurance with his friend Sir Mark Weinberg (qv). Highly secretive (their entries in *Who's Who* are six lines or less), the cousins are amongst the wealthiest individuals in the UK, with Evelyn's fortune in 1992 estimated at £200 million and Jacob's at £154 million. Evelyn was knighted in 1989; Jacob inherited Victor's peerage in

1990. Jacob married in 1961 Serena Mary Dunn: they have three daughters and a son. Evelyn married twice: first in 1966 to Jeanette Bishop, a fashion model (they divorced in 1971 and she died in a Italian mountain tragedy in 1980); secondly in 1973 to Victoria Lou Schott: they have two sons and a daughter. See Philip Beresford, *The Sunday Times Book of the Rich* (1990); Derek Wilson, *Rothschild: A Story of Wealth and Power* (1988).

ROWELL, Sir Herbert Babington
(24 November 1860 - 23 June 1921)

Shipbuilder, born at Carr's Hill, Gateshead, the son of Robert Rowell, a shipbroker, and his wife Jane née Laidlaw, he attended Mill Hill School and completed his education in Switzerland, becoming competent in French and Italian. After a five-year apprenticeship with Wigham Richardson (qv) at Walker-upon-Tyne, he did an advanced course in naval architecture at Glasgow University. He next worked for Sir W G Armstrong, Mitchell & Co at their Walker and Elswick yards, 1883-1891, but moved to R & W Hawthorn-Leslie & Co Ltd in 1891 when Sir Benjamin Browne (qv) appointed him as general manager. Within months he was in complete charge of the construction of a warship. By 1913 he had built over 30 destroyers for the Admiralty. Work increased during the First World War, with the workforce rising from 2,300 to 2,800. When Browne resigned in 1916 Rowell became chairman and managing director. After the war he won orders from Cunard and P & O lines for some of the larger vessels he had long wanted to build at Hebburn. Rowell was a labour hardliner, but promoted innovations (on which he published a few articles) and professional technical education. He sat on a number of government and professional committees and was knighted in 1918. He married, in 1891, Mary Dobree née Robin of Naples; they had two sons and two daughters. See *DBB*.

ROWLAND, (John) David
(10 August 1933 -)

Insurance company executive, born in London, the only child of Cyril Arthur Rowland and his wife Eileen Mary. His father had read for the Bar, but in the depressed 1930s had to work as an insurance inspector. Educated at St Paul's School and Trinity College, Cambridge, David read natural sciences, intending to pursue medicine. But in 1956 he took up an introduction his father (by now prospering with National Employers Mutual) had made to the City insurance brokers Matthews Wrightson. He became a director at the age of 31 and was appointed managing director in 1972. He helped expand the business, so that by 1981, when he became chairman, Stewart Wrightson (as it was then known) was an international broker with 2,700 staff. In 1987 Stewart Wrightson was bought by Willis Faber and Rowland, unhappy with the results of the merger, left in March 1988 to become chief executive of Sedgwick Insurance, Britain's largest independent broker. In January 1993 he became chairman of the troubled insurance group, Lloyd's of London, succeeding David Coleridge (qv). When he took over as its *first* paid chairman (with a salary of £450,000 per annum), Lloyd's had made a £2 billion loss in 1992 and was expected to lose the same amount in 1993. Rowland, with a new chief executive Peter Middleton, is formulating a new business plan - the first ever for Lloyd's - to help ensure its survival. He is involved with the Industrial Society and Templeton College (Oxford Centre for Management Studies). In 1957 David Rowland married Guilia Powell, a musician: they had one son and one daughter. The marriage ended in 1991 when he married Diana Louise Matthews née Dickie, an Islington estate agent. See Jonathan Mantle, *For Whom the Bell Tolls: The Lesson of Lloyd's of London* (1992).

ROWLAND, (Roland Walter) Tiny
(27 November 1917 -)
Industrialist, born Roland Walter Fuhrhop in a British internment camp in the state of Karnataka, India, the son of a German trader and a British mother (named Carton). The family ran an international trading firm in Hamburg. He was educated at a minor public school, Churchers, in Petersfield, Hampshire. During the Second World War (before which he changed his name) he worked in a London shipping agency, joined the army and was also interned. By the late 1940s he was a successful British businessman, wheeling and dealing in companies, but by 1950 had switched to farming and trading in Africa. In 1961 he was asked by Angus Ogilvie (later husband of Princess Alexandra) to manage a derelict company called London & Rhodesian Mining & Land Co (Lonrho). Within thirty years Rowland had built Lonrho into one of the UK's few truly international trading conglomerates with an annual turnover of £5 billion and a workforce of 108,000. Its assets were amongst the most diverse ever assembled by a UK-based group (though 60 per cent of its profits were generated in Africa): they included, *inter alia*, a gold mine in Ghana, a casino in the Bahamas, hotels in Bermuda and the *Observer* newspaper. Despite his liking for secrecy and his reputation as an outsider - he belongs to no clubs and has no *Who's Who* entry - Rowland has regularly hit the headlines. Edward Heath in 1971 described Lonrho as 'the unacceptable face of capitalism'. Rowland has also engaged in a long-running feud with the Fayed brothers

(qv) for control of the House of Fraser and its subsidiary Harrods. He was chief executive of Lonrho and in 1991 (after Edward Du Cann resigned) also became chairman. In 1992 he owned nearly 15 per cent of Lonrho (a stake valued at £114 million) and was paid a salary of £1.6 million, but he was faced with a large sale of assets to cover Lonrho's debts of £1.4 billion. In 1992 Lonrho's dividend was cut for the first time in twenty years and then again in 1993, when profits fell from £205 million to £80 million. There was speculation about his retirement, especially in December 1992 when he sold 43 million of his shares valued at £50 million to an unknown German property developer, Dieter Bock, who joined him as joint chief executive of Lonrho. At the age of 49 he married Josie, the daughter of Lionel Taylor, a former business partner: they have four children. See Tom Bower, *Tiny Rowland: A Rebel Tycoon* (1993); Richard Hall, *My Life with Tiny: A Biography of Tiny Rowland* (1987).

ROWNTREE, Benjamin Seebohm
(7 July 1871 - 7 October 1954)
Promoter, management research and confectionery company chairman, born in York, the third child of Joseph Rowntree (qv), and Emma Antoinette Seebohm. After a Quaker education at Bootham School, York, and Owens College, Manchester, he joined the family confectionery firm in 1889, becoming chairman in 1923 and remaining on the board until 1941. By then Rowntree's was the second largest UK confectioner, but much of Benjamin's energies were directed outside the firm where his Quakerism led him into the search for better management methods. In the inter-war years he initiated the Oxford Conferences for Works Managers, became a member of the Liberal Industrial Inquiry, and established Management Research Groups. He was given an honorary LLD by Manchester University in 1942, and was made a CH in 1931. He married in 1897 Lydia née Potter: they had four sons and one daughter. He left £90,812 gross. See B S Rowntree, *Industrial Unrest: A Way Out* (1922); Asa Briggs, *Social Thought and Social Action: A Study of the Work of Seebohm Rowntree, 1871-1954* (1961); *DBB*; *DNB*.

ROWNTREE, Joseph
(24 May 1836 - 24 February 1925)
Chocolate manufacturer and industrial relations pioneer, born above the family's grocery shop in York, the son of Joseph Rowntree Snr (1801-59) and Sarah née Stephenson. After a Quaker upbringing and education at Bootham, at 16 he became his father's apprentice. In 1869 he joined his younger brother Henry Isaac Rowntree (1838-

83) in a small cocoa and chocolate business. With a mixture of shrewd management, attention to quality and advertising, Rowntree made the firm and its 'Elect' cocoa a household word. When he relinquished the chairmanship in 1923 Rowntree & Co Ltd had a turnover of £3.2 million and 7,000 workers. Rowntree's Quaker and liberal ideals concerning labour welfare and education, profit-sharing, charitable trusts, temperance, and the alleviation of poverty found expression in his business and in his public work in York (for which in 1911 he was made an honorary freeman of the city). Rowntree was twice married: in 1856 to Julia Seebohm (d 1863), daughter of a German Quaker; and in 1867 to Antoinette Seebohm (a first cousin of his first wife), by whom he had two daughters and four sons. He left £220,336 gross. See Joseph Rowntree and Arthur Sherwell, *The Temperance Problem and Social Reform* (1899); Anne Vernon, *A Quaker Businessman: The Life of Joseph Rowntree, 1836-1925* (1958); *DBB*; *DNB*.

ROYCE, Sir Frederick Henry
(27 August 1863 - 22 April 1933)

Motor car and aero-engine manufacturer, born at Alwalton near Peterborough, the son of James Royce, a farmer and mill owner, and Mary née King. His father's attempt to launch a business in London was unsuccessful and his early education and apprenticeship in the Great Northern Railway Co's workshops were interrupted. Eventually, he formed a partnership in Manchester manufacturing electrical equipment, but by 1904 had switched his attention to motor cars. The famous partnership with the salesman, Charles Stewart Rolls (qv), followed in 1906, with Royce appointed chief engineer of the Rolls-Royce Co. An obsessive concern with quality (with little regard for the balance sheet or his own health) was Royce's hallmark. After a breakdown in 1911 due to overwork, ill-health and the shock of Rolls's death, Royce produced his designs (which included aero-engines) in Sussex or France and never visited the factory in Derby again. In 1893 he married Minnie Grace née Punt: they had no children. Royce was appointed OBE in 1918 and created a baronet in 1930. He left £112,598 gross. See Ian Lloyd, *Rolls-Royce: The Growth of a Firm* (1978); Max Pemberton, *The Life of Henry Royce* (1934); *DBB*; *DNB*.

ROYLE, Sir Lancelot Carrington
(31 May 1898 - 19 June 1978)

Multiple food store chairman, he was the younger son of the Reverend Vernon Peter Fanshawe Royle, Church of England clergyman, first master of Elstree School, 1879-99, and headmaster of Stanmore Park School from 1901, and his wife

Eleanor Agnes. He was educated at Stanmore Park, Harrow and the Royal Military Academy, Woolwich. He served in France in the Royal Field Artillery in 1918 and after the Armistice was stationed in Cologne until 1921 when he resigned from the army and joined the management of Van den Bergh Ltd, the Dutch margarine manufacturers and retailers. He remained with this company until 1939, by which time it had twice merged, with Jurgens Ltd in 1927 to form the Margarine Union Ltd and with Lever Brothers Ltd in 1929 to form Unilever Ltd. He briefly returned to the RFA in 1940 but was then appointed to a Treasury committee and afterwards became chairman of the Navy, Army and Air Force Institutes, 1941-53, work for which he was knighted in 1944. Sir Lancelot Royle became chairman of the Home & Colonial Stores Ltd in 1947, remaining in charge until 1958. Founded in 1888, the Home & Colonial Stores had grown rapidly between the wars by acquisition, gaining the Maypole Dairy Co in 1924, Meadow Dairy Co in 1929, and Lipton Ltd in 1931. The group in 1929 formed Allied Suppliers Ltd to handle tea blending and packing and to act as a central buying organisation. Allied Suppliers was also the name given in 1960 to the group's holding company. In 1939 there were 2,986 branches in the group (with probably 15,000 employees), by 1958 there were 4,000 branches (and probably 32,000 employees). Under Royle a new structure was inaugurated, with chairmen of constituent firms sitting on the parent board. In years of shortages and then full employment and rising purchasing power his main achievement lay in creating a unified organisation and a single culture among his senior managers. By 1955 Royle was also managing director of the group and chairman of Liptons. He was chairman of Lipton (Overseas) Ltd, 1959-63, and a director of the British Match Corporation, 1961-68, of Bryant & May, 1961-71, of Liebig's Extract of Meat Co, 1961-68, and of Oxo Ltd, 1961-68. A sprinter of some note, he represented England in the 1924 Olympic Games. Royle married, in 1922, Barbara Rachel, daughter of Henry Haldin KC; they had two sons and a daughter. See Peter Mathias, *Retailing Revolution* (1967); *The Times*, 21 June 1978.

RUSHTON, James Lever
(1871 - 8 March 1936)

Textile machinery manufacturer, born at Bolton, the son T H Rushton (son of a banker), partner of Sir Benjamin Alfred Dobson of Dobson & Barlow, the Bolton textile machinery makers, he was educated at Rugby and Brazenose College, Oxford. He returned to Bolton and trained in the Kay

Street Works of Dobson & Barlow, becoming chairman before the First World War when the firm employed 5,000. His membership of the Institution of Mechanical Engineers suggests that he combined engineering and administrative skills. After Dobson & Barlow merged with five other Lancashire textile machinery manufacturers in 1931, to form Textile Machinery Makers Ltd, Rushton became a TMM director and managing director of Dobson & Barlow, under Sir Walter Preston (qv). Rushton inherited from his father, c. 1906, a 4,000-acre estate near Garstang, between Preston and Lancaster, where he pursued agriculture and shooting. Outside the firm he was an active Anglican, a Conservative and a JP. He married the sister of W J Garnett of Quernmore Park, Lancaster, by whom he had two daughters and a son. See *Bolton Journal and Guardian* 13 March 1936; Ernest Gaskell, *Lancashire Leaders: Social and Political* (ca 1900).

RUSSELL, Major-General George Neville
(19 October 1899 - 24 August 1971)
Nationalised transport industry executive, the son of George Russell, 'of independent means', and his wife Emily Mary née Russell, he was educated at Rugby and the Royal Military Academy, Woolwich. Commissioned into the Royal Engineers, he served between the wars in India, Iraq and Canada. Throughout the Second World War he served on Movements Staff, first with the British Expeditionary Force in France where he directed all road and rail movements, then at GHQ, Middle East as Director of Movements at the battle of El Alamein and the invasion of Sicily, and then in India. He acted as Transport Adviser to the Special Commissioner for South East Asia until 1948 when he was appointed to the Road Transport Executive, one of five executives under the control of the British Transport Commission which was set up by the Transport Act of 1947 to manage the nationalised transport industry. The Road Transport Executive was split in 1949 between passenger and freight transport. Long distance hauliers, operating further than 25 miles, were nationalised and merged as British Road Services. Russell, chairman of BRS, 1948-59, had the job of creating a single organisation from 4,000 separate businesses and operating (at its peak in 1951) 40,000 vehicles. With the election of a Conservative Government in 1951 he was obliged to go into reverse. Under the Transport Act of 1953 General Russell was required to return the greater part of the BRS fleet to private enterprise. This policy was halted in 1956, when BRS employed over 40,000, and Russell had to operate the remaining 16,000 vehicles through five limited companies all trading under the BRS name. Nicknamed 'Cyclone Charlie', General Russell supplied the energy and agility demanded by the enormous tasks set by his changing political masters. He was a member of the Eastern Area Board of the British Transport Commission, 1959-62 (and chairman, 1961-62) and after the BTC was split up in 1962 he served on the British Railways Board. In 1958-59 he was president of the Institute of Transport. Outside business Russell was chairman of the Sutton Dwellings Trust. He was made a CBE in 1943 and a CB in 1946. Curiously, his BRS role went unrecognised. Russell married twice: first, in 1927, to Iris Mills, by whom he had two daughters; secondly, in 1946, to Jocelyn Delia Harvie Bennett, by whom he had a son and two daughters. See *Journal of the Institute of Transport* 28 (1958); *The Times*, 26, 30 August 1971.

S

SAATCHI, Charles
(9 June 1943 -)

SAATCHI, Maurice
(21 June 1946 -)
Advertising agents, both born in Baghdad, the sons of Nathan Saatchi, a prosperous Jewish Iraq textile merchant who emigrated to England in 1947, and his wife Daisy. Charles was educated at Christ's College, Finchley; Maurice at the London School of Economics, where he graduated with a first-class BSc degree in economics. In 1970 they founded Saatchi & Saatchi with £25,000. With Maurice as front man (he became chairman in 1984) and Charles providing the creative drive, they quickly built the largest and one of the best known advertising agencies in the world. It achieved prominence with its work for the Conservative Party (notably its long queue of the unemployed above the caption: 'Labour Isn't Working'). After hitting a peak in the mid-1980s, when they took over three major US agencies, branched into management consultancy, and made bids for the Midland Bank and Hill Samuel, the brothers fell in the subsequent stock market crash and recession and the company only narrowly escaped extinction. Their shares, once worth more than £30 million, became nearly worthless and their wealth now resides largely in Charles's modern art collection. Frenchman Robert Louis-Dreyfus is the chief executive charged with saving the business. Charles in 1973 married Doris Lockhart; Maurice in 1984 married Josephine Hart, by whom he had one son and one stepson. See Ivan Fallon, *The Brothers: The Rise and Rise of Saatchi & Saatchi* (1988); Philip Kleinman, *The Saatchi and Saatchi Story* (1987).

SAINER

SAINER, Leonard
(12 October 1909 - 30 September 1991)
Company lawyer and property company chairman, son of Archer Sainer, a tailor in London's
East End, and his wife Sarah, he was educated at
the Central Foundation and graduated in law from
the London School of Economics in 1929.
Articled to Bullcraig & Davis, solicitors, at a cost
of 500 guineas to his father, his handling of a lease
on the Prince of Wales Theatre in Leicester
Square in 1931 proved momentous. The client
was Charles Clore (qv). Their friendship lasted
until Clore's death and enabled Sainer to buy into
a new partnership, Titmuss, Sainer & Webb
which Sainer, a lifelong diabetic, ran from 1941.
After the war Clore became a much more active
property speculator and Sainer increasingly his
right-hand man — they frequented Annabel's club
in Berkeley Square and shared a passion for horse
racing. Clore's purchase in 1952 of J Sears & Co,
a footwear firm trading as the Trueform Boot Co
and Freeman, Hardy & Willis (which owned
about 900 shops), through a takeover bid, took
Sainer onto the Sears board (he was already director of eight other companies). After Clore emigrated in 1977, Sainer resigned from his law firm
and became chairman of Sears Holdings in 1978.
After Clore's death in 1979 Sainer re-shaped the
Sears group, selling the knitwear, carpet-making
and laundry businesses. He retired from the chairmanship in 1984, when Sears employed nearly
60,000 and earned a net profit of 19 per cent on
capital employed of £968 million. A gentle,
unemotional man, Sainer was a brilliant negotia-
tor with formidable powers of persuasion and
bluff. Like Clore he was a generous benefactor,
particularly towards Jewish and racing charities.
In November 1989 he married his long-standing
companion, Wendy; there were no children. See
David Clutterbuck and Marion Devine, *Clore:
The Man and His Millions* (1987); Charles
Gordon, *The Two Tycoons: A Personal Memoir of
Charles Clore and Jack Cotton* (1984); *The Times*,
2 October 1990.

SAINSBURY, John Davan
Baron Sainsbury of Preston Candover
(2 November 1927 -)
Food retailer and supermarket chain entrepreneur, the son of Alan John Sainsbury (b 1902,
created a peer in 1962) and Doreen Davan
Adams. He is a great grandson of John James
Sainsbury (1844-1928), who founded the family
firm in 1869 as a small dairy and grocery shop in
Drury Lane, London. Educated at Stowe School
and Worcester College, Oxford, he joined the
firm in 1950 (the year it opened its first super-

market), became a director in 1958, and chairman in 1969. Under his leadership Sainsbury's
became the UK's biggest and most successful
supermarket chain, employing 100,000 in 1992.
Between 1969 and 1992 (when he retired as
chairman) the number of Sainsbury supermarkets
rose from 82 to 313, its customers from about 2
million to 7.5 million. Sales grew from £166
million (£1,200 at 1992 prices) to £9,202 million in 1992, while pre-tax profits climbed from
£4.3 million (£33 million at 1992 prices) to
£628 million in 1992 - a compound growth rate
of 24 per cent. The family control about 40 per
cent of the £7.6 billion firm (floated on the
stock market in 1973), yielding the Sainsbury
clan annual dividends of £55 million - enough
to make it the fourth richest family in the UK.
Knighted in 1980, he was made a life peer in
1989 and appointed KG in 1992. He married in
1963 Anya Linden, a former dancer with the
Royal Ballet: they have two sons and one daughter. Chairman of the Royal Opera House, his
family has funded a £50 million wing at the
National Gallery. See *DBB*.

SAINSBURY, David John
(24 October 1940 -)
Food retailer and supermarket chain entrepreneur,
a fourth generation scion of the famous grocer
dynasty and the son of Sir Robert Sainsbury (b
1906) and Lisa née Van den Bergh. After Eton he
studied history and psychology at King's College,
Cambridge, and took a master's degree in business
administration at Columbia University, New York
City, before joining the family firm as finance
director in 1963. Three years later he was awarded
a £12 million block of shares in Sainsbury's as part
of the legal settlement of his father's estate. A
cousin of former chairman, John Sainsbury (qv),
David is the company's largest individual shareholder (with about 21 per cent). In 1988 he
became deputy chairman and succeeded to the
chairmanship in November 1992. More diffident
and more shy than his 'hands-on' predecessor,
David is expected to take a more global view of the
business: at present the group's eyes are firmly on
America, where it has a chain of supermarkets in
the north-east USA. At home expansion is set to
continue northwards, especially in Scotland. When
he took over he had 343 million Sainsbury ordinary shares, worth in 1992 over £1.7 billion and
producing in the previous year £24 million in dividends. The Gatsby Trust - the main vehicle for his
considerable philanthropy - spends the equivalent
of one-third of this income. In 1993 he gave £200
million in shares to the Trust (£11.5 million more
than the combined expenditure on fund-raising of

SAMUEL

the UK's 400 biggest charities since 1991). He has also supported such causes as the London Business School, the Social Democratic Party and educational research. He married in 1973 Susan Carole Reid: they have three daughters. See D J Sainsbury, *Government and Industry* (1981); *idem* (with Christopher Smallwood), *Wealth Creation and Jobs* (1987).

SALMON, Henry
(23 April 1881 - 13 October 1950)

Caterer and food manufacturer, born into a large Jewish family (nine sons and six daughters) of Barnett Salmon and Helena née Gluckstein. After attending the City of London School, he joined the family firm of J Lyons & Co, which had become a household word with its corner tea-shops. He became a managing director in 1909, with special responsibility for the tea division, and also increasingly controlled the property side of the business. In 1941 he became chairman of Lyons, when it employed over 30,000 workers. In 1903 he married his first cousin, Lena, daughter of Isidore Gluckstein: they had two sons and a daughter. He left £43,397. See *DBB*.

SALMON, Sir Isidore
(10 February 1876 - 16 September 1941)

Caterer and food manufacturer, the son of Barnett Salmon, the founder of the catering firm of Salmon & Gluckstein (later J Lyons). Educated privately, he began work in the kitchens of the Hotel Bristol in London and by 1900 was managing Lyons' catering ventures at venues such as the Crystal Palace. He eventually became chairman and managing director of Lyons, which for a time was the largest catering organisation in the world. Unlike other members of the Salmon and Gluckstein families, who shunned publicity, Isidore Salmon was a member of London County Council 1907-25 and Unionist MP for Harrow after 1924. He sat on a string of government committees and was catering adviser to the Army. He was also vice-president of the Board of Deputies of British Jews. He was made CBE in 1920 and knighted in 1933. In 1899 he married Kate Abrahams: they had two sons. See *Times*, 17 September 1941.

SAMUEL, Harold
Baron Samuel of Wych Cross
(23 April 1912 - 28 August 1987)

Property developer, born in Hampstead, London, the son of Vivian Samuel, a master jeweller, and his wife Ada née Cohen, he was educated at Mill Hill School and the College of Estate Management, qualifying as a chartered surveyor. He set up a private practice as an estate agent in Baker Street but

closed this down in order to avoid a conflict of interests with his property company, Harold Samuel Properties Ltd. In 1944 he bought a small property company, Land Securities Investment Trust. Its only assets were three houses and government securities totalling £19,321. By 1952 its assets were worth over £11 million. In 1973 it became the first British property group with assets of more than £1,000 million. These had grown to £3,000 million by 1987 when Samuel died (still in the chair at his death, though having relinquished the managing directorship in 1978). Expansion came in two building booms: the first postwar, the second in the 1960s. During both the property developers tapped huge sums from banks, insurance companies and pension funds to finance builders and contractors, making their profits from dextrous and highly profitable investments and leasing arrangements. In the late 1940s and early 1950s Samuel's LSIT grew by developing offices. He realised he could buy up blocks of flats, requisitioned in wartime for offices, and keep them as offices without having to pay development charges under the Town and Country Planning Act of 1947. Esso House in Stratton Street, Lansdowne House in Berkeley Square and Devonshire House in Piccadilly were examples of this policy. Though not as active a takeover bidder as his main rival Charles Clore (qv), Samuel expanded in part by acquisition. His much publicised but abortive attempt to take over the Savoy in 1953 brought criticism from the City establishment and epitomised two conflicting views of property: the traditionalists' emphasis on longevity of ownership versus the newcomers' perception of property as a commodity. In the 1960s Samuel moved into office development outside London and diversified into shopping centre schemes. His vehicle for the latter was Ravenseft Properties Ltd run by Louis Freeman and Fred Maynard. Initially financed by Samuel he took them over when their success was asssured. Ravenseft developments included schemes in Plymouth, Exeter, Bristol, Coventry, Hull, Sheffield and Swansea. When Jack Cotton, another arch-rival but as flamboyant and sprawling as Samuel was unobtrusive and precise, died in 1964, Sir Harold Samuel (he was knighted in 1963) acquired his City Centre Properties Ltd. From Clore he purchased City & Central Investments. In the property crisis of the early 1970s Lord Samuel (he was created a life peer in 1972) sold off many of his large shopping developments. Outside business he made large donations to the universities (chiefly Magdalene College, Cambridge and University College, London) and to medicine. He served on a number of public bodies including the Land Commission and the Covent Garden Market Authority and he chaired

SAMUEL

the Central London Housing Trust for the Aged. He married, in 1936, Edna Nedas; they had three daughters, one predeceasing him. Lord Samuel's estate was valued at £26 million. See Edward L Erdman, *People and Property* (1982); *The Times*, 1 September 1987.

SAMUEL, Walter Horace
2nd Viscount Bearsted
(13 March 1882 - 8 November 1948)

Oil company executive, the elder and only surviving son of Marcus Samuel (1853-1927), 1st Viscount Bearsted, and Fanny Elizabeth née Benjamin. His father was the founder and for many years the chairman of the Shell Transport & Trading Co. Educated at Eton and New College, Oxford, Samuel succeeded his father as chairman of Shell and was also a director of the family banking business of M Samuel & Co, of Lloyds Bank and the Alliance Assurance Co. He was also a lieutenant for the City of London, a chairman of the Trustees of the National Gallery and a trustee of the Tate. He was awarded the Military Cross in the First World War. He took part, but not as a Zionist, in the conferences of 1938 and 1939 called by the Secretary of State to resolve the Palestine situation. He married in 1908 Dorothea Montefiore Micholls: they had three sons. See *The Times*, 10 November 1948; *DBB* (Marcus Samuel).

SAUNDERS, Ernest (Walter)
(21 October 1935 -)

Drinks company executive, the son of Viennese Jews, Emanuel (Uly) Schleyer and Hanni née David. He came to London in 1938, when his family fled the Nazis. His father, a gynaecologist, set up a practice in London. Educated at St Paul's School, Hammersmith, and at Emmanuel College, Cambridge (MA), where he read law, he opted for business and specialised in the emerging discipline of marketing. He enjoyed a successful career with J Walter Thompson, Beecham, Great Universal Stores and the Swiss multinational Nestlé. He became chief executive of Guinness in 1981 and chairman in 1986. His move to Guinness saw a major restructuring of the ailing brewing combine, which under its chairman, the Earl of Iveagh (qv), had embarked on a disastrous policy of diversification. Saunders, allowed a free hand by Iveagh, initiated a return to the firm's core businesses and infused a more international outlook. Saunders' strategy culminated in the takeovers of the Bells and Distillers spirits groups, which made Guinness the second most profitable beverage company in the world (after Coca-Cola). But the bitter fight for Distillers in 1986 caused the most notorious financial scandal of the decade when Saunders and a

group of multi-millionaire investors, such as Gerald Ronson (qv), were accused and later convicted of false accounting and illegal share rigging. 'Deadly Ernest', as he was known, was sacked as Guinness chairman in 1987 and succeeded by (Sir) Anthony Tennant (qv), and was then sentenced to five years in jail. Protesting his innocence, ill-health won his release after only ten months in 1991. He has since made a swift recovery. He separated from his wife, Carole Anne Stephings, whom he married in 1963: they have two sons and one daughter. See Nick Kochan and Hugh Pym, *The Guinness Affair: Anatomy of a Scandal* (1987); James Saunders, *Nightmare: The Ernest Saunders Story* (1989).

SAVAGE, John Percival
(18 November 1895 - 22 February 1970)

Pharmaceutical company chairman, born in Nottingham, son of Robert Looker Savage, a railway guard, and his wife Mary née Pakes, he was educated at Mundella Grammar School, Nottingham, and joined Boots Pure Drug Co as an office boy in 1911. At headquarters he worked on the retail rather than the manufacturing side of Boots and became an understudy of John E Greenwood, the City-and-Cambridge chartered accountant who headed the retail side after the firm was taken over by L K Lidgett's United Drug Co in 1920. In the mid-1920s Savage was one of the promising young executives sent to the USA for training in American management methods. A strong personality, his position improved after 1933 when John Campbell Boot, 2nd Lord Trent (qv), retrieved the firm from American ownership in negotiations which left Trent estranged from Greenwood. During the Second World War, with Trent absent, Savage became a director in 1941 and effectively ran the firm. Then and thereafter he proved himself outstanding in implementing Trent's policies. His rewards came in 1951 when he was made vice-chairman and in 1953 when Trent chose him as successor. However, Savage's reign as chairman and managing director, 1954-61, proved to be an interregnum between more dynamic leaders. Uneasy in command, his insecurity induced him to shout and swear at subordinates who despised or feared him. To his commercial credit he abandoned the retail policy of simply buying more shops and instead created a two tier system of departmental stores in principal towns and big chemists shops in main secondary centres, despite the litigious opposition of the Pharmaceutical Society. Growth followed: in 1955 the company employed nearly 36,000, in 1959, 40,000 in the UK. Savage married, in 1922, Beatrice Maude Hodgson; they had a son and two daughters. See Stanley Chapman, *Jesse Boot of Boots the Chemist* (1974); *The Times*, 27 February 1970.

SCHICHT, George
(26 April 1884 - September 1961)
Chairman of a major commodities, food and detergents multinational, born at Aussig, Bohemia, the son of Johann Schicht (1855-1907). As soon as he left school, George (originally named Georg) joined the family soap business and became its president. In the 1920s there was a merger between the Schichts and the Dutch margarine firm, Jurgens & Van Den Bergh: they in turn merged with Lever Bros to form Unilever in 1929. In 1930 Schicht settled in the UK as a Unilever director and was naturalised seven years later. During 1932-37 he shared the chairmanship of Unilever with Francis d'Arcy Cooper (qv). In 1937 he moved to the Dutch company of the Group, remaining until his retirement in 1946. In 1909 he married Lena Eckelmann: they had three sons. See Charles Wilson, *The History of Unilever* (2 vols, 1954); *The Times*, 4 September 1961.

SCHOLEY, Sir David (Gerald)
(28 June 1935 -)
Banker, the son of Dudley and Lois Scholey. Educated at Wellington College and Christ Church, Oxford, he began his career as a Lloyd's broker. In 1965 he joined the merchant bank S G Warburg & Co and was groomed for executive responsibility by Sir Siegmund Warburg (qv), the founder of the Bank. Scholey became a director in 1967, deputy chairman ten years later, joint-chairman in 1980, and chairman in 1984. Under Scholey, the Bank's culture began to change from an Establishment outsider to a Bank at the centre of the financial system. S G Warburg was highly successful in the 1980s, pushing its staff up from a few hundred in the founder's day to about 6,000 in 1993. It took over Rowe & Pitman, founded in 1894; Ackroyd & Smithers, one of the two leading stock jobbers before the Big Bang; and Mullens, the long-established Government broker. Scholey built up an impressive client list that included ICI, GEC, Reuters and Reed Elsevier; and the Bank also gave help to the Government, handling a series of big privatisation deals, such as the £5.5 billion British Telecom share issue in 1992. Although Warburg suffered in the recession in 1992 - half year results showed a 35 per cent fall to £51.2 million - Warburg is the most profitable English merchant bank (though still far behind its international competitors, such as Goldman Sachs, Morgan Stanley, and Salomon). The success of Scholey's attempt to make Warburg the most influential merchant bank was signalled in 1992 when he was a strong contender for the Governorship of the Bank of England. He became a non-executive director of GEC in 1992. Scholey was made a CBE in 1976

and knighted in 1987. He married in 1960 Alexandra Beatrix, the daughter of the Hon George and Fiorenza Drew, Canada: they have one son and one daughter.

SCHOLEY, Sir Robert
(8 October 1921 -)
Steel manufacturer, the son of Harold and Eveline Scholey. He was educated at King Edward VII School and Sheffield University (Associateship in Mechanical Engineering). His father was a director of the English Steel Corporation and Scholey followed him into the Sheffield/Rotherham industry by joining Steel, Peech & Tozer (a United Steel subsidiary) as an engineer in 1947. On nationalisation in 1968 (when he was a director and works manager at Steel, Peech & Tozer), United Steel became part of the British Steel Corporation and Scholey joined the board in 1973. He became the right-hand man of first Ian Macgregor (qv) and then Lord Haslam (qv) in the drive to modernise and rationalise the BSC after its disastrous expansion in the 1970s. He became BSC chairman in 1986 - the first career steel man to head the organisation - by which time the BSC had returned to profitability. Between 1980 and 1992 British Steel's workforce was cut from 166,400 to 41,800 with dramatic increases in productivity that in 1990 made it briefly the most profitable steel company in the world (by 1990 it was also amongst the world's top five steelmakers in output). Scholey (nicknamed 'Black Bob') oversaw British Steel's privatisation in 1988 and bowed out in 1992 (with British Steel announcing its first loss of £55 million for seven years), handing over as chief executive to Brian Moffat. In 1946 he married Joan Methley: they have two daughters. He was knighted in 1987 and was president of the Institute of Metals in 1989. See Robert Scholey, 'European Steel: What Future?', *Ironmaking and Steelmaking* 14 (1987); Geoffrey F Dudley and Jeremy J Richardson, *Politics and Steel in Britain, 1967-88: The Life and Times of the British Steel Corporation* (1990).

SCHRODER, Rudolph Bruno
Baron Rudolph Bruno
(14 March 1867 - 10 December 1940)
Merchant banker, born in Hamburg, the son of Johann Rudolph Schroder I (1821-87) and Clara Louise Schroder. After education in Hamburg and military service, he joined the family's Hamburg merchant firm in 1888. In 1892 he was offered a post by his uncle, Baron Sir John Henry William Schroder, who ran the merchant banking firm J Henry Schroder & Co, the London branch of the Hamburg business. Bruno Schroder soon assumed executive control and under him the firm entered

two decades of prosperity: its acceptance business rose from £5 million in 1893 to £11 million in 1913, a sum surpassed only by Kleinwort's. Such was the firm's standing that upon the outbreak of the war, Schroder was swiftly naturalised by the Home Secretary, though his determinedly Anglo-German views meant that the family still suffered abuse. The firm was well placed to benefit from the growth of the American economy in the 1920s and the problems of the German banking system. By 1930 Schroders was the leading London accepting house, though the Central European Banking collapse in the 1930s broke its steady run of prosperity. In 1894 he married Emma Nee Deichmann, the daughter of a Cologne banker: they had two sons and two daughters. He left £502,503. See Stanley D Chapman, *The Rise of Merchant Banking* (1984); Richard Roberts, *A History of Schroders* (1992); *DBB*.

SCOTT, Charles Cuningham

(1867 - 1915)

Shipbuilder, born into the sixth generation of a family of shipbuilders first established at Greenock in 1711, the eldest son of John Scott (1830-1903), he was educated at Fettes College and Edinburgh University. During vacations he worked as an apprentice in the various departments of the yards (there were two in his time), an early graduate of the subsequently popular 'sandwich' system, and in 1890 became assistant engine works manager under his uncle Robert Sinclair Scott. When the firm was converted into a limited liability company in 1900 C C Scott was promoted to assistant general manager and, on the death of his father, was appointed one of the managing directors. When his uncle, R S Scott, died in 1905 he succeeded as chairman, remaining in charge until his own death. Under C C Scott the yards built the first Dreadnought battleship, the *Colossus*, to be launched on the Clyde (in 1910). Further armoured ships followed and engines were installed in others. C C Scott was a member of the Royal Company of Archers and lieutenant-colonel of the 3rd Highland Howitzer Brigade and the Royal Field Artillery. Politically he was a Conservative. C C Scott married, in 1898, the daughter of H E Crum Ewing; they had four daughters. In the firm he was succeeded by his brother Robert Lyons Scott (d 1939). See Anon, *Two Centuries of Shipbuilding by the Scotts at Greenock* (3rd edn, 1950); *The Bailie*, 13 April 1910; *The Times*, 13 February 1915.

SCOTT, Charles James Cater

(17 January 1849 - 19 January 1931)

Dock company executive, son of Alexander Reid Scott of Stokes Hall, Jamaica, and St James's Street,

London, he rose to be a partner in John Cater & Sons, merchant bankers. He became a director of the London & St Katherine Docks Co and by 1888 its chairman. He also chaired the Joint Committee which ran the two major dock companies, the London & St Katherine and the East & West India Dock Co, from 1889. When the two were merged in 1901 to form the London & India Docks Co, Cater Scott (as he was known) was chosen as its first and only chairman. With 4,600 employees (in 1907), 80 per cent of dock accommodation in the Port of London, and a capital of £20 million the LIDC presented old challenges on a new scale. Problems facing London dock companies included the proliferation of large steamships; the consequent movement of some companies eastwards (the East & West India Dock Co opened its Tilbury deep water docks, 26 miles from London Bridge, in 1886); the subsequent surplus dock space close to London; competition from lighters based on river wharves and bonded warehouses in the City and excused from paying dock dues by the free-water clause written into all the dock Acts; complaints from shipowners and London Chamber of Commerce of high charges, poor rail links and a confusing division of authority; and poor labour relations. All of this was investigated in 1900-2 by the Royal Commission on the Port of London to which Cater Scott gave evidence. He recommended a limitation on dock company dividends and an obligation on the companies to provide new facilities. The Commission commended the quality of Cater Scott's evidence but recommended the creation of a public authority to take over all London's docks and wharves. This met sustained opposition until Lloyd George, President of the Board of Trade, concluded from Continental models that docks were preferable to riverside quays and in 1908 made a deal with Cater Scott for the purchase of the LIDC and with parliamentary sanction set up the Port of London Authority. Cater Scott was excluded from the chairmanship of the PLA because it was a public authority. He was a director of a number of other companies, including the United Railways of Havana, the Mexican Railway Co, the Manila Railway Co, the London General Omnibus Co (and chairman, 1912-19), the Underground Electric Railways Co of London (1902-31), and the Westminster Bank. From 1892 he was a director of the North British & Mercantile Insurance Co and its chairman, 1903-26. Scott married, in 1879, Constance, daughter of Major Charles Norris. See *The Times*, 21 January 1931; Joseph G Broodbank, *History of the Port of London* (2 vols, 1921); Theodore C Barker and Michael Robbins, *A History of London Transport* (2 vols, 1963-74).

SHAH

SELF, Sir (Albert) Henry
(18 January 1890 - 15 January 1975)

Chairman of the British Electricity Authority, son of Samuel Adolphus Theodore Self, an omnibus conductor, and his wife Mary Jane née Wills, he was educated at Bancrofts School, Woodford, and in 1907 entered the civil service. By 1919 he had worked in the Board of Trade, the War Office, the General Post Office, the Foreign Office, the Local Government Board and the Ministry of Munitions. Meanwhile he had launched on part-time academic study which saw him amass five undergraduate degrees in science, classics, divinity and philosophy between 1911 and 1934, an MSc in the philosophy of science (1951) and a PhD on philosophical inter-actions between religion and science (1956), all from London University. He was also called to the Bar at Lincoln's Inn in 1922. From 1919 until 1941, when he became director general of the British Air Commission in Washington, he served in the Air Ministry. Sir Henry Self (he was knight-ed in 1939) was appointed permanent secretary to the Ministry of Production in 1942, deputy chair-man of the British Supply Council in Washington in 1945 and permanent secretary to the Ministry of Civil Aviation in 1946. He joined the recently-nationalised electricity industry as deputy chairman of the British Electricity Authority in 1947 and succeeded Lord Citrine (qv) as chairman in 1957, retiring in 1959. Citrine put Self in charge of administration and backed him against the central-ising policies of Sir John Hacking, the other deputy chairman, in charge of engineering. In the power station programme Self introduced competitive tendering (in 1954), had reservations about gradu-ate recruits, (with Citrine) supported the expansion of the nuclear programme in 1956, and made the important proposal for separating the generation and distribution of electricity. Power was firmly decentralised in 1957, when a new Central Electricity Generating Board and twelve existing Area Boards became directly responsible to the Minister of Fuel and Power. Central authority reposed in an Electricity Council of which Sir Henry Self was caretaker chairman while Professor Ronald Edwards was being groomed for the post. Self succeeded in ensuring that the Ministry dealt with the Boards via the Council. His prime weak-ness lay in failing to raise domestic standing and incremental charges in line with long-run costs. Articulate and reflective, Self wrote several pieces about his industrial experience including *Problems of Decentralisation in a Large-Scale Undertaking* (1951). He was made a KCMG in 1942 and a KCB in 1947. Outside business Sir Henry Self was promi-nent in the Modern Churchmen's Union. He mar-ried in 1918 Rosalind Audrey, daughter of Sir John

Lonsdale Otter; they had two sons, Professor Peter J O Self and Hugh Michael Self QC. See Leslie Hannah, *Engineers, Managers and Politicians* (1982); *The Times*, 17 January 1975.

SELFRIDGE, Harry Gordon
(11 January 1858 - 8 May 1947)

Department store retailer, born at Ripon, Wisconsin, USA, the only son of Robert Oliver Selfridge, who ran a dry goods store, and Lois Frances née Baxter. Educated at public school in Jackson, Michigan, he joined the retailing business of Marshall Field in Chicago, becoming general manager in 1886. He reputedly made $1 million working for (and later partnering) Field, but by 1906 he struck out on his own by opening his own store in Oxford Street, London, where he began the 'Americanisation' of the capital's retailing. More interested in showmanship than in finance, Selfridge's business (which became the Gordon Selfridge Trust with £2 million capital in 1926) turned in steady profits until 1925, when they hit a record of £440,000, but in the 1930s his flamboyant and extravagant business methods proved less suit-able. The board forced him to retire in 1939 and he died propertyless. In 1890 he married Rose Amelia Buckingham: they had four children. See H G Selfridge, *The Romance of Commerce* (1918); Reginald Pound, *Selfridge: A Biography* (1960); *DBB*; *DNB*.

SHAH, (Selim Jehane) 'Eddie'
(20 January 1944 -)

Publisher, born in Cambridge, the first of four chil-dren of Moochool and Hazel Shah. His father was a world authority on maritime law; his mother was the daughter of a well-known Cambridge boat builder. His early childhood was spent in India, but on his return to England he attended Gordonstoun (from which he was suspended), Reigate Grammar School and Haywards Heath secondary modern school. His chief interest was sport and his academic record undistinguished. After some theatre work, where he picked up the nickname 'Eddie', he became a production manager on the soap opera *Coronation Street*. In 1974 after experience on a free newspaper published by the *Manchester Evening News*, he launched his own newspaper, the *Sale and Altrincham Messenger*. By 1983 he had built up profits of £600,000 on a £5 million turnover. In that year he came into national prominence with a spectacular battle with the print unions, notably the National Graphical Association, over union recognition at Shah's Stockport Messenger Works. He eventually won and then decided to establish a new non-union national colour newspaper, *Today*. It was a financial disaster and was later sold to Tiny Rowland's (qv) Lonrho and then to Rupert Murdoch. Afterwards

185

SHAW

he continued with the Messenger group, had another unsuccessful try at launching a paper (the *Post*), and dabbled in television, though his golden touch appeared to have deserted him. By 1990 he was planning to concentrate on television production, property development and providing venture capital for small businesses, and was also writing novels. In 1970 he married Jennifer White, a former TV presenter and model: they have two boys and a girl. See Eddy Shah, *Ring of Red Roses* (1991); David Goodhart and Patrick Wintour, *Eddie Shah and the Newspaper Revolution* (1986).

SHAW, Joseph
(1856 - 14 December 1933)
Steam and coal company chairman, son of Joseph Shaw, educated at Malvern and Trinity College, Cambridge, he was called to the Bar at the Inner Temple in 1887. He practised at the Parliamentary Bar for a number of years and became a KC in 1910. Shaw became a director of the Powell Duffryn Co, operating in the Rhymney and Aberdare valleys in South Wales, in 1888, the year the PD board appointed him to a three-man managing committee of control. His fellow members on that committee, Henry Bolden and Graeme Ogilvie, served as PD chairmen but died in office. Shaw was elected chairman in 1897 and continued until 1928, retiring from the PD board in 1930. Under Shaw and his senior manager, Edmund Hann (qv), PD became the largest coal company in South Wales by 1907 when it employed 6,000 and produced four million tons of coal a year. Shaw was also a member of the South Wales and Monmouthshire Coal Conciliation Board and a director of the Great Western Railway Co (of which the PD was a significant customer). He lived for many years at Kentchurch Court near Hereford and latterly at Adderbury House near Banbury. Shaw married twice: first, in 1885, to Charlotte (d 1897), daughter of Sir Philip C Smyly, by whom he had a son and a daughter; second, in 1926, to Constance Isabel, fifth daughter of Sir Philip Smyly. See Anon, *The Powell Duffryn Steam Coal Co Limited, 1864-1914* (1914); A P Barnett and D Willson-Lloyd, *The South Wales Coalfield* (1923); *The Times*, 15, 19 December 1933.

SHAW, Neil (McGowan)
(31 May 1929 -)
Sugar company executive, born in Montreal, the son of Harold LeRoy Shaw and Fabriola Marie Shaw. Educated at Knowlton High School and Lower Canada College, Canada, he became trust officer for the Crown Trust Co in Montreal, 1947-54. He then joined the Canada & Dominion Sugar Co (later renamed Redpath Industries) in Montreal

as a merchandising manager. In 1959 Redpath was taken over by Tate & Lyle, which eventually brought Shaw onto the board of the British-based sugar producer, which was in some trouble in the face of European Commission legislation favouring beet sugar, rather than cane sugar manufacturers like Tate & Lyle. He became chairman of Tate & Lyle in 1981 and was also chief executive, 1986-92 (handing over to Stephen Brown). Shaw recognised that sugar was not the only sweetener customers wanted, so he moved into fructose corn syrup production. In 1988 Tate & Lyle took over Staley Continental (a major American corn wet milling business), another major US sweetener business, Amstar, and later announced the development of an artificial sweetener. Shaw had thus positioned the company to give it a strong place in cane, beet and corn-based sweeteners, and also a foot in the artificial sweeteners market. In 1991 turnover was £3,262 million (pre-tax profit £234 million) and the company had 17,500 workers. When profit fell in 1992 to £190 million, it was the first drop since 1978. It was at that time embroiled in a £150 million takeover bid for the Australian group, Bundaberg Sugar. Shaw also held directorships at Texaco Canada, Scottish & Newcastle Breweries and United Biscuits. He was chairman of Business in the Community in 1991. He married twice: the first in 1952 to Audrey Robinson (dissolved) produced two sons and three daughters; the second was in 1985 to Elisabeth Fern Mudge-Massey. See Philippe Chalmin, *The Making of a Sugar Giant: Tate & Lyle 1859-1989* (1990).

SHEEHY, Sir Patrick
(2 September 1930 -)
Tobacco and insurance company executive, the son of Sir John Francis Sheehy (1889-1949) CSI, and Jean Newton Shrimpton. Educated in Australia and at Ampleforth College, Yorkshire, he served in the Irish Guards, 1948-50, before joining the British-American Tobacco Co. After sales experience in Africa and the West Indies, he became a director in 1970 and chairman in 1976. Like many tobacco manufacturers, British-American Tobacco has needed to diversify, and by 1980 Sheehy had moved the company into perfumes and department stores. After 1982, he further reshaped the company (now renamed BAT Industries, with Sheehy as chairman), shedding some of its acquisitions such as its stores, but adding others such the insurance firms Eagle Star and Allied Dunbar. Nevertheless, BAT (which now employs over 200,000) is still heavily reliant on its famous tobacco brands such as Lucky Strike, Kent and Benson & Hedges: in 1992 BAT's pre-tax profits increased 68 per cent to £1,645 million (from revenue of £22,093 million),

to which tobacco had contributed £1,314 million in trading profit - a record year for tobacco sales. Like other tobacco manufacturers, BAT looks forward confidently to peddling its carcinogens in expanding export markets, such as the Third World and the former Soviet Union, and Sheehy believes 'these are the most exciting times I have seen in the tobacco industry in the last forty years'. In 1993 he announced the appointment of BAT's first chief executive, Martin Brougton, though he set no firm date for his retirement from the chairmanship, having already stayed on longer than his expected departure date in 1991. He was knighted in 1991. In 1964 Sheehy married Jill Patricia Tindall: they have a son and a daughter.

SHEPHERD, Sir William Walker Frederick

(13 October 1895 - 28 February 1959)

Asbestos manufacturer, born in Everton, Liverpool, eldest son of Walker Shepherd, a wine and spirit porter, and his wife Jane née Cramp, he was educated privately. After the First World War, in which he served as an officer in the Cheshire Regiment in France and Palestine, he held several minor commercial posts before joining Turner & Newall, the asbestos manufacturing company formed in 1920 by a merger between Turners of Rochdale and Newalls of Washington near Gateshead. Shepherd became company secretary in 1927, a director in 1931, joint managing director in 1938, and vice-chairman in 1942. He succeeded Sir Samuel Turner (qv) as chairman of Turner & Newall Ltd in 1944. Demand for asbestos products, deriving heavily from the building and motor vehicle trades, was especially strong between the wars and in the 1950s and 1960s. Between 1935 and 1955 the company's UK workforce doubled up to 20,000. These were organised in three groups, processing asbestos in the forms of textiles (Rochdale, Chapel-en-le-Frith in Derbyshire, Leeds, and Dungannon), cement (headquartered at Trafford Park, Manchester) and insulation materials (at Washington, County Durham). Another 20,000 employees worked abroad in mining and manufacturing subsidiary companies in Africa (5), North America (3), India (2) and Brazil (1). Sir Walker Shepherd (he was knighted in 1956) died in office, being found dead on a train in Canada. He was also a director of the London & Globe Insurance Co, the Royal Insurance Co and the District Bank. He was a member of the Millard Tucker Committee on Trading Profits (1949), a governor (and fund raiser) of Manchester University, a benefactor of the Royal College of Surgeons and master of the Worshipful Company of Needlemakers. In 1930 Shepherd married Isabel Cromwell, elder daughter

of Frederick W Ingham; there were no children. See *The Times*, 2, 11 March 1959; *Turner & Newall: The First Fifty Years, 1920-1970* (1970).

SHEPPARD, Sir Allen (John George)

(25 December 1932 -)

Food, drink and retailing company executive, the son of John Baggott Sheppard and Lily Marjorie née Palmer. Educated at Ilford County High School and the London School of Economics (BSc Econ), he qualified as an accountant and spent seventeen years in the car industry, with Ford, Rootes/Chrysler and British Leyland. In 1975 he was headhunted by Grand Metropolitan, the hotel and drinks group founded by Maxwell Joseph (qv), becoming managing director in 1982. During the 1980s GM had diversified into the US health-care market with the acquisition of Quality Care Inc. Sheppard changed this strategy while he was chief executive and chairman, 1986-87, recommending the sale of Quality Care and the resumption of the purchase of core businesses such as Hublein Inc from Nabisco in 1987 and Pillsbury in 1989. The purchase of these US drinks and food firms doubled the size of GM; it then shed its Intercontinental Hotels group in 1988. GM's main divisions and most famous brands now include food (Pillsbury), drink (J & B, Cinzano) and retailing (Burger King). Turnover in 1991 was £8.7 billion with pre-tax profits of £963 million (80 per cent of which are generated abroad) and the group employed 105,000 workers. Sheppard has also served as chairman of the UBM Group, Mallinson-Denny, and the Prince's Youth Business Trust. In 1992 he was asked to help in the Tory Party's management review ordered by John Major. He is twice married: first in 1959 to Peggy Damaris née Jones (dissolved 1980); second in 1980 to Mary née Stewart. He was knighted in 1990. See A J G Sheppard, *Your Business Matters* (1958); Grand Metropolitan, *Facts and Figures 1988: 25 Dynamic and Successful Years* (1988).

SHILLITO, John

(19 January 1832 - 12 February 1915)

Co-operative Wholesale Society chairman, born at Upper Brear near Halifax, the son of George Shillito, a farm labourer, and his wife, Jane, he attended a village dame school and at 14 was apprenticed to a wiredrawer. Afterwards he worked for Gaukroger Bros, card clothing manufacturers in Halifax, staying with them as a foreman until 1883. He joined the Halifax Co-operative Industrial Society in 1861 and in 1870 was first elected to the board of directors of the CWS which had been formed in 1863 under the Industrial and Provident Societies Act of 1862 (the product of co-operators' pressure), allowing one company to invest in another. Shillito retired from the CWS board in 1871 but was re-elected in 1883 and remained until his death, serving as vice-chairman in 1892-95, and chairman, 1895-1915. Under his leadership the CWS continued to move from warehousing to factory processing, a policy established by his predecessor, John T W Mitchell. To the manufacture of biscuits, bread and flour Shillito and his fellow-directors added furniture, clothing, boots, hardware, leather goods, jam, cocoa, tea, tobacco (a controversial move) soap and cutlery. The CWS grew from 14 mills and factories, 6,390 employees and sales of £10.1 million in 1895 to 48 works and factories, 20,994 employees and sales of £31.3 million in 1913. Under Shillito the CWS also made the transition from part-time to professional management, with the appointment of a salaried secretary, Thomas Brodrick (qv), in 1899, and the creation in 1906 of a salaried (£350 per annum) 32-member board of directors. Shillito was president of the Co-operative Congress in 1903. A Liberal, a free-trader and a Unitarian, he remained active almost to the end, visiting Ceylon in his eighty-second year. He married, in 1856, Frances née Sykes; they had four sons and a daughter. See Joyce M Bellamy and John Saville (eds), *Dictionary of Labour Biography* (7 vols, 1972-84) vol 1; Percy Redfern, *The New History of the CWS* (1938).

SHORT, Herbert Arthur
(22 March 1895 - 15 November 1967)
Railway manager, born at Parkstone near Poole, Dorset, son of George Short, foreman railway plate-layer, and his wife Annie Eliza née Masters, he was educated at Bournemouth School and joined the London & South Western Railway Co in 1913. After the First World War, in which he served with the Suffolk Regiment and received the MC, he returned to the LSWR and its post-1922 successor, the Southern Railway. He became docks and marine manager and during the Second World War chaired Southampton Port Emergency Committee, serving also as an officer in the Royal Engineers (Territorial Army). In 1945 he became deputy traffic manager of the Southern Railway and was seconded to the Colonial Office and the Argentine government to advise on transport problems, also visiting Malaya and South America. On the nationalised railways in Britain Short became acting chief officer (docks) of the Railway Executive in 1948 and then chief officer of the North Eastern Region of British Railways in 1950. Under the Transport Act of 1953 six area boards became directly reponsible to the British Transport Commission chaired by General Sir Brian Robertson (qv) and their chief regional managers, like Short on the North Eastern Region, were given authority over their divisional

managers. In 1957 Short went with the BTC team to study railways in the USA. After retiring he became a director of several transport companies in the North East and Dorset. Short married, in 1921, Gladys May née Waterson; they had a son. See T R Gourvish, *British Railways, 1948-73: A Business History* (1986).

SHOWERING, Sir Keith Stanley
(6 August 1930 - 23 March 1982)
Drinks, food and catering manufacturer, born in Shepton Mallet, son of Herbert Showering and Ada Foote. Educated at Wells Cathedral School and Long Ashton laboratories, he joined the family cider business in 1947 at a time of expansion due to the successful marketing of the perry, Babycham. In the 1960s and 1970s he was responsible for running some of the firm's new acquisitions, such as Whiteways and Harveys. In 1975 he became chairman of Allied Breweries into which Showerings had merged: it was the biggest alcohol company in Europe with a sixth of the UK's pubs. On his initiative, in 1979 the group then acquired the old-established food and catering business of Lyons, forming Allied-Lyons, the largest drinks and food company in the UK. Showering was also a vice-chairman of the Guardian Royal Exchange Assurance Co in 1974 and a director of the Bank of England in 1979. He was knighted in 1981. In 1954 he married Marie Sadie née Golden, the daughter of a company director: they had four sons and two daughters. He died at a Bank of England industrial meeting. See *DNB*.

SHUTE, Sir John (Joseph)
(1873 - 13 September 1948)
Cotton industralist, born in Liverpool, the elder son of John J Shute and his wife, Mary. Educated privately and at the Catholic Institute in Liverpool, he entered the cotton broking firm of Reynolds & Gibson. He made rapid progress, having discovered and rectified a series of irregularities which had involved substantial losses, and was made a partner. He succeeded Sir James Reynolds as head of the firm, travelling widely in Europe, the USA, and Africa. He became chairman of Combined Egyptian Mills Ltd (which employed 10,500 in 1935), and was also a trustee and member of the executive of the Empire Cotton Growing Association, chairman of the United Trades Association of Liverpool, and president of the Liverpool Cotton Association. In 1933 he became Conservative MP for the Exchange Division of Liverpool and was knighted in 1935. He had a distinguished military record, winning the DSO in 1916, and retiring from the Army as colonel in 1923. Unmarried, he did much philanthropic work

for children and the Liverpool Repertory Theatre. See *The Times*, 14 September 1948.

SIDDELEY, John Davenport
1st Baron Kenilworth
(5 August 1866 - 3 November 1953)

Motor car and aero-engine manufacturer, born at Chorlton, Manchester, the son of William Siddeley (1837-1911), a hosier, and Elizabeth née Davenport. Educated at Altrincham and Beaumaris in Anglesey, he worked for a number of cycle, tyre and motor car firms, becoming manager of Wolseley Motors (a Vickers' subsidiary) in 1905-9. In 1909 he co-founded the Siddeley-Deasy Motor Co in Coventry, and also manufactured aero-engines during the war. In 1919 the business was bought by the Armstrong, Whitworth group, which eventually (in 1926) brought Siddeley onto the Armstrong head board. In 1935 he sold control of Armstrong-Siddeley to Hawkers (forming Hawker-Siddeley), retiring shortly afterwards. He was a president of the Society of British Aircraft Constructors, 1931-33, and of the Engineering & Allied Employers' Federation, 1934-36, and sometime president of the Society of Motor Manufacturers & Traders. He was made a CBE in 1918, knighted in 1932, and made a peer in 1937. He married in 1893 Sarah Mabel née Goodier: they had two sons and daughters. He left £354,597 net in England. See David Thoms and Tom Donnelly, *The Motor Car Industry in Coventry Since the 1890s* (1985); *DBB*.

SIDGREAVES, Sir Arthur Frederick
(12 June 1882 - 7 June 1948)

Aero-engine and motor car manufacturer, born in Singapore, the son of Sir Thomas Sidgreaves, a chief justice in the colony, and Barbara Catherine née Young. Educated at Downside College, Bath, his early commercial experience was with D Napier & Son, motor car manufacturers. In 1920 he joined Rolls Royce and was its managing director between 1929 and 1946, when turnover at Rolls Royce (UK) Ltd rose from £2.2 million to nearly £34 million. Amongst Sidgreave's achievements was the development of the famous Merlin engine. He was president of the Society of British Aircraft Constructors, 1942-43, and was knighted in 1945. In 1938 he married Dorothy Jessica née Bryant; an earlier marriage to Mable Winter, which produced two sons, had been dissolved. He committed suicide and left £115,888 gross. See Ian Lloyd, *Rolls-Royce* (3 vols, 1978); *DBB*; *DNB*.

SIEFF, Israel Moses
1st Baron Sieff of Brimpton
(4 May 1889 - 14 February 1972)

Chain store retailer, born in Manchester, the son of Ephraim Sieff, a Lithuanian Jew, and Sarah née Saffer. After reading economics and commerce at Manchester University, his early training was with his father's cloth business. In 1915 he joined Marks & Spencer and within two years was on the board of this retailing business, having helped his close friend Simon Marks (qv) gain control. In 1926 Sieff joined Marks & Spencer full time as vice-chairman. He became Simon's 'alter-ego' in the business, and was particularly influential in moulding the firm's social outlook, with its emphasis on benevolent paternalism, and in forging direct links between retailer and manufacturer. When Marks died in 1964, Sieff became chairman, by which time other members of the Sieff family, such as his son Marcus (qv), were on the board. He retired in 1967, when turnover was over £280 million. He was keenly interested in Britain's industrial situation and for many years supported the independent research body, Political and Economic Planning. Zionism was his major public interest and he was a close friend of Chaim Weizmann. He was made a life peer in 1966. In 1910 he married Rebecca, sister of Simon Marks, and had two sons and a daughter. He left £164,808 in the UK. See Asa Briggs, *Marks and Spencer 1884-1984* (1984); *DBB*; *DNB*.

SIEFF, Marcus Joseph
2nd Baron Sieff of Brimpton
(2 July 1913 -)

Chain store retailer, born in Didsbury, Manchester, the younger son of Israel Moses Sieff (qv) and his wife Rebecca. He was educated at Manchester Grammar School, St Paul's, and Corpus Christi College, Cambridge (where he took a second in economics), then served in the Royal Artillery during the Second World War. He joined the family firm, Marks & Spencer, in 1935 and steadily worked his way up the family hierarchy (director 1954, vice-chairman 1965, joint-managing director 1967-83, chairman 1972-84). His term as chairman was marked by extensive merchandize development and the company's expansion overseas. He continued to strengthen Marks & Spencer's commitment to good labour relations with a crusading fervour. Sieff was knighted in 1971 and made a life peer in 1980. Sieff has been a Zionist for over fifty years. He has been married four times: his son from his first marriage, David Daniel Sieff (b 1939), is a director of Marks & Spencer. See Marcus Sieff, *Don't Ask the Price* (1987), *Management the Marks & Spencer Way* (1990).

SIGRIST, Frederick
(1884 - 10 December 1956)

Aircraft engineer and manufacturer, born in Jersey, the son of Edward Sigrist. He joined Tom Sopwith (qv) in 1909, first as auxiliary marine engineer and then as collaborator in the Sopwith Aviation Co. When the company won its first War Office order in 1913, Sigrist became works manager of 100 men. Within five years production was 16,000 aircraft. He was described as a workshop man, who pioneered the greater use of metals in airframes, and nurtured budding designers such as (Sir) Henry Camm. When the firm was renamed the H G Hawker Engineering Co in the 1920s, Sigrist became a director. He stayed with the company through successive reorganisations and eventually became one of the joint-managing directors of the Hawker Siddeley Group Ltd. Ill-health ended Sigrist's involvement in 1939, when he left for Nassau in the Bahamas. He married in 1935 Beatrice Macknight née Burton: they had one daughter. See *The Times*, 12, 13, 14 December 1956.

SIMON, David (Alec Gwyn)
(24 July 1939 -)

Oil company executive, born in London, the son of Roger A D J Simon, an engineer, and Barbara née Hudd. He attended Christ's Hospital, the public school, and then read languages at Caius College, Cambridge, with the help of a British Petroleum Co grant. He joined BP's European marketing division in 1961, taking a BP-sponsored MBA at the European Institute of Business Administration. After several senior posts in marketing, he emerged in 1982 as managing director of BP Oil International. He became a key individual in transforming BP from a government-owned bureaucracy into a more competitive company (for example, in 1987 he was closely involved in the disastrous public flotation of BP shares still owned by the Government). When Sir Peter Walters (qv) retired as chairman in 1990, Simon became deputy chairman and chief operating officer under Robert Horton (qv). Simon's low-key approach made him Horton's natural successor when the latter's more abrasive style and policies failed to produce results at a recession-hit BP. Simon became chairman in 1992 and was immediately faced with a £711 million net loss for the first half of the year, which resulted in a halving of the dividend and future redundancies. Simon, who was made CBE in 1991, is also a non-executive director of Grand Metropolitan. In 1964 he married Hanne née Mohn: they have two sons.

SIMON, Ernest (Emil Darwin)
1st Baron Simon of Wythenshawe
(9 October 1879 - 3 October 1960)

Industrialist, born in Didsbury, Manchester, the son of Henry Simon (1835-99) and Emily née Stoehr. His father's firms - Henry Simon Ltd and Simon-Carves Ltd - were Manchester-based engineering contractors in flour milling and coke oven technology. Educated at Rugby and Pembroke College, Cambridge, Simon joined the business in 1901 and nine years later was chairman. By the mid-1950s (when he retired), Simon-Carves (which went public in 1957 with £4 million capital) had become one of the world's leading engineering firms: employment, for example, grew from 350 in 1910 to 7,802 in 1953. But Simon was equally well known as a committed socialist: a friend of the Fabians, he helped found the *New Statesman*, and became closely involved with the problems of local government in Manchester (of which he became mayor in 1921). He was Liberal MP for Withington (1923-24, 1929-31), but joined the Labour Party in 1946, which brought him a peerage in 1947 (he had been knighted in 1932) and the chairmanship of the BBC 1947-52. He was deeply concerned about world problems of over-population and nuclear armaments, founding the Simon Population Trust and actively supporting the CND. Like his father, he supported scientific education, especially at Manchester University, where he contributed to the building of the Jodrell Bank telescope and provided research fellowships. In 1912 he married Dorothy Shena Potter, the daughter of a shipowner: they had two sons and a daughter. Lord Simon left £397,564. See Anthony Simon, *The Simon Engineering Group* (1953); Ernest Simon, *A City Council from Within* (1926); Mary Stocks, *Ernest Simon of Manchester* (1963); *DBB*; *DNB*.

SINCLAIR, Sir Clive (Marles)
(30 July 1940 -)

Electronics manufacturer and inventor, born at Richmond, Surrey, the son of George William Carter Sinclair, a mechanical engineer, and Thora Edith Ella née Marles. Educated at a number of preparatory schools and St George's College, Weybridge, he worked in publishing before founding Sinclair Radionics in Cambridge in 1962 to market miniature radio and hi-fi kits. He became famous in 1972 for marketing the world's first pocket calculator, the Executive. In 1979 Sinclair Radionics was taken over by the National Enterprise Board. In the same year Sinclair Research was formed and in 1980 its chairman launched the ZX range of home computers: priced under £100, they sold over a million in the first two years. By 1986 intense competition in the UK computer market and the failure of some of Sinclair's projects (notably his C5 electric car) led to the rights of all Sinclair Research products being sold to Alan Sugar's (qv) Amstrad for £5 million. Far more talented as an inventor than as a businessman, Sinclair latest projects include a folding bicycle and a more sophisticated electric car. A chairman of British Mensa, he was knighted in 1983. In 1962 he married Ann née Trevor Briscoe (dissolved 1985): they had two sons and a daughter. See Clive Sinclair, *Practical Transistor Receivers* (1959); Rodney Dale, *The Sinclair Story* (1985).

SINCLAIR, Sir Leonard
(9 June 1895 - 9 August 1984)

Petroleum executive, born in Broughton, Salford, the son of John Sinclair, a Manchester warehouseman, and his wife Mary née Cannan, he was educated at the Higher Grade School, Broughton which he left at the age of 12 to become a boy clerk with Anglo-American Oil Co Ltd. Formed in 1888 as the British subsidiary of John D Rockefeller's Standard Oil Co, this had become the UK's largest importer of paraffin and by 1901 was receiving and storing oil in Trafford Park at the eastern end of the Manchester Ship Canal. The break-up of Standard Oil in 1911 left Anglo-American independent. After the First World War, in which he served with the Royal Welch Fusiliers, the Cheshire Regiment and the Machine Gun Corps, Sinclair returned to Anglo-American and became an authority on petrol, gas and fuel oil. His company was reacquired in 1930 by Standard Oil Co of New Jersey who proceeded in 1938 to open a refinery at Stanlow, near Ellesmere Port on the Ship Canal, in addition to the small refinery at Fawley near Southampton it had acquired in the early 1920s. Sinclair was appointed a director of Anglo-American in 1943, managing director in 1949 and in 1951 chairman also. That year Anglo-American changed its name to Esso Petroleum Co Ltd. After the Second World War, when government policy encouraged the shift of refining from the Middle East to the UK for strategic reasons, Esso built a new refinery at Fawley, with American technical assistance, which started large-scale production in 1951. Initially costing £37 million, it had an annual capacity of 8 million tons in 1956 when Fawley was second only to the Thames estuary as a refining site. Its products were used in the expanding petro-chemicals and plastics industry (major customers in the 1950s being Monsanto Chemicals Ltd and International Synthetic Rubber Co Ltd) as well as for motor vehicle fuel. By the mid-1950s Esso had plants at Purfleet, Avonmouth, Bowling (Glasgow), Mode Wheel (Manchester) and Salt End (Hull), besides Fawley and Stanlow. A new refinery capable of processing 4.5 million tons of crude annually was built at Milford Haven in the late 1950s. Esso Petroleum also controlled British Mexican Petroleum Co, Esso Petroleum Co (Ireland) and Cleveland Petroleum Co. In 1956 the Esso tanker fleet comprised 21 vessels, four of 45,600 tons. At this date the company had 15,000 employees. Esso petrol and oil were marketed through a chain of franchised garages and service stations. Sir Leonard Sinclair (he was knighted in 1955) retired from Esso in 1958. He was a director also of the (American) Esso parent, of several related British petroleum companies and was a part-time member of the British Transport Commission, 1958-61. Sinclair married, in 1926, Mary Levine; they had a daughter. See Duncan Burn, *The Structure of British Industry* (2 vols, 1958); D A Farnie, *The Manchester Ship Canal and the Rise of the Port of Manchester* (1980); *The Times*, 13 August 1984.

SINCLAIR, Robert John
1st Baron Sinclair of Cleeve
(29 July 1893 - 4 March 1979)

Tobacco manufacturer, born in Glasgow, only son of Robert Henry Sinclair, a cotton manufacturer and merchant, and his wife Margaret née McWhannell, he was educated at Glasgow Academy and Oriel College, Oxford. During the First World War he was seconded to the Ministry of Munitions as deputy director of munitions inspection, 1917-19, after being severely wounded at Gallipoli with the King's Own Scottish Borderers. In 1919 he joined Imperial Tobacco, the combination headed by Wills of Bristol and including Players and Churchmans, formed in 1901. From assistant company secretary in 1920, Sinclair became secretary in 1927, a director in 1933, and deputy chairman in 1939. That year he became a member of the prime minister's panel of industrialists. During the Second World War he was director-general of army requirements, 1939-42; member of the Army Council, 1940-42; deputy for the Minister of Production on the Combined Production and Resources Board in Washington, 1942-43; chief executive, the Ministry of Production, 1943-45; and served at the Board of Trade in 1945. Sir Robert (he was knighted in 1941 and made a KCB in 1946) returned to Imperial Tobacco after the war and became chairman in 1947. As Lord Sinclair (he was created a baron in 1957) he retired in 1959 but was made president of Imperial Tobacco, stepping down finally in 1967. During his time the company grew from 33,000 UK employees in 1953 to 46,000 in 1961, its component firms maintaining their long-held market dominance (together producing 90 per cent of British cigarettes). Outside the business of the family-controlled tobacco giant,

Sinclair was pro-chancellor of Bristol University, president of the Federation of British Industries (1949-51), and high sheriff of Somerset (1951). He married, in 1917, Mary daughter of Robert Shearer Barclay of Randfontlin, South Africa; they had two sons. See B W E Alford, *W D & H O Wills and the Development of the UK Tobacco Industry, 1786-1965* (1972); *Daily Telegraph*, 6 March 1979; Anthony Sampson, *Anatomy of Britain* (1962).

SKINNER, Ernest Harry Dudley
(27 July 1892 - 27 August 1985)
Bank and coal industry executive, born in Tottenham Court, London, son of Henry Thomas Skinner, a postal service overseer in the General Post Office, and his wife Harriet née Mead, he was educated privately and entered the Bank of England in 1911 and served as private secretary to the Governor, Montagu Norman (qv), 1929-32; deputy secretary of the Bank of England, 1932-35; and assistant to the Governors, 1935-45. He was closely associated with the Bank of England's involvement in the rationalisation of British industry in the late 1920s and 1930s and its efforts to improve the provision of finance for industry. A close adviser of Norman, Skinner advocated a scheme whereby trade associations in concert with a Whitehall committee, rather than City institutions, would regulate finance for industry. This was rejected and instead two new institutions, the Finance Corporation for Industry and the Industrial & Commercial Finance Corporation (the former for big businesses, the latter for smaller enterprises) were established in 1945, the Bank of England being a shareholder in each and Skinner becoming general manager of the FCI. In 1947 Skinner followed the FCI chairman, Lord Hyndley, to the National Coal Board where Hyndley had become the first chairman. Skinner chaired the Northern Division of the NCB, 1947-50, and then the Durham Division, 1950-57. By 1955 of the NCB's nine divisions Durham ranked third largest in manpower (102,000), third largest by output (25.5 million tons), but seventh in output per manshift. After leaving the NCB Skinner became a member of the Colonial Development Corporation, until 1960. Outside business he was involved in St John's Ambulance work, served on Newcastle Regional Hospital Board (1958-59) and was a regional vice-president of the Northern Counties Amateur Boxing Association. He married, in 1921, Edith Lilian née Stretton; they had a son and a daughter. See William Ashworth, *The History of the British Coal Industry vol 5 1946-1982: The Nationalised Industry* (1986); John Fforde, *The Bank of England and Public Policy, 1941-1958* (1992); *The Times*, 30 August 1985.

SKINNER, Sir Sydney Martyn
(21 July 1864 - 3 March 1941)
Department store manager, left school at 14 and became apprenticed to John Lewis, in Oxford Street. After several appointments he went to the store of John Barker & Co, Kensington, where he eventually became chairman. He transformed the business into a department store of the front rank, employing 6,700 by 1935. He was a past president of the Incorporated Association of Retail Distributors, of the Drapers' Chamber of Trade, and of the Acton Hospital. He was knighted in 1922. In 1902 he married Emiline Madeline, daughter of Samuel Belling. See *Times*, 6 March 1941.

SLATER, James (Derrick)
(13 March 1929 -)
Financier, born in Wembley, north London, the only son of Hubert Slater, owner of a small building and decorating business in Kensington, and his wife Jessica. Educated at Preston Manor County School, he was articled to an accountant and, after National Service, qualified in 1953. After working for a London metal finishing company and an unsuccessful attempt in 1955 to run his own consultancy with friend Kenneth Meyer, in 1956 he joined Park Royal Vehicles as company secretary. This eventually led to a management post at the Associated Equipment Co and in 1963 a deputy sales directorship at the Leyland Motor Corporation Ltd. Meanwhile, Salter acquired a reputation as a share dealer and in 1964 set up Slater Securities Ltd, with his friend and Conservative MP, Peter Walker. Under Slater's chairmanship the company grew phenomenonally in its supposed role as an investment consultancy, industrial conglomerate and bank and became synonymous with Edward Heath's 'New Tories'. But the real speciality of Slater Walker was share manipulation and after the stock market boom faltered in 1970-72 his fortunes rapidly declined. In 1975 Slater Walker collapsed and he resigned, with Walker distancing himself from his partner's excesses. According to the company's biographer: 'While Slater certainly did make money for other people, and himself, in good times, he also lost it for them - and himself - in bad'. Slater is still in demand as a stock analyst, writing books and newspaper articles: he has also written childrens' books. He married in 1965 Helen Wyndham Goodwyn: they have two sons and two daughters. See James Slater, *Return to Go* (1977); Charles Raw, *Slater Walker: An Investigation of a Financial Phenomenon* (1977).

SMALLPEICE, Sir Basil
(18 September 1906 - 12 July 1992)

Transport company executive, born in Rio de Janeiro, Brazil, the son of Herbert Charles Smallpeice, a bank manager, and his wife Georgina née Rust, he was educated at Shrewsbury School and then articled with the London accountants, Bullimore & Co. After qualifying as a chartered accountant in 1930 (and gaining part-time a London BCom the same year) he went into industry with Hoover Ltd, 1930-37; Doulton & Co, as chief accountant and company secretary, 1937-48; and the British Transport Commission, as director of costs and statistics, 1948-50. In 1950 Sir Miles Thomas (qv) recruited him as financial comptroller of British Overseas Airways Corporation, another nationalised and troubled concern. Unassuming, dapper and a man of great integrity, Smallpeice quietly and precisely imposed order on BOAC's accounts. He joined the BOAC board in 1953, becoming deputy chief executive in 1954 and managing director in 1956, head of 18,000 employees. Though he had no aviation or engineering experience he assembled a very able senior management team. He reintroduced the Comet, following the correction of its earlier catastrophic metal fatigue problems, in 1958 and brought into service the Boeing 707 in 1959-60. Relations between government and BOAC management deteriorated following attempts by Smallpeice and his chairman, Admiral Sir Matthew Slattery, to make BOAC profitable by writing off its debt of £80 million, most spent in breaking in British aeroplanes or acting 'in the national interest'. On the basis of a secret report he had commissioned, the Minister of Aviation, Julian Amery, asked Slattery and Sir Basil Smallpeice (he was made a KCVO in 1961) to resign. No match for the politicians, they and three other directors did so, with a widely-shared feeling of injustice. From BOAC Smallpeice in 1964 joined the board of the Cunard Steam-Ship Co (which had formed a joint airline company with BOAC in 1962). Cunard had been run by the Bates (qv) and Brocklebank families but by the 1950s (when it employed 15,000) was suffering from a neglect of modern management techniques. As chairman of Cunard, 1965-71, Smallpeice took radical decisions which brought the company back into profit in mid-1968: management was moved from Liverpool to Southampton; passenger ships were moved from scheduled services to cruising; the loss-making Queen Mary and Queen Elizabeth were retired in 1967; large investments were made in container ship ventures; the Queen Elizabeth 2 was only taken into service after the correction of defects in 1969. When Cunard was taken over by Trafalgar House headed by Nigel Broackes (qv) in 1971 Smallpeice moved to the TH board before accepting the invitation of Duncan Sandys, the new chairman of Lonrho, to be non-executive deputy chairman. Very soon he was in conflict with Roland 'Tiny' Rowland (qv), the managing director. In 1973 Smallpeice and seven other directors resigned from Lonrho. He completely retired from his business posts in 1979. Between 1964 and 1980 he was administrative advisor to the Royal Household. Sir Basil was also a council member of the Insitute of Chartered Accountants, 1948-57, and of the British Institute of Management, 1959-64 and 1965-75 (chairman, 1970-72). In private life he was an Anglican and, in the 1940s, a member of the Christian Frontier Council. Smallpeice married Kathleen Ivey Singleton Brame in 1931; following her death in February 1973 he married in November 1973 Rita Burns, his secretary at Cunards since 1966; there were no children. See Sir Basil Smallpeice, *Of Comets and Queens* (1981); *The Times*, 13 July 1992.

SMITH, Sir Alexander Rowland
(25 January 1888 - 19 April 1988)

Car manufacturer, born at Gillingham, Kent, the son of Alexander James Frederick Smith, a builder, and his wife Martha Pilaster née Challis, he was educated at the Mathematical School, Rochester, and afterwards apprenticed at Humber Ltd in Coventry, qualifying as a jig and tool designer. In 1914 he became manager for the distribution of Ford cars in Bengal, Burma and Assam, based in Calcutta. By 1929 he was back in Britain as general manager of Ford, one of the triumvirate (the others were Patrick Hennessy (qv) and Stanford Cooper) under Sir Percival Perry (qv) responsible for moving Ford's UK manufacturing operations from Trafford Park, Manchester, to a greenfield site at Dagenham, Essex. Begun in 1929, the Dagenham works represented an investment of £2 million in a highly integrated plant which reached full production in 1932 when 25,571 vehicles came off the production line, including the first Ford car specifically designed (by Smith and American engineers) for the British market, the Model Y (retailing at £120). Smith became managing director of Ford of Britain in 1941, the year he went to the USA with a Ministry of Aircraft Production mission. He also managed two shadow factories in Manchester, insisting (against Whitehall scepticism) on using female workers to assemble Merlin engines. By the end of the Second World War the Dagenham plant had made 360,000 fighting and transport vehicles. Sir Rowland Smith (he was knighted in 1944) became chairman of Ford of Britain in 1950, retiring in 1956. His period in office saw growth by acquisition (of Briggs Motor

Bodies in 1952) and internal expansion: employment rose from 16,668 to 45,355, output from 185,124 to 325,291 vehicles, of which the Consul, Zephyr, new Anglias and Prefects, and the Popular (the old Anglia) sold well. By 1956 Ford had just over 30 per cent of the UK vehicle market, exceeded only by the British Motor Corporation (the 1952 merger of Austin and Morris). Smith was also a director of National Provincial Bank and a member of the UK Atomic Energy Authority. In 1948 he joined the Ministry of Pensions standing advisory committee on artificial limbs, and the government committee on procedure for ordering civil aircraft. His hobby was sailing and he lived to be 100. Smith married, in 1913, Janet Lucretia née Baker; they had a son and a daughter. See *The Times*, 22 April 1988; Mira Wilkins and Frank E Hill, *American Business Abroad: Ford on Six Continents* (1964).

SMITH, Clarence Dalrymple
(1869 - 1941)

Iron and steel company executive, the son of a merchant shipowner and MP. Smith became involved in the north-east wire rope business, before entering management (he held his first directorship in 1915) in the Durham iron and steel trades. From 1925 to 1935, he was chairman of the Consett Iron Co Ltd: by 1935 this firm employed 6,914, but during the decade after 1924 it paid no dividends - a reflection of the depressed state of trade and the need for reorganisation at the company. Smith continued as director until 1939, when he retired. He was also a director of his father's firm, Smith's Docks Ltd. He left £45,329. A Conservative and a JP, he was awarded the OBE. See Kenneth Warren, *Consett Iron 1840 to 1980* (1990).

SMITH, The Honourable David John
(20 May 1907 - 26 November 1976)

Newsagent and bookshop company executive, the third son of William Frederick Danvers Smith (qv), 2nd Viscount Hambleden, head of the family firm of W H Smith & Son, and his wife Lady Esther Gore, third daughter of the 5th Earl of Arran. Educated at Eton and Oxford, he had two years of world travel and a short time in the City before entering the family firm in 1930. He became a partner in 1935 and on the death of his brother, William Henry Smith (qv), 3rd Viscount Hambleden, in 1948 he succeeded as governing director (soon re-styled chairman) of the operating company W H Smith & Son Ltd. A year later he became chairman of the newly-formed public holding company, W H Smith & Son (Holdings) Ltd. He remained chairman of both companies

until 1969 and 1972 respectively but stayed on as a director of the holding company. Under his leadership the firm sold the partnership to the public to raise £6 million needed for death duties on his brother's estate; further shifted its retail business from railway bookstalls to large city-centre shops; added gramophone records to the staple merchandise of newspapers, magazines, books and stationery; reorganised the wholesale side into regional groups; moved book distribution from London to a giant purpose-built warehouse with computerised inventory control at Swindon (completed 1967); and opened the chairmanship to non-family members (also in 1967). In 1960 the functions of the two boards were defined, the holding company dealing with high finance and basic policy, the 'limited' board with operational matters. These were radical moves for David Smith, a natural conservative, who adjusted swiftly to the considered opinions of his boards and advisors. The result was rapid growth between 1949 and 1972 when employees increased from 15,312 to 17,514, turnover from £26.2 million to £45.8 million and profits from £1.3 million to £2.5 million (£s indexed at 1950=100). David Smith was a director of Lloyds Bank and of the Union Discount Co of London. Outside business he was lord lieutenant of Berkshire (where he lived), 1959-75; high steward of Wallingford; chairman of the delegacy of King's College, London; and council member of Bradfield College. Smith married, in 1931, Lady Helen Pleydell-Bouverie, daughter of the 6th Earl of Radnor; they had four sons and a daughter. See *The Times*, 27 November 1976; Charles Wilson, *First with the News: The History of W H Smith, 1792-1972* (1985).

SMITH, Sir Harold Charles
(1890 - 6 September 1970)

Gas Council chairman, born in Aston, Birmingham, son of William Henry Smith, stationmaster, and his wife Sarah Betsy née Groscock, he was educated at King Edward VI School, Aston, and entered the gas industry in 1906 when he started in the laboratories of the Birmingham Gas Department. He joined the Worcestershire Yeomanry in 1907, was later commissioned in the Territorial Field Artillery and served throughout the First World War in the Royal Field Artillery. By the mid-1940s Smith was managing director and deputy chairman of the Tottenham Gas Co, one of 700 private or municipal gas companies in the UK. In 1947 he became chairman of the British Gas Council, a body representing several central bodies in the industry, which voted to oppose the Labour government's legislation to nationalise gas. However, once the Gas Act became law in 1948 the BGC voted to implement the enforced takeover as efficiently as possible. Under nationalisation the generation and supply of gas were undertaken by 12 autonomous area boards whose chairmen sat on a new Gas Council established to shape national policies. Smith was appointed deputy chairman of the Gas Council on its inception and then served as chairman, 1952-59. Understanding that reliance on coal limited the industry's growth, he initiated vigorous research into substitutes which, though not immediately fruitful, built up an R & D culture and resources that his deputy and successor Frank Jones (qv) utilised in exploiting North Sea gas. Smith was made a military CBE in 1944 (in the TA he had the rank of colonel) and knighted in 1953. He changed his name by deed poll to Templar-Smith in 1967. In 1917 he married the daughter of Reuben Heaton; they had two daughters. See *The Times*, 10 September 1970; Trevor I Williams, *A History of the British Gas Industry* (1981).

SMITH, Sir Henry Babington
(29 January 1863 - 29 September 1923)
General Post Office executive, the son of Archibald Smith FRS of Jordanhill, Renfrewshire, an eminent mathematician and property lawyer, he was educated at Eton and Trinity College, Cambridge, gaining firsts in both parts of the classics tripos. He entered the Civil Service in 1887, serving as an examiner in the Education Department, as private secretary to the Chancellor of the Exchequer (Goschen), secretary to the British delegates at the Brussels Monetary Conference (1892), and private secretary to the Viceroy of India (Elgin). At the beginning of the Boer War he was Treasury representative in Natal and from 1900 British representative on the council of administration of the Ottoman public debt (president, 1902-3). He returned home in 1903 to become Secretary of the General Post Office, in the tradition of the experienced generalist, rather than a Post Office career administrator. With over 210,000 employees this was the largest business organisation in the UK economy. Babington Smith, still in his forties, discharged his office to the satisfaction of his political masters, both Conservative and Liberal. He represented the GPO and Britain at international telegraphic and postal conferences and at the first radio-telegraphic conference, held in London in 1912. Sir Henry Babington Smith (he was knighted in 1908 and made a GBE in 1920) left the Post Office in 1909 to become president of the National Bank of Turkey, which he was instrumental in forming. In 1914 he was appointed chairman of the Pacific Cable Co (jointly owned by five governments). During the First World War he was on the Anglo-French Commission which negotiated an American loan (1915). On another mission to Washington, headed by Lord Reading in 1918, he was concerned with food aid. Meantime in 1915 he chaired a royal commission on the Civil Service. After the war he chaired the Indian finance and currency committee of 1919 and, in 1921-22, the railway amalgamation tribunal which produced the four railway groups of the interwar years. Smith married, in 1898, Lady Elisabeth Bruce, daughter of the 9th Earl of Elgin; they had four sons and five daughters. See Martin J Daunton, *Royal Mail: The Post Office since 1840* (1985); *The Times*, 1, 2, 3 October 1923.

SMITH, Professor Sir Roland
(1 October 1928 -)
Company director and management consultant, born in Manchester, the son of Joshua Smith, a police sergeant, and his wife Hannah. Educated at Birmingham University, his PhD in 1954 was on the economic history of the Lancashire textile industry. He served as a flying officer in the RAF in 1953. Appointed lecturer in economics at Liverpool University in 1960, he became a director of its Business School in 1963, where he began to build up links with firms such as Esso and RTZ. After 1966, when he became part-time professor of marketing at the University of Manchester Institute of Science & Technology, his lucrative consultancies and non-executive directorships began to multiply. In the 1970s he became involved with businesses ranging from Smith & Nephew to City firms like Midland Bank and Kleinwort Benson. Smith first came to public notice in 1980 when he was invited on to the board of the House of Fraser: until 1986, when the Fayed's (qv) took over, Smith's brief was to keep the predatory Tiny Rowland (qv) of Lonrho at bay. Smith acquired a reputation for dynamism, toughness, coupled with a wry sense of humour, though his touch was far from infallible: the share performance of many of his adopted companies in the 1970s - such as Senior Engineering and Barrow Hepburn - was hardly distinguished. In 1987 he became chairman of British Aerospace, the UK's largest exporter and its second biggest manufacturing company with 110,000 staff. Following two disastrous decisions - the purchase of Rover cars for £150 million and an attempt to convert many of BA's engineering assets into property - BAe's profits slumped from £376 million to under £200 million in 1990-91. After an unsuccessful distress rights issue, Smith in September 1991 was deposed by a boardroom coup. Named in 1990 as Britain's busiest businessman, he still held about ten directorships including the chairmanship of his beloved Manchester United football club. Smith was knighted in 1991. He

SMITH

married Joan née Shaw in 1954. See Ivan Fallon and James Strodes, *Takeovers* (1987).

SMITH, William Frederick Danvers
2nd Viscount Hambleden
(12 August 1868 - 16 June 1928)

Newspaper-distribution and stationery company proprietor, born at Filey, Yorkshire, the younger and only surviving son of William Henry Smith II (1825-91), the 'Son' in W H Smith & Son and a well-known statesman, and his wife, Emily née Danvers, he was educated at Eton and New College, Oxford, gaining a third in history in 1890. The following year he succeeded his father as head of the family firm. During his time the business grew from something over 4,000 to over 12,000 employees. Much credit for this expansion must go to Charles Harry St John Hornby (qv) whom Freddie Smith (as he was known) recruited in 1892. When the hard-pressed railway companies sought to increase their income from W H Smith & Son contracts in the 1890s, Smith gave his backing to Hornby's proposal to spread their assets out of railway bookstalls and into urban bookshops. By 1906 Smith & Son had 200 such bookshops, in the long term saving themselves from the decline which overtook the railways. Freddie Smith, a devout Anglican and epitome of the Christian gentleman, saw the establishment of company superannuation and pension funds in the mid-1890s. Outside the firm he was chiefly interested in philanthropic work, especially London's voluntary hospitals (pre-eminently King's College Hospital). During the First World War he served in Gallipoli and Egypt (1915-16) with the Royal 1st Devon Yeomanry. He inherited his mother's peerage (created after the death of his father) on her death in 1913. Smith married, in 1894, Lady Esther, daughter of Arthur Gore, 5th Earl of Arran; they had three sons and two daughters. See *The Times*, 18, 19, 20 June 1928; Charles Wilson, *First with the News: The History of W H Smith, 1792-1972* (1985).

SMITH, Sir William George Verdon
(1876 - 19 February 1957)

Aircraft manufacturer, born in London, the eldest son of William George Smith (d 1889), he was brought up after his father's death by two maternal uncles, George (qv) and Samuel White, Bristol stockbrokers and pioneers of electric tramways, motor buses and aircraft. He entered the stock-broking firm and specialised in preparing legislation for tramway undertakings. In 1901 he became secretary of the London United Tramways (promoted and chaired by his uncle George) but in 1911 returned to the Bristol Tramways & Carriage Co Ltd as assistant to the managing director, becoming managing director himself in 1916 on the death of his uncle, then Sir George White. He became a director of the Bristol Aeroplane Co (founded in 1910 by Sir George White) in 1927 and chairman a year later, retiring in 1955. The peacetime contraction of the 1920s reversed in 1934 when rearmament started. At Bristol Aeroplane, one of the first-rate aircraft constructors on the Ministry list, the workforce rose from 4,300 in 1934 to 8,000 in 1935 and 14,000 in 1938, peaking during the Second World War at 58,000. In 1955, in post-Korean War peacetime, the firm employed 21,000. The company's board was dominated by the White family, gentlemanly kin who found it nigh-impossible to control or accept their brilliant aero engine designer, Roy Fedden (responsible for the Bristol Jupiter engine). Bristol Aeroplane made none of the five most successful British aircraft of the Second World War. In the following decade it built at Filton the giant Brabazon airliner, a commercial flop, and the Britannia, another, much more successful, turbo-prop. Sir George Verdon Smith (he was knighted in 1946) was a director of the Western National Omnibus Co (and its chairman), Lloyds Bank and Bristol Gas Co. A Conservative and a Presbyterian, he married, in 1911, Diana Florence (d 1928), elder daughter of M Anders; they had a son, Reginald (qv), and a daughter. Smith married secondly Hilda Beatrice née Jackson-Barstow in 1934. See Charles Harvey and Jon Press (eds), *Studies in the Business History of Bristol* (1988); *The Times*, 20 February 1957.

SMITH, William Henry
3rd Viscount Hambleden
(25 July 1903 - 31 March 1948)

Newspaper distributor and bookseller, the eldest son of William Frederick Danvers Smith ('Freddy'), 2nd Viscount Hambleden (d 1928), and Lady Esther (Caroline Georgiana) Gore. William H Smith ('Billy'), was educated at Eton and New College, Oxford, and then entered the business, W H Smith, founded by his great-great grandfather towards the end of the eighteenth century. Billy was head of the firm from 1928 until his death, ably assisted by C H St John Hornby (qv): a difficult period, which nevertheless saw turnover rise from about £4 million to £10 million and the workforce from 12,000 to 14,000. W H Smith became a public company on Hambleden's death, a move prompted by death duties of £6.1 million payable on his estate of £8.1 million (most of it being assets of W H Smith & Son Ltd). He married in 1928 Lady Patricia Herbert, only daughter of the 5th Earl of Pembroke: they had three sons and two daughters. See *The Times*, 1, 5, 6, 9 April 1948; Charles Wilson, *First With the News: The History of W H Smith 1792-1972* (1985).

SNAPE, Thomas Henry
(1849 - 11 July 1929)
Early twentieth-century managing director at John Hetherington & Sons, textile machine makers and a limited company since 1894. Located at the Vulcan, Phoenix and Ancoats works, Manchester, Hetheringtons employed 4,200 in 1907. In the 1890s Hetheringtons were in the forefront of floating contractors' spinning companies as one way of developing their markets; the policy, by creating competition, aroused the ire of existing spinners. Snape was also chairman of the Soudan Mill Co Ltd, registered in 1903 and running 267,500 spindles in three mills at Middleton in 1921: another example of the linkage between machine makers and spinners. Snape died at Withington in his eightieth year. See *Manchester Guardian*, 13 July 1929; Mike Williams with D A Farnie, *Cotton Mills in Greater Manchester* (1992)

SOLOMON, Sir Harry
(20 March 1937 -)
Food manufacturer and distributor, the son of Jacob and Belle Solomon. Educated at St Albans School and the Law Society School of Law, he qualified as a solicitor in 1960 and then ran his own practice. In 1975 he co-founded Hillsdown, merging his own property interests with the meat businesses of David Thompson (qv). In 1980 Solomon resigned from his law firm as Hillsdown began a period of rapid expansion: in ten years the two men bought 284 new businesses (many of which were bought from the receiver, but soon responded to streamlined management) and borrowed £600 million. Profits rose from £116,000 to £110 million. Hillsdown specialised in producing chickens, bacon, eggs and vegetables, usually sold with various supermarket brand labels attached. After 1987, two years after Hillsdown was floated as a public company, Thompson began selling his shareholding and left the business, leaving Solomon as chairman. Between 1987 and 1992 Hillsdown's turnover increased from £3,038 million to £4,656 million, pre-tax profits from £108 million to £186 million. In 1991 the group employed over 48,000. In 1992, after Hillsdown's share priced halved after a £218 million rights issue flopped, Solomon announced he would relinquish the posts of chief executive and chairman by April 1993 in favour of Sir John Nott. Solomon was knighted in 1991. He married in 1962 Judith Diana Manuel: they have one son and two daughters.

SOOTHILL, Ronald Gray
(19 August 1898 - 18 August 1980)
Asbestos manufacturer, the son of the Reverend Alfred Soothill, a United Methodist minister and from 1905 principal of Ashville College, Harrogate,

and his wife, H E Gray, daughter of the Reverend Richard Gray, he was educated at Ashville College, and Mill Hill School. He served in the Royal Artillery, 1917-18, and afterwards went to Jesus College, Cambridge, taking a degree in mathematics and economics. From Cambridge he went straight to Cadbury Bros Ltd, training as a manager in the large-scale organisation, 1922-28. He joined Turner & Newall Ltd in 1928, becoming a main board director under fellow-Methodist Sir Samuel Turner (qv) in 1942. He was made a joint managing director, with Harry Hanson in 1949, deputy chairman in 1958 and, when Sir Walker Shepherd (qv) died suddenly, chairman in 1959. He retired in 1967 and was made honorary president until 1973. Under his leadership the company continued to meet the demand for asbestos materials from the building and motor vehicle trades, but it stabilised its labour costs by holding its global employment figure at 40,000 between 1955 and 1965. Soothill was a director of the District Bank, Royal Insurance Co, William Mallinson & Sons, Liverpool & London & Globe Insurance Co, London & Lancashire Insurance, and Tube Investments. He sat on the Committee of Inquiry into Shipping, 1967-70 and was a member of the court of Manchester University and chairman of the governors of Ashville College. He married, in 1926, Thelma, eldest daughter of Edwin J Bird; there were no children. See *The Times*, 21 August 1980.

SOPWITH, Sir Thomas Octave Murdoch
(18 January 1888 - 17 January 1989)
Aircraft manufacturer, born in Kensington, London, the son of Thomas Sopwith Jr (1838-98), an engineer and lead mining entrepreneur, and Lydia Gertrude née Messiter. After attending Seafield Engineering College, Tom Sopwith used his inheritance to indulge his taste for motor cars, boats and, increasingly, aeroplanes. In 1912 he founded the Sopwith Aviation Co at Kingston-upon-Thames to manufacture his own designs, with the help of Frederick Sigrist (qv). It flourished during the First World War, but in the 1920s it was reorganised as the Hawker Engineering Co with Sopwith as chairman of a talented design team. By 1935 Sopwith had merged with other leading makers to form the Hawker Siddeley Aircraft Co Ltd and the firm was poised to make a vital contribution to the war effort with aircraft such as the Hurricane. Sopwith was chairman, a post he held until 1963: by which time his group was one of the two main UK airframe manufacturers, capitalised at £43.7 million with 127,000 employees. He was chairman of the Society of Aircraft Constructors, 1925-6; awarded a CBE in 1918; and was knighted

in 1953. Sopwith was twice married: in 1914 to the Hon Beatrix Mary Leslie Hore-Ruthven (d 1930); and in 1932 to Phyllis Brodie, by whom he had a son. See Bruce Robertson, *Sopwith - The Man and His Aircraft* (1970); DBB.

SORRELL, Martin (Stuart)
(14 February 1945 -)

Marketing services entrepreneur, born in London, the son of Jack Sorrell, a prosperous Jewish electrical retailer, and his wife Sally. He attended Hasmonean, a Jewish school in Hendon, before reading economics at Cambridge University (second class BA) and taking an MBA at Harvard. In 1968 he joined Glendinning Associates as a marketing trainee, then in the early 1970s gained further experience with Mark McCormack and James Gulliver (qv). He made his first £1 million as a finance director, 1977-86, for the Saatchi brothers (qv). In 1985 he became a major partner in WPP (Wire & Plastic Products), an obscure maker of wire baskets. Within four years Sorrell made WPP Britain's second biggest marketing services company after Saatchi's: by 1988 sales were £547 million and profits £40 million. Sorrell launched an aggressive campaign of acquisitions in the USA, where he bought the J Walter Thompson Group in 1987 for $500 million; then in 1989 took over the Ogilvy Group (despite David Ogilvy's description of him as 'an odious little jerk [who has] never written an advertisement in his life'). Like many of the Thatcherite heroes of the 1980s, Sorrell's empire did not fare well in the recession of the early 1990s: in 1992 WPP had debts of $1 billion, which it had to reschedule for the second time. Sorrell married in 1971 Sandy Finestone: they have three sons. See Judi Bevan and John Jay, *The New Tycoons* (1989); Tom Lloyd, *Entrepreneur!* (1992).

SOUTHGATE, Colin Grieve
(24 July 1948 -)

Computer software and electronics company executive, the son of Cyril Alfred Southgate and his wife Edith Isabelle. Educated at the City of London School, he joined International Computers Ltd (later ICL) in 1969 and a year later founded Software Services. In 1980 Southgate's company was absorbed into BOC Computer Services Division, of which he became chief executive. In 1983 he joined Thorn EMI Information Technology and two years later was Thorn's managing director. In 1987 he became chief executive of Thorn EMI and has also been chairman since 1989. Under Southgate Thorn has been transformed from a sprawling and declining conglomerate associated with electrical fittings and light bulbs, into a business dominated by its music and TV rental interests. EMI Music (to which

Southgate has added in 1992 the Virgin music business of Richard Branson (qv) for £500 million) is now the third biggest record company in the world and Thorn also has an international rental business and interests in lighting, electronics and security systems. Under Southgate turnover has risen from £2,939 million in 1988 to £3,954 million in 1992 (with pre-tax profits of £225 million and £255 million, respectively), with a workforce of over 53,000. Southgate also holds non-executive directorships at Lucas, Prudential and Powergen. In 1962 he married Sally Patricia Mead: they have two sons and two daughters.

SPENCER, Sir Henry Francis
(8 April 1892 - 31 May 1964)

Iron and steel merchant and manufacturer, born at Sedgley, Staffordshire, son of Henry Francis Spencer, a boat loader, and his wife Alice, he left school at 13 and went to work in a foundry. At 22 he was a self-made iron and steel merchant and by the early 1930s H F Spencer & Co Ltd was a major distributor of steel sheets, especially to the motor vehicle industry. In 1935 his business became associated with Richard Thomas & Co, a leading tin-plate manufacturer headed by Sir William Firth (qv), and Spencer joined as sheet sales controller. The firm merged with Baldwins in 1944 to become Richard Thomas & Baldwins. Spencer became commercial general manager in 1948, director in 1949, assistant managing director in 1951 and managing director in 1953, initially under Ernest Lever (qv) as chairman. Knighted in 1963, he died in office at a difficult time for the government-owned RTB, which employed 25,000 in 1955. In the mid-1950s the Macmillan government decided to subsidise a new strip steel mill in South Wales (and another in Scotland) to meet future demand. On a greenfield site and in record time Spencer built the giant integrated works at Llanwern near Newport, costing £150 million, producing 1.4 million tons of steel a year and employing 6,000 people. Rising costs and a slump in world steel demand meant that it opened in 1962 to face virtual bankruptcy and only by 1965 (after Spencer had died) was it able to pay its way. The works were named after him. Spencer, a discreet supporter of nationalisation, was a council and executive committee member of the British Iron and Steel Federation and a vice-president of the British Institute of Management. He married, in 1916, Ethel May née Southall; they had one daughter. See *The Times*, 2, 4, 6, 11 June 1964; John Vaizey, *The History of British Steel* (1974).

SPENCER, Sir Thomas George
(1888 - 29 February 1976)

Cable manufacturer, the son of Thomas and Mary Spencer. Educated at the Polytechnic and the Royal Ordnance School, Woolwich, he joined the engineering staff of Western Electric Co Ltd in 1907. He later became chief cable engineer and was closely associated with the development of long-distance telephone systems. Later, as director of cable manufacture, he supervised the building of factories and organised the production of the first long-distance telephone cables in twelve European countries. In 1930 he became European director of manufacture for International Standard Electric Corporation, of which his company had become a part, and was managing director of Standard Telephone & Cables Ltd (the company's new name) from 1932 to 1957. He was chairman of STC from 1951 to 1965, when the firm expanded rapidly (employment grew from nearly 8,000 in 1935 to nearly 23,000 in 1955). In 1943 he founded the Telephone Communication Engineering & Manufacturing Association, of which he served as chairman and life president. He was a member of the governing body of Woolwich Polytechnic from 1939 and its chairman from 1949 to 1952. Knighted in 1946, he was made a knight commander of St Gregory in 1958 for communications services to the Vatican. He was twice married: first in 1914 to Grace Adelaide Player, by whom he had one son; second, in 1953 to Ethel Bailey (Ethel Bilsland, FRAM), the youngest daughter of James Bilsland. See Peter Young, *Power of Speech: A History of Standard Telephones and Cables, 1883-1983* (1983).

SPENCER, Victor Albert Francis Charles
1st Viscount Churchill
(23 October 1864 - 3 January 1934)

Railway company chairman, only son and heir of Francis George Spencer, 2nd Baron Churchill of Whichwood, and his wife Jane, daughter of the 2nd Marquess Conyngham, he was educated at Eton and the Royal Military College, Sandhurst, being commissioned into the Coldstream Guards in 1884 and retiring as a subaltern in 1889. He succeeded his father as Lord Churchill in 1886 and from 1889 until 1905 was a lord-in-waiting, holding numerous other Court appointments. He was created a viscount in 1902. In the House of Lords he served as a Conservative whip for many years. In 1908 he succeeded Alfred Baldwin as chairman of the Great Western Railway Co, remaining in the chair until his death. Employing 70,000 in 1907, the GWR was still expanding before the First World War with the opening of shorter routes from Paddington to Taunton and to Birmingham and from Bristol to Birmingham. After the merger of the country's 130

railways into four groups in 1922 the GWR came to employ over 95,000 by 1935. Churchill was a conscientious chairman whose political and Courtly connections reinforced the GWR's proud image as a premier railway company. In the City he was also a director of the British Overseas Bank (chairman for ten years), the Grand Union Canal Co, the Peninsular & Oriental Steam Navigation Co and the British India Steam Navigation Co. He married twice: first, in 1887, to Lady Verena Maud Lowther, daughter of the 3rd Earl of Lonsdale, by whom he had two sons and two daughters, and whom he divorced for desertion in 1927; second, in 1927, to Christine McRae née Sinclair by whom he had a son and a daughter. See *The Times*, 4 January 1934.

SPRIGGS, Sir Franks Spencer
(29 March 1895 - 11 June 1969)

Aircraft manufacturer, born at Kettering, Northamptonshire, the son of William Samuel Spriggs, a caterer, and his wife Katharine née Jackson, he was educated at Westbourne School and in his late teens moved to London where he became an office boy for T O M Sopwith (qv) in 1913. During the First World War he moved into Sopwith's workshops and built up a detailed knowledge of aeroplane production. From 1920 until the early 1930s, a time of meagre demand for aircraft, Spriggs worked for Sir W G Armstrong Whitworth Aircraft Ltd (and after 1926 its successor under J D Siddeley (qv)). In 1933 Spriggs was again working for Sopwith, as general manager and director of Hawker Engineering Co Ltd. When Sopwith acquired Gloster Aircraft Co the following year he installed Spriggs as chairman. In 1936 the Air Ministry rated Glosters as among the best managed aircraft manufacturers. In addition to these posts, by 1939 Spriggs was managing director of six firms belonging to the Hawker Siddeley Aircraft Co (organised in 1935). It was Spriggs and Sopwith who promoted the development of the Hawker Hurricane fighter aircraft as a 'private venture' (a company design, not an Air Ministry specification). By 1943 he had succeeded Sopwith as chairman of all the companies in the Hawker group except the parent company. In effect he was executive chairman and as such shared with Sopwith the credit for managing a wartime labour force which exceeded 100,000 and which produced over 40,000 aircraft (including the highly successful Avro Lancaster bomber and the Hawker Hurricane fighter) and over 50,000 engines. Glosters built the first aircraft to fly with a Whittle jet engine (15 May 1941) in recognition of which Spriggs was knighted (and further honoured with a KBE in 1948). His long tenure as managing director of Hawker Siddeley under Sopwith's chairmanship ended when he

retired in 1958. Spriggs was not well known outside the company boardroom. He married, in 1920,
Amy Gladys Spratley (d 1967), the daughter of a
builder; they had two daughters. See *DBB*.

SPURRIER, Sir Henry
(16 June 1898 - 17 June 1964)
Motor vehicle manufacturer, born at Leyland,
Lancashire, son of Henry Spurrier II, a mechanical
engineer, and his American wife Jessie née Albro,
Henry Spurrier III was educated at Repton School
and then began an engineering apprenticeship with
Leyland Motors Ltd. This had been formed in 1907
from the Lancashire Steam Motor Co in which his
father and grandfather (Henry Spurrier I), also an
engineer, had financial interests. After the First
World War (in which he served in the Royal
Flying Corps as a pilot lieutenant in the Middle
East) he rejoined Leyland Motors which briefly
digressed into private car production. After the
chief engineer, J Parry-Thomas was killed in 1923
Henry Spurrier II took the firm back into heavy
vehicle manufacture: refurbishing over 3,000 RAF
Leyland 3-ton lorries re-purchased from the War
Department (and sold again by Leyland at a substantial loss) and then developing a range of heavy
diesel vehicles between 1925 and 1939. These
included the L-type bus chassis of which 4,000
were built by 1928, taking the company into profit
again. The T-types which first appeared in 1927,
particularly the Titan double-decker bus and the
Bison, Buffalo and Hippo lorries, further met a rising demand for road passenger and goods vehicles
which transformed the British landscape between
the wars. Henry Spurrier III, assistant manager,
1930-42, specialised in overseas sales. As general
manager, 1942-49, he oversaw the wartime production lines at Leyland which made over 10,000
tank engines and 3,000 medium and heavy tanks
(Centaur, Cromwell, Comet). Employment rose
from 6,000 in 1935 to a wartime high of 11,000.
Henry Spurrier III became managing director in
1949 and chairman in 1957, holding both posts
until a brain tumour forced his retirement in 1962-
3. Between 1947 and 1963 the company expanded
remarkably, with turnover rising from £13 million
to £172 million and the workforce from 8,500 to
54,000. Much of this came from acquisitions:
Albion Motors of Glasgow in 1951, Scammell
Lorries of Watford in 1955, Associated Commercial
Vehicles (which included Maudslay, Thornycroft
and Crossley) in 1962. Assisted by Stanley
Markland (qv) and Donald Stokes (qv), Sir Henry
Spurrier (he was knighted in 1955) diversified
Leyland into mass passenger car production by tak-
ing over the ailing Coventry-based Standard
Triumph in 1961: his last major strategic move.

Reserved, thrifty, honest and wholly dedicated to
the family firm based at Leyland, an old textile
community, Spurrier had few involvements beyond
his firm and his hobbies of shooting and sailing. He
was a part-time member of the Iron and Steel
Board from 1958 and a director of the District
Bank. He married, in 1920, Winifred Mary née
Cope; they had two daughters. See *DBB*; Graham
Turner, *The Leyland Papers* (1971).

STAMP, Josiah Charles
1st Baron Stamp of Shortlands
(21 June 1880 - 16 April 1941)
Statistician and railway company chairman, born in
Kilburn, London, the son of Charles Stamp, a
cheesemonger, and Clara Jane née Evans. After
attending Baptist schools (later becoming a leading
Methodist), he joined the Inland Revenue in 1896
where hard work and his statistical ability (he was
awarded an external first class honours and DSc
degree at London University) earned him promotion to the Board of Inland Revenue by 1914. His
major achievement was the creation of Excess
Profits Duty. In 1919 he accepted an offer from
Lord McGowan (qv) to join Nobel Industries as a
finance director. In 1926 he became an executive
of the London Midland & Scottish Railway, soon
succeeding W G Granet (qv) as chairman. Both at
Nobel and the LMS Stamp introduced modern
management and accounting procedures. Known as
the 'busiest man in Britain', Stamp was much in
demand as an expert economist (a director of the
Bank of England, he served on the Economic
Advisory Committee and the Dawes and Young
Committees), besides being a prolific writer and
powerful spokesman for the railways. His influence
in Government was reflected in a steady stream of
honours: CBE 1918, KBE 1920, GCB 1935, and a
peerage 1938. He received numerous honorary
degrees and was president of seven professional
societies. He married Olive Marsh, daughter of a
Greenwich builder, in 1903. They and one of their
four sons were killed in a London air raid. He left
£163,549. See J C Stamp, *British Incomes and
Property* (1916); J Harry Jones, *Josiah Stamp: Public
Servant* (1964); *DBB*; *DNB*.

STANLEY, Albert Henry
Baron Ashfield of Southwell
(8 August 1874 - 4 November 1948)
Transport executive, born at New Normanton,
Derby, the son of Henry Knattriess (later changed
to Stanley), a coach painter, and Elizabeth née
Twigg. His early education and career was in
America, where he became a railway manager,
returning to London in 1907 as representative of
American interests in the Underground Electric

Railways of London Ltd. By 1914 he had become the outstanding figure in London transport and had been knighted. During the First World War he was president of the Board of Trade, elected as Unionist MP for Ashton-under-Lyme, and in 1920 given a barony. Returning to dominate the capital's transport with Frank Pick (qv) as his chief of staff, in 1933 he became chairman of the newly-formed London Passenger Transport Board, a post he held until 1947. He was a founder and president of the Institute of Transport. In 1904 he married Grace Lowrey Woodruff of Detroit: they had two daughters. He left £59,971. See Theodore CBarker and Michael Robbins, *A History of London Transport* (2 vols, 1963-74); *DBB*; *DNB*.

STEDEFORD, Sir Ivan Arthur Rice
(28 January 1897 - 9 February 1975)
Engineering company executive, born in Exeter, one of the four sons and seven children of the Reverend Charles Stedeford, minister in the Bible Christian Methodist Church (and president of the United Methodist Church in 1928-29), and his wife Emma Jane née Rice, he was educated at the denomination's Shebbear College, north Devon, and King Edward VI Grammar School, Birmingham. Apprenticed to the Wolseley Tool & Motor Co Ltd, a Vickers subsidiary at Aston, Birmingham, 1913-16, and then serving in the Royal Naval Air Service as an observation officer, 1917-19, Stedeford went into the motor trade after the war and had his own business until 1928. He then joined his father-in-law's firm, Tubes Ltd, as sales director. Registered in 1897, operating from the Climax Works at Aston, and managed by John Herbert Aston JP of Henley-in-Arden, in 1928 Tubes Ltd was one of the nine subsidiaries, all in the Birmingham area, of Tube Investments Ltd (a merger of 1919 between five firms making, chiefly, ferrous tubes, including Tubes Ltd). Stedeford's father-in-law, J Herbert Aston, was a main board director of TI and Arthur Chamberlain (qv) was chairman. By 1935 TI had 21 subsidiaries and employed 15,000. In 1935 Stedeford became a joint managing director of Tubes; in 1936 a managing director of TI; and by 1943 a director of 18 of the subsidiaries in the TI group. From 1942 until he retired in 1963 he was both chairman and managing director of TI. After the war the company grew rapidly, chiefly by acquisition, with 36 UK operating companies, £50 million capital employed and 32,000 employees in 1952; and 60 UK subsidiaries, £160 million capital employed and 65,000 employees in 1961. The denationalisation of steel in 1953 offered the chance of vertical growth and TI purchased their first steel company, Round Oak Steel Works. Under the tall and

reserved Sir Ivan Stedeford (he was knighted in 1954 and made a GBE in 1961) TI was restructured before 1955 into a multidivisional company with seven divisions (steel tube, aluminium, cycle, electrical, engineering, steel, general, and an export organisation). Stedeford kept TI at the forefront of technical innovation, with TI's radioactive research group working on radioisotopes and tracer techniques in 1954 and TI's technological centre installing an IBM 650 computer in 1957. Stedeford's successful takeover bid for British Aluminium in 1957-58, made jointly with the American firm Reynolds Metals, was seen as a triumph for Midlands manufacturers over City financiers. Sir Ivan Stedeford was a director of the Commonwealth Development Finance Corporation (1953), Atlas Assurance Co, National Provincial Bank (1948-64) and then the National Westminster Bank (1964-69) and a governor of the BBC (1951-55). He was a member of several public bodies including the committee of inquiry into the BBC (1949-50), the UK Atomic Energy Authority (1954-59), the executive council of the Department of Scientific and Industrial Research (1950-52) and an advisory group on the British Transport Commission (1960) which he chaired. He married, in 1923, Gwendoline Edith Aston; they had three daughters. See George Bull and Anthony Vice, *Bid for Power* (1961); Ronald S Edwards and Harry Townsend, *Business Enterprise* (1958); Idem, *Business Growth* (1966); *The Times* 11 February 1975.

STEEL, Gerald
(15 February 1895 - 14 September 1957)
Steel manufacturer, born in Ecclesall, Sheffield, the son of Henry 'Harry' Steel (1863-1920) and Maggie née Wyatt. His grandfather was one of the founders of the Rotherham steelmakers, Steel, Peech & Tozer, which later became part of the United Steel Companies, of which his father was chairman, 1918-20. Educated at Charterhouse and Oriel College, Oxford, he served in Africa during the war, and then joined United Steel after his father's death. After a spell in India, he became general manager in 1932 of United Steel subsidiary, Samuel Fox of Stocksbridge, which he guided into alloy steel production. After 1941 he became the right-hand man of Sir Walter Benton Jones (qv) in the drive to modernise United Steel. In 1950 he became general managing director, at the beginning of a decade when United Steel acquired a reputation as one of the most efficient and progressive of UK steel companies. It was also one of the largest, with a workforce in 1955 of about 34,000 (amongst the top 25 UK companies). During 1953-60 capital expenditure was £80 million: profits rose

from £9,136,000 in 1954 to £22,582,000 in 1960. Gerald Steel devoted much attention to personnel and industrial training: he was the first chairman of the British Iron and Steel Federation's Training Committee and served on the Social and Industrial Council established under the chairmanship of the Archbishop of Canterbury. He was also a vice-president of the Iron and Steel Institute. In Sheffield he was a former church burgess and chairman of the Sheffield Church Extension Committee, and a JP from 1941. he became a CBE in 1956, but illness and death denied him the chairmanship of United Steel and the office of Master Cutler. He married in 1922 Ruth née Crawshaw: they had two sons and two daughters. He left £40,837 gross. See Jonathan Boswell, *Business Policies in the Making: Three Steel Companies Compared* (1983); Ronald Peddie, *The United Steel Companies* (1967); *DBB*.

STEIN, Cyril
(20 February 1928 -)
Gambling and hotel chain operator, the son of Jack Stein and Rebecca née Selner. In 1957 Stein and his group of investors acquired control of Ladbroke, the betting shop chain that was named after the village where it was established. It had kept a low profile for 70 years because of the UK's gambling laws. In 1963 off-track betting was legalised and three years later Stein became chairman, prior to the company's flotation in 1967. By 1971 it had 660 betting shops, but Stein began a programme of diversification into property and hotels. In 1972 he entered the real estate market with the acquisition of the London & Leeds Development Corporation and Ladbroke also entered the lodgings business. Some projects were disastrous - such as an attempt to run casinos that was aborted in 1979 - but Stein's purchase of the 91-hotel Hilton International chain for £645 million in 1987 made Ladbroke the largest hotel operator in the world (four years later Hilton hotels were valued at £2.5 billion). Ladbroke also runs the Texas Homecare (DIY) chain. In 1991 Ladbroke's turnover was £3,785 million (pre-tax profit £210 million) and the group employed over 53,000 workers. The collapse in property values hit Ladbroke in 1992, when pre-tax profits fell to £40.1 million, but the company has paid a dividend every year since its flotation. Stein married in 1949 Betty Young: they have two sons and a daughter.

STEPHENSON, William Lawrence
(13 January 1880 - 7 May 1963)
Chain store chairman, born at Scarborough, the son of Frederick James Stephenson, works manager

in a small upholstery firm, and his wife Eliza née Toder; he was educated in Hull and at 17 was apprenticed to Edwin Owen, owner of a general merchandising firm in Birmingham supplying dry goods to American department stores. The energy and flair which made Stephenson Owen's chief buyer before he was 30 greatly impressed Frank W Woolworth (1852-1919). When Woolworth established a British subsidiary he recruited Stephenson to assist his cousin Fred Moore Woolworth. F W Woolworth & Co Ltd (a private company) opened their first store in Liverpool in 1909. By 1914 they had 44 such stores, all selling a wide range of cheap luxury and household goods at low fixed prices in large open stores. High turnover on low margins produced the profit. When Fred Woolworth died in 1923 Stephenson succeeded him as managing director. He was soon adding to the one hundred stores, choosing freehold properties on prime high street sites. In June 1931 the firm, now with 494 branches in Britain, was floated as a public company, amid accusations of insider trading which Stephenson wholly rejected. He became chairman (still under the American parent which retained 52 per cent of the ordinary shares), though relinquished the managing directorship in 1932. Expansion continued to be financed from profits and by 1940 (when the firm had a trading surplus of over £8 million) 768 stores were open. During the Second World War Stephenson was Director General of Equipment in the Ministry of Aircraft Production. He retired from the Woolworths board in 1948 when profits were £9.6 million. Uninterested in politics, Stephenson outside business was preoccupied by his family and yachting. He married, in 1909, Lillian, daughter of Joseph Drake, a Shipley provision merchant. They had a son and three daughters. Stephenson left an estate valued at £3.49 million. See *DBB*.

STERLING, Jeffrey Maurice
Baron Sterling of Plaistow
(27 December 1934 -)
Shipping and property company executive, the second of three children of Harry and Alice Sterling (originally Steinberg). His father was a semi-ortho-dox Jew who developed a publicly-quoted entertainments company, Sterling & Michaels, by the 1950s. Educated at Reigate Grammar School, Preston Manor County School and the Guildhall School of Music, he worked for Paul Schweder & Co (Stock Exchange) between 1957 and 1963. In 1969 he began building up his own group - the Sterling Guarantee Trust - which brought him to the attention of Lord Inchcape, who was looking for new managerial talent for the Peninsular & Oriental Steam Navigation Co. In 1980 Sterling

joined the P & O board, helped to fend off a threatened takeover by Nigel Broackes's Trafalgar House (owner of Cunard), and became chairman in 1983. Two years later the Guarantee Trust's extensive property interests were absorbed into P & O. Sterling then diversified further into property, with the purchase of Stock Conversion in 1991 and a half share in Laing Properties. It also operates the housebuilding firm Bovis. In the 1990s P & O is by far the largest British shipping company and one of the biggest UK property companies - not necessarily a good position in 1992; and there will also be competition from the Channel Tunnel. Turnover rose from £2,920 million in 1987 (pre-tax profit £274 million) to £4,897 million in 1991 (pre-tax profit £217 million). It employed about 70,000 in 1992. The Zeebrugge ferry disaster in 1987 and his fervent support for Margaret Thatcher have ensured Sterling's high profile. He served as special adviser to the Secretary of State for Industry, 1982-3. He was also a member of the British Airways Board, 1979-82, and of the board of European Ferries after 1985. He has been closely involved as governor with the Royal Ballet and its School. Awarded a CBE in 1977, Sterling was knighted in 1985 and made a life peer in 1991. He was president of the General Council of British Shipping, 1990-91. He married in 1985 Dorothy Ann Smith: they have one daughter. See David and Stephen Howarth, *The Story of P & O* (1986).

STERLING, Sir Louis Saul
(16 May 1879 - 2 June 1958)
Industrialist, born in New York, who was a newspaper boy until he came to England in a cattle boat with about £6 in his pocket. He took a job in the gramophone trade and later became managing director of the Columbia Gramophone Co (later Electrical & Musical Industries - EMI), controlling HMV, Columbia, and Marconiphone. He was also a director of S G Warburg Ltd. A noted philanthropist, by 1956 his gifts over 30 years totalled £1.5 million. He donated his rare book collection to London University, which named a room of the Library after him. In 1919 he married Cissy, daughter of Isaac Stevens. See *The Times*, 3 June 1958.

STEVENS, Marshall
(18 April 1852 - 12 August 1936)
Industrial estate developer, born at Plymouth, eldest son of Sanders Stevens, a shipbroker from a line of men in the shipping trades, and his wife Emma Ruth née Marshall, he was educated at the Mansion House, Exeter, and entered the family business, T J & S Stevens, in about 1868. He moved to Garston, just outside Liverpool, in 1877

and set up as an independent steamship agent. He discovered that the railway companies had established monopoly powers over transportation between Liverpool and Manchester. When in 1882 Daniel Adamson, the Manchester engineer, projected a ship canal from the Mersey to Manchester, Stevens became Adamson's lieutenant and then provisional manager of the Manchester Ship Canal in 1885 and general manager, 1891-97. After the Canal opened in 1894 Stevens negotiated with the railways for lower rates, securing them in 1897. That year he accepted an offer from E T Hooley, the company promoter,to become general manager of the newly-projected Trafford Park Estates Ltd, formed to transform a deer park of two square miles into an industrial estate, eventually the largest in Europe. Paid £2,500 a year, Stevens realised that such a park, by linking firms and factories to Manchester rather than Liverpool, could enable the Canal to reach the traffic targets it initially failed to attain. He succeeded, but not easily. As managing director, 1897-1929, and as chairman, 1912-29, he attracted new industries to the North West which, in the long term, helped to spare the region from industrial desolation. Among those firms locating at Trafford Park were several American companies, like Westinghouse Electric (in 1899), Ford (in 1911) and Kelloggs (in 1924). By 1935 180 firms were at Trafford Park and the aggregate value of the estate rose from £900,000 in 1896 to £100 million in 1936. Stevens, a Unionist, was MP for Eccles, 1918-22. He married, in 1873, Louisa Blamey; they had six sons and a daughter (d in infancy). The fourth son, T H G Stevens, succeeded his father as a managing director (1924-54) and chairman (1955-61) of Trafford Park Estates. See *DBB*; D A Farnie, *The Manchester Ship Canal and the Rise of the Port of Manchester* (1980).

STEWART, Andrew Graham
(22 August 1901 - 7 May 1964)
Steel manufacturer, born at Baillieston, Scotland, the son of John Graham Stewart (qv), he was educated at Winchester and Pembroke College, Cambridge, where he took an engineering degree. In 1924 he joined Stewarts & Lloyds, the Scottish and Midlands steel tube makers where his father was chairman. He spent seven years on the shopfloor learning the practicalities of steel and tube making. He was appointed a director in 1931 and general managing director in 1932, later having special responsibility for labour relations at the new works at Corby. Under Sir Allan Macdiarmid (qv), Stewart was in charge of wartime tube and shell production at Stewarts & Lloyds, which totalled nearly a million shell cases and projectiles. He became deputy chairman in 1943 and chairman and

general managing director in 1945 on the death of Macdiarmid. Graham Stewart remained in charge of Stewarts & Lloyds until his own death, opposing vigorously the short experience of nationalisation, 1949-53, and overseeing very substantial growth, from 14,000 employees in 1935 to 42,000 in 1955 and approaching 59,000 in 1964. Graham Stewart was also a director of Tube Investments and of the United Steel Cos; and a president of the British Iron and Steel Federation in 1955, part-time member of the Iron and Steel Board, 1956-61, and president of the British Employers' Confderation, 1952-54. He married, in 1929, Barabel Greig; they had three sons and two daughters. See Frederick Scopes, *The Development of Corby Works* (1968); *The Times*, 9, 15 May 1964.

STEWART, John Graham
(1862 - June 1925)

Iron and steel tube manufacturer, one of the four sons and five children of Andrew Stewart (1832-1901), a Glasgow tube manufacturer who moved to Coatbridge in 1867, and his wife Jane née Cuthbert, James Graham Stewart and his brother Thomas Cuthbert Stewart were taken into the family firm following the death of an uncle in 1886. Meeting a growing demand for gas and water pipes and boiler tubes, the Stewarts grew by taking over rivals and in 1890 merged with the Clydesdale Iron & Steel Co to form a public company, A & J Stewart & Clydesdale Ltd, the largest firm in the Scottish tube trade. To forestall their major rivals in England the Stewarts took over James Menzies & Co of Rutherglen in 1898, bringing their employment up to 6,000. When Lloyd & Lloyd Ltd of Birmingham and Halesowen purchased a Clydeside tube maker in 1900 the rivals opted for negotiations rather than a price war. The two firms merged in 1903 to form Stewarts & Lloyds Ltd, employing over 10,000 in 1907 and producing half the UK's mainstream tube products by 1914. John Graham Stewart served as the first chairman until his death. The firm's direction lay with a group of half a dozen directors, rather than with Stewart alone, and they took years to make major strategic moves, like backward integration into iron ore and coal mining with the purchase of the North Lincolnshire Iron Co in 1918, Alfred Hickman Ltd in 1920 and a south Yorkshire colliery from Messrs J & J Charlesworth in 1923. John Graham Stewart was primarily a tube maker, not an iron and steel manufacturer, but had the wisdom to bring forward a talented accountant, Allan Macdiarmid (qv), and to bring in a practical steelmaker, Charles Atha, when their skills were needed. Stewart's son, Andrew Graham Stewart (qv) also chaired the company. See Jonathan Boswell, *Business Policies in the Making: Three Steel Companies Compared* (1983); *DSBB*; Frederick Scopes, *The Development of Corby Works* (1968).

STEWART, Sir Percy Malcolm
(9 May 1872 - 27 February 1951)

Building materials manufacturer, born at Hastings, the son of (Sir) Halley Stewart (1838-1937), oil cake manufacturer, and Elizabeth née Atkinson. After attending a number of schools, such as the Royal High School in Edinburgh, he joined his father in about 1900 in taking over a Bedfordshire cement and brickmaking plant. Stewart played an important role in rationalising the UK's cement and brick industry: the former through Associated Portland Cement Manufacturers, formed in 1912; the latter through the London Brick Co, formed in 1923. From 1924 Stewart was chairman of both these conglomerates, thus controlling two major sources of UK building materials. Growth was steady: for example, he trebled LBC's £1 million capital and brick production rose from 475 million in 1923 to 2,000 million in 1954. He was made an OBE in 1918 and awarded a baronetcy in 1937. He retired in 1945. He married twice: first to Cordelia Rickett, daughter of a businessman and Liberal MP; second to Beatrice Maud Pratt. There was a son and daughter from both marriages. He left £541,869 gross. See Richard Hillier, *Clay that Burns* (1981); *DBB*; *DNB*.

STEWART-LIBERTY, Arthur Ivor
(11 January 1916 - 11 July 1990)

Retail and design firm chairman, born at Great Missenden, the son of Captain Ivor Stewart-Liberty and Evelyn Katherine née Phipps. His father was the nephew and heir of Sir Arthur Lasenby Liberty (1843-1917), founder of Liberty's department store in Regent Street, London, famous for its clothes, furnishings, and Far Eastern fabrics. Educated at Winchester and Christ Church College, Oxford, he joined the family firm in 1946 and became chairman in 1952. Until his retirement in 1981, Arthur Stewart-Liberty strove to maintain the traditional Liberty image, while introducing new lines (his Art Nouveau Lotus collection was a striking success in the 1960s). Undaunted by a hunting accident in 1964 that left him paralysed from the waist down, he expanded Liberty internationally in Europe, America and - where it all began - in the Far East. Between 1952 and 1981 Liberty's capital increased from £200,000 to £2.5 million; turnover from £2 million to £23 million. He married twice: first in 1942 to Rosabel Fynn Fremantle (by whom he had two sons and one daughter before the marriage was dissolved in 1953); second in 1955 to Elizabeth Stuart (they had one daughter).

His two sons, 'Mr Richard' and 'Mr Oliver', continue the family involvement in Liberty's. See Stephen Calloway (ed), *The House of Liberty* (1992).

STIRLING, John Anderson
(8 February 1893 - 4 January 1982)

Scottish Co-operative Wholesale Society executive, born at Barrhead, near Glasgow, the son of George Stirling, an employee of the local firm of Shanks (sanitary ware manufacturers), who was also on the board of management of the Barrhead Co-operative Society, and his wife Anne Moncrieff Anderson. He attended the local school, working part-time as a milk boy for the Barrhead Society and joined the SCWS in 1913 as a clerk in the accountant's department of the Glasgow head office. During the First World War he served with the 2nd Lowland Field Ambulance Corps, the 5th Highland Light Infantry and the London Scottish, 1914-18, in Gallipoli, the Middle East and France. He returned to the SCWS in 1919 and took courses in bookkeeping and accountancy, a teacher's diploma with the London Chamber of Commerce and in the 1923 examinations for the fellowship of the London Association of Accountants (later merged with the Association of Certified and Corporate Accountants) was placed third. At the SCWS he was consequently moved to the audit department, simultaneously acting as secretary of the Co-operative Convalescent Homes Ltd, 1923-32. Later he was appointed an assistant accountant. Nominated by Tillicoultry Society he was elected to the SCWS board in 1943 and was the sole Scottish retail representative on the National Mutual Aid Committee, set up to assist Societies heavily damaged by war bombing. He was elected SCWS secretary (equivalent to CEO) in 1949, succeeding Robert Leckie (qv). He retired in 1959, the year he was president of the Co-operative Congress, the highest honour bestowed by the movement. During his secretaryship the SCWS experienced relatively little growth, having nearly 14,000 employees in 1955, compared to over 12,000 in 1935. Stirling never moved from his birthplace where he became a director of the Co-operative Society, secretary of the YMCA for some years, and a longstanding member of Arthurlie Church of Scotland (where he indulged his fondness for choral singing and was active in the Boys Brigade). He married, in 1926, Nina McConnachie, a schoolteacher in Paisley; they had one daughter. See *Co-operative Review* (January 1959); *Scottish Co-operator,* 12 September 1959.

STOKES, Donald Gresham
Baron Stokes of Leyland, Lancashire
(22 March 1914 -)

Motor vehicle manufacturer and salesman, born at Bexley, Kent, the only son of Harry Potts Stokes, an electrical engineer, and Marie Elizabeth née Yates. Educated at Blundell's public school, Tiverton, in 1930 he realised a boyhood ambition by joining Leyland Motors, the bus and lorry makers based near Preston, as an engineering apprentice. He soon discovered that his expertise lay in selling and in 1946 took charge of the firm's export department. After his appointment as Leyland's general sales and service manager, he made the company more sales oriented and helped it move into the manufacture of private cars. He became managing director of Leyland in 1963, following Sir Henry Spurrier's (qv) retirement, and then chairman in 1967. By then the firm had become British Leyland after the takeover of British Motor Holdings, making Stokes head of one of the largest motor vehicle firms in the world with a turnover approaching £1,000 million per annum. It was also one of the most unwieldy, with 77 UK factories, 66 overseas plants and 185,000 workers, and Stokes had only a limited success in solving its management problems. In real terms the company went into decline, leading to a Government inquiry (the Ryder Report, 1975), which was critical of Stokes. He was effectively dismissed and became BL president. He was knighted in 1965 and became a life peer in 1969. He was president of the Society of Motor Manufacturers and Traders, 1961-62, and president of the Institution of Mechanical Engineers in 1972. He married in 1939 Laura Elizabeth Courteney, daughter of Frederick Lamb: they have one son. See P J S Dunnett, *The Decline of the British Motor Industry* (1980); *DBB.*

SUGAR, Alan (Michael)
(24 March 1947 -)

Computer and electrical goods manufacturer, born in Hackney, London, of Jewish parents: Nathan, a semi-skilled worker in the garment trade, and Fay née Apple. A genuine East-End barrow-boy, Sugar left secondary school at 16 and began buying and selling electrical goods, founding A M S Trading Co (General Importers) - the forerunner of Amstrad plc - in 1968. Amstrad initially produced hi-fi products, but in 1984 - four years after its public flotation - Amstrad introduced its first personal computer and established itself as amongst the most profitable of all British firms. Amstrad's turnover mushroomed from £8.8 million in 1980 to £626 million in 1989; pre-tax profits from £1.4 million to £76 million. But an economic recession curtailed Amstrad's growth and Sugar - whose personal fortune is estimated to have slipped from £432 million to £80 million - attempted to restructure the company by moving into other markets for consumer electronics, such as satellite dishes. But the attempt to find another blockbuster product like computers has so far proved unsuccessful. Amstrad recorded an unprecedented loss for 1992 (which saw shares fall to 27p from a peak of 220p) with Sugar offering £113 million (30p a share) to buy the company and return it to private ownership - an offer which the shareholders rejected in December 1992. Some of the £34 million he made from his earlier sale of Amstrad shares he has invested in Tottenham Hotspur FC. He married Ann Simons in 1968: they have two sons and a daughter. See David Thomas, *Alan Sugar: The Amstrad Story* (1990).

SUMMERS, Henry Hall
(1865 - 1945)

Sheet steelmaker, born in Chester, the second youngest son of John Summers (1822-76), who had established a cut nail business (for clogs) in Stalybridge, Lancashire. Educated at Malvern College and Owen's College, Manchester, he worked as a coal merchant and an enamel sign-maker, until his three elder brothers allowed him to join the business as a partner in 1889, when the firm was losing about £1,000 a year. He began expanding the business, importing steel sheets from America and the Continent, and in 1894 began producing galvanised sheet. The firm - which became a limited company in the 1890s as John Summers & Sons Ltd - soon expanded into the largest galvanised sheet makers in the UK. In 1902 Summers built a bar mill and open-hearth steel plant at Hawarden Bridge. By 1908 the headquarters of the firm was moved from Stalybridge to Shotton, Cheshire, where it also produced its own steel. In 1913 Summers became chairman and remained so until 1937. In 1920 he added pig iron and coal to the company's products when he purchased the Shelton Steel & Iron Co, Stoke-on-Trent. Mindful of US advances in sheet steel in the inter-war period, in 1937 he sanctioned the installation of hot and cold continuous strip mills at the firm, the result of an agreement with the Mesta Machine Co of Pittsburgh. Under Summers (who retired as chairman in 1937, but remained as president) steel sheet production had reached 300,000 tons per annum by 1945; while the number of workers had increased from 450 in 1889 to 15,600 in 1946. He left £37,048 and his youngest son, (Sir) Richard Felix Summers (qv), took over as chairman. See Andrew Reid, *Continuous Venture* (1948); Kenneth Warren, *The British Iron and Steel Sheet Industry Since 1840* (1970).

SUMMERS, Sir Richard Felix
(10 December 1902 - 6 February 1977)

Steel manufacturer, younger son of Henry Hall Summers (qv), ironmaster of Cornist Hall, Flint, he was educated at Shrewsbury and Clare College, Cambridge, joining the family firm in 1925. The first family iron and steelworks had been established by his great grandfather, John Summers (1822-76), at Stalybridge a few miles east of Manchester in 1860. His grandfather, James Woolley Summers (1849-1913), registered the firm of John Summers & Sons Ltd in 1898 and laid down the first steelworks at Queens Ferry on the Dee near Chester in 1902. His father had made the firm a major producer of sheet steel. Richard Summers trained in the works, became a director in 1930, managing director in 1936 and chairman in 1938, retiring in 1971. Following a brief period of nationalisation, 1949-53, the Summers family re-purchased the business. The firm's workforce stood at 12,500 in 1955. Growth came chiefly from a massive expansion at Shotton, west of Queens Ferry, where a new steelworks was built in 1953, employing 10,000 and producing a million tons of steel (sheets) a year by 1958. Outside the firm Sir Richard Summers (he was knighted in 1962) was president of the British Iron and Steel Federation in 1960 and a director of the United Steel Cos, Steetley & Co, the District Bank, the Royal Insurance Co, the Liverpool & London & Globe Insurance Co, and a Midland area board member of the British Transport Commission. He was high sheriff for Flintshire 1944-45. He married, in 1925, Evelyn née Irvine; they had four sons. See *Iron and Coal Trades Review*, 20 April 1953; Andrew Reid, *Continuous Venture* (1948); *The Times*, 8 February 1977.

SWASH, Stanley Victor
(29 February 1896 -)

Chain store executive, born in Cardiff, son of Alfred Walter Swash, a schoolmaster (later a JP and local authority education officer), and his wife Sylvia Alice Dawson née Marshall, he was educated at Llandovery College, Carmarthen, and St John's College, Oxford where his course in mathematics was interrupted by the First World War. He served in the Royal Field Artillery, 1915-19, retiring as a battery commander with the MC and bar and severe wounds. After completing his Oxford degree he worked briefly for the Ministry of Pensions and in 1921-24 was a lieutenant instructor in the Royal Navy. He joined F W Woolworth & Co Ltd in 1924, one of the few degree-educated managers (most were ex-grammar school boys) hired by William Lawrence Stephenson (qv) who had just become managing director. Still belonging to its American parent, the firm was converted from a private into a public company in 1931. Swash, remembered for not swearing and leaving parties early, was given charge of merchandise in the metropolitan district in 1934, running 8 out of the company's 36 depots. Meantime he studied law and was called to the Bar at Lincoln's Inn in 1938, no doubt assisting his promotion to director in 1939. During the Second World War he commanded 57 County of London Home Guard Battalion with the rank of lieutenant-colonel. He became chairman of Woolworths in 1951, retiring in 1955. With the relaxing of rationing and the growth of the UK economy in the 1950s consumer incomes and expenditures rose. Woolworths, which focused on the middle and lower sections of the variety goods market, grew appreciably, from 761 stores in 1950 to 912 stores (and 60,000 employees) in 1955. Net profit per store rose from £6,708 in 1950 to £11,930 in 1955. After retiring Swash held several public appointments: membership of the Milk Marketing Board, 1957-63, of the Horticultural Marketing Advisory Council in 1958, and chairmanship of the BOAC-BEA committee of enquiry, 1963-64. He married twice, first, in 1924, to Florence Kathleen Moore (divorced, 1955), by whom he had three sons and a daughter; second, in 1955, to Jane Henderson. By 1980 he had retired to Malta. See T W Cynog-Jones, 'Retail Giants: No 11, F W Woolworth & Co Ltd' *New Dawn* 1963.

SWAYTHLING, David (Charles Samuel Montagu)
4th Baron Swaythling
(6 August 1928 -)

Banker and tobacco company executive, the elder son of the Stuart Albert Samuel (third baron) Swaythling (1898-1990) and Mary Violet, elder daughter of Major Levy DSO. After attending Trinity College, Cambridge (where he read law, then switched to English literature), he joined Samuel Montagu & Co, the London bank founded by his great-grandfather. Determined to succeed at the bank, where his father had not been a notable success, at 41 he achieved his ambition of becoming chairman. In 1973, after Montagu's was absorbed by the Midland Bank, Swaythling moved on to run Orion Bank, a loss-making consortium bank, which he succeeded in turning around by 1979. A spell with Merrill Lynch and J Rothschild Holdings followed, before he was asked to be deputy chairman and chairman-elect of Rothmans International, whose board he had sat on for 20 years. In 1988 he became chairman of this tobacco multinational that had been founded in 1972 under the South African Rembrandt group (but has been

in existence in one form or another for over 80 years). Since he took over the chairmanship, Rothmans' pre-tax profits have increased from £339 million to £565 million. Turnover in 1992 was £6,253 million and the group employed 30,000, making it one of the top five tobacco companies in the world (with brands such as Rothman and Carreras, and substantial holdings in Dunhill and Cartier Monde). Not surprisingly Swaythling opposes the anti-smoking lobby and also any legislation to restrict tobacco advertising. He is a director of the *Daily Telegraph* and was on the board of LWT for 21 years, having been involved in its formation. He describes himself as a Tory wet and a 'lobster-eating Jew', who does not believe in the mumbo-jumbo of religion. In 1951 he married Christiane Francoise Ninette, the daughter of Edgar Dreyfus of Paris: they have one son and one daughter (and one daughter is deceased). See *Rothman Company History* (1986).

SWIRE, Sir Adrian (Christopher)
(15 February 1932 -)

SWIRE, Sir John (Anthony)
(28 February 1927 -)

Shipping company entrepreneurs, the sons of John Kidston Swire (d 1983) and Juliet Richenda. They were the fifth generation to enter John Swire & Sons, the shipping and merchanting firm that had been founded in Liverpool in 1816. Both attended Eton and University College, Oxford. John then served in the Irish Guards in Palestine, joined the family business in Hong Kong in 1950, and eventually became chairman, 1966-87. After 1987 he was honorary president. Adrian was in the Coldstream Guards from 1950 to 1952 and later served with the RAF Volunteer Reserves and the Royal Hong Kong AAF. He joined Swire's in the Far East in 1956, became deputy chairman in 1986-7, and succeeded his brother as chairman in 1987. The Swire brothers sit on the board and control 65 per cent of John Swire & Sons, which is still a privately-owned London-based company. The business now embraces shipping, airlines and Kentucky Fried Chicken. Some 80 per cent of profits come from a key share in the Hong Kong-based Swire Pacific group, which itself owns half the Cathay Pacific airline. Recession and the Gulf War hit Cathay's profits in 1991 and political uncertainty over the Chinese takeover of Hong Kong will add to the Swire's future problems. Nevertheless, their fortune was estimated at £600 million in 1992. Adrian was a director of Brooke Bond, 1972-82, and serves on various shipping bodies (in 1982 he became, for example, chairman of the International Chamber of Shipping). John was director of Royal Insurance, 1975-80, British Bank of the Middle East, 1975-79, and adviser to the Hong Kong & Shanghai Banking Corporation after 1969. Adrian was knighted in 1982; John in 1990. Adrian married in 1970 Lady Judith Compton: they had two sons and a daughter. John married in 1961 Moira Cecilia Ducharne: they also have two sons and a daughter. See *DBB* (John Swire, 1825-1898).

SYKES, Sir Alan John
(11 April 1868 - 21 May 1950)

Textile bleacher, born at Cheadle, Cheshire, the second son of Thomas Hardcastle Sykes (1833-1901), bleacher, and Mary née Platt, from the textile machine family. Educated at Rugby and Oriel College, Oxford, in 1890 he joined the family firm of Sykes & Co. In 1900 the firm became part of the Bleachers' Association (a merger of 60 businesses), of which Sykes became chairman in 1916. He had great success in expanding the Association (the workforce had reached about 15,000 in 1925, and dividends averaged about 15 per cent during 1918-26) and paid particular attention to employee welfare. This prosperity was to be steadily eroded during the remainder of his life (he died still in office), when he was joined at the helm by Sir William Clare Lees (qv). Sykes was a prominent figure in Stockport affairs (in 1910-11 he was mayor) and a leading Conservative in the north-west (he was MP for Knutsford between 1910 and 1922). He had a taste for Freemasonry, the Volunteers and yellow Rolls Royces, though he never married. He was awarded a baronetcy in 1917. He left £186,365 gross. See *Concerning the Bleachers' Association* (1925); *DBB*.

SYKES, Richard (Brook)
(7 August 1942 -)

Pharmaceutical company executive, born near Huddersfield, the youngest of the three children of a carpenter. Educated at Royds Hall Grammar School, he left at 16 to work at Huddersfield Royal Infirmary in the pathology laboratories. He moved to London, attending Paddington Technical College, Chelsea College, and Queen Elizabeth College, London University, where he took a first-class honours degree in microbiology. His subsequent PhD at Bristol University, partly funded by the pharmaceutical company, Glaxo, was in the field of antibiotics. In 1972, after 14 years in research, he joined Glaxo to produce antibiotics effective against resistant strains. Four years later he moved to the American firm, Squibb, to extend this research further. In 1986 he rejoined Glaxo as second in command to the research director Sir David Jack, succeeding him in 1987. In 1993 Sykes

became Glaxo's chief executive and deputy chairman to Sir Paul Girolami (qv), after the previous holder of those posts, Dr Ernest Mario (an old colleague of Sykes's from Squibb), had resigned after differences with Girolami over the company's future strategy. Sykes now directs the largest UK drug company (and the second largest in the world), which in 1992 had a turnover of £4,096 million (a 21 per cent increase on the previous year), pre-tax profits of £1,427 million and 45,000 workers. With Glaxo's profits assured in the short term by the phenomenally successful Zantac (an ulcer drug) and new treatments for migraine, asthma and the side-effects of cancer therapy, one of Sykes's major tasks will be to lay the foundations of Glaxo's success beyond the year 2,000 when the patents on Zantac expire. Like Girolami, who rejected Mario's idea that Glaxo should move into the 'over the counter' market, Sykes is apparently committed to the strategy that has made Glaxo so successful: organic growth, fuelled by the development of its own drugs, which are aimed at the prescription market and sold at a premium price. Sykes's wife, Janet, is also a scientist: they have a son and a daughter. See Matthew Lynn, *Merck v Glaxo: The Billion-Dollar Battle* (1991).

SZARVASY, Frederick Alexander
(1875 - 3 July 1948)

Financier, probably born in Hungary, the son of Alexander Szarvasy, a banker. Little is known of his early years until he came to London in about 1901. Shortly before the First World War, he went into the new issue and company promotion business with his own company, the British Foreign & Colonial Corporation Ltd. With a reputation as a company doctor, in the inter-war years he assisted Dunlop Rubber (where he had a seat on the board), Marconi's Wireless Telegraph Co, Beardmore's and Amalgamated Anthracite Collieries Ltd (of which he became chairman until his death). He was also chairman of the Anglo-French Banking Corporation and on the boards of several other finance houses. Keenly interested in music and art, he was chairman of the Covent Garden Opera Syndicate. In 1921 he married Kate Muriel Rhona, daughter of Augusto Saavedra of the French Consular Service. He left £371,491. See *DBB*.

T

TATE, George Vernon
(21 April 1890 - 30 September 1955)

Sugar manufacturer, the third son of G B Tate and a grandson of Sir Henry Tate Bt, who gave the Tate Gallery to the nation. Educated at Winchester and Trinity College, Oxford, he began his business career with a City stockbrokers. Awarded the Military Cross in the First World War, he joined the sugar manufacturing firm founded by his grandfather - Henry Tate & Sons. The amalgamation with Lyle's came in 1921 and two years later he was elected to the board of the combined enterprise. For some years he worked at the refinery at Victoria Docks on the Thames, and in 1929 became vice-chairman of the firm. He was elected chairman in 1937, succeeding C E L (Lord) Lyle (qv). Tate & Lyle was by then the leading UK sugar refiner, employing about 7,000 workers. Tate's tasks included dealing with the reorganisations and losses caused by German wartime bombing; and fighting the threat of nationalisation after the war. He was elected president of the company on the death of Lord Lyle, only a year before his own demise. He married in 1922 Evelyn Victoria Ann née Chandler: they had two daughters. See Philippe Chalmin, *The Making of a Sugar Giant: Tate & Lyle, 1859-1989* (1990).

TEARE, Andrew Hubert
(8 September 1942 -)
Extractive and minerals company executive, the son of Arthur Hubert Teare, a Methodist minister, and Rosalind Margaret Baker. Educated at Kingswood School, Bath, and University College, London (where he read classics), he joined Turner & Newall in 1964. After a spell at Cement Roadstone, 1972-3, he worked for the Rugby cement group, where he was managing director, 1984-90. In 1990 he became chief executive of ECC (formerly English China Clays), the world's leading kaolin company and major supplier of calcium carbonates. Teare's strategy has been to focus the company more clearly on industrial minerals (for paper manufacture and ceramics) and construction materials (such as precast concrete), shedding its housing division and moving the head office to London away from its old base in Cornwall, where the bulk of its clays and its emotional home were located. In 1991 ECC integrated the recently acquired Georgia Kaolin and also carried out a major restructuring in the UK. In 1992 ECC's turnover was £966 million (pre-tax profit £86.2 million) and it had a workforce of 10,500. Teare is also a non-executive director of the NFC and a president of the National Council of Building Material Producers. He married in 1964 Janet Nina Skidmore: they have three sons.

TEMPLE, Nicholas
(2 October 1947 -)
Computer company executive, the son of Leonard Temple and Lily Irene née Thornton. Educated at King's School Gloucester, he joined IBM as a sys-

tems engineer in 1965. He worked on the introduction of IBM System/360 and became an expert in operating systems and telecommunications. In 1981 he moved to IBM's headquarters in New York as a software consultant: two years later he was appointed laboratory director in Germany, and by 1986 was group director of the services sector. The following year, he moved to IBM's European headquarters in Paris as vice-president responsible for systems and products (the first non-American to head European product development). He returned to the UK at the beginning of 1991 as general manager and was appointed chief executive in 1992, succeeding Sir Anthony Brian Cleaver (qv). Nick Temple has the responsibility for a fundamental change in the direction of IBM (UK): it recorded a pre-tax loss of £616 million in 1992, a five-fold increase on a loss of £124 million in the previous year, against a background in which its global parent lost $5 billion in 1991 - the largest in corporate history at that time. He is married with a son and two daughters.

TENNANT, Sir Anthony (John)
(5 November 1930 -)
Brewer, the son of Major John Tennant and Hon Antonia, daughter of Lord Charnwood. Educated at Eton and Trinity College, Cambridge, his early business training was in marketing at Mather & Crowther, 1953-66, before running his own consultancy. He joined the brewery firm of Trumans in 1970, becoming managing director of Watney Mann & Trumans in 1976, until 1982. In 1983 he was appointed chairman of Grand Metropolitan's drinks subsidiary, International Distillers & Vintners Ltd. Tennant joined Guinness in 1987 in the aftermath of the Ernest Saunders' (qv) scandal, following a bitter, but successful, battle for Distillers. While Saunders' and Guinness's names were being dragged through the courts, under Tennant the company quietly set about digesting its prey. Distillers was renamed United Distillers, its marketing organisation was replaced and its products were repositioned at the higher-priced end of the market. Guinness also expanded abroad, buying, for example, Spain's largest brewer in Seville. Guinness's turnover grew from £2,272 million in 1987 (pre-tax profit £408 million) to £4,667 million in 1991 (pre-tax profit £956 million): by then the group employed 23,000. Tennant became chairman of Guinness in 1989 and retired at the end of 1992, handing over to Tony Greener (qv). He became a non-executive director of the International Stock Exchange in 1991 and joined the board of Christie's International in 1993. He married in 1954 Rosemary Violet Stockdale: they have two sons. He was knighted in 1992.

TETT, Sir Hugh Charles
(28 October 1906 -)

Petroleum executive, born in Heavitree, Exeter, Devon, elder son of James Charles Tett, a draper's traveller, and his wife Florence late Windsor née Lihou, he was educated at Hele's School, Exeter, University College Exeter, and Imperial College of Science and Technology (as it became). He joined the Anglo-American Petroleum Co (Esso Petroleum Co from 1951) in 1928 and became manager of its technical department in 1935. During the Second World War he served on the technical advisory committee of the Petroleum Board and as a lieutenant-colonel with the Combined Intelligence Sub-Committee, 1944-45. Afterwards he chaired the council of the Institute of Petroleum, 1947-48. At Anglo-American he was managing director of Anglo-American Research Ltd, 1947-49, general manager, marketing, of Anglo-American, 1949, director of Esso Petroleum Co, 1951, and chairman, 1959-67, in succession to Sir Leonard Sinclair (qv). During his chairmanship the company shrank in terms of employment (from about 15,000 in 1955 to 12,600 in 1966) and engaged in a fierce petrol price war which involved trading stamps and heavy advertising, Esso's interest being promoted by 'Tiger in the Tank' adverts. After leaving Esso Sir Hugh Tett (he was knighted in 1966) became a director of Pirelli General Cable Works Ltd and of Bristol Composite Materials Ltd. He was a member of the Council for Scientific and Industrial Research, 1961-64; the advisory council of the Ministry of Technology, 1964-67; and of the Economic Development Committee for the Motor Manufacturing Industry (chairman, 1967-69). Tett was pro-chancellor of Southampton University, 1967-79. He married three times: first, in 1931, to Katie Sargent (d 1948), by whom he had a daughter; secondly, in 1949, to Joyce Lilian née Mansell (d 1979), by whom he had a daughter; thirdly, in 1980, to Barbara Mary née Mackenzie. See WW 1963, 1980, 1986.

THOMAS, Richard
(1838 - 28 September 1916)

Tinplate manufacturer, the son of Richard Thomas, secretary and manager of the Bridgwater Gas Works, he was educated at the Wesleyan College, Taunton, and then had a variety of jobs before he entered the tinplate trade in 1863 as cashier to the Melyn Works, Neath. After a false start, with the formation of the Ynyspenllwch Iron & Tinplate Co Ltd in 1865, he set up on his own in 1871, leasing works at Lydney and forming Richard Thomas & Co. He added works at Lydbrook in 1875 and converted the business to a limited company in 1884. When Richard Beaumont Thomas, the eldest of his sons, became managing director in 1888, Richard Thomas made the first of a series of acquisitions during a downturn in trade which saw his company become the largest tinplate manufacturer in South Wales by 1899. In 1909 he had over 7,000 employees and when he died over 11,000 (operating 133 out of 530 tinplate works in South Wales, together with associated collieries, marketing agencies and steel works). Richard Thomas married in 1859 and had five sons and a daughter. See DBB; Walter E Minchinton, The British Tinplate Industry: A History (1957).

THOMAS, William Miles Webster
Baron Thomas of Remingham, Berkshire
(2 March 1897 - 9 February 1980)

Motor industry executive and airline chairman, born at Cefn Mawr, near Ruabon, Denbighshire, the only child of William Henry Thomas, a retired furniture dealer, and his wife Mary Elizabeth née Webster; his father died when he was a year old and he was raised by his mother, being educated at Ruabon Grammar School and King Edward VI School, Bromsgrove. His engineering apprenticeship, commenced in 1913, was ended by the First World War in which he started as despatch rider and ended as a test pilot with the Royal Flying Corps in Baghdad (with a DFC). Following four years as a journalist with The Motor and other Iliffe motoring magazines, he was recruited by William Morris (qv) in 1923 to become an adviser on sales promotion. He became a director and chief sales executive of Morris Motors Ltd in 1927, director and general manager of Wolseley Motors (a Morris subsidiary) in 1934, managing director of Wolseley in 1937 and vice-chairman and managing director of Morris Motors in 1940. Knighted in 1943 for his services in tank production for the war effort, he became estranged from Lord Nuffield. In 1947 he resigned from the Nuffield Organisation and soon after was appointed deputy chairman of the new state-owned British Overseas Airways Corporation. He took over as chairman in 1949 (at £7,500 a year plus £1,000 expenses and a car - less than he received with Morris) and stayed in office until 1956. He found an over-staffed and inefficient organisation. With the aid of key senior managers like Basil Smallpeice (qv) he slimmed BOAC down from 24,100 staff to 16,500 within three years and installed improved management systems. As a public relations man, he succeeded in improving BOAC's self-image. BOAC's motley fleet of older aircraft he replaced with Argonauts, Constellations, Stratocruisers and Britannias, though his initiative in introducing the world's first jet-powered commercial airliner, the Comet, in 1952 was confounded in 1953 by a series of disasters, due to metal fatigue, which it took four years to rectify. By 1956 BOAC had just become profitable. Thomas resigned from BOAC over disagreements with his political master, Harold Watkinson, the new Minister of Transport and Civil Aviation in 1955. Thomas was chairman of the American-owned Monsanto Chemicals Ltd, 1956-63; chairman of Britannia Airways from 1963; and a director of the Sun Insurance Office, Sun Alliance Insurance, the Dowty Group and the Thomson Organisation. He served on various public bodies including the Development Corporation for Wales, 1958-67; the Welsh Economic Council, 1965-66; the Welsh Advisory Committee for Civil Aviation, 1961-66; and the National Savings Committee, 1965-72 (chairman, 1965-70). He was made a life peer in 1971. Thomas wrote numerous articles and two books, including his autobiography, *Out on a Wing* (1964). He married, in 1924, Hylda Nora née Church, formerly William Morris's secretary; they had a son and a daughter. See *DBB*.

THOMPSON, David (Brian)
(4 April 1936 -)
Food industrialist and property developer, born into a Suffolk farming background, the son of Bernard Thompson and Rosamund Dee. He was educated at Haileybury and ISC. In 1974 he co-founded Hillsdown (named after Thompson's luxury north London home), merging the meat interests inherited from his father with the property business of (Sir) Harry Solomon (qv). Hillsdown, which produces food products for supermarkets, grew rapidly in the 1980s. Thompson was chairman between 1974 and 1984 and then became joint-chairman, handing over increasingly to Solomon. After 1987 Thompson sold out his stake in Hillsdown for £300 million and moved into property. His son, Richard, runs the family company, Thompson Investments, and he also bought into a small estate agency, Glentree. Renamed Union Square, it lost £10.5 million in the year to the end of March 1991. Thompson, a shy man, also has extensive racing interests in Newmarket. See Philip Beresford, *The Sunday Times Book of the Rich* (1990); William Kay, *Tycoons: Where They Came From and How They Made It* (1985).

THOMPSON, Sir Peter (Anthony)
(14 April 1928 -)
Transport company executive, born at Monkseaton near Tyneside, the son of Herbert Thompson, who ran a men's outfitters in Newcastle, and his wife Sarah Jane. Educated at Royal Drapers School, Bradford Grammar School and Leeds University, where he read classics and history, in 1952 he was

recruited by Unilever as a management trainee. He moved to GKN in 1962, then worked as a transport controller at Rank and British Steel. In 1972 he joined British Road Services Ltd, a subsidiary of the National Freight Corporation. NFC was a troubled, state-owned loss-making enterprise, but Thompson organised a £53 million employee buy-out of the business in 1982. It proved a resounding success: NFC's market capitalisation rose from £7.5 million to nearly £900 million by the time it was listed on the Stock Exchange in 1989. The workforce grew from 23,000 in 1982 to 33,000 in 1989, as the NFC became the UK's largest employee-owned company. Thompson himself progressed from his early socialism, through a period of disillusionment with nationalised industries, to 'participative, communicative, sharing, employee-focused management'. Thompson was chief executive, 1982-84, and chairman, 1982-91, when James Watson (qv) took over. Thompson was knighted in 1984. He married in 1958 Patricia Anne Norcott (d 1983): they had one son and two daughters. He married secondly Lydia Mary Kite née Hodding, by whom he had two daughters. See Peter Thompson, *Sharing the Success: The Story of NFC* (1989).

THOMSON, Sir Adam
(7 July 1926 -)
Airline operator, born in Cathcart, a suburb of Glasgow, the son of Frank Thomson, a railwayman, and Jemina Rodgers. Educated at Rutherglen Academy, Coatbridge College and the Royal Technical College, Glasgow, he became a pilot in the Fleet Air Arm, 1944-47. In the 1950s he was a flying instructor and commercial pilot with firms such as BEA, West African Airlines and Britavia. In 1961 he and a group of friends founded Caledonian Airways as a charter airline. It grew modestly with leased aircraft until 1970, when its takeover of British United Airways helped the airline (now renamed British Caledonian) become the biggest independent carrier in the UK. Thomson became chairman and chief executive. After a promising start in the 1970s, by the early 1980s BCal's profitability was undermined by a series of factors: the Falklands War and international terrrorism, which disrupted air traffic; the decline in the world oil industry, which hit routes into Texas, Scotland and Saudi Arabia; and - according to Thomson - the Government's shielding of its competitor British Airways in the run up to privatisation. In 1986 BCal made a loss of £19.3 million (this was despite disposals of £25.4 million). In 1987 BCal was bought by British Airways for £237 million, after the Lord King and Sir Colin Marshall (qqv) had fended off a bid - favoured by Thomson and BCal

- from Scandinavian Airline Systems (SAS). Thomson stepped down and was said to have received about £3 million for his shares and options. Thomson also served as a director of Williams & Glyn's Bank, the Royal Bank of Scotland and Otis Elevators. Since 1988 he has been chairman of Gold Stag. Appointed CBE in 1976, he was knighted in 1983. Thomson married in 1948 Dawn Elizabeth Burt: they have two sons. See Adam Thomson, *High Risk: The Politics of the Air* (1990).

THOMSON, Roy Herbert
Baron Thomson of Fleet
(5 June 1894 - 4 August 1976)

Newspaper, radio and television proprietor, born in Toronto, Canada, elder of the two sons of Herbert Thomson, a barber, and his wife Alice Maud née Coombs, he was educated at Jarvis Street Collegiate School, Toronto, studied bookkeeping for a year and then worked in Toronto as a clerk-salesman for ten years. An avid reader of rags-to-riches romances, he determined to become a millonaire. His career, with its recurring failures and remarkable success, exemplified that of any Horatio Alger hero. At the age of 25 he took his wife and two small daughters to a 640-acre prairie farm only to discover that he hated farming. Within months he sold out at a loss. He failed again in 1925, in a partnership with his brother Carl and his brother-in-law, selling motor supplies. He tried selling radios, first in Ottawa, then northwards at North Bay, even more difficult with the onset of the Depression. However, when Thomson discovered that Canada's radio stations were too far away he decided to build his own radio station at North Bay. With credit and engineering help he had station CFCH on the air and earning advertising revenues by 1931. By the end of 1944 he had eight radio stations and five newspapers. He moved back to Toronto, still expanding his empire. By the early 1950s he was beginning to look abroad. In 1952 he bought the *Scotsman* and moved to Scotland in 1954, leaving his son Kenneth to run his Canadian business, to which television stations were now being added. Knowing the commercial potential of television ('just like having a licence to print your own money', he observed), Thomson set up Scottish Television Ltd and secured the Central Scotland ITV contract in 1956. Without his bid the Independent Television Authority would have lacked a Scottish contractor until 1958, thereby slowing the development of the ITV network. Advised by James Coltart, former manager of Beaverbrook's (qv) *Glasgow Evening News*, he negotiated from Gomer Berry (qv) the purchase of most of the Kemsley newspapers, including the *Sunday*

Times, in 1959. Distinguished by his accent and his pebble glasses (he suffered from myopia), Thomson became a well-known figure in Britain. Lord Thomon (he was made a baron in 1964) gained *The Times* in 1966 when he agreed with Gavin Astor, Lord Astor of Hever, to set up a joint company, Times Newspapers, to control both *The Times* and the *Sunday Times*. The Thomson Organisation would own 85 per cent, the Astor family 15 per cent: an arrangement to meet the scrutiny of the Monopolies and Mergers Commission. In his role as a newspaper proprietor Thomson resolutely refused to be drawn into editorial matters. What he failed to understand, and what infuriated him, were the idiotic overmanning practices of the Fleet Street printers. Thomson expressed his views with characteristic courage and candour in his autobiography *After I Was Sixty* (1975). Besides newspapers and television, the Thomson Organisation had investments in the booming North Sea oil industry. In North America his major acquisition in the 1960s was the Brush Moore group of newspapers in the USA. Thomson founded the £5 million Thomson Foundation, a training centre for media professionals, in 1962. Much interested in the needs for mass media and understanding the commercial potential of the Third World and the East, he visited African countries, India, the USSR (in 1964) and toured China in 1972. He died in Toronto. Thomson married, in 1916, Edna Irvine (she died of cancer in 1951); they had two daughters and a son, Kenneth. See Bernard Sendall, *Independent Television in Britain* (2 vols, 1982-83); *The Times*, 5, 10, 13 August 1976.

THORNTON, Sir Ronald George
(21 July 1901 - 17 July 1981)

Banker, the son of Henry George Thornton, whose untimely death prevented him from going to university, he was educated at St Dunstan's College, Catford, and at 18 joined Barclays Bank. Briefly in the inspection department and at Birmingham head office, he spent most of his career at the Lombard Street branch, London, becoming a manager there in 1940. He became an assistant general manager in 1943 and a general manager in 1946, reaching senior general manager before he retired in 1961. He was then appointed a director of Barclays and vice-chairman, 1962-66. Knighted in 1965, he was a director of the Bank of England, 1966-70, the first career clearing banker in this position. While at Barclays he worked for 30 years with Anthony William Tuke (qv). In the 1950s, when Barclays was the largest clearing banker with over 20,000 employees, he chaired a Committee of London Clearing Bankers committee which dealt with the Cheque Act of 1957 (eliminating the need to endorse cheques) and with evidence to the Radcliffe inquiry into the workings of the monetary system, 1957-59. He saw the appointment of the first woman branch manager, the first incursion by an English bank into hire purchase, and the launching of personal loans. He sat on the Committee of Inquiry on Decimal Currency (strongly advocating the pound as the basic unit) and was a prominent member of the Export Council for Europe, 1960-64. As a progressive chairman of the Banking Information Service, 1962-66, he activated an internationally-admired bank education service. He was a director of the Friends Provident & Century Life Office, the Century Insurance Co, Century Insurance Trust Ltd, and United Dominions Trust Ltd, 1962-71. Thornton married, in 1927, Agnes Margaret née Masson; they had a son and a daughter. See *Spread Eagle* April 1966; *The Times*, 22 July 1981.

TOMBS, Sir Francis (Leonard)
Baron Tombs of Brailes
(17 May 1924 -)
Industrialist, born in Walsall, the son of Joseph and Jane Tombs. Educated at Elmore Green School, Walsall, he left at 16 to begin a lifelong career in engineering by joining the General Electric Co, taking an economics degree at Birmingham College of Technology in his spare time. Tombs' early experience was with the electricity industry: with Birmingham electricity department, 1946-47, and with the British Electricity Authority, 1948-57. After working as a general manager at GEC at Erith, Kent, 1958-67, and as a director at James Howden in Glasgow, 1967-68, Tombs joined the South of Scotland Electricity Board in 1969. At the SSEB he was appointed chairman, 1974-77, and then accepted Tony Benn's invitation to chair the Electricity Council. He resigned from the post three years later when the Conservatives scrapped the Council's Labour-inspired plans for revamping the industry. In the 1980s he chaired both the Weir Group and Turner & Newhall, before accepting the chairmanship of aero-engine maker Rolls-Royce in 1985. He stayed at RR until 1992, when he was succeeded by Sir Ralph Robins (qv) - a period of uneven profitability for the company, partly a reflection of costly development programmes and the disruptions caused by the Gulf War and the recession. He was chairman of the Engineering Council, 1985-88; president of the Institution of Electrical Engineers, 1981-2; and also chaired the Advisory Council of Science and Technology (1987-90), advising Government on its research priorities and the extent of its involvement with international projects. In 1949 he married Marjorie Evans: they have three daughters. Tombs was knighted in 1978 and created a life peer in 1990.

TOMPKINS, (Granville) Richard (Francis)
(15 May 1918 - 6 December 1992)
Trading stamps entrepreneur, brought up in north London, the son of Richard and Ethel May Tompkins. He attended Pakeman Street LCC School in Holloway, north London, leaving at the age of 13 as a self-confessed dunce. He qualified as an engineering draughtsman, but had a succession of humble jobs either side of the Second World War, which he spent with the Home Forces. After the war he set up a small printing firm, but his business breakthrough came after a visit to the USA in the mid-1950s, where he had seen the impact of trading stamps. In 1958 he launched Green Shield Stamps in London: after a slow start the idea took off in the 1960s, when Tompkins was helped by a deal with Sir John Cohen (qv) of Tesco. Tompkins held 97 per cent of the shares in the Green Shield company, which at its peak employed 5,000. The stamps familiarised consumers with catalogue shopping, which Tompkins exploited with the founding of the Argos discount chain in 1973 (he sold it in 1979 to BAT for £25 million). The inflation of the 1970s killed trading stamps and by 1980 (when he founded the Tompkins Foundation for his charitable work) his career was effectively over. But by then Tompkins had made his fortune: at his death he was reputed to be worth £50 million. He was married twice: he parted from his first wife, whom he had married during the Second World War, in 1962 (they had two daughters). In 1970 he married the model Elizabeth Nancy Duke: they had one daughter. See Philip Beresford, *The Sunday Times Book of the Rich* (1990).

TUGENDHAT, Sir Christopher
Baron Tugendhat
(23 February 1937 -)
Industrialist, the elder son of Dr Georg Tugendhat (1898-1973), an Austrian Jewish emigré, who later became a governer of the London School of Economics and a founder of the Manchester Oil Refinery Group. His mother, Maire Littledale, was an Irish catholic. Educated at Ampleforth College and Caius College, Cambridge, he became a journalist with the *Financial Times* between 1960 and 1970. He then held the safest Conservative seat in the country (Cities of London and Westminster) between 1970 and 1974, before becoming an EEC British commissioner in Brussels under Roy Jenkins. In the 1970s and 1980s Tugendhat also sat on the boards of oil companies and television companies, served as a director at Commercial Union and the BOC Group and as deputy chairman of the National Westminster Bank. One of his most eventful posts was as chairman of the Civil Aviation

Authority between 1986 and 1991, when he
defused publicity over 'near misses', oversaw the
British Airways takeover of British Caledonian, and
masterminded new investments in air traffic control. In 1991 he became chairman of Abbey
National (with Peter Birch (qv) as his chief executive), in time to see the first drop in its profits since
its conversion from building society to a bank. In
1992, with a workforce of 18,000 and a stock market value of £3.3 billion, Abbey National had sales
of £744 million and pre-tax profits of £270 million. One of his first decisions at Abbey National
was to offer for sale its unsuccessful estate agency
business, which was responsible for losses and write
downs of £226 million since its inception in 1987.
In 1967 Tugendhat married Julia Lissant Dobson:
they have two sons. He was knighted in 1990. See
Christopher Tugendhat, *Oil: The Big Business*
(1968), *The Multinationals* (1971).

TUKE, Anthony William
(24 February 1897 - 12 June 1975)
Clearing banker, born at Saffron Walden, Essex,
the son of William Favell Tuke - chairman of the
Quaker-inspired Barclays Bank - and his wife Eva
Marian née Nockolds. Educated at Winchester, he
joined the bank in 1919 and after steadily rising
through the executive ranks became chairman
between 1951 and 1962. During that decade
Barclays became the UK's largest bank and Tuke,
despite his conservatism (he was known as the 'Iron
Tuke'), oversaw some revolutionary changes in
banking, such as computerisation. He married in
1919 Agnes Edna née Gannaway and they had
three sons, one of whom, Anthony Favill Tuke,
survived him and became chairman of Barclays in
1973. He left £167,369. See Anthony William
Tuke (with Richard J H Gillman), *Barclays Bank
Ltd, 1926-1969* (1972); *DBB*.

TURNBULL, Sir George (Henry)
(17 October 1926 - 22 December 1992)
Motor vehicle industrialist, educated at King Henry
VIII School, Coventry, and Birmingham
University (BSc mechanical engineering). Turnbull
became an apprentice in the Coventry car industry
in 1941 and rose rapidly through the ranks at
Standard Triumph, which later became part of
British Leyland. In 1973 Turnbull became managing director of this last ditch attempt to save the
UK's only surviving mass producer of cars and
trucks. But after disagreements with Lord Stokes
(qv), in 1974 Turnbull left to direct the little-
heard-of Hyundai Motors of South Korea, which
he made a world force. From 1977 to 1979 he
worked with the Iran National Motor Co in
Tehran, before returning to Coventry as head of

Talbot UK. In 1984 he became managing director
at Inchcape and in 1986 chairman and chief executive. Although Inchcape was a sprawling international trader, Turnbull returned to the automobile
fold, for Inchcape sells more than 180,000 cars a
year in more than 20 countries. Ironically - in view
of Turnbull's reputation (he was once described as
the best leader British Leyland never had) and his
commitment to the UK car industry - Turnbull
reinforced Inchcape's involvement in cars and his
new company became a major distributor for
Toyota (which by 1990 had acquired a 5 per cent
holding in Inchcape). Under Turnbull, Inchcape's
profits grew from £86 million to £185 million: by
1992 the firm's market capitalisation stood at £2
billion (amongst the top 50 UK firms), with a
turnover in the previous year of £3,635 million
and a workforce of nearly 37,000. Knighted in
1990, at the end of 1991 Turnbull retired through
ill-health, and the chairmanship was resumed by Sir
David Orr, with Charles Mackay as chief executive. From 1982 to 1984 he was chairman of the
Society of Motor Manufacturers; and after 1987
chairman of the Industrial Society. Turnbull married in 1950 Marion Wing: they had one son and
two daughters. See Stephanie Jones, *Two Centuries
of Overseas Trading: The Origins and Growth of the
Inchcape Group* (1986).

TURNER, Sir Samuel
(18 February 1878 - 23 December 1955)
Asbestos manufacturer, the son of Robert Turner,
one of the three sons of Samuel Turner I, cotton
spinner of Spotland, Rochdale, who added asbestos
works to the cotton mills of their father. Samuel
Turner III was educated at schools in England,
Germany and Switzerland and then entered the
family firm. This was headed by his uncle Samuel
Turner II (1840-1924, knighted in 1914) who was
senior partner in the cotton mills of S Turner & Co
Ltd, the asbestos works of Turner Bros Ltd and
chairman of Turner & Newall Ltd, the merger of
1920 between Turner Bros and Newalls, magne-
sium manufacturers of Washington near Gateshead.
The company grew substantially in the interwar
years in response to demand for asbestos products
for the building and motor vehicle industries.
Samuel Turner III became a director of Turner &
Newall in 1920, deputy chairman and then chairman in 1929, remaining in office until 1944. In the
mid-1930s he was also a joint managing director.
By 1935 the firm comprised a group of 30 operating companies, 22 in the UK, and employed about
10,000, presumably over 7,000 in the UK. The
UK companies processed asbestos in the forms of
textiles, cement and insulation materials. The foreign subsidiaries, in South Africa, Southern

Rhodesia and the USA, mostly mining companies, were acquired to safeguard supplies of raw asbestos. Samuel Turner III recorded in *WW* for 1935 that he 'entered upon a business career at the age of 18, and since then devoted entire time to that and to travel incidental thereto' suggesting that he had much to do with the overseas subsidiaries. Sir Samuel Turner (he was knighted in 1938) was vice-chairman of the District Bank, 1942-49. He was high sheriff of Lancashire in 1930, made a free-man of Rochdale in 1937, served as president of the Devonshire Royal Hospital, Buxton in 1938-39, as well as a member of the court of governors of Manchester University, which he endowed with a new dental hospital and school in 1937. Rochdale received various gifts from Sir Samuel Turner and his family including Denehurst Park, his father's home. Turner wrote two books, *Eclipse or Empire* (with H B Gray, 1916) and *From War to Work* (1918). In his early adulthood Samuel Turner III ran the Sunday School at the Baillie Street chapel, Rochdale, where the Turner family were pillars of the United Methodist Free Churches (United Methodist Church from 1907, Methodist Church from 1932). He married, in 1902, Jane née Fielden; they had a son and a daughter. See *The Times*, 24 December 1955; *United Methodist Magazine* (1914).

U

URQUHART, Lawrence McAllister
(24 September 1935 -)
Oil company executive, the son of Robert and Josephine Urquhart. Educated at Strathallan and King's College, London (where he read law), he joined Price Waterhouse & Co, 1957-62. He was employed by Shell International Petroleum in 1962-64, then worked for PA Management Consultants, Charterhouse and TKM, before returning to the oil industry to work for Burmah Oil in 1977. Burmah (renamed Burmah Castrol in 1990) had run into grave difficulties in the mid-1970s, but it was rescued by a team led by (Sir) Alastair Down. Urquhart became managing director of Burmah Castrol 1985-88, then chief executive, and finally chairman in 1990. He continued restructuring the company, establishing new group directors which reflected the importance of its lubricants (Castrol's products account for about two-thirds of the group's earnings). In 1991 Burmah Castrol's turnover was £2,352 million (pre-tax profit £165 million) and it employed over 24,000 workers (75 per cent of whom work out-side the UK). Urquhart in 1992 was an independent director of the ECC Group, Scottish Widows Fund and Life Assurance Society, and Premier Consolidated Goldfields. He was also a member of the South Western Regional Health Authority. He married in 1961 Elizabeth Catherine Burns: they have three sons and one daughter. See T A B Corley, *A History of the Burmah Oil Company, 1886-1966* (2 vols, 1983-88)

V

VALLANCE, Iain David Thomas
(20 May 1943 -)
Telecommunications executive, the son of Edmund Thomas Vallance and his wife Janet Davidson. His Scottish parents both worked for the Post Office, his father later becoming director of the organisation in Scotland. Educated at Edinburgh Academy, Dulwich College, Glasgow Academy and Brasenose College, Oxford, and London Graduate School of Business Studies (MSc), he joined the Post Office as Assistant Postal Controller in 1966. After various executive posts in finance and planning at the Post Office and its successor (after privatisation in 1984) British Telecom, Vallance became chairman of BT in 1987 after Sir George Jefferson, inaugural chairman of the privatised company, was forced out in a public row over efficiency and service. He has instituted a cor-porate shake-up which will reduce jobs by 50,000 in five years (in 1992 BT employed 175,000) and give BT a more international identity. Under Vallance has occurred BT's abandonment of the name British Telecom and its yellow logo, replacing it with a red and blue Pan-like piper. Service and repair times have also improved drastically and so have profits (a 14 per cent leap in 1990-91, with pre-tax profits over £3 billion) and the chairman's salary (to £374,000). Not all of this has proved popular, though Vallance argues that BT needs all the cash it can get for global expansion and opposes Government interference. In 1992 he was appointed a non-executive director of the Royal Bank of Scotland. In 1967 he married Elizabeth Mary McGonnigill, who has been a visiting professor at London University: they have one son and one daughter.

VANSITTART, Guy Nicholas
(8 September 1893 - 3 February 1989)
Motor vehicle company chairman, youngest of the three sons of Captain Robert Arnold Vansittart OBE, FRGS and his wife Alice née Blane, he was educated at Eton and Trinity College, Oxford, where he read history. He was commissioned in the Indian Army in 1913 and served with the Central India Horse regiment until 1922, reaching the rank of captain. His brother, Robert Gilbert, attained eminence in the Foreign Office as chief diplomatic adviser to the Foreign Secretary, 1938-41, and was created Baron Vansittart in 1941. Guy Vansittart joined the Institute of Directors in 1939 when he

recorded one directorship, of Vauxhall Motors Ltd, the British subsidiary since 1925 of General Motors Corporation in the USA. By 1943 he was additionally a director of AC-Sphinx Sparking Plug Co Ltd, Associated Ethyl Co Ltd, Delco-Remy & Hyatt Ltd and Frigidaire Ltd, divisions of General Motors Ltd (the British subsidiary of the American parent). After the war he was still a director of these companies, except Associated Ethyl, and was additionally a director of General Motors Ltd. In 1948 he became chairman of Vauxhall Motors Ltd and by 1955 was also chairman of General Motors Ltd. He retired from both posts in 1958-59. At Vauxhall Motors he seems to have played a figurehead role for the business was run at a strategic level by its American owners and at the works level by managers like Charles Bartlett (qv) and Walter Hill. After retiring from the Vauxhall board Vansittart turned to insurance and investment companies for a business income. In 1961 he was a director of R H Heal & Co Ltd, Copthall Holdings Ltd, Pekin Syndicate Ltd and Perthpoint Investment Ltd. In 1963 he was a director of Perth Point Investments Ltd, Copthall Holdings Ltd, Anglo-Continental Investment & Finance Co Ltd, Padley & Venables Ltd, and Kreglinger & Co. Vansittart lived at Cholsey Grange, Ibstone, Buckinghamshire, where shooting and riding were his recreations. He married, in 1922, Margaret Helen, daughter of Sir Henry Procter of Great Amwell, Hertford, formerly Bombay merchant and YMCA promoter; they had three daughters.

VERDON-SMITH, Sir (William) Reginald

(5 November 1912 - 21 June 1992)

Aeroplane company executive, the son of Sir William G Verdon Smith (qv). The family owned, along with their cousins the Whites - relatives of Sir George White (qv) - the Bristol Aeroplane Co. Educated at Repton and Brasenose College, Oxford, he gained a first in jurisprudence and the Vinerian Law Scholarship. He was called to the Bar, but responded to his father's request to join the Bristol Aeroplane Co in 1938. By 1942 he was on the board of the firm, which, although it had gone public in 1935 with a capital of £1.5 million and employed 50,000, was still family-controlled. In 1952 he was managing director and chairman, 1955-68, succeeding his father who had held the post for 25 years. Under Verdon-Smith, family ownership and control were gradually diluted as the business was absorbed into the developing UK aircraft industry by a series of mergers (with Armstrong Siddeley Motors in 1959, the British Aircraft Corporation (BAC) in 1960, and rivals Rolls Royce in 1966). Verdon-Smith became chairman of the BAC's hold-

ing company between 1969 and 1972 (having survived a scandal in 1968 concerning excess profits at Bristol Siddeley Engines), combining the post with a banking career (he was a director of Lloyds Bank between 1951 and 1983 and chairman of Lloyds Bank International, 1973-79). In 1946-48 he was the youngest ever president of the Society of British Aircraft Constructors. He was concerned throughout his career to give Britain better-educated engineers and managers. He raised money for a new chair in aircraft engineering at Bristol University and became the University's Pro-Chancellor. He served on a succession of government committees and inquiries in the 1950s and 1960s. His knighthood in 1953 was for his contribution to employment training. He married in 1946 Jane Hobbs, by whom he had one son and one daughter. See Charles Gardner, *British Aircraft Corporation: A History* (1981).

VESTEY, Samuel George Armstrong
3rd Baron Vestey of Kingswood
(19 March 1941 -)

VESTEY, Edmund Hoyle
(19 June 1932 -)

Meat importers and retailers and cousins and heirs to a business empire that was founded in the late nineteenth century by (Baron) William Vestey (1859-1940) and (Sir) Edmund Hoyle Vestey (1866-1953). The Liverpool-based Vesteys, aided by a burgeoning demand from the industrialising cities and developments in refrigeration and shipping, built up cattle ranches, cold storage facilities and butcher's shops around the world. Samuel was the only son of the late Captain the Honourable William Howarth Vestey and Pamela Helen Fullerton née Armstrong; Edmund the only son of Ronald Arthur Vestey and Florence Ellen McLean. Samuel was educated at Eton and was with the Scots Guards before joining Union International, the main Vestey company; Edmund was also educated at Eton and was with the Queen's Bays until he joined the business. They are presently chief executives of Union International (Samuel is director and Edmund has been chairman since 1988), with Timothy Vestey (son of Edmund) as managing director. The Vesteys are one of the richest families in the UK, reckoned to be worth £1.5 billion in 1990. Union International entered the 1990s employing 23,000 world-wide and with over a thousand Dewhurst butcher's shops in the UK. It made some £27 million profits on £1.4 billion turnover in 1989, but overcapacity in the meat industry by 1991 hit profits and the group had debts of £460 million. It made a loss of nearly £20 million in 1990 and more than £100 million in

1991. For the first time the Vesteys recruited an outsider as chief executive - Terry Robinson, an accountant from the Lonrho board. By 1993 he had returned the business to profitability, selling 700 of its butcher's shops and reorganising the business. The Vesteys' fortune is alleged to have fallen by £500 million. Lord Vestey is twice married: first in 1970 to Kathryn Mary Eccles (dissolved 1981, two daughters); second in 1981 to Celia Elizabeth Knight (two sons). Edmund married in 1960 Anne Moubray, daughter of General Sir Geoffry Scoones: they have four sons. Both live is some style, mix with the Royal family and have a taste for hunting and polo. The ability of the family to evade income tax completely through offshore trusts brought them some notoriety in the 1980s. See Philip Knightley, *The Vestey Affair* (1981); *DBB*.

VICKERS, Albert
(16 September 1838 - 12 July 1919)

VICKERS, (Thomas Edward) Tom
(9 July 1833 - 19 October 1915)
Steel and armaments manufacturers, both born in Sheffield, the sons of Edward Vickers (1804-97) and Anne née Naylor. Their father was a miller, who later launched the Vickers' steelmaking dynasty in Sheffield in the early nineteenth century; their mother was the daughter of a local steelmaker. Tom attended Sheffield Collegiate School and then received technical training in Germany, at Neuwied-on the-Rhine; Albert was educated privately and then studied at Hamel-on-the Weser. Tom (usually known as Colonel Tom, because of his assocation with the local militia) had joined the business by the age of 21, masterminding its expansion to the River Don Works in the 1860s. Tom became chairman of Vickers in 1873, when the business employed about a thousand men. Albert joined Vickers in 1854, gaining experience in the US market. The brothers complemented each other: Tom the technologist; Albert the business diplomat and strategist. Towards the end of the nineteenth century, they steered Vickers into the arms trade, acquiring a string of UK and foreign subsidiaries that turned the company into an integrated, though diverse, arms conglomerate that vied with W G Armstrong as Britain's leading arsenal. In 1909 Tom resigned as chairman, handing over to Albert, who held the post until 1918. By 1914 Vickers's issued share capital was almost £6 million; the average annual profits since 1897 had been £589,391. By 1918 only Coats, Lever Bros and Imperial Tobacco surpassed it in capital size. Tom boasted that Vickers could build a battleship from start to finish: however, this dependence on armaments proved a liability in the 1920s. Both

men shunned publicity. Tom was a Conservative, a magistrate, served as Master Cutler in 1872, and was created CB in 1898. Albert's influence as armourer-statesman is shown by the award of several foreign decorations, such as the Order of the Rising Sun in Japan. Tom married in 1860 Frances Mary Douglas (1841-1904), the daughter of a London surgeon; they had two sons and four daughters. Albert in 1861 married a Bostonian, Helen Horton Gage, by whom he had three children. After her death he married in 1875 Edith née Foster: they had a son and two daughters. Tom left £117,347; Albert £774,686. See John D Scott, *Vickers: A History* (1962); Clive Trebilcock, *The Vickers Brothers* (1977).

VILLIERS, Sir Charles (Hyde)
(14 August 1912 - 22 January 1992)
Industrialist, the son of Algernon Hyde Villiers and Beatrix Paul (later Lady Aldenham). Born into a famous and patrician family, his ancestors included Barbara Villiers, mistress of Charles II. Educated at Eton and New College, Oxford, in 1931 he became assistant to the Reverend Tubby Clayton of Toc H before taking up a merchant banking post with Glyn Mills in 1932. In 1936 he joined the Grenadier Guards, later serving in Special Operations during the Second World War and winning the MC. He resumed his banking career in the City with J Henry Schroder Wagg in 1948, before assisting the Labour Government as managing director of the Industrial Reorganisation Corporation between 1968 and 1971. After a spell as chairman of Guinness Mahon & Co, between 1976 and 1980 he was appointed chairman of the British Steel Corporation in succession to Monty Finniston (qv). Faced with a state industry in headlong decline, after the expansionism of Lord Melchett (qv) (also a merchant banker) and Finniston had foundered, Villiers began a cutback of jobs and investment, and introduced a 'Steel Contract' to devolve management. But though he was well-intentioned, his gentleman-amateur image and his BSC U-turn lost him the support of the Government during the 1980 steel strike and his departure was unmourned. Under Villiers the BSC's workforce fell from about 208,000 to 166,000; and its losses had reached £1,784,000 million by 1980. The public credit and the blame for the revolution he had initiated at the BSC fell on his successor, Ian MacGregor (qv). Villiers left to head the job creation subsidiary, BSC (Industry), which was a notable success. He was also on the board of several merchant banks and government bodies. He was knighted in 1975. Villiers married first in 1938 Pamela Constance Flower, by whom he had a son. On his second marriage in 1946 to

VIRANI

the Belgian resistance heroine, Countess Maire Jose de la Barre d'Erquelinnes (by whom he had two daughters), he embraced Catholicism. See Charles Villiers, *Start Again, Britain* (1984); Geoffrey F Dudley and Jeremy J Richardson, *Politics and Steel in Britain 1967-1988: The Life and Times of the British Steel Corporation* (1990).

VIRANI, Nazmudin Gulamhusein
(2 March 1948 -)

Property and leisure company entrepreneur, born in Uganda, the son of Gulamhusein Virani and his wife Fatma. Educated at the Aga Khan School, Kampala, he left Uganda in 1972 and settled in the UK, where he immediately bought a supermarket in Dulwich. Working eighteen hours a day, seven days a week, he built up a chain of 19 supermarkets by the mid-1970s, and then moved into hotel and pubs. His master company was Control Securities, which Virani moulded into £240 million enterprise, the largest Asian-owned business in Britain. Amongst the investors Virani attracted was Gerald Ronson (qv). But Virani did not survive the property crash after 1987. In the fallout of the BCCI scandal in 1992, Virani was charged on 14 counts of fraud. He and his two brothers resigned from the board of Control, which was in refinancing talks with its bankers. An Ismaili Moslem, Virani married in 1970 Yasmin Abdul Rasul Ismail: they have two sons and one daughter.

W

WALKER, George (Alfred)
(14 April 1929 -)

Property developer and entrepreneur, born into a working-class family in the East End of London, the son of William James Walker and Ellen née Page. His father was a brewery drayman; his mother a shorthand typist. Educated at Jubilee School, Bedford, Essex, at 14 he began a colourful career: first as a porter in Billingsgate fish market, then as a professional boxer, before spending a two-year spell in prison for a warehouse robbery. In the 1960s he managed his brother Billy's career as a top British heavyweight (the 'Blond Bomber') before moving into business. Trading on Billy's name, in London the brothers set up a chain of Billy's Baked Potato outlets: they sold out in 1969 for £¼ million and bought their first greyhound track. It was the start of Brent Walker, the company which Walker expanded in the 1980s to include casinos, fruit-machine operations, pubs, leisure centres, betting shops, golf courses and marinas - all with the help of the banks. Brent Cross Shopping Centre, London's Trocadero and Brighton Marina were among the most notable sites. Walker himself was

reputed to have amassed a personal fortune of £40 million. In 1989, the banks helped Walker acquire the William Hill betting shops from Grand Metropolitan for £685 million. But Brent Walker (with debts of £468 million and assets of only about £25 million) folded when the property boom collapsed at the end of the 1980s and the company only narrowly escaping extinction. In 1992 Walker was ousted by the banks. In the following year, while attempting to resurrect his fortunes selling cigarettes in the former Soviet Union, he was charged with theft and false accounting at Brent Walker involving £12.5 million. Walker was made a freeman of the City of London in 1978. He married in 1957 Jean Maureen, the daughter of Georgie Hatton, an Essex garage owner: they have one son and two daughters.

WALKER, Sir Herbert Ashcombe
(16 May 1868 - 29 September 1945)

Railway manager, born at Paddington, London, the son of George Stephen Walker (a future MD) and Ellen Frances née Ley. After attending North London Collegiate School and St Francis Xavier's College, Bruges, he joined the London & North Western Railway in 1885. Walker progressed at the LNWR, but he was attracted by a better offer from the London & South Western, which he joined in 1912 as general manager. Before his retirement in 1937, he transformed the L & SWR's suburban network with electrification and dealt effectively with the problems posed by the formation of the Southern Railway group in 1922. During the First World War he became chairman of the Railway Executive Committee under the Board of Trade and was subsequently knighted in 1915 and then made KCB in 1917. He married twice: first in 1895 to Ethel Griffiths (d 1909), a solicitors' daughter; second in 1910 to Lorina, a widow of A Shields of the Stock Exchange. He left £38,059. See Cuthbert Hamilton Ellis, *The South Western Railway* (1956); DBB.

WALKER, Jack
(c 1930 -)

Steel stockholder and airline operator, the son of the owner of a sheet metal business in Blackburn. He left school at 14 and took over the family business, C Walker & Sons, on his father's death in 1951. Jack Walker moved the firm out of sheet metal and into steel stockholding. In 1956 sales were £46,000; by 1988 they were £623 million with £48 million profits and the group had 3,400 employees. Walker had expanded the business by buying the stockholding operations of Tube Investments in 1983; then three years later he bought GKN Steelstock for £50 million, making

218

his firm the largest steel stockholder in the UK. In 1989 Walker himself sold out to British Steel for £330 million. Jack and his brother and business partner, Fred, shared the proceeds from the highest sum ever paid for a private British company. Jack based himself in Jersey, where the two brothers are concentrating on running Walker's Jersey European Airlines, on which he has spent some £30 million. One of the richest individuals in the UK with a fortune estimated at £360 million (enough to place him amongst the 20 richest in the land), Walker shuns publicity. However, his attempt to transform Blackburn Football Club into a force in British league football (he has spent £2.5 million on players and lured Kenny Daglish to become manager) has brought him into the limelight. See Philip Beresford, *The Sunday Times Book of the Rich* (1990).

WALKER, Philip Gordon
(9 June 1912 -)
Paper and insurance company chairman, one of the six sons and eight children of William Walker, oil and grease manufacturer of Hanley in the Potteries and a prominent local Methodist, and his wife Kate Blanche née Dixon, he was educated at Epworth College, Rhyl and then trained as a chartered accountant with Bourner, Bullock & Co of Stoke-on-Trent, 1929-35. He worked in his father's firm, Walkers (Century Oils) Ltd, 1935-40, afterwards returning to a professional firm of accountants, Layton-Bennett, Billingham & Co where he was a partner, 1944-51. In this capacity he encountered Albert E Reed & Co, paper manufacturers with mills in the West of England and Kent, for whom his firm acted as consulting accountants. Walker became a close friend of Clifford Dommett Sheldon, Reeds' energetic and innovative vice-chairman and managing director, and was with him in the USA when he suddenly died in 1950. Though not an engineer, in contrast to Sheldon, Walker was very familiar with the industry and was appointed managing director in 1951, nominated by the ailing chairman, (Albert) Ralph Reed (1884-1958). Walker, at Reeds until 1963, and his board moved relatively away from the newsprint market and more into cellulose tissues (they made the first British Kleenex handkerchief in 1952) and packaging. Despite problems of foreign competition arising from GATT and EFTA, Reeds' workforce rose from 5,000 in 1950 to 16,700 in 1960 and 26,000 in 1964-65. Walker left when Cecil King (qv) absorbed Reed's into his International Publishing Corporation. After Reed's, Walker was chairman and managing director of Philblack Ltd, 1963-71; chairman of Sun Life Assurance Society Ltd, 1971-82 (executive chairman, 1976-82); and

chairman of Chapman Industries PLC, 1968-83. He was also a part-time member of the Monopolies and Mergers Commission, 1963-65; member of the Performing Right Tribunal, 1971-83; and member of the Restrictive Practices Court, 1973-83. Walker married twice: first, in 1938, to Anne May (marriage dissolved), by whom he had a son and two daughters; secondly, in 1962, to Elizabeth Oliver.

WALLACE, William
(10 May 1891 - 21 October 1976)
Chairman of confectionery manufacturing company, born in Sunderland, the son of James Wallace, then working in a firm of solicitors (and qualifying in 1895 at the age of 36), and his wife Alice née Donkin; William was educated locally and privately at Argyle House School, until he was 16 and was then articled to his father who had set up his own practice in 1903, specialising in shipping law. After his father's death in 1911 he went on to qualify as a solicitor in 1912, attaining first-class honours. During several years' practising in Newcastle-upon-Tyne he became interested in social work and, influenced by Benjamin Seebohm Rowntree (qv), joined the Ministry of Reconstruction, 1917-19. In 1919 he joined Rowntrees at York as assistant to Seebohm Rowntree, then labour director, and established the company's profit sharing scheme. He became secretary to the finance director in 1924 and then administrative secretary in the chairman's office in 1929, completing a training which led to the company secretaryship at the end of 1929. Wallace joined the board of Rowntree & Co Ltd in 1931, serving as deputy chairman, 1944-52, and chairman, 1952-57. His term at the top, with the company employing 19,000 in 1955, saw the transition from family to professional management. He was president of the Cocoa, Chocolate and Confectionery Alliance Ltd, 1951-53; member of the grand council of the Federation of British Industry; lay member of the Restrictive Practices Court, 1958-60; and founder member of the British Institute of Management. He also sat on various Rowntree family trusts. Wallace wrote *Business Forecasting and Its Practical Application* (1927), on the strength of which he was awarded a London University MCom; *Enterprise First* (1946); and *Prescription for Partnership* (1959). For the Liberal Party he anonymously wrote *We Can Conquer Unemployment* (1929). Raised a Congregationalist, he was identified with the Society of Friends in middle life. Wallace married, in 1918, Nancie E Hancox; they had a son and two daughters. See *The Times*, 23 October 1976; William Wallace, *"I Was Concerned": The Autobiography of William Wallace* (1985).

WALTERS, Sir Peter (Ingram)
(11 March 1931 -)

Petroleum company executive, born in Birmingham, the son of Stephen Walters and Edna née Redgate. He attended King Edward's School and Birmingham University (BCom). After military service, he joined British Petroleum in 1954, working in international oil supply and development and regional management. He was appointed managing director in 1973 and was amongst those BP directors who favoured a policy of diversification into coal, minerals and information technology as a solution to the oil crisis of the 1970s. This was not successful and after heavy losses in 1981 of £600 million in its European oil, chemical and shipping businesses, plus considerable duplication in the US (where it part-owned Standard Oil) Walters was appointed chairman and began reversing the policy of diversification, selling off BP's coal, IT and minerals interests. He retired in 1990 and was succeeded by Robert Horton (qv). He is currently a non-executive director of SmithKline Beecham, deputy chairman of Thorn EMI and non-executive chairman of Blue Circle. He became deputy chairman of the Midland Bank in 1990 and chairman the following year. He was knighted in 1984. In 1960 he married Patricia Anne née Tulloch: they have two sons and one daughter.

WANLESS, Derek
(29 September 1947 -)

Banking executive, the son of Norman Wanless, a Blue Circle cement store manager in Newcastle upon Tyne, and his wife Edna née Charlton. He won a scholarship to a direct grant school, Newcastle Royal Grammar, and then attended King's College, Cambridge, where he took a first in mathematics and was a senior wrangler. The Natwest Bank had supported him with a scholarship at Cambridge and he began his career with them in 1970. After attachment to a former finance director, Wanless became a planning manager at 28. He was an area manager in Newcastle in the 1980s and became a director of Natwest in 1991. After working as chief executive of UK financial services, 1990-92, he became group chief executive of Natwest in 1992. He married in 1971 Vera West and they have one son and four daughters.

WARBURG, Sir Siegmund George
(30 September 1902 - 18 October 1982)

Banker, born at Urach, southern Germany, the only child of Georg Siegmund Warburg, a Jewish landowner, and Lucie née Kaulla. Educated at the Humanistic Gymnasia of Reutlingen and then of Urach, at 17 he joined the family firm of M M Warburg & Co, one of the leading German private banks. He became partner in 1930, but three years later, with Hitler's rise to power, he moved to London and founded a finance company - the New Trading Co Ltd - which in 1946 adopted the name of S G Warburg & Co Ltd. Over the next 35 years Warburg's not only won recognition, but became London's foremost merchant bank. Warburg, who was naturalised in 1939, was knighted in 1966. He retired to Switzerland in 1973. He married in 1925 Eva Maria née Philipson: they had a son and a daughter. See Jacques Attali, *A Man of Influence* (1986); Stanley Chapman, *The Rise of Merchant Banking* (1984); *DNB*.

WARING, Sir Arthur Bertram
(12 June 1893 - 2 March 1974)

Manufacturer of electrical engineering components, born in Manchester, the son of Bennett Morton Waring, a wholesale jeweller, he was educated privately. His training as a chartered accountant, completed in 1920, was interrupted by the First World War, in which he joined the Lancashire Fusiliers, was commissioned in the field and served as a captain with the 29th Division at Gallipoli. In 1922 Waring became the first qualified accountant on the staff of Joseph Lucas Ltd, the Birmingham electrical components manufacturer headed in the interwar years by Oliver Lucas and Peter Bennett (qv). By 1924 Waring was company secretary. He proved adept at applying the policies of Lucas and Bennett who left day-to-day management to him. Waring became joint general manager in 1931 and a director in 1935 when the company employed 20,000. During the Second World War he operationally managed 40,000 employees in 33 factories. He became joint managing director with Bennett (the chairman) in 1948 and then chairman in 1951. He remained in charge until 1969 when he became honorary president. Under Sir Bertram Waring (he was knighted in 1960) the company was transformed from a Birmingham business producing accessories for the motor industry into an international group with interests spreading into aviation components and industrial engineering. In 1951 its sales of £42.5 million made £928,297 net profit; in 1969 sales of £251 million, worldwide, made £16.7 million pre-tax profit. Employment numbers rose from 45,000 in 1955 to 65,000 in 1966. Waring held many presidential posts in the Birmingham engineering trades and in the motor industry, including the Motor Industry Research Association and the Birmingham and District Engineering and Allied Employers' Association. He was life member of the court of governors of Birmingham University and a past president of the Birmingham branch of the British Legion. Waring married in 1927 Muriel née Columbell, daughter of a motor trader; they had a son. See *DBB*; Harold Nockolds, *Lucas: The First 100 Years* (2 vols, 1976-78).

WARNER, Sir Lionel Ashton Piers
(30 April 1875 - 22 November 1953)

Port manager, born at Bedford, the son of Major Ashton C Warner of the 20th Hussars, he was educated at Marlborough and, after a short time with the Great Western Railway at Abergavenny, worked for the London & North Western Railway Co, 1893-1914, first at headquarters at Euston, then as outdoor assistant to the superintendent at Preston and in 1910 as goods superintendent at Liverpool. In 1913 he became divisional superintendent for the north, based at Manchester, but in 1914 accepted the invitation to become assistant general manager of the Mersey Docks & Harbour Board with a view to succeeding the general manager, Alfred Chandler. During the First World War Warner was secretary of the Liverpool Co-ordination Committee, formed to harmonise the naval, military and civil requirements of the port; in 1915 he went with Sir Thomas Royden, a leading Liverpool shipowner, to deal with congestion in French channel ports; and in 1916 he joined the Ministry of Shipping as director of the ports branch. He became general manager of the MDHB in 1920. Stern but shrewd, Warner introduced the function of the top professional manager to the MDHB whose board members were unused to the division between directorate and senior management. He worked closely and amicably with Richard Durning Holt (qv) who later became his chairman. Sir Lionel Warner (he was knighted in 1936) retired in July 1941. He married twice: first, in 1904, to Nina Mary née Liddon, by whom he had two sons (one killed in the RAF in 1940) and a daughter; second, in 1945, Margaret Elizabeth, widow of S Bryce Newbery. See Stuart Mountfield, *Western Gateway: A History of the Mersey Docks and Harbour Board* (1965); *The Times*, 23 November 1953.

WARTER, Sir Philip Allan
(31 December 1903 – 14 April 1971)

Film and television company chairman, the third son of William Henry Warter, Folkestone wharfinger and director of British & Foreign Wharf Co Ltd, he was educated at the Oratory School, Edgbaston, Birmingham, and then entered the family firm. By 1929 he was managing director of British & Foreign Wharf Co. After war broke out he became director of warehousing in the Ministry of Food in 1940, and controller-general of factory and storage premises at the Board of Trade, 1942-45, for which he was knighted in 1944. He was adviser to the Board of Trade on industrial estates,

1945-46. Meanwhile he had married the daughter of John Maxwell (1877-1940), chairman of the Associated British Picture Corporation, operator of Elstree Studios (which produced nearly 200 films in the 1930s) and a chain of nearly 500 cinemas. On his father-in-law's death he became chairman of ABPC. In 1954, with the creation of the Independent Television Authority, he took ABPC into the new medium of communication, against the wishes of his deputy chairman Eric Fletcher (qv), and formed ABC Television, fourth largest of the 14 independent television companies in 1965. When ABC and Rediffusion, run by John Spencer Wills (qv), merged to form Thames Television in 1967, Warter became chairman, heading one of the five richest of the television companies. Warter resigned from ABPC and Thames in 1969 when he lost a takeover battle against EMI who paid £63 million for APBC (of which Warter remained president). ABPC employment between 1955 and 1965 remained at 12,500-13,000. Sir Philip Warter was a part-time member of the British Transport Commission, 1958-62, and its deputy chairman (at £6,000 a year) under Dr Richard Beeching (qv), 1961-62. After the BTC was broken up in 1962 Warter was appointed chairman of the Transport Holding Co, formed to manage the road haulage and passenger services legacy of the BTC. At one time Sir Philip Warter was a director of Thomas Cook & Son. He married, in 1929, Katherine Scott Maxwell; they had one daughter. See T R Gourvish, *British Railways, 1948-73: A Business History* (1986); Bernard Sendall, *Independent Television* (2 vols, 1982-3); *The Times*, 15 April 1971.

WATERSTONE, Timothy (John Stuart)
(30 May 1939 -)

Bookseller, the son of Malcolm Waterstone and Sylvia Sawday. Educated at Tonbridge School, he read English at St Catherine's College, Cambridge, before working in Calcutta for his father's tea-broking company, and then as marketing manager with Allied Breweries. His association with the book trade began in 1973 when he joined W H Smith, working in distribution. Eight years later he was fired for failing to establish a profitable American operation and as a response opened his own bookshop in the Brompton Road, London, in 1982. Ten years later Waterstone had 86 bookstores, which had revolutionised the book trade, with their thoughtful layout, large selection of high-quality titles, book readings and signings, and informed staff. In 1989 he sold out to W H Smith for £42 million (with his share at £9 million), promising to retire as chief executive in 1993, but remaining on the board until May 1994. Waterstone will spend most of that time in America setting up a US Waterstone chain (by 1992 there were already stores in Boston and Chicago). He has also been deputy chairman of Sinclair Stevenson Ltd since 1989. Waterstone is married to Mary Rose Alison: he has six children from two previous marriages. See Julian Critchley, *Some of Us* (1992).

WATES, Norman Edward
(12 January 1905 - 21 July 1969)

Builder and contractor, born in Streatham, London, the son of Edward Wates, a house furnisher, and his wife Sarah née Holmes. Educated at Emmanuel School, Wandsworth, in 1923 he joined his father, who by then had begun building houses around Streatham. By 1928 he and his brothers, Ronald and Allan, took control of the business, which grew from a small house builder to a large-scale London property developer. The firm undertook contract work for local authorities and for the Government (war work, for example, included the construction of Mulberry harbours). A family-owned private company, Wates reflected Norman's preoccupation with working conditions and new technologies: he reduced casual labour, maintained a high safety record, improved management techniques (he was involved in the creation of the London Business School) and undertook projects with religious charities. He left £703,279. He married Margot Irene Sidwell: they had three daughters and three sons, one of whom, Sir Christopher Wates, is presently chairman of the still privately controlled company. See *DBB*; *DNB* (Neil Edward Wates).

WATKINS, James William
(4 September 1890 - 12 January 1959)

Railway manager, one of at least two sons and a daughter of William Watkins, a railway company official, and his wife Mary, he had a scholarship place at Tewkesbury Grammar School which he left at 14 to become a clerk with his father, then stationmaster on the Midland Railway at Ashchurch, Gloucestershire. In 1914 he enlisted as a private in the 5th Battalion, the Gloucestershire Regiment, was commissioned on the field in the Lancashire Fusiliers and rose to the rank of lieutenant-colonel, commanding their 2nd Battalion and winning the DSO, MC and four mentions in despatches. He returned to the Midland Railway Co after the First World War and served at Derby where by 1942 he was divisional superintendent of operations. He held the same post at Crewe, still on the London, Midland & Scottish Railway (formed in 1922), 1944-48. After nationalisation he

was appointed operating superintendent of British Railways, London Midland region, headquartered at Euston. He became chief regional officer of the London Midland region at a salary of £3,750 in 1951 (chief regional manager after the reorganisation of 1953) and a full-time member of the British Transport Commission in 1956, dying in office. Watkins was widely admired and respected as a humane and caring manager who was actively involved in many regional staff organisations, from cricket to horticulture. He married, in 1918, Ethel Mary Price (d 1953); they had three daughters. See T R Gourvish, *British Railways, 1948-73: A Business History* (1986); *The Times*, 13, 16 January 1959.

WATSON, James (Kenneth)
(16 January 1935 -)

Transport company executive, born in Watford, the son of James Watson, a small businessman, and his wife Helen. A product of what he has described as a lower middle class family, he was educated at Watford Grammar School and Stanford University, California. He trained as an accountant and found his first job in industry at Richard Tompkins' (qv) Green Shield Stamp operation as financial controller. He moved on to the Lex Group and then in 1968 to Times Furnishings, where he took financial responsibility for the firm's clothing, furnishing and property interests. In 1970 he joined British Road Services Ltd, a subsidiary of the transport group NFC. The latter was a domestic, state-owned loss-maker, which was about to be transformed by Sir Peter Thompson (qv) into a highly profitable employee-owned operation. By 1977 Watson was NFC's director of finance, becoming deputy chairman in 1985 and chairman in 1991. With revenues of over £1.5 billion and a workforce of over 33,000, the Bedford-based NFC is listed on the stock market and is the UK's largest employee-owned company. One of the architects of the employee-buy-out, Watson has been described by Thompson as having 'all the physical attributes of a City man, silver-haired, sauve, blue-suited with a white collar over a striped shirt', and viewing anywhere north of Watford as a spiritual and cultural wilderness. Watson married in 1959 Eileen Fay Waller: they have two sons and one daughter. See Peter Thompson, *Sharing Success: The Story of NFC* (1989).

WATSON, William
(1843 - 4 October 1909)

Merchant and shipping company chairman, born in South Carolina, the second son of Stephen Watson, he was educated privately and then entered the cotton broking business, alternating between Charleston, SC, and Liverpool. He settled in Liverpool in the mid-1870s and became a prominent figure on the Liverpool Cotton Exchange, serving as president of the Cotton Association in 1886-87. He headed the firms of Watson & Co in Liverpool and Watson & Hill and Watson, Wood & Co at Charleston and Memphis, 1872-1902. For a short time he was a member of the Mersey Docks & Harbour Board, 1892-93, a brevity perhaps not unrelated to his appointment as director of the Cunard Steam Ship Co in 1892. Certainly the Cunard board were then very unhappy with the MDHB because of the inadequate facilities available at Liverpool for the larger (12,000 gross tons) passenger vessels Cunard were then introducing. Watson became deputy chairman of Cunard in 1902, and chairman (in succession to George Burns, 2nd Baron Inverclyde) in 1905. In his short four-year rule, Watson saw the arrival of a new scale of passenger liners, the 31,000 ton *Lusitania* and the 32,000 ton *Mauretania*, both introduced in 1907 and again straining relations with the MDHB. Abroad Watson faced fierce competition from the Morgan and Continental alliance of shipowners. The downward spiral in transatlantic passenger rates was halted in 1908 when Watson, Albert Ballin of Hamburg-Amerika and other shipowners patched up a cartel agreement. It lasted about three years. Watson was also a director and latterly chairman of the Royal Insurance Co and a director of the North & South Wales Bank, the Standard Marine Insurance Co and a number of other companies. He was a deputy lieutenant of Cheshire and a politically-inactive Conservative. Watson married Jane Stock née Bower. See *The Times*, 5 October 1909; Francis E Hyde, *Cunard and the North Atlantic, 1840-1973* (1975).

WATT, William Warnock
(6 July 1890 - 19 May 1963)

Chemical company executive, educated at Whitehill School, Glasgow, he joined Ogston & Tennant Ltd, soap manufacturers of Renfrew and Aberdeen, becoming their chairman and managing director, 1929-34. After O&T were absorbed by Unilever, Watt was vice-chairman of Lever Bros Ltd, 1935-37. He moved to the British Oxygen Co Ltd as managing director in 1939, remaining until 1956. During the Second World War he was president of the Institute of Welding, 1941-42, and of the British Acetylene Association, 1942-43. From 1939 he chaired the arc welding electrode section of the British Electrical and Allied Manufacturers' Association and was a member of the Treasury advisory business (organisation and methods) panel, 1941-60. BOC, which employed 13,000 in the

UK and 7,000 abroad by 1956, produced industrial and medical gases, needed in steel welding (in motor vehicle manufacturing, shipbuilding, construction especially) and in hospitals. After retiring Watt sat on the Admiralty Commission, Admiralty requirements in material, 1956-57. He was also a governor of the Hammersmith group of hospitals, 1956-60, and a member of the board of management of the London Postgraduate Medical School, 1957-60. He was created a CBE in 1958. Watt married twice: first, in 1919, to Margaret Mitchell Arnott (d 1940), by whom he had a son and a daughter); second, in 1952, to Erica Constance Dalgleish. See *The Times*, 21 May 1963.

WATTS, Sir Philip
(30 May 1846 - 15 March 1926)

Director of Naval Construction, the son of John Watts, JP, the principal assistant to John Fincham, master shipwright of Portsmouth Dockyard, he came from a long line of men associated with naval construction. After an apprenticeship in Portsmouth Dockyard, Watts passed through the Royal School of Naval Architecture and Marine Engineering at South Kensington as an Admiralty pupil, qualifying in 1870. Promoted to the grade of constructor in 1883 he was moved to Chatham Dockyard but left the Admiralty in 1885 to become chief naval architect and managing director of the Elswick-upon-Tyne shipyard of Sir W G Armstrong Mitchell & Co. He was given a seat on the board of Armstrongs where Sir Andrew Noble (qv) was the dominant force. Watts designed and supervised the building of many of the 116 warships and 420 cargo and passenger steamers built by Armstrongs, 1852-1907. Combining speed and gun-power, his ships (of up to 15,000 tons) were bought by many foreign navies and substantially contributed to the Japanese navy which defeated the Russian fleet in 1905. When, in 1902, Sir Philip H White, the Director of Naval Construction at the Admiralty and Watts' predecessor at Elswick, resigned, Watts was appointed in his place. By 1907 Britain's naval dockyards employed nearly 26,000 (mostly civilians) on warship construction and maintenance. By the time Sir Philip Watts (he was knighted in 1905) retired in 1912 he had overseen the introduction into the Royal Navy of the 12-inch gun, 18,000 ton Dreadnought class of battleship, and its successors, in the naval race with Germany that led to the First World War. From 1912 Watts was adviser on naval construction to the Admiralty Board. He was prominent in the Insitution of Naval Architects, a member of the Institution of Civil Engineers, president of the Shipbuilding Employers Federation and involved in similar bodies in the North East. His honours included the FRS and two doctorates. Watts was a Freemason, an active member of the volunteer movement (with the rank of colonel of the 1st Northumberland Royal Garrison Artillery) and sent a six-gun battery and ammunition column from Elswick to the Boer War. He married in 1875, Elsie Isabelle née Simonan; they had two daughters. See *Shipbuilder* 2 (1907-8); *The Times*, 16 March 1926; Kenneth Warren, *Armstrongs of Elswick* (1989).

WEDGWOOD, The Honourable Josiah
(20 October 1899 - 5 May 1968)
Pottery manufacturer, born at Newcastle upon Tyne, the son of (Baron) Josiah Clement Wedgwood 'Josiah IV' (1872-1943), then training as a naval architect, and Ethel née Bowen. Educated at Bedales and the London School of Economics (PhD Econ, 1928), he joined Josiah Wedgwood & Sons in 1927 as company secretary, becoming managing director in 1930. In 1947 he became chairman, the firm having become a public company in 1945, and held the post until 1967. He supervised the firm's move to a new factory at Barlaston, introduced new designs and to further his quest for 'good pots' and 'happy potters' introduced profit-sharing (his published PhD had attacked inherited wealth) and other worker's schemes. Between 1938 and 1967 sales rose from £200,000 to £3.25 million. In 1919 he married Dorothy Mary née Winser: they had three children, but the couple lived apart for many years. The Honourable Josiah Wedgwood left £300,351. See Josiah Wedgwood, *The Economics of Inheritance* (1929, reprinted 1939); John Wedgwood, *A Personal Life of the Fifth Josiah Wedgwood* (1979); *DBB*.

WEDGWOOD, Sir Ralph Lewis
(1874 - 5 September 1956)
Railway manager, born at Barlaston Lea, Stoke-on-Trent, the third surviving son of Clement Francis Wedgwood (of the famous pottery dynasty) and Emily Catherine née Rendel. Educated at Clifton College, Bristol, and Cambridge, where he took a first-class degree in moral philosophy, he decided to break with the pottery tradition and joined the North Eastern Railway in 1897. Groomed as heir apparent by general manager G S Gibb, Wedgwood advanced steadily to become chief general manager of the London & North Eastern Railway in 1923 (he was knighted the following year). Recession characterised his tenure of office (he retired in 1939), but he moulded the LNER into an effective, decentralised organisation which was well-publicised with the record-breaking runs

of Nigel Gresley's (qv) *Mallard*. He was in demand as an expert witness and in other industries (for example, as a member of the Central Electricity Board); he also maintained close links with the Arts. He married in 1906 Iris Veronica Pawson and had two children: one is the historian Dame Veronica Wedgwood. He left £52,171 gross. See Ralph Lewis Wedgwood, *International Rail Transport* (1946); *DBB*; *DNB*.

WEEKS, Ronald Morce
Baron Weeks of Ryton in the County of Durham
(13 November 1890 - 19 August 1960)
Glass, engineering and aircraft companies executive and chairman, born at Helmington Row, County Durham, the son of Richard Llewellyn Weeks, a mining engineer, and his wife Susan Helen Walter née McIntyre, he was educated at Charterhouse and Gonville and Caius College, Cambridge where he took a third in natural sciences and in 1912 was recruited by Pilkington Bros Ltd as a trainee. At St Helens he joined the Territorial Army and during the First World War gained a regular commission in the Rifle Brigade, winning the DSO, MC and bar and three mentions in despatches, retiring as a brevet major. Returning to Pilkingtons, Weeks became Cowley Works manager in 1920, a director in 1928 and chairman of the company's executive committee in 1939 (briefly). Besides running the Cowley Hill and Doncaster plants, he concerned himself with technical and management training matters. The Second World War saw him rise rapidly, from battalion commander in the TA to lieutenant-general and Deputy Chief of the Imperial General Staff responsible for organisation and equipment, 1942-45. For a few months in 1945 he was deputy military governor and chief of staff on the Control Commission in Germany. At the end of the war, in August 1945, he returned to Pilkingtons. However, a new and able generation of the family, led by William Henry Pilkington (qv) was now in charge and Sir Ronald Weeks (he was made a KCB in 1943) accepted an offer with prospects from Vickers Ltd. He became a director of Vickers in 1945, deputy chairman in 1946 and chairman in 1949. Combining skills as an administrator and leader of men, with experience of industrial and military organisation and a strong and determined (and autocratic) character, he was soon much involved in Vickers strategic management. His major decision, made in 1955 when the company employed 70,000, was to split Vickers into three operating companies, for engineering, shipbuilding and aircraft. Lord Weeks (he was made a baron in 1956) retired in 1956 but remained on the Vickers and Pilkington boards until his death. He

held a number of other directorships including Royal Exchange Assurance and the Westminster Bank. From 1956 he was chairman of the Finance Corporation for Industry. He was much interested in education and management education. Weeks married twice, first, in 1922, to Evelyn Elsie Haynes, daughter of Henry Haynes of Nottingham; second, in 1931, following the death of his first wife, to Cynthia Mary Cumming daughter of J W Irvine, a stockbroker. He had two daughters. See *DBB*; Theodore C Barker, *The Glassmakers. Pilkington: The Rise of an International Company, 1826-1976* (1977); John D Scott, *Vickers: A History* (1963).

WEINBERG, Sir Mark (Aubrey)
(9 August 1931 -)
Life assurance entrepreneur, born in South Africa, the son of Philip and Eva Weinberg. His Latvian-born father, a life insurance agent, died when he was 2. Educated at King Edward VII School, Johannesburg, he read law at Witwatersrand University. Since the political climate was uncongenial and a South African law degree was not much use elsewhere, he responded to the advice of Professor Jim Gower (the academic who mater-minded self-regulation in London's financial market) and re-qualified with a Master's degree at the London School of Economics. After another spell in South Africa, in 1961 he returned to the UK and founded Abbey Life: capitalised at £50,000, Weinberg sold it three years later to ITT for £110,000, staying on to manage it until 1970. In 1971 he borrowed £1 million and took a 10 per cent stake in Hambro Life, which he launched at the suggestion of Hambros Bank. He took over Allied, one of the large unit trust groups and Dunbar, the small private bank, and renamed the group Allied Dunbar. As managing director, 1971-83, and chairman after 1984, Weinberg ushered in hard-sell and aggressive marketing techniques. He sold Allied Dunbar to BAT in 1986 for £664 million, taking a seat on the BAT board until 1989. He immediately founded J Rothschild Assurance, with his close friend Jacob (Lord) Rothschild (qv). Weinberg is a prolific fund-raiser and servant of charities. In 1985 he and Sir Hector (Lord) Laing (qv) formed The Per Cent Club, to encourage companies to give at least half a per cent of their profits to a charity of their choice (in 1993 the club has over 500 major corporate members and raises about £100 million annually). Weinberg married first in 1961 Sandra le Roith, the daughter of a Johannesberg architect (she died in 1978 from a brain tumour); then in 1980 Anouska Hempel, the ex-actress who owns the glamorous Blake's Hotel in London. He was knighted in 1987. See Maurice Victor Blank and M Weinberg, *Take-Overs and Mergers* (1962, 4th edition 1980).

WEINSTOCK, Arnold
Baron Weinstock of Bowden
(29 July 1924 -)
Electronics manufacturer, born in north London, the son of Polish immigrants Simon Weinstock, a tailor, and his wife Golda. Having attended state schools, in 1944 he took a second-class honours degree in statistics at the London School of Economics. After National Service in 1947 he became an assistant in a Mayfair estate agency, and then in 1954 joined Michael Sobell - another Polish Jew, whose daughter, Netta, Weinstock had married in 1949 - to found Radio & Allied Industries. Weinstock was the managing director of Radio & Allied, which thrived in the television boom of the 1950s, and which by 1963 had taken over the ailing General Electric Co by reverse takeover. Weinstock headed GEC as managing director (a post he has held ever since, eschewing the title of chairman) and embarked on a policy of ruthless cost and labour cutting, while laying the foundation for a much larger company with the takeovers of AEI and English Electric in 1967-68. In the 1960s and 1970s Weinstock became one of the most successful and publicised British businessmen, though GEC was to be criticised in the 1980s for its conservative stance, its notorious cash mountain (that reached £1.5 billion) and problems with the government-sponsored Nimrod early warning defence system. But by the 1990s Weinstock's business had grown even larger with the takeover of Plessey, Ferranti's defence wing, and with links with European giants such as Siemens. With a turnover of £9,435 million in 1992 (pre-tax profit £829 million) and a work-force of 105,000 (75,000 in the UK), GEC is twice the size of Racal, the UK's second biggest electronics group. Weinstock's personal fortune is estimated at over £90 million. He has a daughter and a son, Simon, who is on the board of GEC and may succeed his father. Weinstock was knighted in 1970 and made a life peer in 1980. See Robert Jones and Oliver Marriott, *Anatomy of a Merger: A History of GEC, AEI and English Electric* (1970).

WEIR, William Douglas
1st Viscount Weir of Eastwood
(12 May 1877 - 2 July 1959)
Industrialist, born in Glasgow, the son of James Weir and Mary née Douglas. Educated at Allan Glen's School and Glasgow High School, he joined the family's marine-engineering business, G & J Weir, at 16. He became managing director in 1902 and under him the business thrived, particularly on Admiralty contracts for its auxiliary machinery and pumps. During the First World War, however, Weir moved into public service, resigning as managing director in 1915 (though he remained as

chairman until 1953) when Lloyd George invited him to join the Ministry of Munitions. Weir became particularly influential in the planning, supply and strategic use of airpower, emerging from the war as Minister of Air. Believing that 'the next war is likely to be a war of aircraft', until his resignation in 1938 he used his influence to prepare the British response to German rearmament. He was also concerned with problems of sugar supply, electricity and North Atlantic shipping and held directorships at ICI, Shell and Lloyds Bank. By 1958 the Weir group was capitalised at £6.8 million, with a net profit the following year of £1.7 million. He was knighted in 1917, awarded a peerage in 1918, made GCB in 1934, and accepted a viscountcy in 1938. See William J. Reader, *Architect of Air Power: The Life of the First Viscount Weir of England, 1877-1959* (1968); *DBB*; *DNB*.

WELLCOME, Sir Henry Solomon
(21 August 1853 - 21 July 1936)

Pharmaceutical manufacturer, born in Almond, Wisconsin, USA, the son of Solomon Cummings Wellcome (1827-76), a farmer and Adventist preacher, and Mary née Curtis. After attending a log-house school he graduated from the Philadelphia College of Pharmacy in 1874, before forming a partnership in England with fellow graduate Silas Burroughs in 1880. With their combined abilities - Burroughs in administration and Wellcome's in selling - Burroughs, Wellcome & Co prospered. After Burroughs's death in 1895, Wellcome took complete control: he expanded overseas and made a heavy research commitment by establishing several laboratories. In 1924 the many branches of the business were consolidated into the Wellcome Foundation Ltd (capital £1 million), when Wellcome's close personal involvement lessened: but he ensured through his will that the Foundation continued his work in medical research and in the history of medicine. He was knighted in 1932. In 1901 he married Gwendoline Maud Syrie, daughter of the philanthropist Dr Thomas J Bernardo: before the marriage was dissolved in 1916 they had one son. Wellcome left £3,014,473. See H S Wellcome, *The Story of Metlakahtla* (1887); Helen Turner, *Henry Wellcome: The Man, His Collection and His Legacy* (1980); *DBB*; *DNB*.

WEMYSS, Randolph Gordon Erskine
(11 July 1858 - 17 July 1908)

Coalmine owner, the elder son of James Hay Erskine Wemyss, landed proprietor in East Fife, and his wife Augusta Millicent Anne Mary Kennedy née Erskine, his father died when he was 5 and his inherited estates were managed by trustees including his mother. Wemyss was educated at Eton and then toured the USA in 1879, returning determined to develop the mining potential of his lands which had been modestly mined since the seventeenth century. He built a private railway, the Wemyss & Buckhaven Railway, to link his East Fife villages and pits to the North British Railway at Thornton. Then he broke the NBR's monopoly by building, with legislative sanction, a new dock at Methil from which East Fife coal could be exported. With this counter (Methil dock was opened in 1887 and sold with the WBR to the NBR two years later) Wemyss secured the lower freight rates that made it economical for him to develop his coalmines. In 1894 he floated the Wemyss Coal Co which by 1908 was producing 1.4 million tons of coal a year and employing about 4,600 men. Bad relations with the NBR (of which Wemyss was a director, 1889-99) continued as Wemyss resisted the NBR's drive to monopolise the railway network in Fife and to concentrate its dock investments in Burntisland in West Fife, rather than in Methil, Wemyss's outlet, in East Fife. A Unionist, he was prominent in the local government of Fife. Wemyss married twice: first, in 1884, to Lady Lillian Mary Paulet, who divorced him after a much publicised court case in 1898; second, in 1899, to Lady Eva Cecilia Margaret Wellesley. After the second marriage he took his yacht to South Africa and made a derringdo contribution to the Boer War. He had a son and two daughters. See *DSBB*.

WEST, Sir Frederick Joseph
(17 April 1872 - 14 November 1959)

Gas engineer and Manchester Ship Canal Co chairman, born at Maidstone, second son of John West (1839-1922), then engineer to the local gas undertaking and inventor of a machine for stoking gas retorts which he formed a company to manufacture in 1874, and his second wife Mary Ann née Law; his father moved to Manchester in 1880, as chief engineer to the corporation. Frederick entered West's Gas Improvement Co, his father's firm (moved from Maidstone to Albion Works, Miles Platting in Manchester in 1884, when his father went independent), and in 1922 succeeded his father as chairman of the company which contracted mainly for carbonising plant but also for whole gasworks. From 300 employees in 1899 the firm grew to 1,100 in 1922. A Conservative, Frederick West was elected a City councillor in 1905, an alderman in 1920 and lord mayor in 1924. He became a Corporation director of the Manchester Ship Canal Co in 1917 and served as chairman, 1933-50, resigning in 1933 from the City Council to secure election as a shareholders' director. With the 1930s depression and renewed competition from Liverpool after the opening of the East Lancashire Road in 1933, the Ship Canal experienced a long period of difficulty. Employment fell from about 11,500 in 1935 to about 6,000 in 1955 (with a third of them, the dockers, being employed by the National Dock Labour Board). A director of Manchester Liners, 1942-55, he chaired the Port of Manchester committee of the Chamber of Commerce. Concerned with industrial education, he was chairman of the governing body of Manchester College of Technology and sat on the court of Manchester University. Knighted in 1936, he was made a KBE in 1943 and GBE in 1947. See Douglas A Farnie, *The Manchester Ship Canal and the Rise of the Port of Manchester* (1980); *The Times*, 16 November 1959.

WESTINGHOUSE, George
(6 October 1846 - 12 March 1914)
Electrical and railway equipment manufacturer, born at Central Bridge, New York, the son of George Westinghouse, manufacturer of farm implements at Schenectady, NY, and his wife Emeline née Vedder, he was educated at local schools. After an adventurous youth he joined his father and became a prolific inventor, taking out his first patent in 1865. In 1869 he invented the air brake and organised the Westinghouse Air Brake Co to manufacture this and the Union Switch & Signal Co to make his electrical signal control system of 1882. Both substantially improved the safety and efficiency of railways. His Westinghouse Electric Co manufactured electrical generating equipment utilising alternating current and capable of long distance power transmission. This led to a legal and commercial battle with Thomas Edison. Westinghouse won the legal tussle but lost the commercial one when Edison General Electric merged with Thomson-Houston Electric Co in 1892 to form a new giant rival, the General Electric Co. Both Westinghouse and GE of America set up subsidiaries in England where the electrical engineering industry was retarded by the Electrical Lighting Act of 1882 (which gave local authorities power to purchase electricity undertakings within 21 years). British Westinghouse Electric & Manufacturing Co was formed in 1899 when George Westinghouse visited England to finalise his investment at Trafford Park, Manchester, the new industrial estate being developed beside the Ship Canal by Marshall Stevens (qv). On 30 acres of a 130-acre site, an American-designed factory for the manufacture of steam engines, gas engines and steam turbines was opened in 1902 (the same year that GE's British Thomson-Houston smaller plant started at Rugby). It employed 3,000 men initially. British Westinghouse did not show a profit on the £4.5 million total invested in Trafford Park until 1907 when 5,000 were employed. The market for railway electrification proved hard to expand in Britain. There were management problems, despite the preparatory work done by Westinghouse in sending 40 British managers to the USA for training in American methods. Westinghouse, who infrequently visited Britain, therefore sent over two lieutenants, Newcomb Carlton and Philip A Lange, to sort matters out in 1906. They did so by writing down capital, curbing extravagance, firing executives, effecting an internal reorganisation, selling off part of their Trafford Park site and by raising a £250,000 mortgage on Trafford Park in the City of London. Meantime, the American parent went into bankruptcy and George Westinghouse resigned from the British Westinghouse board in 1909, being succeeded by John Annan Bryce, banker and MP. Westinghouse married, in 1867, Marguerite Erskine née Walker of Delaware County, NY; they had a son. See John Dummelow, *1899-1949* (1949) John N Ingham, *Biographical Dictionary of American Business Leaders* (4 vols, 1983); ; Robert Jones and Oliver Marriott, *Anatomy of a Merger: A History of GEC, AEI and English Electric* (1970).

WESTON, Garfield Howard
(28 April 1927 -)
Chairman of a food manufacturing and distribution conglomerate, born in Canada, second eldest of the three sons and six daughters of Willard Garfield Weston (qv) and his first wife Reta Lila née Howard; he was brought from Toronto to England at the age of 8 and educated at Sir William Borlase School, Marlowe, New College, Oxford, and Harvard University. He started in his father's business empire as managing director of Ryvita in 1951, and then managing director of Weston Biscuits, Australia to 1954. He became vice-chairman of Associated British Foods in 1960 and chairman of Weston Holding Inc in 1965. He succeeded his father as chairman of Associated British Foods in 1967 and as chairman of Fortnum & Mason in 1978. By 1992 ABF ranked the ninth largest in Europe's food industry and 41st among the UK's largest companies: with a turnover of £3,510.4 million, pre-tax profits of £332.4 million, total assets of £1,865.4 million and nearly 54,000 employees. Notably, it still had a relatively low long-term debt (£160.8 million). Garry (as he is known), in running the non-North American side of the Weston family multinational business (his younger brother Galen runs the North American operation), has deliberately avoided debt

and by 1990 had a cash mountain of £1.1 billion. In contrast to his father, he has emphasised internal expansion rather than growth by acquisition. Some of his father's acquisitions have been sold, like the Fine Fare supermarket sold to Dee Corporation in 1986 at the peak of investor interest in food, for £1.4 billion. He has maintained profitability by investing heavily in order to remain a low-cost producer in factory baking. In over 20 years as chairman he has made only one major acquisition, that of British Sugar which cost around £880 million in November 1990 (thereby diminishing his cash pile by that amount). With the family controlling ABF (holding about 63 per cent of the equity) he has the freedom to develop long-term strategies without worrying unduly about dividend levels and possible takeover - in contrast to many of Britain's big businesses. Consequently, though he employs 6,000 less than his father did in 1962, his 1992 turnover is about twice that of 1962 (in real terms). More low-profile than his father, and discreet to the point of secretive (not least for personal security reasons), Garry Weston is reputedly worth £1.7 billion, and therefore the fifth richest person in the UK, most of his wealth is in family shareholdings controlled by family-owned charitable trusts. Though still a Canadian citizen Garry Weston was one of Mrs Thatcher's close industrial advisers in the 1980s and was contributing £100,000 a year to the Conservative Party in 1990. He married, in 1959, Mary Ruth, daughter of Major-General Sir Howard Kippenberger; they have three sons and three daughters. See *Independent on Sunday*, 25 November 1990.

WESTON, Willard Garfield
(26 February 1898 - 22 October 1978)

Food manufacturer, wholesaler and retailer, eldest son of George Weston, who inherited from his father and ran what became Toronto's largest bakery (later diversifying into biscuit production), and his wife Emma Maude, he was raised as a strict Wesleyan Methodist and educated at Harbord Collegiate Institute, Toronto. After serving in France in the Canadian Engineers during the First World War, and on leave visiting British biscuit factories, he returned to Canada determined to make British quality biscuits by less costly production methods. He did so and when his father died in 1924 he succeeded as president of George Weston Ltd, with about 200 employees. During the depression he acquired businesses at low prices and in ten years his companies had total sales of C$365 million. In 1934 he discreetly started operations in Britain when he bought the biscuit division of Mitchell & Muil of Aberdeen, paying for the business with non-voting preference shares in the

parent firm. He moved Mitchell & Muil's production to Edinburgh, lowered prices and still made a profit. That same year he acquired, by his favoured method, the west London bakery, Chibnalls Bakeries Ltd. A string of other acquisitions followed and by 1938 his business, Allied Bakeries (formed 1935), had at least 22 bakeries, 189 retail shops, profits of £300,000 on an issued capital of £1.89 million, and a workforce of 4,000. After the Second World War, during which Weston was MP (Conservative) for Macclesfield, the growth of Allied Bakeries continued. He unified the bakeries under the Sunblest trade name in 1949. He bought Fortnum & Mason (1951), the Aerated Bread Co and a string of other companies. In the 1950s he opened his Fine Fare chain of supermarkets. The late-1950s saw a race against Ranks and Spillers to acquire bakeries after the millers refused to give volume discounts to Weston and he went abroad for his flour. Weston changed the group's parent company name to Associated British Foods Ltd in 1960. In 1961 it controlled over 110 bakeries producing bread, biscuits and cakes, margarine and cooking fats; 2,850 shops; employed 60,000 people; and had a turnover of £183 million (1962). In Canada the firm also grew rapidly and secretively during the 1950s and 1960s. In Australia and Africa its subsidiaries became some of the largest food processors. Garfield Weston retired in 1967, after the death of his first wife, passing the ABF chairmanship to his second son Garry (qv), leaving himself as president. A devout evangelical Christian, he was positive, optimistic and dedicated to work, but was also autocratic, ruthless, and cunning. He shunned public position and publicity (even in Parliament in six years he spoke but once). His preoccupation with the Commonwealth made him an opponent of the European Common Market. Garfield Weston married twice: in 1921 to Reta Lila née Howard by whom he had three sons and six daughters; second, in 1972, to Marguerita Martin de Montoya, a Spanish lady. See *DBB*; T W Cynog-Jones, 'Retail Giants. No 18: The Weston Bakery and Food Group' *New Dawn* 1963.

WHARTON, The Right Honourable John Lloyd
(18 April 1837 - 11 July 1912)

Railway company chairman, born at Aberford, Yorkshire, the only son of John Thomas Wharton, of Dryburn, Durham, and Aberford, and his wife Mary née Jacob, he was educated at Eton and Trinity College, Cambridge and was called to the Bar at the Inner Temple in 1862. He pursued a political career, sitting as MP (Conservative) for Durham, 1871-74, and for the Ripon division of the West Riding of Yorkshire, 1886-1906. He was sworn of the Privy Council in 1897. Wharton was elected a director of the North Eastern Railway in 1880 and chaired its traffic committee, 1895-1906. He succeeded Sir Edward Grey (who resigned his seat to become Foreign Secretary) as chairman of the NER in 1906. At that date the company employed about 48,000 and its management was headed by Alexander Butterworth (qv). The chairman's role does not seem to have been very significant. Wharton was recalled as concerning himself with staff welfare and the St John Ambulance Association in particular. Both his grandfathers were Anglican clergymen and Wharton married, in 1870, the daughter of another: Susan Frances (d 1872), daughter of the Reverend A Duncombe, by whom he had a daughter. See *North Eastern Railway Magazine* (August 1912); Robert J Irving, *The North Eastern Railway Company, 1870-1914: An Economic History* (1976).

WHITBREAD, Francis Pelham
(16 October 1867 - 29 October 1941)
Brewer and brewing trade association leader, the third son of Samuel Whitbread (1830-1915), brewer and Liberal MP for Bedford, and Lady Isabella Charlotte, daughter of the Third Earl of Chichester. Educated at Eton and Trinity College, Cambridge, Frank (as he was known) qualified as a barrister in 1891 and the following year joined the family brewing firm, one of London's largest, as managing director. He helped Whitbread's through the difficult years before 1914, when the demand for beer declined, but in the inter-war period he found a wider role as chairman of the Brewers' Society and of the National Trade Defence Association. He harmonised relations between brewers and retailers, opposed the temperance movement, and advanced rationalisation in the industry. He filled all the major elective posts in the industry (such as president of the Institute of Brewing, 1913-15) and also continued the family's social work tradition. He married in 1894 the Honourable Ida Madeleine Agnes, daughter of the 4th Lord Sudeley: they had a son and a daughter. He left £243,653. See Kevin H Hawkins and C L Pass, *The Brewing Industry: A Study in Industrial Organisation and Public Policy* (1979); Nicholas B Redman, *The Story of Whitbread plc 1742-1990* (1991); *DBB*.

WHITE, Sir George
(28 March 1854 - 22 November 1916)
Tramway promoter and aeroplane manufacturer, born at Kingsdown, Bristol, the son of Henry White, a painter and decorator, and Eliza née Tippetts. Educated at St Michael's Boy School, at 15 he became a junior clerk in the solicitor's office

of Stanley & Wasbrough, whose involvement with tramway promotion led in 1874 to the formation of Bristol Tramways Ltd. White became a leading figure in the firm and eventually in the transport affairs of Bristol and other cities: due to him Bristol had one of the first electric tramway systems in Britain and towards the end of his career he established the first viable UK aeroplane manufacturing firm - the forerunner of the famous Bristol Aeroplane Co. He was also involved with railways, docks and shipping, notably the Taff Vale Railway, the Avonmouth and Sharpness Docks, and the Great Western Shipping Co. A leading figure in Bristol's commercial life, he became a city councillor and JP: his baronetcy in 1904 was awarded for public service. In 1876 he married Caroline Rosena née Thomas: they had two children. He left £185,579. See Charles Harvey and Jon Press, *Sir George White of Bristol 1854-1916* (1989); *DBB*.

WHITE, George Stanley Midleton
(11 April 1913 - 31 March 1983)
Aircraft and car manufacturer, grandson of Sir George White 1st Bt (qv), the founder of Bristol Aeroplane Co, and the son of Sir George Stanley White 2nd Bt (1882-1964) and his wife Kate Muriel née Baker, he was educated at Harrow and Magdalene College, Cambridge, where he studied engineering under W S Farren, subsequently director of the Royal Aircraft Establishment. He returned to the family firm and trained with engineers like Roy Fedden, the brilliant aero-engine designer, under his father's cousin Verdon Smith (qv) the BAC chairman. By 1940 George White was general manager of the company and Beaverbrook's contact there. In the mid-1950s, when BAC employed 21,000, he was managing director. In the post-war years he had much to do with the production of the Bristol Freighter but became more interested in the Bristol Car Co which he ran and then owned. In 1960 the BAC's aircraft side merged with the aircraft interests of Vickers and English Electric to form the British Aircraft Corporation in which his contemporaneous relative Sir Reginald Verdon-Smith (qv) played a major part and management shifted to a very different team. George White was also a member of the Bristol stockbroking firm of George White & Co, founded by his grandfather. In 1969 Sir George White (he succeeded as 3rd Bt in 1964) was seriously injured in a road accident and had to retire. He married, in 1939, Diane Eleanor née Collins; they had a son and a daughter. See Charles Gardner, *British Aircraft Corporation: A History* (1981). Charles Harvey and Jon Press (eds), *Studies in the Business History of Bristol* (1988); *The Times*, 8 April 1983.

WHITE, Vincent Gordon Lindsay
Baron White of Hull
(11 May 1923 -)

Multinational corporate entrepreneur, the son of Charles White and Lily May née Wilson. Educated at De Aston School, Lincolnshire, he joined his father's publishing business - Welbecson - but left in 1940 to join the Army's Special Operations Executive in the War. He returned to become chairman of Welbecson in 1947 and in the 1950s became friends with (Lord) James Hanson (qv), whose younger brother he had met in the war. White and Hanson became partners when their respective businesses were taken over by the Hull-based Wiles Group. But later they bought out Wiles and renamed the business the Hanson Trust in 1969. Hanson is now one of the largest and most successful of British (and American) businesses, famous for buying and selling companies like commodities. White's major contribution has been to organise the US side of the operations called Hanson Industries. He arrived in New York in 1973 with $3,000 capital, using as his first office a room in Manhattan's Pierre Hotel. By the end of the 1980s Hanson had built a $6 billion conglomerate in low-technology businesses (his first purchase was a fish processing firm), with White's fortune estimated at £75 million. White is also a non-executive director of British Airways. A favourite of the gossip columnists, his interests include yachting, flying and horse-racing (he has sponsored the English Derby). In 1974 he married the actress Virginia North (one son): he has two daughters from a former marriage. He was knighted in 1979 and became a life peer in 1991. See Ivan Fallon and James Strodes, *Takeovers* (1987).

WHITELAW, William
(15 March 1868 - 19 January 1946)

Railway transport executive, the son of Alexander Whitelaw (1823-79), of Gartshore, Dumbartonshire, and Barbara Forbes Lockhart. His father had developed mineral resources in the south-west of Scotland. Educated at Harrow and Trinity College, Cambridge, he made a brief excursion into politics and carried the seat for the Conservatives in 1892 (though he was defeated at the next general election in 1895, which effectively ended his political career). He specialised in directorships of railway companies: the Highland Railway, 1898-1912; the North British Railway, 1908-22 (vice-chairman, 1910-12, and chairman, 1912-22); and London & North Eastern Railway, 1923-38 (chairman). As chairman of the LNER, he directed an organisation which employed 171,339 in 1935. It was the most severely hit by depression of all the groups, since it relied most heavily on freight for revenues. Whitelaw was also a director of the Bank of Scotland and of the Forth Bridge Railway Co. Like other members of his family, Whitelaw was an ardent supporter of the Church of Scotland. He married in 1890 Gertrude née Thompson: they had two daughters. He left £731,736. His grandson is the Rt Hon William Whitelaw MP, the former cabinet minister. See *DSBB*.

WHITELEY, William
(29 September 1831 - 21 January 1907)

Department store owner, born at Agbrigg, near Wakefield, Yorkshire, the son of William Whiteley, a corn factor, and his wife Elizabeth née Rowland, he left school at 14 and after two years on an uncle's farm was articled for seven years to Harnew & Glover, the largest drapers in Wakefield. After seeing the Great Exhibition of 1851 he envisioned a giant emporium for London and moved there in 1855. For eight years he shifted between retail and wholesale businesses increasing his savings from £10 to £700. He opened his first shop in 1863 in Bayswater and by 1872 had extended it into a large department store employing nearly 700 in the shop and 1,000 outside the premises. Whiteley, nicknamed the 'Universal Provider', claimed to supply everything from a pin to an elephant. By 1906 Whiteley's shops, farm and factories employed 6,000 and had a turnover of £1 million, with 10 per cent profit. Whiteley, however, was a harsh paternalist, running a fines system that employed seven staff. Despite his public image, as a respectable evangelical Churchman, married (to a sales assistant, Harriet Sarah née Hill, in 1867) with two sons and two daughters, and forever extolling his assistants to greater industry and honesty, he and a financier friend had a long-running liaison with two sisters in Brighton. Suspicious, Whiteley's wife left him in 1881 (when his income was divulged as £15,000). On 21 January 1907 a man claiming to be Whiteley's illegitimate son, Horace George Rayner, entered Whiteley's office and shot him dead. At the Old Bailey trial 4,000 petitions and 180,000 signatures were submitted in Rayner's defence (he was imprisoned until 1919). See *DBB*.

WILLIAMS, Clement (Hilton)
(1877 - 22 June 1963)

Food manufacturer, born in Reading, the son of Bullivant Williams (qv), a manager and later director of the local biscuit firm of Huntley & Palmers. Educated at Marlborough College, aged 19 Clement followed his father into Huntley & Palmers, two years before the business became a limited company. During the First World War he served in France and attained the rank of major. After a year in the City studying business methods, in 1926 he was appointed general manager of

Huntley & Palmers, became a director four years later, and managing director in 1933 (two years later the business had 7,245 employees). He resigned the post in 1945, remaining on the board until 1948, when he became the first director to retire from the board. He also served as vice-chairman of Wokingham District Council and of Reading Conservative Association. In 1957 he was made an MBE. He married in 1921 Margaret née Deare, the widow of a friend: she and a daughter survived him. See T A B Corley, *Huntley & Palmers of Reading 1822-1972* (1972); *Reading Standard*, 28 June 1963.

WILLIAMS, Leonard John
(7 August 1894 - 18 December 1975)

Banker, born at Bideford, Devon, son of Charles Williams, an ironmonger, and his wife Lily née Thorne, he was educated at Bideford Grammar School and then entered the National Provincial Bank as an apprentice at Southampton in 1911. He was transferred to the Advance Department, at London head office, and then to Nottingham where he was accountant at the National Provincial and Smiths Bank branches. After a short time as an inspector, Williams returned to the Advance Department as controller in 1928. He became joint chief controller in 1930 and head of the advance department with the rank of assistant general manager in 1939. He was promoted to joint general manager in 1943 and chief general manager in 1951, a post from which he retired in 1956. Spanning war and post-war years, Williams' tenure was mainly concerned with reconstruction of bank premises and then with expanding to meet the demands of growing markets in the 1950s. In 1955 the National Provincial, with 11,000 employees, was the smallest of the 'Big Five' banks. Williams was a director of the National Provincial Bank, 1956-69, and a vice-president of the Institute of Bankers for that period. He was a director of Ranks Hovis McDougall Ltd, 1956-72, and of the City of London Real Property Co Ltd, a subsidiary of Harold Samuel's (qv) Land Securities Investment Trust, 1956-69. Williams was a benefactor of the Royal College of Surgeons and was made an honorary FRCS in 1968. He married, in 1923, Doris (d 1965), daughter of Arthur Mayall; they had two sons. See *The Natproban* 1952, 1956.

WILLIAMS, Thomas Edward
Baron Williams of Ynyshir
(26 July 1892 - 18 February 1966)

President of the Co-operative Wholesale Society, born at Ynyshir, in the Rhondda, the son of William Williams, a miner, and his wife Mary, he was educated at Porth County School and at 13 started in the office of the Ynyshir & Wattstown

Co-operative Society. Joining the Amalgamated Union of Co-operative Employees, he represented them on the Porth Trades and Labour Council when he was 18. Soon after, he gained a Glamorgan County Council scholarship to take the two-year diploma in economics and political science at Ruskin College, Oxford. He moved to London in 1914 as a clerk in the general office of the Royal Arsenal Co-operative Society. His time there was interrupted by the First World War in which he served in the Middlesex Regiment, from which he was invalided out early in 1918. Williams became prominent in the RACS, serving on its political purposes committee, 1929-35, and as a member of the joint committee of London co-operative societies. In 1934 he was elected as a director of the CWS. Salaried and full time, he served continuously on the main CWS board's grocery committee during the 1930s and 1940s. As director of the New Zealand Produce Association Ltd, and in the interests of other concerns, he travelled widely. During the Second World War he served on the Ministry of Food's tea distribution committee. Meantime Williams was active in politics: member of London County Council, 1932-35; member of the national executive of the Labour Party, 1931-35; and a Labour parliamentary candidate. Under the Labour government of 1945-50 Williams became a part time member of the London Transport Executive. In 1948 he was created a baron. The following year he became a member of the central executive of the Co-operative Union. Lord Williams was president of the CWS Ltd, 1951-57, during which he sat on the first of four postwar committees of enquiry assembled to examine and recommend improvements in the structure of the CWS. In 1952-53 he was president of the Co-operative Congress, the movement's highest honour. Williams married, in 1921, Lavinia Northam; they had a daughter. See *Co-operative Review* (February 1952); William Richardson, *The CWS in War and Peace, 1938-1976* (1977).

WILLIAMS, (William) Bullivant
(1834 - 19 March 1917)

Biscuit manufacturer, born in Reading, younger son of the proprietor of the stage coach which ran between Reading and London, he left school at 14 and followed his brother Charles into a clerkship with Huntley & Palmers Ltd, the family firm's market having been lost to the railways. In the 1860s he made annual but not very successful sales trips to the Continent. By 1874 William Bullivant Williams was the confidential manager for the seven partners in the biscuit-making business, with access to all the books except their private ledger. When the company became a public limited liability company in 1898 he was appointed the first non-Palmer director and placed in charge of the firm's general administration. By 1907 he was managing director administering 6,500 employees. Bullivant Williams was a devout and generous member of St Peter's Church, Caversham, where he lived. He married, in 1870, the daughter of William Parker JP of Bourne, Lincolnshire; they had five children. See T A B Corley, *Quaker Enterprise in Biscuits: Huntley & Palmers of Reading, 1822-1972* (1972); *Reading Standard*, 24 March 1917.

WILLS, Sir George Alfred
(3 June 1854 - 11 July 1928)

Tobacco manufacturer, born at Kingsdown, Bristol, the eldest son of Henry Overton Wills III, tobacco manufacturer, and his wife Alice née Hopkinson, he belonged to the third generation in the family firm of W D & H O Wills. Raised a Congregationalist and educated at Mill Hill School, he entered the family firm in 1872, becoming factory manager in 1875 and an exceptionally skilled tobacco leaf buyer. Under the chairmanship of his uncle, William Henry Wills (qv), and with the co-operation of three brothers, especially Herbert (Harry) Wills (1856-1922), he turned the firm into a highly profitable business. Its foundation was the American-invented Bonsack cigarette-making machine, rights to which George negotiated in 1883, and the use of manufacturers' brand names. 'Woodbine' cigarettes, at 1d for five, appeared in 1888, produced in a new factory at Bedminster, Bristol. George Wills became an original director of Imperial Tobacco Co in 1901 and succeeded his uncle, Lord Winterstoke, as chairman in 1911, retiring in 1924 with the title of president. He was also a director of the Great Western Railway and British American Tobacco. Like his father, one of nine Wills family millionaires who died before him, Sir George Wills (he was made a baronet in 1923) was enormously generous to Bristol, especially its university and hospitals; he was also generous to Nonconformist causes. Shy and retiring, his main interest was organ music, appreciating and performing. In 1878 Wills married Susan Brittan Proctor, daughter of Robert Proctor, a Clifton manure merchant; they had a son and four daughters, one of whom became the wife of the Bishop of Bath and Wells. Sir George Wills left £10 million. See B W E Alford, *W D & H O Wills and the Development of the UK Tobacco Industry, 1786-1965* (1973); *DBB*.

WILLS, Gilbert Alan Hamilton
1st Baron Dulverton of Batsford
(28 March 1880 - 1 December 1956)

Tobacco manufacturer, second son of Sir Frederick Wills, 1st Bt, one of the clan of Bristol tobacco manufacturers, and his wife, Anne, elder daughter of the Reverend James Hanilton, he was educated privately and at Magdalene College, Oxford. He spent a year in the Wills factories in Bristol learning about tobacco and cigarette processing but left the business in 1908 to be ADC to the Lord-Lieutenant of Ireland for four years, indulging his passion for fox hunting. He succeeded to the baronetcy on the death of his father in 1909 and in 1912 entered parliament as Unionist MP for Taunton. He served throughout the First World War with the Royal North Devon Yeomanry and the Machine Gun Corps, at Gallipoli and on the Western Front, becoming a battalion commander, retaining his parliamentary seat throughout the war. Although returned as Coalition Unionist MP for Weston-super-Mare in 1918, and becoming a PPS to the Postmaster-General, Sir Gilbert Wills retired from parliament in 1923 having been made a member of the executive committee of the Imperial Tobacco Co. The following year he succeeded his cousin, Sir George Wills (qv), as chairman of Imperial Tobacco, retiring in 1947 when he was made president. Lord Dulverton (he was created a baron in 1929 for public and political services) was largely a figurehead at Imperial Tobacco. His self-confessed major achievements for the business were the formation of the Tobacco Trade Association in 1931 and the establishment of the company's contributory pension scheme. He was a director of the British American Tobacco Co and of the Great Western Railway. A multi-millionaire (he left £4.268 million; in real terms less than his father's estate of £3.05 million), like other members of his family he was a munificent benefactor of the city of Bristol. A JP of Somerset and Gloucester, he was high sheriff of Gloucestershire in 1928. He married, in 1914, Victoria May, third daughter of Rear-Admiral Sir Edward Chichester, 9th Bt; they had three sons. See B W E Alford, *W D & H O Wills and the Development of the UK Tobacco Industry, 1786-1965* (1973); *The Times*, 3 December 1956.

WILLS, Sir John Spencer
(10 August 1904 - 28 October 1991)

Transport and television company chairman, elder of two sons of Cedric Spencer Wills, an Australian in the iron trade, and his wife Cecile Charlotte née Dravers; his parents divorced in 1908 and he was educated at Cleobury Mortimer College and Merchant Taylors School. His mother was unable to support him beyond the age of 17 so he then advertised for a job in *The Times*. The advertisement brought a secretarial post with Emile Oscar Garcke (1856-1930), the German-born founder of British Electric Traction, registered in 1896 to promote electric tram systems in Britain. By the 1920s it was in the bus business. After a year or so living with the Garcke family, Wills was found a job in BET headquarters. In 1926 he became general manager of the East Yorkshire Motor Services Ltd, a BET operating subsidiary, strengthening his prospects by marrying Garcke's daughter in 1936. Wills became a main board director in 1939 and managing director in 1946, at which date BET subsidiaries ran 9,000 buses with gross receipts of £25.89 million and employed about 100,000 people. Threatened by nationalisation, in 1947 Wills and his chairman Harley Drayton (qv) took BET into cable broadcasting by buying Broadcast Relay Co, known as Rediffusion, with interests in the UK and several colonies. Wills became chairman and managing director. When independent television was launched in 1954 Rediffusion joined with Associated Newspapers, chaired by the 2nd Viscount Rothermere, to form Associated Rediffusion which won the London weekday franchise. After two years of losses Rothermere sold Associated's interests for £1.65 million. A month later A-R was in profit. Wills became chairman of BET in 1966 and the following year A-R lost its franchise. BET retained an interest in television by investing in Thames Television, the 1967 merger between Rediffusion and ABC Television headed by Sir Philip Warter (qv). In 1966, when BET employed around 70,000, mostly in transport, Harold Wilson's Labour government proposed nationalising the bus industry. Wills therefore sold the BET's 34 bus companies to the government's Transport Holding Co (which became the National Bus Co in 1968) for a basic price of £35 million. Deprived of the BET's main business activity, Wills invested the proceeds in a series of diversifications which turned BET into a business support services group. Some £11.4 million was spent on new shares in Rediffusion Ltd; £4.5 million on Initial, the laundry business; £6 million on Grayston Plant Ltd, plant hire business; £8 million on Murphy Bros Ltd, a Leicester-based mining and contracting business; and several more businesses. Wills retained the holding in Thames Television, which lost its franchise in October 1991. He was knighted in 1969 for his services to industry and the arts (the London Symphony Orchestra, the Royal Opera House and the Royal Shakespeare Theatre were major beneficiaries of his support). Sir John Wills retired as managing director of BET in 1973 and as director and chairman in 1982. Wills married, in 1936, Elizabeth Drusilla Alice Clare Garcke; they

had two sons, one of whom, Nicholas (qv) later became chairman of BET. See Roger Fulford, *The Sixth Decade, 1946-1956* (1956); *Independent*, 12 November 1991; G E Mingay, *Fifteen Years On: The BET Group, 1956-1971* (1973); Bernard Sendall, *Independent Television in Britain* (2 vols, 1982-83); *The Times*, 5 November 1991.

WILLS, Nicholas (Kenneth) (Spencer)
(18 May 1941 -)

Support services company executive, the son of (Sir) John Spencer Wills (qv) and Elizabeth Garcke. His father was a director (and later chairman) of the British Electric Traction Co. Educated at Rugby and Queen's College, Cambridge, he joined BET in 1970 from the bankers Morgan Grenfell. His first job was as manager of BET's investment trusts. He was appointed a BET director in 1975, became managing director in 1982 and was chief executive between 1985 and 1991 (handing over to John Clarke). He has been chairman of BET since 1991. The company, which began to diversify from the transport business under Harold 'Harley' Drayton (qv), is now heavily involved with distribution, security services, personnel, cleaning (the famous hand-towel business, 'Initial', is a subsidiary), and plant hire. Between 1987 and 1991 BET's turnover increased from £1,692 million to £2,790 million (pre-tax profits from £157 million to £217 million) and the group now has over 124,000 workers (92,000 in the UK). Wills has been on the boards of several financial houses - National Mutual Life, Colonial Securities Trust, and Globe Investment Trust - and has also served on several public bodies, such as Business in the Community and the Prince's Youth Business Trust. He married first in 1973 Hilary Ann née Flood: they had two sons and two daughters before the marriage was dissolved. His second marriage in 1985 was to Philippa Trench Casson by whom he had a daughter.

WILLS, William Henry
Baron Winterstoke of Blagdon
(1 September 1830 - 29 January 1911)

Tobacco manufacturer, born in Bristol, the second and only surviving child of William Day Wills, tobacco manufacturer and one of the founders of the Bristol firm of W D & H O Wills, and his wife Mary née Steven, he was educated at Mill Hill School and University College, London. Ill-health deflected him from a career as a barrister and he became a traveller for the family firm. He was admitted to a one-sixth partnership in 1858 and in 1865 became, with his cousin Henry Overton Wills III (1828-1911), responsible for running the business. He moved from active management to the chairmanship in 1880, backing his nephews led by George Alfred Wills (qv) in their pursuit of new technology and branded products. When the flamboyant James Buchanan Duke (1856-1925) attempted to bring his American Tobacco Co into British markets in 1901, Sir William Henry Wills (he was made a baronet in 1892) headed counter moves which merged 13 UK tobacco firms to form the Imperial Tobacco Co (with W D & H O Wills receiving £7 million of the £12 million paid for the 13 constituents). Sir William Henry Wills, chairman of Imperial Tobacco from 1901 until his death, then negotiated an international trading agreement with Duke which split world tobacco markets between American Tobacco, Imperial Tobacco and the jointly-owned British American Tobacco Co. William Henry Wills' net annual income rose from £10,000 in 1880 to £200,000 in 1902. For many years he was a director of the Great Western Railway and Phoenix Assurance Co. A devout Congregationalist, Wills was prominent in the public life of Bristol and sat in parliament as a MP (Liberal) for Coventry, 1880-85, and for Bristol East, 1895-1900. He made substantial benefactions to Bristol, its art gallery and university especially, and to various Nonconformist causes. Highest of his many honours was his peerage, created in 1906. Wills married, in 1853, Elizabeth Stancombe (d 1896); there were no children. At his death Lord Winterstoke left over £2.5 million. See B W E Alford, *W D & H O Wills and the Development of the UK Tobacco Industry, 1786-1965* (1973); *DBB*.

WOLFSON, Sir Isaac
(17 September 1897 - 20 June 1991)

Retail industry magnate, born in Glasgow the son of Solomon Wolfson, a Jewish immigrant from Bialystok in Poland who owned a picture framing business in Glasgow, and his wife Necho née Wilemson, he was educated at Queens Park School, Glasgow (as a fee-paying pupil). At 14 he started working for his father becoming a traveller, initially in Scotland. He moved to London in 1920, selling clocks, mirrors and upholstery covers from premises in Old Street. His father-in-law, Ralph Specterman, the wealthy proprietor of a string of suburban cinemas, provided financial backing for his early business ventures. In 1930 Wolfson supplied 500 clocks to a Manchester mail order company, Great Universal Stores, run by three brothers, Abraham, George and Jack Rose (a contraction of Rosenson, the family being Jewish immigrants from Lithuania). Wolfson was recruited as chief buyer and when the business ran into difficulties during the slump, with GUS share prices tumbling in 1932, Wolfson bought a large stake (reputedly

£250,000 worth, money mostly provided by Sir Archibald Mitchelson, later GUS chairman) in GUS, of which he became joint managing director with George Rose. Rose left in 1934 leaving Wolfson in command. He tightened controls and finances so that the losses of 1932 were transformed into a profit of £333,536 in 1933. Over the next decade Wolfson expanded GUS largely by acquisition. Fast-talking, impassively-faced, with a quick mind and a retentive memory, he 'read balance sheets as other men might read thrillers'. Some companies he bought with GUS finance, some (like Drages, a furniture retailing store which he transformed into a finance company) with his own money. Many were companies in difficulty, nearly all had unrealised potential. More were added during the Second World War. Wolfson took the firm into hire purchase furniture retailing in 1934, but mail order based in Manchester and London was GUS's principal activity, supported by furnishing. In the 1950s high street store chains were brought into the group, in women's wear (eg Leslie's Stores in South Wales and Morrisons Holdings, a chain of 268 fashion shops) and men's wear (eg Masters & Co (Clothiers), Rego Clothiers and Town Tailors). By the 1960s the group comprised over 250 companies, in mail order, furnishings, drapery, clothing, shoes, food, travel and property in the UK, together with several foreign subsidiaries in retailing and some oil interests in Israel. GUS assets rose from just over £686,000 in 1932 to £1.98 million in 1938 to £16 million in 1948. Employment soared from 1,000 in 1929 to 7,000 in 1938 to 60,000 in 1955 and 70,000 in 1965. Wolfson became chairman in 1945 and, starting in 1952, ensured that the family retained control of the business by issuing non-voting shares when going to the market for fresh capital. His son became joint chairman in 1981 and Sir Isaac (he was made a baronet in 1962) finally stepped down in 1987, when GUS employment was down to 44,000. Management reorganisation followed a business credit agreement of 1986 with Harris Queensway, whose chairman Sir Philip Harris (qv) joined the GUS board. Critics had pointed to the lack of initiative on the High Street and over-reliance on cash holdings. In private Wolfson was devoted to his family and his faith. A devout and Orthodox Jew, he neither smoked nor drank and lived without personal ostentation. Universities, the medical profession and the state of Israel were the main beneficiaries of his great philanthropy (his lifetime gifts being around £100 million). The Wolfson Foundation, which disbursed £42.8 million between 1955 and 1980, funded two postgraduate colleges named after him, one each at Oxford and Cambridge. He retired to Israel to his palatial home in the grounds of the Weizman

Institute at Rehovot where he died. He married, in 1926, Edith Specterman (d 1981); they had one son, Leonard Gordon, later Baron Wolfson (qv). See Stephen Aris, *The Jews in Business* (1970); T W Cynog-Jones. 'Retail Giants, Nos 1-2: GUS' *New Dawn* (1963); *Daily Telegraph*, 21 June 1991; *The Independent*, 22 June 1991; *The Times*, 21 June 1991.

WOLFSON, Leonard Gordon
Baron Wolfson of Marylebone in the City of Westminster
(11 November 1927 -)

Retailer, the son of Isaac Wolfson (qv) and Edith Specterman. Educated at King's School, Worcester, he became a director of Great Universal Stores, of which his father was chairman, in 1952. He has been GUS chairman since 1966, working full-time without a chief executive, but overseeing three managing directors. He controls the Wolfson Foundation (of which he was a founder trustee), which owns more than 50 per cent of the GUS voting shares, and also makes large donations to medical and scientific bodies (for which he has been awarded numerous honorary degrees). By 1992 GUS had a turnover of £2,597 million with pre-tax profits of £459 million, and employed nearly 30,000. Highly secretive, with strong links with the Conservative Party, Wolfson was knighted in 1977 and created a life peer in 1985. He married in 1949 Ruth née Sterling: they have four daughters.

WONTNER, Sir Hugh (Walter Kingwell)
(22 October 1908 - 25 November 1992)

Hotelier, the son of Arthur Wontner, a distinguished actor. His mother was an actress, who gave up the stage when her three children were born. Brought up in London, he was educated at Oundle and in France before joining the secretarial staff of the London Chamber of Commerce before he was 20. Wontner became secretary of the Hotels and Restaurants Association in London in 1933 and five years later became assistant to (Sir) George Reeves-Smith, the managing director of the Savoy Hotel in London since 1901. Wontner began a lifetime's service with the Savoy Group: a director in 1940, he became managing director of the Savoy Hotel, 1941-79, chairman 1948-84, and was president at his death. He steered the Savoy and the group's other hotels - such as Claridges, the Berkeley and the Connaught - through the Second World War and established an unashamed commitment to excellence, style and luxury, regardless of the cost. He also defended the Savoy from a number of takeover bids, which began in the 1950s, from the likes of Harold Samuel (qv), (Sir) Charles Clore (qv) and (Sir) Maxwell Joseph (qv). His annual battles with Charles Forte (qv), who criticised

the Savoy's dismal profit record, were particularly acrimonious. Trusthouse Forte eventually gained 69 per cent of the Savoy's equity, but only 42 per cent of the voting rights. A five-year truce was declared in 1989, with Forte failing to gain control. Besides running the Savoy, Wontner was adviser to the Royal Household and was also closely involved with the Corporation of London, becoming alderman, sheriff and Lord Mayor. Most at home in formal or ceremonial garb, he was a master of several livery companies, such the Feltmakers' and the Clothmakers' Companies (though he preferred the company of women). He was also chairman of the Savoy Theatres, 1948-92; and was a trustee of the Opera Trust. Wotner was knighted in 1972 and made GBE in 1974. In 1936 he married Catherine Irvin: they had two sons and one daughter. See Stanley Jackson, *The Savoy a Century of Taste* (1989).

WOODALL, Sir Corbet
(27 August 1841 - 17 May 1916)

Gas engineer, consultant and manager, born in Liverpool, youngest of the three sons of William Woodall, manager of the Liverpool gas works, and his wife Martha née Basson, he was educated at the Crescent School, run by the Congregationalists (who had his lifelong allegiance), but left early to join his eldest brother William in managing the Burslem gas works. He moved to London in 1859 and worked in several gas works management posts, succeeding his mentor Robert Morton after 1869 as chief engineer of the Phoenix Co, one of the largest in the country. Woodall became so successful as a consulting gas engineer that when the Phoenix was acquired by the South Metropolitan Co, headed by George Livesey (qv), in 1880, he retired from his £1,600 a year job to devote all his time to consultancy. In the engineering institutions he became a member of the Civil Engineers in 1877, the Mechanical Engineers in 1882 and in 1878 was elected president of the British Association of Gas Managers. He was elected a director of the Gas Light & Coke Co in 1897 and its governor (chairman) in 1906. The GLCC, the monopoly supplier of gas in London north of the Thames, was the largest gas company in the world, supplying annually 21.5 million cubic feet of gas (over 12 per cent of British consumption) and employing 15,000 people. Woodall promoted Livesey's co-partnership schemes in the GLCC workforce. He also followed the South Metropolitan in bringing the price of gas down, to 2s 6d per 1,000 cubic feet in 1912. He was knighted in 1913, the year he presided over the Institution of Gas Engineers. Woodall married, in 1865, Anne Whiteman; they had five daughters and five sons. See *DBB*.

WORKMAN, Francis
(16 February 1856 - 14 November 1927)
Shipbuilder, born in Belfast, youngest of 15 children of Robert Workman, partner in the firm of J & R Workman muslin manufacturers, and his wife Jane née Service, he attended the Royal Belfast Academical Institution until he was 17 when he was apprenticed in the Belfast shipbuilding firm of Edward Harland and Gustav Wolff. In 1877 he started his own four-acre yard on the north bank of the River Lagan and in 1880 entered into partnership with a young Scot, George Clark (qv) who possessed capital, talent and links with the shipping industry. By 1900 the firm of Workman, Clark & Co had ten building berths with a maximum length of 700 feet and two engine works on a 50-acre site. In 1907 they employed 8,000. From 1910 Workman, a Unionist, became more involved in political and municipal affairs, serving as high sheriff of Belfast in 1913 and of County Down in 1917. He was also active in the Presbyterian Church in Ireland. In 1920 he helped to arrange the takeover of Workman, Clark by the Northumberland Shipping Co and assented to the issue of a fraudulent prospectus which led to a stressful trial in 1927 that hastened Workman's death. He married Sarah MacCausland; they had a son and a daughter. See *DBB*.

WRENCH, The Right Honourable Frederick Stringer
(4 November 1849 - 7 June 1926)
Chairman of Irish lace business, only son of the Reverend Frederick Wrench, rector of Stowting, Kent, he was educated at Haileybury and Exeter College, Oxford. Here he met Henry Bellingham (later the 3rd baronet) with whom he spent long vacations in County Louth and fell in love with Bellingham's sister. He became an Irish land agent, advocating the sale of estates. In 1887 he became Land Commissioner in Ireland, based in Dublin, selling an increasing number of estates after the Land Purchase Act of 1891. He had a detailed knowledge of Ireland and its agriculture and involved himself in numerous agricultural societies and pursuits (his hobbies were shooting, stalking, travelling, photography and breeding pedigree stock). In this context he promoted rural industries and became involved in the Irish Lace Depot. Established in 1893-94 by Lady Aberdeen, this was an agency for marketing the household-made lace goods made by Irish wives and daughters and offering training in lace-making. By 1900 it had sales of over £23,000 and by 1906 it gave work to 5,000 people scattered across the country. A JP for Cavan, Fermanagh, and Monaghan, Wrench was made a Privy Councillor for Ireland in 1902. Following the civil war in Ireland after the First

World War, Wrench retired with his wife to Hythe, near his birthplace. In 1872 Wrench married Charlotte Mary, third daughter of Sir Alan K Bellingham, 2nd Bt; they had a son and two daughters. See Department of Agriculture and Technical Instruction for Ireland, *Ireland: Industrial and Agricultural* (1902); *The Times*, 8 June 1926.

WRIGHT, Arthur Fitzherbert
(August 9 1865 - 6 January 1952)
Iron company chairman, the eldest son of Francis Beresford, of Warwick, and Adeline Francis Henrietta née Fitzherbert. Educated at Harrow and Trinity College, Cambridge (BA 1887), he became a director and secretary of the Butterley Iron Co. In 1900 he married the Honourable Daisy Isabel, daughter of Robert Chichester, 3rd Baron Moncrieff. He was a JP for Derbyshire. See John Venn and J A Venn, *Alumni Cantabrigienses* (6 vols, 1956-54).

WRIGHT, George Maurice
(6 September 1879 - 18 October 1956)
Department store manager, the son of William Wright (1847-1935), a builder's foreman of Wandsworth, and Lucie Louise Loutine Bidault. He was articled to the London firm of Hibberd, Bull & Co and qualified as an accountant in 1903. In 1911 he joined the accountant (Sir) Alfred Cornelius Roberts in the partnership of A C Roberts, Wright & Co in the City of London. Roberts held several government posts in the First World War, including assistant director-general of army clothing, and he was probably influential in Wright's departure from the partnership in 1916 to join the department store, Debenham's. Described as a brilliant accountant, Wright became a director of Debenham's and with Sir Frederick Richmond (qv) steered the company through the difficult 1920s (when the financial speculator, Clarence Hatry (qv), bought a block of Debenhams' shares) and the depression of the 1930s. He became chairman of Debenhams between 1952 and 1956, when the firm employed about 11,000, had 110 stores and assets of £36 million (but with an issued capital, unchanged since 1934, of only £6.2 million). Wright married twice and had one daughter by his first wife. He left £237,000. See Maurice Corina, *Fine Silks and Oak Counters: Debenhams 1778-1978* (1978).

WRIGHT, Sir William Charles
(12 January 1876 - 14 August 1950)
Sheet steel and tinplate manufacturer, born in Ladywood, Birmingham, the son of John Roper Wright and his wife Jessie Eliza née Wilson. His father was an engineer and future chairman of Baldwins Ltd, the famous iron and steel firm, and

this led directly to Charles Wright's appointment in 1907 as manager of the Port Talbot steelworks. At the beginning of the First World War he was appointed by Lloyd George to supervise the supply of steel - work recognised with a CB in 1918 and a KBE in 1920. He succeeded his father as chairman of Baldwins in 1925 in time to oversee the merger of the steel interests of Baldwins with Guest Keen & Nettlefolds in 1930. Six years later he became chairman of Guest Keen Baldwins when reforms were needed in the structure of the UK steel and tinplate industry. This resulted in Baldwins merger with Richard Thomas in 1944, forming the Steel Co of Wales in 1947 (when Wright resigned as chairman of GKB). He succeeded his father as baronet in 1926 and was made a GBE in 1943. In 1898 he married Maud, daughter of Isaac Butler, a business partner of the Wrights: there were no children. He left £270,323. See Kenneth Warren, *The British Iron and Steel Sheet Industry since 1840* (1970); *DBB*.

Y

YATES, Harry James
(16 November 1873 - 28 August 1955)
Gas appliance manufacturer, born at Aston, Birmingham, the son of Henry Edwin Yates, edge tool manufacturer, and his wife Annie née Bott. The family lived comfortably: when Harry was twelve his father equipped a workshop where he experimented with electricity. In 1893 his father bought him the appliance business of Arden Hill, just when the market for gas cookers was beginning to grow very quickly. Yates combined entrepreneurial drive with interest in applied research throughout his life. Within a few years he amalgamated his firm with John Wright, the largest gas appliance firm, and this formed the core of the Radiation group of companies established in 1919. Wright and later Radiation set up research laboratories headed by academically-trained scientists before the gas supply industry was greatly interested in appliances, and vastly improved cooker performance by introducing the oven thermostat in 1923. By the late 1930s Radiation employed around 10,000. While the main output was for the gas industry, constituent companies also made electric, oil and solid fuel appliances, and were consistently profitable in the interwar years, profits rising from £160,000 in 1922 to £292,000 in 1931 and £327,000 in 1937. Throughout his business career Yates promoted makers' associations and cartel arrangements to protect manaufacturers' profits. He was a founder member of the Federation of British Industries which advocated a larger role for businessmen in government in order to curb bureau-

cratic waste. Retiring in 1939, he was the outstanding figure in the gas appliance business between the wars. In his youth he was an amateur racing car driver and held a pilot's licence. Keen on photography he also sponsored and perhaps engaged in X-ray research. Harry Yates was married and had two sons, one of whom followed him into the appliance business (the other was an architect). See Francis Goodall, 'The British Gas Appliance Industry, 1875-1939' (London PhD, 1992).

YOUNG, Sir James Reid
(2 December 1888 - 6 September 1971)
Steel and armaments manufacturer, the son of the Reverend Dr Young, a Church of Scotland minister at Paisley, and his wife Janet née Reid, he was educated at Paisley Grammar School and Glasgow University. He trained as a chartered accountant and by 1920 had enough experience to be appointed chief accountant to Vickers Ltd. With steelworks at Sheffield, a naval yard at Barrow and various other interests capable of producing all manner of fighting vessels from battleships to submarines, and also guns, machine guns, shells and aircraft, the company had played a major role in the armaments industry before and during the First World War. After the war Vickers diversified into electrical technology, its major investment being in British Westinghouse Electrical Co, jointly purchased with the Metropolitan Carriage, Wagon & Finance Co of Dudley Docker (qv) in 1918. However, this new policy of acquisitions was hindered by the absence of any Vickers accounts for the period 1914-20, despite 200 accountancy staff on the payroll. Young's job was to clean up this mess, which he did, starting by sacking half the accountants. Company secretary by 1935, Young was subsequently promoted to director of Vickers-Armstrongs Ltd (following the merger between the two armaments giants in 1927) in 1936 and director of Vickers Ltd, the parent company, in 1937. Under the chairmanship of Sir Ronald Weeks (qv) Young was managing director of Vickers, 1952-54, and chairman of Vickers-Armstrongs at the same time. Weeks was the man who dominated Vickers in the 1950s, Sir James Young (he was knighted in 1951) his chief executive officer in reshaping the structures organising the activities of a 70,000-strong workforce. From 1941 until 1954 Young was chairman of the advisory panel, organisation and methods division at HM Treasury. He married, in 1918, Margaret Boyd, daughter of Dr William Walker; they had a son and a daughter. See Richard P T Davenport-Hines, *Dudley Docker: The Life and Times of a Trade Warrior* (1984); John D Scott, *Vickers: A History* (1962).

YOUNG, David Ivor
Baron Young of Graffham
(27 February 1932 -)

Industrialist, born and brought up in a north London Jewish community, the son of Joseph and Rebecca Young. His grandfather had emigrated from Lithuania; his father was a small businessman, first in flour then in children's clothing. Educated at Christ's College, Finchley, he left at 16 to work for his uncle in a solicitor's office while taking a law degree in the evenings at University College, London. For five years after 1956 he worked for Great Universal Stores as Isaac Wolfson's (qv) private assistant (his cousin had married Leonard Wolfson), before founding his own property company, Eldonwall. In the 1960s this company developed industrial estates and became one of the largest private property developers. In 1970 he sold out to Town & Country, but stayed in the property business with his friend Jeffrey Sterling (qv). Badly hit by the crash of 1973, Young rebuilt his career in the UK and USA and then entered Conservative politics in 1979. He became adviser to the Secretary of State for Industry, joined the Cabinet in 1984, and was appointed Secretary of State for Employment in 1985. He became Secretary of State for Trade & Industry in 1987, where his 'sweeteners' deal with Sir Roland Smith (qv) over the sale of the car firm Rover to British Aerospace proved controversial. In the time-honoured tradition, he left the DTI in 1989 and in the following year became chairman of a leading UK company, Cable & Wireless. In 1992 this firm, which is heavily involved in the telephone networking business, had a turnover of £3,176 million (pre-tax profits of £643 million) and a workforce of 39,000. Young is also a director of Salomon Inc and Salomon Bros International Ltd. He married in 1956 Lita Marianne Shaw: they have two daughters. He became a life peer in 1984. See David Young, *The Enterprise Years* (1990).

CROSS-REFERENCES TO TITLED PERSONS

Aberconway, see McLaren
Aldenham, see Gibbs
Allerton, see Jackson, William Lawies
Anslow, see Mosley
Ashfield, see Stanley
Bearsted, see Samuel, Walter Horace
Beaverbrook, see Aitken
Bessborough, see Ponsonby
Camrose, see Berry
Chandos, see Lyttelton
Chilston, see Akers-Douglas
Colgrain, see Campbell
Cowdray, see Pearson
Crawford, see Lindsay
Dulverton, see Wills, Gilbert Alan Hamilton
Ebury, see Grosvenor, Robert Wellesley
Hambleden, see Smith
Harlech, see Ormsby-Gore
Hartwell, see Berry

Hollenden, see Morley
Inchcape, see Mackay
Invernairn, see Beardmore
Kemsley, see Berry
Kenilworth, see Siddeley
Kylsant, see Philipps
Masham, see Cunliffe-Lister
Northcliffe, see Harmsworth, Alfred Cahrles
Nuffield, see Morris
Riverdale, see Balfour
Rothermere, see Harmsworth, Harold Sidney
Stalbridge, see Grosvenor, Richard de Aquila
Strathalmond, see Fraser, William Milligan
Templar-Smith, see Smith, Harold Charles
Trent, see Boot
Wardington, see Pease
Wargrave, see Goulding
Waverley, see Anderson
Winterstoke, see Wills, William Henry

COMPANY INDEX

Abbey National	Bellman, Charles Harold; Birch, Peter Gibbs; Tugendhat, Christopher Samuel
Alfred McAlpine	McAlpine, Alfred James
Allied Bakeries	Weston, Willard Garfield
Allied Dunbar	Weinberg, Mark Aubrey
Allied Newspapers	Berry, James Gomer
Allied-Lyons	Holden-Brown, Derrick; Jackaman, Michael Clifford John; Showering, Keith Stanley
Amalgamated Anthracite Collieries	Cope, Alfred; Szarvasy, Frederick Alexander
Amalgamated Cotton Mills Trust	Fairfax, Albert Kirby
Amalgamated Press	Berry, John Seymour; Berry, William Michael
AMEC	Cockshaw, Alan
Amstrad	Sugar, Alan Michael
Anglo-Persian Oil Co	Cadman, John; Fraser, William Milligan
Argyll	Grant, Matthew Alistair; Gulliver, James Gerald
Armstrong (Sir W G), Whitworth & Co	Cruddas, William Donaldson; Noble, Andrew; Siddeley, John Davenport
Army & Navy Co-operative Society	Grosvenor, Robert Wellesley
Arthur Balfour & Co	Balfour, Arthur
Asda	Norman, Archibald John
Asprey's	Asprey, John Rolls
Associated Biscuit Manufacturers	Palmer, Charles Eric; Williams, Clement Hilton
Associated British Foods	Weston, Garfield Howard; Weston, Willard Garfield
Associated British Picture Corporation	Fletcher, Eric George Molyneaux; Warter, Philip Allan
Associated Electrical Industries (AEI)	Dannatt, Cecil; Lusk, William Clardy; Lyttelton, Oliver; Pole, Felix John Clewett
Associated Newspapers	Harmsworth, Alfred Charles William

COMPANY INDEX

Associated Portland Cement Manufacturers	Earle, George Foster; O'Hagan, Henry Osborne; Reiss, John Anthony Ewart; Stewart, Percy Malcolm
Associated Television (ATV)	Grade, Lew
Austin Friars Trust	Hatry, Clarence Charles
Austin Motor Co	Austin, Herbert; Engelbach, Charles Richard Fox
Austin Reed	Reed, Austin Leonard
Babcock & Wilcox	Dewrance, John; Fraser, William Lionel; Hague, Charles Kenneth Felix; McKinstry, Archibald
Bank of England	George, Edward Alan John; Leigh-Pemberton, Robert Robin; Norman, Montagu Collet; Richardson, Gordon William Humphreys
Barclays Bank	Buxton, Andrew Robert Fowell; Quinton, John Grand; Thornton, Ronald; Tuke, Anthony William
Barclays Hotels	Barclay, David; Barclay, Frederick
Barker (John) & Co	Skinner, Sydney Martyn
Barlow Clowes	Clowes, Peter
Bass	Prosser, Ian Maurice Gray
Bayer (Charles) & Co	Bayer, Charles
Beardmore (William) & Co	Armstrong, Oliver Carleton; Beardmore, William; Lithgow, James
Beecham Group	Lazell, Henry George Leslie
Bernard Matthews PLC	Matthews, Bernard
Birmingham Small Arms Co (BSA)	Docker, Bernard Dudley Frank; Rogers, Hallewell
Birtwistle & Fielding	Birtwistle, Albert; Birtwistle, Arthur
Bleachers Association	Cross, Herbert Shepherd; Lees, William Clare; Sykes, Alan John
Body Shop	Roddick, Anita Lucia
Bolckow, Vaughan & Co	Johnson-Ferguson, Jabez Edward
Booker	Caine, Michael Harris
Boots	Blyth, James; Boot, Jesse
Boot's Pure Drug Co	Boot, John Campbell; Savage, John Percival
Bowater	Bowater, Eric Frederic Vansittart
Bradford Dyers Association	Douglas, George; Robinson, Thomas
Brent Walker	Walker, George Alfred
Bristol Aeroplane Co	Smith, William George Verdon; White, George; White, George Stanley Midleton
British Aerospace	Cahill, John Conway; Day, Judson Graham; Smith, Roland
British Aircraft Corporation	Verdon-Smith, William Reginald
British Airways	King, John Leonard; Marshall, Colin Marsh; McFadzean, Francis Scott
British American Tobacco (BAT)	Sheehy, Patrick
British & Commonwealth Holdings	Gunn, John Humphrey
British Broadcasting Corporation (BBC)	Cadogan, Alexander George Montagu; Jacob, Edward Ian Claud; Reith, John Charles Walsham
British Caledonian Airways	Thomson, Adam
British Coal	Clarke, John Neil

COMPANY INDEX

COMPANY INDEX

Lucas Industries	Bennett, Peter Frederick Blaker; Gill, Anthony Keith; Messervy, Roney Godfrey Collumbell; Waring, Arthur Bertram
Lucas (Joseph)	Bennett, Peter Frederick Blaker
Lyons (J) & Co	Gluckstein, Isidore Montague; Salmon, Henry; Salmon, Isidore
Manchester Collieries	Burrows, Robert Abraham; Ramsden, Joseph
Manchester Ship Canal Co	West, Frederick Joseph
Marks & Spencer	Greenbury, Richard; Marks, Simon; Rayner, Derek George; Sieff, Israel Moses; Sieff, Marcus Joseph
Maxwell Communications Corporation	Maxwell, Ian Robert
Mersey Docks & Harbour Board	Gladstone, Robert; Holt, Richard Durning; Robinson, Montague Arnet; Warner, Lionel Ashton Piers
Messenger Group	Shah, Selim Jehane (Eddie)
Metal Box Co	Barlow, Robert; Ducat, David
Metropolitan Amalgamated Rly Carr & Wagon	Docker, Frank Dudley
Midland Bank	Edington, William Gerald; Holden, Edward Hopkinson; Hyde, Frederick; McKenna, Reginald; McMahon, Christopher William; Pearse, Brian Gerald; Ormsby-Gore, William George Arthur
Midland Railway	Granet, William Guy; Paget, George Ernest
Morley, I & R	Morley, Samuel Hope
Morris Motors	Morris, William Richard
Mountleigh	Clegg, Ronald Anthony
Mowlem	Beck, Edgar Philip
Mullard Co	Eriks, Sierd Sint
National Coal Board (NCB)	Bowman, James; Browne, Edward Humphrey; Ezra, Derek; Haslam, Robert; Holmes, Noel Galway; Houldsworth, Hubert Stanley; Parker, Ronald William; Rees, David Morgan; Ringham, Reginald; Robens, Alfred; Skinner, Ernest Harry Dudley
National Freight Corporation	Thompson, Peter Anthony; Watkins, James Kenneth
National Provincial Bank	Campbell, Colin Frederick; Cornwall, Ernest; Robarts, David John; Williams, Leonard John
National Westminster Bank	Alexander, Robert Scott; Wanless, Derek
Naval Dockyards	Bryant, Frederick; Johns, Arthur William
Next	Davies, George William
North British Locomotive Co	Lorimer, William; Reid, Hugh
North British Railway	Jackson, William Fulton
North Eastern Railway	Butterworth, Alexander Kaye; Wharton, John Lloyd
North Staffordshire Railway	Mosley, Tonman; Phillipps, William Douglas
Ocean Coal Co	Davies, David
Pasolds Ltd	Pasold, Eric Walter
Patons & Baldwins	Forrester-Paton, Alexander; Procter, William Thomson

COMPANY INDEX

Rothmans International — Swaythling, David Charles Samuel Montagu

Rothschilds — Rothschild, Evelyn Robert Adrian de; Rothschild, Nathaniel Charles Jacob

Rowntree — Rowntree, Benjamin Seebohm; Rowntree, Joseph; Wallace, William

Royal Dockyards — Marshall, James Brown; Watts, Philip

Royal Mail Group — Philipps, Owen Cosby

Royal Ordnance Factories — Donaldson, Hay Frederick

Rubery Owen & Co — Owen, Alfred George Beech; Owen, Ernest William Beech

Rylands & Sons — Carnelley, William; Rhodes, Edward

S G Warburg — Scholey, David Gerald; Warburg, Siegmund George

Saatchi & Saatchi — Saatchi, Charles; Saatchi, Maurice

Sainsbury — Sainsbury, David John; Sainsbury, John Davan

Savoy Group — Wontner, Hugh Walter Kingwell

Schroders — Schroder, Rudolph Bruno

Scottish Co-operative Wholesale Society — Beaton, Neil Scobie; Davidson, John Martin; Leckie, Robert Walker; Maxwell, William; Pearson, John; Stirling, John Anderson

Scott's Shipbuilding & Engineering Co — Brown, James; Scott, Charles Cuningham

Sears Holdings — Clore, Charles; Maitland-Smith, Geoffrey; Sainer, Leonard

Selfridge's — Selfridge, Harry Gordon

Shell Transport & Trading — Cohen, Robert Waley; Godber, Frederick; Holmes, Peter Fenwick; Samuel, Walter Horace

Simon-Carves — Simon, Ernest Emil Darwin

Sinclair Research — Sinclair, Clive Marles

Singer & Co — Bullock, William Edward

Singer Manufacturing Co — Baxter, James; Park, Franklin Atwood; Rickey, Walter Josiah

Sir James Joicey & Co — Joicey, James

Slater Walker — Slater, James Derrick

Smith (S) & Sons — Gordon-Smith, Ralph

Smith (W H) & Son — Awdry, Charles; Hornby, Charles Harry St John; Hornby, Michael Charles St John; Hornby, Simon Michael; Smith, David John; Smith, William Frederick Danvers; Smith, William Henry

SmithKline Beecham — Bauman, Robert Patten

Sock Shop International — Mirman, Sophie

South Eastern & Chatham Rly — Akers-Douglas, Aretas; Bonsor, Henry Cosmo Orme

South Metropolitan Gas Co — Livesey, George Thomas

Southern Railway Co (SR) — Holland-Martin, Robert Martin; Walker, Herbert Ashcombe

St James's Club — de Savary, Peter John

Standard Life — Galpin, Rodney Desmond

Standard Motor Co — Dick, Alick Sydney

Standard Telephones & Cables (STC) — Gill, Frank; Spencer, Thomas George

Stanton Ironworks Co — Crompton, John Gilbert

Staveley Coal & Iron Co — Markham, Charles Paxton

Steel Co of Scotland — Lorimer, William

COMPANY INDEX